Beverage Literature:
A Bibliography

compiled by

A. W. Noling

The Scarecrow Press, Inc.
Metuchen, N.J.   1971

Ref. 016.663
N71

2637

Table of Contents

iii

Preface

The Hurty-Peck Library of Beverage Literature

The library as it stands today grew from a rather specialized collection of material to one of the world's largest libraries on beverage literature. Books on soft drinks and soft drink flavors were collected for quite a few years before any attempt was made to obtain books on any other types of beverages. This was natural as the company's primary interest was in learning as much as possible about its own field. Serious efforts to collect beyond the soft drink field began in the late 1950's when the compiler relinquished his responsibilities as chief executive officer of the company and subsequently had the time to devote to the finding and obtaining of all kinds of beverage literature.

The need for more information on the source and processing of the materials required for beverage production became apparent as the search for soft drinks literature (and that of the flavoring which went into them) deepened. This led into the fields of brewing, fermenting, distilling and rectifying, which in turn led to collecting books on beer and ale, wine, spirits, etc. and their manufacture. It was only a short step to add to the search the literature on beverages usually associated with food, such as coffee, tea, and chocolate.

At this writing, the library is housed in the Hurty-Peck plant in Southern California. Material is shelved by subject and then in alphabetical order by author within the subject. A card catalogue is available with cards for the author, title and subject. A vertical file is also maintained. This material is divided into 128 categories with special emphasis on soft drinks and flavoring.

The Hurty-Peck library is intended to provide a permanent place for the many pieces of beverage and related material still in existence. It is available for research purposes in any of the various aspects of the subject. The library is known to hold more titles (in English) than any

other single library--not excepting the Library of Congress
and the British Museum Library.   There are close to 5, 000
titles now on the shelves, including those from the collection
of the late George B. Beattie, noted English beverage trade
journal contributor and technical analyst.

Up to the present time little attention has been given to
collecting incunabula as such for the library.   Research into
the area of old writings suggests that there are about 350
such titles (in English) published prior to 1800 which have
not been obtained.   Of these, about 25 were printed in the
16th century and 100 others were printed during the 17th
century.   Some of these will be acquired.   The library is
kept current with the purchase of all drink books as they are
published.

Many books now in the library have been acquired for
the purposes of preservation rather than for present day technical use.   Similar to many collections of books these provide a source for facts on the semi-modern history of some
phase of the broad beverage field.

Some titles in the library may seem, on the surface,
to be unrelated to the beverage field.   A part of these came
into the library by accident when they were obtained as part
of a large number of volumes classed by the seller as pertaining to the subject.   These have been scrutinized closely
and those included do add something to the overall picture of
beverage literature.   The library holds another number of
titles of general technical nature which are not included in
this bibliography.   They represent background material for
the technical researcher.

Some of the books in the library are reprints as the
originals are sometimes very difficult, if not impossible, to
obtain.   The reprints satisfy the primary purpose of the
library--to provide information on beverages.   One of the
difficulties in locating the missing out-of-print material is
the dearth of dealers who specialize in this and allied fields.
Among the few who do are the Corner Book Store in New
York City, Elizabeth Woodburn in Hopewell, New Jersey, and
John Lyle in Devon, England.   Not since the days of Orange-
Judd in New York and the Dahl's in Stamford, Connecticut,
has any publisher placed extra emphasis on beverage literature.

It is quite likely, although no authentic figures are
available, that many more books in some categories of

beverage literature have been published in languages other
than English.   Wine books in French and Italian, and German
books on beer and brewing are the best examples.   Perhaps
this situation applies more to out-of-prints than to current
literature.   For instance, a study of the card catalogue of
the University of California Library at Berkeley, which has
a comprehensive collection in the wine category (over 500
entries), shows more than 55% in languages other than
English.   The Hurty-Peck library has attempted to confine
its collecting efforts to one language and practically all of
the titles on the shelves are in English.

The list of books in the library is growing daily although
the rate of acquisition is decreasing.   Most of the missing
titles are long out-of-print and consequently are rare.   Efforts to obtain copies are continuing constantly.   They must
wait, however, until someone offers the books to the second-
hand book market.

Newell Myres, librarian of the Bodlein Library at
Oxford pointed out recently:

> Make no mistake about it, we are in the last
> generation to see books of earlier centuries than
> the nineteenth in at all common supply in the book-
> shops and auction rooms of the world.   The high
> proportion of such books which find their way into
> permanent institutional possession rather than into
> the temporary keeping of private collectors makes
> it certain that the limited supplies cannot last very
> long.

Perhaps this is good reason to make the effort now to build
the Hurty-Peck Library into a permanent repository in this
long-neglected beverage literature field.

Introduction

The student of beverages or beverage products may have been impressed with the apparent lack of literature relating specifically to the subjects of drinks and drinking. The truth is, a substantial amount is available, but it is located sometimes in widely separated spots. The need for a guide to the literature prompted the compilation of this bibliography. A source of information on the many titles in existence and their locations, this listing of beverage-related literature is intended as a working guide for the serious inquirer. Inclusions and omissions of some semi-related literature are predicated on this intended use.

Publications included in this bibliography fall into a number of major classifications or categories. These classes are detailed in the section entitled "Description of Subject Categories." Comment on some of them might be helpful to the user of this book.

The largest and fastest growing section of beverage literature is that on wine. Numerous books on wine in English are being published each year; such literature in other languages might be as prolific or even more so. Books on wine in French and Italian make up the majority of entries in some of the libraries with better than average collections on the subject. This bibliography lists almost 1200 titles on wine, wine-making, grapes and grape-growing, mostly in English.

On such subjects as coffee, tea, chocolate, and fruits emphasis has been placed, for inclusion, on the titles which relate in some substantial way to the use of such products as, or in, beverages. Some books on culture, planting, growing, and other related areas have been included, however. A greater number of such botanical and technical titles can be found in the card catalogues of the larger libraries. All of the principal books, both out-of-print and current, published on the technology of manufacture of the base products are included in the bibliography. Almost all of them contain some historical and background

material of value to anyone interested in those products when
used in beverages.

A fair number of cookbooks which recommend themselves
for their close relation to beverage literature are included.
There are, of course, untold thousands of others which deal
largely with solids and not with liquids and are not pertinent to
a bibliography of beverage literature.   Quite a few cookbooks
have been written around a single type of beverage such as coffee, chocolate, beer, wine, and spirits when used in cooking;
they are all listed.   It is interesting to note that during the 16th
and 17th centuries the only published information on beverages
was in books on cooking, confectionery and housekeeping. These
covered such subjects as brewing, fermenting and distilling in
the home with details of the processes used in making beer,
wine and spirits.   Practically no commercial production of
beverages took place in those days.

The bibliography lists only a limited number of titles of
books published on the subject of inns and taverns although they
have a close connection with the subject of drinks and drinking.
Many of the excluded titles dwell on food and lodging more than
on liquid refreshment.   Those selected are the ones, in the
opinion of the compiler, which have importance on the areas of
the use and history of beverages and the customs pertaining to
them in the public houses.

Books on temperance have, like cookbooks, been published in the thousands over the centuries.   Those selected for
the bibliography lean largely to the physical side of the use and
make-up of beverages rather than to the moral or spiritual side.

The inclusion of foods and fruits as categories of
beverages stems from the fact that most soft drink types,
as well as many alcoholic beverages, derive their main or
secondary flavors from them.

A reasonable number of titles of miscellaneous reference books useful to the producers or fabricators of various
types of beverages are included.   In some of the secondary
areas of this category only a few representative titles have
been listed as most of them have too broad an application.
Microscopes are an example.   They are an adjunct of the
manufacture of beverages and beverage ingredients but not of
first importance to beverage literature.   The card catalogues
of the major technical libraries all have comprehensive list-
ings of titles on these fringe topics although they are not

necessarily catalogued as referring to beverages.

In some of the categories less obviously connected with beverages, books have been listed only when the title or main subject matter particularly recommends them as a beverage reference. Among them are those of confectionery and ices (including ice cream); food and food products (sugar, for example); flavorings; perfumery. The card catalogues of all of the major libraries have been analysed for appropriate titles to include in these classifications.

There are a considerable number of titles which do not apply solely to any one type of beverage, its manufacture, or use. These have been difficult to classify. Other "hard to type" titles touch on a number of fields--cookery, flavoring, perfumery, fruits, foods, for example--in the same volume. These are often valuable references to the manufacture and use of beverages. Such books have been placed in the general or "catch-all" category of drinks and drinking.

It has been the endeavor of the compiler to set forth in the author list the essential details of each entry including the full name of the author, the full title, name and location of the publisher, date of publication, number of pages, description of the content when the title does not make it clear, and other things such as the appearance of illustrations, bibliographies, glossaries, etc. Also noted is the location of one copy if the title is not in the Hurty-Peck Library. Often this is the place where a copy was first seen and does not necessarily mean that a copy of the volume cannot be seen in other collections. The selection of location was usually based on its accessibility and strength of holdings in the beverage field. Of the titles with no location designation, the majority are found in the Hurty-Peck library. A small percentage of those with non-designated locations, however, are in two categories: publications whose information came from a library's catalogue, but which cannot be found on a library shelf (many of the books in the British Museum were destroyed during World War II, for example); and publications whose information came from other bibliographies. The latter materials have not been located and the hope of getting more information rests solely with used-book dealers and personal correspondence. The number involved is minor.

While extensive efforts have been made to do a complete descriptive job in the listing of all of the books, in

some cases this has not been possible.   For some of the
titles the source has been antiquarian book-dealer lists.
These often omit some details.   As the lists may be old, or
the books sold, it has been impossible to obtain the missing
information.   As was mentioned above, some entries for
books not in the library have been taken from the subject
catalogues of various other libraries and are judged by
their librarians to relate to beverages.   It has not been
possible for the compiler to see all of those books.   For all
of the books in the Hurty-Peck Library, the information is
complete.

The title listing section of the bibliography provides
only a short title and the author's last name and initials.
This information will allow the reader to refer to the author
list and obtain full details on the book and its location.
Similarly the subject listing is also abbreviated with author
name and initials and a short title.   Reference to this sub-
divided list will provide proper entry into the author list
for further information on any particular book in any
category.

It has not been considered to be in the scope of this
bibliography to include a listing and description of various
editions of the same out-of-prints.   Numerous reference
sources can be consulted if such information is desired.
Among them are Bitting's Gastronomic Bibliography; Simon's
three bibliothecas--Gastronomica, Bacchia and Vineria;
Vicaire's Bibliographie Gastronomique, to mention a few.
These sources are helpful in learning more about some
16th, 17th and 18th century titles, many of which are in
languages other than English.   Around 400 of such titles,
mostly in English, are listed and described and about one-
fourth of them can be found in the Hurty-Peck Library.

There are many thousands of pieces of beverage
literature material, mostly unavailable now, which have
been published in the form of essays, lectures, manuscripts,
commercial or trade reports, acts of legislatures, technical
bulletins, pamphlets, magazine articles, clippings, periodicals, etc. Although they are in the field of beverage
literature, it is not possible to list them all in this volume.
The Hurty-Peck Library contains some of the more important ones and the Library of Congress and the British Museum Library have catalogued many more.   This bibliography
describes a fair number.

Some other book titles are only of indirect or incidental value to the subject of beverages. Most of these are so general in their application that description of them has been omitted. Also there are many works on subjects such as the origin or source and production of materials, microbiology, chemistry of products, processes, etc. These, while having some relation to the manufacture of beverages, are too general and technical for this specialized bibliography. Any good technical card catalogue will list them. In some cases a book has been included which has some relation to a major beverage field although it may lie in some other literary area, such as the novel.

The names of a substantial number of libraries, both public and private, specializing in beverage titles or having better than average collections are listed in the appendix. Some quiet people, no doubt, have outstanding collections but have not made them known. Antiquarian book dealers, who know of most of them, are reticent about disclosing the names of their clients, whether private collectors or libraries.

A list of standard reference books which were consulted has also been appended to this volume. Some reference to beverage literature has been found in almost all of them. Nearly all of the larger libraries have these reference works. The list of bibliographies, dictionaries, glossaries, etc. will be a source of further information in a specific category. Reference to this subject-divided list will give the author and title of books containing such helps. This can lead to more detailed information which might be contained in periodicals, reports, bulletins, lectures and magazine articles not listed in this bibliography.

The compiler recognizes that any interested student of beverage literature may know of some titles which are not included and should be. It is practically impossible to be aware of all titles even though years have been devoted to the project. At the same time others will find many titles in these pages which they had not known before. It is hoped that this work will fill a need in the long-neglected field of beverage literature.

A. W. Noling

Explanation of Abbreviations Used

ABCB	American Bottlers of Carbonated Beverages. Washington
Amer.	American Book Service. Beverage book-list. New York
ANL	Australian National Library. Canberra, Australia
Argosy	Argosy Book Catalog. New York
ASDI	American Soft Drink Industry. Riley
B & F	Bibliography of Food. Baker & Foskett, 1958
BG	Bibliotheca Gastronomica. Simon
BM	British Museum Library. London
BV	Bibliotheca Vineria. Simon
Barton	Barton Distilling Co. Bardstown, Ky.
Baron	Brewed in America
Beach	Apples of New York
Berkeley	Univ. of Calif. at Berkeley
Bird	Catalogue of Library. London (Section titled: "Institute of Brewing")
Bitt	Gastronomic Bibliography. K. A. Bitting
Bodleian	Oxford University Library
Booknoll	Book list from Booknoll Farm. Hopewell, N. J.
Bourbon Inst.	Bourbon Institute Library. New York
Brady	Brady Wine Library. Fresno State College, Calif.
Brown	Culinary Americana
Carson	Social History of Bourbon
CBI	Cumulative Book Index
Chap.	Brewing. A. G. Chapman, 1912
Ck. Li.	Check list books on grapes, etc. Amerine, 1949-1959. Also with Wheeler, 1938-1948
Cooper	References Ancient and Modern to Literature on Beer and Ale
Corn.	Corner Book Store Lists. N. Y.
Crerar	John Crerar Library at Illinois Inst. Technology. Chicago
Dahls	Dahls Publ. Co. Stamford, Ct.
Davis	Univ. of Calif. at Davis, Calif.
Ell.	Pleasures of Table. Ellwanger
Fitch	Mineral Waters of US and American Spas.

Forbes	Short History of Distillation
Fuller	Grape Culturist. 1864
F. & W.	Ex. Food & Wine Exhibition. Rare Books Catalogue, 1961
GATC	Great Amer. Trade Cats. Romaine
GBPOL	Great Britain Patent Office Library. London. (Now BM)
Greenwood	Classified Guide to Technical and Commercial Books
Haz	Old Cookery Books. Hazlitt
H-P or HPLBL	Hurty-Peck Library of Beverage Literature
Hudson	Development of Brewing Analysis
IB	Institute Brewing Library. London
Kirkby	Evolution of Artificial Mineral Water
Knapp	Cocoa and chocolate, 1920
Jagendorf	Folk Wines, 1963
Janes	Red Barrel
Jordon	Jordon Wine Co. Toronto
LC	Library of Congress
Low	David Low, Bookseller. Oxford
Lucia	Wine as Food & Medicine
Lyle	Book List of John Lyle. Exeter, Devon
Maggs	Food & drink through ages. Maggs Bros.
Mathias	Brewing Industry of England 1700-1830
Mitch	Mineral & Aerated Waters. C. A. Mitchell
Money	Cultivation and manufacture of tea.
Napa	Napa Valley Wine Library. St. Helena, Calif.
Northe	Book list. J. N. Northe, Oklahoma City
Novak	Non-intoxicants, 1922
NYPL	New York Public Library
Ox	English Cookery Books. A. W. Oxford
Peddie	Subject Index for Books Publ. before 1880.
PLOSA	Public Library of So. Australia, Adelaide
POSL	Patent Office Scientific Library. Washington
Riley	John Riley Collection. Washington
Sch.	Schenley Library Bibliography.
Scho	Schoellhorn-Biblio Braueusens
Shand	Book of French Wines and Other than French
STC	Short Title Catalog. Pollard
Stopes	Malt and Malting
Sub-G	Subject Guide to Books in Print
Ukers	All about Coffee (or Tea)
UCLA	Univ. Calif. Los Angeles
USBA	US Brewers' Ass'n. Library
US Cat.	United States Catalog
Vic	Vicaire's Bibliographie Gastronomique

W & FS	Wine, Food Society Library
WI	Wine Institute Library. San Francisco
WTC	Wine Trade Club. London
Walford	Book lists. G. W. Walford, London
Warner	Liquor cult and its culture
Wellman	Coffee, Botany, etc.

AUTHOR LIST

Author List
(Items without location symbols
can be found in Hurty- Peck Library)

L'Abbe, Lucien
    The liquor dealer's silent assistant.   n p 1895.
    38p.   LC
Abbott Laboratories.   Chemical Marketing Div. Brominated
    oils (basic formulas for) Bulletin no. 337 North Chicago,
    Ill., 1961. 8p.

_____.
    Sucaryl sweetened beverages.   Bulletin no. 142 North
    Chicago, Ill., c1960.   8p.
Abdullah, Achmed and Kenny, John
    For men only.   A cookbook.   New York, G.P. Putnam's
    Sons.   c1937.   205p.
Abrahamson, E.M. and Pexet, A.W.
    Body, mind and sugar.   Key to understanding alcoholism,
    etc. New York, Henry Holt and Co. 1955. 206p. References.
Accum, Frederick
    Guide to the Chalybeate spring of Thetford.   London,
    C. Green, 1819.   159p.   Illus-engraving.

_____.
    A treatise on adulterations of food, and culinary poisons.
    London, Longman, Hurst, Rees Orme and Brown, 1820.
    372p.

_____.
    A treatise on adulterations of food and culinary poisons.
    The fraudulant sophistication of bread, beer, wine,
    spiritous liquors, tea, coffee, etc.   2nd edition.
    Philadelphia, AB'M Small.   Vol. II from Mallinkrodt
    Collection of Food Classics.   269p.

_____.
    A treatise on the art of brewing exhibiting the London
    practice of brewing porter, brown stout, ale, table beer,
    etc.   London, Longman, Hurst, Rees, Orme and Brown,
    1820.   268p.

_____.
    Treatise on the art of making wines from native fruits.
    London, Longman, Hurst, Orme, Rees and Brown.
    1820.   92p.   NYPL

Acker, Merrill and Condit
>Price list of wines and liquors, no. 101. New York,
September 12, 1877. 4p.

Ackroyd, William
>The history and science of drunkenness. London and
Manchester, Simpkin, Marshall and Co., and Tubbs,
Brook and Chrystal, 1883. 128p. Illus.

Acton, Bryan and Duncan, Peter
>Making mead, metheglin, hippoccras, melomel,
pyment, cyser. Andover, Amateur Winemaker, 1965.
56p. Illus.

——————.
>Making wines like those you buy. Second impression.
Andover, Amateur Winemaker, 1964. 80p. Illus.

Acton, B.
>See Duncan, Peter and Acton, Bryan.
Progressive winemaking.

Acton, Miss Eliza. (Revised by Hale, Mrs. S.J.)
>Modern cookery in all its branches.
Philadelphia, John E. Potter and Co., n d (entered in
1860). 418p.

Adair, Adele
>Kitchenette cookery. London, Denis Archer, 1932.
143p.

Adair, Arthur H., joint author
>See Toye, Nina. Drinks--long and short.

——————.
>See Toye, Nina and Adair, A.H. Petits and grand
verres choix des meilleurs cocktails

Adam (Brother)
>See Brother Adam. Mead.

Adams, Georgian
>See Chatfield, Charlotte and Adams, Georgian.
Proximate composition of American Food Materials

Adams, Leon D.
>The commonsense book of drinking. New York, David
McKay Co., Inc., 1960. 210p. Dictionary of terms.

——————.
>The commonsense book of wine. New York, David
McKay Co., Inc., c1958. 178p.

Adcock, Garnet I.
>See Jusfrute, Ltd. Aerated water manufacturers' hand
book. Introduction by G.I. Adcock.

——————.
>Brewing for cordial makers. Another Jusfrute Bottler's
Aid. Gosford, NSW, Australia. Published by Jusfrute,
Ltd., (1937). 60p. Illus.

—————————.
Cordial Makers' Syrups. Another Jusfrute Bottler's
Aid. Gosford, NSW, Australia, n d 87p.

—————————.
The Jusfrute Book. A text book of aerated water
manufacture. Gosford, NSW, Australia. Published by
Jusfrute Co., 1937. 166p. Illus. 2nd edition, 1957.
166p. Illus.

—————————.
Pasteurization for cordial makers. Another Jusfrute
Bottler's Aid. Gosford, NSW, Australia. Published
by Jusfrute Co., n d 20p. Illus..

—————————.
Preservatising beverages--simply explained. Gosford,
NSW, Australia. Jusfrute, LTD., n d 8p.
Addison, Joseph
    The trial of the wine-brewers. An essay. San
    Francisco. Printed by John Henry Nash, 1930. 18p.
Addison, William
    English Spas. London, B.T. Batsford, Ltd., 1957.
    152p. Illus.
Ade, George
    The old-time saloon; not wet--not dry, just history.
    New York, Long, R. and Smith, R.R., c1931. 174p.
    Illus.
Adkins, T.F.
    Nautical Cookery Book (The). 4th edition. Glasgow,
    James Brown and Son, 1907. 163p.
Adkins, William S.
    The National Soda Fountain Guide. St. Louis. National
    Druggist, 1913. 192p.
Adler, H.R.
    Adler's hand book for the retail liquor dealer. Chicago.
    H.R. Adler. 112p. Illus.   LC
Adlum, John
    A memoir on the cultivation of the vine in America,
    and the best mode of making wine. 2nd edition . . .
    Washington. Printed for the author by W. Greer, 1828.
    179p. Vocabulary.

—————————.
On making wine. Georgetown, D.C., James C. Dunn,
printer, 1826. 36p.
                                (Notre Dame University)

23

"Adrian"
    Cocktail fashions of 1936.   London, Simpkin Marshall,
    1936.   (Heath- Good drinks)
Agg- Gardner, J. T.
    Compulsory Temperance, London, Chapman and Hall
    Ltd. , 1884.   15p.
Agricultural Chemists, Association of
    Methods of analysis.   Official and tentative of the
    Association of Agricultural Chemists.   Washington,
    Revised to November 1, 1919.   417p.   1930, 593p.
    1935, 710p.
Aiken, George D.
    Pioneering with fruits and berries.   New York,
    Stephen Daye Press, 1936.   94p.   Illus- photos.
                                (Brady Library- Fresno State College)
Ainsworth- Davis, James Richard
    Cooking through the centuries.   New York, E. P.
    Dutton and Co. , 1931.   242p.   Illus.   Short list of
    books.   LC
Airkem, Inc.
    Odors and sense of smell.   A bibliography 320 B. C.
    to 1947.   New York, 1952.   342p.   Bibliography Crerar
Akenhead, D.
    Vitacultural research, London, Empire Marketing
    Board Bulletin, no. 11, 1928.   70p.   Bibliography
                                                                    GBPOL

Alanne, Eero
    Observations on the development and structure of
    English wine- growing terminology.   Published in
    Memoires de la Societe Neophilologique de Helsinki
    XX, 1959.   55p.
Alcott, William Andrus
    Tea and coffee . . . Boston, New York, G. W. Light,
    1839.   174p.   Illus- drawings.

_____.
    Tea and coffee: their physical, intellectual and moral
    effects on the human system.   With notes and additions
    by Nelson Sizer.   New York, Fowler and Wells, 1884.
    118p.
Alderton, Geo. E.
    Treatise and handbook of Orange- Culture in Auckland,
    New Zealand.   Wellington, Published by authority of
    the government, 1884.   76p.
Aldin, Cecil
    Old inns.   London, William Heinemann Ltd. , 1930.
    149p.   Illus.

24

Alexander, Helen Cadbury
    Richard Cadbury of Birmingham.   London, Hodder and
    Stoughton, 1906.   448p.   Illus.
Alexander, Jerome
    Colloid chemistry.   2nd edition.   London, Chapman and
    Hall, 1925.   208p.   Illus.   Bibliography- Glossary.
Alexander, Russell George
    Plain plantain.   Country wines, dishes, from a 17th
    century household manuscript receipt book.   Ditchling,
    Sussex, S. Dominic's Press, n d 98p.
Alexis of Piedmant (pseud. for G. Ruscelli)
    Secrets of Alexis.   London, 1559.   BM
Allardt, Erik - Touko Markkanen - Martti Takala
    Drinking and drinkers.   Alcohol research in the
    northern countries.   Helsinki, The Finnish Foundation
    for alcohol studies, 1957.   162p.   References.
Allen, Benjamin
    Natural history of chalybeat and purging waters of
    England.   London, S. Smith and B. Walford, 1699.
    185p.   BM

_____.
    Natural history of mineral waters of Great Britain.
    London, published by author, 1711.   104p.   BM
Allen, Frank W.
    Apple growing in California.   Circ. 178 California
    Agricultural Extension Service Berkeley.   Published by
    College of Agriculture, University of California, 1951.
    paged by sections total 75p.   Illus.
Allen, Herbert Warner
    Claret.   London, T. Fisher Unwin, 1924.   44p.   map.

_____.
    Mr. Clerihew-Wine merchant.   London, Methuen and
    Co., 1933.   277p.

_____.
    A contemplation of wine.   London, Michael Joseph,
    1951.   232p.

_____.
    Gentlemen, I give you--wine!   London, Faber and Faber,
    1930.   38p.

_____.
    Good wine from Portugal.   London, Sylvan Press, 1957.
    59p.   Illus.

A history of wine; great vintage wines from the Homeric age to the present day. New York, Horizon Press, 1962. 307p. Illus.

Natural red wines; with report on the red wines of America, by Frank Schoonmaker. London, Constable, 1951. 320p. Glossary of wine terms.

Number three Saint James's Street; a history of Berry's, the wine merchants. London, Chatto and Windus, 1950. 269p. Illus.

The romance of wine. New York, E. P. Dutton, 1932. 264p. Illus.

Rum. The Englishman's spirit. Criterion Miscellany no. 34. London, Faber and Faber, 1931. 32p.

. . . Sherry, with an appendix on shippers and a folding map. London, Constable and Co., Ltd., 1933. 117p.

Sherry and port. London, Constable, 1952. 215p.

See Friends of Wine (The) publisher. Summer wine coolers. London n d contains "On mixing of wine cups" by Allen, H. Warner.

Through the wine-glass . . . . London, Michael Joseph, 1954. 244p.

White wines and cognac. London, Constable, 1952. 278p.

The wines of France. London, Unwin, 1924. 261p.

The wines of Portugal. New York, McGraw-Hill Book Company. Produced by George Rainbird Ltd., London, 1963. 192p. Illus.

Allen, Mrs. Ida Cogswell (Bailey)
Ida Bailey Allen's wines and spirits cook book; 456 recipes, 81 menus, complete index. New York, Simon and Schuster, 1934. 366p.

———— Mrs. Allen's Book of Sugar Substitutes.
Boston, Small, Maynard and Company, 1918. 92p.

———— When you entertain. What to do and how. Atlanta,
The Coca-Cola Co., 1932. 124p. Illus.

Allen J. Fiske
The culture of the grape. Boston, Button and Went-
worth printers, 1847. 55p. Illus.

———— A practical treatise on the culture and treatment of
the grape vine. Third edition. New York, C.M.
Saxton, 1855. 330p. Illus. Copy 1957.

Allen, Paul W.
Industrial fermentations. New York. The Chemical
Catalog Company, 1926. 424p.

Allen, Percy
Burgundy: The splendid Duchy. London, Frances
Griffiths, 1912. 302p. Illus.

Allen, R.L. MD
A historical, chemical and theurapeutical analysis of
the principal mineral fountains at Saratoga Springs.
Third edition rev. Saratoga Springs, B. Huling, 1853.
72p.

Allen, W.J.
Citrus Culture. Farmers' Bulletin no. 90, December
1914. Sydney, Department of Agriculture, New South
Wales, 1915. 96p. Illus.

Allport, Noel L.
The chemistry and pharmacy of vegetable drugs.
London, George Newnes Limited, 1943. 264p. Illus.

D'Alonzo, C. Anthony
The drinking problem, and its control. Houston,
Texas, Gulf Publishing Co., 1959. 130p.

Alpers, William C. and Kennedy, Ezra, J.
The Era Formulary, New York, D.O. Haynes and
Co., 1914. 521p. 1928. 521p.

Althaus, Julius
Spas of Europe, London, Trubner and Co., 1862.
494p.   (Riley Memorial)

Altshul, I.D.
Drinks as they were made before prohibition. Santa
Barbara. Published by author, 1934. 51p.   LC

27

Alwood, Wm B. and Davidson, R.J. and
Moncure, W.A. P.
 The chemical composition of apples and cider.
 Washington, Bureau of Chemistry, Department of
 Agriculture, Bulletin no. 88, 1904. 46p.
Alwood, William Bradford
 . . . A study of cider making in France, Germany,
 and England with comments and comparisons on
 American work . . . . Washington, Government
 Printing Office, 1903. 114p. Illus. Works of
 Reference.
Amateur, Anne (pseud)
 Home-brewed wines and unfermented beverages for all
 seasons of the year. New York, Scribner, 1921. 28p.
Amateur winemakers National Guild of Judges
 Judging home-made wines, n p (Hertford) Published
 by the Guild, n d., (1964). 28p. Illus.
American Academy Political and Social Science
 Regulation of the liquor traffic. Philadelphia. The
 annals of the American Academy of Political and
 Social Science. Vol. XXXII, no. 3, November 1908.
 471-652 pages.
American Bottlers Carbonated Beverages
 Air in bottled carbonated beverages. Washington,
 1958. 21p.
—————————.
 See Noling, A.W.
 Beverage Flavoring Materials in the bottled carbonated
 beverage industry.
—————————.
 Beverage production and plant operation. Washington.
 Bound volume of training course texts. 21 sections,
 1948 edition. Not paged consecutively.
—————————.
 Bibliography. A.B.C.B. Research Fellowship and
 Technical Publications. Washington, n d to 1945. 7p.
 1951. 9p.
—————————.
 Bottle washing (information bulletin concerning)
 Washington, 1950. Various authors. Paged by section.
—————————.
 See Buchanan, J.H. and Levine, Max
 Bottle washing and its control in the carbonated
 beverage industry.

‾‾‾‾‾‾ Bottling plant maintenance. Washington, 1939.
Various authors, paged by sections.

‾‾‾‾‾‾ Bottling plant sanitation. Washington, 1955, Various
authors, paged by sections.

‾‾‾‾‾‾ Cost survey and suggested operating budgets for the
carbonated beverage industry. A.B.C.B. Educational
Bulletin no. 2 (revised edition) Washington. Prepared
by Arthur E. Low and Co., Chicago, July 1932. 34p.

‾‾‾‾‾‾ Customer checking of beverage bottles - some preliminary ideas. Washington, 1961. 7p.

‾‾‾‾‾‾ The development of improved beverage cases.
Washington, 1961. 10p. Illus.

‾‾‾‾‾‾ See Priestley, Joseph
Directions for impregnating water with fixed air.
Originally London, Johnson, J., 1772.

‾‾‾‾‾‾ A discussion of the one trip container.
Washington, 1961. 24p.

‾‾‾‾‾‾ Dissolving caustic before addition to bottle washer
(Schemes for). Washington, (by Korab, Harry E.),
1950. 7p. Illus. drawings.

‾‾‾‾‾‾ Facts about soft drinks. A.B.C.B. Public Information
Series. Washington, n d c1954, unpaged.

‾‾‾‾‾‾ Food and nutritional values of bottled carbonated
beverages. Washington, reprinted 1950. 7p.

‾‾‾‾‾‾ Growth and economic status of the bottled soft drink
industry. A statistical summary. Washington, 1957.
11p.

‾‾‾‾‾‾ Health and liquids. Washington, 1943. 7p.
Bibliography.

‾‾‾‾‾‾ See Riley, John J.
A history of the American soft drink industry; bottled
carbonated beverages, 1807-1957.

_____ .
How to protect stainless steel beverage processing
equipment from corrosion. Washington, 1957. 9p.

_____ .
Improving Maintenance operations. Washington, 1953.
6p.

_____ .
Industrial Relations Guide. Washington, n d, ca1959.
32p.

_____ .
Insect control in the beverage plant. Washington, 1960.
6p.

_____ .
Leasing vs owning of trucks and equipment. Washington,
1959. 12p.

_____ .
List of references to authoritative writings on the
carbonated beverage industry. Compiled by Home
Economics Department, Washington, 1929 edition.
12p. typed copy.

_____ .
See Bolte, Arthur, H. and Low, Arthur E.
Management and cost control in the carbonated coverage
industry.

_____ .
Management for profit in the bottled soft drink industry.
Washington, 1958-1959.
Report No. 1. Creating a strong organization.
c1958. 31p.
Report No. 2. Running an efficient plant.
c1959. 28p.
Report No. 3. Building up sales
c1959. 44p.
Report No. 4. Controling costs.
c1959. 28p.
Report No. 5. Planning for growth.
c1959. 32p.

_____ .
Manual for profit planning for the bottled carbonated
beverage industry. Washington, prepared by Stevenson,
Jordan and Harrison, Inc., N.Y., 1950. 50p.

_____ .
See Medbury, Henry E. Editor.
The manufacture of bottled carbonated beverages.

30

_____. Memorandum on sweetening agents for carbonated beverages. Washington, n d ca1940 (by Levine, Max.) 9p. References on sugar.

_____. See Korab, Harry E. Microbiological aspects of one-trip glass bottles as used by the carbonated beverage industry.

_____. Modern water treatment. Washington, 1951. Various authors, paged by section.

_____. See Riley, John J. Organization in the soft drink industry. A history of the American Bottlers of Carbonated Beverages.

_____. Petition for exemption of bottled carbonated (non-alcoholic) beverages from ingredient labeling under the F.F.D. & C. Act of 1938, Washington, July 28, 1939, before Secretary of Agriculture. 28p.

_____. Plant Operation Manual. A series of discussions. Washington, 1939 and 1940, paged by sections.

_____. Sanitary Code. extra part to ABCB Training Course. Washington, c1945. 16p.

_____. See Riley, John J. Scientific and medical origin of carbonated waters.

_____. Shop notes for soft drink bottling plant operators. Washington, c1946. 148p.

_____. See Toulouse, J.H. and Levine, Max. Suggestions for maintaining quality and uniformity of bottled carbonated beverages.

_____. See Levine, Max and Toulouse, J.H. Suggestions on elimination of spoilage in the carbonated beverage industry.

_____. Sunlight and soft drinks. Washington, 1956. 7p.

_____ .
Technical problems of the bottled carbonated beverage
manufacture. Washington.
1947 edition 59p.
1950 edition 75p.
1954 edition 89p.
1959 edition 111p.

_____ .
Training Course in beverage production and plant
operation. Washington, ca1946-1948.
1. Chemistry, physics and micro-organisms. 33p.
2. Product uniformity and spoilage prevention. 31p.
3. Sanitary maintenance. 11p.
4. Beverage colors. 22p.
5. Acidulants and preservatives. 15p.
6. Beverage flavoring materials. 29p.
7. Sweetening agents. 31p.
8. Syrups and syrup making. 27p.
9. The syrup room. 20p.
10. Water for beverage bottling. 20p.
11. Outline of water treating methods. 16p.
12. Theory of refrigeration and water cooling. 31p.
13. Carbonic gas and carbonation. 15p.
14. Beverage carbonating equipment. 13p.
15. Beverage manufacturing equipment. 25p.
16. Bottles and crowns. 20p.
17. Bottle washing and its control. 33p.
18. Bottle washing equipment. 17p.
19. Cost determination. 20p.
20. Cost controls in the beverage plant. 17p.
21. The bottling plant for the bottled carbonated
    beverage industry. 20p.

_____ .
Truck Operational data. Washington, 1959. unpaged
(52).

_____ .
See Buchanan, J.H. and Levine, Max. The testing
of washing solutions.

_____ .
Unflavored carbonated and mineralized waters.
Washington, 1939. Various authors. paged by
sections.

_____ .
The use of invert syrup. Washington, 1947, (by
Medbury, Henry E.) 10p. List of literature cited.

———
See McClellan, Walter S.
The utilization of ingested carbon dioxide, and
bibliography: physiological values of carbon dioxide and
carbonation of liquids.

———
See Millis Advertising Company.
What is wrong with the bottled carbonated beverage
industry.
American Bottlers' Protective Ass'n.
Souvenir volume, being an account of The Tenth Annual
Convention held in Baltimore, October 11-14, 1898.
Published in Baltimore 1899. The Crown Cork and
Seal Company, 1899. 99p. plus. Illus.
American Brewing Academy, Chicago
Tenth anniversary reunion, alumni and former students,
American brewing academy of Chicago, from the
thirtieth day of September to the third day of October,
nineteen hundred and one, at Chicago, Illinois. Chicago
Blakely printing company, 1901. 248p. Illus.
American Burtonizing Co.
Brewing water; its defects and their remedy. New York,
printed by Peck and Durham, 1909. 46p.   LC
American Can Company
Canned Food Manual. Prepared for U.S. Army. New
York, published by American Can Co., 1942. 104p.
Illus.

———
The Canned food reference manual. New York, 1939.
242p. Bibliography. 1943. 552p. Illus.

———
A history of packaged beer and its market in the United
States. New York, 1969. 31p. Illus--drawings.

———
Manual for institutional canning. Research Division.
Book no. 170, Maywood, Illinois, 1946. 152p.
multigraphed.

———
Summer patterns of American beer consumption 1961.
New York, c1962. 36p. Illus.

———
Technical aspects of cans and the canning of carbonated
beverages. n p n d (1955). 8p.
American Coffee Growers Ass'n
Coffee growing by proxy. New York, 1895. 30p.
Illus.   LC

American Food Journal Institute
   Bibliography of nutritive values of chocolate and cocoa.
   n p (Prepared for Hershey Chocolate Co.) n d (1925).
   64p.   Bibliography   LC
American Honey Institute
   Old Favorite Honey Recipes.   Madison, Wisc.
   Published by American Honey Institute.   c1945.   52p.
American Medical Ass'n
   Accepted foods and their nutritional significance.
   Description of products accepted by AMA.   Chicago,
   Council of Foods AMA, 1939.   492p.
American Perfumer and Aromatics
   First documentary edition.   (New York).   Moore
   Publishing Company, 1960.   285p.   Illus.
American Pharmaceutical Association of
unofficial preparations.
   ✓The National Formulary.   n p   Published by the
   Association, 1888.   176p.   3rd edition, 1906.   267p.
   5th edition, 1926.   546p.
American Pharmaceutical Ass'n.
   Pharmaceutical Recipe Book.   n p Published by The
   American Pharmaceutical Ass'n.   1929.   454p.
American School of Classical Studies at Athens
   Amphoras and the ancient wine trade.   Princeton,
   N.J., 1961.   40p.   Illus-photos.
American Society of Brewing Chemists
   Methods of analysis.   Madison, Wisc., Various
   dates.

_____.
   Official and tentative methods of analysis of the
   society.   Chicago.   Various dates.   (Various locations).
American Soda Fountain Co.
   American dispensers book.   (Cover title How to make
   a soda fountain pay.)   Boston, 1903.   176p.   Illus-
   photos.
American Soda Fountain Company
   American Soda Book of receipts and suggestions.
   Boston.   Published by the company.   n d ca1907.
   263p.   Illus.

_____.
   Book of instructions and sundry catalogue.   Philadelphia,
   n d ca1901.   289p.   Illus-photos, engravings.

_____.
   Catalog no. 96.   n p (Boston), n d 94p.   POSL

34

American Soft Drink Journal
Bottler's Reference and data issue. Atlanta, 24th
edition, March 15, 1962. 202p. Illus.
American Spice Ass'n
See Lane, Betty
A.B.C. of spice cookery (The).
American Spice Trade Ass'n.
A history of spices. New York, 1960. 16p.
Suggested reading on spices

_____.
How to use spices. New York, 1958. 48p. Illus.

_____.
A manual of spices. New York, n d 15p.

_____.
Spices; what they are--where they come from. New
York, 1959. 16p. Illus.

_____.
A treasury of spices. Edited by Lester W. Jones.
New York, 1956. 224p. Illus-photos.
American Sugar Refining Co.
Annual Report. 1930; 1931; 1932; 1933; 1935.
New York. Pages various.
Amerine, Maynard Andrew
A check list of books and pamphlets on grapes and wine
and related subjects, 1938-1948, by Maynard A. Amerine
and Louise B. Wheeler. Berkeley. University of
California Press, 1951. 240p. Bibliography. Also
1960-1968 (Amerine alone). Davis. 65p.

_____.
See Joslyn, M.A. and Amerine, M. A.
Commercial production of brandies.

_____.
Joslyn, Maynard Alexander, . . . Commercial
production of dessert wines.

_____.
. . . Commercial production of table wine. M.A.
Amerine and M.A. Joslyn. . . . Berkeley, University
of California, 1939. 143p. Selected references.

_____.
See Joslyn, Maynard Alexander & M.A. Amerine
Dessert, appetizer and related flavored wines. The
technology of their production.

_____.
See Ough, C.S. and M.A. Amerine
Effects of temperature on wine making.

Amerine, Maynard A. and A. J. Winkler
Grape varieties for wine production.   Circular 356
Berkeley, 1943.   15p.   WI

———.
Laboratory procedures for enology.   Davis,
California.   Various dates.   various pagination.   NYPL
Amerine, Maynard A. and E. B. Roessler
Sensory evaluation of wines.   San Francisco, Wine
Institute, 1965.   26p.   Multigraphed.   Selected
References

———.
A short check list of books and pamphlets in English
on grapes, wines and related subjects 1949-1959, with
the assistance of the Research Librarians of the
University Library, Davis, San Francisco, 1959.   61p.
Photocopy.
Amerine, Maynard Andrew and Maynard Alexander Joslyn
Table wines; the technology of their production in
California.   Berkeley, University of California Press,
1951.   397p.   Illus.   Literature cited.
Amerine, Maynard Andrew and W. V. Cruess
Technology of wine making.   Westport, Conn.   The
Avi Publishing Co., 1960.   709p.   Illus. Bibliography.
Amerine, Maynard Andrew
Wine.   Reprinted from Scientific-American for August
1964.   San Francisco, W. H. Freeman and Co., 1964.
12p.
Amerine, Maynard Andrew and V. L. Singleton
Wine, an introduction for Americans.   Berkeley,
and Los Angeles.   University of California Press,
1965.   355p.   Illus. Supplementary reading.
Amerine, Maynard A. and George L. Marsh
Wine making at home.   San Francisco.   Wine
Publications, 1962.   31p.   Illus.   References.
Ames, Richard
Search after claret.   Various editions.   A poem in
4 books.   London, 1691.   18p.   BM
Amoy Canning Co.
The story of ginger.   Hongkong, 1950.   12p.   Illus.
Amsdon, Edward
Complete system of bookkeeping for brewers, etc.
London, Published by author.   1906.   50p.   BM

———.
Guide to brewer's bookkeeping.   London, Published by
author, 1881.   113p.   BM

36

—————·
Mineral water manufacturers' guide to bookkeeping,
Published by author. London, 1882.
25p.   BM
Amsinck, George S.
Practical brewings, London, Published by author, 1868.
160p.   BM

—————·
Statistical returns of brewers, victuallers, beersellers,
etc., London, Published by author, 1873.   7p.   BM

—————·
Statistics relating to the brewing trade.   London,
Published by author, 1865.   21p.   BM
Anderson, Dwight
The other side of the bottle.   New York, A. A. Wyn,
Inc., 1950.   258p.
Anderson, Frederick
Handbook of modern cocktails.   Stamford, Conn., J. O.
Dahl, 1934.   48p.   LC

—————·
Modern cocktail manual of 168 drinks.   Stamford,
Conn.   The Dahls, n d ca1935.   64p.
Anderson, Graham
Jottings on coffee-its culture in Mysore.   Bangalore,
Caxton Press, 1879.   144p.   NYPL
Anderson, Josephine
See Isel, Harry and Josephine Anderson.   Blending
at its best.   LC
Anderson, Oscar E. Jr.
The health of a nation.   Harvey W. Wiley and the fight
for pure food.   Chicago.   Published for the University
of Cincinnati by University of Chicago Press, 1958.
333p.   Notes.
Anderson, Russell
One hundred famous cocktails; the romance of wines and
liquors, etc.   New York, Kenilworth Press, 1934.   46p.
Illus.   LC
Andrae, E. H.
Guide to the cultivation of the grape vine in Texas
and instructions for wine-making.   Dallas, 1890.
                            Hedrick-Grapes of New York
Andre, G. G.
Spon's encyclopedia of industrial arts, manufactures,
raw commercial products.   London, E. and F. Spon,
1882.   2142p.   (2 vol.)   (Crerar)

Andrea, A. Louise
  Home bottling, drying and preserving.   London, C.
  Arthur Pearson, Ltd., 1920.   124p.

————.
  Home canning, drying and preserving.   Garden City,
  Doubleday, Page, 1918.   150p.
Andreae, Percy
  The prohibition movement, in its broader bearings
  upon our social, commercial and religious liberties.
  Chicago, Felix Mendelsohn, 1915.   421p.
Andree, John the Elder
  Account of the Tilbury water.   London, M. Jenour,
  1737.   38p.   various editions.   BM
Andrup, Ernst
  Nogle Bidrag Til Pasteuriseringens historie.   (The
  history of pasteurization).   In Danish Saertryk
  Brygmesteren NR, 1954.   With English translation
  printed in Brewers' Guardian, 1955.   103p.   Illus.
Andrews, W.
  Over the tea cups,   Hull, 1700.   Ukers-All about tea
Angostura Bitters, Ltd.
  For home use.   4th edition, Port-of-Spain, Trinidad,
  B.W.I., n d ca1932.   45p.   Illus--drawings.
  10th edition, 1946.   46p.   Illus--drawings.

————.
  One hundred prize winning West Indian recipes.
  Published by the company.   n p (Trinidad), n d.
  76p.
Angostura Wuppermann Corp.
  Angostura.   Recipe book.   Norwalk, Conn., n d
  ca1926.   48p.

————.
  The Angostura Cook Book.   New York, 1961.
  48p.   Illus.

————.
  Angostura recipes.   New York, 1934.   38p.   Illus.

————.
  Professional mixing guide.   New York
  Various editions and dates.
Anheuser-Busch, Inc.
  Hops . Rice . Malt.   St. Louis, c1965.   24p.   Illus-
  drawings in color.   Historical.

————.
  How to handle and serve bottled and draught beers
  St. Louis, 1942.   40p.   Illus.   LC

———— .
See Krebs, Roland
Making friends is our business. 100 years of
Anheuser-Busch.

———— .
Men, materials and equipment. St. Louis, 1942.
40p. Illus.   LC

———— .
Proper handling of Anheuser-Busch draught. St.
Louis, n d. 12p. photocopy.

———— .
Who has not heard of Budweiser beer?
St. Louis, 1909. 10p. Illus.
Anstie, Francis E.
On the uses of wines in health and disease. New
York, J. S. Redfield, publisher, 1870. 84p.

———— .
Stimulants and narcotics, their mutual relations with
special researches on the action of alcohol, aether and
chloroform in the vital organisms. Philadelphia.
Lindsay and Blakiston, 1865. 414p.
Anthony, Daniel
The guaging inspector and measurers assistant.
Providence, printed by Muller and Hutchins, 1817.
76p.   (Duke Univ.)
Anthony, Norman and O. Soglow
The drunk's blue book. Revised edition. New York,
Frederick A. Stokes, 1939-1940. 88p. plus 24 Illus.
1933, same.
Anthony, Norman
Here's how! New and rev. ed. By Judge, jr.,
[pseud.] New York, The John Day Company, (1927).
63p. Illus.

———— .
Here's how again! by Judge, jr. [pseud.] New York,
The John Day Company, (1929). 63p. Illus.

———— .
See Judge, Jr.
Noble experiments. The third volume in the famous
Here's How! series.
Antrobus, H. A.
History of Assam Company. Edinburgh, Constable,
1858. 501p.   LC
Applegreen, John
Applegreen's barkeeper's guide; or how to mix drinks.
Chicago, The Hotel Monthly, 1899. 56p. Illus.   LC

Appert, M.
The art of preserving of all kinds of animal and
vegetable sunstances for several years. London,
Black, Parry and Kingsbury, 1812. Reproduced as
Volume I from Mallinkrodt Collection of Food
Classics. St. Louis, Mo. n d. 164p.
Applegreen, John
Applegreen's Bar Book or how to mix drinks. Third
edition. Hotel Monthly, Chicago, 1909. 89p.
Appleton, John Howard
Beginners' handbook of chemistry. New York,
Chautauqua Press, 1888. 256p.
Appleyard, Alex
About home-made wines. London, Thorsons Publishers
Ltd., 1966, 61p.
_____.
Make your own wine. London, Athene, 1953? 61p.
London, Leslie J. Speight, n d same
d'Appligny, Le Pileur
Instructions sur l'art de faire la biere. Paris. Chez
Serviere, 1783. Volume contains Parmentier - Methode
conserver les grains, etc. 1784. In French.
Instructions, 255p. Methode, 100p.
Arakelian, K. Inc.
Correct service of Madera wines and brandies. Madera,
California, n d. unpaged (24), Illus.
Arbuthnot, John, MD
An essay concerning the nature of aliments and the
choice of them, according to the different constitutions
of human bodies, etc. The fourth edition to which are
added practical rules of diet. London, H. & R.
Tonson, 1756. 365p.
Arctander, Steffen
Perfume and flavor chemicals. (Aroma Chemicals).
Montclair, N.J., Published by author, 1969. 2 vol.
unpaged. (Chemicals numbered). Literature cited.
_____.
Perfume and natural flavoring materials. Elizabeth,
N.J., Published by author, 1960. 736p. Illus-photos.
Bibliography.
Arechabala, Jose S A
On its 75th anniversary, 1878-1953. Havana, 1954.
unpaged (76), Illus.
Armitage, George T.
Hawaiian hospitality.   (CBI 1949-1952)

40

Armstrong, Charles S.
    Tea culture in Ceylon.   Colombo, A.M. and J.
    Ferguson, 1887. 10p.   BM
Armstrong, J. and Virgil I. Partch
    VIP's new bar guide. n p n d, ca1962.
                                 (Subject guide)
Armstrong, Rev. Lebbeus
    The temperance reformation, its history, etc., New
    York, Fowler and Wells, 1853. 408p.
Arnold of Villanova
    The earliest printed book on wine. (Translated by
    Henry E. Sigerist), New York, Schuman's, 1943.
    Facsimile of original dated 1478. 44p. plus facsimile.
Arnold, Edwin Lester Linden
    Coffee: its cultivation and profit. London, Whittingham,
    1886. 270p. Illus.

––––––––.
    Coffee planting in Southern India. London, Sampson
    Low and Co., 1881. 2 vol.   BM
Arnold, John Paul
    History of brewing in the United States. Chicago.
    Published on pages 69-150 of American Brewing
    Academy - Tenth Anniversary Reunion, 1901. 81p.

––––––––.
    History of the brewing industry and brewing science
    in America, prepared as part of a memorial to the
    pioneers of American brewing science, Dr. John E.
    Siebel and Anton Schwarz; begun by the late John P.
    Arnold, completed by Frank Penman. Chicago, 1933.
    259p. List of writings of Dr. Siebel; Bibliography of
    writings of Anton Schwarz.

––––––––.
    Home-made beverages and vinegars, temperance and
    light drinks. Theoretical hints and practical methods
    with over 170 formulas. . . . Chicago, North Chicago
    Printing Co., 1918. 72p.

––––––––.
    Origin and history of beer and brewing; from prehis-
    toric times to the beginning of brewing science and tech-
    nology; a critical essay. Chicago, Alumni Ass'n of
    the Wahl-Henius Institute of Fermentology, 1911.
    411p. Illus.
Arroyo, Rafael
    Studies on rum. Research Bulletin no. 5. University
    of Puerto Rico. Agricultural Experiment Sta. Rio
    Piedras, P.R., 1945. 272p. Literature cited.

Arthur, Stanley Clisby
Famous New Orleans drinks and how to mix 'em.
Nouvelle Orleans, Harmanson, 1937. 96p. Illus.
1938. Third printing.
Arthur, T. S.
The bar-rooms at Brantly, or the great hotel specula-
tion. Philadelphia, The John C. Winston Co., entered
1877. 437p.

_____.
Grappling with the Monster or the curse and cure of
strong drink. New York, John W. Lovell and Co.,
entered 1877. 320p.

_____.
Six nights with the Washingtonians; and other temperance
tales. Philadelphia, T. B. Peterson and Bros., entered
1871. 536p.

_____.
Ten Nights in a bar-room - and what I saw there. n p
Winston, entered 1854. 353p.
Asbury, Herbert
See Thomas, Jerry
The Bon-Vivant's Companion: or, How to mix drinks.
Ash, Douglas
How to identify English drinking glasses and decanters,
1680-1830. London, G. Bell and Sons Ltd., 1962.
200p. Illus.

_____.
How to identify English silver drinking vessels 600-
1830. London, G. Bell and Sons Ltd., 1964. 159p.
Illus.
Ash, John
Experiments and observations to investigate by chemical
analysis the medical properties on mineral waters of Spa
and Aix-la-Chapelle, in Germany, etc., London, J.
Robson and J. Clarke, 1788. 400p.   BM
Ash, O. M.
Ceylon tea from the bush to the teapot. Colombo,
1930.   (Ukers-All about tea)
Ashton and Green, Ltd.
On the use of slate in breweries. London, 1891. 24p.
Askinson, George William
Perfumes and their preparation. Containing complete
directions for making handkerchief perfumes, smelling-
salts . . . cosmetics, hair dyes, and other toilet
articles . . . New York, N. W. Henley and Co., 1907.
812p. Illus-engravings. 5th edition, 1922. 392p.
Illus-engravings.

Association of American Railroads
    Beverages. Report of committee. Washington, D.C.
    1946. 184p. Illus.   LC

——————.
    Report on beverages. Washington, 1947. 54p.   LC
Association of Teachers of Domestic Subjects
    A.T.D.S. Cookery Book (The). London, 1940-1941.
    117p.
Atchison, Topeka and Santa Fe Railway Company
    Wine of California; the stirring story of a great
    American industry. Chicago, printed by the Regen-
    steiner Corp., 1937. 35p. Illus.
Atherton, Emmet (pseud)
    Here's how. Seattle, Pacific Publications, 1933. 108p.
Atiyeh, Wadeeha
    Scheherazade Cooks! New York, Gramercy Publishing
    Co., 1960. 189p.
Atkins, O.A.
    See Standard Bottling and Extract Co. O.A. Atkins,
    President. The Standard Soda Water Flavors.
Atkinson, Ame and Grace Holroyd.
    Practical cookery. 6th edition. Leeds, Nutt and Co.,
    Ltd., n d 222p. 15th edition, n d (214p.)
Atkinson, F.E. and Dorothy Britton and A.W. Moyls
    Fruit juices, cider and wines. Summerland, C.B.
    Canada. S P 24 Research Branch, Canada, Dept.
    of Agriculture, 1961. 42p. Illus.
Atkinson, John
    The humour of drinking, by John Aye (pseud) . . .
    London, Universal Publication, Ltd., 1934. 282p.

——————.
    Wine wisdom, a simple and concise guide on what to
    buy and how to serve, by John Aye (pseud) . . .
    London, Universal Publications, Ltd., 1934. 114p.
    Glossary.
Atkinson, R.W.
    Chemistry of saki-brewing. Tokyo. Memo of
    Science Dept. of Tokyo, University no. 6., 1881.
    73p.   NYPL
(Atkyns, Arabella)
    The Family Magazine. London, J. Osborn, 1747.
    305p. 3rd edition.
Attfield, John
    Water and water supplies and unfermented beverages.
    London, International Health Exhibition Handbook. W.
    Clowes and Son, 1884. 113p.   NYPL

Atwater, W.
   Physiological aspects of the liquor problem; investiga-
   tions made and under the direction of W.O. Atwater,
   John S. Billings, H.P. Bowditch, R.H. Chittenden and
   W.H. Welch. Volume I. Boston and New York,
   Houghton Mifflin, 1903. 396p.

Auchter, E.C. and H.B. Knapp
   Orchard and small fruit culture. 3rd edition. New
   York. John Wiley and Sons, Inc., 1937. 627p.
   Illus-photos.

Aucken, I.
   Dictionary of scientific cocktail making. London,
   Published by author, 1964. 52p.

Aufhammer, G., Pierre Bergal, F.R. Horne
   Barley varieties - EBC. (European Brewery Conven-
   tion). 2nd edition, Amsterdam, Elsevier Publishing
   Co., 1958. 159p. Illus.

Augenstein, Moritz
   Manual of instructions for brewers and distillers.
   Washington, Printed by Judd and Detwiler, 1872.
   169p.   LC

Ault, R.G. and E.J. Hudson
   Report on the brewing, malting and allied processes.
   A literature survey prepared for the Institute of Brewing.
   London, 1953. 34p. 1955, 28p.

Aurand, L.W.
   See Triebold, Howard O. and Leonard W. Aurand
   Food composition and analysis.

Austin, Alma H.
   The romance of candy. New York, Harper and Bros.,
   1938. 234p.

Austin, Cedric
   The science of wine. London, University of London
   Press, 1968. 216p. Illus--drawings.

Austin, Nichols and Co.
   Wine and liquor handbook . . . Brooklyn, N.Y.,
   1936. 96p. Illus.

Australian Wine Board
   Wine, 1788-1939. Adelaide, 1939. 21p.   (PLOSA)
_____.
   See Norris, Sheila
   Your life is more pleasant with wine.

Axe, Emerson W.
   See MacLaren, Hale
   Be your own guest.

44

Axtell, Frank P.
The standard coffee code. New York, Publisher, 1905.
144p.
Aye, John
Wine wisdom; a simple and concise guide on what to
buy and how to serve. London, Universal Publications,
Ltd., n d 114p.
Aylett, Mary
Country Wines. London, Odhams Press, 1953. 192p.
Illus.

_____.
Encyclopaedia of home-made wines. London Odhams
Press, (1957). 192p.
Aylett, Mary and Olive Ordish
First catch your hare. A history of the recipe makers.
London, Macdonald and Co., Ltd., 1965. 242p. Illus-
plates. References.

B., A.
Some account of the rise and progress and present state
of the brewery. London, J. Robinson, 1757. 21p.
(GBPOL)
B. (E.)
A treatise on the virtues of whisky considered in its
physical and political uses with a word or two concern-
ing brandy and rum. Dublin, 1750. 8p.   LC
B., (J.) Writing master
In praise of tea. A poem. Canterbury, Published
by author, 1736. 11p.   BM
B. (R.)
The perfumers legacy or the companion to the toilet.
(by a retired perfumer). London, Kent and Richards,
1850. 72p.   BM
Baar, Stanley
The beverage distilling industry. Boston, Bellman
Publishing Co., 1947. 47p. Illus. Bibliography   LC
Bacchus
Brewer's Guide for the Hotel, Bar and Restaurant.
Valletta Series. Hints on the manufacture of beer,
wines, spirits and liquors. n p. Printed by St.
Giles Printing Works, Norwich. n d. 185p.

Bacchus and Cordon Bleu
New guide of the hotel, bar, restaurant, butler and chef.
London, 1885. 496p.
Bacci, Andreae
De naturali, vinorum historia de vinis Italiae. Romae,
Nicholai Mutis, anno 1595. (In Italian). 369p.
Bachchan, Harivanshrai
The house of wine. (Madhushala). London, The
Fortune Press, 1950. (Poetry). 46p. Illus.
Bagenall, B.W.
Descendents of the pioneer winemakers of South
Australia, Adelaide Published by author, 1946. 27p.
(Mitchell Library, Sydney)
Bagnall, A. Gordon
Wines of South Africa. An account of their history,
production and nature. Paarl, South Africa, K.W.V.
Paarl, South Africa, 1961. 95p. Illus.
Baildon, Samuel
Tea in Assam, Calcutta, W. Newman and Co., Ltd.,
1877. 65p.   BM

_____ .
The tea industry in India, etc., London, W.H. Allen
and Co., Ltd., 1882. 248p.   BM
Bailey, Alfred
The mixologist . . . a complete and up-to-date guide
for the business establishment and home buffet.
Denver, Published by author, 1934. 130p. Illus.   LC
Bailey, E.H.S. and Herbert S. Bailey
Food Products, their chemistry, and use. 3rd revised.
Philadelphia, P. Blakiston Sons Co., 1928. 563p.

_____ .
The source, chemistry and use of food products.
Philadelphia, Reprinted June 1920. P. Blakeston's Son
and Co. 541p. Illus.
Bailey, L.H.
American grape training. An account of the leading
forms now in use in training the American grapes.
New York. The Rural Publishing Co., 1893. 95p.
Illus.

_____ .
The principles of fruit-growing with applications to
practice. New York, The Macmillan Company, 1926.
432p. Illus.

————— Pruning manual. New York, Macmillan and Co., 1942.
407p. Illus-engravings-drawings.
(Brady library-Fresno State Col.)

————— Sketch of the evolution of our native fruits. New York,
Macmillan, 1898. 472p. Illus-photos-drawings.
Bibliography. (Brady library-Fresno State Col.)
Bailey, N.
Dictionarium Domesticum being an new and compleat
household dictionary. London, C. Hitch and C. Davis,
1736. unpaged.
Bailey, R. Douglas
The Brewer's Analyst. London, Kegan Paul, Trench,
Trubner and Co., Ltd., 1907. 423p. Illus.
Baines, Maud
What to drink. London, G.W. Daniel and Co. First
aids to health no. 25, 1936. 22p. BM
Baird, Dr. Irving
See Cossley-Batt, Dr. Jill and Dr. Irvin Baird.
Elixir of Life.
Baker, Charles Henry, Jr.
The ESQUIRE Culinary Companion. New York, Crown
Publishers, 1959. 320p.

————— The gentlemen' companion. Contents-Vol. 1. being
an exotic cookery book. Col. 2. being an exotic
drinking book. New York, Crown Publishers, 1946.
2 volumes. 1951.

————— The South American gentleman's companion. Contents-
1. Being an exotic cookery book; or, Up and down the
Andes with knife, fork, and spoon. 2. Being an exotic
drinking book; or, Up and down the Andes with jigger,
beaker, and flask. New York, Crown Publishers, 1951.
Baker, E. Alan and Foskett, D.J.
Bibliography of food. Select international bibliography
of nutrition, food and beverage technology and distribu-
tion 1936-56. New York, Academic Press Inc., 1958.
331p.
Baker, George M.
The Temperance drama; etc., series of dramas. Boston,
Lee and Shepard, Entered 1873. pages various.
Baker, Julian L.
The brewing industry. London, Methuen, 1905. 178p.
Illus.

Baker, Walter and Co.
An account of the manufacture and use of cocoa and chocolate in ancient and modern times. Dorchester, Mass. n d ca1876. 24p.

————— .
Baker's Best chocolate recipes. Dorchester, Mass., 1932. 60p. Illus-photos.

————— .
Best chocolate and cocoa recipes. Dorchester, Mass. (General Foods), 1931. 60p. Illus-colored photos.

————— .
See Parloa, Miss.
Chocolate and cocoa recipes.

————— .
Chocolate and cocoa recipes by Miss Parloa. Dorchester, Mass, 1914. Contains also homemade candy recipes by Janet McKenzie Hill. 64p. 1910. 64p. Illus-drawings.

————— .
The Chocolate Plant (Theobroma Cacao) and its products. Dorchester, Mass., 1891. 40p. Illus-photos, drawings.

————— .
See Parloa, Miss Maria
Choice recipes.

————— .
Choice recipes by Miss Maria Parloa. Dorchester, Mass., c1892. 40p. Illus.

————— .
Choice receipts. Dorchester, Mass. c1904. 64p. Illus-photos.

————— .
Choice receipts. (by Miss Parloa), Dorchester, Mass., 1893. 31p. Illus-drawings.

————— .
Cocoa and chocolate. A short history of their production and use. New edition. Dorchester, Mass., 1899. 72p. Illus-photos. 1904, 69p. Illus. 1910, Revised, 69p. Illus. 1917, Revised, 123p. Illus.

————— .
Description of the educational exhibit of cocoa and chocolate. Dorchester, Mass. The Barta Press, 1915. 39p. Illus.   LC

_____ Famous chocolate recipes. Dorchester, Mass. General
Foods Corporation, 1936. 64p. Illus- photos.

_____ Famous chocolate recipes. Selected by Frances Lee
Barton, New York. Consumer Service Dept. General
Foods Corp., 1936. 64p. Illus.

_____ Famous recipes for Baker's chocolate and breakfast
cocoa. Dorchester, Mass., 1928. 64p. Illus.

Bakewell, Frederick G.
Great Facts. A popular history of the most remarkable
inventions during the present century. New York, D.
Appleton and Co., 1860. 307p. Illus.

Balch, A.W. and Co.
Price list of wines and liquors. New York, 1898.
30p.

Bald, Claud
Indian tea: its culture and manufacture. Being a text
book on the cultivation and manufacture of tea. 4th
edition. . . . Calcutta, Thacker, Spink and Co., 1922.
397p. Illus.

Baldwin, Leland D.
Whiskey rebels. Pittsburg. University of Pittsburg
Press, 1939. 326p.   LC

Balfour, Mrs. Clara Lucas
Confessions of a decanter. London, no. publisher,
n d ca1865. 64p.   (Brady Library- Fresno State Col.)

_____ Morning dewdrops or the juvenile abstainer. New and
revised edition. London, United Kingdom Band of Hope
Union, n d, ca1898. 286p. Illus.

Balfour, Jean
Cocktail fare. London and Glasgow, Collins Nutshell
Books, 1963. 128p.

Ball, Samuel
An account of the cultivation and manufacture of tea in
China: derived from personal observation during an
official residence in that country from 1804 to 1826; and
illustrated by the best authorities, Chinese as well as
European: with remarks on the experiments now making
for the introduction of the culture of the tea tree in
other parts of the world. ... London, Longman, Brown,
Green and Longmans, 1848. 382p. Illus.

49

Balzer, Robert Lawrence

Adventures in wine, legends, history, recipes. Los
Angeles, Ward Ritchie Press, 1969. 114p. Illus-
photos.

———————.

California's best wines. Los Angeles, W. Ritchie
Press, 1948. 153p.

———————.

The pleasures of wine. Indianapolis, Bobbs-Merrill
Co., Inc., 1964. 319p. Illus.

Bamber, Edward F and M Kelway

Account of the culture and manufacture of tea in India
from personal observation. Calcutta, T.S. Smith,
1866. 92p. BM

———————.

A textbook on chemistry and agriculture of tea including
the growth and manufacture. Calcutta, Low Publishing
Co., 1893. 258p. (National Agricultural Library)

———————.

Kingsford, Arthur Charles and M. Kelway Bamber.
Report on the tea industries of Java, Formosa and
Japan.

Bancks, Rev. Gerard W.

Mead, and how to make it. Fourth edition. London,
Published by author, n d ca1900. 15p.

Bangs, John Kendrick

Coffee and repartee. New York, Harper and Brothers,
1893. 123p. Illus.

Banning, Kendall

The squire's recipes; being a reprint of an odd little
volume as done by Kendall Banning. Chicago, Brothers
of the Book, 1912. 36p.

Baralt, Blanche Z. de

Cuban Cookery. Havana, Molina and Cia., n d, 168p.

Barber, C.A.

Tropical Agriculture Research in the Empire. London,
His Majesty's Stationary Office, 1927. 77p.

Barber, Edith M.

The Party sampler. New York, Sterling Publishing
Co., 1951. 63p.

Barclay, J.

The arts of brewing and distillation. London, William
Cole, n d ca1810. 70p.

Barclay, Jas. and Co., Ltd.
Corby's presents ten superb recipes. Peoria, Ill.,
n d, 24p. Illus.
Barclay Perkins and Co., Ltd
Anchor Magazine, 150th year commemoration, 1781-
1931, Vol. 11 no. 6., London, 1931. 111p. Illus.

————————.
Three centuries. The story of our ancient brewery.
Southwark, London, Harley Publishing Co., Ltd., 1951.
28p. Illus-photos, drawings.
Bareau, Paul Louis Jean
Cocoa, a crop with a future. Bournville, England,
Cadbury Bros., 1953. 89p. Illus.
Barham, Joseph F.
Considerations on the late act for continuing the
prohibition of corn in the distillery. London, James
Ridgeway, 1810. 72p.   BM
Baring, Francis
The principle of the commutation act established by
facts. I ondon, J. Sewell, 1786. 62p.
Barker, George M.
A tea planter's life in Assam, Calcutta, Thacker,
Spink and Co., 1884. 247p. Illus.
Barker (J.H.) and Co.
One hundred fountain formulas, Brooklyn, 1899. 78p.
Jllus.   LC
Barker, Ralph E.
Small Fruits. New York, Rinehart and Co., 1954.
90p.
Baker, Julian, L.
See Jones, G. Cecil and Baker, Julian L.
Original gravity tables.
Baker, Oliver
Black Jacks and Leather Bottles. Being an account of
some of the leather drinking vessels in England, etc.,
no. 217, autographed. Stratford-on-Avon, 1921. 190p.
Illus.
Barnard, Alfred
The noted breweries of Great Britain and Ireland . . .
London, Sir J. Causton and Sons, 1889-91. 3 vols.
Illus-engravings. H.P. Library has: v. 1, 2.

————————.
The whiskey distilleries of the United Kingdom. London,
Harper's Weekly Gazette, 1887. 457p.   (Davis)

Barnes, Albert
The complete bartender. The art of mixing cocktails,
punches, egg noggs . . . and all plain and fancy drinks
in the most approved style. Philadelphia, Crawford
and Co., 1884. 64p. 1890, 64p.
Barnes, Alison
Successful entertaining for the modern hostess.
London, C. Arthur Pearson, Ltd., 1963. 159p.
Barnett and Foster
Aerated beverages (including cordials, brewed beers,
etc.), and all about them. London, published by
Barnett and Foster, 1910. 117p. Illus.

_____.
Catalogue of mineral water and ice making machinery
and appliances. London, 1912. 136p. Illus.

_____.
General catalogue no. 645. London, 1927. 160p.
Illus-photos.

_____.
Instructions for erecting and working B and F patent
improved aerated water and beer carbonating machinery.
London, 1897. 131p. Illus.

_____.
Recipes for the manufacture of aerated waters, cordial,
etc., London, 1899. 121p.

_____.
Some syrup suggestions. London, n d, ca1948.
1 page.
Baron, Stanley
Brewed in America: a history of beer and ale in the
United States. Boston, Little, Brown and Co., 1962.
424p. Illus. Bibliography.
Barratt, Stuart
See Haszonics, Joseph J. and Barratt, Stuart
Wine Merchandising.
Barrett, E.R.
The truth about intoxicating drinks. London, National
Temperance Publication Depot. n d ca1890. 226p.
Barrett, Otis Warren
The Tropical Crops. A popular treatment of agricult-
ure in tropical regions, etc. New York, The Mac-
millan Co., 1928. 445p. Illus.
Barron, Archibald F.
Vines and vine-culture: being a treatise on the
cultivation of the grape vine; with descriptions of the
principal varieties . . . . London, Pollett, 1883. 240p.
4th edition, London, Barron, 1900. 202p.

Barron, Harry
Distillation of alcohol. Louisville, Published by J.W. Seagram, 1944. 115p.   (Davis)
Barry, Sir Edward
Observations, historical, critical, and medical, on the wines of the ancients. And the analogy between them and modern wines. With general observations on the principles and qualities of water, and in particular on those of Bath . . . London, T. Cadell, 1775. 479p.
Barry, P.
Barry's Fruit Garden. New edition. New York, Orange Judd Co., 1911. 516p.

————.
The fruit garden; a treatise. New York, Charles Scribner, 1851. 398p. Illus.
Bartholomew, Elbert T. and Sinclair, Walton B.
The Lemon Fruit, its composition, physiology and products. Berkeley and Los Angeles, University of California Press, 1951. 163p. Illus. Literature cited.
Bartow, Mary
See Miller, Carey D. ; Bazore, Katharine, Mary Bartow. Fruits of Hawaii, description, nutritive value, and recipes.
Bartrum, Edward
The book of pears and plums. London, and New York, John Lane, 1903. 96p.   LC
Bass, Ratcliff and Gretton Ltd.
Bass. The story of the world's most famous ale. Burton-on-Trent, n d ca1927. 38p. Illus.
Batchelor, Denzil
For what we are about to receive. (Food and drink). London, Herbert Jenkins, 1964. 210p.
                    (Brady Library- Fresno State Col.)

————.
Wines great and small. London, Cassell and Co., 1969. 190p.
Bate, Robert B.
Tables for Bate's patent saccharometer. London, Published by author, 1823. 10p.   BM

————.
Tables of the weight of spirits in the imperial measure, etc. London, 1825. 14p.   (GBPOL)

Bater, Claude H.
   Brewing calculations. London, E. and F. Spon., 1897.
   340p.   BM
Battam, Anne
   Collection of scarce valuable receipts together with
   directions for making several sorts of wine. London,
   Published by author, 1750. 198p.   BM
Battershall, Jesse P.
   Food adulteration and its detection. New York, E. & F. N.
   Spon and Co., 1887. 328p. Bibliography.
Battiscombe, Esther Georgina
   English picnics. London, Harvil Press, 1949. 212p.
   Illus.   BM
Baumgartner, John G. and Hersom, A. C.
   Canned Foods. An introduction to their microbiology.
   4th edition. London, J. and A. Churchill Ltd., 1956.
   291p. Illus. References.
Baverstock, James H.
   Hydrometrical observations and experiments in the
   brewery. London, Printed for author and sold by G. G.
   L. Robinson and J. Robinson, 1785. 104p. Contains also--
   Short address--on the prejudices against breweries
   1807. 18p.

_____ .
   Observations on the state of the brewery and on the
   saccharine quality of malt. Alton, Hants, 1813.
   pages 478 to 494.

_____ .
   Practical observations or prejudices against the brewery
   with hints to sugar colonists. London, White and
   Cochrane, 1811. 68p.   BM

_____ .
   A short address to the public on the prejudices against
   the breweries. Farnham, 1807. Printed but not for
   sale by J. B. Rutter. Bound with Baverstock-Hydrometical
   observations. London, 1785. 18p.
Baverstock, James, H., F. S. A.
   Treatises on brewing, with notes and an introduction
   containing a biographical sketch of the author, and two
   papers on specific gravity, including an account of the
   various hydrostatical instruments which have been used
   in the brewery; and on malting. London, G. and W. B.
   Whittaker, 1824. 333p.
Baxter, W. H.
   Repeal of the malt tax and brewer's license duty, etc.
   London, 1874. 41p.   (Stopes)
54

Bayard, Luke
    The Wine Guide. Reprinted from Wine Magazine,
    London.
    Vol. 1. 58p. Illus-drawings.
    Vol. 2. 71p. Illus. n d .
    Vol. 3. 71p. Illus. 1965. n d
    Vol. 4. 71p. Illus. 1966. n d
    Vol. 5. 66p. Illus. 1968. n d
    Vol. 6. 63p. Illus. 1969. n d
Baylies, William
    Practical reflections on the uses and abuses of Bath
    waters. London, A. Millar, 1757. 254p.   BM
Bayly, Hugh Wansey, Editor
    What we drink. Various authors. London, William
    Heinemann. Issued under the authority of the Scientific
    Committee of the True Temperance Ass'n., 1930.
    128p.
Baynard, Dr. Edward
    See Floyer, John (First part-1702). Baynard, Dr.
    Edward (Second part-1706). History of cold bathing both
    ancient and modern.
Bazore, Katherine
    See Miller, Carey D. and Bazore, Katherine
    Fruits of Hawaii.

_____.
    See Miller, Carey D.; Bazore, Katharine, Bartow,
    Mary. Fruits of Hawaii. Description, nutritive
    value, and recipes.

_____.
    Hawaiian and Pacific foods. New York, M. Barrows
    and Co., 1949. 290p. References
Beach, Frederick H.
    3 point 2 and what goes with it. (beer). New York,
    Published by author, 1933. 31p. Illus.   LC
Beach, S.
    New and complete cellar book for homemade wines.
    London, T. Traveller. 34p.   BM
Beach, S.A. et al.
    The Apples of New York. Report of the New York
    Agricultural Experiment Station for the year 1903.
    Albany, 1905. 1st of the series. 2 vols. 409, 360.
    Illus-colored plates.
Beach and Clarridge
    B. and C. book of hot soda formulas. Boston, 1891.
    27p.   LC

———— Beach and Clarridge, makers of concentrated extracts, fruit juices, essential oils, etc. Boston, 1890. 8p. Illus. LC

Beadel, J.
Instructions for making beer and ale in all temperatures especially adopted for tropical climates. (Scho)

Beadle, S. C.
Soda fountain guide. Winnepeg, Hall Printing Co., 1920. 41p. BM

Beal, E. A., MD
The Information Readers-number 1. Food and beverages. Boston, 1893. 281p.

Beale, John
Treatise of cyder and perry. 1665-67. (Mathais)

Beam, William
See Leffmann, Henry and Beam, William
Select methods in food analysis.

Bear, J. W.
The vitacultural resources of Victoria. Melbourne, Muller and Slade, 1893. 30p.
(State Library of Victoria)

Beard, George M.
Eating and drinking. New York, G. P. Putnam and Sons, 1871. 180p. NYPL

———— Stimulants and narcotics. New York, G. P. Putnam and Sons, 1871. 155p.

Beard, James Andrews
Hors d'oeuvre and canapés, with a key to the cocktail party. New York, M. Barrows and Co., c1940. 189p. Illus.

Beardsall, Francis
Treatise on the natural properties and composition of ancient and modern wines. London, Published by author, 1839. 54p. (Harvard University)

Beasley, Henry
The Druggist's General Receipt Book, etc. 6th American ed. Philadelphia, Lindsay and Blakiston, 1868. 495p.

Beastall, William
A useful guide for grocers, distillers, etc.,--making and managing all kinds of wines and spiritous liquors. New York, Published by author, 1829. 340p.

Beattie, George B.
A B C of soft drinks business. London. Series of
articles in Soft Drinks Trade Journal from February
1958-January 1962. Pages not continuous. Dictionary.

———·
American Cream Sodas. London. Published in Soft
Drinks Trade Journal from January 1953 to March 1953
in section RECIPE CORNER. Insertions nos. 61 through
63.

———·
A brief history of soft drinks. London. Published
in Soft Drinks Trade Journal. February 1953 to
October 1954, in 10 sections.

———·
Cola Drinks. American Type. London. Published in
Soft Drinks Trade Journal from September 1952 to
December 1952 in Section RECIPE CORNER. Insertions
nos. 57 through 60.

———·
Factory arrangement. Sydney. Published in Australian
Cordial-Maker and Brewer. April 1956 to July 1956, in
4 sections.

———·
Flavoured Cordials. London. Published in section
RECIPE CORNER in Soft Drinks trade Journal from
April 1953 to October 1954. Insertions no. 64 to
82 inclusive.

———·
Grapefruit. London. Published in Soft Drinks Trade
Journal from May 1951 to September 1951. London
in section RECIPE CORNER. Insertions nos. 41
through 45.

———·
Herbal Drinks-operational techniques. London.
Published in Soft Drinks Trade Journal from April 1952
to August 1952 in section RECIPE CORNER. Insertions
nos. 52 through 56.

———·
See "Pyramid" (George B. Beattie). The mechanical
side of mineral water manufacture.

———·
"Pyramid" (George B. Beattie). Mineral water spoilage
prevention.

‗‗‗‗‗‗‗‗‗‗.
Plant for the smaller bottler. London. Published in
Soft Drinks Trade Journal from March 1955 to December
1955. in 12 parts (parts 1 and 2 missing from H.P.
Library).

‗‗‗‗‗‗‗‗‗‗.
Small bottlery problems. Sydney. Published in
Australian Cordial-maker and Brewer in August 1956
and November 1956, in 2 parts.

‗‗‗‗‗‗‗‗‗‗.
Soft drink flavours. Their history and characteristics.
London. Published in Perfumery and Essential Oil
Review. December 1956 to November 1964, in 30
sections each on separate flavour or subject.
References.

‗‗‗‗‗‗‗‗‗‗.
The soft drinks bottler. Volume I. London. The
Mineral Water Trade Review Co., Ltd., 1950. 146p.
Illus.

‗‗‗‗‗‗‗‗‗‗.
The soft drinks bottler. Volume II. London. Published
by The National Association of Soft Drinks Manufacturers,
1958. 204p. Illus. Dictionary.

‗‗‗‗‗‗‗‗‗‗.
Spa Waters. London. Published in Soft Drinks Trade
Journal from October 1951 to January 1952 in section
RECIPE CORNER. Insertions nos. 46 through 49.

‗‗‗‗‗‗‗‗‗‗.
Squashes. Sydney. Published in Australian Cordial-
maker and brewer, from March 1953 to June 1953. in
4 parts.

‗‗‗‗‗‗‗‗‗‗.
What the young bottler should study. London. Published
in Soft Drinks Trade Journal October 1954 to August
1957. 25 parts (7, 8, 9, missing from H.P. Library)
Beatty-Kingston, W.
Claret, its productions, etc., 1895.
(Massel-Applied Wine Chemistry and Technology)
Beaumont, Thomas
An essay on the nature and properties of Alcoholic
Drinks. London, Simpkin, Marshall and Co., 1838.
48p.
Beaven, E.S.
Barley, Fifty years of observation and experiment.
London, Duckworth, 1947. 394p. Illus. Bibliography.

Beck, Bodog, F.
   Honey and health; a nutrimental, medicinal and historical commentary. New York, McBride, 1938. 272p.
   Illus. Bibliography.
Beck, E. James
   The aesthetics of wine. The history of wine in
   Australia. Cover title-Wine, its history, culture and
   making. Sydney, Rhinecastle Wines Pty Ltd., 1945.
   unpaged (59). Dictionary of wine.
Beck, Fred
   The Fred Beck Wine Book. New York, Hill and Wang,
   1964. 242p. Illus. Glossary.
Beck, Hastings
   Meet the Cape wines. Capetown, Purnell and Sons,
   1955. 41p. Illus.
Becker, Kurt
   See Ruff, Donald G.
   Bottling and canning of beer, by Donald G. Ruff and
   Becker, Kurt.
Beckett, Mrs. E.
   Fruit bottling and preserving. London, George Newnes,
   n d ca1918. 31p.   BM
Beckett, Edwin
   The Book of the Strawberry with sections also on the
   raspberry, blackberry, loganberry and Japanese wine-
   berry. London, John Lane, 1902. 83p.
Beckwith, A. R.
   The vintner's story. Sydney, Oswald Ziegler, 1959.
   35p.   ANL
Beckwith, Edward Lonsdale
   Practical notes on wine. London, Smith, Elder and
   Co., 1868. 106p.
Beddoes, Thomas
   Considerations of the medical use of factitious airs.
   Bristol, Bulgin and Posser, 1794. 95p.   BM
Bedel, A.
   Traitè complet de la fabrication des liqueurs, etc.
   Paris, Garnier Frères, 1899. (in French). 384p.
   Illus.
Bedford, John
   Pewter. Collectors Pieces no. 6. London, Cassell
   and Company Ltd., 1965. 64p. Illus.
   _____ .
   Toby jugs. London, Cassell and Co., 1968. 64p.
   Illus-photos.

59

Bedoukian, Paul Z.
Perfumery synthetics and isolates. New York, Van Nostrand, 1951. 488p. Bibliographical references.

Beebe, Lucius, Morris
Snoot if you must. New York, D. Appleton-Century Co., 1943. 296p. Illus.

_____.
The Stork Club bar book. New York, Toronto, Rinehart and Co., 1946. 186p.

Beech, Frederick, Walter
See Pollard, Alfred, and Beech, Frederick Walter. Cider-making.

_____.
Homemade wines, syrups and cordials. London, National Federation of Women's Institutes, 1964. 126p.

_____.
Wines and juices. London, Hutchison, 1961. 180p. Bibliography.

Beecher, Lyman
Six sermons on the nature, occasions, signs, evils, remedy of intemperance. Belfast, The Ulster Temperance Society, 1830. 98p.

Beedell, Suzanne
Wine making and home brewing. London, Sphere Books Ltd., 1969. 189p. Illus-drawings.

Beeton, Isabella M. Mrs.
The Book of Household Management, new edition. London, Ward, Lock and Tyler, (1869). 1139p.

Beeton, Isabelle, M. Mrs.
Jam making, etc., and homemade wines. London, Ward, Lock and Co., 1924. 128p.
(Cleveland Public)

Beilenson, Edna
The ABC of wine cookery. Mount Vernon, N.Y., Peter Pauper Press, 1957. 61p. Illus.

_____.
The Christmas Stocking Book. Mount Vernon, N.Y., Peter Pauper Press, 1957. 60p. Illus.

_____.
Holiday punches, party bowls, and soft drinks. Mount Vernon, N.Y., Peter Pauper Press, 1953. 61p. Illus.

Beilenson, Peter
Aquavit to zombie; basic and exotic drinks. Mt. Vernon, N.Y., Peter Pauper Press, 1957. 60p. Illus.

————. The holiday drink book. Mt. Vernon, N.Y., Peter Pauper Press, 1951. 61p. Illus.

————. King of Hearts drink book. Mount Vernon, N.Y., Peter Pauper Press, 1955. 63p. Illus.

————. Merrie Christmas drink book. Mount Vernon, N.Y., Peter Pauper Press, 1955. 63p. Illus.

Belanger, Emil J.
Drug and specialty formulas. Brooklyn, Chemical Publishing Co., 1941. 307p.

————. Modern manufacturing Formulary. New York, Chemical Publishing Co., 1958. 399p.

Bell, Agrippa Nelson
Climatology and mineral waters of the United States. New York, W. Wood and Co., 1885. 386p. Illus.

Bell, Archibald
Inquiry into the policy and justice of the prohibition of the use of grain in distilling. Edinburgh, A. Constable and Co., 1808. 109p.   BM

Bell, B.
See Dorozynski, Alexander and Bibiane Bell
The Wine Book. Wines and wine making around the world.

Bell, James
The Chemistry of Foods. London, Chapman and Hall, 1881 and 1883. 2 vols. part 1. 120p. part 2. 179p.

Bell, John
The mineral and thermal springs of the United States and Canada. Philadelphia, Parry and McMillan, 1855. 394p.   LC

————. On baths and mineral waters. Philadelphia, H.H. Porter, 1831. 532p.   LC

Bell, Joseph
A treatise on confectionery. Newcastle, Published by author, 1817. 223p.   BM

Bell, William M.
Wm. M. Bell's "Pilot", 3rd edition. Chicago, Published by author, 1918. 248p.

Bellew, John
Fermented goods. London, Maclaren, 1950. 183p.
                    BM

Hilaire

Belloc, Joseph Hilary Pierre
   Advice. (Hilary Belloc's) on wine, food and other
   matters. London, Harvill Press, 1960. 37p.
Bellows and Co., Inc.
   A catalogue of fine wines and spirits. Third edition.
   New York, c1949. 28p.
Belt, T. Edwin
   Preserving winemaking ingredients. Andover,
   Hampshire. Amateur Winemaker, n d (1968). 118p.
   Illus- drawings.
Belth, George and J. Mitchell Fain
   Household guide to wines and liquors. New York,
   Bellson Syndicate, 1934. 48p.   LC
Beman, David
   Mysteries of the trade. Boston, printed for author,
   1825. 152p.   NYPL
Benjamin, Count of Rumford
   Of the excellent qualities of coffee and the art of making
   it in the highest perfection. London, T. Cadell and
   V. Davies, 1812. Pages 155 to 207. Illus-engravings.
Bennett, H. Editor in chief
   The Chemical Formulary. Volume II. New York, D.
   Van Nostrand Co., Inc., c1935. 570p. Vol. 3. 566p.
   1936. Vol. 5. 676p. 1941.

_____.
   Formulas for Profit. Cleveland and New York, The
   World Publishing Co. 1943. 632p.

_____.
   Money- making Formulas. Cleveland, World Publishing
   Co., c1939. 638p.

_____.
   New formulas for profit. Cleveland and New York,
   World Publishing Co., c1941. Previously published
   as Chemical Formulary Volume V. 674p.

_____.
   Practical emulsions. A handbook of emulsions
   emulsifiers and methods of formulating and making
   emulsions of practical value in industry. Brooklyn,
   Chemical Publishing Co., 1943. 462p. Illus.
Bennett, R.
   Bennett's guide to winemakers, brewers, distillers, etc.
   containing tables arranged to specific gravity, etc.,
   Cincinnati, Published by author, 1852. 48p.
                                           (Cincinnati Public)

Benson, Carl (pseud)
Anacreontics. (Poetry about drinking) (By Charles
Aster Bristed.) New York, Privately printed, 1872.
75p.   NYPL
Benson, John
The licensed victualler's instructor and spirit dealer's
companion, Liverpool, 1854. 48p.   (Dealer's List)
Benson, John (Liverpool)
The spirit and licensed victualler's guide. London,
George Philip and Son, 1878. 368p. tables.
Benstead, C.R.
Hic, Haec, Hock! A low fellow's grammer and guide
to drinking, etc. London, Frederick Muller Ltd.,
1934. 212p. Illus. Bibliography.
Bentley, Iris
Wine with a merry heart. New York, Comet Press
Books, 1959. 30p. Illus.
Benwell, W.S.
Journey to wine in Victoria, Melbourne, Sir Isaac
Pitman and Sons, 1960. 120p. Illus. Glossary.
Bergal, P.
See Aufhammer, G., Bergal, Pierre, Horne, F.R.
Barley varieties - EBC.
Bergeron, Victor Jules
Bartender's guide, by Trader Vic (pseud).
Garden City, N.Y., Doubleday, 1947.   437p.   Illus.

_____.
Trader Vic's Book of food and drink, with an intro-
duction by Lucius Beebe. Garden City, New York,
Doubleday and Co., Inc., 1946. 272p. Illus.
Berghausen, E. Chemical Co.
Flavor literature. Cincinnati, various dates.
Folder of various pieces.
Bergman, Torbern, Olof
Om Luftsyra. (On acid in air - which see). Stock-
holm, Almquist and Wikesell, 1956. (in Swedish.)
127p. Illus.

_____.
On acid of air; excerpt from KVA 1773. Treatise on
bitter, seltzer, spa and pyrmont waters and their
synthetical preparation; excerpt from KVA 1775. Tobern
Bergman as pioneer in the domain of mineral waters by
Uno Boklund. Stockholm, Almqvist and Wiksell, 1956.
128p. Illus. Bibliography.

Berkeley, Tom
    We keep a pub. London, Hutchinson, 1955. 224p.
    Illus.
Berliner, J.J. and Staff
    A Berliner research report on wine and fermented fruit
    products . . . . New York, J.J. Berliner, (1936).
    50p. manuscript.

——————   Encyclopedia of alcoholic essence formulas. New York,
    1945.   LC

——————   Survey on beverages. New York, n d ca1938. 52p.

——————   Syrup formulas. New York, n d. 30p.

——————   Wines, New York, 1955. 64p.   (Davis)
Berling, E.M.
    Art in confectionery and pastry. New York, E.M.
    Berling, 1930. 196p.
Berman, Louis, MD
    Food and character. London, Methuen and Co., Ltd.,
    1933. 384p.
"Bernard"
    One hundred cocktails. How to mix them. London,
    W. Foulsham and Co., Ltd., 1958. 96p.
Bernard, Bertram M.
    Liquor laws in 48 states. New York, Oceana
    Publications, 1949. 87p.   (Los Angeles Public)
Bernhard, William
    The book of 100 beverages. London, Houlston and
    Stoneman, 1850. 64p.

——————   The book of One Hundred beverages for family use.
    New York, C.S. Francis and Company, 1853. 63p.
    1855, same.
Berry, C.J.J.
    Amateur winemaker's recipes. Andover, Hants,
    Amateur Winemaker Magazine, 1968. 124p. Illus-
    cartoons.

——————   First steps in winemaking. 19th impression. Andover,
    Hants, Amateur Winemaker, n d. 109p. Illus.
    Wine Vocabulary. 2nd edition, 163p. Illus., 2nd
    impression. 2nd edition (1968), 160p. Illus., 5th
    impression.

Hints on home brewing. Seventh impression, Andover, Hants, Amateur Winemaker, 1962. 21p. Illus. Brewing Vocabulary.

Home brewed beers and stouts. 2nd impression, Andover, Hampshire. Published by Amateur Winemaker, (1963). 63p. Illus. 2nd edition, 1966. 97p. Illus-drawings, Canadian edition. Brewing Vocabulary.

Making wine is not difficult. Andover. Published by Andover and District Winemakers' Circle, n d, ca1964. 8p.

One hundred thirty new wine making recipes. Sixth impression, Andover, Hants, Amateur Winemaker, 1961. 82p. Illus.

See Turner, Bernard C.
The winemaker's companion; a handbook for those who make wine at home, by B. C. A. Turner, and C. J. J. Berry.

Winemaking with canned and dried fruit. Andover, Hampshire, Amateur Winemaker, 1968. 83p. Illus-drawings. Advertising.
Berry, Charles Walter
In search of wine . . . London, Constable, 1935. 389p.

A miscellany of wine. London, Constable and Co., 1932. 104p.

Viniana. 2nd edition, rev. and enl. London, Constable 1934. 161p. Illus-plates. 1st edition, 1929. 1st edition, New York, Knopf, 1930.
Berry, Riley M. Fletcher
Fruit Recipes. Manual of the food values of fruit and nine hundred different ways of using them. Garden City, New York, Doubleday-Page, 1911. 341p.
Berry Brothers and Rudd Ltd.
Tokay. London, Berry Bros., (1933). 29p. tables.

A wine cellar book. . . . New York, Buckingham, c1934. 31p. Illus.

Berry-Smith, F
Grape growing in the home garden. New Zealand, Dept.
of Agriculture, Bull. no. 291. Auckland, Dept. of
Agriculture, 1957. 15p. Illus.

_____.
Vitaculture, 1958.
(Massel-Applied wine chemistry and Technology)
Beverage Research Bureau
A manual on beers, wines and liquors for everybody.
Alliance, Ohio, 1934. 32p.   LC
Beveridge, N.E.
Cups of valor. Harrisburg, Pa., Stackpole Books,
1968. 106p. Illus-drawings.
Bewley, Richard (pseud)
A treatise on air, etc. London, 1791. 2 vol.   BM
Bickerdyke, John (pseud)
The curiosities of ale and beer. Author-Cook, Charles
Henry. London, Field and Tuer, n d, ca1886.
449p. Illus.
Biddle, Anthony Joseph Drexel
The land of the wine; being an account of the Madeira
Islands at the beginning of the twentieth century and
from a new point of view. Philadelphia, London,
D. Biddle, 1901. 2 v. Illus. Philadelphia, G.W.
Jacobs, c1901.

_____.
The Madeira Islands. . . . London, Hurst and Blackett,
Ltd.; Philadelphia and New York, D. Biddle, 1900.
2 v.   LC
Bienfang, Ralph
The Subtle Sense. Norman, Okla., University of
Oklahoma Press, 1946. 157p. Bibliography.
Biggle, Jacob
Biggle Berry Book. Philadelphia, Wilmer Atkinson Co.,
1913. 143p. Illus-Colored plates.

_____.
Biggle Orchard Book. Philadelphia, Wilmer Atkinson
Co., 1906. 144p. Illus-colored Plates.
Bijur, George
Wines with long noses. London, Hampton Hall Press,
1951. 31p. Illus.
Binkley, Robert C.
Responsible Drinking. New York, Vanguard Press,
1930. 215p.

66

Bioletti, Frederick, T.
   Bench grafting resistant vines. Sacramento. California
   Experiment Station Bulletin no. 137, 1900. 38p.
                                                        NYPL

———— .
   The best wine grapes of California. Sacramento,
   University of California, Bulletin no. 193, 1907.
   19p.   NYPL

———— .
   Elements of grape growing in California. Calif. Agri.
   Extension Service Circular no. 30. Berkeley, Univ.
   of California, 1929. 37p. List of Publications

———— .
   Grape culture in California. Berkeley, Univ. California
   Agri. Bulletin no. 197, 1908. 60p.
                              (Los Angeles Public)

———— .
   Manufacture of dry wines in hot countries. Sacramento.
   Univ. Calif. Bulletin no. 167, 1905. 66p.   WI

———— .
   New method of making dry red wines. Sacramento.
   Univ. Calif. Bulletin, no. 174, 1906. 36p.   WI

———— .
   New wine cooling machine. Sacramento, Univ. Calif.
   Bulletin no. 177, 1906. 27p.   WI

———— .
   The principles of wine-making. Sacramento, W.W.
   Shannon, 1911. 396-442p. Illus.

———— .
   See Grazzi-Soncini, G.
   Wine. Classification-winetasting-qualities and defects.
   Trans. by F.T. Bioletti.

———— .
   Wine making on a small scale. San Francisco, 1935.
   24p.   (St. Louis Public)
Birch, George
   Handbook of gauging at breweries, and distilleries and
   of the saccharometer. Wolverhampton, Whitehead
   Bros., 1894. 133p.   BM
Birch, Lionel
   The story of beer. London and Burton-on-Trent.
   Truman, Hanbury, Buxton and Co., Ltd., 1951. 96p.
   Illus.
Bird, A.E.P. and Turner, William
   Cocktails, their kicks and side-kicks. New York,
   Published by authors, 1930. 28p. Illus.   LC

Bird, William
French wines; a practical guide for the cellarman, wine-butler and connoisseur. Paris, Havas, 1955. 77p. Illus.

——— A practical guide to French wines. Paris, Three Mountains Press, n d, 80p. maps.

Bird, William H.
Catalog of the London section of the Institute of Brewing library. London, Published by the Institute, 1914. 43p. BM

——— A history of the Institute of Brewing. London, Published by The Institute of Brewing, 1955. 139p. Illus.

Birkett, E.
The Golden wine of Old Britain. London, Published by author, 1952. 122p. Illus.

Birkett, Edmund Lloyd, Ed.
Thomson's conspectus of the British pharmacopoeias. 17th edition. London, Longman, Brown, Green and Longmans, 1852. 214p.

Birmingham, Frederic A. Ed.
See Esquire.
Drink book, edited by Frederic A. Birmingham.

Bishop, George
The booze reader. A soggy sage of a man in his cups. Los Angeles, Sherbourne Press, 1965. 288p. Illus. Bibliography

Bishop, J. Leander
History of American manufacturers. Philadelphia, E. Young and Co., 1864. 2 vol. LC

Bishop, Jim
The Glass Crutch. The biographical novel of William Wynne Wister. New York, Doubleday, Doran and Co., 1945. 309p.

Bitting, A. W.
Appertizing or art of canning; its history and development. San Francisco, The Trade Pressroom, 1937. 852p. Illus.

Bitting, Katharine Golden
Gastronomic Bibliography. San Francisco, Published by author, 1939. 718p. Illus.

Black, Henry Campbell
A treatise on the laws regulating the manufacture and
sale of INTOXICATING LIQUORS. St. Paul, West
Publishing Co., 1892. 711p.
Black, William
A practical treatise on brewing and on storing of beer
deduced from forty years' experience. London, Smith
Elder and Co., Cornhill, 1835. 148p. Illus-drawings.

_____.
A practical treatise on brewing based on chemical and
economical principles; with formulae for public brewers,
and instructions for private families. London, Longman,
Brown, Green and Longmans.
Third edition, much enlarged and improved, 212p. 1844.
Fourth edition, 249p. 1849.
Fifth edition, 249p. 1854.
New edition, 249p. 1866.
1870, 249p.
Blackford, A. S.
See Cruwell, G. A. and A. S. Blackford.
Brazil as a coffee growing country.
Blackpool and District Mineral Water Mfgrs and
Bottler's Trade Protection Ass'n
Memorandum and articles of an Association 1901.
20p. Also Bye-Laws of the Association, 1903. 8p.

_____.
Annual reports 25th meeting 1926 , 44p; 29th 1930, 40p;
30th 1931, 38; 31st 1932, 32p; 32nd 1933, 32p; 33rd 1934,
32p; 34th 1935, 32p; 35th 1936, 32p; 37th 1938, 32p;
38th 1939, 32p; 39th 1940, 32p; 40th 1941, 32p.
Blair, Henry William
Temperance movement. Conflict between man and
alcohol. Boston, William E. Smythe Co., 1888.
583p.
Blair, R. E.
See Shear, S. W. and Blair, R. E.
California Fruit Statistics and related data.
Blake, George
Strictures on the new mode of brewing, etc. London,
J. Johnson, 1791. 128p.   BM

_____.
Theoretical and practical remarks on G. Blake's system
of malting and brewing. London, Printed for the author,
1817. 84p.   BM

Blake, John Henry
Tea hints for retailers. . . . Denver, Williamson-
Haffner, 1903. 275p. Illus.
Blake, W. H.
The Brewer's Vade-Mecum. London, The Brewers
Journal, 1902. 279p.
Blaser, Werner
Japanese temples and tea-houses. New York, F. W.
Dodge Corp., 1957. 156p. Illus. Bibliography.   LC
Bleasdale, John Ignatius
On Colonial wines. Melbourne, Stilwell and Knight,
1867. 24p.   ANL

Pure native wine considered as an article of food and
luxury. Adelaide, Andrews, Thomas and Clark, 1868.
28p.   ANL
Blencowe, Ann B.
The receipt book of Mrs. Ann B. Blencowe. London,
The Adelphi Guy Chapman, 1925. 60p.
Bliss, R.
Remarks and experiments on the different types of
brewing. Oxford, printed by N. Bliss, 1807. 68p.
                                                    (Crerar)
Blits, H. I.
Professor H. I. Blits' methods of canning fruits and
vegetables by hot air and steam and berries by the
compounding of syrups, etc. With new edition and
supplement. Milwaukee, Northwestern Publishing Co.
n d, ca1893.
Blochman, Lawrence Goldtree
Here's how! A round-the-world bar guide. With con-
tributions by members of the Overseas Press Club.
New York, New American Library, 1957. 192p.
Bloomfield, William
The servant's companion, or practical housemaid's
and footman's guide. London, J. R. Blonsell, n d,
ca1820. 32p.
Bloomhardt, F. B.
See Lockhart Ernest E. and Bloomhart, Fred B.
A survey of world literature on coffee.
Blout, Jessie Schilling
A brief economic history of the California wine-growing
industry. San Francisco, Bureau of Markets, Calif.
State Dept. Agri., 1943. 21p.

Blue Seal Extract Co., Inc.
　　Beverage Flavor Handbook and Catalog.　Cambridge,
　　Mass., 1953.　63p.　Illus.
Blumenthal, M. L. Ed.
　　The bottler's helper; a practical encyclopaedia for the
　　bottler of soft drinks, compiled from the contribution
　　of over seven hundred bottlers; Philadelphia,
　　Blumenthal Bros., 1907.　312p.
Blumenthal, Saul
　　Food manufacturing.　A compendium of food information
　　in the canning, flavoring, beverage, confectionery,
　　essence, etc., industries.　Brooklyn, Chemical
　　Publishing Co., 1942.　664p.　Bibliography.

————————— ·
　　Food Products.　Brooklyn, N. Y., Chemical Publishing
　　Co., 1947.　986p.　Bibliography.

————————— ·
　　See Fiene, D. E. and Blumenthal, Saul.
　　Handbook of food manufacturing.
Blumenthals Ltd.
　　Let's have a party.　Booklet issued by Ayala
　　Champagne, Croizet Brandy and Rocher Liqueurs.
　　London, n d, 20p.
Blunier, O.　Editor
　　The Barkeeper's Golden Book.　The exquisite book of
　　American drinks.　Zurich, Morgarten-Verlag ag Zurich,
　　1935.　(English-Français-Deutsch).　276p.　Illus.
　　List of mixed drinks.
Blunno, Michele
　　Notes on winemaking.　Sydney, New South Wales,
　　Department of Agriculture, Farmer's Bulletin no. 19,
　　1897.　13p.　　　　　　　　　　　　　　　　ANL
Blunt, Edmund M.
　　The merchant and seaman's expeditious measurer, etc.
　　New York, Published by author, 1825.　196p.
Blyth, Alexander Wynter
　　The Analysis of foods and the detection of poisons.
　　(A manual of practical chemistry).　New York, William
　　Wood and Co., 1878.　468p.　Notes.

————————— ·
　　Foods: their composition and analysis.　3rd edition.
　　London, Charles Griffin and Co., 1888.　640p.
　　Bibliography.　4th edition, 1896.　735p.　Bibliography.
　　1903.　616p.

Blythe, Samuel
The Old Game. A retrospect after three years on the
wagon. New York, George H. Doran Company, 1914.
68p.
Board of State Viticultural Commissioners.
Report for 1893-1894. Sacramento State Office, 1894.
208p.
Board of Trade
Report on the census of production for 1954. Volume
9, Industry L. Soft drinks. British wines and cider.
London, HMSO, 1958. 10p.
Bode, Charles Gustav.
Wines of Italy. New York, McBride, 1956. 135p.
Illus.
Bodington, C
Wines of the bible. (Lecture on temperance). London,
S.P.C.K., 1887. 31p. BM
Boeglin, C.A.
Sundaes, ices and cream sodas. How to make them.
London, Published by author, 1927. 119p. NYPL
Bogen, Emil and Hisey, Lehman W.S.
What about alcohol? Los Angeles. Published by
Angelus Press for the Scientific Education Committee,
1936. 112p.
Bogert, L. Jean
Dietary uses of the banana in health and disease.
Berkeley, California. Research Department United
Fruit Co., N.Y., 1942. 67p. Illus.
Boireau, Raimond
Wines, their care and treatment in cellar and store.
Sacramento, California State Board of Vitacultural
Commissioners, 1889. 148p. NYPL
Boles, J.N.
See Hoos, Sidney, and Boles, J.N.
Oranges and orange products. Changing economic
relationships.
Bolitho, Hector
The wine of the Douro. London, Sidgwick and Jackson,
1956. 23p. Illus-plates.
Bolling, Robert, Jr.
Sketch of vine culture. n p, 17--? 108p.
(National Agricultural Library)

Bolte, Arthur H.
  Management and cost control in the carbonated beverage
  industry, by Arthur H. Bolte . . . and Arthur E. Low
  . . . in cooperation with the Cost accounting committee
  of the American bottlers of carbonated beverages. Rev.
  ed. Washington, D. C., American Bottlers of
  Carbonated Beverages, 1936. 172p.
Bolton, Mary
  Homemade wines, confectionery and sweets. London,
  W. Foulsham and Co., Ltd., 1957. 128p.
Bon Viveur
  See Cradock, John
  An A. B. C. of wine drinking.

  _____ .
  Bon Viveur's London and the British Isles. London,
  Andrew Dakers Limited, 1955. 256p.
Bonham, Wesley A.
  Bonham's guide for soda dispensers. Chicago,
  Published by author, entered 1894. 47p. Illus.
Bonynge, Francis
  The future wealth of America--agricultural advantages
  of cultivating tea, coffee and indigo. New York,
  Published by author, 1852. 242p.   LC
Book Club of California
  Bonanza Banquets. San Francisco. (J.H. Jackson,
  Ed.), no. 13 in the series, 1950. Unpaged (12parts)

  _____ .
  The vine in early California. San Francisco. The Book
  Club of California, 1955. Unbound folders in portfolio.
Boorde, Andrew
  Breviary of helthe. London, Imprinted by Wyllyam
  Hyddleton, 1547. 2 parts.   BM
Booth, Abraham
  On the natural chemical properties of water and of
  various British mineral waters. London, George
  Wightman, 1830. 196p.   BM
Booth, David
  . . . The art of brewing . . . Published under the
  superintendence of the Society for the diffusion of useful
  knowledge. London, Baldwin and Cradock, 1829. 64p.
  Illus.

  _____ .
  The art of brewing. London, parts 1 and 2, Baldwin
  and Cradick, 1829. Parts 3 and 4, London, F.J.
  Mason, 1834. Parts 1 and 2, 64p., parts 3 and 4, 56p.
  Illus.

———— .
The art of wine-making, in all its branches. To which
is added an appendix concerning cider and perry.
London, F.J. Mason, 1834. 123p. Illus.
Booth, George C.
The Food and Drink of Mexico. A collection of authentic
recipes collected from the many regions of Mexico.
Los Angeles, The Ward Ritchie Press, 1964. 190p.
Illus.
Booth's Distilleries Ltd.
An anthology of cocktails. London, n d ca1920. 50p.
Illus.
Boothby, William T.
"Cocktail Bill" Boothby's World drinks and how to mix
them; the standard authority as originally compiled by
Hon. Wm. T. Boothby . . . completely revised and
greatly enlarged into a unabridged encyclopedia of all
popular beverages. San Francisco, Printed by the
Recorder Printing and Publishing Co., 1934. 270p.

———— .
Cocktail Boothby's American bartender. 2nd edition.
San Francisco, The San Francisco News Co., 1900-
100p.   LC

———— .
"Cocktail Bill" Boothby's World drinks and how to
prepare them. San Francisco, Boothby's World Drinks
Co., 1930. 160p. Cover title SWALLOWS.

———— .
The world's drinks and how to mix them. San
Francisco, Pacific Buffet, 1908. 139p.
Boots Pure Drug Co., Ltd
Saccharin. Its uses in foods and beverages of all
kinds and in pharmacy. Nottingham, n d ca1954.
26p.
Borden's Condensed Milk Co.
Drinks and dishes. New York, 1907. 16p.
                                                    (Brown University)
Borella
The court and country confectioner, etc., distilling,
making fine flavoured wines. London, G. Riley and
A. Cooke, 1770. 271p.   LC
Borella, S.P.
See Harris, Henry G. and Borella, S.P.
All about ices, jellies, creams and conserves.

Bosdari, C. de
   Wine of the Cape.   Cape Town, A.A. Balkema, 1955.
   95p.   Illus.
Bose, Dhirenda K.
   Wine in ancient India.   Calcutta, K.M. Conner and Co.,
   1922.   51p.   (Berkeley)
Boswell, Peyton
   Wine makers manual; a guide for the home wine
   maker and the small winery.   New York, Orange Judd,
   1944.   96p.   Illus.   Bibliography.   1952, 96p.   Illus.
   Bibliography.
Boulestin, Xavier Marcel
   What shall we have to drink?   London, W. Heinemann,
   Ltd., 1933.   85p.
Bourbon Institute
   The Bourbon Chef.   New York, n d, Volume 2.   21p.
Bourke, Arthur, Ed.
   Winecraft; the encyclopaedia of wines and spirits.
   London, Harper and Co., 1935.   182p.
Bowen, Harvey E.
   The mixer.   San Francisco, Select Publications, 1933.
   16p.   LC
Bower, J.A.
   Simple methods of detecting food adulteration.   London,
   Society for promoting Christian Knowledge, 1895.
   118p.   LC
Bowers, Edwin F.
   Alcohol.   Its influence on mind and body.   New York,
   Grosset and Dunlop, 1916.   207p.
Bowker, Dr. H.L. and Co.
   Price list and descriptive catalogue of extracts, colors,
   etc., for soda water beverages, etc., Third edition.
   Boston, n d ca1879.   40p.
Boyes, E.
   How to obtain an ideal cup of coffee, its cost and
   value.   London, Published by author, 1898.   16p.   BM
Boyle, Peter
   The Publican and spirit dealer's daily companion.   5th
   edition.   London, Printed and sold by P. Boyle, (1800).
   148p.

————————.
   The publican's daily companion.   London, 1794.   106p.
                                                         NYPL
Boyle, Robert
   Short memoirs for the natural experimental history of
   mineral waters.   London, Printed for S. Smith, 1684.
   112p.   LC

Bradford, Sarah
  The Englishman's wine. The story of port. London,
  Macmillan and Co., Ltd., 1969. 208p. Illus-photos.
  Bibliography.
Bradford, William
  Brewery Construction. Paper for Brewers Congress.
  London, Carlton Chambers, 1885. 21p.
Bradley, Mrs. Alexander Orr
  Beverages and sandwiches for your husband's friends.
  (By one who knows.) New York, Brentano's, 1893.
  48p.   LC
Bradley, Alice V.
  Tables of food values. Peoria, Ill., Charles A.
  Bennett, 1956. 322p. (General Foods Research Libr.)
Bradley, Edith and May Crooke
  The Book of fruit bottling. Chapters on fruit drying,
  homemade wines and cider making, etc. London,
  John Lane, 1907. 97p.
Bradley, James Frederick
  Cocktails, wines and liquors. New York, Bradley
  Enterprises, 1934. 63p. Illus.   LC
Bradley, Richard
  Country housewife. London, D. Browne, 1727. 187p.
                                                          BM

_____.
  Dictionarie Oenonmique. (wine), 1725. Folio.   BM
_____.
  Short historical account of coffee, London, 1716.
                                                    (Wellman)

_____.
  The virtue and use of coffee, with regard to the plague,
  and other infectious distempers. London, Printed by
  E. Mathews, 1721. 34p.   LC
Bradshaw, B.
  Bradshaw's dictionary of mineral waters. London,
  Trubner and Co., Many editions from 1882 to 1904.
  372p.   BM
Bradshaw, Penelope
  Bradshaw's valuable family jewel. London, Published
  by author, 1748. 48p.   LC
Bragato, R.
  Viticulture in New Zealand. (with special reference to
  American vines). Wellington, Government Printing
  Office, 1906. 60p.   (PLOSA)

Brande, W.
The Town and Country Brewery Book, or everyman his
own brewer. London, Dean and Munday, n d, ca1840.
284p.
Brande, William T.
Experiments to ascertain the state in which spirit exists
in fermented liquors. London, W. Bulmor and Co.,
1811. 11p.   BM
Brandimbourg, Gabriel
Guide des Bals et Soirees. (American and English
drinks). Biarritz. L'Imprimerie A Peria, 1907.
(In French). 31p.
Brandt, Johanna
The Grape Cure. 10th edition. New York, Published
by The Order of Harmony, 1928. 220p.

_____.
The grape cure, for cancer and other diseases.
Published in South Africa, 1948. 94p.
Brannt, William, Theodore
Animal and Vegetable fats and oils (A practical treatise
on). 2nd edition revised and in great part rewritten.
Philadelphia, Henry Carey Baird, 1896. 2 vol.
Vol. 1, 528; vol. 2. 728, Illus.

_____.
A practical treatise on the manufacture of vinegar and
acetates, cider and fruit wines. . . . Philadelphia,
Baird, 1890. 478p. Illus.
1900, 2nd edition. 1901, 2nd edition. London, Low,
Marston.

_____.
See Deite, Carl, 1838.
A practical treatise on the manufacture of perfumery;

_____.
A practical treatise on the raw materials and the dis-
tillation and rectification of alcohol, and the preparation
of alcoholic liquors, liqueurs, cordials and bitters.
Philadelphia, H.C. Baird and Co., London, S. Low,
Marston, Searle and Rivington, 1885. 330p. Illus-
drawings.
Brannt, William Theodore and Wahl, William H.
The Techno-Chemical Receipt Book. Philadelphia,
Henry Carey Baird, 1888. 495p. 1889, 495p. 1917,
495p.

_____ .

See Thausing, Julius
The theory and practice of the preparation of malt and
the fabrication of beer, with especial reference to the
Vienna process of brewing . . . by Julius E. Thausing.

Brasseries de Pilson Enterprise Nationale
Pilson Urquell. Pilson Tchecoslovaquie, n d.
unpaged (20), Illus.

Bratby and Hinchliffe, Ltd.
The practical mineral water maker. 4th edition.
Manchester, 1903. 95p.

Brathwait, Richard
The law of drinking. (Solome disputation theoretike and
practike briefely shodowing..) Edited by W. Brian
Hooker. New Haven, 1903. (Originally published in
London, 1617.) Published by Hooker. 107p.

Braum, Emil
Frozen gems and dainty dishes. Recipes for the
general use of fine and fancy drinks, plain and fancy
soda waters, syrups, etc. Kansas City, Mo. Review
Publishing Co., 1896. 66p.   LC

Bravery, H.E.
Amateur wine-making. London and Glasgow, William
Collins Sons and Co., 1964. 160p. Illus.

_____ .

Home brewing without failures. London, Max Parrish,
1965. 160p. Brewing Vocabulary.

_____ .

Home wine-making. London, Arco Publications, 1968.
112p. Illus-photos.

_____ .

Home wine-making without failures. London, Max
Parrish, 1958. 114p. 1964, 221p.

_____ _ .

The simple science of wine and beer making. London,
Macdonald and Co., Ltd., 1969. 168p. Illus-drawings.

_____ .

Successful winemaking at home. New York, ARC
Editions, 1962. 151p. Illus.

Brazil, Departamento Nacional do Cafe.
ABC of coffee. Rio de Janeiro. National Coffee
Department of Brazil, 1911. 24p. Illus.   LC

Brazil. Departmento Nacional do Cafe.
See Costa Neves. A story of "King Coffee".

Brazilian Coffee Institute
Coffee and Brazil. New York, n d ca1960. unpaged (24), Illus..
Brazilla Company (The)
No title Soda fountains and supplies. Minneapolis, n d, ca1920. 32p. Illus.
Bredenbek, Magnus.
What shall we drink? Popular drinks, recipes and toasts. New York, Carlyle House, 1934. 215p. Illus.
Breen, Herbert
How to stop drinking. New York, Henry Holt and Co., 1958. 183p. Bibliography.
Breen, Mary and Lawson, Arthur
The weekend companion. New York, George W. Stewart, 1940. 372p.
Brenner, Felix
500 recipes. Cocktails and mixed drinks. London, Paul Hamyln, 1964. 95p. Glossary.
Brenner, M.W.
see Hackstaff, B.W. and Brenner, M.W.
An analysis of packaging costs in the brewing industry.
Bretzfield, Henry
Liquor marketing and liquor advertising. New York, Abelard-Schumann, 1955. 262p. Illus. Glossary.
Breuckmann, Franz Ernst
A treatise on coffee and a condemnation of its use. Brunswick, 1727. (Ukers-All about coffee)
Brévans, J. Moréal de.
The manufacture of liquors and preserves. New York, Munn, 1898. 200p. Illus.
Brewers Association of Canada.
Brewing in Canada. Ottawa, April 1965. 142p. Bibliography.
Brewers' Digest
Buyers' Guide and Directory. Chicago, 1965. 106p. Illus.
Brewers' Guild
See Incorporated Brewers' Guild
Brewing scientific reviews.
Brewers' Industrial Exhibition
Essays on the malt liquor question. Published in New York, by Francis Hart and Co., for the exhibition, 1876. 40p. Illus.

Brewers' Institute S. A.
    see Van Niekerk, J. A. H.
    A survey of the control of alcoholic beverages in other
    countries.
Brewers' Journal and Hop and Malt Trade's Review
    Brewer's Journal Centenary Number. London, 1965.
    330p. Illus.
Brewery and bottling Engineer's Ass'n.
    British Brewery and soft drinks equipment. London,
    Published by author and Food Machinery Ass'n, 1964.
    119p. 1965, 118p.
Brewster, H. Pomeroy
    The coffee houses and tea gardens of old London.
    Rochester, Post Express Printing Co., 1888. 42p. LC
Briant, Lawrence
    Laboratory text book for brewers. London, Published
    by author, 1884. 323p. Illus.
    2nd edition, 1898, 356p. Fell and Briant
    3rd edition, 1911, 443p. Fell and Briant
Bridgeman, Thomas
    Fruit cultivators manual. New York, Published by
    author, Various editions. Various paginations.
                                    (Napa and others)
Bridges, Milton Arlanden
    Food and beverage analysis. Philadelphia, Lea and
    Febiger, 1935. 246p. 1950, 412p. 3rd edition,
    Bibliography.
Briggs, John
    Treatise on the machinery used in making and prepara-
    tion of soda water, 1871.
                        (Mitchell- Mineral & aerated waters)
Briggs, Richard
    The English art of cookery according to the present
    practice, etc. 3rd edition. London, Printed by
    G. G. and J. Robinson, 1794. 564p.
Bright, William
    Bright on the grape question. (Bright's single stem,
    dwarf and renewal system of grape culture).
    Philadelphia, Published by author, 1860. 121p. NYPL
Brillat-Savarin, Jean Anthelme
    A handbook of Gastronomy. Boston and New York,
    Houghton-Mifflin, 1915. 394p.

    The physiology of taste or meditations on transcendental
    gastonomy. Translation from the French Physiologie du
    gout. New York, Boni and Liveright, 1926. 360p.

Bristol Brewery Georges and Co., Ltd
One hundred and fifty years of brewing 1788-1938.
Souvenir book. Bristol, 1938. 99p. Illus.
British Dairy Farmer's Association.
Dairy Show Catalogue. London, 1959. 447p.
British Standards Institution
Specifications for caramel for use in food stuffs. London,
British Standard no. 3874, 1965. 8p.
Briton-Jones, H.R.
The diseases and curing of cocao. London, Macmillan
and Co., 1934. 161p. Illus-photos. Bibliography.
Britton, Dorothy
see Atkinson, F.E. and Britton, Dorothy and Moyls,
A.W.
Fruit juices, cider and wines.
Broadbent, Humphrey
Domestick coffee man shewing the true way of preparing
and making chocolate, coffee and tea. London, T.
Carll; T. Bickenton, 1722. 26p.   BM
Broadbent, J.M.
Wine tasting. London, Wine and Spirit Publications
Ltd., 1968. 78p. Glossary of tasting terms English-
French-German.
Brock, R. Barrington
Outdoor grapes in cold climates. Viticultural Research
Station Report No. 1 Oxted, Surrey, 1949. 71p. Illus.

_____.
Progress with vines and wines. Viticultural Research
Station Report No. 3 Oxted, Surrey, 1961. 64p. Illus.

_____.
Starting a vineyard. Report No. 4 from the Vita-
cultural Research Station, Oxted, Surrey, 1964. 78p.
Illus.
Broadner, Joseph, Howard M. Carlson, Henry T.
Maschal, Editors.
Profitable food and beverage operation. Second edition.
New York, Ahrens Publishing Co., 1955. 424p. Illus.
Bibliography. 1951 - 1st ed. 395p.
Brody, Iles
The Colony. Portrait of a restaurant and its famous
recipes. London, Jarrolds Publishers-London Ltd,
1946. 192p.
Bronner, Stanley
See Washburne, George B. and Bronner, Stanley
Beverages de luxe.

Brookes, Richard
 Natural history of chocolate-being an account of the
 cocoa, tree, etc., London, 1725. 95p.   BM
Brooks, Colin
 Tavern Talk.   London, James Barrie, 1950.   197p.
Brooks, James
 Whiskey Drips.   A series of interesting sketches
 illustrating the operations of whiskey thieves, etc.
 Philadelphia, William B. Evans and Co., entered 1873.
 348p.   Illus.
Brooks, Johnny
 My 35 years behind bars; memories and advice of a
 bartender, including a liquor guide.   New York,
 Exposition Press, 1954.   136p.   LC
Brooks, R.O.
 Critical Studies in the legal chemistry of foods.
 New York, Chemical Catalog Company, 1927.   280p.
Brooks, Reid M. et al.
 Register of new fruit and nut varieties, 1920 to 1950.
 Berkeley, Univ. of California, 1952.   206p.
                    (Brady Library-Fresno State College)
 _____ . and Claron O. Hesse
 Western fruit gardening.   Berkeley, University of
 California Press, 1953.   287p.   Illus-drawings.
                    (Brady Library-Fresno State College)
Brother Adam
 Mead.   London, Reprint from Bee World, 1953.   6p.
Brown, Adrian J.
 Brewing and modern science.   Cantor Lectures.
 London, Royal Society of Arts, 1911.   44p.

 _____ .
 Laboratory studies for brewing students.   London,
 Longmans, Green, and Co., 1904.   193p.   Illus.
Brown, Alex
 The coffee planter's manual.   Colombo, "Ceylon
 Observer Press", 1880.   242p.   LC
Brown, Alfred J.
 I bought a hotel.   London, Williams and Norgate,
 1950.   275p.
Brown, B. Meredith
 The Brewer's Art.   2nd edition, London, Published for
 Whitbread and Company, Ltd., by Naldrett Press Ltd.,
 1949.   58p.   Illus.-plates in color.   Bibliography.

Brown, Bob
Homemade Hilarity. Country drinks both hard and soft.
Weston, Vt., The Countryman's Press, 1938. 16p.
Brown, Chas. W.
Standard cyclopedia of recipes. Chicago, Frederick
J. Drake and Co., 1907. 449p.
Brown, Cora Lovisa (Brackett)
The wine cook book . . . by the Browns; Cora, Rose
and Bob. Boston, Little, Brown and Co., 1941.
462p. 1934 - same.
Brown, Cora, Rose and Bob
The wining and dining quiz. New York, D. Appleton
Century Co., 165p.   LC
Brown, Eleanor and Bob
Culinary Americana. Cookbooks 1860 through 1960.
New York, Roving Eye Press, 1961. 417p.
Bibliography.
Brown, Ernest and Hunter, H. H.
Planting in Uganda. London, Longmans, Green and
Co., 1913. 176p. Illus.
Brown, Harold T.
See Thorpe, Edward and Harold T. Brown
Report on determination of original gravity beers by
distillation process.
Brown, Florence Isabella
The bartender's friend; a compilation of the best in
mixicology from reliable sources, both new and old,
and particularly from the formulary of the famous old
Grand opera house bar, Syracuse, New York, by
A mixer [pseud], with the collaboration of Patrick W.
Guinee . . . New York, N.Y., Jarmor Publishing Co.,
1933. 170p. Illus.
Brown, Helen Evans
A book of appetizers. With a number of drinks by
Philip S. Brown. Los Angeles, 1958. unpaged (163).
Brown, Horace T.
Reminiscences of fifty years' experiences of the
application of scientific method to brewing practice.
London, Printed by Harrison and Sons, 1916. 82p.
Brown, John Hull
Early American beverages. Rutland, Vt. Charles
E. Tuttle Company, 1966. 171p. Illus-photos.
Bibliography- Glossary.

Brown, Neail W.
   Liquor dealer's and bartender's companion. New York,
   1865. 44p.   (Yale University)
Brown, O. Phelps
   The complete herbalist. London, Published by author,
   1875. 504p.
Brown, Philip S.
   See Brown, Helen Evans
   A book of appetizers. With a number of drinks by
   Philip S. Brown.
Brown, Robert Carlton
   Let there be beer! By Bob Brown. New York, H.
   Smith and R. Haas, 1932. 321p. Illus.
Brown, W. Jann
   See Liebowitz, Daniel and Brown, W. Jann and Olness
   Marlene
   Cook to your heart's content on a low-fat, low-salt
   diet.
Browne, Charles
   The Gun Club drink book. New York, Charles
   Scribner's Sons, 1939. 190p. Illus. 1941, same.
Browne, Edith A.
   Cocoa. (Peeps at Industry). London, A and C
   Black Ltd., 1920. 88p. Illus-photos.
      _____.
      . . . Tea. London, A and C Black, 1912. 88p.
   Illus-photos.
Browne, Peter. Bishop of Cork and Ross
   Of drinking to memory of the dead. Dublin, 1713.
   Numerous others. 44p. Other places.   LC
Browne, W. Aloysius and Browne, C.W.
   Get back to nature and live. (The "Walpole" Botanic
   Guide to Health.) "A nature healing book worth its
   weight in gold." Southampton (England). Published
   by the authors. n d, (1931). 132p.
Brownen, George
   See Skrine, Edward H. and Brownen, George
   The tea we drink.
Brownrigg, William
   Use of knowledge of mephetic exhalations. An
   experimental inquiry into mineral elastic spirit con-
   tained in Spa water, etc. London, 1766. 28p.   BM
Bruce, Charles A.
   Account of the manufacture of black tea as practiced at
   Suddeya in upper Siam. Calcutta, G.H. Hutmann, 1838.
   18p.   BM
84

_____ Report on the manufacture of tea and on the extent
and produce of tea platations in Assam.   London, 1910.
India Tea Ass'n, Calcutta, Bishops College Press, 1839.
36p.   BM
Bruce, Edwin M.
Detection of the common food adulterants.   3rd edition.
New York, D. Van Nostrand, 1917.   88p.
Brunswick-Balke-Collender Co.
A book of recipes.   How to mix fancy drinks
BARTENDER'S GUIDE.   New York, (1933).   40p.   Illus.
Brunswyke, J.
Vertouse boke of distyllacyon, 1527.   BV
Bruun, Kettil
Drinking behavior in small groups.   Alcohol research
in Northern Countries.   An experimental study.
Helsinki, The Finnish Foundation for Alcohol Studies,
1939.   132p.   References.
Bruun, Kettil and Ragnar Hauge
Drinking habits among northern youth.   Helsinki, Publ.
no. 12., The Finnish Foundation for Alcohol Studies,
1963.   97p.   References.
Bryan, A. Hugh
Maple-Sap Syrup: its manufacture, composition, and
effect of environment thereon.   Washington, U.S.
Dept. Agriculture, Bureau of Chemistry no. 134, 1917.
110p.   Bibliography.
Bryant, William Baily
Nineteenth century handbook on the manufacture of
liquors, wines and cordials without the aid of distil-
lation.   Also the manufacture of effervescing beverages
and syrups, vinegar and bitters.   Owensboro, Ky.,
Industrial Publishing Company, 1895.   310p.
Advertising matter.
Buchan, William D.
Cautions concerning cold bathing and drinking mineral
waters.   London, A. Strahan and Cadell, T., 1786.
20p.   BM
Buchanan, J.H. and Levine, Max
Bottle washing and its control in the carbonated
beverage industry.   ABCB Educational Bulletin no. 1
(Revised edition).   Washington, Published by Amer.
Bottlers Carbonated Beverages.   Reprint 1936.   33p.
Illus.

_____.
The testing of washing solutions. ABCB Educational
Bulletin No. 1. Washington. Published by American
Bottlers of Carbonated Beverages, 1929. 8p.
Buchanan, Robert
 The culture of the grape and wine-making. Cincinnati
Fifth edition, Moore, Wilstach, Keys and Co., 1856.
142p. Sixth edition, 1860, 142p. Eighth edition, 1865,
142p.
Buck, Tom
But Daddy! (Teaching the young about alcohol). New
York, William Morrow and Company, 1967. 219p.
Buckingham, Sir. J.
(A few) Facts about Indian tea. London, India Tea
Ass'n, 1910. 31p.   BM
Buckingham, James Silk
History and progress of the temperance reformation,
in Great Britain, etc. London, Partridge, Oakey and
Co., 1854. 160p.
Buell, J. S.
The cider makers' manual. Buffalo, Haas and Kelley,
1869. 174p. Illus.
Buell, O. D. and Haughey, J. T.
100 and 10 most popular American drinks, etc.
Kansas City, Printed by Palmer Printing Co., 1934.
unpaged.
Bullock, Thomas
The ideal bartender. St. Louis, Buxton and Skinner
Printing and Stationery Co., 1917. 53p.
Bulos, Monsieur
Art of wine making. See Fisher, S. I - Observations
on the character of the European vine.
Bumstead, George
Specimens of a bibliography of old books and pamphlets
illustrative of the mug, glass, loving cup, bottle, etc.
Diss. (England), 1885. 144p.   NYPL
Bunting, J. J.
See Shillington, D. F. and Bunting, John J. compilers.
Bunting's book on breakfast beverages.
Bunton, John
See Hall, James J. and Bunton, J.
Wines.
Bunyard, Edward Ashdown
The anatomy of dessert with a few notes on wine.
London, Chatto and Windus, 1933. 217p.

Bunyard, Edward and Lorna
The Epicure's Companion. London, J.M. Dent and
Sons Ltd., 1937. 539p. Illus.

Bunyard, George
Apples and pears. London, J.C. and E.C. Jack,
1911. 115p. Illus.

Bunyard, George and Owen Thomas
The Fruit Garden. The Country Life Library.
London, George Newnes Ltd., 1904. 507p. Illus.

Burbidge, F.W.
The book of the scented garden. London, John Lane-
the Bodley Head Ltd., 1923. 96p. Illus.
Bibliography.

Burgess, A.H.
Hops. Botany, cultivation and utilization. London,
Leonard Hill, 1964. 300p. Illus. Bibliography.

Burgess, Rev. H.T.
Fruit of the vine. Adelaide. South Australian Total
Abstinance League, 1878. 138p.
(State Library of Victoria)

Burgoyne, Burbidges and Co.
Notes on the manufacture of aerated waters, cordial,
brewed beers, etc. London, Published by the
company, n d. 132p. plus 32.

Buring, H.P.L.
Australian wines: 150th anniversary of the wine industry
of Australia. Sydney, Federal Vitacultural Council
of Australia, 1938. 15p. (State Library of Victoria)

Buring, Leo Ltd.
Art of serving wine. Sydney, 1935. 32p.
(Boston Public)

Burke, Harman Burney
Burke's complete cocktail and drinking recipes, etc.,
New York, Books, Inc., 1934. 93p.
1936, 125p. c1936, 125p. c1941, 93p.

——————
Cocktail and tastybite recipes. Boston, Samuel Ward
Mfg. Co., 1934. 93p.

Burke, Thomas
The book of the inn; being 200 pictures of the English
inn from the earliest times to the coming of the railway hotel. London, Constable, 1927. 401p. Illus.

——————
The English Inn. London, Longmans, Green, 1930. 187p.
Illus. 1931, 186p. Illus. 1940, 189p. Illus.

_____. Will someone lead me to a pub? London, George
Routledge and Sons Ltd., 1936. 84p. Illus.

Burnett, The Joseph Company
About vanilla. Boston, 1900. 44p.

_____. Dainty and artistic desserts. Menus and special
recipes by Mrs. Janet M. Hill. Boston, n d. 38p.

Burns Bottling Machine Works
Burns Master Air-Free Bottling system. For the
progressive bottler, by William W. Burns, Sr.
Baltimore, Published by the Company, 1941. unpaged.
Illus.

_____. Twenty years plus Burns equals profits to you.
Baltimore, Published by the Company, 1939. 47p.
Illus.

Burns, Dawson
Christendom and the drink curse, etc., London,
Partridge and Co., 1875. 333p.

_____. Temperance history. London, National Temperance
Publication Bureau, (1890). 2 volumes 463, 511.

_____. Temperance in the Victorian age. London, The Ideal
Publishing Union, 1897. 208p.

Burns, Jabez
The "Spice-Mill" companion. Compendium of valuable
receipts, with many historic and curious facts in relation to coffee, spices, etc. New York, 1879. 102p.
                                                        LC

Burt, S. H. Compiler
The Universal Household Assistant. New York, S. H.
Moore and Co., 1885. 510p.

Busby, James
Australian farmer's and land owner's guide to the
profitable culture of the vine in New South Wales.
London, Smith Elder and Co., 1839. 192p.   ANL

_____. Grapes and wine. Visit to the principal vineyards of
Spain and France, etc., New York, C. S. Francis and
Co., 1848. 166p.   LC

_____. Journal of a recent visit to the vineyards of Spain and
France, etc. Philadelphia, Jacob Snyder Jr., 1838.
177p.

———— Manual of plain directions for planting and cultivating vineyards and for making wine in New South Wales, Sydney, R. Mansfield, 1830. 96p.   ANL

———— Treatise on the culture of the vine and art of making wine. Sydney, R. Howe, 1825. 250p.   BM

Busch Products Co.
Practical direction, receipts and processes for production of various kinds and qualities of liquors, etc. New York, 1933. 94p.   (Yale Univ.)

Bush, Baron de and Bush, Richard Arthur
Recipes for the manufacture of aerated and mineral waters and cordials. Third edition. London, Published by W. J. Bush and Co., 1890. 70p. 4th edition, 1894. 94p. 5th edition, 1897. 106p.

Bush, Richard Arthur
Recipes for the manufacture of liqueurs, spirits, etc. Third edition. London, W. J. Bush and Co., 1892. 25p. Illus.

Bush, Raymond
A fruit-growers diary. London, Faber and Faber Ltd., 1950. 248p. Illus.

———— Harvesting and storing garden fruit. Cider, etc., home-made wines. London, Faber and Faber, 1947. 162p.

———— Soft fruit growing. Harmondsworth, England, Penguin Books, 1944. 175p. Illus-photos, drawings.

———— Tree fruit growing. Volume I-Apples. Volume II-Pears, quinces, stone fruits. Harmondsworth, England, Penguin Books, 1943. 167, 158p. Illus-photos, drawings.

Bush, W. J. and Co.
See Pocock, J.
The brewing of non-excisable beers.

———— Bush catalogue and book of reference for the bottler. New York, 1950. 67p.

———— Centenary Album. 1851-1951. London, Published by the Company. A pictorial record of Bush world-wide development, establishments and personalities during 100 years of progress, 1951. unpaged.

———— Citrus juice compounds for the soft drinks industry. London, 1952. 32p. Illus.

———— Export price-list no. 2. London, 1947. 109p.

———— General Price List no. 1. London, 1949. not paged consecutively.

———— Liqueur Compounder's Handbook (The) of recipes for the manufacture of liqueurs, alcoholic cordials, and compounded spirits. Eighth edition, revised and enlarged. London, 1921. 57p. Illus.

———— Practical recipes for the manufacture of aerated beverages, cordials, non-alcoholic brewed beers, carbonated mineral waters, etc., Seventh edition. London, 1909. 183p. 1916, 173p. 1925. 177p.

———— Price list for the soft drinks industry. London, 1957. 25p.

———— Price list of essential oils, etc. New York, May 1918. 40p.

———— Products for the beverage trades. Special edition Brewers' Exhibition, London, 1947. 20p. 2nd edition, 1950, 56p. 3rd edition, 1951, 55p. 4th edition, 1954, 52p.

———— Products for the soft drinks industry. 5th edition. London, 1957. 72p.

———— Recipes for manufacture of liqueurs, alcoholic cordials, spirits, etc. Fifth edition. London, 1899. 33p.

———— See Skuse's complete confectioner, etc.
Bush and Son and Meissner.
    Illustrated descriptive catalogue of American grape vines. A grape growers' manual . . . 3rd edition. St. Louis, Studley, 1887. 153p. Illus.
Bushman, J. S.
    Burton and its bitter beer. London, W. S. Orr and Co., 1853. 179p.   BM

Butler, Frank Hedges
  Wine and the wine lands of the world, with some account
  of places visited. London, T. Fisher Unwin Ltd., 1926.
  271p. Illus.
Butler, W. C.
  Butler's modern practical confectioner. Manchester,
  A Heywood, 1898. 97p.   BM
Butterfield, H. M.
  Bush berry culture in California. Berkeley. Circular
  no. 80 California Agricultural Extension Service.
  College of Agri. University of California, 1942. 62p.
  Illus.
Butterfield, Herbert E.
  The scientific manufacture of jams and allied products.
  Watford, Herts, Published by the author, June 1926.
  36p.
Buzzo-Cardozo of Hollywood
  Hollywood's favorite cocktail book. Hollywood, n d.
  40p. Illus.
Byfield, T.
  The artificial spaw, or mineral waters to drink, etc.
  London, Published by author, 1684. 70p.   LC
Bynum, Lindley Davis
  California wines; how to enjoy them. Los Angeles,
  H. H. Boelter Lithography, 1955. unpaged. Illus.
Byrn, M. La Fayette
  The complete practical brewer. Instructions, art of
  brewing, ale, beer and porter; and small beers, root,
  sarsaparilla, etc. Philadelphia, Henry Carey Baird,
  1852. 199p.

——————————.
  The complete practical distiller, etc. Philadelphia,
  Henry Carey Baird, 1866. 198p. Illus-drawings.
  8th edition, 1871, 217p. Illus.
Byrne, E.
  Guaging, Liverpool, Sheppard and Co., 1887. 83p. BM
Byrne, Oliver
  Practical, complete and correct gager. (The). London,
  A. H. Bailey and Co., 1840. 328p.   BM
Byron, O. H.
  The modern bartenders' guide, or fancy drinks and how
  to mix them. New York, Excelsior Publishing House,
  1884. 114p.   LC
Bywaters, Herbert W.
  Modern methods of cocoa and chocolate manufacture.
  Philadelphia, Blakiston Sons and Co., 1930. 316p.
                                                          NYPL
                          91

C. (P.)
>   Discourse on the preparation, preservation, etc., of
>   malt liquors.   London, J. Oswald, 1733.   94p.
>   GBPOL
Cadbury Brothers Ltd.
>   Bournville, the factory in a garden.   Pictorial
>   description of making chocolate and the place where it
>   is made.   n p.   Bournville, Cadbury Brothers Ltd., nd.
>
> _____
>   Cadbury's of Bournville.   The building of a modern
>   business.   Produced by the Publication Department at
>   Bournville, n d.   31p.   Illus-photos, drawing.
>   2nd edition, 1949.   24p.   Illus.
>
> _____
>   See Bareau, Paul.
>   Cocoa: A crop with a future.
>
> _____
>   Cocoa and chocolate.   From grower to consumer.
>   Bournville, 2nd impression.   Publication Department,
>   1949.   16p.   Illus-photos.   Revised 1959-28p.   Illus-
>   photos.
>
> _____
>   See Wood, G. A. R.
>   Cocoa growing in India.
>
> _____
>   See Wood, G. A. R.
>   Cocoa growing in Venezuela, Columbia and Ecuador, etc.
>
> _____
>   See Anon
>   Cocoa growing costs.   (Reprints).
>
> _____
>   See Anon.
>   Cocoa Grower's Bulletin.   From no. 1 August 1953
>   through no. 7 Summer 1969.
>
> _____
>   See Urquhart, D. H.
>   Cocoa in some countries of South-East Asia and
>   the Pacific.   Ceylon-Hawaii-Thailand-Malaya-Papua- and
>   New Guinea- The Fiji group.
>
> _____
>   Education and training in office and factory.   Some
>   Bournville schemes.   Bournville, 1948.   24p.   Illus-
>   photos.

———•—— Industrial Challenge. The experience of Cadburys of Bournville in the post-war years. Contents- Account of developments in making chocolate during the last 10 years. London, 1964. 92p. Illus-photos.

———•—— See Urquhart, D. H.
Prospects for cocoa growing in Uganda and Zanzibar.

———•—— See Urquhart, D. H. and Dwyer, R. E. P.
Prospects of extending the growing of cocoa in Papua and New Guinea.

———•—— See Urquhart, D. H.
Prospects of the growing of cocoa in the British Solomon Islands with notes on Malaya, Ceylon and Java.

———•—— See Urquhart, D. H. and Wood, G. A. R.
Report on a visit to the cocoa zone of Bahia, Brazil.

———•—— See Urquhart, D. H.
Report on an investigation into the prospects for growing cocoa and oil palms in India.

———•—— See Wood, G. A. R.
Report on cocoa growing in the Dominican Republic Mexico, Guatemala and Costa Rica.

———•—— See Urquhart, D. H.
Report on the cocoa industry in Sierra Leone. And notes on the cocoa industry of the Gold Coast.

———•—— See Urquhart, D. H.
Report on the cocoa industry in the French Ivory Coast.

———•—— See Urquhart, D. H.
Report on the expansion of the cocoa industry in Jamaica.

———•—— See Urquhart, D. H.
Report on the possibilities of cocoa-growing in the protectorate of Nyasaland.

———————.
See Deverson, H. J.
The tree of the Golden Pod. The story of cocoa
farmers and chocolate workers.

Cadbury, Richard
Cocoa: all about it. By "Historicus" (pseud). London,
S. Low, Marston and Co., 1892. 99p. Illus. plates.

Cain, Arthur H. (Dr.)
Young people and drinking. The use and abuse of
beverage alcohol. New York, Fifth impression. The
John Day Company, 1963. 96p. Suggested Reading.

Caladonia Springs.
Folder of The Grand Hotel Company of Caladonia
Springs. Title page, WELL? Ontario, Canada n d,
ca1905. 16p. Illus.

California. Agricultural Extension Service.
San Bernardino County.
Wine in cooking. San Bernardino, University of
California, n d. unpaged (16), Illus.

California. Board of state viticultural commissioners.
Annual report; appendix A. Grape syrup. Sacramento,
1893. 15p. Illus.

California Fruit Growers Exchange
Bottlers Handbook for the use of EXCHANGE bottlers
juices. Ontario, California, c1938. 53p. Illus.

California Fruit Growers Exchange
Products Department
Exchange Citrus Pectin. 2nd edition. Ontario,
California, 1934. 63p. paper cover. 4th edition,
1941, 117p. 6th edition, 1954, 146p.

California. State Board of Horticulture.
Annual Report. (fruit), 1891. 488p.

California. State Fair and Exposition.
Wine awards. (Sacramento), 1961. 31p.

Calkins, Alonzo
Opium and opium appetite with notices of alcoholic
beverages, cocoa, tea, coffee and the like. Philadelphia, J. B. Lippincott and Co., 1871. 390p.

NYPL

Calkins, Raymond
Substitutes for the saloon. An investigation made for
the Committee of Fifty. Boston and New York,
Houghton Mifflin and Co., 1901. 397p. Bibliography.

Callahan, Genevieve.
The New California Cook Book. New York, M.
Barrows and Co., 1960. 373p.

94

Callow, Edward
    Old London Taverns. Historical, descriptive and
    reminiscent. London, Downey and Co., Ltd., 1899.
    354p. Illus.
Calvert Distillers Company
    Party Encyclopedia. The House of Calvert. n p, 1960.
    96p. 1963, same.
Cambiaire, Celestin Pierre
    The Black Horse of the Apocalypse. Wine, alcohol
    and civilization. Paris, Librairie Universitaire J.
    Gambier, 1932. 486p.
Cameron, Sheila Mac Niven
    Homemade ice cream and sherbets. Rutland, Vt.
    Charles E. Tuttle and Co., 1969. 56p.
Camp, Charles D. Laboratories
    Book of formulas and manufacturers guide. (Flavors).
    Chicago, 1921. 150p.   LC
Camp, John
    Oxfordshire and Buckinghamshire pubs. London,
    B. T. Batsford Ltd., 1965. 175p. Illus.
Campbell, Andrew
    The book of beer. London, D. Dobson, 1956. 304p.
Campbell, Clyde H.
    Campbell's book. A manual on canning, pickling and
    preserving. Third edition. Chicago, Vance Publishing
    Corp., 1950. 222p. Illus.

_____.
    Campbell's Book of canning, preserving pickling.
    Revised edition. Chicago, Vance Publishing Co., 1945.
    856p. Bibliography.
Campbell, Ian Maxwell
    Reminiscences of a vintner. London, Chapman & Hall,
    1950. 276p. Illus.

_____.
    Wayward tendrils of the vine. London, Chapman and
    Hall, 1948. 210p.

_____.
    Wine: Post-war problems and possibilities, 1941.
            (Massel-Applied Wine Chemistry and Technology)
Campbell, Lute E.
    Campbell's tea, coffee and spice manual. Los
    Angeles, Published by author, 1920. 180p.   LC
Campbell, William T.
    Big Beverage. (Fiction). Atlanta, Tupper and Love,
    1952.

Campbell Soup Company
   Proceedings Flavor Chemistry Symposium.   Camden,
   N. J., 1961. 229p. Illus.
Canada Dry Ginger Ale Co., Inc.
   See Moore, Roy M.
   Down from Canada came tales of a wonderful beverage.
Canada Dry Corp.
   How to be a cordial host, New York, n d. 16p.
                                                 (Brown Univ.)

—————— .
   The Masterly touch. New York, 1934. 44p. Illus.
Candler, Charles Howard
   Asa Griggs Candler. Emory University, Georgia, 1950.
   487p. Illus. Bibliography.
Capper, W. Bently
   Licensed houses and their management. The Trade
   Encylopedia. London, Caxton Publishing Co., n d,
   ca1927. 3 volumes 252, 278, 300. Illus.

—————— .
   See Moral, Julian J.
   Progressive catering. A comprehensive treatment of
   food, cookery, drink, catering services and management.
Caradeuc, H. de
   Grape culture and winemaking in the South. Augusta,
   Ga., Aiken Vine Growing Ass'n, 1859. 23p. (Davis)
Card, Fred W.
   Bush-Fruits. A horticultural monograph of raspberries,
   blackberries, dewberries, currants, gooseberries,
   and other shrublike fruits. 5th edition. New York,
   Macmillan Co., 1911. 537p. Bibliography.
Cardelli, M.
   Manuel du Limonadier et du Confiseur. Paris, 6th
   edition. A la librairie Encyclopedique de Roret. (In
   French). 280p.
Carling, Thomas Edward
   The complete book of drink; a guide to the buying,
   storing, service and selling of all alcoholic liquors.
   London, Practical Press, 1951. 208p. Dictionary
   of terms.

—————— .
   Wine. Thumbnail sketches of wines of the world, etc.
   London, Barrie and Rockliff, 1960. 56p.

—————— .
   Wine aristocracy; a guide to the best wines of the
   world. London, Rockliff, 1957. 136p.

_____. Wine drinker's aide-memoire. Tutle page-WINE DATA.
Canterbury, Practical Press, 1959. 35p.

_____. Wine etiquette, etc., Whitstable, Published by author,
1949. 39p.   BM

_____. Wine lore; a critical analysis of wine dogma. London,
Practical Press, 1954. 55p. Illus. Glossary.

_____. Wine-wise. How to know, choose and serve wine.
Second edition, Canterbury, no publisher, 1949. 65p.
Carlisle, Donald Thompson
Wining and dining with rhyme and reason, by D.T.
Carlisle and Elizabeth Dunn. New York, Minton,
Balch and Co., 1933. 128p. Illus. Bibliography.
Carlsberg Breweries
Book of Carlsberg. (The). Carlsberg Breweries,
Carlsberg, Denmark, 1946. unpaged, Illus.
Carlsberg Bryggerierne
(The Carlsberg Breweries), Copenhagen, 1927. 85p.
Illus.
Carlson, A.J. et al.
Studies on the possible intoxicating action of 3.2 per
cent beer. Chicago, University of Chicago Press,
1934. 85p. Bibliography   LC
Carlson, H.M.
See Brodner, Joseph, Carlson, Howard, and Marchal,
Henry T. Editors
Profitable food and beverage operation.
Carnell, P.P.
A treatise on family wine making, etc. London,
Sherwood, Neely and Jones, 1814. 158p.
Carpenter, G.A.
See Hope, G.D. and Carpenter, G.A.
Some aspects of modern tea pruning.
Carpenter, P.H. and Harrison, C.J.
The manufacture of tea in northeast India, Calcutta,
Printed at Catholic Orphan Press, 1927. 42p.
                          (National Agriculture Library)
Carpenter, William B.
On the use and abuse of alcoholic liquors, in health
and disease. London, Charles Gilpin, 1850. 283p.

_____. On the use and abuse of alcoholic liquors, in health and disease. Boston, Prize essay published for Massachusetts Temperance Society by Wm. Crosby and H. P. Nichols, 1851. 264p.

_____. Use and abuse of alcoholic liquors (prize essay on) in health and disease. Philadelphia, Henry C. Lea, 1866. 178p.

Carrico, G.
Art of mixing drinks. Chicago, Reilley and Lee, 1938. 230p.   CBI

Carroll, Robert S.
What price alcohol? A practical discussion of the causes and treatment of alcoholism. New York, The Macmillan Co., 1942. 362p.

Carosso, Vincent P.
The California wine industry, 1880-1895; a study of the formative years. Berkeley, University of California Press, 1951. 241p. Bibliography.

Carson, Gerald
The social history of bourbon; an unhurried account of our star-spangled American drink. . . . New York, Dodd, Mead, 1963. 280p. Illus. Glossary, Chapter notes.

Carswell, D and C
Scots weekend book. London, G. Routledge and Sons, 1936. 503p.   LC

Carter, Charles
Complete city and country book. London, H. Bettesworth and C. Hitch, 1732. 280p.   BM

Carter, Henry
The control of the drink trade. London, Longmans, Green and Co., 1918. 323p. 2nd edition, 1919, 343p.

Carter, J. A.
Confessions of a bartender. Los Angeles, Published by author, 1947. 80p.

Carter, W.
Cook and confectioner's guide. London, Bailey and Co., 1800. 260p.   BG

Carter, Youngman
Drinking Bordeaux, London, Hamish Hamilton Ltd., 1966. 95p. Illus. Bibliography.

_____. Drinking Burgundy. London, Hamish Hamilton, Ltd. 1966. 91p. Illus. Glossary.

98

‾‾‾‾‾‾ Drinking champagne and brandy. London, Hamish
     Hamilton, 1968. 96p. Illus-photos.
Caruba, Rebecca
     Cooking with wine and high spirits. New York, Crown
     Publishers, 1963. 155p.
Cary, Samuel F.
     The liquor manufacture and traffic. New York,
     Brognard and Co., 1849. 12p.   NYPL

‾‾‾‾‾‾ The National Temperance Offering. New York, R.
     Van Dien, entered 1855. 320p.
Casanave, Armand
     Practical manual for the culture of the vine in the
     Gironde. Sacramento. California Vitaculture
     Commission, 1885. 61p.   NYPL
Casey, Edward M.
     The Mixologist and compounder. San Francisco.
     California Publishing Co., 1889. 302p.   LC
Cassagnac, Paul de.
     French wines. London, Chatto and Windus, 1930.
     242p. Illus. New York, Dutton, n d.
Castella, Hubert de.
     Handbook on vitaculture for Victoria. Melbourne,
     Robert S. Brain, government printer, 1891.
                         (James-Wine in Australia)
Castella, F. de
     Home wine making. Melbourne, 1921. 24p.
                                        PLOSA
Castella, Hubert de
     John Bull's vineyard. Melbourne, Sands and Mac
     Dougall, Ltd., 1886. 263p.   (University of Illinois)
Catts-Patterson Co., Ltd.
     Proposed plan for the development of the Australian
     wine industry. Melbourne, 1929. 12p.
                         (State Library of Victoria)
Cauchois, F.A. and Co., Compiler
     Over the black coffee. History, etc., New York, n d.
     ca1905. 108p.
Caux, J.W. de
     Licensed victualler's vade mecum. Great Yarmouth,
     J. Buckle, 1905. 68p.   BM
Cavallo, Tiberius
     Essay on medical preparation of factitious airs.
     London, C. Dilly, 1798. 256p.   BM

Cavan, Sherri
　　Liquor license. An ethnography of bar behavior.
　　Chicago, Aldino Publishing Co., 1966. 246p.
Cave, Henry W.
　　Golden tips. A description of Ceylon and its great tea
　　industry. Third edition. London, Cassell and Company,
　　1904. 476p. Illus. 1900, 474p.
Cave, Peter L.
　　Best drinking jokes. London, Wolfe Publishing Co.
　　1969. 64p.
Cazaubon, D.
　　Treatise and practical guide of the apparatus for the
　　fabrication of gaseous drinks, sparkling wines, etc.
　　Paris, Printed by A. Henninger, 1876. 132p.
　　　　　　　　　　　　　　　　　　　(Boston Public)
Central Food Technological Research Institute
　　Mango. Monograph for industry. No. 1. Mysore,
　　1962. 59p.

―――――― .
　　Papaya. Industrial monograph No. 2. Mysore, 1963.
　　41p.
Cerwin, Herbert
　　Famous recipes by famous people. San Francisco,
　　Lane Publishing Co., 1940. 62p. Illus-drawings.
Chace, E.M.; Loesecke, Von H.W. and Heid, J.L.
　　Citrus Fruit Products. Washington, Circular no. 577
　　U.S. Dept. Agriculture, November 1940. 47p.
　　Literature cited.
Chadwick, William A.
　　A practical treatise on brewing, etc. London, Whit-
　　taker and Co., 1835. 62p.　　　　　　　　　　BM
Chafetz, Morris E. and Demone, Jr., Harold W.
　　Alcoholism and society. New York, Oxford University
　　Press, 1962. 319p. Bibliography.

―――――― .
　　Liquor: the servant of man. Boston, Little Brown
　　and Co., 1965. 236p. Selected reading list.
Chain Store Research Bureau
　　The future of the soft drink industry. Studies of five
　　large franchise firms. New York, n d, ca1939. 53p.
Chakravarty, Taponath
　　Food and Drink in ancient Bengal. Calcutta, P.
　　Chakravarty, 1959. 72p. Bibliography.
Chaloner, Len
　　What the vintners sell. London, H. Cranton, 1926.
　　159p. Illus.

Chamberlain, Arthur
    Speeches in Leeds, Cardiff and Hull in favour of main-
    taining free--direction for the licensing justices---.
    n p, March, 1904. 38p.
Chamberlain, Bernard Peyton
    A treatise on the making of palatable table wines,
    recommended to gentlemen, especially in Virginia, for
    their own use. Charlottesville, Va., Priv. print. for
    the author, 1931. 97p.
Chamberlain, Narcissa G. and Narcisse
    The Flavor of France in recipes and pictures. New
    York, Hastings House, 1962. 232p. Illus.
Chamberlain, Samuel
    Bouquet de France. New York, Gourmet, 1952. 619p.
                                                          LC
Chambers, Amelia
    Ladies best companion. London, J. Cooke, 1800.
    196p.   BM
Chambers, F. T.
    See Strecker, Edward A. and Chambers, Jr., Francis T.
    Alcohol, one man's meat.
Chambers, Mary D.
    One-piece dinners. Boston, Little, Brown, and Co.,
    1924. 188p.
Chamney, Montfort
    The story of the tea leaf. Calcutta, The New Indian
    Press, n d, ca1931. 78p.
Champin, Aime
    Vine grafting. Sacramento, California Vitacultural
    Commissioner's report no. 2. Appendix no. 3, 1883.
    134p.   NYPL
Champion, William
    The Maltster's Guide. Being a statement from long
    experience of the best means of making malt. London,
    Printed by A. Bedford and A. Robins, Southwark,
    1832. 204p.
Chancellor, Charles Williams
    Treatise on mineral waters and seaside resorts,
    descriptive and medical. Baltimore, J.B. Piet and Co.,
    1883. 160p.   LC
Chandler, S.E. and Mc Ewan, J.
    Tea, its culture, manufacture and commerce. London,
    1913.   (Torgasheff-China as tea producer)
Chandler, William H.
    Fruit growing. Boston, Houghton Mifflin, 1925. 777p.
                                                          LC

Chang, Stephen S.
See Anon. Flavors and spices and flavor characterization.
Chapin and Gore, Compiler
Manual. What to use. How to mix. How to serve. Chicago, Chapin and Gore Publishers, 1935. 72p.
Chapman, Alfred Chaston
Brewing. . . . Cambridge, England, University Press; New York, G. P. Putnam's Sons, 1912. 130p. Illus. Bibliography.

_____.
The hop and its constituents. London, The Brewing Trade Review, 1905. 99p. Illus-drawings.

_____.
The industry of brewing. London, 1911. 19p. (Bird)
Chapman, Thomas
The cyder-maker's instructor. London, Green and Russell, 1762. 28p.   LC
Chappaz, George and Henriot, Alexandre
The champagne vine country and champagne wine. Epernay, Moet and Chandon, n d, ca1920. 32p. Illus.
Chappius, B.
See Fisher, S. I.
Observations on the character and culture of the European vine.
Chaptal, Jean A. C. et al.
Treatise upon wines. Charleston, S. C. J. H. Sargent, 1823. 166p.   (Boston Public)
"Charles"
See Reinhardt, Charles Nicholas
"Cheerio!" A book of punches and cocktails.

_____.
The Cocktail Bar. London, W. Foulsham and Co., Ltd. 1960. 159p.
"Charles" formerly of Delmonicos.
Punches and cocktails (Book of) New edition revised and enlarged. New York, Arden Book Company, 1934. 53p.
Charles, C. (Charles Nicholas Reinhardt)
Bartender's guide. Chicago, Nelson Hall, publ. 1949. 177p.   CBI
Charleton, Rice
Treatise on Bath waters. Bath. . . T. Boddley, 1754. 74p.   (Univ. of Missouri)

Charleton, Walter
  Two discourses. (of the mysteries of vintners.)
  London, Printed by R.W. for William Whitwood, 1669.
  230p.   LC
Charley, Vernon, L.S.
  See The Cider Factory, Plant and layout.

——————.
  See Warcollier, Georges
  The principles and practice of cider-making.

——————.
  Recent advances in fruit juice production. London,
  Commonwealth Bureau of Horticulture and plantation
  crops. February 1950. 176p. References.
Charlotte
  Let's have a party. Watford, Herts, Bruce Publishing
  Co., Ltd., 1946. 77p. Illus.
Charrington's Brewery
  See Strong, L.A.G.
  A brewer's Progress 1757-1957.
Charters, James (Jimmie the Barman)
  This must be the place!. London, Herbert Joseph Ltd.,
  1934. 300p. Illus.
Chase, A.W.   MD
  Dr. Chase's Recipes. Ann Arbor, R.A. Beal, 1870.
  384p. Library has 12 editions.
Chase, Edithe Lea
  Waes Hael; the book of toasts. . . . By Edithe Lea
  Chase and Capt. W.E.P. French. . . . New York,
  Crafton, 1905, 303p. Illus.
Chase, Emily
  The pleasures of cooking with wine. London, Peter
  Davies, 1960. 243p.
Chase and Sanborn
  Coffee. Boston, n d, ca1884. 64p.

——————.
  The tea table. Boston, Vol. 1.-no. 1, May 1890,
  Published quarterly by authors. 16p. Illus.

——————.
  "To the household". Sixth edition. Boston, 1889.
  unpaged (48). Illus.
Chatfield, Charlotte and Adams, Georgian
  Proximate composition of American Food Materials.
  Washington, U.S. Department of Agriculture. Circular
  549., 1940. 89p.

Chatfield, Charlotte and McLaughlin, Laura I.
Proximate composition of fresh fruits. Washington,
U.S. Dept. Agriculture, Circular no. 50, 1931. 19p.

Chatt, Eileen M.
Cocoa: cultivation, processing, analysis. New York,
Inter-science Publishers, 1953. 302p. Illus. Bibliography.

Cheek-Neal Coffee Co.
The story of coffee and how to make it. (Maxwell
House Coffee). Nashville, Tenn., 1925. unpaged
(16).

Cheever, George B.
Defense in abatement of judgement for an alleged libel
in the story entitled "Inquire at Amos Giles' Distillery".
New York, Leavitt, Lord and Co., 1836. 112p.

"Chemist and Druggist"
See Anon.
Art of dispensing. (The). Methods and processes
involved in compounding prescriptions.

Cheney, Ralph Holt
Coffee; a monograph of the economic species of the
genus Coffea L. New York, The New York
University Press, 1925. 244p. Illus. Bibliographies.

Chenoweth, Walter W.
Food Preservation. A textbook for student, teacher,
home-maker and home factory operator. New York,
John Wiley and Sons, 1930. 344p. Illus.

———— How to preserve food. Boston, Houghton Mifflin Co.,
1945. 289p.

Cheraux, Dr. M.T. Puckett
The daughter of an alcoholic. New York, Pageant
Press, 1960. 73p.

Cherrington, Ernest H. Ed. and Comp.
The Anti-Saloon League Year Book 1910. Westerville
Ohio, Published by The Anti-Saloon League of America.
256p. 1932-33, 233p.

———— History of the anti-saloon League. Westerville, Ohio,
The American Issue Publishing Co., 1913. 161p.

Chester, Thomas
Carbonated beverages. The art of making, dispensing,
and bottling soda-water, mineral-waters, ginger-ale
and sparkling liquors. New York, P.H. Reilley,
Printer, 1882. 108p. Illus.

Chesterton, G.K.
  Wine, water and song. 19th edition. London, Methuen
  and Co., Ltd., 1945. 60p. Illus.
Chicotte, Pedro
  Mis 500 cocktails. Madrid, Editorial Pueyo, 1933.
  (In Spanish). 298p.
Child, Samuel
  Every man his own brewer. A small treatise explain-
  ing the art and mystery of brewing porter, ale, two-
  penny and table beer, etc. 3rd edition. No publisher,
  n d, London, 21p. 1794. 4th edition. J. Ridgeway,
  20p.
  _____.
  Practical treatise explaining the art and mystery of
  brewing porter, ale, two-penny and table beer.
  (Every man his own brewer). Fifth edition. London,
  J. Ridgeway, 1798. 24p. 7th edition, 1799. 29p.
Chiris, Antoine
  See Antoine Chiris Company
  Whole sale Price List. Essential oils, etc.
Chocolate Manufacturers Ass'n of the USA
  The story of chocolate. Washington, 1960. 31p.
  Illus. Bibliography.
Chodowski, A.T.
  Wine, its use and abuse: wines of the bible. Sydney,
  1920. 16p.   PLOSA
  _____.
  Wine, its use and abuse: the fermented wines of the
  bible. Christ Church, N.Z. Christ Church Press,
  Ltd., 1893. 22p.   (National Library, Wellington)
Chorlton, William
  The American grape growers guide. New York, C.M.
  Saxton and Co., 1856. 171p. Illus. 1860, C.M.
  Saxton, Barker and Co., 204p.
  _____.
  The American grape grower's guide intended especially
  for the American climate. New York, Orange Judd,
  1865. 204p. 1899, 211p. Illus. new edition.
  _____.
  Chorlton's grape growers' guide. Same as above.
  _____.
  The cold grapery. New York, J.C. Riker, 1852.
  95p. Illus.

Christ, Edwin R. and Fish, F.R.
    That book about wine. Burbank, S.D. Privately
    printed, 1955. 31p.   (Univ. of Missouri)
Christian, Russell
    Sherry, London, 1881.   (Jeffs- Sherry)
Christie, A.W.
    See Cruess, W.V. and Christie, A.W.
    Laboratory Manual of Fruit and Vegetable Products.
Chubb, W.P.
    Receipt book or Oracle of Knowledge containing nearly
    one thousand useful receipts with directions for making
    British wine. London, J. Smith, 1825. 230p.
Church, A.H.
    Food. A brief account of its sources, constituents and
    uses. London, Chapman and Hall Ltd., 1889. 252p.
Church, Mary Ellen
    ✓The American guide to wines. Chicago, Quadrangle
    Books, 1963. 272p. Illus.
Church, Ruth Ellen
    Mary Meade's Magic recipes for the electric blender.
    Indianapolis, Bobbs-Merrill, 1952. 256p.
Churchill, S.D.
    All sorts and conditions of drinks. (Price list of
    wine merchants of Cardiff). London, 1893.
                         (Wine Trade Club)

Churchill, Creighton
    A notebook for the wines of France: a wine diary or
    cellar book listing the nine hundred most important
    French wines and/or their vineyards, with space for
    the wine drinker's own records and notations. . .
    New York, Knopf, 1961. 387p. Illus. Bibliography.

————————
    The world of wines. New York, The Macmillan Co.,
    1964. 271p. Glossary-Bibliography.
Claiborne, Craig, Editor
    New York Times Cook Book. New York, Harper and
    Row, 1961. 717p. Illus.
Clair, Colin
    Of herbs and spices. London, Abelard-Schuman Ltd.,
    1961. 276p. Illus-drawings (color). Bibliography.
Clark, George and Son Ltd.
    Brewing. A book of reference. London, n d, (1936).
    6 parts (volumes)-paged consecutively. 275p.

————————
    Technical sugar data. London, n d, ca1950. unpaged
    (47).

Clark, Herbert
   Beer gravity tables. Heckmondwike, 1884. unpaged
   (28).
Clarke, A.
   . . . Flavouring materials, natural and synthetic.
   London, H. Frowde and Hodder and Stoughton, 1922.
   166p. Illus.
Clarke, Ebenezer
   The worship of Bacchus a great delusion. 2nd edition.
   London, James Clarke and Sons, 1877. 86p. Illus.
Clarke, Eddie
   King cocktail. Shaking again with Eddie. London, 1954.
   88p.   BM

_____ .
   Practical bar management. London, Practical Press
   Ltd., 1954. 161p. Illus. Glossary.

_____ .
   Shaking in the 60's. London, Cocktail Books Ltd.,
   1963. 256p. Illus.

_____ .
   Shaking with Eddie. London, Published by author,
   1948. 51p.   CBI
Clarke, Mrs. Edith
   Plain cookery recipes. 2nd series Vol. 11. London,
   William Clowes and Sons. (National Training School
   of Cookery), 1927. 146p.
Clarke, Edward W.
   Brewery bookkeeping. Chicago, H.C. Rich and Co.,
   1898. 181p.   Crerar
Clarke, Frank K.
   Make your wine at home. London, Elek Books Limited,
   1969. 86p. Illus-drawings.
Clarke, J. Harold
   Small fruits for your home garden. Garden City, N.Y.,
   Doubleday and Co., Inc., 1958. 372p. Illus.
Clarke, Nick
   Bluff your way in wine. London, Wolfe Publishing Ltd.,
   1967. 63p. Maps. Glossary
Clarke, Ronald
   Food colours. London, British Food Manufacturers
   Industries Research Ass'n. Private circulation, 1952.
   9p.   BM
Clarke, T.E.B.
   What's yours? The student's guide to Publand. London,
   Peter Davies, 1938. 165p. Illus.

Clarke, William
Clarke's complete cellar manual and publican and innkeeper's practical guide, and wine and spirit director
and assistant. London. Sherwood, Gilbert and Piper,
1851. 264p. (Simon-Private Library)

_____.
Publican and Innkeeper's Practical guide, etc. London,
Sherwood, Gilbert and Piper, 1829. 264p. Illus-
engravings.
Clarkson, Charles
Instructions for brewing porter and stout. London,
1853. 16p. Bird
Clarkson, Rosetta E.
Herbs. Their culture and uses. New York, The
Macmillan and Co., 1942. 226p. Illus.
Clausen, Henry Jr.
Souvenir of 25th convention of United States Brewers
Association. Address by Clausen, New York, 1885.
40p. Illus.
Clayton, David and Langdon, David
Wake and die! London, Allan Wingate, 1952. 112p.
Illus.
Cleland, Charles
Abstracts of the several laws that are now in force,
relating to the importation and exportation of wines.
Into and out of Great Britain. London, Printed for
the author, 1737. 172p. LC
Cleland, Elizabeth
New and easy method of cookery. Edinburgh, Published
by author, 1759. 232p. BM
"Clements"
Homemade wines, liquors and vinegars. London,
W.H. Allen and Co., 1888. 35p.
Clerck, Jean de.
A textbook of brewing. London, Chapman and Hall,
1957-58. Vol. 1.-1957, 587p. Illus. Vol. 2.- 1958,
650p. Illus.
Cleveland, Bess A.
California Mission Recipes. Rutland-Tokyo. Charles
E. Tuttle, 1965. 141p. Illus.
Clifford, F.S.
A romance of perfume lands or the search for Capt.
Jacob Cole. Boston, Clifford and Co., 1881. 295p.
Illus.

Clifton, Francis
   State of Physick, ancient and modern, briefly considered.
   (Food and drink). London, W. Bowyer, 1732. 192p.
                                                        BM
Clinch, George
   English hops. A history of cultivation and preparation
   for the market from the earliest times. London, Mc-
   Corquordale and Co., Ltd., (1919). 120p. Illus.
   Bibliography.
Clinkard, Charles Ernest
   The uses of juice extracted from raw fruits and
   vegetables. Auckland, C.E. Clinkard and Co., 1946.
   32p.   (National Library, Wellington)
Clotho (Pseud)
   Prosit; a book of toasts. San Francisco, P. Elder,
   1904. 134p. Illus.
Clubb, Henry S.
   The Maine Liquor Law: its origin, history and results
   including a life of Hon. Neal Dow. New York, Fowler
   and Wells, 1856. 430p.
Coan, Titus Munson
   Home uses of mineral waters. Published in Harper's
   New Monthly Magazine, 1888. pages 719 to 726.
   clippings.
Cobb, Gerald
   Oporto, older and newer. Published by author at
   Ancora and Meanstroke, 1965-66. 110p. Illus-photos.
Cobb, Irvin Shrewsbury
   Irvin S. Cobb's own recipe book. Louisville and Balti-
   more, Frankfort distilleries, 1934. 52p. Illus.
   1936, 51p. Illus.

_____ .
   Red likker. New York, Cosmopolitan Book, 1929.
   339p.
Cobbett, William
   Cottage Economy. Hartford, Silas Andrus and Son,
   1848. 158p. Illus.
The Coca-Cola Co.
   Coca-Cola Bottler (The). April 1959. 50th Anniversary
   issue. Atlanta, Vol. 5. no. 1., included a reprint of
   Volume 1., no. 1., dated April 1909. 238p. Illus.

_____ .
   A guide for proper cup machine operation. Atlanta,
   1949. 49p. Illus.

———— Opinions, orders, injunctions and decrees relating to unfair competition and infringement of trade-mark. First edition. Atlanta, 1923. 648p. Illus.

———— The Refresher Magazine of the Coca-Cola Company. 75th Anniversary Edition. Atlanta, 1961. 91p. Illus.

Cochran, Thomas C.
    The Pabst Brewing Co. The history of an American business. New York, New York University Press, 1948. 451p. Illus. Bibliography.

Cockburn, Ernest
    Port wine and Oporto. London, Wine and Spirit Publications Ltd., (1940). 132p. Illus-photos. Glossary.

Cocks, C.
    Bordeaux: its wines and the claret country. London, Longman, Brown, Green and Longmans, 1846. 215p.

Codman, Charles R.
    Years and years; some vintage years in French wines. Boston, S.S. Pierce Co., 1935. 27p. Bibliography.

Codman, R.S.
    Vintage dinners, etc. Boston, Privately printed, 1937. 129p. Illus.   LC

Codman, Mrs. Theodora Larocque
    Was it a holiday. Boston, Little, Brown, 1935. 235p. Illus.

Coffee Brewing Institute, Inc.
    There's a story in your coffee cup. New York, 1963. 32p. Illus.

Coffin, Robert Barry.
    Ale in prose and verse, by Barry Gray (pseud), and John Savage. New York, Russell's American Steam Printing House, 1866. 97p. Illus.

Cogan, Thomas
    The haven of health. London, Henry Middleton for W. Norton, 1584. 284p.   BM

Coghill, J.A.
    Cocktail recipes, 1923. 94p.   (Brisbane Public)

Cohan, Erwin
    "Here's How" by Clegg, pseud. Philadelphia, Columbia Publishing Co., 1933. 106p.   LC

Coit, J. Eliot
Citrus Fruits. An account of the citrus fruit industry
with special reference to California requirements and
practices and similar conditions. New York, Macmillan
and Co., 1915. 520p. Bibliography. 1922, same.
Coker, Margaret R.
See Mirrlees, Emily Lina and Coker, Margaret Rosalys
Wishful cooking.
Colam, E.E.F.
Practical milk bar operation, catering and ice cream
making. Foreword by Arthur T.E. Binsted dated June
1946. London, No publisher mentioned (Attwood and Co.,
Ltd., London), n d. 193p. Illus. Bibliography.
Colborne, R.S.
Synthetic aromatics, perfumes, isolates. Washington,
Hobart Publishing Co., 1947. 73p.   Berkeley
Colburn, Frona Eunice Wait
In old vintage days. San Francisco. Printed by John
Henry Nash, 1937. 178p.
Colchester-Wemyss, Sir Francis
The pleasures of the table. 2nd edition. London,
James Nisbet and Co., Ltd., 1962. 276p.
Cole, Ann Kilborn
Fine food, wine and pickled pine. The story of
Coventry Forge Inn. New York, David McKay
Company, Inc., 1962. 211p.
Cole, Mary
Ladies complete guide. Includes the complete brewer.
London, 1791. 460p.   NYPL
Cole, S.W.
The American Fruit Book; containing directions for
raising, propagating, and managing fruit trees, shrubs
and plants; with a description of the best varieties of
fruit, etc. Boston, John P. Jowett and Co., 1850.
288p.
Colin, Jane
Herbs and spices for health and beauty. London,
Arlington Books, 1962. 96p.
Collier, Jim
CHEERS! New York, Avon Book Division, Hearst
Corporation, 1960. 144p. Illus. Bibliography.
Collier, Joseph
Experiments and observations on fermentation and the
distillation of ardent spirit. Papers read February and
November 1797. n p, No publisher. pages 243 to
274. Illus.

Collingwood, Francis and Woollams, John
    The Universal Cook. London, J. Scatcherd and J.
    Whitaker, 1792. 451p. Illus.
Colman, Julia
    The catechism on beer. New York, National
    Temperance Society and Publication House, 1885. 32p.
Colmenero, de Ledesma Antonio
    Chocolate - or an Indian drinke. (could be same as
    "A curious treatise of the nature and quality of
    chocolate"). English edition. London, 1685.
    11 leaves.   BM

    Curious treatise on the nature and quality of chocolate.
    English edition. London, 1640. 21p.   BM
Colvin, D. Leigh
    Prohibition in the United States. A history of the
    prohibition party and the prohibition movement. New
    York, George H. Doran Company, 1926. 678p.
Colyer, Frederick
    See Scamell, George
    Breweries and maltings: their arrangement, construction,
    machinery and plant.
Combrune, Michael
    An essay on brewing with a view of establishing the
    principles of the art. London, R. and J. Dodsley,
    1758. 214p.   Crerar

    The theory and practice of brewing. London, J. and J.
    Dodsley, etc., 1762. 298p.
Comite Interprofessionel du Vin do Champagne
    The Champagne wine. Epernay, France. n d. 31p.
    Illus.
Commissioner of Agriculture
    Annual report of the commissioner of agriculture, for
    the year 1878. Washington, Government Printing Office
    1879. 608p.
Commissioner of Patents
    Abridgements of specifications. Class 14 Beverages.
    (excepting tea, coffee, etc.).
    1. Period - 1877-1883. London, 1894. 82p.
    2. Period, 1884-1888. London, 1896. 74p.

    Abridgement of specifications. Class 14 Beverages
    except tea, coffee, and the likes.
    1. Period - 1889-1892. London, 1898. 74p.
    2. Period - 1893-1896. London, 1899. 84p.

————. Abridgements of specifications relating to brewing, wine-making, and distilling alcoholic liquids, 1634-1866. London, 1881. 552p.

————. Abridgement of specifications relating to preparing and cutting cork; bottling liquids; securing and opening bottles, etc., 1777-1866. London, 1872. 341p. Also Part II - 1867-1876. London, 1884. 379p. Also Part III- 1877-1883. London, 1885. 348p.

————. Abridgements of the specifications relating to the preservation of food. 1691-1855. London, 1857. 46p.

————. Abridgements of specifications relating to unfermented beverages, aerated liquids, mineral waters, and etc., 1774-1866. London, 1877. 134p. Part II - 1867-1876. London, 1883. 112p.

Compton, Henry
Chocolate and cocoa. Information book. How things are obtained. 3rd edition. London, The Educational Supply Ass'n, Ltd., 1957. 63p. Illus.

Compton, Herbert
Come to tea with us. London, Anti Tea Duty League, 1905. 124p.   BM

Concklin, Jerry
The bartender; or How to mix drinks. New York, R.K. Fox, 1888. 56p. Illus.   LC

Conant, James Bryant, Editor
Pasteur's study of fermentation. Cambridge, Mass. Harvard University Press, 1952. 57p.

Conil, Jean
For epicures only. London, T. Werner Laurie Ltd., 1952. 181p. Illus.

Considine, John H.
The Buffet Blue Book. 322 Mixed drinks. Chicago, Published by author, 1912. unpaged.

Consumer Union
The Consumers Union report on wines and spirits; ratings, recommendations, and buying guidance covering wines, whiskies, gins, vodkas, rums, brandies, and cordials. Mount Vernon, N.Y., Consumers Union of U.S., 1962. 158p.

Consumers Union of U.S.
  Wines and liquors (Consumers Union reports on).
  Second edition. New York, 1939. 125p.
Continental Can Company
  A B C of canning soft drinks. New York, n d,
  ca1955. unpaged (20).
Cook, A.H., Editor
  Barley and malt. Biology, biochemistry, technology.
  New York, Academic Press, 1962. 740p. Illus.
  References.
Cook, Charles Henry
  The curiosities of ale and beer: an entertaining history.
  (Illustrated with over fifty quaint cuts). By John
  Bickerdyke (pseud). London, Field and Tuer, 1889.
  449p. Illus.
Cook, Fred S. Ed.
  The wines and wineries of California. Volcano,
  California, "The California Traveller", (1969). 80p.
  Illus-photos. Vocabulary-wine.
Cook, L. Russell
  Chocolate production and uses. New York, Magazines
  for industry, 1963. 463p. Illus. Bibliography.
Cook, O. P.
  Shade in coffee culture. Bulletin no. 25, U.S. Dept.
  Agriculture. Washington, Government Printing Office,
  1901. 79p. Illus-photos.
Cook, Philip
  A wine merchant's assessment of Burgundy. London,
  Ridley's Limited, (1968). 28p. Illus-photos.
Cook, Richard
  Oxford night caps, a collection of receipts for making
  various beverages used in the University . . . London,
  The Peppercorn Press, 1931. 31p.
Cook and Bernheimer and Co. (Trade Catalog)
  Liqueurs fines. New York, (1891). Unpaged. Illus-
  colored photos.
Cook and Confectioner
  See The Complete Cook, J.M. Sanderson. The
  Complete Confectioner, Parkinson.
Cooke, Charles Wallwyn Radcliffe
  A book about cider and parry. 2nd edition. London,
  H. Cox, 1898. 120p.
Cooke, Matthew
  Injurious insects of the orchard, vineyards, etc.
  Sacramento, H.S. Crocker and Co., 1883. 472p.
  Illus-drawings.   (Brady Library-Fresno State Col.)

Cooley, Arnold James
    Handbook of perfumes, cosmetics and other toilet
    articles. Philadelphia, J.B. Lippincott and Co., 1873.
    804p.
——————.
    The toilet and cosmetic arts in ancient and modern
    times, etc. London, R. Hardwicke, 1866. 804p.
Coombs, James H.
    Bar Service. A non-technical manual for male and
    female bar-staff. Careers behind the bar. Volume I.
    London, Barrie and Rockliff, 1965. 248p. Illus.
    Glossary.
Cooper, A. Distiller
    The complete domestic distiller. A new edition
    corrected and revised. London, Thomas Tegg, 1826.
    276p.
Cooper, Ambrose
    The complete distiller. London, P. Vaillant, 1758.
    266p. New enlarged, 1803 Vernon Hood, 277p.
Cooper, George
    The modern domestic brewer. London, sold by
    Sherwood, Neeley, and Jones, 1811. 51p.   LC
Cooper, Isabella M.
    References, ancient and modern to the literature on
    beer and ale. New York, United Brewers Industrial
    Foundation, 1937. 31p. Bibliography.
Cooper, Raymond Westervelt
    The drama of drink. Its facts and fancies through
    the ages until now. Andover, Mass., Drama of Drink
    Distributors, 1932. 365p.
Cope, F.J.
    See Saunders, Wm.
    An essay on the culture of the native and exotic grape
    and both sides of the grape question, etc.
Coppinger, Joseph
    The American practical brewer and tanner. New York,
    Printed by Van Winkle and Wiley, 1815. 246p.   LC
Corbett, Edmund V. Compiler
    The libraries, museums and art galleries year-book,
    1964. London, James Clarke and Co., Ltd., 1964.
    556p.
Corbyn, Theophilus N.
    The compounder's pocket remembrancer; a treatise on
    manufacture of liquors, syrups, cordials, etc.
    Philadelphia, Published by author, 1888. 206p.   LC

Cordley and Hayes
　　Catalog of XXth Century coolers. New York,
　　Published by the company, 1920. 44p. Illus.
Cordon Bleu
　　See Bacchus and Cordon Bleu
　　New guide of the hotel, bar, restaurant, butler and
　　chef.
Cornelius, Dr.
　　Howitt, William (See)
　　The Student-life of Germany. From ms of Dr.
　　Cornelius. Philadelphia, Carey and Hart, 1842. 467p.
C (osens), F.W.
　　Sherryana, by F.W.C. London, Fleet Street, 1887?.
　　54p.
Cosnett, Thomas
　　The footman's directory and butler's remembrancer.
　　London, Simpkin and Marshall, and Henry Colburn,
　　1825. 288p.
Cossley-Batt, Dr. Jill and Baird, Dr. Irvin
　　Elixir of Life. Seattle, Washington, Python Publishing
　　Co., 1935. 116p.
Costa Neves
　　A story of "King Coffee". Rio de Janeiro. National
　　Coffee Department of Brazil, 1938? 63p. Illus.
Costello, Louisa S.
　　Summer amongst the Bocages and the vines. London,
　　Richard Bentley, 1840. 98p.　　　　　　　　　BM
Cotar, Charles
　　A treatise on the mineral waters of Vichy for the use
　　of practitioners. London, Lewis, 1913. 208p. Illus.
Cottam, H.
　　Tea cultivation in Assam. Colombo, 1877. 75p.
　　　　　　　　　　　　　　　　　　　　　　　GBPOL
Cotten, C.B.
　　Formula of New York, Philadelphia and Baltimore
　　manufacturers of wines and liquors. Cincinnati,
　　Published by author, 1851. 36p.　　　　　　　LC
Cotter, Oliver
　　Adulteration of liquors. With a description of the
　　poisons used in their manufacture. See what you drink.
　　Drink no more. Brooklyn, Published by author,
　　Entered 1874. 45p. Illus.

Cotton, Leo, Editor
 Old Mr. Boston; Deluxe Official Bartender's Guide.
 Boston, Mr. Boston, Distiller. 2nd printing 1935. 160p.
 3rd print -- Ben Burk, Inc., 1936., 160p.
 4th print -- Ben Burk, Inc., 1940., 160p.
 5th print -- Ben Burk, Inc., 1941., 160p.
 6th print -- Burke Bros. Distilleries., 1946., 160p.
 7th print -- Burke Bros. Distilleries., 1948., 160p.
 8th print -- Burke Bros. Distilleries., 1949., 160p.
Couche, Donald D.
 Modern detection and treatment of wine diseases.
 London, Published by author, 1935. 98p.   BM
Couling, Samuel
 History of the temperance movement in Great Britain
 and Ireland. London, William Tweedle, 1862. 374p.
Country Associations
 Wines, spirits for all occasions. London, 1954. 64p.
                                                  BM
Country Brewers Society
 64th Annual Report, 1885-1886. London, 15p.
Courtenay, J.M. de
 The Canada vine grower. Toronto, James Campbell
 and Son, 1866. 58p.   (Toronto Public)

_____ .
 The culture of the vine and emigration. Quebec, Joseph
 Durveau, 1863. 55p.   (Public Archives of Canada)
Courtney, Marion
 Cocktail Companions. Chicago, Wilcox and Follett
 Company, 1954. 95p.
Coville, Frederick V.
 Directions for blueberry culture. Bulletin no. 974.
 U.S. Dept. Agri. Washington, Government Printing
 Office, 1921. 24p. Illus- 29 plates.
Cox, Harry
 The wines of Australia. London, Hodder and Stoughton,
 1967. 192p. Illus-photos.
Cox, Helen
 The Food, Flowers and Wine cookbook. Flowers, by
 Stuart Mc Hugh. Wines, by George Dowglass. London,
 Odhams Books Ltd., 1964. 224p. Illus.
Cox, Henry Edward
 The Chemical analysis of foods. Philadelphia, P.
 Blakiston's Son and Co., 1926. 323p.
Cox, Henry Edward and Pearson, David
 The Chemical analysis of foods. New York, Chemical
 Publishing Co., 1962. 476p.

Cox, John
See M'Ewen, George
The culture of the peach and nectarine. Edited and
enlarged by John Cox.
Coxbie, Thomas
See Peedle, Thomas and Coxbie, Thomas
Fallacy of water drinking.
Coxe, John Redman
The emporium of Arts and Sciences. Volume 2.
Philadelphia, Joseph Delaplaine, 1812. 240p.
Coxe, William
A view of the cultivation of fruit trees and management
of orchards and cider, etc. Philadelphia, M. Carey
and Son, 1817. 253p. Illus- drawings.
Cozzens, Fred C.
Cozzens Wine Press (Periodical). First series nos.
1 to 12. July 20, 1854 to May 20, 1855. New York.
96p. each issue 8 pages bound in one volume.
Advertising.
Craddock, Harry
The Savoy cocktail book. London, Constable, 1930.
287p. Illus.
1934, New and enlarged edition. New York, Simon
and Schuster, 1934.
1930, same New York, Richard Smith Inc.
1965, 251p. London, Constable and Co.
Cradock, John (Von Viveur, pseud.)
An A.B.C. of wine drinking. London, Frederick
Muller, 1954. 96p. Illus.

_____.
Wining and dining in France with Bon Viveur. London,
Putnam, 1959. 225p.
Crafts, Dr. and Mrs. Wilbur F. and Misses
Mary and Margaret W. Leitch
Intoxicating drinks and drugs in all lands and times.
Revised 10th edition. Washington, The International
Reform Bureau, 1909. 287p. Illus.

_____.
Intoxicants and opium. In all lands and times. a 20th
century survey on intemperance, based on a symposium
of testimony from 100 missionaries and travelers.
Revised 6th edition. Washington, The International
Reform Bureau, 1904. 288p. Illus.

Crahan, Marcus Esketh
Early American inebrietatis. Review of the development of American habits in drink and the national bias and fixations resulting therefrom. Los Angeles, The Zamorano Club, 1964. 62p. Bibliography.

Craig, Elizabeth
Beer and vittels. London, Museum Press, 1955. 196p.

―――――. Bubble and Squeak. London, Chapman and Hall Ltd., 1936. 165p.

―――――. See Cookery. Elizabeth Craig's Household Library. 256p.

―――――. A cook's guide to wine. London, Constable, 1959. 176p.

―――――. See Anon. One thousand household hints. Elizabeth Craig's Household Library. London, Collins, 1950. 248p.

―――――. Sip softly. London, Published by The National Association of Soft Drinks Manufacturers, Ltd., n d. 10p. paper cover.

―――――. Wine in the kitchen, n p, no publisher, n d. 8p.

―――――. Wine in the kitchen. London, Constable and Co., Ltd., 1934. 136p.

―――――. Woman wine and a saucepan. London, Chapman and Hall, 1936. 189p.

Cramer, Pieter J. S.
Review of the literature on coffee research in Indonesia. Turriallo, Costa Rica, Inter-American Institute of Agricultural Sciences, 1957. 262p.   LC

Cramond, W.
On Scots drink. 2nd edition. Elgin, "Courant and Courier" Office, 1896. 36p.   PLOSA

Crampton, Charles Albert
Fermented alcoholic beverages, malt liquors, wine and cider. Washington, U.S. Dept. Agriculture Bulletin no. 13, 1887. 52p.   LC

Crane, E.J.; Patterson, Austin M. and Marr, Eleanor B.
A guide to the literature of chemistry. 2nd edition.
New York, John Wiley and Sons, Inc., 1957. 397p.

Crane, Rev. J.T.
Arts of intoxication. The aim and results. New York,
Carleton and Lanahan, 1871. 264p.

Crane, M.B.
See Hall, Sir A. Daniel and Crane, M.B.
The Apple

Crang, Alice
Preserves for all occasions. Harmondsworth, Penguin
Handbook, 1948. 160p. Illus.

Crawford, Iain
Make me a wine connoisseur. London, The Dickens
Press, 1969. 64p. Illus- maps.

————
Wine on a budget. London, Paul Hamlyn, 1964. 96p.
Glossary.

Crawley, Alfred Ernest
Dress, drinks, and drums, edited by Theodore
Bestermann. London, Methuen and Co., Ltd., 1931.
274p. Bibliographical foot- notes.

Creek, Douglas
Cocktails for amateurs. Torquay. Devenshire Press,
1948. 21p.   BM

Cresta Blanca Wine Co.
Nature smiled. . . and there was Cresta Blanca.
Los Angeles, Cresta Blanca Wine Co., Inc., 1944.
108p. Illus.

Crewe-Jones, F.
Two hundred fifty recipes for delicious drinks. New
York, Waverly Press, 1927. 64p.   NYPL

Crewel, Dr.
Every man his own brewer. London, John Henry, 1768.
256p.   (Institute of Brewing)

Crichton, David Alexander
The Australasian fruit culturist. Melbourne, Alex.
McKinley and Co., 1893. 2 volumes 314, 435. Illus.

Crichton, Robert
The secret of Santa Vittoria. (Wine). A novel, New
York, Simon and Schuster, Inc., 1966. 447p.

Cristiani, Richard S.
Perfumery and kindred arts. A comprehensive treatise on perfumery. Containing a history of perfumes, a complete detailed description of the raw materials and apparatus used in the perfumer's art . . . With an appendix, giving directions for making domestic wines, cordials . . . Philadelphia, H. C. Baird and Co., 1877. 308p. Illus.

Criticos, George
The life story of George of the Ritz, as told to Richard Viner. London, Heinemann (William) Ltd., 1959. 238p. Illus.

Crocker, E. C.
Flavor. New York, McGraw Hill Book Co., 1945. 172p. Illus. Bibliography.

Crockett, Albert Stevens
Old Waldorf bar days; with the cognomina and composition of four hundred and ninety-one appealing appetizers and salutary potations; also, a glossary for the use of antiquarians and students of American mores. New York, Aventine Press, 1931. 242p. Illus.

———. The old Waldorf-Astoria bar book . . . . New York, Dodd, Mead, 1934. 177p.

———. The old Waldorf-Astoria bar book with amendments due to the repeal of the XVIIIth. New York, Published by Crockett, 1935. 177p. Illus. Glossary

Croft, John
A treatise on the wines of Portugal. York, Printed by A. Ward for J. Todd, 1788. 31p.   LC

Croft-Cooke, Rupert
Madeira. London, Putnam, 1961. 224p.

———. Port. London, Putnam, 1957. 219p.

———. Sherry. New York, Alfred A. Knopf, 1956. 210p.

———. Wine and other drinks. London and Glasgow, Collins Nutshell Books no. 6., 1962. 160p.

Crole, David
Tea; a textbook of tea planting and manufacture . . . London, Crosby Lockwood, 1897. 242p. Illus. Footnotes.

Croly, Mrs. J. C.
   Jennie June's American cookery book. New York, The
   American News Co., 1870. 379p.
Crombie, Max, Editor
   The infidel grape. An anthology in miniature IN
   PRAISE OF WINE. Northwood, Middlesex, Knights
   Press, Ltd., n d. 23p. Illus-drawings.
Crombie, Max (compiler)
   The Wassail Bowl. An anthology in miniature of
   conviviality. Northwood, Middlesex, Knights Press Ltd.,
   n d, ca1930. 24p. Illus.
Cronk, Anthony
   English hops glossary. West Malling, St. Leonard's
   Press, 1959. 32p. Glossary.   GBPOL
Crook, James King
   The mineral waters of the United States and their
   therapeutic uses to which is added an appendix on
   potable waters. New York and Philadelphia, Lea
   Brothers and Co., 1899. 588p.
Crook, W. (publisher)
   New relation of use and virtue of tea. London, 1685.
   35p.   BM
Crooke, May
   See Bradley, Edith and Crooke, May
   The Book of Fruit Bottling. Chapters on fruit drying,
   homemade wines and cider making, etc.
Crooker, Joseph Henry
   Shall I drink? Boston, The Pilgrim Press, 1914.
   257p.
Crookes, William
   On the manufacture of beet-root sugar in England and
   Ireland. London, Longmans, Green and Co., 1870.
   290p.
Crosfield, Joseph and Sons Ltd.
   Brewing in the Soviet Union. Warrington, England,
   Published by Crosfield, 1962. 89p. (33 figures.)
Crosfill, John
   Historical survey of the temperance question. Birming-
   ham, The Templar Printing Works, 1920. 139p.
Crosland, Thomas W. H.
   The beautiful teetotaler. London, Century Press, 1907.
   156p.   BM

Cross, Charles
The American compounder; or Cross' guide for retail
liquor dealers . . . giving cost and profits of whiskies,
secrets of compounding and blending, and general
information pertaining to the liquor business. St.
Louis, (1899). 150p. Illus.

Cross, Marcus E.
The mirror of intemperance. Philadelphia, John T.
Lange, 1849. 240p.

Crotch, W. Walter
The complete year book of French quality wines,
spirits and liqueurs. Paris, M. Ponsot, 1947. 1230p.
Illus. Vocabulary.

Crouch, A. C.
See Elliot-Godsave, G. and Crouch, A. C.
The Thames. Southend to Kingston. Book number one,
of Riverside Taverns and Inns.

Crowley, Charles E.
A complete ritual of conviviality, hospitality and hilarity
well concocted from recipes gathered along the beaten
and unbeaten paths of man. New York, Humor Publishing Corp. 1933. 79p. Illus.   LC

Crown Cork and Seal Co., Inc.
The story of Crown Cork and Seal. Philadelphia, n d,
ca1959. 26p.

Croze, Austin de.
What to eat and drink in France; a guide to the
characteristic recipes and wines of each French
province, with a glossary of culinary terms. London,
and New York, F. Warne and Co., Ltd., 1931. 332p.
Glossary.

Cruess, William V.
Commercial Fruit and Vegetable Products.
A textbook for student, investigator and manufacturer.
New York, McGraw-Hill, 1924. 530p. References.
3rd edition, 1948. 906p.

_____ .
Joslyn, Maynard A. and Cruess, W.V. (see).
Elements in winemaking.

Cruess, William V. and Irish, J.H.
Fruit beverage investigations. University of California
Publications. College of Agri. Agricultural Experiment
Sta. Bull. no. 359., April 1923, Berkeley, University
of California Press. Pages 526-568. Illus-photos.

See Irish, John H.
Fruit juices and fruit juice beverages.
Cruess, William Vere, et al
↗ Laboratory examination of wines and other fermented
products. With M.A. Josyln and L.G. Saywell.
New York, Avi Publishing Co., 1934. 111p. Illus.
Cruess, William V. and Christie, A.W.
Laboratory Manual of fruit and vegetable products.
New York, McGraw-Hill, 1922. 109p. Selected
References.

——————.
Preparation of fruit juice in the home. Berkeley, Univ.
California Circular no. 65., 1932. 15p.   WI

——————.
↗ The principles and practice of wine making. 2nd
edition. New York, The Avi Publishing Co., 1947.
475p. Illus. Selected references. same, 1934.

——————.
See Amerine, M.A. and Cruess, W.V.
Technology of wine making.
Cruwell, G.A. and Blackford, A.S.
Brazil as a coffee growing country. Colombo, A.M.
and J. Ferguson, 1878. 150p.   NYPL
Culinary Arts Institute
Ice cream and cool drinks. (Subject guide, 1960).

——————.
The Mixer, Handmixer and Blender Cookbook. By the
Staff of Home Economists. Chicago, Spencer Press
Inc., 1954. 256p.
Culver, John Breckenridge
The gentle art of drinking. New York, Ready Reference
Publishing Co., 1930. 60p.
Cunningham, J. and W. Co.
Directions for managing strong beer exported to
America, Etc. Glasgow, 1767. Ms. (Brown University)
Cunynghame, Francis
Reminiscenses of an epicure. London, Peter Owen
Limited, 1955. 156p.
Curtis, Joseph Henry
As long as there is a single apple tree left, New
England can never be made bone dry. Boston, Published
by author, 1917. 63p. List of authors and books. LC

Curtis, Kenneth J.
The soft drinks industry legal handbook. 2nd edition. London, Published by The National Association of Soft Drinks Manufacturers, Ltd., 1963. 457p.

Cusmano, G.
Dizionario di Viticulture ed Enologia. Milano, Fratelli Dumolard, Editori, 1889. (In Italian). 304p. Dictionary.

Cussler, Margaret and De Give, Mary L.
'Twixt the cup and the lip. Psychological and Socio-Cultural factors affecting food habits. New York, Twayne Publishers, 1952. 262p. Illus.

Cust, Lady (The Honorable)
The invalid's own book. Recipes. New York, D. Appleton and Company, 1853. 144p.

Cutten, George B.
The psychology of alcoholism. London and Felling-on-Tyne. Walter Scott Publishing Co., 1907. 357p. Illus-photos, drawings.

D. (N.)
The virtues of coffee. London, Printed by W. G. 1663. 8p.   BM

Dahl, Joseph Oliver
Soda fountain and luncheonette management. Third printing. Stamford, Connecticut, Dahl Publishing Co., 1945. 228p.

_____.
Soda fountain management. Stamford, Connecticut, Dahls, n d, ca1937. 350p.   LC

Dahlgren, Bror Erik
Cacao. Chicago, Feild Museum of Natural History, 1923. Pages 25 to 38. Illus.

_____.
Coffee. Chicago, Field Museum of Natural History, 1938. 43p. Illus.

Dahlman, Wilhelm
Tafelwasser. Limonaden und Brausen. (In German). Leipzig, Fachbuchverlag, 1959. 122p. Illus.

Daiches, David
Scotch Whisky. Its past and present. London, Andre Deutsch, 1969. 168p. Illus-photos, engravings, Bibliography.

Daly, Tim
Daly's bartenders' encyclopedia. Worcester, Mass.,
T. Daly, 1903. 115p. LC
Dambaugh, L. N.
Coffee frontier in Brazil. Gainesville, Florida.
University of Florida, 1959. 59p. (Cornell Univ.)
Damblon, Heinrich
New method in manufacture of chocolate, cocoa powder
and confectionary. Cologne, Joseph Hofer, 1939.
155p. NYPL
Dane, Frederick
Sketch of the growth and history of tea and the science
of blending particularily adapted to Canadian trade.
Toronto, Mail Job Printing Co., 1891. 116p.
(Toronto Public)
Daniels, W. H.
The temperance reform and its great reformers. New
York, etc. Nelson and Phillips, 1879. 686p.
Same, published by Phillips and Hunt.
Daraio, John P.
Healthful and therapeutic properties of wine, beer,
whiskey, bitters, liquors in general. New York, no
publisher, 1937. 112p. LC
D'Armand, F.
Art of fine wine drinking. 1903.
(Massel- Applied wine chemistry and technology)
D'Armand, F. Jr.
Key to the trade (wine). Sacramento, H. S. Crocker
and Co., printer, 1865. 70p. UCLA
Darrow, Clarence and Yarros, Victor S.
The prohibition mania. A reply to Irving Fisher and
others. 2nd edition. New York, Boni and Liveright,
1927. 254p.
Darwin, Bernard
See Anon.
Receipts and relishes being a vade mecum for the
epicure in the British Isles.
Daughters of the American revolution. Massachusetts. Col.
Timothy Bigelow chapter, Worcester.
A book of beverages; being recipes secured from those
housewives most notable for their skill in the preparation
of choice and delectable beverages for winter nights and
summer noons . . . Worcester, Mass., 1904. 37p.

"Davenports" of Bath Row
Fifty years of progress. Being a description of the
House of Davenport. (Beer). Birmingham, 1935. 56p.
Illus.
Davey, Norman
The hungry traveller in France. London, J. Cape,
1931. 296p. Illus.
David, William K.
Secrets of wise men, chemists and great physicians.
Chicago, Published by author, 1889. 125p.
Davidson, James W.
The Island of Formosa. Past and present. History,
resources, people and commercial prospects. Tea,
camphor, sugar, etc. London and New York, Mac-
millan and Co., also Kelly and Walsh Yokohama,
etc., 1903. 720p. Illus.
Davidson, R.J.
Alwood, Wm. B. and Davidson, R.J. and Moncure,
W.A.P. (See)
The chemical composition of apples and cider.
Davidson, William R.
The wholesale wine trade in Ohio. Columbus, Ohio.
Ohio State University, 1955. 94p.   NYPL
Davies, Frederick
Drinks of all kinds, hot and cold, for all seasons, by
Frederick Davies and Seymour Davies. London, J.
Hogg, 1895. 148p.

_____.
Temperance drinks for summer and winter. A book
of recipes. London, Ward, Lock, Bowden and Co.,
1892. 121p.
Davies, John of Leeds, England
The innkeeper and butler's guide, or, A directory in
the making and managing of British wines; together with
directions for the managing, colouring and flavouring
of foreign wines and spirits. 5th edition. Leeds,
Printed by G. Wilson, 1807. 200p. 1809, 199p.
printed by W. Preston and Co.
Davies, John B.
The Butler, by an experienced servant. London,
Houlston and Stoneman, 1855. 108p.   BM
Davies, Samuel E.
An English butler's canapes, salads, sandwiches, drinks,
etc., New York, The Hirschler Books,, 1916. 109p.
Davies, Seymour
See Davies, Frederick
Drinks of all kinds, hot and cold, for all seasons.

Davis, Adelle
Let's eat right to keep fit. New York, Harcourt, Brace
and Co., 1954. 322p.

Davis, J. Irving
A beginner's guide to wines and spirits. London, S.
Nott Ltd., 1934. 93p. Illus. Glossary.

Davis, Kate B.
See Wachtmeister, The Countess Constance and Kate
Buffington Davis.
Practical vegetarian cookery.

Davis, S. F.
History of the wine trade. London, The Wine and
Spirit Ass'n of Great Britain, Inc., 1969. 19p.

Davis, Thomas
Mineral waters. Price list and invoice (Invoice in
long hand). London, 1759. 1 page loose

Davison, Eloise
Beer in the American home. New York, United
Brewers Industrial Foundation, 1937. 29p. Acknow-
ledgments

Dawson, Charles Carroll
Saratoga: its mineral waters, and their use in preventing and eradicating disease, and as a refreshing
beverage. New York, Russell Brothers Printers, 1874.
640p. Illus.

Day, Samuel Phillips
Tea, its mystery and history. London, Simpkin,
Marshall and Co., 1878. 92p. Illus.

Dayl, Barry
The world of fragrance. Hollywood, California, World
Fragrance, 1959. 188p. Illus.   LC

Deane, Albert B.
The licensed victuallers' official annual legal text book,
diary and almanac for the year 1913. London, Published
by The Licensed Victuallers' Central Protection Society
of London Ltd., 1913. 331p. Illus.

Deane, Edmond
Spadecrene Anglia or the English Spa fountain. Bristol,
Simpkin, Marshall, Hamilton, Kent, 1922. Reprint of
1626. 138p.   (Brisbane Public)

Dearden, Joseph
A brief history of the ancient and modern Tee-Totalism
with a short account of drunkenness. Preston, J. Livesay, 1838. pages various.

Death, James
The beer of the bible. London, Trubner and Co. With
a visit to an Arab brewery, notes on the oriental
ferment products, etc., One of the leavens of Exodus.
London, Trubner and Co., 1887. 179p. Illus.

————.
The defects of beer, n p London, n d, (1889), typed
56p. loose
Deering, C.
Muscadine grapes. Washington, U.S. Farmer's
Bulletin no. 1785, 1938. 37p.   BM

————.
See Husmann, G.C. and Deering, C.
The muscadine grapes.
Dees, Francis, T.R.
Young tea planter's companion. London, Swan,
Sonnenschein, Lowery and Co., 1886. 100p.   BM
Defay, Stefen G.M.
Professional bar management. London, 1955. 112p.
                                    (Wine and Food Society)
DeGive, M.L.
See Cussler, Margaret and DeGive, Mary L.
'Twixt the cup and the lip.
DeGouy, Louis Pullig
The cocktail hour. New York, Greenberg, 1951.
386p.

————.
Cooking with apple brandy. Stamford, The Dahls, 1931.
63p.   NYPL

————.
Derrydale game cook book. New York, Greenberg,
1950. 308p.   LC

————.
The master chef's best! appetizers, snacks, punches,
and cocktails. Greenlawn, N.Y., Harian Publications,
1954. 173p.   LC

————.
Soda Fountain Luncheonette drinks and recipes. Stamford, Connecticut, J.O. Dahls, 1940. 237p.
Deighton, Len
Drinks-man-ship. Town's album of fine wines and
high spirits. London, Haymarket Press Ltd., 1964.
133p. Illus.

Deite, C.
   A practical treatise on the manufacture of perfumery.
   From the German by William T. Brannt.   Philadelphia,
   H. C. Baird, 1892.   358p.
Dejean, M.
   Traite raisonne de la distillation ou la distillation
   reduite en principes.   4th edition.   Paris, P. F. Didot,
   1777.   (In French.)   461p.
Delavan, E. C.
   Adulterations of liquors.   New York, Brognard and Co.,
   American Temperance Repository, n d, ca1840.   12p.

   ─────────
   Temperance essays, and selections from different
   authors.   Albany, Van Benthuysen's Steam Printing
   House, 1865.   268p.   4th edition, 1869, 312p.
Delderfield, Eric R.
   A brief guide to inn signs.   4th edition.   Exmouth,
   Devon.   The Raleigh Press, 1932.   36p.

   ─────────
   More about inn signs.   Exmouth, Devon, The Raleigh
   Press, 1953.   40p.   Illus.
Delineator Home Institute
   . . . Beverages for parties.   New York, Delineator
   Service, 1929.   28p.   Illus.   LC
De Lisser and Co.
   Book of formulas.   For the manufacture of carbonated
   beverages.   "Red Book".   New York, 1889.   17p.
Demko, Dr. Charles
   Growing grapes in Florida.   State of Florida Dept. of
   Agri.   Bulletin no. 63.   Tallehassee, June 1957.   26p.
   Illus- photos.
Demone, Harold W.
   See Chafetz, Morris E. and Demone, Jr., Harold W.
   Alcoholism and Society.
Denison, Merrill
   The Barley and the Stream.   The Molson Story.
   Toronto, McClelland and Stewart Ltd., 1955.   398p.
   Illus.
Denman, James Lemoine
   A brief discourse on wine embracing an historical and

descriptive account of the vine, etc. London, Published
by J. L. Denman, 1861. 138p.

_____.
Pure wine and how to know it. London, Spottiswoode
and Co., 1869. 39p.   NYPL

_____.
The vine and its fruit, more especially in relation to
the production of wine: embracing an historical and
descriptive account of the grape, its culture and treatment in all countries, ancient and modern, drawn from
the best authorities, and incorporating a brief discourse
on wine. 2nd edition. rev. and enl. London, Longmans,
Green, 1875. 518p. Illus. maps.

_____.
What should we drink? An inquiry suggested by Mr. E.
L. Beckwith's 'Practical notes on wine.' London,
Longmans, Green, 1868. 120p.

_____.
Wine and its adulterations. London, Spottiswoode and
Co., 1867. 34p.   BM

_____.
Wine and its counterfeits . . . London, Briscoe and
Co., printers, 1876. 59p.

_____.
Wine as it is drank in England, and as it should be,
pure, wholesome and refreshing. London, Chifferial,
1865. 39p.   (Harvard Univ.)

_____.
Wine, the advantages of pure and natural wine, etc.
London, Published by author, 1865. 31p.   BM
Dennis, C. B.
A background to mead making. 4th edition. Ilford,
Essex. Published by Central Association of bee-keepers.
1961. 20p. Illus.
Denniston, G.
Grape culture in Steuben County. 1865.
                                        (Listed in Peddie)
Depew, Chauncey M. Ed.
One hundred years of American Commerce. New York,
D. O. Haynes and Co., 1895. 678p. Illus.

Despeissis, A.
The handbook of horticulture and vitaculture of Western Australia. 2nd edition. Perth Government Printer, 1903. 620p. Illus.

The vineyard and the cellar. Sydney, Dept. Agriculture Bulletin, 1894. 61p. BM

Desrosier, Norman W.
The technology of food preservation. Revised and augmented. Westport, Conn. AVI Publishing Co., 1963. 405p. Illus.

Dettori, Renato G.
. . . Italian wines and liqueurs. Rome, Federazione Italiana Produttori ed esportatori di vini, liquori ed affini, 1953. 158p. Illus.

Deutsche Brauerei Ausstellung.
Offizieller Katalog. Munich. (German Brewers Ass'n official catalog-exhibition), 1951. 364p.

Deverson, H.J.
The tree of the Golden Pod. The story of cocoa farmers and chocolate workers. (Bournville), (Cadbury Brothers, Ltd), n d. 36p. Illus-(color)-photos, drawings.

De Voto, Bernard
The Hour. Boston, Houghton Mifflin Company, 1951. 84p. Illus-drawings.

Dewey, H.T. and Sons Co.
Fiftieth anniversary 1857-1907. (wine). New York, 1907. 32p.

Dewey, Mrs. Suzette
Wines for those who have forgotten and those who want to know. Chicago, The Lakeside Press, 1934. 97p. Illus.

DeWitt, William A.
Drinking and what to do about it. New York, Grosset and Dunlap, 1952. 186p. Bibliography.

Dexter, Philip
Notes on French wines. Boston, Privately printed, 1933. 76p. NYPL

Dicey, Patricia Compiler
Wine in South Africa. A select Bibliography. University of Cape Town-School of librarianship, 1951. 29p. multigraphed copy, Bibliography.

Dick, William B.
Dick's book of toasts. New York, Dick and Fitzgerald, 1883. 172p.

_____ .
Encyclopedia of practical receipts and processes containing over 6400 receipts. New York, Dick and Fitzgerald, entered 1872. 607p.

Dickey, James M.
The devil's mortgage cancelled. Monon, Indiana. Published by author, 1899. 220p.

Dickinson, Denis and Goose, P.
Laboratory inspection of canned and bottled foods. London and Glasgow, Blackie and Son Ltd., 1955. 148p.

Dietz, F. Meredith and Deitz, Jr., August
Gay Nineties Cook Book. Richmond, Va. The Dietz Press, 1945. 318p.

Didier, Jacob A.
The reminder; an up-to-date, bartenders' vest pocket guide; how to mix drinks at the present time. Binghamton, New York, 1934. 178p.   LC

Digby, Sir Kenelm
Choice and experimental receipts in physick and chirurgy, etc. (Soft drinks). London, H. Brome, 1668. 308p.   BM

_____ .
The Closet of Sir Kenelme Digby opened. (London, Printed for E.C. and H. Broome, 1669). Volume VI from Mallinkrodt collection of Food Classics. St. Louis, 1967, a reprint. 312p.

_____ .
The closet of Sir Kenelm Digby, knight, opened; newly edited, with introduction, notes, and glossary, by Anne Macdonell. London, P.L. Warner, 1910. 291p. Glossary.

Dignadice, N.D.
Vocational guide in approved coffee cultivation practices. Manila, 1959. 49p.   (Cornell University)

The Diners' Club Magazine
The Diners' Club drink book. New York, Regents American Pub. Corp., 1961. 287p. Illus. Glossary.

Director, Anne
Art of Wine Cookery (The). London, Arco Publications, 1960. 190p.

———————— . The standard wine cook book.   Garden City, N.Y.,
   Garden City Books, 1948.   218p.
Dixon, Bernard
   Redox methods.   Reprinted from the Journal of the
   Incorporated Brewers' Guild, n p, 1939.   24p.   Illus.
Dobell, Daniel
   The art of brewing practically exemplified.   Instructions
   to brew--ales, stout, porter, and India pale ales.
   London, Reed and Pardon, n d, ca1850.   47p.
Doblache, Guillermo
   My first trip to Villa Nueva.   London, Reprinted from
   Bonfort's Wine and Spirit Gazette, 1896.   Also Lil'
   Ras'h'l, 1897.   15p. and 13p.
Dobson, Matthew
   A medical commentary on fixed air.   London, Printed
   for T. Cadell, 1787.   172p.   LC
Dobyns, Fletcher
   The amazing story of repeal.   An expose of the power
   of propaganda.   Chicago and New York, Willett, Clark
   and Co., 1940.   457p.
Dodd, George
   British manufactures.   Series IV and V.   London,
   Charles Knight and Co., 1845.   218 and 224p.

———————— . Nature's gifts and how to use them.   London, Ward
   Lock and Co., n d, ca1840.   283p.   Illus.
Dodds, Susanna W.
   Health in the household or hygenic cookery.   New
   York, Fowler and Wells, 1884.   602p.
Dodge and Olcott, Inc.
   The changing world of food.   New York, 1957.   36p.
   Illus.

———————— . Flavor department Bulletin 130 Suggestions for preparing
   flavor bases for summer drinks, home drink concentrates nectars, etc.   New York, n d.   28p.

———————— . Reference book and catalog of flavors and seasonings.
   New York, 1956.   68p.   Illus.

———————— . The story of an unique institution.   150th anniversary
   book.   New York, Privately printed by Dodge and
   Olcott, 1948.   95p.

———————•
Vanilla extracts, flavors, and sugars, etc. Bulletin
125, New York, n d. 17p.
Dodoens, R.
A Nievve Herball. London, 1578.   BV
Dods, Mistress Margaret
The Cook and Housewife's Manual. 4th edition rev.
and enl. Edinburgh and London, Published by Oliver
and Boyd, Simpkin and Marshall, 1829. 552p.

———————•
See Johnstone, Christian Isobel
The cook and housewife's manual: a practical system
of modern domestic cookery and family management . . .
Dominion Brewers Ass'n.
Facts on the brewing industry in Canada. Ottawa,
1948. 127p. Illus. Bibliography.
Don, R. S.
Wine, London, The English Universities Press
Limited, 1968. 202p. Illus-drawings. PROUNCIATION
GUIDE
Donovan, E.O.
On the question whether alcohol is the product of
fermentation or distillation, 1814.   (Scho)
Donovan, Michael
The Cabinet Encyclopedia. Domestic Economy Volume I.
New edition. London, Longman, Orme, Brown, Green,
and Longmans and John Taylor., 1837. 376p.

———————•
. . . Domestic economy. London, Printed for Long-
man, Brown, Green and Longmans and J. Taylor, 1842.
2 vols.
Doran, Dr.
Table traits with something on them. (Drinks and
drinking). London, Richard Bentley, 1854. 547p.
                    (Brady Library-Fresno State Col.)
Doran, James M.
The elementary chemistry of whiskey manufacture.
Washington, Distilled Spirits Institute, 1936. 16p.
Doran, Mrs. Roxana Brook, Compiler
Prohibition punches, a book of beverages. Philadelphia,
Dorrance and Co., Inc., 1930. 93p. Illus.
Dorchester, Daniel
The liquor problem in all ages. New York, Phillips
and Hunt, 1884. 656p.

Dorf, B. B. and Company
Cordial cocktail confidences. New York, n d, ca1929.
24p. Illus.
Dornot, C. C.
Wine and spirit merchants own book together with
the most approved methods of making British wines.
London, 1855. 136p.   GBPOL
Dorr, Rheta Childe
Drink; Coercion or control. New York, Frederick
A. Stokes, Co., 1929. 330p.
Doring, Paul
Money-saving formulas (The Home Book of).
Philadelphia, The Blakiston Co., 1946. 440p.
Dorozynski, Alexander and Bell, Bibiane
The wine book. Wines and wine making around the
world. New York, Golden Press, 1969. 310p.
Illus-photos.
Dossie, Robert
An essay on the spiritous liquors with regard to their
effects on health. London, n d, ca1735. 50p.   BM
Dougharty, John
The general guager: or, the principles and practice
of guaging beer, wine and malt, etc. Third edition.
London, James Knapton, 1719. 240p. 6th edition,
1750. 420p. John and Paul Knapton.
Doughty, Charles M.
Travels in Arabia Deserta. 2 volumes. London,
Jonathan Cape Ltd., and The Medici Society Ltd.,
1924. 623, 690, Illus. Glossary.
Douglas, Auriel
The International Hangover book. Los Angeles,
Price-Stern-Sloan, 1968. 95p. Illus-drawings.
Douglas, William
The House of Shea. Winnepeg, Manitoba, Published
by the House, 1947. 109p. Illus-photos.
Douglass, Earl L.
Prohibition and commonsense. New York, Alcohol
Information Committee, 1931. 310p.
Douglass, E. M.
See McCarthy, Raymond G. and Douglass Edward M.
Alcohol and social responsibility. A new educational
approach.
Dowd, Mary T. and Jameson, Jean D.
Food, its composition and preparation. 2nd edition.
New York, John Wiley and Sons, 1925. 177p.
Glossary.

Douglass, George
    See Cox, Helen. The food flowers and wine cookbook.
Dowling, A. F.
    Indian tea. Calcutta, 1880.   (Ukers-All about tea.)
_____.
    Tea notes. Calcutta, 1886.   (Ukers-All about tea.)
Down, P.
    See Turner, B. C. A. and Down, Peter
    Behind the wine list.
Downey, A. J.
    Australian grape growers manual for the use of
    beginners. Melbourne, Robertson, 1895.   70p.
                                                        PLOSA
Downing, A. J.
    The fruits and fruit trees of America; or the culture,
    propagation, and management, in the garden and
    orchard, etc. New York and London, Wiley and
    Putnam, 1845.   594p.
Downman, Francis
    Not claret. London, Richards, 1937.   96p.
Dows, C. D. and Co.
    Descriptive catalogue and price list of soda water
    apparatus. Boston, 1873-74.   73p.   Illus.
Doxat, John
    Booth's handbook of cocktails and mixed drinks.
    London, 1966. Booth's Distilleries Ltd., Pan Books
    Ltd., 1966.   191p.   Bibliography.
Drahota, Rudolf
    A treatise on the manufacture of liquors, syrups,
    cordials, and bitters.   Cover title DRAHOTA'S
    RECEIPTS. Includes Fabrication von Liqueuren
    (In German), 8th edition. Philadelphia, No Publisher,
    1891.   94p.
Drake, Francis S.
    Tea leaves being a collection of letters, etc. relating
    to shipment of tea to American colonies in year 1773
    by East India Tea Co., Boston, A. O. Crane, 1884.
    375p.   Illus.
Drake, Samuel Adams
    Old Boston taverns and tavern clubs. With account of
    "Cole's Inn", etc., by Walter K. Watkins. Boston,
    W. A. Butterfield, 1917.   124p.   Illus-map.

Dreesbach, Philip
  Beer bottlers' handy book . . . containing . . . many
  figuring examples, tables, bookkeeping forms and
  steaming charts. Chicago, Wahl-Henius Institute,
  1906. 765p. Illus.
Drennen, Mrs. G. T.
  Tea gardens of South Carolina. Published in DIXIE,
  a monthly magazine. Vol. III, No. 7. Baltimore 1900
  7p. Illus.
Drex, A.
  A B C of wines, cocktails and liqueurs. New York,
  Crown Publishing Co., 1933. 46p. Illus.   LC
Drinkwater, Caleb
  How to serve wine and beer. Cleveland. The Watkins
  Publishing Co., 1933. 80p. Illus.   LC
Driscoll, John Francis
  The bartender's friend. Chicago, Published by author,
  1933. 64p.   LC
_____.
  The drink master; how to prepare and mix all popular
  American alcoholic drinks, etc. Chicago, L.M.
  Driscoll, 1934. 64p. Illus.   LC
Driver, John
  Letters from Madeira in 1834 (wine). London, Long-
  man and Co., 1836. 85p.
                          (Brady Library-Fresno State Col.)
Driver, Sydney C.
  Some principles of the wine trade. London, L. Upcett
  Gill, 1909. 65p.   BM
Druggists Circular (The).
  The Druggists Circular Formula Book. New York,
  1915. 242p.
Druit, Robert
  Report on the cheap wines from France, Italy,
  Austria, Greece and Hungary, etc. London, 1865.
  Henry Renshaw, 1865. 179p. 2nd edition, 1873- 180p.
Drummond, Jack C. and Wilbraham, Anne
  The Englishman's food. Five centuries of English diet.
  London, Jonathan Cape, 1964. 574p. Illus.   BM
Dubelle, George H.
  "Non Plus Ultra" (The). Soda Fountain requisites of
  modern times. New York, Spon and Chamberlain, 1893
  160p.

_____.
Soda fountain beverages. A practical receipt book for druggists, chemists, confectioners and venders of soda water. Comprising a selected list of 500 drinks including the latest novelties. 3rd edition rev. and enl. New York, Spon and Chamberlain, 1905. 154p. 1911. 4th edition, 1917.

Dubois, Raymond and Wilkinson, Percy W.
New methods of grafting and budding as applied to reconstitution with American vines. Melbourne, Robert S. Brain Government Printer, 1901. 72p.

_____.
Trenching and subsoiling for American vines. Department of Agriculture, Viticultural Station, Rutherglen, Victoria. Robert S. Brain Government Printer, Melbourne, 1901. 171p. Illus.

Du Breuil, A.
Vineyard culture, improved and cheapened. Trans. by E. and C. Parker with notes and adaptations to American culture by John A. Warder. Cincinnati, Ohio, 1867. Robert Clarke and Co., 1867. 337p. Illus- drawings.

Du Breuil, M.
The Thomery system of grape culture. From the French. New York, Geo. E. Woodward, 1880? 60p. Illus.

Du Brow, Maxwell
Cocktails for two thousand. New York, 1951. Illus. unpaged. Recipes numbered.

Dubrunfaut, Augustin Pierre
A complete treatise on the art of distillation . . . also the whole art of rectification, in which is particularly treated the nature of essential oils . . . From the French of Dubrunfaut. By John Sheridan. To which is prefixed, The Distillers' practical guide, by Peter Jonas, with genuine recipes for making rum, brandy, Hollands' gin, and all sorts of compounds, cordials, and liqueurs. 4th edition. London, Sherwood, Gilbert and Piper, 1830. 532p. Illus.

Duckwall, Edward Wiley
Canning and preserving of food products with bacteriological techniques. Pittsburg, Published by author, 1905. 478p.

Duffy Malt Whiskey Co.
Duffy's pure malt whiskey. Medicine for all mankind,
Rochester, N.Y., 1904. 32p. Illus.
Duffy, Patrick Gavin
Bartender's Guide (The Standard), Garden City, N.Y.
Perma Books, 1951. 244p. 1955, 254p. Glossary.
1960, paperback.

The official mixer's manual; the standard guide for
professional and amateur bartenders throughout the
world. Garden City, N.Y., Blue Ribbon Books, 1940.
326p. Illus. 1934. New York, R. Long and
R. Smith. 299p. Illus.
Dufour, John James
American vine-dresser's guide, being a treatise on the
cultivation of the vine, and the process of wine
making adopted to soil, etc., of United States.
Cincinnati, Printed by S.J. Browne, 1826. 314p.
Illus.   LC
Dufour, Philippe Sylvestre
The manner of making of coffee, tea, and chocolate, etc
London, W. Crook, 1685. 116p. Illus.   LC
Dugdale, J.N.
How to keep healthy in the tropics. Chapter on Use
and abuse of alcohol. Singapore, Malaya Publishing
House, Ltd., 1930. 153p.
Dulcken, H.W.
The book of German songs. London, Ward and Lock,
1856. 324p. Illus.
Dumbra, Carl Dominick
Forward American wines, including wine producers
formulae. Sacramento, 1942. 2 vol. Illus.   LC
Dumont, Louis
How you can make wines, etc. Secrets of good wine
making revealed; making of dry table wines from
grapes, berries and other fruits. Santa Rosa, Calif.,
F.H. Eaton, 1955. 8p.   (Milwaukee Public)
Duncan, Dr. Daniel
Wholesome advice against the use of hot liquors,
particularly coffee, cocoa, tea, etc. London, H.
Rhodes, 1706. 280p.   NYPL
Duncan, Peter
See Acton, Bryan and Duncan Peter. Making mead,
methoglin, hippocras, melomel, pyment, cyser.

_____. See Acton, Byron and Duncan, Peter.
Making wines like those you buy.

Duncan, Peter and Acton, Bryon
Progressive winemaking. Andover, Hants, Amateur
Winemaker, 1967. 425p.

Dunlop, John
Artificial drinking usages of North Britain. Greenock,
K. Johnston, 1836. 122p.   NYPL

_____. On the wine system of Great Britain. Greenock, R. B.
Lusk, 1831. 57p.   NYPL

_____. The philosophy of artificial and compulsory drinking
usage in Great Britain and Ireland; containing the
characteristic, and exclusively national, convivial laws
of British society. 6th edition of the Scottish usages,
with large additions. London, Houlston and Stoneman,
1839. 331p.

Dunn, Helen, Compiler
Celebrity recipes. New York, Grayson
Publishing Co., 1958. 234p. Illus.

Dunn, James B.
Adulteration of liquors with a description of the
poisons used in their manufacture. New York,
National Temperance Society and Publication House,
1869. 24p.   LC

Duplais, Pierre
A treatise on the manufacture and distillation of alcoholic liquors. To which are added the United States
internal revenue regulations for the assessment and
collection of taxes on distilled spirits. Philadelphia,
H. C. Baird, 1871. 743p. Illus.

Dupont, Eugene T.
The Romance of Flowers. New York, Romance of
Flowers, n d. 32p.

Du Pont de Nemours, Alicia
The cultivation of vineyards in southwestern France.
New York, Brentano's, 1920. 273p. Illus.   LC

Dupré, August
On elimination of alcohol. London, Reprinted from
Proceedings of Royal Society Publication no. 133, 1872.
                                                   BV

———— See Thudichum, John Louis William. A treatise on
the origin, nature, and varieties of wine; being a
complete manual of viticulture and oenology. By J. L. W
Thudichum, M. D., and August Dupré. . .

Duranty, Walter
See Loos, Mary and Duranty, Walter
Return to the vineyard. (A novel).

Durfee, Charles H.
Should you drink? New York, The Macmillan Co.,
1954. 152p.

———— To drink or not to drink. New York, Longmans,
Green and Co., 1937. 212p. Bibliography.

Durr, Alfina
Fashions in drinks. San Pedro, California, Kreiger
Printing Co., 1933. 28 leaves. LC

Durvelle, J. P.
The preparation of perfumes and cosmetics. London,
Scott, Greenwood and Son, 1923. 419p. Illus.

Dussauce, Hippolyte
A practical guide for the perfumer: being a new treatise
on perfumery the most favorable to beauty without being
injurious to the health, comprising a description of the
substances used in perfumery, and the formula of more
than one thousand preparations . . . Philadelphia, H.
C. Baird, London, Trubner and Co., 1868. 376p.

———— Treatise on the coloring matters derived from coal tar.
Philadelphia. Henry Carey Baird, 1863. 196p.

Dutton, Thomas
Food and drink rationally discussed. London, H.
Kimpton, 1894. 124p. BM

Dwyer, Eleanor
Caviar to cordial; a book of recipes, by Eleanor and
Vincent Dwyer. Detroit, Sign of the Mermaid, 1935.
129p.

Dwyer, R. E. P.
See Urquhart, D. H. and Dwyer, R. E. P.
Prospects of extending the growing of cocoa in Papua
and New Guinea.

Dyal, Sukh
Tropical Fruits. Growing, fruit juices, syrups,
drying, etc. New York, Chemical Publishing Co., Inc.,
1942. 258p. Illus.

Eakin, John R.
Rudiments of grape culture. Little Rock, Ark., 1868.
81p. Davis
Eales, Mary
The Complete confectioner. London, R. Montagu, 1742.
203p. NYPL

_____.
Eales receipts. (Ices). London, H. Moore, 1718.
100p. (Cornell University)
Earle, Alice Morse
State-coach and tavern days. New York, The Mac-
millan Co., 1901. 449p. Illus.
Earle, Maude
Sickroom cookery and hospital diet. London, Spottis-
woode and Co., Ltd., 1910. 246p.
Eastwood, B.
A complete manual for the cultivation of the cranberry.
New York. C.M. Saxton and Co., 1856. 120p. Illus-
engravings.
Eaton, E.L.
Winning the fight against drinking. Cincinnati, Jennings
and Graham, 1912. 344p.
Eberle, E.G.
Soda water formulary. Dallas, Texas Druggist, 1902.
231p. NYPL
Eberlain, H.
See Richardson, A.E. and Eberlein, Donaldson H.
The English inn, past and present.
Ebert, Albert E.
See Hiss A. Emil and Albert A. Ebert
The new standard formulary.
Ebert, Albert E. and Hiss, Emil A.
The Standard Formulary. Second and revised edition
Chicago, G.P. Engelhard and Co., 1897. 500p.
Echols, P. and Sons Proprietors
The Bedford Alum and Iodine Springs near New London,
Bedford County, Virginia. Philadelphia, 1867. 30p.
Eden, T.
Tea. 2nd edition. London, Longmans, 1965. 205p.
Illus.
Edmonds, George
The country brewer's assistant and English vintner's
instructor. London, 1749. 134p. GBPOL

Edmunds, W. of Hereford
On wines. New way of making wines from herbs, fruits
and flowers. London, 1767. 190p.   BM

Edwards, Mrs.
Edwards (Mrs.) cookery book. London, T. Werner
Lewis, 1913. 303p.   BM

Edwards, Henry of Hoxton
Collection of old English customs and bequests. London
J.B. Nichols and Son, 1842. 267p.   NYPI

Edwards, Walter N.
The beverages we drink. London, Ideal Publishing
Union Ltd., 1898. 220p. Illus.

Edwards, William MacArthur
How to mix drinks. Philadelphia, David McKay Co.,
1936. 102p. Illus.

Ehret, George
Twenty-five years of brewing, with an illustrated history
of American beer, dedicated to the friends of George
Ehret. New York, The Gast Lithograph and Engraving
Co., 1891. 120p. Illus.

Eichenlaub, John E. MD
Dr. Eichenlaub's home tonics and refreshers for daily
health and vigor. Englewood Cliffs, N.J., Prentice-
Hall Inc., 1963. 224p.

Eichler, Fr. A.
A treatise on the manufacture of liquors syrups,
cordials and bitters, including instructions for making
vinegars, cider, wines, punch essences, etc., 6th
edition. Philadelphia, Ashenbach and Miller, 1884.
Section 1. 94p. in English
Section 2. 116p. in German to pg. 210.
Title EICHLER'S RECEIPTS.

Eichler, Lillian
The new book of etiquette. New York, Garden City
Publishing Co., 1940. 508p.

Ellet, Mrs.
The practical housekeeper. New York, Stringer and
Townsend, 1857. 599p.

Elivin, R.F.
Essay toward improvement of brewing, 1835.
(Listed in Peddie)

Elliot, John
An account of the nature and medicinal values of the
principal mineral waters of Great Britain and Ireland.
Description of Dr. Nooth's apparatus and Dr. Preistley's
experiments on air. Second edition. London, J.
Johnson, 1789. 296p.

Elliot, Robert H.
Gold, sport and coffee planting in Mysore, Westminster. Archibald, Constable and Co., 1894. 480p.
fold-in map.

Elliot-Godsave, G. and Crouch, A.C.
The Thames. Southend to Kingston. Book number
one of Riverside Taverns and Inns. Croydon, Surrey
The Constitutional Press Ltd., 1964. 80p. Illus.

Elliott, Cyril
Distillation in practice. London, E. Benn Ltd., 1925.
188p. Illus.   LC

Elliott, E.C. and Whitehead, F.J.
Tea planting in Ceylon. Fort, Colombo and London,
Times of Ceylon, 1926. 278p. Illus. Photos,
drawings.

Elliott, F.R.
The Western fruit book or American fruit growers'
guide. New York, A.O. Moore and Co., 1859.
528p.

Elliott, Virginia
Quiet drinking; a book of beer, wines and cocktails
and what to serve with them. New York, Harcourt,
Brace and Co., 1933. 112p. 4th printing.

_____.
Shake 'em up! A practical handbook of polite drinking.
by Virginia Elliott and Phil D. Stong. New York,
Brewer and Warren, 1930. 80p. Illus.

Ellis, Mrs.
A voice from the vintage. New York, D. Appleton
and Co., 1843. 32p.

Ellis, Aytoun
The essence of beauty. A history of perfume and
cosmetics. London, Secher and Warburg, 1960. 200p.
Illus.

_____.
The Penny Universities. A history of the coffee houses.
London, Secker and Warburg, 1956. 290p. Illus-
photos-drawings.

Ellis, Charles
    Origin, nature and history of wine. London, Published
    by F.S. Ellis, 1861. 56p.   NYPL
Ellis, John
    An historical account of coffee. London, John Ellis
    and E. and C. Dilly, 1774. 71p.   NYPL
Ellis, John
    The fruit of the vine. (Unfermented or fermented,
    which?). New York, The National Temperance Society
    and Publication House, 1893. 128p.

———— The New Christianity. New York, Published by the
    author, 1887. 511p.

———— Pure wine - fermented wine and other alcoholic drinks
    in the light of the new dispensation. New York,
    Published by author, 1880. 48p.

———— A reply to the Academy's review of "The wine question
    in light of new dispensation". New York, Published by
    author, 1883. 270p. (Brady Library-Fresno State Col.

———— A review of Rev. Edward H. Jewett's "Communion
    Wine". Mt. Joy, Penna., J.R. Hoffer, 1889. 38p.

———— The wine question in the light of the new dispensation.
    New York, Published by the author, 1882. 228p.
(Ellis, William)
    The compleat cyderman, etc., by experienced hands,
    etc. London, R. Baldwin, 1754. 133p.

———— Country housewife's family companion. London, J.
    Hodges, 1750. 379p.   NYPL

———— A practical farmer. (London). Thomas Astley, Stephen
    Austen, 1732. 171p.   BM
Ellis, William (Brewer)
    The new art of brewing and improving malt liquors.
    London, 1761. 228p.   BM
Ellwanger, George H.
    Meditations on gout with a consideration of its cure
    through the use of wine. New York, Dodd, Mead
    and Co., (1897). 208p.

———————— .
The pleasures of the table. An account of gastronomy from ancient days to present times. New York, Doubleday, Page and Co., 1902. 477p. Illus. Bibliography

Elwell, Fayette H.
Brewery accounting. New York, Published by U.S. Brewing Ass'n, 1934. 161p.   LC

Elsdon, G.D.
Edible oils and fats. Their substitutes and adulterants. New York, Van Nostrand Co., 1926. 521p. Illus.

Elville, E.M.
English tableglass. Revised edition. London, Country Life Limited, 1960. 275p. Illus. Bibliography.

Elworthy, Reginald T.
See Satterly, John and Elworthy, Reginald T. Mineral springs of Canada.

Elyot, Sir Thomas
The Castle of Healthe. (The Castell of Helth). London, T. Berthelet, 1533. 86 leaves.   BM

Embleton, Wm. K.
From plantation to cup. History Dwinell-Wright Co., Boston, Privately printed by Pneumatic Scale Co., 1924. 39p. Illus.

Embury, David A.
The fine art of mixing drinks. New York, Doubleday and Co., (Garden City), 1949. 372p.
Second edition, 1952, 372p.
Third edition, 1958, 400p.

Emerson, Edward Randolph
Beverages, past and present; an historical sketch of their production, together with a study of the customs connected with their use. New York and London, G.P. Putnam's Sons, 1908. 2 v.

———————— .
A lay thesis on Bible wines. New York, Merrill and Baker, 1902. 63p.

———————— .
The story of the vine. New York and London, G.P. Putnam's Sons, 1902. 252p.

Emerson, Haven
Alcohol, Its effects on man. New York, D. Appleton Century Co., Inc., 1934. 114p. SOURCES OF INFORMATION.

_____ Alcohol and man. The effects of alcohol on man in
health and disease. New York, The Macmillan Co.,
1932. 450p. References.

Empire Tea Market Expansion Board
A new essay upon tea, addressed to the medical
profession wherein are shown: 1. a part of its history,
2. its effect on the human frame. 3. the rules for
choosing and serving what is best. London, 1936.
39p. Illus.

Engel, Leo
American and other drinks. London, Tinsley Brothers,
n d, ca1886. 73p. Illus.

Enkema, L. A.
Acids. Comparative uses of various types in soft
drinks. Indianapolis. Hurty-Peck and Co., 1951. 8p.
(Tables)

_____ Bottlers prepare--protect your beverages against off-
season changes. Indianapolis, Hurty-Peck and Co.,
1949. 25p.

_____ Root beer. How it got its name, etc., Indianapolis,
Hurty-Peck and Co., 1952. 10p. Illus-drawings.

_____ Syrup making for cup venders. Indianapolis, Hurty
Peck and Co., 1948. 31p. Illus-drawings.

_____ Use of benzoate of soda as a preservative. Indianapolis, Hurty-Peck and Co., 1949. 8p. Illus-
drawings.

Ensslin, Hugo R.
Recipes for mixed drinks. New York, Published
by author, 1916. 63p.

Entholt, Dr. Hermann
The Ratskeller in Bremen. Bremen, G. Winters,
1930. 70p. Illus.

Erlanger, Baba and Daren Pierce.
Compleat Martini Cook Book (The). New York,
Random Thoughts Publishing Co., 1957. 32p.

Ermitano (pseud)
Shillingsworth of Sherry. London, Sociedad de
alamencenistas de vinos Espanoles, 1874. 155p.   BM

Erneholm, Ivar
    Cacao production in South America. Gothenberg. Med-
    delande fran, Goteborg hogskolas geografiska Kustitution,
    1948. 279p. Bibliography.   LC
Errington, R.
    See Johnson, George W. and Errington, Robert
    The grape vine.
Erskine, John
    Prohibition and christianity. Indianapolis, The Bobbs-
    Merrill Co., 1927. 319p.
Escritt, L. B.
    The Small Cellar. London, Herbert Jenkins, 1960.
    192p. Illus-photos. Bibliography.
Esquire
    Drink book, edited by Frederic A. Birmingham. New
    York, Harper, 1956. 310p. Illus. 1957, London,
    Frederich Muller.
Ettlinger, John
    How to make home-bread ale, n p. (Providence, R.I.),
    1961. 8p.
Evans, George G.
    What shall we drink? Philadelphia, Published by
    author, 1877. 46p.   LC
(Evans, Len) Cellarmaster of The Bulletin
    Guide to Australian Wines. (Sydney), The Bulletin,
    1966. 84p.
Evans, Ray
    Whiskey salesman's handbook. Duluth, 1953. (Carson)
Everest, Arthur E.
    See Perkin, Arthur G. and Everest, Arthur E.
    Natural organic colouring matters.
Evers, Clifford F.
    Tressler, Donald K. and Evers, Clifford F. (See)
    The freezing preservation of foods.

_____.
    Tressler, Donald K., Evers, Clifford F. and Long, Lucy
    (See)
    Into the freezer-and out.
Evelyn, John
    The French Gardiner. London, H. and John Crooke,
    1669. Bound with John Rose, The English Vineyard
    vindicated. 294p. Illus.

<u>   .</u>
<u>   </u>Sylva, or a discourse of forest trees, etc. with
Pomona; or an appendix concerning fruit trees in relation to cider; also Kalendarium Hortense of the Gardiner's
almanac. London, Jo. Martyn and Ja. Allestry, 1670.
247, 60, 63. Illus.

Fabre, Jean H. C.
    Analysis of wines and interpretations of analytical re-
    sults, etc. 2nd edition n p, No publisher listed, 1945.
    128p.   (Davis)
<u>   .</u>
<u>   </u>The secret of everyday things. New York, Century Co.,
    1923. 381p.
Fachuri, Antonio Pandelli
    Bacchus joins Lucullus: art of eating and drinking.
    London, Mc Corquodale and Co., 1934. 61p. Illus. LC
Fadiman, Clifton
    Dionysus; a case of vintage tales about wine. New
    York, McGraw-Hill, 1962. 309p. Illus.
Faes, Dr. H. Director
    Lexique Viti-Vinicole International. Paris, F. Rouge
    and Cie., 1940. (Français-Italian-Espagnol-Allemand).
    278p.
Fain, J. Mitchell
    See Belth, George and J. Mitchell Fain. Household
    guide to wines and liquors.
Fairburn, William Armstrong
    Man and his health: liquids. New York, The Nation
    Press Inc., 1916. 537p. Illus. Bibliography.   LC
Fairchild, Lee
    The Tippler's Vow. New York, Crosscup and Sterling,
    1901. unpaged.   (Bourbon Institute Library)
Fairfax, Arabella
    The family's friend, or the whole art of cookery made
    plain and easy. Printed for author, 1753. (Oxford)
Fairrie, Geoffrey
    Sugar. Fairrie and Co., Liverpool, 1925. 233p.
    Bibliography.
Faissole, C. A.
    The restauranteers' handbook. New York, Harper
    and Bros., 1938. 149p.   LC

Falconer, William
Account of the efficacy of the agua mephitica, alkalines,
etc., London, 1789. 3rd edition. 163p.   BM

_____.
Account of the use and application and success of Bath
waters in rheumatic cases. Bath, W. Megler, 1795.
72p.   NYPL

_____.
Essay on Bath waters. Bath, 1770. 275p.   BM

_____.
A practical dissertation on Bath waters. Bath, G.G.J.
and G. Robinson, 1790. 188p.
Fallon, J.T.
Handbook of Australian vines and wines. Melbourne,
Murray Valley Vineyard, 1874. 49p.   ANL

_____.
The Wines of Australia. London, Unwin, 1876. 47p.
                                                          PLOSA
Fanshowe, E.L.
See Rathbone, W. and Fanshowe, E.L.
Liquor legislation in U.S. and Canada.
Farkas, Alexander
Perfume through the ages. A brief history of the
civilizing influence of fragrance. New York,
Psychological Library, Publishers, 1951. 25p.
Farley, James
New and complete cellar book or butler's assistant.
London, Whittaker and Co., 6p.   BM
Farley, John
The London art of cookery. London, J. Fielding,
1785. 459p.   NYPL
Farmar, F.C.
Guide to Farmar's wine and spirit merchant's rule.
Liverpool, Published by author, 1909. 75p.   BM
Farmer, Fannie Merritt
Food and cookery for the sick and convalescent. Boston,
Little, Brown, 1911. 289p. Illus.
Farmer, J.A.
International sweetmaker and confectioner. Capetown,
No publisher, 1956. 75p.
Farmers Weekly (The)
Farmhouse Fare. 2nd edition. London, Hulton Press,
1945. 160p.

_____ .
Home-made country wines. Recipes from Country House-
wives collected by The Farmers weekly. London,
Hulton Press Ltd., 1956. 71p. 1955, 72p.

Farrow and Jackson, Limited
Recipes of American and other iced drinks. London,
n d. 78p. Illus.

Faulkner, Frank
The art of brewing; practical and theoretical . . . .
London, F.W. Lyon, 1876. 199p.

_____ .
Malting, brewing, vinegar-making and distilling.
London, 1885.   (Stopes-in press)

_____ .
The theory and practice of modern brewing. A rewritten and much enlarged edition of "The art of Brewing"; with a complete and fully illustrated appendix,
specially written for the present period. 2nd edition.
London, F.W. Lyon, 1888. 396p. Illus-plates.

Fawcett, William
Banana (The). Its cultivation, distribution and com-
mercial uses. Introduction by Sir Daniel Morris.
Published under auspices of the West India Committee.
London, Duckworth and Co., 1913. 287p. Illus.

Fedden, Marguerite
The nurse's invalid cookery book. London, "Rad-
clyffes", n d. 110p.

Feery, William C.
Wet drinks for dry people. A book of drinks based
on the ordinary home supplies. Chicago, Bazner Press,
1932. 59p.   LC

Fehlandt, August F.
A century of drink reform in the United States.
Cincinnatti, Jennings and Graham, 1904. 422p.

Feldman, Herman
Prohibition, its economic and industrial aspects. New
York, D. Appleton and Co., 1927. 415p.

Felker, P.H.
The Grocers' Manual. . . . containing a full description
of all the goods sold by the trade. 2nd edition. St.
Louis, The Grocer Publishing Co., Entered 1879.
312p.

Feltham, Leonard R.
Service for soda fountain, ice cream parlours and milk
bars. London, Haywood and Co., "Confectioners Union".
1936. 185p.   BM

Fenton, F.
    The bible and wine. 2nd edition. London, Partridge,
    1907. 125p.   PLOSA
Fenton, Rev. Samuel
    The excellent properties of salted brandy as most
    efficacious medicine and sedative. 2nd edition. London,
    Simpkin Marshall and Co., 1865. 72p.
Feret, Edouard
    . . . Bordeaux and its wines classed by order of merit.
    3rd English edition. Bordeaux, Feret and Fils,
    1899. 828p. Illus. maps. Tables.
Ferguson, John
    Coffee planter's manual for both Arabian and Liberian
    species. 4th edition. London, A.M. and M.J.
    Ferguson, 1898. 320p.   NYPL
Fessler, Julius H.
    The art of wine making and wine vinegar. Berkeley,
    Published by Berkeley Yeast Laboratory, 1941. 8p.

    Guidelines to practical winemaking. Oakland, 1965.
    98p.   (Brady library- Fresno State Col.)
Feuchtwanger, Lewis
    Fermented liquors: a treatise on brewing, distilling,
    rectifying, and manufacturing of sugars, wines, spirits,
    and all known liquors, including cider and vinegar.
    New York, Published by the author, 1858. 218p.
    Illus.
Field, Edward
    The Colonial Tavern. A glimpse of New England town
    life in the 17th and 18th centuries. Providence,
    Preston and Rounds, 1897. 296p.
Feuerheerd, H.L.
    The gentleman's cellar and butler's guide. London,
    Chatto and Windus, 1899. 91p.   NYPL
Field, S.S.
    The American drink book. New York, Farrar,
    Straus and Young, 1953. 282p. Illus.
Field, Sara Bard
    The vintage festival. Play pageant celebrating the vine
    in autumn at St. Helena, California. San Francisco,
    Book Club of California, 1920. 24p.   (Napa)
Field, Thos. A.
    Pear culture. A Manual for the propagation, planting,
    cultivation and management of the pear tree. New York,
    Orange Judd and Co., 1866. 286p. Illus- engravings.

Fielding, Sir Charles (Agricola)
Food. London, Hurst and Blackett Ltd., 1923. 255p.
Fiene, Dr. F. and Blumenthal, Saul
Handbook of food manufacture. Abridged edition. New
York, Chemical Publishing Co.,, 1938. 208p.
Filby, Frederick A.
A history of food adulteration and analysis. London,
George Allen and Unwin, 1934. 269p. Bibliography.
Finch, John D.
See Hastings, Samuel D. Ed.
The people versus the liquor traffic. Great speeches of
John B. Finch.
Finch, Jos. S. and Co.
The merry mixer. Schenley, Pa., 1940. unpaged (24),
Illus.

_____
The Wilkin Family Home Cooking Album. Schenley,
Penna., 1935. 48p. Illus.
Finch, Robert James
A world-wide business (Cadbury-cocoa). Birmingham,
Cadbury Brothers, 1948. 47p. (Brisbane Public)
Finchett, Thomas
Crosland's cordial and liqueur maker's guide and
publican's instructor. London, T.A. Dewdney, n d,
ca1890. 32p.
Finck, Henry T.
Food and flavor. New York, The Century Co., 1913.
594p.
Findlater, Mackie, Todd and Co., Ltd.
Findlater's the home of Treble Diamond.
Wine and liquor price list. London, n d, ca1923. 14p.
Fink, Robert B. Jr.
Cooking with rum. Stamford. The Dahls, 1937. 54p.
(Brown Univ.)
Finn, Timothy
Pub games (The Watney Book of). London, Queen
Anne Press, 1966. 125p. Illus-drawings.
Finnemore, Horace
The essential oils. London, E. Benn, Ltd., 1926.
880p. Illus.
Firestone, Clark B.
Bubbling waters. New York, McBride, 1938. 296p.
Illus. Bibliography.

Firmenich and Cie.
Technical booklet AROMATIC CHEMICALS.
Descriptive booklet of synthetic aromatics and raw
materials for perfumery. Geneva, 1949. 95p.

Firth, R.H.
See Notter, J. Lane and Firth, R.H.
Practical domestic hygiene

Fischer, Ing. Walther
Factworterbuch fur Braurei und maltzerei. Nurnberg,
Verlag Hans Carl, 1955. English - Deutsch, Deutsch -
English, 174p. and 159p.

Fisher, Mrs.
Prudent housewife. London, 1750. 136p.   LC

Fisher, Irving
The "Noble Experiment". New York, Alcohol Information Committee, 1930. 492p.

_____.
Prohibition at its worst. New York, The Macmillan
Co., 1926. 255p.

Fisher, Mary Frances Kennedy
A cordial water. Boston, Little, Brown and Co.,
1961. 178p.

_____.
Here let us feast. New York, The Viking Press,
1946. 491p.

_____.
The story of wine in California. Berkeley, University
of California Press, 1962. 125p. Illus.

Fisher, Mary Isabel
Liqueurs, a dictionary and survey; with sections on
spirits, aperitifs, and bitters. Westminster. London,
Meyer, 1951. 87p. Illus. Dictionary.

Fisher, S.I.
Observations on the character ond culture of the
European vine. Also Manual of the Swiss vigneron
by Mons. Brun Chappuis and Art of wine making by
Mons. Bulos. Philadelphia, Ley and Biddle, 1834.
244p.

Fisher and Son
The Derbyshire instruction book , how to brew
splendid ale. London, n d, ca1850. 16p.

Fisk, F.R.
See Christ, Edwin R. and Fisk, F.R.
That book about wine.

Fisk, Walter W.
The book of ice-cream. New York, The Macmillan Co.,
1921. 302p.

Fiske, John
Tobacco and alcohol. New York, Leypoldt and Holt,
1869. 163p.

Fitch, William Edward
Mineral waters of the United States and American spas,
Philadelphia and New York, Lea and Febiger, 1927.
799p. Illus. Bibliography, References.

Fitchett, Laura Simkins
Beverages and sauces of colonial Virginia, compiled
by L. S. F. Richmond, Va. William Byrd Press,
1938. 110p.

Flagg, William J.
Three seasons in European vineyards: treating of vine-
culture; vine disease and its cure; wine-making and
wines, red and white; wine-drinking, as affecting
health and morals. New York, Harper, 1869. 332p.
Illus.

Flanders, Charles R.
Gourmet au Vatel. An authoritative guide to the proper
selection, handling, mixing and serving of wines and
liqueurs. Boston, M. F. Foley Co., 1934. 119p.

Fleishmann Co.
Excellent recipes for baking raised breads; also
directions for making summer drinks. Cincinnati,
1914. 48p.   (Boston Public)

Fleishmann Distilling Corp. (The)
Fleishmann's mixers' manual. New York, n d, 16p.
1947, 24p. Illus.

Fleishman, E. M.
Modern luncheonette management. Stamford, Conn.
Dahls, 1947. 166p.   (Seattle Public)

_____ .
Modern luncheonette management. Planning, layout,
employee training, operation. 2nd revised ed. New
York, Ahrens Publishing Co., Inc., 1955. 127p.

Fleischman, Joseph
The art of blending and compounding liquors and wines
and valuable information concerning whiskies in bond.
New York, Dick and Fitzgerald, 1885. 68p.

Fleming, James
Readings for winter gatherings. London, The Religious
Tract Society, 1870. 1254p.

Fletcher, C. R. L.
    See Sadler, E. and Fletcher, C. R. L.
    Wine ghosts of Bremen.
Fletcher, H. R.
    Instructions to brew real beer at home.   London, 1916.
    32p.   BM
Fletcher, S. W.
    Strawberry growing.   New York, Macmillan Co.,
    1922.   325p.   Illus-photos, drawings.
Fleury, R. de.
    1700 cocktails for the man behind the bar.   London,
    William Heinemann Ltd., 1934.   211p.

———————— .
    1800 and all that.   Drinks ancient and modern.   London,
    The St. Catherine Press, 1937.   334p.   (2094 recipes)
Flexner, Marion W.
    Cocktail-supper Book.   New York, M. Barrows and Co.,
    1955.   255p.
Flint, George Elliot
    The whole truth about alcohol.   New York, The Mac-
    millan Co., 1919.   294p.
Flockhart, W. B.
    Pure Indian tea or the tea we drink.   London, Rose-
    mont Press, 1905.   41p.   BM
Florida Citrus Commission
    Citrus fruit in health and disease.   Published for the
    medical profession.   Second edition.   Lakeland,
    1956.   31p.   Illus.   References.
Florida Citrus Exchange
    Florida's Food Fruits.   Seeldsweet Oranges and grape-
    fruit, n p.   Florida Citrus Exchange, 1919.   32p.
Flower, Barbara and Rosenbaum, Elisabeth
    The art of cooking by Apicius.   London and New York,
    Peter Nevill Ltd., 1958.   259p.   (translation of original
    of 1498).
Flower, Richard
    Observations on beer and brewers in which the
    inequalities, injustice and impolicy of the malt and beer
    tax are demonstrated.   Cambridge, 1802.   32p.   BM
Floyd, Robert Mitchell
    Songs of the apple tree with kith and kin.   Boston, Press
    of Walker Young and Co., 1900.   95p.
Floyer, Sir John
    Galenic art of preserving old men's health.   London,
    Medicina Gerocomica, 1724.   491p.   BM

Floyer, John (First part-1702)
Baynard, Dr. Edward (Second part-1706)
 History of cold bathing both ancient and modern. 2nd
 edition. London, Sam Smith and Benjamin Walford,
 1706. 192p. (1st part), 240p. (2nd part).
Focatiis, A. de.
 The main source of alcoholism in the United States
 and suggested remedial legislation. New Orleans,
 Hauser Printing Co., 1915. 30p.
Fogelsonger, M. I.
 The secrets of the liquor merchant revealed; or, The
 art of manufacturing the various kinds and qualities
 of brandies, whiskies, gins, rums, bitters, wines,
 cordials, syrups, etc., by the use of the different
 essential oils, essences, etc. Alpena, Michigan, Mc-
 Phail and Ferguson, printers, 1898. 122p.
Folim, Otto
 Preservatives and other chemicals in foods: their use
 and abuse. Cambridge, Mass., 1914. 60p.
Folsom, Anne
 The care and training of husbands. New York, Duell,
 Sloane and Pierce, 1950. 61p.   LC
Food Engineering.
 Bottler's and Glass Packers' Handbook. New York,
 McGraw-Hill Publishing Co., n d, 1951. 54p. Illus.
Food Industries.
 Successful quality control in food processing.
 New York, McGraw-Hill Publishing Co., 1930. 147p.
 Illus. Reprints of articles.
Food Standards Committee
 Report on soft drinks. London, Her Majesty's
 Stationary Office, 1959. 19p.
Foord, Alfred Stanley
 Springs, streams and spas of London; history and
 associations. London, Unwin, 1910. 351p. Illus.
Foot, Frederick Norman
 Coffee, the beverage; designed as a handbook of informa-
 tion for the coffee trade and others interested in the
 subject of coffee. New York, The Spice Mill Publishing
 Co., 1925. 205p. Illus.
Foote, E. J.
 Will you take wine? A guide to the purchase, serving
 and appreciation of wines, cocktails, spirits, and liqueur
 London, Putnam, 1935. 72p.

Foote, H.E.
   See Sivitz, Michael and Foote, H. Elliott.
   Coffee processing technology.
Foote and Jenks Incorporated
   The calculator for bottlers.   Jackson, Mich., n d,
   1940.   22p.
   4th edition, 1946.   28p.
   6th edition, 1955.   34p.
   7th edition, 1962.   38p.
Forbes, Bertha A.
   Money making hints for soda fountains.   New York,
   D.O. Haynes and Co., 1907.   97p.   LC
Forbes, Ellert
   Wines for everyman.   London, H. Joseph, Ltd., 1937.
   191p.
Forbes, Patrick
   Champagne: the wine, the land and the people.   London,
   Victor Gollancz Ltd., 1937.   492p.   Illus-photos.
   Bibliography.
Forbes, R.J.
   Short history of the art of distillation.   Leiden, E.J.
   Brill, 1948.   405p.   Illus.   Bibliography.

--------- .
   Studies in ancient technology.   Volume III.   Leiden,
   E.J. Brill, 1955.   268p.   Bibliography.
Ford, John C.
   Man takes a drink.   Facts and principles about alcohol.
   New York, P.J. Kenedy and Sons, 1955.   120p.
   Bibliography.
Ford, William
   A practical treatise on malting and brewing.   London,
   Published by author, 1849.   334p.
Forgeot, P.
   See Poupon, Pierre and Forgeot, Pierre
   A book of burgundy.
Fornachon, J.C.M.
   Bacterial spoilage of fortified wines.   Adelaide.
   Australian Wine Board, 1943.   126p.   (Univ. Illinois)

--------- .
   Studies on the sherry flor.   Adelaide, Australian Wine
   Board, 1953.   139p.   Bibliography.
Forrest, D.M.
   A hundred years of Ceylon Tea, 1867-1967.   London,
   Chatto and Windus, 1967.   320p.   Illus-photos.
   Bibliography.

Forrester, G. P.
    See Wooley, S. W. and Forrester, G. P.
    Pharmaceutical formulas. Being "The Chemist and
    Druggist" book.
Forrester, Joseph James
    The Oliveira prize essay on Portugal. (wine). London,
    J. Weale, 1853. 290p. Illus.   LC

_____
    Port and the wines of Portugal, 1845.   (Shand)

_____
    Wine trade of Portugal. Proceedings of a meeting.
    London, Pelham and Richardson, 1845.   BM

_____
    A word or two on port wine. London, T. Whittaker,
    1848. 19p.   BM
Forsyth, J. S.
    The farmer, maltster, distiller and brewer's practical
    memo book. London, D. Cox, 1824. 132p.
                                              (Yale Univ.)

Forsyth, William
    A treatise on the culture and management of fruit
    trees. Third edition. London, T. N. Longman and
    O. Rees, 1803. 523p. Illus.
Fort, J. V.
    Let's talk beer. Springfield, Mo. Mycroft Press,
    1958. 147p.
Fort, Lyman M.
    See Harkness, Kenneth M. and Lyman M. Fort
    Alcohol; its uses and abuses. A syllabus for schools.
Fortune, Robert
    A journey to the tea countries of China: including Sung-
    lo and the Bohea hills, etc., London, John Murray,
    1852. Spine and cover - Tea districts of China and
    India. Fancy title page - Visit to the tea districts of
    China and India. 398p. Illus.

_____
    Report on the present condition and future prospects
    of tea cultivation in northwest provinces. Calcutta,
    1857. 114p.   GBPOL

_____
    Report on the tea plantations of northwest provinces.
    Agra. Secundra Orphan Press, 1851. 15p.
                             (National Agricultural Library)

160

———— . The tea-districts of China and India, or two visits
to the tea countries of China and the British tea
plantations in the Himalaya, etc. in 2 volumes.
3rd edition. London, John Murray, 1853. 315, 298
Illus.

Fosdick, Raymond B. and Scott, Albert L.
Toward liquor control. New York, Harper and
Brothers., 1933. 220p. Bibliography.

Foster, A. E. Manning "Diner-out".
Dining and wining. London,
Geoffrey Bles, n d. 118p.

———— . Through the wine list, by "Diner-out".
London, Geoffrey Bles, 1924. 112p.

Foster, Charles
Home winemaking. London, Ward Lock and Co.,
Ltd., 1969. 64p. Illus-photos, drawings.

Foster, David S.
Inns, taverns, alehouses, coffee-houses in and around
London. Westminster. Reference Library, 1900.

BM

Foster, William
Short history of cooper's company. (Worshipful
Company of Coopers). London, Published by Co.,
1944. 146p. BM

Foster and Ingle
Gatherings from the wine-lands. London, Published
by authors, 1855. 192p.

———— . Wine, what is it? London, 1856. BM

Fothergill, Anthony
A new experimental inquiry into the nature and qualities
of Cheltenham water. Bath. Printed by R. Cruttwell,
1788. 122p. LC

Fothergill, John
Confessions on an Innkeeper. London, Chatto and
Windus, 1938. 311p. Illus.

———— . An Innkeeper's diary. London, Chatto and Windus,
1931. 294p. Illus.

———— . My three inns. London, Chatto and Windus, 1949.
239p. Illus.

Fougner, Selmer
 Along the wine trail. New York, The Sun Printing
 and Publishing Ass'n, 1934-1937. 5v.

_____.
 Along the wine trail; wines of the world. New York,
 The Sun, 1934. 108p.

_____.
 Baron Foughner's bar guide. Detroit, no publisher,
 1910. Scroll
Fowler, George
 How to bottle. Quarter century edition. Reading.
 George Fowler, Lee and Co., 1925? 144p.
Fowler, Nathaniel C.
 Stories and toasts for after dinner. New York, A.L.
 Burt Co., 1914. 216p.
Fox, Helen Morganthau
 Gardening with herbs. For flavor and fragrance.
 New York, Macmillan Co., 1933. 334p. Bibliography.
Foy, C.F.
 The principles and practice of ale, beer and stout
 bottling. Edited by Arthur T.E. Binsted. London,
 Binsted and Sons, 1955. 279p. Illus.
Foyles, Christina
 Party book. London, John Gifford, 1968. 255p.
 Illus-photos.
Francatelli, Charles Elme
 The Cook's Guide and Housekeeper's and Butler's
 Assistant. London, Richard Bentley, 1861. 512p.
 Glossary.
Francis, Grant R.
 Old English drinking glasses, their chronology and
 sequence. London, Herbert Jenkins, 1926. 222p.
 Illus.   BM
Francis Draz and Co.
 A glimpse of a famous wine cellar in which are
 described the vineyards of Marne and the methods
 employed in making champagne. New York, Francis
 Draz, 1906. (Unpaged). Illus.
Frandsen, J.H. and Markham, E.A.
 The manufacture of ice creams and ices. New York,
 Orange Judd, 1919. 315p.
Franklin, Fabian
 The A B C of prohibition. New York, Harcourt,
 Brace and Co., 1927. 150p.

162

What prohibition has done for America. New York, Harcourt Brace and Co., 1922. 129p.

Franklyn H. Mortimer
A glance at Australia in 1880 or Food from the South. (Including wine). Melbourne. The Victoria Review Publishing Co., Ltd., 1881. 414p.

Franklin Brewery
History of beer and Quaker beer, 1916.
(Davison-beer in American home)

Franz, Arnulf
The new wine book-information and directions for making wine from grapes, raisins, oranges, berries, etc., Los Angeles, Western Beverage Corp., 1934. 57p. Illus.   LC

Franz, J. C. A.
Treatise on mineral waters (A). London J. Churchill, 1842. 156p.

Fraser, Samuel
American fruits. Their propagation, cultivation, harvesting and distribution. New York, Orange Judd Publishing Co., 1924. 888p.

The strawberry. New York, Orange Judd Publishing Co., 1926. 120p. Illus-photos.

Fraser, W. M.
The recollections of a tea planter. London, The Tea and Rubber Mail, 1935. 181p.

Frazier, William Carroll
Food microbiology. New York, McGraw-Hill Book Co., 1958. 472p. Illus photos-drawings. References.

Frederick, Mrs. Christine
Hershey's Helps for the hostess. Hershey, Penna. Hershey Chocolate Co., 1934. 48p. Illus-drawings.

Free, James L.
Just one more. New York, Coward Mc Cann, 1955. 207p.   (Brisbane Public Library)

Freeland, J. M.
The Australian Pub. Melbourne, Melbourne University Press, 1966. 229p. Illus-photos.

Freeman, Harry H.
Retail liquor dealers' guide of information. Chicago, 1912. 96p.   LC

Freels, S. C.
The X-ray; or, Compiled facts and figures of unequaled interest to the retail liquor dealer; or the art of buying, rectifying, reducing, blending, compounding, preserving and selling all wines and liquors common to the traffic. San Francisco Press of H.S. Crocker Co., 1900. 96p. Illus.

Freeman, Jefferson Davis
Confederate Cook Book. Reprint of 1863. Harriman, Tenn. Pioneer Press, 1961. unpaged (28).

French, John
The art of distillation: or, A treatise of the choicest spagyrical preparations, experiments, and curiosities, performed by way of distillation. The London-distiller, exactly and truly showing the way (in words at length, and not in mysterious characters and figures) to draw all sorts of spirits and strong-waters; together with their virtues, and other excellent waters. London, Printed by E. Cotes for T. Williams, 1667. 293p. Illus.

————————.
The London distiller--the way to draw spirits and strong waters, etc. London, Thomas Williams, 1667. 43p.

French, Richard Valpy
The history of toasting; or, Drinking of healths in England. London, National Temperance Publishing Depot, 1881. 104p.

————————.
Nineteen centuries of drink in England. 2nd edition. enl and rev. London, National Temperance Publication Depot, 1890. 898p. Bibliography.

French, Capt. W.E.P.
See Chase, Edith Lea
Waes Hael; the book of toasts. By Edithe Lea Chase and Capt. W.E.P. French.

Friedman, Jacob
Friedman's common-sense candy teacher. Chicago, Jonas B. Bell, 1906. 359p.

Friends of wine
Short guide to wine. London, The Friends of Wine, n d, ca1956. 19p.

Friends of Wine (The) Publisher
Summer wine coolers. London, Contains "On mixing of wine cups" by H. Warner Allen, n d. unpaged (8), Illus.

Fries, Alex and Bro., Inc.
Manual for compounders, rectifiers and cordial manufacturers. Cincinnati, Published by the Company with Fries and Bro. New York, 1933. 48p.

Fries and Fries, Inc.
Manual for compounders. Formulae for making beverages. Cincinnati, n d, ca1937. 258p.

Fries Brothers
Manual. (Liquor), Cincinnati, 1934. 63p.
(Toledo Public)

Fritsch, J.
Manual Pratique de la Fabrication des Eaux et Boissons Gazeuses. Paris, Librairie Generale Scientifique et Industrielle, H. Desforges, 1906. (In French), 349p. Illus.

Fritzsche Bros., Incorporated
Catalogue essential oils, aromatic chemicals, fine drugs and fruit flavors. New York, n d, ca1931. 47p.

_____.
Flavors and spices and flavor characterization. Flavors by Edmund H. Hamman; spices by Ernest Guenther, 18p.; flavor characterizations by Stephen S. Chang, 11p.; Reprinted from Kirk-Othmer ENCYCLOPEDIA OF CHEMICAL TECHNOLOGY, New York, Published by Fritzsche Bros., 1966.

_____.
Fritzsche's manual, containing practical formulas and suggestions for the application of essential oils, essences and aromatic products for the preparation of liquors, cordials, flavorings, etc. New York, Fritzsche Brothers, 1897. 117p.

_____.
Guide to the flavoring ingredients as classified under the Federal Food, Drug and Cosmetic Act. New York, November, 1966. 84p.

_____.
Perfumer's handbook and catalog. New York, 1944. 266p. Illus. Bibliography.

———— Pharmaceutical flavor guide; and supplement no. I.
New York, 1957. 49, 16 Illus.

Fritzsche Bros. , Inc. , 1871-1936.
Pictorial record of present. New York,
1936. (unpaged).

———— Price List 1915. (Branch of Schimmel and Co. ,
New York. 26p.

———— Wholesale price list. New York, December 31, 1940.
28p.

Froedtert Malt Corporation
A motivation research study of beer consuming habits.
Milwaukee, 1955. 32p. Illus.

Frost, S. Annie
Our new cook book. Philadelphia, American Publishing
Co. , 1883. 454p.

Froude, Charles C.
Right food the right remedy. New York, Brentanos,
1924. 306p.

Frumkin, Lionel
Science and technique of wine (The). London, H. C.
Lea and Co. , Ltd. , 1965. 230p. Wine tasting
Glossary.

Fujita, Y.
Fundamental studies in essential oils. West Lafayette,
Indiana. Published by Purdue University, 1951. 627p.
(Purdue University)

Fukukita, Yasunosuke
Tea cult of Japan. An aesthetic pastime. 3rd edition.
Board of Tourist Industry, Japanese Government
Railways, 1937. 76p. Illus. Bibliography.

Fuller, A. H.
Bottle washing. Volume 3 of Jusfrute Handbooks
for the Soft Drink Industry. Gosford, N. S. W.
Australia. Jusfrute, Ltd. , n d, (1967). 60p. Illus-
drawings.

———— Jusfrute handbook for soft drink industry. 1. factory
design and layout. 2. plant sanitation. Gosford,
N. S. W. n d, ca1968. 91p. Illus-photos, drawings.

———— Water treatment. Volume 2 of the Jusfrute Handbooks
for the Soft Drinks Industry. Gosford, N. S. W. Australia
Jusfrute Ltd. , n d, (1967). 40p. Illus-drawings.

Fuller, Andrew, S.
  The grape culturist. A treatise on the cultivation of
  the grape. New York, Published by author, 1864.
  262p. Illus.
  1866, 7th thousand Orange Judd and Co.
  1867, 282p. Orange Judd and Co.
  1899, 282p. Orange Judd and Co.

—————— .
  The small fruit culturist. New York, Orange Judd
  Co., 1867. 276p.
Fulton, James Alexander
  Peach Culture. New revised edition. New York,
  Orange Judd Co., 1910. 204p.
Funk, Wilfred
  If you drink. New York, Wilfred Funk, Inc., 1940.
  170p. Illus.
Furnas, C.C. and Furnas, S.M.
  The story of man and his food. New York, The New
  Home Library, 1937. 364p. Notes.

—————— .
  The Life and Times of THE LATE DEMON RUM.
  New York, G.P. Putnam and Sons, 1965. 381p.
  Illus. Bibliography.
Furnivall, Frederick James, Ed.
  Boke of nurture by John Russell, 146p. ca1460;
  Boke of nurture by Hugh Rhodes, 28p. 1577; Boke of
  Keruynge by Wynkyn de Woorde, 56p. 1513. London,
  R. Curzon, 1867.   NYPL

—————— .
  The book of quinte essence (perfumery). London,
  Early English Text Society, 1899. 31p.   BM
Furness, Rex
  The fermentation industry. London, Ernest Benn,
  1924. 19p.   BM

Gaige, Crosby
  Crosby Gaige's Cocktail guide and ladies' companion.
  M. Barrows and Co., 1941. 223p. Illus.

—————— .
  The standard cocktail guide, a manual of mixed drinks
  written for the American host. New York, M.
  Barrows and Co., 1944. 128p. Illus.

Gairdner, Meridith
Essay on the natural history, origin, composition and
medicinal effect of the mineral and thermal springs.
Edinburgh, no. Publisher 1832. 420p.   BM

Gale, Hyman, Ed.
The how and when, published and edited by Hyman Gale
and Gerald F. Marco. 2nd edition. Chicago, Marco
Importing Co., 1940. 224p. Illus. 3rd edition, 1945.
224p.

Galland, Antoine
Treatise on the origin of coffee. London, 1695.
(Ukers- All about coffee)

Gallobelgicus (pseud)
Wine, Beere, Ale and Tobacco: a seventeenth century
interlude. Chapel Hill, N.C., The University, 1915.
54p.   LC

Gammick, Charles H.
The bartender and the way to a man's heart. New
York, C.J. Mooney, 1900. 120p. Advertising matter.
LC

Gardiner, Alfred G.
Life of George Cadbury. London, Cassell and Co.,
Ltd., n d, ca1923. 308p. Illus- photos.

Gardiner, Grace
See Steel, F.A. and Gardiner, G.
The Complete Indian housekeeper and cook.

Cardner, John, Editor
The brewer distiller and wine manufacturer.
Philadelphia, P. Blakiston Son and Co., 1883. 278p.
Illus. reprint 1902, London, J. and A. Churchill.

Gardner, Victor, R.
The cherry and its culture. New York, Orange, Judd
Publishing Co., 1930. 128p. Illus.

Gardner, William Howlett
Food acidulants. New York, Allied Chemical Corp.,
1966. 185p. References.

Gardner and Son
Price list. Wine and spirit merchants, maltsters.
The Brewery, Little Coggeshall, Essex, n d, ca1910.
12p.

Garey, Thomas A.
Orange cultivation in California with an appendix on
grape culture. San Francisco. Published for author,
1881. Part on grape by L.J. Rose. 227p.   Davis

Garnett, Thomas MD
    A treatise on the mineral waters of Harrogate, contain-
    ing the history, etc. Eighth edition. Knaresborough,
    G. Wilson, 1829. 176p.
Garnsey, William
    Garnsey's new wine tables. London, 1797. folio   BM
Garrett, Franklin
    Coca-Cola 1886-1962. A chronological history. Atlanta,
    Published by Coca-Cola Co., 1962. 8p.
Garrett, Paul
    The art of serving wine. Norfolk, Va., Garrett, 1905.
    48p. Illus.
Garrow, Alan B.
    Sideboard and cellar. Toronto, Musson Book Co.,
    1950. 128p.   (Toronto Public)
Garvin, Fernande
    French wines. New York, Le Comite National des
    Vins de France, 1960. 64p. Illus-maps. Glossary.
Gattefossé, René Maurice
    Formulary of perfumery and of cosmetology. London,
    L. Hill, 1952. 252p.
Gavin, Clark
    Here's how. The how to do it book of home entertain-
    ing. New York, Liquor Publishing Co., 1951.
    128p. Illus. Glossary.
Gay, John
    Wine, a poem. A type facsimile reprint of 1708.
    London, Dulau and Co., Ltd., 1926. 14p.
Gayon, U.
    Studies on wine-sterilizing machines. Melbourne.
    Department of Agriculture Vitacultural Station,
    Rutherglen, Victoria, 1901. 103p.
Gayre, G. R.
    Wassail! in mazers of mead. London, Phillimore,
    1948. 176p. Illus. Notes.
Gazan, M. H.
    Flavours and essences; a handbook of formulae.
    London, Chapman and Hall Ltd., 1936. 115p. Illus.
Gee, Philip
    Scotch whisky. Questions and answers. Edinburgh,
    Published for The Scotch Whisky Ass'n, 1957. 55p.
Gelleroy, William
    The London cook. London, S. Crowder, 1762. 486p.
                                                     BM

General Foods Corp.
My party book of tested chocolate recipes, n p, 1938.
26p. Illus- photos.

Gennery- Taylor, Mrs.
Easy made wine and country drinks. Kingswood, Surrey
Elliott Rightway Books, 1959. 124p.

Gervinus, Georg Gottfried
The art of drinking. A historical sketch. New York,
United States Brewers Ass'n, 1890. 23p.   LC

Gesner, Conrad
A newe booke of distillattyon of waters. London,
1559. 463p.   BM

——————
Newe Jewell of Healthe. London, H. Denham, 1576.
                                                           BM

Geysius, Joh. Jacobus
Parastota, Fabylam Monte Fiasconium, etc. Altdorffi,
1680. (Reprint?), (In Latin). 44p.

De Giacomi, de. Ed.
Food Directory, 1954. Westminster, London, Tothill
Press Limited. 522p.

Gibbs, Ed.
Have a drink! (New York) no publisher (Distributed
by Licensed Beverage Institute), 1955. 122p. Illus.

Gibbs, W. M.
Spices and how to know them. Buffalo, N. Y,
Matthews- Northrup, 1909. 179p. Illus.

Gibson, Joseph W.
Scientific bar- keeping. Buffalo, E. N. Cook and Co.,
1884. 42p.   LC

Gibson, W. C.
See Taylor, Bert L. and Gibson, W. C.
The log of the water wagon.

Gilbey, Sir Walter
Notes on alcohol. Second edition. London, Vinton and
Co., 1904. 32p. Illus.

Gilbey, W. and A. Ltd.,
The Compleat Imbiber. A centenary exhibition of
drinking through the centuries. London, 1957.
(unpaged), 311 exhibits described. Illus.

——————
A complete list of wines, spirits and liquors, etc.
London, 1889. 49p. Illus.

Gilbey, Walter and Alfred
    Book of prices. London, 1870. 28p. (Boston Public)
_____.
    Treatise on wines and spirits of the principal producing
    countries. London, 1869. Unpaged (64).   GBPOL
Gildemeister, E. and Hoffman, Fr.
    The volatile oils. Written under auspices of
    Schimmel and Co., Leipzig. Trans. by Edward
    Kremers, Madison, Wisc. Milwaukee, Pharmaceutical
    Review Publishing Co., 1900. 733p. Illus. 1922,
    3 vol. New York, J. Wiley and Sons.
Giles, Rev. Charles
    The convention of drunkards: a satirical essay on
    intemperance, etc. New York, Published "by request"
    1899. 126p.
Giles, John
    Ananas. London, Printed for author, 1770. 56p.   LC
Giles, Samuel
    The brewer's meteorological and statistical guide.
    London, Longman, Green, Longmans and Roberts,
    1861. 123p.
Gill, J. Thompson, Manager
    The Practical Confetioner. Chicago, Confectioner and
    Baker Publishing Co., Entered 1881. paged by parts
    not consecutive. 5th edition, 1890. 6th edition, 1890.
Gillespie, Jerry L.
    The drinking driving man's diary. Newport Beach,
    California. Rush and Lehmann, 1969. 59p.
Gillett, W.E. Manufacturer and Importer
    Selling price list. (Flavors). Chicago, n d, (1900).
    4p.
Gilliland, R.B. and Harrison, G.A.F. and Knight, E.C.
    Brewing malting and allied processes. A literature
    survey prepared for the Institute of Brewing. n p,
    (London), 1956. 30p.
Gillman, A.W. and Spencer, S.
    Brewer's materials. London, 1876. 65p. Stopes
Gilmour, Andrew
    Our drinks, or the nature and physical effects of
    fermented liquors as an ordinary beverage. London,
    W. Tweedie, 1856. 92p.   (Indiana Univ.)
_____.
    Sacramental wines. Glasgow, C. Gallie, 1849. 64p.
                                            NYPL

171

Gilpin, George
    Tables for reducing quantities of weight in any mixture
    of spirits and water. London, 1794. 110p.   GBPOL
Ginrum Alpha Co.
    See Anon
    The Legend of Liqueurs, wines and spirits.
Ginsberg, Ben
    Let's Talk Soft Drinks.   The story of a great industry.
    Springfield, Mo.   The Mycroft Press, 1960.   139p.
Girtin, Tom
    Come landlord!   London, The Quality Book Club, n d.
    256p.
Givaudan-Delawanna Inc.
    The Givaudan Index.   Specifications of synthetics and
    isolates for perfumery.   New York, 1949.   378p.
    2nd edition, 1961, 431p.
Glasgow and District Licensed Trade Defense Ass'n.
    Summary of Scottish Licensing laws.   (Glasgow), 1968.
    20p.
Glass Manufacturers Federation, Publishers
    Glass containers. London, n d. 50p. Illus. Reading
    List.
Glasse, Hannah
    Art of cookery made plain and easy.   1747 and on.
    Many editions, mostly London.   (many places).

_____ Compleat confectioner. London, 1760. 225p. many
    editions.   LC
Glauber, Johann Rudolf
    Description of new philosophical furnaces, or, a
    new art of distilling.   London, printed by Richard
    Coats for Tho. Williams, 1651.   452p.   LC
Glendinning, R.
    Practical hints on the culture of the pineapple.   London,
    Longman and Co., 1839.   55p.   Illus-drawings.
Glenlivit Distillery
    Glenlivit, being the annals of Glenlivit Distillery founded
    by George Smith in 1824.   Aberdeen, 1964.   40p.
    Illus.
Glenmore Distilleries
    See Wilson James Boone
    The spirit of old Kentucky.
Gloeckner, John T.
    Standard mixer; The American bartenders' guide.
    Pittsburgh, Standard Mixer Publishing Co., 1918.   93p.
                                                        LC

172

Glover, Robert Mortimer
On mineral waters: their physical and medicinal
properties. London, Henry Renshaw, 1857. 375p.
Illus.
Glozer, Liselotte F. and William K.
California in the kitchen. An essay upon, and a check
list of California imprints in field of gastronomy
from 1870?-1932. (Berkeley), Privately printed, 1960.
43p. Illus. Bibliography.
Gneisieau, Arthur
How to brew beer and make wine. Los Angeles, Auto
Brew, 1963. 16p.
Gobright and Pratt
The Union Sketch-Book. A reliable guide. New York,
Pudney and Russell, 1860. 168p.
Goddard, Gloria and Wood, Clement
Let's have a good time tonight. An omnibus of party
games. New York, Grosset and Dunlap, 1932. 304p.
Illus.
Godwin, George
Hansons of Eastcheap. The story of the house of
Samuel Hanson and Son Ltd., 1747-1947. London,
Privately printed for Hanson. 99p. Illus.
Goeldner, Charles R. Compiler
Automatic merchandising. A selected and annotated
bibliography. Published by American Marketing Ass'n
with National Automatic Merchandising Ass'n. Series no.
9, n p, 1963. 47p. Bibliography.
Goettier, Dr. Hans
Lexikon der spirituosen, und alkoholfreien getranke,
industrie. Berlin, Carl Knoppke Gruner Verlag und
Vertrieb, 1958. (In German). 561p. Dictionary.
Goettsche, H. C.
Brewery accounting. 2nd edition, no place. Printed
by Donnelly in Crawfordsville, Indiana, 1934. 279p.
Goffinet, Sybil
Cream, butter and wine. London, Andre Deutsch, 1955.
120p.
Gold, Alex, Ed.
Wines and spirits of the world. London, Virtue and Co.,
Ltd., 1968. 708p. Illus-photos. Glossary.
Golding, Louis and Simon, Andre L. Eds.
We shall eat and drink again. A wine and food
anthology. London, Hutchinson, n d, ca1941?
275p. Illus.

Gomez, Gabriel
Cultivation and preparation of coffee. Mexico.
Typographical office of the Dept. of fomento,
colonization and industry, 1894. 148p. Illus.   LC
Gonzalez Byass and Co., Ltd. Jerez, Spain.
Old sherry; the story of the first hundred years of
Gonzalez Byass and Co., 1835-1935. London, Sir
Joseph Causton and Sons, Ltd., 1935. 155p. Illus.
Good Housekeeping Institute
Preserves, pickles, salads and homemade wines.
London, National Magazine Co., 1942. 117p. Illus.
Gooderham and Worts Ltd.
A souvenir of Canadian International Fair. (Liquor).
Toronto, n d, ca1938. unpaged (32), Illus.

_____.
What is whiskey? Bulletins one through nine,
Chicago, 1935. unpaged.
Goodson, Anthony, Compiler
London's Friendly Inns and Taverns. London,
Regency Press, 1965. 112p. Illus.

_____.
More friendly inns in and around London. London,
Regency Press, 1965. 176p. Illus.
Goodwin, Harriet
How to cook with wine. London, Angus and Robertson,
1960. 127p. Illus.
Goodwyn, Henry
The brewer's assistant. London, 1796. 234p.   BM
Goold, Joseph
Aërated waters and how to make them; together with
receipts for non-alcoholic cordials, and a short essay
on the art of flavouring. London, J.G. Smith, 1880.
118p.
Goosmann, Justis Christian
The carbonic acid industry; a comprehensive review of
the manufacture and uses of CO_2. Mineral waters and
other beverages. Methods of carbonating and bottling.
Chicago, Nickerson and Collins Co., 1906. 368p.
Illus.
Gordon, Ernest
The anti-alcohol movement in Europe. New York,
etc. Fleming, H. Revell Co., 1913. 333p.
Gordon, Ernest Barron
When the brewer had the stranglehold. New York,
Alcohol Information Committee, 1930. 276p.
References.   LC

Gordon, Harry Jerrold
Gordon's cocktail and food recipes. Boston, C.H.
Simonds Co., 1934. 125p.
Gordon, Jean
The art of cooking with roses. New York, Walker
and Co., 1968. 159p.

_____ .
Coffee recipes. Customs. Facts. Fancies. Wood-
stock, Vermont and St. Augustine, Fla., 1963. 96p.
Illus. Bibliography.

_____ .
Orange Recipes. Woodstock, Vermont Red Rose
Publications, 1962. 101p.

_____ .
Rose Recipes. Woodstock, Vermont. Red Rose
Publications, 1959. 100p.
Gordon, Leslie, Ed.
The new crusade including a report concerning
prohibition etc. Compiled by Jackson-Babbitt Inc.,
Cleveland, The Crusaders Inc., 1932. 283p.
Bibliography.
Gordon, Robert I.
Cocktails and snacks. (By Robert and Anne London).
Cleveland, World Publishing Co., 1953. 236p. Illus.
Gore-Browne, Margeret
Let's plant a vineyard. London, Mills and Boon Ltd.,
1967. 59p. Illus.-drawing, photos.
Gorham, Maurice
Back to the local. London, P. Marshall, 1949. 126p.
Glossary of terms commonly used in connection with
London pubs.

_____ .
The Local. London, Cassell and Co., Ltd., 1939.
51p. Illus. Glossary.
Gorham Co.
The Gorham Cocktail book. New York, 1905. 47p.
Gottlieb, David and Rossi, Peter H.
A bibliography and bibliographic review of food and
food habit research. Library Bulletin no. 4. Quarter-
master Food and Container Institute, Chicago, January,
1961. 112 pages. Bibliography.
Goudiss, C. Houston
Give the grape its rightful place. New York, Privately
printed. (The People's Home Journal), 1921. 17p.

Gouffe, Jules
    The Book of Preserves.   London, Sampson, Low Son and
    Marston, 1871.   333p.
Gough, John B.
    Autobiography and personal recollections (Temperance).
    Springfield, Mass., Bill Nichols and Co., 1869.   552p.
    1871.
                .
    ―――――Sunlight and shadow.   Hartford, Ct. Worthington and Co.,
    1882.   542p. (Temperance)
Gould, F. L.
    See Bottles and Bins recipes. (Anon).
Gould, H. P.
    Peach-growing.   New York, The Macmillan Co.,
    1918.   426p.   Illus-photos.
Gould, Wilbur, A. Dr.
    Quality control clinic.   Chicago, 1957.   Published by
    Food Packer (Vance Publishing Co.), n d, ca1957.
    32p.   Illus.
Graham, C.
    On lager beer.   London, 1881.   26p.   GBPOL
Graham, G.
    See Mottram, V.H. and Graham, George
    Hutchinson's Food and the principles of dietetics.
Graham, Harry Crusen
    . . . Coffee.   Production, trade, and consumption by
    countries.   Washington, Govt. Print. Off., 1912.
    134p.   Bibliography.
Graham, James
    A new plain rational treatise on the true nature and
    uses of Bath waters.   London, R. Cruttwell.   1789.
    48p.   (Berkeley)
Graham, M.E. Comp.
    Wine and Food Society of Southern California; a
    history with a Bibliography of A.L. Simon, Los Angeles,
    The Society, 1957.   60p.   PLOSA
Graham, Stirling
    Melrose, Honey of Roses.   n p.   Records and Golds-
    borough, Inc., 1944.   95p.   Illus.
Graham, William of Vare
    Art of making wine from fruits and flowers.   London,
    Printed for W. Nicoll, 1750.   Various editions in many
    places.

Gramp, G., and Sons, Ltd., Rowland Flat, Australia
100 years of wine-making. Adelaide, S. Australia.
Gillingham, 1947. (unpaged). Illus.
Grange, Cyril
The complete book of home food preservation. 3rd
edition. London, Cassell Ltd., 1949. 305p.
Grant, C.W.
Manual of the vine. Ionia, N.Y., Published by author,
1864. 115p. (New York Agri. Exp. Sta. Geneva)
Grant, E.B.
Beet-Root sugar and cultivation of the beet. Boston,
Lee and Shepard, 1867. 158p.
Grants of St. James Ltd.
A gateway to wine. London, 1964. 76p. Illus.
Supplementary Glossary.
Granville, August B.
The spas of England and principal seabathing places.
MIDLAND SPAS, London, Henry Colburn, 1841. 324p.
Illus.

_____.
The spas of England and principal seabathing places.
NORTHERN SPAS, London, Henry Colburn, 1841. 423p.
Illus.

_____.
The Spas of England and principal seabathing places
SOUTHERN SPAS, London, Henry Colburn, 1841.
paged from Midland Spas, p. 327 to 640- Illus.

_____.
The Spas of Germany. Second edition. London,
Henry Colburn, 1839. 516p. Illus.

_____.
The spas of Germany revisited, 1843. 578p. BM
Grapewin, Charley
The Flowing-Bowl. n p. Privately published, 1933.
17p. Illus.
Gratrix, Dawson
In pursuit of the vine. London, H. Jenkins, 1953.
227p. Illus.
Gratz, Herman
The making of ice creams, ices, etc. Revised 2nd
edition. Philadelphia, published by author, 1912. 92p.
Gray, Arthur, Comp.
The little tea book. New York, The Baker and Taylor
Co., 1903. 99p. Illus.

‎——— Over the black coffee. New York, Baker and Taylor
1902. 108p.

‎——— Toasts and tributes. New York, Rohde and Haskins,
1904. 301p.

Gray, Barry (pseud)
See Coffin, Robert Barry. Ale in prose and verse.

Gray, Grace Viall
Every step in canning. Chicago, Forbes and Co.,
1920. 253p.

Gray, James
After repeal; what the host should know about serving
wines and spirits, proper glassware and cocktail
recipes. St. Paul, Brown Blodgett Co., 1933.
32p. Illus.   LC

Gray and Co., Brewers
Observations on the vinous fermentation. . .
advantages to the process of brewing. London,
Published by Messrs. Gray, 1823. 30p.

Grazzi-Soncini, G.
Wine. Classification-wine tasting, qualities and
defects. Trans. by F. T. Bioletti Sacramento,
State Office, 1892. 57p.

Green, Herbert W.
Mixed drinks. A manual for bar clerks. Indianapolis,
Frank H. Smith, 1895. 168p.

Green, Martin and White, Tony
Guide to London pubs. London, Heinemann Ltd.,
1965. 179p. Illus.

Green, Samuel B.
Amateur fruit growing. A practical guide to the
growing of fruit for home use and the market.
Minneapolis, Farm, Stock and Home Publishing Co.,
1894. 129p. Illus-engravings.

‎——— Popular fruit growing. Prepared especially for
beginners and as a textbook for schools and colleges.
St. Anthony Park, Minn. Webb Publishing Co., St.
Paul, Minn., 1910. 328p. Illus-photos.

Green, S. H.
Beer gravity tables. London, Sheppard Cooper and
Co., 1912. 43p.   BM

Greenberg, Emanual and Madeline
    Whiskey in the kitchen. Indianapolis and New York.
    The Bobbs-Merrill Co., Inc., 1968. 315p.
Greenberg, Leon A.
    The definition of an intoxicating beverage. New
    Haven, Reprint from Journal of Studies on Alcohol
    Vol. 16, no. 2. 316-325, June 1955. unpaged (12)
    Bibliography.
Greenfield, W.S.
    Alcohol: its use and abuse. Health primer. New
    York, D. Appleton and Co., 1892. 95p. List of
    authorities.
Greenhalgh, Mollie
    See Hardwick, Michael and Mollie Greenhalgh.
    The jolly toper.
Greenish, Henry George
    The microscopical examination of food and drugs,
    London, J. and A. Churchill, 1903. 321p. Illus.
Greenleaf, A.B.
    See Rosenbloom, Morris Victor.
    Bottling for profit; a treatise on liquor and allied
    industries.
Greenleaf, Sidney S.
    See Peninou, Ernest P. and Greenleaf, Sidney S.
    A directory of California wine growers and wine
    makers in 1860.

_____.
    See Peninou, Ernest and Sidney Greenleaf
    Winemaking in California.
Greenwood, Arthur
    Public ownership of the liquor trade. London, Leonard
    Parsons, 1920. 185p.
Greenwood, Edgar, Comp.
    Classified guide to technical and commercial books.
    London, Scott, Greenwood and Co., 1904. 216p.
Greenwood, Raymond
    The vintage at Chateau Monbousquet. The story of a
    vineyard and the making of wine. London, B.M.
    and J. Strauss Ltd., (Wine dealers), n d, (1966).
    unpaged (16), Illus.
Green and Green Inc.
    Green and Green presents flavors of distinction. Price
    List no. 54, Houston, Texas, n d, (1954). 18p.

Greg, Thomas Tylston
Through the glass lightly. Essays on wine. London,
J. M. Dent and Co., 1897. 143p.   BM
Gregg, Thomas
Handbook of fruit culture. New York, Fowler and
Wells, 1857. 163p.   LC
Gregor, M.
Notes upon pure and natural wines. London, 1869. BV

_____.
Notes upon pure and natural wines of Hungary. London,
1871.   BV
Gregory, T. C.
See Herstein, Karl M. and Gregory, Thomas C.
Chemistry and technology of Wines and Liquors.
Grew, Nehemiah
Treatise on the nature and abuse of bitter purging salt
contained in Epsom, and other such waters. London,
1697. 64p.   BM
Griesediek, Alvin
The Falstaff story. 2nd edition. St. Louis, n p,
1952. 367p. Illus.
Grieve, Maud
Culinary herbs and condiments. London, William
Heinemann Ltd., 1933. 203p.
Griffin, John Joseph
The chemical testing of wines and spirits. London,
J. J. Griffin and Sons, 1872. 150p. Illus.
Griffith, William
Report on tea planting upper Siam. Calcutta, 1838.
85p.   BM
Griffiths, Sir Percival
The history of the Indian tea industry. London,
Weidenfeld and Nicolson, 1967. 730p. Illus-photos.
Bibliography.
Griffiths, T. M.
Non-secret formulas. St. Louis, Published by author,
1897. 513p. 1910, 514p.
Grindal, Martin
Warm beer, a treatise with observations on cold water,
etc. London, printed for T. Reed, 1724. 50p.   BM
Grindon, Leo H.
Fruits and fruit-trees. An index to the kinds valued
in Britain. Manchester, Palmer and Howe, 1885.
328p. Illus.

Grindrod, Ralph Barnes
Bacchus. An essay on the nature, causes effects and
cure of intemperance. New York, J. and H. G. Langley,
1843. 512p.
Grinstead, Raymond M.
Modern handbook of wine and liquor control. Stamford,
Conn., no. 29, The Dahls, n d, 1945. 48p.
Griswold, Frank Gray
French wines and Havana cigars. New York,
Dutton's Inc., 1929. 101p.   LC

———•——— The Gourmet. New York, Duttons, Inc., 1933.
121p. Illus-photos.

———•——— Old Madeiras. New York, Duttons, 1929. 65p.
Grohusko, Jacob Abraham
Jack's manual on the vintage and production, care and
handling of wines, liquors, etc. New York, A. A.
Knopf, 1933. 234p.

———•——— Jack's Manual on the vintage, care and handling of
wines, liquors, etc. 4th edition. New York, Published
by author, n d. 151p.
Grommes and Ulrich
Special price list of whiskies, wines, etc. Chicago,
1915. 36p. Illus.
Groote, Melvin de.
Manufacture of emulsion flavors. Reprinted from
American perfumer and essential oil review. New
York, 1920. 27p.
Gross, Emanuel
Hops in their botanical, agricultural and technical
aspects. London, Scott Greenwood Co., 1900. 341p.
                                                              LC
Gross, Gwen
Bar of chocolate. (a child's book). London, Long-
mans Green, 1957. 17p.   BM

———•——— A cup of coffee. (Child's book). London, Longmans,
Green, 1957. 17p.   BM
Grossman, Harold J.
Beverage dictionary. Stamford, Conn. J.O. Dahl,
1938. 59p.

Grossman's guide to wines, spirits and beers. New
York, Sherman and Spoerer, 1940. 404p. Illus.
1943, New York, Scribner's, 404p. Illus.
1955, New York, Scribner's, 427p. Illus. Bibliography.

Practical bar management. New York, Ahrens
Publishing Co., 1959. 160p. Illus.

Groves, Philip W.
Microbiology. Volume 1 of Jusfrute handbooks for the
soft drink industry. Gosford, N.S.W. Australia, n d,
1966. Jusfrute, Ltd., 60p. Illus.

Groves and Whitnall, Ltd.
The history of a brewery, 1835-1949. Salford and
Manchester, 1949. 32p. Illus.

Grubb, Norman H.
Cherries. London, Crosby Lockwood and Son, Ltd.,
1949. 186p. Illus-colour plates. Authorities quoted.

Grubbs, V. W.
Practical prohibition. Greenville, Texas., T.C.
Johnson and Co., 1887. 383p.

Gudeman, Jon
See McCord, William and Joan McCord with Jon
Gudeman
Origins of alcoholism.

Guenther, Ernest
The essential oils. New York, Van Nostrand, 1948-52.
6 v. Illus. Bibliographies.

See Flavors and spices and flavor characterization.
See Fritzsche Bros.

Lemon oil production around the world. Reprinted
from perfumery and essential oil record. New York,
Fritzsche Brothers, Inc., October 1963-February 1964.
59p. Illus-photos. References.

Guidott, Thomas
Apology for the Bath, London, 1705. 115p.   BM

Collection of treatises relating to the city and water
of Bath. London, 1725. 6 parts.   BM

A discourse of Baths and the hot waters there. London,
Henry Brome, 1676. 200p. Illus-drawings.

Guinee, Patrick
See Brown, Florence Isabella
The bartender's friend.
Guinness, Arthur and Son and Co., Ltd.
Guide to St. James's gate brewery.   Dublin, 1928.
106p. Illus. 1931, 106p. Illus.

—————·
Guinness's Brewery.   Dublin, 1919. 16p. Illus.
also loose postcards.

—————·
Guinness, Dublin, (cover title). n d, 62p. Illus.
small.
1939, 62p. Illus.
1948, 70p. Illus.
(1952), 70p. Illus.
n d, 64p. Illus (in German),
Assorted postcards 16p. Illus. A morning in Dublin.

—————·
Physiological aspects of alcoholic beverages. A review
of recent research, including new studies on Guinness
Stout. no. 1. The metabolism of alcohol, Dublin
1938. References. 4p.
Gunn, Neil M.
Whisky and Scotland. London, George Routledge and
Sons Ltd., 1935. 198p.
Gunter, William
Confectioner's Oracle (Gunter's). London, Alfred
Miller, 1817. 122p.   BM
Guthrie, William
Remarks on burgundy, claret, champagne. London,
Simpkin, Marshall and Co., 1889. 38p.   BM
Gutmann, Edward
The watering places and mineral springs of Germany,
Austria, and Switzerland. New York, D. Appleton and
Co., 1880. 331p. Illus-engravings.
Gutteridge, William
The Ne Plus Ultra of assaying, weighing and valuing
spiritous liquors. London, 1827-1828. 2 vol.   BM
Guyer, William
The merry mixer; or Cocktails and their ilk; a booklet
on mixtures and mulches, fizzes and whizzes. New
York, J.S. Finch and Co., 1933. 63p. Illus.
New York, Pepper, 1933. 63p.
New York, Stagg, 1933. 63p.

Guyot, Jules
Cultivation of the vine and wine-making. Melbourne,
Walker, 1865. 108p.   ANL
————————.
Growth of the vine and principles of winemaking.
Melbourne, Leader Office, 1896. 28p.
                                   (State Library of Victoria)
Guynn, Stephen
See Lloyd, F.C.
The art and technique of wine. Edited by Stephen Gwynn.
————————.
Burgundy. London, Constable, 1934. 144p.
Gyrogy, Paul
The fine wines of Germany and all the world's wine
lore. Berlin, Paul Funk Berlin West, 1965. 172p.
Dictionery form. German, English dictionery of
contents. Works of reference.

H. (M)
The coffee drinker's manual   (Listed in Peddie)
————————.
The young cooks monitor or directions for cookery
and distilling. London, 1683.   BM
Haarer, A. E.
Coffee growing. London, Oxford Univ. Press, 1963.
127p. Illus. Glossary.
————————.
Modern coffee production. 2nd revised and enlarged.
London, Leonard Hill Books Ltd., 1962. 495p.
Illus. References.
Haarlem, J.R.
Variety tests for grapes for wine. Toronto, 1954.
151p.   (Davis)
Haas, John I. Inc.
Yakima Golding Hop Farms. Washington, D.C. 1960.
82p. Illus-photos.
Hack, F.
Home brewed wines and beers, 1934.
           (Massell-Applied Wine Chemistry and Technology)
Hackett, F. Michael
English Cottage Wines. The art of making wine in the
home. Morpeth, English Cottage Wine Co., 1960. 53p.

184

Hackstaff, B.W. and Brenner, M.W.
    An analysis of packaging costs in the brewing industry.
    A study by Schwarz Laboratories. Sponsored by Glass
    Container Mfg's Institute. Reprinted from American
    Brewer May 1964. Mount Vernon, N.Y., 1964. 15p.
    9 charts.
Hackwood, Frederick William
    Good cheer. The romance of food and feasting. London,
    T. Fisher Unwin, 1911. 424p. Illus.

————————.
    Inns, ales, and drinking customs of old England.
    London, T.F. Unwin, 1909. 392p. Illus.
Haggard, Howard W. and Jellinek, E.M.
    Alcohol explored. Garden City, N.Y., Doubleday
    Doran and Co., 1942. 297p. Selective references.

————————.
    Devils, drugs and doctors. New York, Blue Ribbon
    Books, 1929. 405p.
Hahnemann, Samuel
    Treatise on the effects of coffee. Louisville, Bradley
    and Gilbert, 1875. 35p.   LC
Haig, Alexander
    Diet and food. 6th edition. London, J and A
    Churchill, 1906. 139p.
Haimo, Oscar
    Cocktail and wine digest. Enciclopedia y guia para
    la casa y el bar. New York, International Cocktail
    wine and spirits Digest, Inc., Edicion Espanola, 1946.
    176p. Illus.

————————.
    Cocktail and wine digest; encyclopedia and guide for
    home and bar. New York, No publisher, 1945. 125p.
    Illus-drawings, 1950, 143p.

————————.
    Cocktail digest (from private notes). Brooklyn,
    Printed by the Comet Press, Inc., 1943. 95p. Illus.
Haimo, Oscar (of the Hotel Pierre)
    Cocktail digest. New York, Published by the author,
    Printed by Comet Press, 1943. 95p.
Halasz, Zoltan
    Hungarian wine through the ages. Budapest, Corvina
    Press, 1962. 185p. Illus. Bibliography.
Hale, D. Everett
    Cook with beer; real old-country cooking. New
    York, Vintage Press, 1957. 56p. Illus.

‾‾‾‾‾‾ It's smart to cook with beer; 200 recepes for cooking
with beer. Belleville, N.J., Published by author,
1949. 115p.

Hale, Mrs. S. T.
See Acton, Miss Eliza (Revised by Mrs. S.J. Hale)
Modern cookery in all its branches.

Hale, William J.
Prosperity beckons. Dawn of the alcohol era.
Boston, The Stratford Co., 1936. 201p.

Hales, Stephen
Experiments on Chalybeate or Steel waters. London,
1739.   BM

‾‾‾‾‾‾ A friendly admonition to the drinkers of gin, brandy,
and other distilled spiritous liquors, etc. Appendix
by an eminent physician, to such as may be desirious
to break off that odious and fatal habit of drinking
drams. 5th edition with additions. London, B. Don
bookseller, 1754. 43p.

‾‾‾‾‾‾ Statical essays. (Mineral water). London, 1738. 2
vol.   BM

Hall, Sir A. Daniel and Crane, M.B.
The Apple. London, Martin Hopkinson, Ltd., 1933.
235p. Bibliography and glossary.

Hall, A. George, Ed.
Invitations to dine in London and Greater London.
London, Gray's Inn Press, 1956. 372p. Illus.

Hall, E. Hepple
Coffee taverns, cocoa houses and coffee palaces. Their
rise, progress and prospects: with a directory. London,
S.W. Partridge and Co., (1879). 118p. Illus-engraving
Advertising.

Hall, Harrison
The distiller . . . Adapted to the use of farmers and
distillers. 2nd edition enl. and improved. Philadelphia,
Published by the author, 1818. 338p. Illus-plates.

Hall, Irene S.
See Morgan, Agnes Fay and Irene Sanborn Hall
Experimental food study.

Hall, James J. and Bunton, John
Wines. London, W. and G. Foyle, Ltd., 1961.
93p.

Hall, S. C.
The trial of Sir Jasper a temperance tale in verse.
London, Virtue, Spalding, and Daldy, n d, ca1872.
64p.
Hall, T.
Queen's royal cookery. London, C. Bates and A.
Bettesworth, 1709. GBPOL
Hall and Nahler
Six best cellars. New York, Dodd Mead, 1919. 106p.
NYPL
Hallett, Elizabeth Hughes
Elizabeth Hallett's Hostess book. Edinburgh, John
Grant Booksellers Ltd., 1948. 400p.
Hallgarten, Peter
Liqueurs. London, Wine and Spirit Publications Ltd.,
1967. 135p. Illus- photos.

—————.
See Simon, S. P. E. and Hallgarten, Peter
The Wineograph chart.
Hallgarten, S. Fritz
Alsace and its wine gardens. London, Andre Deutsch,
1957. 187p. Illus.

—————.
See Simon, Andre Louis.
The great wines of Germany and its famed vineyards.
Andre I. Simon S. F. Hallgarten.

—————.
Rhineland wineland; a journey through the wine districts
of western Germany. London, P. Elek, 1951. 199p.
Illus. Works of reference.

—————.
Rhineland wineland. London, Arlington Books, 1965.
319p. Illus.
Halsey, S. M. M.
See Smith, Jacqueline Harrison and Sue Mason Maury
Halsey, compilers.
Famous old recipes. (cookery).
Ham, (J.) of Westeokers, Somerset
Instructions for brewing by new method from unmalted
corn. London, Sherbourne, 1822. 33p. BM

—————.
Manufacture of cider and perry reduced to rules.
Sherbourne, 1827. 62p. GBPOL

Ham, John
The theory and practice of brewing from malted and unmalted corn and from potatoes. London, W. Simpson and R. Marshall, 1829. 104p. Illus.

Hamel-Smith, Harold
Some notes on cocoa planting in the West Indies. London, Published by author, 1901. 70p.

Hamilton, Alexander V.
The household cyclopedia of practical receipts and daily wants. Springfield, Mass. W.J. Holland and Co., 1875. 423p.

Hamlin, Chas. E. and Warren, Chas.
Hamlin's formulas or every druggist his own perfumer. Baltimore, Edward B. Read and Son, 1885. 141p.

Hamman, E.H.
See Fritzsche Bros.
Flavors and spices and flavor chacterization.

Hammell, George M. Ed.
The passing of the saloon. An authentic and official presentation of the anti-liquor crusade in America. Cincinnati, Ohio, 1908. The Tower Press, 436p. Illus. Bibliography.

Hammond, H.
Notes on wine and vine culture in France. Beech Island, S.C. Published by author, 1856. 21p.   NYPL

Hampson, John
The English at table. London, William Collins, 1944. 48p. Illus-drawings.

Hampton, F.A.
The scent of flowers and leaves. London, Dulau and Co., 1925. 135p. Bibliography.

Hamway, Jonas
An essay on tea. 32 letters to two ladies, n p, n d, ca1757.   (Wine and Food Society)

Hance Brothers and White
Advice and help. (Soda fountains). Philadelphia, 1891. 64p.   LC

—————
Hance's pure fruit juices. Philadelphia, n d ca1884. unpaged (12).

—————
Pure fruit juices. (catalogue). Philadelphia, 1889. 96p.   LC

Hancock, George Charles
Report on the composition of commoner British wines
and cordials (alcoholic and non-alcoholic). London,
H.M. Stationary Office, 1924. 58p.   LC
Haney, Jesse and Co.
Steward and barkeeper's manual (Haney's). A complete
and practical guide for preparing all kinds of plain and
fancy mixed drinks and popular beverages. New York,
1869. 67p.   LC
Hankerson, Fred Putnam
The cooperage handbook. Brooklyn, N.Y., Chemical
Publishing Co., 1947. 182p. Illus. Glossary of
terms.
Hanly, J. Frank and Stewart, Oliver Wayne, Editors
Speeches of the flying squadron, Indianapolis, Published
by Hanly, Stewart, Poling and Landrith, n d, ca1915.
420p.
Hann, George E.
Some notes on the technical study and handling of wines.
London, 1948. 82p.   (Davis)
Hansen, Emil Chr.
Practical studies in fermentation being contributions to
the life history of micro-organisms. London, Spon;
New York, Spon and Chamberlain, 1896. 277p.
Hansen, Jens P.
Wine in the bible. Evanston, Ill., Signal Press, n d,
ca1955. 22p.
Hanson, R.
Short account of tea and tea trade, 1876.
                                       (Listed in Peddie)
Hantke's Brewers' School and Laboratories.
Letters on brewing. Milwaukee, 1902-1905. Five
volumes. (In English-German). Paged by sections,
Illus.
Haraszthy, Agostin
Grape culture, wines, and winemaking with notes upon
horticulture and agriculture. New York, Harper and
Brothers, 1862. 420p. Illus.
Hardinge, G.N.
Development and growth of Courage's brewery.
London, Published by Courage, 1933. 54p.   BM
Hardman, William
The wine-growers and wine-coopers' manual. With
plans and alcoholic tables. London, Tegg, 1878. 166p.

Hardwick, Homer
　Winemaking at home. New York, W. Funk, 1954.
　253p. Illus. Glossary.
Hardwick, Michael and Greenhalgh, Mollie
　The jolly toper. London, H. Jenkins, 1961. 126p.
　Illus- drawings.
Hardy, John
　The retail compounder or publican's friend. London,
　n d, ca1795.　　　　　　　　　　　　　　　　BM
Hardy, Thomas
　Note on the vineyards of America and Europe.
　Adelaide, Henn., 1885. 134p. (Los Angeles Public)

————————.
　A vigneron abroad. Adelaide, South Australia Register,
　1899. 34p.　　　　　　　　　　　　　　　　　ANL
Hardy, Thomas and Sons, Ltd., Adelaide, Australia
　The Hardy tradition; tracing the growth and development
　of a great winemaking family through its first hundred
　years. Adelaide, T. Hardy, 1953. 50p. Illus.
Hargreaves, William
　Alcohol and man or the scientific basis of total
　abstinence. New York, The National Temperance
　Society and Publication House, 1885. 224p.

————————.
　Alcohol and science or alcohol and what it is and what
　it does. London, W. Nicholson and Sons, n d, ca1875.
　252p.

————————.
　Our wasted resources; the missing link in the
　temperance reform. New York, The National
　Temperance Society and Publication House, 1876.
　201p.

————————.
　Malt liquors; their nature and effects. Philadelphia,
　1877. 8p.　　　　　　　　　　　　　　　　　　LC
Haring, Frank
　Knowing alcoholic beverages. New York, Liquor Store
　Magazine, 1961. 116p. Illus.
Harington, Sir John
　The Englishman's doctor or School of Salerne. London,
　1609.　　　　　　　　　　　　　　　　　　　BM
Harington, John E.M.
　Tea in Europe. Hitchin, Garden City Press, 1904.
　64p.　　　　　　　　　　　　　　　　　　　BM

Harkness, Kenneth M. and Fort, Lyman M.
Alcohol; its uses and abuses. A syllabus for schools.
Mitchell, South Dakota, Educator Supply Co., 1935.
107p. Reference materials list.
Harland, M.
See Herrick, Christine Terhune and Harland, Marion.
Consolidated library of modern cooking and household
recipes. Vol. V, Beverages, etc.

_____.
See Herrick, Christine Terhune and Harland, Marion.
Modern domestic science Vol. V. Beverages, etc.
Harler, Campbell R.
The culture and marketing of tea. 2nd edition. London,
New York, Oxford University Press, 1956. 263p.

_____.
Tea growing. London, Oxford University Press, 1966.
162p. Illus-photos.

_____.
Tea manufacture. London, Oxford University Press,
1963. 126p. Illus. Glossary.
Harper, Charles G.
Historic and picturesque inns of old England. London,
Ed., J. Burrow and Co., 1927. 172p. Illus.
Harrington, T.S.
See Hornsby, Jack H. and Harrington, Thomas S.
Successful liquor retailing.
Harris, A.J.
The license-holder's handy guide. 8th edition. Bristol,
1912. W.C. Hemmons, Central Printing Works.
64p. 18th edition, 1930-55p.
Harris, Florence La Ganke
Flavor's the thing. New York, M. Barrows and Co.,
1939. 319p. Illus.
Harris, Henry G. and Borella, S.P.
All about ices, jellies, creams and conserves. London,
Maclaren and Sons, 1920. 200p.
Harris, Robert
Drunkard's Cup. (A sermon). Bernard Alsop, 1626.
29p.   BM
Harris, Wm.
Brewers' accounts. (A lecture on). Dublin, The Paper
and Printing Co., of Ireland Ltd., n d, (1893). 72p.
Harrison, Appolos W.
Perfumery, its history, character and use. Philadelphia,
1953. 32p. Illus.   LC

191

Harrison, C.J.
  See Carpenter, P.H. and Harrison, C.J.
  The manufacture of tea in northeast India.
Harrison, Godfrey
  Bristol Cream. London, Batsford, 1955. 162p. Illus.
Harrison, Michael
  Beer cookery; 101 traditional recipes. London, Spearman, 1953. 143p. Illus.
Harrop, Joseph
  Monograph on flavoring extracts with essences, syrups, and colorings. Also, formulas for their preparation. Colombus, O., London, Harrop and Co., 1891. 161p.
Harry and Wynn
  See Mc Elhone, Harry
  Barflies and cocktails. Over 300 cocktail recipes by Harry and Wynn.
"Harry's of Ciro's. (Harry Mc Elhone)
  A B C of mixing cocktails. London, n d, Odhams Press Ltd., n d. 110p.
Hart, James
  Diet for the diseased. London, R. Allot, 1633. folio.
                                                          BM

Hart John Hinchley
  Cacoa; a manual on the cultivation and curing of cacao. London, Duckworth, 1911. 307p. Illus.
Hart, Madge Amelia, Comp.
  Eating and drinking, a miscellany. London, S. Low, Marston and Co., Ltd., 1947. 232p. Illus.
Hartley, Arthur
  The bottling of English beers. London, The Brewing Trade Review, 1906. 217p.
Hartley, Dorothy
  Food in England. London, McDonald and Co., 1969. 676p. Illus-drawings.
Hartley, Joseph
  The wholesale and retail wine and spirit merchant's companion. London, Published by author, 1835. 208p.
  _____.
  The wine and spirit merchant's companion. 2nd edition. London, Simpkin, Marshall and Co., 1843. 228p. same (different binding)
Hartley, Walter N.
  Fermentation and distillation. London, 1884. 26p.
                                                          (Bird)

192

Hartman, Dennis
    Wines and liqueurs, what, when, how to serve.
    Washington, Congressional Press, Inc., 1933. 23p. LC
Hartman, George
    Hartman's curiosities of art and nature of the true pres-
    erver and restorer of health. London, Printed for A.C.
    and G. Hartman, 1682. 384p.   BM

―――――――.
    The family physitian. London, H. Hill, 1696. 528p.
                                                     BM
Hartman, Louis Francis and Oppenheim, A.L.
    On beer and brewing techniques in ancient Mesopatamia.
    Baltimore, American Oriental Society, 1950. 55p.
    Illus.   LC
Hartong, B.D. Comp.
    Elsivier's dictionary of barley, malting and brewing.
    In six languages. Amsterdam, Elsivier Publishing Co.,
    1961. 669p. Bibliography.
Hartshorne, Albert
    Antique drinking glasses. (Former title old English
    Glasses). New York, Brussel and Brussel, 1968.
    490p. Illus-engravings, drawings.

―――――――.
    Old English glasses. An account of glass drinking
    vessels in England, from early times to the end of the
    eighteenth century. London and New York, E. Arnold,
    1897. 490p. Illus.
Harvey, E.S.
    See Parker, Milton, Harvey, E.S. and Stateler, E.S.
    Elements of food engineering.
Harvey, John and Sons Limited
    Harvey's wine guide. Bristol, 1948. 48p. Illus-photo,
    maps.

―――――――.
    Wine list. 2nd edition. 1963-1964, Harvey's of Bristol.
    92p. Illus.

―――――――.
    Wine list decorations. Bristol, 1961-1963. 100p. Illus.
Haskell, G.
    Wines, liqueurs and brandies. (In vino veritas). London,
    Published by author for private circulation only, 1922.
    94p.

―――――――.
    Account of various experiments for the production of new
    and desirable grapes. Ipswich, Mass. No Publisher,
    1877. 18p.   (Davis)

Hasler, G. F.
>Wine service in the restaurant. Professional guide for the sommelier. London, Wine and spirit Publications Ltd., 1968. 81p. Illus-photos.

Hassan, Badrul
>Drink and drug evil in India. Madras, Ganish, 1922. 161p. LC

Hassell, Arthur Hill
>Adulterations detected. London, Longman, Brown, Green, Longmans, and Roberts, 1857. 712p.

———.
>Food and its adulterations, etc. London, Longman, Brown, Green and Longmans, 1855. 659p.

Hassell, Arthur Hill
>Food: its adulterations, and the methods for their detection. London, Longmans, Green and Co., 1876. 896p.

Hastings, Milo
>Physical culture food directory; a rating of foods for vitality, growth, reduction and energy and for the prevention of constipation. New York, MacFadden, 1925. 151p. Tables.

Hastings, Samuel D. Ed.
>The people versus the liquor traffic. Great speeches of John B. Finch. Chicago, Published by literature committee R.W.G. Lodge, I.O. of G.T., 1882. 285p. 1883, 285p.

Haszonics, Joseph J. and Barratt, Stuart
>Wine Merchandising. New York, Ahrens Book Co., 1963. 214p. Illus.

Hatch, Edward White
>The American wine cook book. New York, G.P. Putnam's Sons, 1941. 315p. Illus. Glossary.

Hatfield, W.E.A. (Workers Educational Ass'n).
>Hatfield and its people. Book 3 Pubs and Publicans. The story of Hatfield's breweries, inns and alehouses. May 1960. 32p. Illus.

Hatton, Joseph
>Cocoa. London, Barclay and Fry, 1892. 22p. BM

Hauge, R.
>See Bruun, Kettil and Ragnar Hauge
>Drinking habits among northern youth.

Haughey, J.T.
>See Buell, O.D. and Haughey, J.T.
>110 most popular American drinks, etc.

Hausbrand, E.
Principles and practice of industrial distillation. New
York, John Wiley and Sons, 1926. 300p.

Hauser, Benjamin Gayelord
Here's how to be healthy. New York, Tempo Books
Inc., 1934. 48p.   LC

Hauser, Isaiah L.
Tea; its origin, cultivation, manufacture and use.
Chicago and New York, Rand, Mc Nally and Co., 1890.
27p.   LC

Hausner, A.
The manufacture of preserved foods and sweetmeats.
London, Scott, Greenwood and Son, 1912. 238p.

Hawker, Charlotte
Chats about wine. London, Daly and Co., 1908. 158p.
1907, same.

——————— .
Wine and wine merchants. London, 1909.   BV

Hawkes, George
The publican's guide for reducing spirits. (Bermondsey)
Published by author, n d, ca1890. 88p.

Hawkes, S. N.
Historical notes on beer and brewing. London, 1850.
15p.   GBPOL

Hawkins, J.
Treatise on natural and artificial mineral waters.
Philadelphia, R. Wright, 1823. 48p. (Kentucky Univ.)

Hay, William Howard, MD
Health via food. East Aurora, N.Y., Health Foundation,
1934. 317p.

Hay, William Ltd.
The story of ginger. Hull, n d, 15p. Illus.

Hayman, E. N.
A practical treatise to render the art of brewing more
easy. 2nd edition. London, Longman, Hurst, Rees
Orme, and Brown, 1823. 123p. Illus-engravings.

Hayne, Arthur P.
Control of temperature in wine fermentation. Berkeley,
University of California Agricultural Sta. Bulletin no.
117, 1897. 19p.   UCLA

Haynes, E. Barrington
Glass through the ages. Hammondsworth, Middlesex,
Penguin Books, n d, 1948. 240p.

Hayes, Joseph J.
The inside tip to the man that came back, the bar
tender. New York, Printed by Imperial Press, 1933.
96p.   LC

Hayward- Tyler and Co., Ltd.
Aerated water machinery and bottlers' appliances.
List "E". London, n d, ca1927. 179p, Illus-photos.
n d, ca1929, 128p. Illus.-photos.
Haywood, Mrs. Eliza
A new present for serving maid. London, Printed for
A Pearch, 1771. 272p.   LC
Haywood, J. K.
Mineral waters of the United States. Washington,
Government Printing Office, 1905. 100p.
Haywood, Joseph L.
Mixology; the art of preparing all kinds of drinks.
Wilmington, Del., Press of the Sunday Star . . . 1898.
54p.   LC
Hazelmore, Maximilian
Domestic economy, also the complete brewer. London,
J. Creswick and Co., 1794. 392p.   NYPL
Hazelton, Nika Standen
Chocolate! New York, Simon and Schuster, 1967.
93p.
Hazlitt, W. Carew
Old cookery books and ancient cuisine. London,
Elliott Stock, 1902. 271p. Bibliography.
Head, Brandon
The food of the gods. A popular account of cocoa.
London, Johnson, 1903. 109p. Illus.
Healy, Maurice ("Prattler")
A bibulography of memorabilia, trivia jocose jocoseria
and other odd notes upon wine and its lore. A supple-
ment to his paper on "Irish Wine". London, Private
circulation only, 1927. 10p.
Healy, Maurice
Claret and the white wine of Bordeaux. London,
Constable, 1934. 165p.

_____.
Stay me with flagons; a book about wine and other
things. Annotated by Ian Maxwell Campbell and with
a memoir by The Rt. Hon. Sir Norman Birkett.
London, Michael Joseph, 1950. 262p.
Heaton, Nell St. John
A calendar of food and wine, compiled by Nell Heaton
and André Simon. London, Faber and Faber, 1949.
268p. Illus.

Heath, Ambrose
Dining out. How and what to order. What to drink,
etc. London, Eyre and Spottiswood, 1936. 106p.
Glossary.

———— Good drinks. London, Faber and Faber, 1939. 239p.
Illus. Bibliography.

———— Homemade wines and liqueurs; how to make them.
New York, Wehman, 1956. 96p. 1961, same.
London, Herbert Jenkins.
Heath, Ambrose and Cottington D. D. Taylor, Compilers.
National Mark Calendar of Cooking. Compiled for
The Ministry of Agriculture (London), 1936. 128p.
Heaten, Nell St. John
Cooking with wine. Second edition. London, Faber
and Faber, 1963. 144p. Illus. Glossary.

———— Wines, mixed drinks and savouries. London, Arco
Publications, 1962. 160p.
Heaton, Vernon
Cocktail party secrets. Kingswood, Surrey, Elliot
Right Way Books, 1968. 125p.

———— A pub of your own. The right way to manage it.
Kingswood, Surrey, Elliott Right Way Books, 1964.
122p.
Heddle, Enid Moodie
Story of a vineyard, Chateaux Tahbilk, Melbourne, The
Hawthorne Press, 1968. 73p. Illus-drawings.
Hedrick, Ulysses Prentice
Cyclopedia of hardy fruits. New York, The Macmillan
Co., 1922. 370p. Illus-Glossary.

———— Fruits for the garden. New York, Oxford Univ. Press,
1944. 171p.   LC

———— Grapes and wines from home vineyards. London, New
York, Oxford University Press, 1945. 326p. Illus.

———— A history of agriculture in the State of New York.
Geneva, N.Y., New York Agricultural Experiment Station.
1933. 450p.

—————— A history of horticulture in America to 1860. New
York, Oxford University Press, 1950. 551p. Illus.
Bibliography.

—————— Manual of American grape-growing. New York, Mac-
millan, 1919. 458p. Illus.
Hedrick, Ulysses Prentice et al
The Cherries of New York. Report of the New York
Agricultural Experiment Station for the year 1914.
Albany, 1915. (4th of series). 371p. large size
colored plates. Bibliography and references.

—————— The Grapes of New York. Report of the New York
Agricultural Experiment Station for the year 1907.
Albany, 1908. (2nd of series). 564p. Illus-colored
plates. Bibliography and references.

—————— The Peaches of New York. Albany, N.Y. J.B. Lyon
Co., printers. Report of the New York Agricultural
Experiment Station for the year of 1916, 1917. (5th
of series). 541p. Illus-colored plates. Bibliography
and references.

—————— The Pears of New York. State of New York Department of Agriculture. 29th Annual Report. Volume 2.
Part II. Albany, N.Y., J.B. Lyon and Co., printers,
1921. 636p. Illus.

—————— The Plums of New York. Report of the New York
Agricultural Experiment Station for the year 1910.
Albany, 1911. (3rd of series). 616p. Illus-colored
plates. Bibliography and References.

—————— The small fruits of New York. Albany, Report of the
New York Agricultural Experiment Station for the year
ending June 30, 1925. 614p. Illus-color plates.
Bibliography and references.
Heering, Peter F.
Peter F. Heering. The History of a Danish Firm
during 125 years. Copenhagen, 1943. 46p. Illus.
Hehner, Otto
Alcohol tables, proof spirit. London, J. and A.
Churchill, 1880. 21p.   GBPOL

Heid, J. L.
    See Chace, E. M. Loesecke, H. W. von, and Heid, J. L.
    Citrus Fruit Products.
Heine and Co.
    Perfumers raw materials, essential oils, etc. New
    York, March 1914. 32p.
Heinz, H. J. Co.
    Nutritional Data. Third Edition. Published by H. J.
    Heinz Company, Pittsburg, 1956. 157p.
Held, John Jr.
    Peychaud's New Orleans cocktails. New Orleans,
    A. V. and J. Solari Ltd., 1935. unpaged (32), Illus.

_____.
    Ye Olde Mixer-Upper. Olde wood cut recipes. New
    York, Hillcrest Distilling Co., 1935. 24p. Illus.
Helmont, Jean Baptiste van
    A tennery of paradoxes (nativity of tarter in wine).
    London, Printed by J. Fisher for W. Lee, 1650. 144p.
                                                        LC
Helwig, Ferdinand C.
    See Smith, Walton Hall and Helwig, Ferdinand C.
    Liquor. The servant of man.
Hemlow-Merriam and Co.
    Fruit growers manual . Auburn, California, 1901.
    78p.   LC
Hemphill, Rosemary
    Fragrance and flavor. The growing and use of herbs.
    Sydney, Angus and Robertson, Ltd., 1959. 107p. Illus-
    drawings.
Henderson, Alexander
    The history of ancient and modern wines. London,
    Baldwin, Cradock and Joy, 1824. 408p.
Henderson, Bruce Upton
    Pop's master mixer. Honolulu, K. Stone, 1946. 186p.
    Illus.   LC
Henderson, J. A. and W. E.
    Account of tea cultivation in Ceylon. Colombo, Times
    of Ceylon Printing Works, 1893. 38p.   BM
Henderson, James Forbes
    Startling profits from wine making, in combination with
    the wine, spirit, and aerated water trades. 2nd edition.
    Dundee, W. and D. C. Thomson, 1897. 110p.

Henderson, Mary E.
   Diet for the sick; a treatise on the values of foods,
   their application to special conditions of health and
   disease, and on the best methods of their preparation.
   New York, Harper, 1885. 234p. Illus.
Henderson, Robert
   An inquiry into the nature and object of the several
   laws restraining and regulating the retail sale of
   alcohol, beer, wine and spirits. London, 1817.
   144p.   BM
Henderson, W. A.
   Housekeeper's instructor or universal family cook.
   London, Printed by J. Stratford, 1804. 448p.   LC
   _____ .
   Modern domestic cookery. New York, Leavitt and
   Allen, 1857. 360p.
Henderson, Yandell
   A new deal in liquor. A plea for dilution. Garden
   City, Doubleday, Doran and Co., 1934. 239p.
Henius, Max
   See Wahl, Robert
   American handy-book of the brewing, malting and
   anxiliary trades . . . by Robert Wahl, Ph.D., and
   Max Henius, Ph.D.
   _____ .
   . . . Danish beer and continental beer gardens;
   illustrated lecture by Max Henius at the annual conven-
   tion U.S. Brewers' association in Atlantic City,
   N.J., October 2d, 1913. New York, United States
   Brewers' Association, 1914. 51p. Illus.
Max Henius Memoir Committee
   Max Henius. A biography. Chicago, 1936. (400
   copies-copy no. 200). 221p. Illus.
Hennessy, Jas. and Co.
   Gift of taste. (cognac). Printed in Paris, n d.
   unpaged (24), Illus.
   _____ .
   Hennessy is everywhere. n p, n d. 16p. Illus.
Henninger, Otto
   The reliable bartenders' guide: drinks as they are
   made in the leading cafes. New York, Needham Press,
   1917. 98p.   LC
Henri, Monsieur, Wines, Ltd., Brooklyn, New York
   Your guide to the imported wines of Monsieur Henri.
   Brooklyn, 1960. 48p. Illus.

Henriot, A.
   See Chappaz, Georges and Henriot, Alexandre
   The Champagne vine country and champagne wine.
Henry, B.S.
   Studies of yeasts and the fermentation of fruits and
   berries of Washington. Bulletin of University of
   Washington, n d, ca1936. 90p.
Henry, Thomas
   Account of preserving water at sea, directions for
   preparing mephetic julep. London, 1781. 43p.   BM
─────────.
   Experiments and observations on ferments and
   fermentation. London, 1773. Warrington, 1785.
                                      Harvard University
Henry William
   The elements of experimental chemistry. 10th edition.
   2 volumes. London, Baldwin, Cradock and Joy, 1826.
   666p and 721p. Illus-plates.
Henseler, Hugo and Bernard Weichsel
   Wir Mixen. (cocktails). Leipzig. Veb Fachbuchverlag,
   1963. (in German). 198p. Illus.
Henshaw, Dennis
   Brush your teeth with wine. London, Hammond,
   Hammond Co., 1960. 284p. Illus.
Herbert, James
   Art of brewing India pale ale and export ale, stock
   and mild ales, porter and stout. Burton-upon-Trent.
   Published by author, 1866. 48p.
Herbemont, N.
   A treatise on the culture of the vine. Baltimore,
   Irving Hitchcock, 1833.   BG
Herod, William P.
   An introduction to wines; with a chapter on cordials and
   aperitives. New York, Fortuny's, 1936. 63p.
   Bibliography.
Herrick, Christine Terhune. Editor in Chief and Harland,
Marion
   Consolidated library of modern cooking and household
   recipes. Vol. V. Beverages, etc. New York, R.F.
   Bodmer Co., 1905. 293p. Illus.
─────────.
   Modern domestic science Vol. 5. Beverages, etc.
   Chicago, Debower-Chapline Co., 1908. 293p. Illus.

Herisko, Clarence
     Drinks and snacks for parties. New York, Imperial
     Publishing Co., 1960. 96p. Illus.
Hershey Chocolate Corp.
     The story of chocolate and cocoa. Hershey, Penna.
     1964. 31p. Illus.
Hersom, A. C.
     See Baumgartner, John G. and Hersom, A. C.
     Canned foods. An introduction to their microbiology.
Herstein, Karl M.
     Chemistry and technology of wines and liquors. M.
     Herstein and Morris B. Jacobs, 2nd edition. New
     York, D. Van Nostrand Co., 1948. 436p. Illus. 1935.
Herstein, Karl M. and Gregory, Thomas C.
     Chemistry and technology of wines and liquors. New
     York, D. Nav Nostrand and Co., 1935. 360p. Illus.
     Bibliography.
Herter, Rudolph Bruno
     Back to work; an old industry leads the way (Brewing).
     Chicago, F. A. Brewer and Co., 1933. 31p. Illus.
                                                        LC
Hesse, C. O.
     See Brooks, Reid M. and Hesse, Claron O.
     Western fruit gardening.
Hester, John
     These oils, water, extractions or essences. London,
     1585. 1p. Manuscript note.   Vanderbilt University
Hetherington, Thomas
     See Shevlin, James and Hetherington, Thomas.
     Alcoholic spirit testing.
Heuckmann, Dr. Wilhelm and Vom Endt, Rudi
     The grafted wine. (Italy), n p. No Publisher, n d.
     16p. Illus.
Hewitt, Charles
     Chocolate and cocoa, its growth and culture. London,
     Empire Marketing Board no. 7., 1862. 88p.   BM
Hewitt, John Theodore
     Chemistry of winemaking. London, 1928. 56p. NYPL
_____.
     Synthetic colouring matter, etc. London, Longmans
     Green and Co., Ltd., 1922. 405p.   NYPL
Hewitt, Robert Jr.
     Coffee: its history, cultivation, and uses. New York,
     D. Appleton and Co., 1872. 102p. Illus.

Heyne, Ernest B.
Complete catalogue of European vines, with their synonyms and brief description. San Francisco, Pacific Press Office, 1881. 63p. (Berkeley)

Heywood, Thomas
Philocathonista or Drunkard opened, etc., London, J. Raworth, 1630. 91p. BM

Higby, Ralph H.
See Kessler, Edward Joseph
Practical flavoring extract matter.

Higgins, Bryan
Analysis of the Tilbury alterative water. London, 1786. (Kirkby)

Higgins, Bryan
Experiments and observations relating to acetous acid, fixable airs, etc. London, T. Cadell, 1786. 353p. LC

_____.
Fragment of the 4th part of Dr. Higgins observations and advices for the improvement of--sugar and rum. London, 1803. 63p. BM

_____.
Observations and advices for the improvement and manufacture of Muscovado sugar and rum. St. Jago de la Vega. Printed by A. Aileman, 1797. 2 parts. BM

Hilgard, Eugene W.
Reports on experiments on fermenting red wines and related subjects during the years of 1886-7. Sacramento, State Office Publication, 1888. 48p. (Davis)

Hill, Brian
Inn-signia. 2nd edition. London, Published for Whitbread and Co., Ltd., by Naldrett Press, Ltd., 1949. 58p. Illus. Bibliography.

Hill, Ernestine
Water into gold. Melbourne, Robertson and Mullens, 1937. 328p. Illus.

Hill, Mrs. Jane M. (Mc Kenzie)
See Burnett, Joseph Company
Dainty and artistic desserts.

_____.
Canning, preserving and jelly making. Boston, Little, Brown and Co., 1919. 197p.

Hill, M.F.
Planters' progress. The story of coffee in Kenya.
Nairobi. The Coffee Board of Kenya, 1950. 210p.
Illus-photos.

Hill, Polly
The Gold Coast cocoa farmer. London, Oxford
University Press, 1956. 139p. Bibliography.   LC

Hillar, Elizabeth O.
The calendar of sandwiches and beverages. Joliet,
Illinois, P.E. Volland Co., 1915. unpaged (60).

Hills, William M.
Small fruits. Their propagation and cultivation including
the grape. Boston, Cupples, Upham and Co., 1886.
138p. Illus-engravings.

Hills Bros.
The art of coffee-making. San Francisco, 1957.
26p.

Hilsebusch's Henry William
Hilsebusch's thorough course of rectifying and compounding. Providence, Gem Publishing Co., 1906.
55p.

_____ .
Knowledge of a rectifier. Providence, R.I., The
Gem Publishing Co., 1903. 130p. 3rd edition, 1904,
130p.

Hind, Herbert Lloyd
Brewing; science and practice. New York, J. Wiley
and Sons Inc., 1938-1940. 2 v. Illus.plates.

Hindley, Charles
Tavern anecdotes and sayings including the origin of
signs. London, Tinsley Brothers, 1875. 414p. Illus.

_____ .
The true history of Tom and Jerry. London,
Published by author, n d, ca1887. 216p. Illus-
Vocabulary.

Hinton, C.L.
Fruit pectins, their chemical behaviour and jellying
properties. New York, Chemical Publishing Co., 1940.
96p. References.

Hiram-Walker and Sons.
A plot against the people. An attempt to pervert the
food law. Fourth edition. Walkerville, Ont. 1911,
116p.

Hires, Charles E. Co.
   Jingle jokes for little folks. Malvern, Pennsylvania,
   1901. unpaged (12), Illus.

_____.
   Recipes for the manufacture of flavoring extracts,
   etc. Philadelphia, Published by The Charles E.
   Hires Co., 1894. 46p.
Hirsch, Irving
   Manufacture of whiskey, brandy and cordials. Newark,
   N.J., Sherman Engraving Co., 1937. 183p. Illus.
Hirsch, Joseph
   The problem drinker. New York, Duell, Sloan and
   Pearce Inc., 1949. 211p.
Hirschfeld, Al
   Manhattan oases. New York's 1932 speak-easies; with
   a gentleman's guide to bars and beverages. New York,
   Dutton, 1932. 82p. Illus.
Hirschfeld, Albert Martin
   The standard handbook on wines and liquors. New
   York, W.C. Pepper and Co., 1907. 61p.
Hiscox, Gardner D. and O'Connor, T. Sloane Editors
   Fortunes in formulas. New York and Boston, Books,
   Inc., 1939. 861p. 1957, 867p.

_____.
   Henley's Twentieth Century book of recipes. New York,
   The Norman W. Henley Publishing Co., 1910, 787p.
   1916, 807p. 1919, 807p. 1928, 809p. 1933, 809p.
   1937, 883p. 1945, 867p.
Hisey, LW.S.
   See Bogen, Emil and Lehmann, W.S. Hisey
   What about alcohol?
Hispanus, Petrus (John XXI Pedro Juliano Popa)
   Treasure of health. London, Willyam Coplande, 1558.
                                                    BM
Hiss, A. Emil
   See Ebert, Albert E. and Emil, Hiss, A.
   The standard formulary.
Hiss, A. Emil and Ebert, Albert A.
   The Standard Manual of soda and other beverages.
   Chicago, G.P. Engelhard, 1897. 257p. 1901, 10th
   edition, 242p. 1902, 10th edition, 242p. 1904, Revised,
   258p. 1906, Revised, 258p.

_____.
   The new standard formulary. Chicago, G.P.
   Englehard Co., 1910. 1256p.

Historicus (pseud)
    See Cadbury, Richard
Hitchcock, Edward
    An essay on alcoholic and narcotic substances.
    Amherst J.S. and C. Adams and Co. Published
    under direction American Temperance Society, 1830.
    48p.

————. History of a zoological convention held in Central
    Africa. Fitchburg, Mass. George Trask, 1863.
    126p.
Hitchcock, Thomas
    A practical treatise on brewing, etc. London,
    No Publisher, 1842. 71p. Illus-fold-out drawing.
Hitt, Thomas
    Treatise of fruit trees (A). 2nd edition. London,
    Printed for author, 1757. 392p. Illus-drawings.
Hoare, A.H.
    Commercial apple growing. Revised edition, London,
    The Bodley Head, 1948. 288p. Illus-photos.
    References.
Hoare, Clement
    Descriptive account of an improved method of planting
    and managing roots of grape vines. London, Long-
    man, Brown, Green and Longmans, 1844. 81p.

————. A practical treatise on the cultivation of the grape vine.
    Second edition. London, Longman, Rees, Orme,
    Green and Longman, 1837. 210p.
Hobson, Richmond Pearson
    Alcohol and the human race. 3rd edition. New York,
    Fleming H. Revell Co., (1919). 205p.
Hocker El Curtis
    Alcoholic beverage encyclopedia. San Francisco.
    Printed by Sterret William, Inc., 1941. 155p.
                                    (Oakland Public)
Hockings, Albert John
    Queensland garden manual. Directions for cultivation
    of garden, orchard and farm and cultivation of--
    coffee, tea, fruits, etc., 2nd edition. Brisbane,
    Published by author, 1875. 200p.
Hodges, Elisabeth
    The story of glass. Bottles and containers through
    the ages. New York, Sterling Publishing Co., Inc.,
    1960. 47p. Illus.

Hofer, A. F.
Grape growing, a simple treatise on the single pole
system. New York, 1878. 32p.   LC
Hoffman, F.
New experiments and observations on mineral waters.
London, 1731. 246p.   GBPOL
Hoffman, Friederich
Treatise on the nature of aliments or foods.   Davis
and Reymers. 1761.   (Bitting)
Hoffman, J. W.
Cyclopedia of foods.   Condiments and beverages.
London, Simpkin, Marshall and Co., n d, ca1890.
306p.
Hoffman, Fr.
See Gildemeister, E. and Hoffman, Fr.
The volatile oils.
Hoffmann, Henry
The 'Count' reminisces, presenting in authentic, concise
form the famous drink mixing recipes and data, by
"Count" Henry Hoffmann . . . Saint Louis, 1933.   34p.
Hogg, Anthony, Editor
Wine mine.   Autumn 1962.   Horsham, Sussex Peter
Dominic Ltd., 1962.   144p.   Illus.
Summer 1965, 144p.   Winter 1965, 160p.
Summer 1966, 144p.   Winter 1966, 160p.
Summer 1967, 144p.   Winter 1967, 160p.
Also 1961, 112p.
Hogg, Robert
The apple and pear as vintage fruits.   Hereford,
Jakeman and Carver, 1886.   247p.

————————   .
The Fruit Manual: a guide to the fruits and fruit trees
of Great Britain.   Fifth Edition, London, Journal of
Horticulture Office, 1884.   759p.
Hoggson, Thomas
The Squire's homemade wines, 1765.   Decyphered and
transcribed by Noble Foster Hoggson.   Newly published
by Charles Edmund Merrill, New York 1924.   Pynson
Printers.   37p.   small 1524 copies made.   Have no.
776, 867, 1247.
Holbrook, M. L.
Eating for strength.   New York, Wood and Holbrook,
1877.   157p.   (Brown)

Holden, Edgar A.
    History of vitaculture and winemaking in Australia.
    Sydney, n d.   (Location Unknown)
Holding, Emmie Mary
    What shall we drink?   London, Sheldon Press, 1946.
    20p.   BM
Holland, Vyvyan
    Drink and be merry.   London, Victor Gallanz, 1967.
    173p.
Hollenback, G. N.
    See Hoynak, P. X. and G. N. Hollenback
    This is liquid sugar.   2nd edition.
Hollingworth, H. L.
    Influence of caffein on mental and motor efficiency.
    Archives of Psychology.   Edited by R. S. Woodworth
    No. 22, April, 1912.   Columbia contributions to
    philosophy and psychology.   Vol. XX, no. 4.   New York,
    Science Press, 1912.   166p.
Hollingworth, H. L. and Poffenberger, Jr., A. T.
    The sense of taste.   New York, Moffat, Yard and Co.,
    1917.   200p.
Hollingworth, John
    The modern extracter; a complete treatise for the
    making of extracts, flavors, syrups and sundries,
    especially prepared for the soda bottling, soda fountain
    and ice cream trades.   Pittsburgh, Pa., The Extracter
    Co., 1923.   179p.   Illus.
Holm, John
    Cocoa and its manufacture.   London, Printed in Here-
    ford, 1874.   24p.   GBPOL
Holmes, Joseph
    Series of prize essays on practical brewing, etc.
    reprinted from Holmes Brewing Trade Gazette, Leeds,
    Joseph Holmes.
    Green cover, 1879, 140p. and 46p.
    Green cover, n d , 140p. and 46p.
    Red cover, 1879, 140p. and 46p.
Holt, Anne
    A life of Joseph Priestley.   London, Oxford University
    Press, 1931.   221p.   LC
Holyrod, Grace
    See Atkinson, Amy and Holroyd, Grace.
    Practical cookery.

_____ .
See Atkinson, Amy and Holroyd, Grace
Practical cookery.
Homan, J. A.
Prohibition, the enemy of temperance. Cincinnati,
The Christian Liberty Bureau, 1909. 116p. NYPL
Honig, Pieter, Ed.
Principles of sugar technology. New York, Elsivier
Publishing Co., 1953. 767p. Illus.
Hooker, W. B.
See Brathwait, Richard.
The law of drinking.
Hooper, Egbert Grant
The manual of brewing: scientific and technical. Fourth
edition. London, Sheppard and St. John, 1891. 366p.
Illus. 2nd edition, 1882, 251p. Illus.

_____ .
Manuel de Brasserie. Bruxelles, Typographie et
Lithographie AD, Mertens, 1892. (In French). 394p.
Hooper, J. W.
Hooper's Western fruit book. Cincinnati, Moore,
Wilstach, Keys and Co., 1857. 333p.
Hooper, Mary
Little Dinners. 22nd edition. London, Kegan Paul,
Trench, Trubner and Co., 1891. 265p.

_____ .
Nelson's Home Comforts. 8th Edition, London, G.
Nelson, Dale and Co., 1887. 124p.
Hoos, Sidney and Seltzer, R. E.
Lemon and lemon products. Changing economic
relationships. 1951-1952. Bulletin 729, Calif.
Agri. Exp. Sta. College of Agri. _Univ. of Calif.
Berkeley, 1952. 78p.
Hoos, Sidney and Boles, J. W.
Oranges and orange products. Changing economic
relationships. Bulletin 731, Calif. Agri. Exp. Sta.
College of Agri. Univ. of Calif., Berkeley, 1953.
68p.
Hooton, Caradine R.
What shall we say about alcohol? New York, Nash-
ville, Abington Press, 1960. 127p.
Hope, G. D.
Report on certain aspects of the tea industry of Java
and Sumatra. Calcutta, India Tea House Publication
no. 2. Criterian Printing Works, 1916. 122p.
(National Agricultural Library)

Hope, G. D. and Carpenter G. A.
Some aspects of modern tea pruning. Calcutta, India
Tea Ass'n, Publ. no. 1., 1914. 56p.
Hope, W. H. St. John
On the English medieval drinking bowls and on other
vessels such as standing cups, chalices, etc., West-
minster, communicated to the Society of Antiquaries,
1887 and later dates. 65p. Illus-photos.
Hopkins, Albert Allis
Homemade beverages, the manufacture of non-alcoholic
drinks in the household. New York, The Scientific
American publishing Co., 1919. 232p. Illus.

_____.
The Scientific American Cyclopedia, etc., New York,
Munn and Co., 1892. 675p. 22nd edition, 1903, 629p.
1911, 1077p.
Hopkins, Reginald Haydn.
Biochemistry applied to malting and brewing, by
Professor R. H. Hopkins and Civilingenier B. Krause.
London, G. Allen and Unwin, Ltd., 1937. 342p.
Hoppe, A. L.
See Mueller, C. C. and Hoppe, A. L.
Pioneers of mixing cognac, etc.

_____.
See Mueller, C. E. and Hoppe, A. L.
Pioneers of mixing gin, etc.

_____.
See Mueller, C. C. and Hoppe, A. L.
Pioneers of mixing Irish and Scotch whiskys.

_____.
See Mueller, C. C. and Hoppe, A. L.
Pioneers of mixing liqueurs and cordials.

_____.
See Mueller, C. C. and Hoppe, A. L.
Pioneers of mixing rums.

_____.
See Mueller, C. C. and Hoppe, A. L.
Pioneers of mixing whiskeys, ryes and bourbons.

_____.
See Mueller, C. C. and Hoppe, A. L.
Pioneers of mixing wines.
Horne, Eric (Butler)
What the butler winked at. (Written by himself).
London, T. Werner Laurie Ltd., 1924. 281p.

210

Horne, F. R.
    See Aufhammer, G., Bengal, Pierre and Horne, F. R.
    Barley varieties, EBC. (European Brewery Convention).
Hornickel, Ernst
    The great wines of Europe. London, Weidenfield and
    Nicolson, 1965. 229p. Illus.
Hornsby, Jack H. and Harrington, Thomas S.
    Successful liquor retailing. Second edition. New
    York, Pickwick Press, 1959. 137p. Illus. Glossary.
Horsfield, Thomas
    Essay on the culture and manufacture of tea in Java,
    etc., London, 1841. 52p.   GBPOL
Horsley, Sir Victor and Sturge, Mary D.
    Alcohol and the human body. London, Macmillan and
    Co., 1909. 344p. Glossary.
Horton, C. H. Compiler and Editor
    The mineral water trade Year Book. Published by
    The National Union of Mineral Water Manufacturers'
    Associations Ltd., 1939. 194p.
Horton, Donald
    Functions of alcohol in primitive societies: a cross-
    cultural study. n p, Reprinted from Quarterly
    Journal of Studies on Alcohol, September 1943. 320p.
    Bibliography   LC
Hospitality Guild
    Catalog of 500 books on foods and beverages.
    Stamford, Dahls, 1935. 67p.   NYPL
Hough, Henry Beetle
    An alcoholic to his sons. New York, Simon and
    Shuster, 1954. 245p.
Houghton, A. G.
    Brewing and malting in Australasia. Melbourne,
    Alfred Lawrence and Chicago, H. C. Rich. 141p.
                    (Fleishman Malting Co. Chicago)
Houghton, John
    Art of brewing, 1707.   (Scho)
Houlston and Stoneman
    See Confectioner (The).

_____.
    Cooper (The). History and instructions. London,
    Houlston and Stoneman. Cover title, Houlston and Sons
    Industrial Library, n d, 88p.
Housekeeper, A.
    Home-brewed ale; or plain instructions, etc. London,
    G. and J. Robinson, 1804. 71p.

Hovey, Charles M.
   Fruits of America. Boston, D. Appleton, 1851. 2 vol.
   Illus. LC
Howard, Maria Willett
   Lowney's cook book. Boston, Walter M. Lowney and
   Co., 1907. 367p. Bibliography.
Howe, B.B. and A.H.
   Manual of liquor tests, 1925. (U.S. Catalog 1928)
Howe, Robin
   Wine and food Society's guide to soups. London, The
   Society, 1967. 198p. Illus-photos, drawings.
Howe, Sonia E.
   In quest of spices. London, Herbert Jenkins Limited,
   1946. 268p. Illus-Bibliography.
Howell, George Coes
   The case of whiskey. Altadena, Calif., Published by
   author, 1928. 238p.
Howell, Reginald
   See Stevenson, Wm. and Howell, Reginald
   S and H gallonage table.
Howitt, William
   The Student-life of Germany. From ms of Dr. Cornelius.
   Philadelphia, Carey and Hart, 1842. 467p.
Hoy, Albert Harris, MD
   Eating and drinking. The alkalinity of the blood, the
   test of food and drink in health and disease. Chicago,
   A.C. Mc Clurg and Co., 1896. 304p.
Hoynak, P. X and Hollenback, G.N.
   This is liquid sugar. 2nd edition. Yonkers, N.Y.
   by Corn Products Co., Refined Syrups and Sugars, Inc.
   1966. 250p. Illus.
Hu, Tun Yuan
   The liquor tax in U.S. 1791-1947. New York,
   Graduate School of Business, Columbia Univ., 1950.
   188p. LC
Hubbell, M.H.
   Art of mixing then. (By Samuel Pepys, pseud).
   Buffalo Published by author, 1933. 31p.
                                     (Buffalo Public)
Hubler, Ethel
   Dragons in the wind. Los Angeles, The National
   Voice, 1940. 48p.
Hudson, E.J.
   See Auit, R.G. and Hudson, E.J.
   Report on the brewing, malting and allied processes.

212

Hudson, J.R.
Development of brewing analysis. A historical review.
London, The Institute of Brewing, 1960. 102p.
Hudson, William
Wines of Italy. (Wines in relation to wines of Italy,
a lecture). London, 1888. 33p.   BM
Huggett, Henry E.V.
RHENISH. A paper on Rhine wines. London,
Privately printed, 1929. Autographed, 199 copies.
no. 83. 41p.
Huggins, James D.
Hints to peasant proprietors and others engaging in the
cultivation of cocoa. Port of Spain. Franklins Electric
Printery, 1908. 24p.   BM
Hughes, A.
Cyprus wines. An island industry. London, Cyprus
Wine Board, n d. 12p. Illus.
Hughes, E.
Treatise on the brewing of beer. Uxbridge. Published
for author, 1796. Reproduced 1941. 47p.   LC
Hughes, John
An itinerary of Provence and the Rhone. (wine).
London, Cawthorn. 1822. 267p.   BM
Hughes, John F.C.S.
Ceylon coffee, soils and manures. London, Straker
Bros., Co., 1879. 154p.   NYPL
Hughes, L.E.
Licensed victualler's manual or every publican his own
stocktaker. Manchester, Abel Heywood, 1885. 52p.
                                                 (Greenwood)
Hughes, Mary B.
Every woman's canning book. Third printing. Boston,
Whitcomb and Barrows, 1918. 96p.
Hughes, Osee
Introductory foods. 3rd edition. New York, The
Macmillan Co., 1955. 551p. Illus. References.
Hughes, William
American Physitian (The). Treatise on roots and plants.
London, J.C. and W. Crook, 1672. 159p. (Crerar)

_____ .
Compleat vineyard. London, Will Crook, 1665. 29p.
                                                        BM
Hughey, George Washington
Beer as a beverage. New York, National Temperance
Society and Publication House, 1880. 21p.   LC

Hughson, D.
    See Henderson, W.A.
    Modern Domestic Cookery.
Hugill, J.A.C.
    Sugar. London, Cosmo Publications and Tate and Tate
    Ltd., 1949. 64p. Illus.
Huie, James
    Abridgement and excise duties. 3rd edition. Edinburgh,
    No Publisher mentioned, 1818. 893p.
Hull, Edmund C.P.
    Coffee, its physiology, history and culture, Madras,
    1865. 208p.   NYPL

———.
    Coffee planting in southern India and Ceylon. Being
    a 2nd ed., rev. and enl., of "Coffee, its physiology,
    history, and cultivation." London, New York, E. and
    F.N. Spon, 1877. 324p.
Hulton, Henry Francis Everard.
    Beer, (a lecture). London, 1934. 33p.   LC
Hume, H. Harold
    Citrus fruits and their culture. New York, Orange-
    Judd Co., 1913. 587p. List of citrus literature.

———.
    The cultivation of citrus fruits. New York, Mac-
    millan Co. 1934. 561p.
Hume, Rosemary
    Party food and drink. New and completely revised
    edition. London, Chatto and Windus, 1957. 126p.
Humphrey, Heman
    Parallel between intemperance and the slave-trade.
    New York, John P. Haven, n d, ca1835. 19p.
Hunt, Ezra M.
    Alcohol; as a food and medicine. New York, National
    Temperance Society and Publication House, 1877, 137p.
Hunt, Peter, Compiler
    Eating and drinking. An anthology for epicures,
    Ebury Press, 1961. 320p. Illus. Acknowledgments.
Hunt, Ridgely, Comp.
    The saloon in the home; or, A garland of rumblossoms,
    compiled by Ridgely Hunt and George S. Chappell. New
    York, Coward-McCann, Inc., 1930. 95p. Illus.
Hunt, T.C.
    See Langmead, Frederick and Hunt, T.C.
    Review of the effects of alcohol on man.

Hunter, A.
    Receipts in modern cookery with a medical commentary.
    New edition.   London, John Murray, 1820.   262p.
Hunter, Herbert
    The barley crop.   London, Crosby Lockwood and Son,
    Ltd., 1952.   179p.   Illus.
Hunter, H. H.
    See Brown, E. and Hunter, H. H.
    Planting in Uganda.
Huntington, Richard Thomas
    Bar management and beverage profits.   Stamford, Conn.
    The Dahls, 1938. 110p. 1938. Illus. List of Beverage
    books and magazines.

_____ .
    Beverage Service.   Stamford, Conn.   no. 43.   The
    Dahls, n d, (1935).   62p.   Dictionary.
Hurst, J. B.
    See Jelf, E. A. and Hurst, C. J. B.
    The law of innkeepers.
Hurty-Peck and Co.,
    See Enkema, L. A.
    Acids.   Comparative uses of various types in soft
    drinks.

_____ .
    See Noling, A. W.
    Aromatic chemicals.

_____ .
    See Noling, A. W.
    Beverage base inventory control.

_____ .
    See Noling, A. W.
    Beverage bases.

_____ .
    See Noling, A. W.
    Beverage Flavors.

_____ .
    A bibliography of books and booklets on beverages, their
    history and manufacture.   Compiled by A. W. Noling.
    Indianapolis, 1961.   55p.   Illus.

_____ .
    See Enkema, L. A.
    Bottlers prepare--protect your beverages against off-
    season changes.

——————.
See Towey, John M.
Cherry.   Information about industry and flavor.

——————.
See Noling, A.W.
Cloudy beverages.   What they are and how to handle
them.

——————.
See Noling, L.J.
Grape.   Information about grapes, history, uses, etc.

——————.
See Noling, A.W.
History and Hurty-Peck and Company.   Its first 50
years.   1903-1953.

——————.
How to make syrup for soft drinks.   Pictures showing
step by step procedure.   Indianapolis, 1953.   15p.
Illus.

——————.
Ice and Ice-cold Tall-One.   A proposal to American
Service Co., from Hurty-Peck and Co., by A.W.
Noling.   Indianapolis, March 1, 1929.   Paged by
sections.

——————.
See Noling, L.J.
Lemon.   Information about lemons and lemon processing.
A discussion of lemon beverage flavors and the different
types of lemon soft drinks.

——————.
See Noling, A.W.
Measuring the acid content in soft drinks.

——————.
See Noling, A.W.
Measuring sugar content of syrup and beverages.

——————.
See Towey, John M.
Orange.   Information about different varieties, etc.

——————.
See Enkema, L.A.
Root beer.   How it got its name, etc.

——————.
See Pfafflin, Henry C.
Suggested bottlers syrup formulas using other than cane
or beet sugar.

———————.
See Noling, A.W. and Towey, John M.
Sunstruck off-flavor in soft drinks.

———————.
See Enkema, L.A.
Syrup making for cup venders.

———————.
See Enkema, L.A.
Use of benzoate of soda as a preservative.
Husenbeth, Frederick C.
Wine merchant, Bristol, Guide for a wine cellar.
London, Effingham Wilson, 1834. 133p. (Davis)
Hussmann, George Charles Frederick
American grape growing and wine making. With
contributions from well-known grape growers, giving
a wide range of experience. New York, Orange-Judd
1880. 243p. Illus. 1883, 310p. Illus., 1888, 269p.
Illus., 1896, 269p. 4th Edition, Illus.

———————.
The cultivation of the native grape, and manufacture
of American wines. New York, G.E. and F.W. Woodward, 1866. 192p. Illus. 1870, same. 1866, Illus,
191p. American News Co.

———————.
Grape culture and winemaking in California. A practical
manual for the grape-grower and wine-maker. San
Francisco, Payot, Upham, 1888. 380p. Illus.
Husmann, George Charles Frederick and C. Deering.
The muscadine grapes. Washington, Dept. Afri.
Bulletin no. 273, 1913. 64p.   BM
Husmann, George Charles Frederick
Some uses of the grapevine and its fruit. Washington,
1904. In USDA Yearbook, 1904. 17p. Illus.   LC
Hutchinson, Peggy
. . . Do's and don'ts of wine making. With a special
section of herb and hedgerow tonic wines for pleasure
and health. 150 completely new recipes. London, W.
Foulsham, 1959. 120p.

———————.
. . . Home-made sparkling wine secrets. London, W.
Foulsham, n d, 128p.

———————.
Home-made wines; how to make them, by Peggy
Hutchinson and Mary Woodman. London, W. Foulsham,
1958. 92p.

_____. Making soft drinks with Peggy Hutchinson. London, W. Foulsham and Co., Ltd., 1960. 92p.

_____. . . . More Peggy Hutchinson's home-made wine secrets. London, W. Foulsham, 1959. 128p. Illus.

_____. Peggy Hutchinson's home-made wine secrets. London, W. Foulsham Co., 1960. 124p.

_____. . . . Tonic wine-making secrets. London, W. Foulsham, 1960. 94p.

Hutchinson, W.H. and Son, Inc.
Into Hutchinson's second century. Chicago, 1950. 25p. Illus.

Hutchison, William G.
Songs of the vine. With a medley for malt-worms. London, A.H. Bullen, 1904. 300p.

Hutton, Isaac G.
The vigneron; an essay on the culture of the grape and the making of wine. Washington, Published by author, 1827. 60p.   LC

Hutton, John Bradley
The Book of Vodka. Birmingham (England). Published by J. and J. Vickers and Co., Ltd., 1964. 12p. Illus-photos.

Huxley, Gervas
Talking of tea. London, Thames and Hudson, 1928. 108p. Illus.

Hyams, Edward S.
√Dionysus. A social history of the wine vine. London, Thames and Hudson, 1965. 381p. Illus.

_____. The grape vine in England. London, The Bodley Head, 1949. 208p. Illus.

_____. Grapes under cloches. London, Faber and Faber, 1952. 133p. Illus. Glossary.

_____. Vin; the wine country of France. London, Newnes, 1959. 208p. Illus.

_____. Vineyards in England. . . . London, Faber and Faber, 1953. 229p. Illus.

218

————— The wine country of France. Philadelphia, Lippincott,
1960. 208p. Illus. LC
Hyatt, Thomas Hart
Hyatt's hand-book of grape culture; or, why, where,
when, and how to plant and cultivate a vineyard,
manufacture wines . . . San Francisco, Bancroft,
1867. 279p. Illus.
Hyatt, Woolf, Charles
Food, drink and drug frauds and the law of adulteration.
A guide for shoppers and sellers. London, The
Gutenberg Press Ltd., n d, ca1903. 272p.

————— Truth about things. London, Gutenberg Press, n d.
158p. LC
Hydraulic Press Mfg. Co.
Mount Gilead equipment and supplies for cider, vinegar
and grape juice manufacturers, etc., Mount Gilead, Ohio,
1924. 44p. Illus.

————— Net price list of equipment and supplies for cider,
grape juice manufacturers, etc., Mount Gilead, Ohio,
1922. 48p. Illus.

Ibbetson, Alexander
. . . Tea from grower to consumer. London, Sir I.
Pitman and Sons, Ltd., 1910. 114p. Illus.
n d, ca1924. Illus.
Idris, T. H. W.
Notes on essential oils. With special reference to their
composition, chemistry and analysis. With tables of
constants. London, Geo. Du Boistel and Co., 1898.
193p.
Ice Cream Merchandising Institute
Let's sell ice cream. Published by the Ice Cream
Merchandising Institute, Inc., Washington, D.C. 1947.
306p.
Imperial College of Tropical Agriculture
A report on cacao research. St. Augustine, Trinidad,
B.W.I., 1945-1951. 132p. Illus.
Imperial Economic Committee
Wine report no. 23. London, 1932. 92p.
(Brisbane Public)

Incorporated Brewers' Guild
  Brewing scientific reviews.   London, Brewers' Guild
  Publishing Co., (Jenkyn Griffiths), Ed., by A Clark
  Doull, 1949.   379p.   Illus.
India.   Council of Scientific and Industrial Research
  Essential oils and aromatic chemicals.   New Delhi,
  1958.   174p.   LC
Ingram and Royle
  Natural mineral waters, their properties and uses.
  London, 1886.   68p.   GBPOL
Institute (The)
  Good Housekeepings book of cool drinks.   New York,
  Hearst Corp.   Food editor Dorothy B. Marsh, 1953.
  24p.   Illus.
Institute of Brewing.
  The brewing industry research foundation.   Nutfield,
  Surrey, 1952.   34p.   Illus.

  _____.
  See Gilliland, R. B. and Harrison, G. A. F. and
  Knight, A. C.
  Brewing malting and allied processes.   A literature
  survey prepared for the Institute of Brewing. 30p. 1956.

  _____.
  See Hudson, J. R.
  Development of brewing analysis.   A historical review.

  _____.
  Journal of The Institute of Brewing.   Containing the
  transactions of the various sections, together with
  abstracts of papers.   Published in other journals, etc.
  Edited by Arthur R. Ling.   London, Harrison and Sons.
  Vol. XII, 1906, 780p.
  Vol. XIII, 1907, 768p.
  Vol. XIV, 1908, (Vol. 5 New Series), 647p.
  Vol. XVI, 1910, (Vol. 7 New series), 690p.
  Vol. XVIII, 1912, (Vol. 9 New series), 732p.

  _____.
  See Preece, I. A.
  Malting brewing and allied processes. . . .

  _____.
  Transactions of the Institute of Brewing Volume VII,
  1893-1894.   London, J. S. Phillips, 1894.   254p.
Insull, Thomas
  See Redmayne, Paul and Insull, Thomas
  Cocoa and chocolate.   Men and women at work.

International Bureau of the American Republics
    Coffee. Extensive information and statistics.
    Washington. Government Printing Office, 1902. 108p.
    Bibliography.   LC
International Federation of Fruit Juice Producers
    Analyses. Analytical methods of determining fruit juice
    content. Wadenswil, Switzerland, 1962. (In English-
    French-German). Paged by sections. Illus-drawings.

    _____.
    New Results in Science and technology of fruit juices.
    Wageningen (Holland), Juris-Verlag Zurich, 1961. (In
    German-French-English), 187p.
von Isokovics, Alois
    Modern aromatic chemicals. Monticello. N.Y.,
    Synfleur Scientific Laboratories, 1932. 48p.
    Bibliography.
Iverson, John R.
    Liquid Gems. A book of drinks for the fastidious
    drinker. n p, (San Francisco), No Publisher, 1937.
    121p.
International Library Directory.
    A world directory of libraries. 2nd edition. London,
    A.P. Wales Organization, 1966-1967. 1204p.
Invictus
    Guide to the soda fountain. London, Merritt-Hatcher
    Ltd., n d, ca192-, 90p. Illus.
Irish, John H.
    See Cruess, W.V. and Irish, J.H.
    Fruit beverage investigations.

    _____.
    Fruit juice concentrates. Bulletin no. 392. Berkeley,
    University of California, College of Agriculture, 1931.
    20p. Illus.

    _____.
    Fruit juices and fruit juice beverages. Univ. of Calif.
    College of Agri. Agricultural Experiment Sta.,
    Circular no. 313, Berkeley, 1928. 64p. Illus-photos.

    _____.
    Fruit juices and fruit juice beverages. Revised by W.V.
    Cruess. Berkeley, U. of California College of Agri.
    Experiment Sta., Circular 313, 1932. 61p. Illus.
Irving, Washington
    Old Cristmas in Merrie England. Mount Vernon, N.Y.,
    Peter Pauper Press, n d. 60p. Illus.

Irwin, J. A.
Hydrotheraphy at Saratoga. A treatise on natural
mineral waters. New York, 1892. Cassell Publishing
Co., 1892. 270p.

Irwin-Harrissons and Crosfield
A trip to the Keemun tea district. New York, 1919.
14p.   LC

Isel, Harry and Josephine Anderson
Blending at its best; thousands of new creations.
(alcoholic products). Galesburg, Ill., Published by
authors, 1952. 127p.   LC

Izaak, Alexander
Distilled spirits industry and contributions to distilling
science. n p, no publisher, n d, ca1928.   (Carson)

Jack, Florence B.
Cookery for every household. London, T. C. and E. C.
Jack Ltd., 1919. 711p.

_____ .
Good Housekeeping invalid cookery book. London, Good
Housekeeping Magazine, 1938. 128p.

_____ .
Homebrewed wines and beers including cordials and
syrups. Milwaukee, Casper, 1934. 56p.
                              (Cincinnati Public)

_____ .
One hundred drinks and cups. London, Country Life,
1927. 52p.   BM

_____ .
One hundred home-brewed wines including cordials,
beers and syrups. London, Country Life Ltd., 1928.
56p. Third impression, 1931.

Jackson, George H.
The medicinal value of French brandy. Montreal,
Published by author, 1928. 315p. Illus.

Jackson, Henry.
An essay on bread; etc., to which is added an appendix;
explaining the vile practices committed in adulterating
wines, cider, porter, punch, vinegars and pickles.
London, J. Wilkie, 1758. Vol. IV from the Mallinkrodt
Collection of food classics. 55p. photo-process
1966.

————————.

An essay on British isinglass intersperced with hints
for further improvement of malting, brewing, fermenting,
etc. London, J. Newbury, 1765. 94p.   (Davis)
Jacob, H.E.
    Grape growing in California. Revised by A.J. Winkler.
    Berkeley, Circular no. 116, California Agriculture
    extension service-University of California, 1950. 80p.
    Illus.
Jacob, Heinrich Eduard
    Coffee; the epic of a commodity. New York, The
    Viking Press, 1935. 296p. Illus. Bibliography.

————————.

    The saga of coffee, the biography of an economic product.
    London, G. Allen and Unwin Ltd., 1935. 384p.
    Illus.
Jacob, Morris Boris
    Chemical analysis of food and food products. New York,
    Van Nostrand, 1938. 537p.   LC

————————.

    The chemistry and technology of food and food products.
    New York, Interscience Publishers, 1944. 952, 890
    Illus.

————————.

    See Herstein, Karl M.
    Chemistry and technology of wines and liquors.

————————.

    Manufacture and analysis of carbonated beverages. New
    York, Chemical Publishing Co., 1959. 333p. Illus.
    Bibliography.

————————.

    Synthetic food adjuncts; synthetic food colors, flavors,
    essences sweetening agents, preservatives, stabilizers,
    vitamins and similar food adjuvants. New York, D.
    Van Nostrand Co., 1947. 335p. Bibliographical foot notes.
Jacquelin, Louis
    The wines and vineyards of France. Louis Jacquelin
    and Rene Poulain. London, Paul Hamlyn, 1962. 416p.
    Illus.
Jacoutot, Auguste
    Chocolate and confectionery manufacture. London,
    MacLaren and Sons, n d, ca1900. 211p. Illus.
Jacquin, Charles et Cie
    Jacquin's Cordials. Philadelphia, n d, ca1936.
    unpaged (36). Illus.

Jagendorf, M. A.
Folk wines, cordials, and brandies. Ways to make
them, together with some lore, reminiscences, and wise
advice for enjoying them. New York, Vanguard Press,
1963. 414p. Illus. Glossary.

Jahrbuch, 1955
Gesellschaft fur die Geschichte und Bibliographie des
Brauwesens E.V. Berlin, 1955. (In German). 237p.
Bibliography.

James, Daniel J.
Evolution of the glass container industry. Fayetteville,
Ark. (Thesis), 1956. 23p. LC

James, Norah C.
Cooking in cider. Kingswood, Surrey, The World's
Work (1913) Ltd., 1952. 64p.

James Walter
Antipasto. Melbourne, Georgian House, 1957. 100p.

_____.
Barrel and Book, a wine-maker's diary. Melbourne,
Georgian House, 1949. 100p. Illus.

_____.
The fear of wine. Sydney, 1953. 24p.
(Mitchell Library, Sydney)

_____.
The gadding vine. Melbourne, Georgian House, 1955.
118p. Illus.

_____.
Nuts on wine. Melbourne, Georgian House, 1952.
85p. Illus.

_____.
What's what about wine: an Australian wine primer.
Melbourne, Georgian House, 1953. 45p. Illus.

_____.
Wine; a brief encyclopedia. New York, Knopf, 1960.
208p. Illus.

_____.
Wine growers diary. Melbourne and Sydney. Lothian
Publishing Co., 1969. diary (unpaged), Illus-photos.

_____.
Wine in Australia; a handbook. Melbourne, Georgian
House, 1952. 166p. Illus. Bibliography.
Revised Edition, 1955, 168p. Illus.
1962, London, Phoenix House, 148p. Illus.

_____.
A word-book of wine. London, Phoenix House, 1959.
208p. Illus.

Jameson, John and Son Limited
"Soverigne Liquor". A brief investigation into the making and maturing of good Irish whiskey. Dublin, 1950. unpaged (28), Illus.

Janes, Hurford
The Red Barrel. A history of Watney Mann. London, John Murray, 1963. 226p. Illus. Bibliography.

Jank, Jas. J.
Spices: their botanical origin: their chemical composition; their commercial use. 4th edition. np. No publisher, 1924. 181p. Illus.

Japan Tea Syndicate (The)
Facts about tea. Yokohana and Hiogo, Japan, n d, ca1890. 18p. Illus.

Jaques, George
A practical treatise on the management of fruit trees. Of the most valuable fruits for general cultivation adapted to the interior of New England. Worcester, Erastus N. Tucker, 1849. 256p.

Jacques, Harry Edwin
How to know the economic plants. Dubuque, Iowa. William S. Brown and Co., 1958. 174p. Illus-Glossary.

Jarrin, W.A.
The Italian Confectioner. London, Routledge, Warne and Routledge, 1861. 288p.

Jarvis, D.C.
Arthritis and folk medicine. London, Pan Books Ltd., 1960. 159p.

Jayne, Dr. D. and Son Inc.
Jayne's Bartender's Guide. Philadelphia, 1934. 152p.

_____ .
Red J. Jay Bartenders Guide. Philadelphia, n d, ca1933. 152p.

Jeannes, William
Gunter's Modern Confectioner. London, John Camden Hotten, 1861. 224p.

Jeffrey, Ernest John
Brewing; theory and practice. 3rd edition. London, N. Kaye Co., 1956, 414p. Illus.

Jeffs, Julian
Sherry. London, Faber and Faber, 1961. 268p. Illus-Glossary-Sources.

Jelf, E.A. and Hurst, C.J.B.
The law of innkeepers. London, Horace Cox, 1904.
144p.
Jellinek, E.M.
Alcohol addiction and chronic alcoholism. Effects of
alcohol on the individual Vol. 1. New Haven, Yale
University Press, 1942. 336p. Bibliography.

_____ .
See Haggard, Howard W. and Jellinek, W.M.
Alcohol explored.
Jellinek, Paul
The practice of modern perfumery. London, L. Hill,
1956. 219p.
Jenks, James
The complete cook. London, 1 768. 364p.   BM
Jensen, H.R.
Chemistry flavouring and manufacture of chocolate
confectionery and cocoa. Philadelphia, P. Blakiston
and Co., 1931. 406p. Illus.
Jensen, Lloyd B.
Man's Foods. Nutrition and environments in food
gathering times and food producing times. Champaign,
Ill., The Garrard Press, 1953. 278p. References.
Jerez Industrial
Sherry as seen by the British. Collection "Sherry
in the world". Edit. Jerez Industrial. Jerez de la
Frontera, Spain, n d. 57p.
Jermyn, David
The story of gin. London, The House of Booth's
n d, ca1965. 8p.
Jessey, Henry
The Lord's loud call to England, etc., also odious sin
of drinking health. London, Published by H.J. 1660.
40p.   (Univ. Chicago)
Jessie, Jill Eve
Perfume album. New York, Perfume Production Press,
1951. 158p. Illus. Bibliography.
Jewett, Charles
A forty years' fight with the DRINK DEMON. New
York, National Temperance Society and Publ. House,
1872. 407p.
Jewett, Edward H.
The Two-Wine theory. "Comminion wine". New
York, E. Steiger and Co., 1888. 176p.

Jillson, Willard Rouse
Early Kentucky distillers 1783-1800. Louisville, The
Standard Printing Co., 1940. 63p.
Jimmy (pseud).
Green cocktail book. London, T. Werner Laurie,
1938. 96p. BM
Jimmie, The Barman
See Charters, James (Jimmie the Barman)
This must be the place!.
"Jimmy" Late of Ciro's, London
Cocktails. Philadelphia, David McKay Co., n d. 96p.
Joelson, Annette
The memoirs of Kohler of the K.W.V. London, Hurst
and Blackett Ltd., 1946. 128p. Illus.
JOHN
"Happy Days!" A book of good cheer, of cocktails,
drinks and how to mix them. New York, Felshin
Publishing Co., 1931. 96p.
Johns, Bud
The ombibulous Mr. Mencken. San Francisco,
Synergistic Press, 1968. 63p. Illus-photos.
Johnson, Charles
Modern brewery plant. Bristol, 1889. 35p. GBPOL
Johnson, Eli
Drinks from drugs. A startling exposure of the tricks
of the liquor trade. Chicago, Revolution Temperance
Publishing House, 1881. 86p. Illus. LC
Johnson F. Ernest and Warner, Harry S.
Prohibition in outline. New York, The Methodist
Book Concern, 1927. 102p. Bibliography.
Johnson, George W. and Errington, Robert
The grape vine. (Gardener's Monthly), London, R.
Baldwin, 1847. 2 vol. Illus-drawings.
(Brady Library-Fresno State Col.)
Johnson, Grove
The Australian Brewing Student's Manual. Melbourne,
The Australian Brewers' Journal (Alfred Lawrence),
1917. 213p.

_____.
History of brewing studies. Melbourne, 1917. 213p.
ANL

_____.
Practical studies for winemaker, brewer and distiller.
Perth, Imperial Printing Co., 1939. 91p. WI

_____ The student's manual of yeast culture. London,
Published by the author, (1908), 188p.
Johnson, H. A. Co.
Catalog of everything for the baker, confectioner and
ice cream maker. Boston, n d, ca1917. 200p. Illus.
Johnson, Harry
The new and improved illustrated bartenders guide, etc.
New York, Published by author, 1900. 268p. Illus.

_____ New and improved illustrated bartender's manual, etc.
New York, Published by author, 1888. 197p. Illus.
1900, Revised, 268p. Illus. (Guide).
Johnson, Hugh
The best of vineyards is the cellar. Contains a
Section "Lunching and dining in London", London,
Hedges and Butler (wine dealer). 1965. Unpaged (44),
Illus. (Cover title "1667")

_____ The Pan book of wine. Articles from House and
Garden. Revised edition. London, Pan Books, Ltd.,
1964. 176p. Illus. Bibliography.

_____ Wine. London, Thomas Nelson and Sons Ltd., 1966.
264p. Illus.
Johnson, O'Neal
See Meserole, H. H. H. and Johnson, O'Neal
Ice cream at the drug store soda fountain.
Johnson, R.
Bottling of naturally matured beers. Reprinted from
Brewers' Guardian. London, 1955. 19p. Illus.
Johnson, R. J.
Notebook for tea planters. Colombo, R. Johnson and
Co., 1861. (Forrest - 100 years Ceylon tea)
Johnson, Samuel
Indulgence in wine. St. Catharines, Ont. Modern
Publications Reg'd., 1966. (Reprint of original 1825
London). 21p.
Johnson, Smith and Co.
Homebrewed wines and beers and bartenders' guide.
Racine, Wisc., n d, ca1910. 32p.
Johnson, W. H.
Cocoa. Its cultivation and preparation. London, John
Murray, 1912. 186p. Illus-photos.

228

Johnson's Saccharum Co., Ltd.
On the economical production of brewer's worts. London
n d. 6p.
Johnston, E. and Co., Ltd.
One hundred years of coffee. London, Published by the
company, 1942. 40p. Illus.
Johnston, J.C.
Citrus fruit for the home orchard. Circ. 409 rev.
Calif. Agri. Exp. Sta. extension service. Berkeley,
Published by Div of Agri. Sciences Univ. of Calif.,
1953. 15p. Illus. Recommended reading.

——————— .
Citrus growing in California. Circular 426 Calif. Agri.
Exp. Sta. Extension Service. Berkeley, Published by
Div. of Agri. Sciences, Univ. of Calif., 1954. 43p.
Illus.
Johnston, James F.W.
The Chemistry of common life. Edinburgh, and
London, William Blackwood and Sons, 1855. 2 volumes
352p, 466p.
Johnstone, Christian Isobel
The cook and housewife's manual: a practical system
of modern domestic cookery and family management
. . . The 6th ed., rev. and enl.: to which is added,
a comprehensive treatise and domestic brewing. By
Mistress Margaret Dods (pseud), . . . Edinburgh,
Oliver and Boyd, 1837. 491p. Illus.
Jonas, Peter
The Distiller's Guide. Third Edition. London, Sher-
wood. Neely and Jones, 1818. page heading
A KEY TO THE DISTILLERY. 292p.

——————— .
Distillers Practical guide. 4th edition. London, Sher-
wood, Gilbert, and Piper, 1830. 283p. (Bound with
John Sheridan Comp. Treat Art of Distillation).

——————— .
Distiller's, wine and brandy merchant's vade mecum.
Hull, Published by author, 1808. BG

——————— .
The theory and practice of guaging. (Jonas's art of
guaging improved). New edition by W. Tate, London,
Sherwood, Neely and Jones, 1823. 392p.
Jones, Charles
See Quinn, Elton L. and Jones, Charles. Carbon dioxide.

Jones, G. Cecil and Baker, Julian L.
Original gravity tables. Published by the Brewers
Journal, London, n d. large card.
Jones, H. Williams
What will you take to drink? An account of the compo-
sition and effects of certain drinks in common use, etc.
London, John Kempster and Co., (1875), 29p.
Jones, Howard
Alcoholic addiction. A psycho-social approach to
abnormal drinking. London, Tavistock Publications,
1963. 209p. Bibliography.
Jones, Idwal
High Bonnet. A novel of Epicurean Adventure, New
York, Prentice-Hall, Inc., 1945. 184p.

_____.
Vines in the sun, a journey through the California
vineyards; New York, W. Morrow, 1949. 253p.
Illus.

_____.
The vineyard. (a novel). New York, Duell, Sloan and
Pearce Inc., 1942. 280p.
Jones, John MD
Arte and science of preserving bodie and soule in
healthe. (Food and drink). London, Henry G.
Bynneman, 1579. 1 leaf.   BM
Jones, Karl B.W.
Tea manufacture in Southern India. Madras, United
Planters Ass'n, 1937. 180p.   BM
Jones, Marie A. (Revised by)
Publications and patents U.S. Citrus Products Station
Winter Haven, Fla. May 1956. 34p.
Jones, Tom
Henry Tate 1819-1899. (Food Products). London,
Tate and Lyle Ltd., 1960. 32p. Illus. Bibliography.
Jones, Trevor of the Tea Bureau
Tea. London, Educational Supply Ass'n, 1958. 89p.
(Fleishman Research Library)
Jones, Vincent
East Anglia Pubs. London, B.T. Batsford and Co.,
1965. 152p. Illus.
Jordon, Stroud
Chocolate evaluation. Assisted by Katheryn E. Lang-
will. New York, Applied Sugar Laboratories, Inc.,
1934. 225p. References-Bibliography.

Jordan, Stroud and Katheryn E. Langwill
Confectionery analysis and composition. Chicago, The Manufacturing Confectioner, 1946. 116p.

Jordan, Joseph V.
Simple facts about wines--spirits, liqueurs, etc. Los Angeles, Los Angeles School of Bartending, 1937. 90p.

Jordan, Rudolf
Quality in dry wines through adequate fermentations, etc. San Francisco, Printed by Pernau Publishing Co., 1911. 146p. Illus.   LC

Jorden, Edward
Discourse of natural Bathes and mineral waters. London, 1632. 92p.   BM

Josephy, Helen, and McBride, Mary Margeret
Beer and skittles. A friendly guide to Modern Germany. New York - London, G.P. Putnam's Sons, 1932. 272p. Illus.

Joslyn, Maynard Alexander
Commercial production of dessert wines. Berkeley, Calif. Univ. of California Press, 1941. 186p.

_____.
See Cruess, William Vere.
Laboratory examination of wines and other fermented fruit products, by W.W. Cruess . . . M.A. Joslyn . . . and, L.G. Saywell.

_____.
See Amerine, Maynard Andrew.
Table wines; the technology of their production in California, by M.A. Amerine and M.A. Joslyn.

Joslyn, Maynard Alexander and Amerine Maynard Andrew
Commercial production of brandies. Bull. 652, Univ. of Calif., 1941. 80p. Illus.

_____.
Dessert, appetizer and related flavored wines. The technology of their production. Berkeley, University of California division of Agricultural Sciences, 1964. 483p. Illus. Literature cited. General references.

Joslyn, Maynard A. and Cruess, W.V.
Elements in winemaking. Berkeley, Circular no. 88, 1934. 64p.   BM

Joslyn, Maynard Alexander and Marsh, G. L.
Utilization of fruit in commercial production of fruit
juices. Berkeley, Univ. of Calif. College of Agriculture
1937. 63p. Selected list of references.
Judd, Deane B
Colorimetry. Washington, National Bureau of
Standards, (Circular 478), March 1, 1950. 56p.
Illus-drawings. References.
Jude
Medicinal and perfumery plants and herbs of Ireland
Dublin, M. H. Gill, 1933. 124p. Illus.
Judge, Jr. (Norman Anthony)
Here's How! New York, Leslie-Judge Co., 1927.
62p.

—————.
Noble experiments. The third volume in the famous
Here's How! series. New York, John Day Co., 1930.
63p.
Judson, Helena, Ed.
Light entertaining; a book of dainty recipes for special
occasions. Sandwiches, beverages, candies, chafing
dish recipes. New York, The Butterick Publishing
Co., 1910. 68p. Illus.
Judson, Lewis B.
Units of systems of weights and measures. Their
origin, development and present status. Washington,
National Bureau of Standards (Circular 570), May 21,
1956. 29p. Illus.
Jullien, André
The topography of all the known vineyards; containing
a description of the kind and quality of their products,
and a classification. London, G. and W. B. Whittaker, 1824. 248p. Vocabulary.

—————.
Wine merchants companion. London, W. Anderson,
1825. 107p.   NYPL
Juniper, William
Law of drinking. San Francisco, Herbert and Peter
Faley, 1935. 27p. (Brady Library-Fresno State Col.)

—————.
A merry, ingenious, and diverting work entitled Liber
compotorum felicium: or, The true drunkard's delight.
London, Unicorn Press, 1933. 375p.

Jusfrute Ltd.
See Adcock, G. I.

_____.
Aerated water manufacturers' hand book.   Introduction
by G. I. Adcock.   Gosford, N. S. W. n d, ca1932,
Jusfrute Ltd.   28p.

_____.
See Fuller, A. H.
Bottle washing.

_____.
See Fuller, A. H.
Jusfrute handbook for soft drink industry.

_____.
Jusfrute schools, topic sheets, n p. (Gosford, NSW),
n d, (1963).   Unpaged (96) sheets.

_____.
Technique without tears.   Another Jusfrute bottler's
aid.   Gosport, N. S. W. n d, ca1948, Jusfrute Ltd.
20p.
No. 2, n d, ca1949, 8p.   Illus.
No. 3, n d, ca1950, 24p.   Illus.

_____.
See Fuller, A. H.
Water treatment.   Volume 2 of the Jusfrute Handbooks
for the Soft Drinks Industry.
Justin., Margeret M.: Rust, Lucile Osborn and Vail, Gladys
R.
Foods.   An introductory college course.   3rd ed., Boston,
Houghton, Mifflin Co., 1948.   723p.

K., G. A.
Clarets and Sauternes: Classed growths of the Medoc
and other famous red and white wines of the Gironde.
London, The Wine and Spirit Trade Record, 1920.
398p.   Illus.
K. W. V. Public Relations Dept.
Entertaining with wines of the Cape.   Paarl, 3rd ed.
1968.   79p.   Illus-drawings.   1959, 48p.   Illus.

_____.
A handbook on wine.   (For retail licensees).   Cape
Town, n d.   78p.   Illus-photos, Glossary wine terms.

233

_____ . Planning a wine and cheese party. Suider Paarl
Cape, 1967. 16p. Illus-drawings.

_____ . A survey of wine growing in South Africa, 1963-1964.
Suider Paarl, Cape, 1964. 56p. Illus-card cover.
1964-1965, 56p. Illus.
1965-1966, 56p. Illus.
1966-1967, 56p. Illus.
1967-1968, 52p. Illus.
1968-1969, 54p. Illus.
K.W.V. Paarl
See Bagnall, A. Gordon
Wine of South Africa. An account of their history,
production and nature.
Kahn, Allen Ray
Sugar. A popular treatise. Los Angeles, U.S.
Sugar Publications Co., 1921. 78p.
Kahn, E.J. Jr.
The Big Drink. The story of Coca-Cola. New York,
Random House, 1960. 174p.

_____ . The Universal Drink. (Coca-Cola). Published in the
NEW YORKER, February 14 to March 7, 1959, New
York. 4 installments paged by month.
Kahn, Gordon
See Hirschfeld, Al
Manhattan oases. New York's 1932 speak-easies; with
A gentleman's guide to bars and beverages, by Gordon
Kahn.
Kakuzo, Okakura
The Book of Tea. A japanese harmony of art culture
and the simple life. Second edition, Sydney, Angus
and Robertson, Ltd., 1935. 102p. Illus.

_____ . The Book of Tea. Edited and introduced by Everett
F. Bleiler. New York, Dover Publications Inc., 1964.
76p.
Kallett, Arthur and Schlink, F.J.
100,000, 000 guinea pigs. New York, Grosset and
Dunlap, 1935. 30th printing. 312p.
"Kappa"
Bartender's guide to the best mixed drinks. Revised
edition. Tokyo, Japan, n d, Kasuga Boeki, K.K.
(In Japanese and English). 143p..

Kappeler, George J.
Drinks and how to mix them. Akron, Ohio. Saalfield
Publishing Co., 1911. 150p.   LC

_____.
Modern American drinks; how to mix and serve all
kinds of cups and drinks. New York, The Merriam
Co., 1895. 120p. Akron, Ohio, Saalfield, 1895.
Karpman, Benjamin
The alcoholic woman. Washington, D.C. The Linacre
Press, Sponsored by Washington Institute of Medicine
Research Foundation, 1948. 238p. case histories.
Kaufman, William I.
The tea cookbook. Garden City, N.Y., Doubleday
and Co., 1966. 192p. Illus-photos.

_____.
The coffee cookbook. Flavorful robust recipes for
every course-plus history, legend and lore. Garden
City, Doubleday and Co., Inc., 1964. 191p. Illus.
Keable, Benjamin Bayley
Coffee, from grower to consumer. London, New York,
Pitman, (1922). 122p. Illus.
Keeble, Richard
Surrey Pubs. London, B.T. Batsford, Ltd., 1965.
148p. Illus-drawings.
Keane, Eva
The Penfold Story. (Wine). Sydney, Oswald L.
Ziegler, n d, (1951). 78p. Illus.
Kearney, Paul W.
Toasts and anecdotes. New York, E. J. Clode, 1923.
299p.
Keating, Lawrence A.
Men in aprons. "If he could only cook." New York,
M.S. Mill Co., Inc., 1944. 186p.
Keech, J.
Grape grower's guide. Auburn, N.Y., W.J. Moses,
1869. 15p.   LC
Keegal, E.L.
Tea manufacture in Ceylon. Colombo, Tea Research
Institute of Ceylon, 1958. 179p. Illus. Bibliography,
                              (Harler-Tea Manufacture)
Keegan, Louis M.
Food values for calculating diabetic and nefritic diets.
New York, Macmillan, 1926. 106p.   LC

Keen, G. Alan, etc.
Here's How. Being a new symposium of recipes of good cheer. A dictionary for the wine connoisseur, etc. London, Victoria Wine Co., Ltd., n d. 61p. Illus.

Keen, W.
Coffee cultivation in Ceylon, 1871. (Money)

Keene, James B.
Handbook of hydrometry. London, 1875. 60p. BM

————.
A handbook of practical guaging. Philadelphia, Henry Carey Baird, 1868. 108p. Illus. 1st American from 2nd London edition. 4th London Edition, F. Pitman, 108p. n d,

Keir, David
The Younger Centuries. The story of William Younger and Co., Ltd., 1749-1949. (Beer). Edinburgh, 1951. 110p. Illus.

Keir, Ursala
The vintage. New York, Sloane, 1953. 307p. WI

Keitel, Adolph
Government by the brewers? Chicago, Appersley and Co., 1918. 84p. Illus. LC

Keller, William B.
The beer and ale bottlers' manual. New York, No publisher, 1893. 112p. Illus. LC

————.
Keller's bottlers' handbook, comprising the bottling laws of the different states. New York, National Bottlers' Gazette, 1884. 96p. Advertising matter. LC

Kelley, William J.
Brewing in Maryland, Baltimore, Published by author, 1965. 735p. Illus.

Kelly, Alex C. MD
The vine in Australia. Melbourne, Sands Kenny and Co., 1861. 215p. Illus.

————.
Wine-growing in Australia., and the teaching of modern writers on vine-culture and wine-making. Adelaide, E. S. Wigg, 1867. 234p.

Kelphick, Levy S.
Eat and drink to live. San Francisco, 1886. 22p.
(Brown Univ.)

Kelway, M.
    See Bamber, Edward F. and Kelway, M.
    Account of the culture and manufacture of tea in India
    from personal observation.
Kelynack, T.N.
    The drink problem of today in its medico-sociological
    aspects. New York, E.P. Dutton and Co., 1916.
    318p.
Kelynack, T.N. and Kirkby William
    Arsenical poisoning in beer drinkers. London,
    Bailliere, Tindall and Cox, 1901. 125p. Illus.
    Bibliography.
Kemble, H.R.
    See Weiss, Harry B. and Kemble, Howard R.
    They took to the waters.
Kemp, James F.
    The mineral springs of Saratoga. Albany, University
    of the State of New York, 1912. 79p.
Kendo, T.A.
    Treatise on silk and tea cultivation and other Asiatic
    industries adapted to soil and climate of California.
    San Francisco, A. Roman and Co., 1870. 73p.
                            (National Agricultural Library)
Kendrick, S.G.
    The preparation of flavoured mineral waters. London,
    Barnett and Foster Ltd., n d, 1937. 47p. Illus.
Kennedy, Ezra, J.
    See Alpers, William C. and Kennedy, Ezra, J.
    The Era Formulary.
Kenny, John
    See Abdullah, Achmed and Kenny, John.
    FOR MEN ONLY. A cookbook.
Kenrick, William
    The new American orchardist. Boston, Carter, Hendee
    and Co., and Russell, Odiorne and Co., 1833. 423p.
Kenwood, Henry R.
    Public health laboratory work. 6th edition. London,
    H.K. Lewis, 1914. 418p.
Kent and Waverly Breweries
    Over a century of brewing tradition. The story of
    Tooth and Co., Ltd. Sydney, Published by Kent and
    Waverly Breweries, (1953). 78p. Illus.
Kent, J.C.
    An essay on the nature, the end and the means of
    imitation in the fine arts. London, Smith, Elder and
    Co., 1837. 468p.

Kent, Rockwell
    To Thee! A toast in celebration of a century of
    opportunity and accomplishment in America; 1847-1947.
    Written and illustrated by Rockwell Kent. Manitowoc,
    Wisconsin, Rahr Malting Co., 1946. 59p. Illus-
    drawings.
Kentish, Thomas
    The gauger's guide and measurer's manual. London,
    Dring and Page, 1861. 346p.
Kepner, Charles David and Soothill, Jay Henry
    The Banana Empire. A case study in American
    imperialism. New York, The Vanguard Press, 1935.
    392p. Abridged Bibliography.
Kercht, J.S.
    Improved practical culture of the vine especially in
    regular vineyards. Sydney, W. Baker, 1843. 44p.
                                                    PLOSA
Kerr, Norman Shanks
    Inebriety or Narcomania, its etiology, pathology, treat-
    ment and jurisprudence. 3rd edition. New York,
    J. Selwin Tait and Sons, 1894. 605p.

    _____.
    Wines: scriptural and ecclesiastical. London, National
    Temperance Publ. Depot, 1887. 166p.

    _____.
    Wines of the bible, London, National Temperance
    Publicity Bureau, 1885. 12p.   BM
Kessler, Edward Joseph
    Practical flavoring extract maker, a treatise on the
    manufacture of the principal flavoring extracts, in
    accordance with the requirements of the food laws of
    the United States. First edition by E.J. Kessler . . .
    rev. and expanded by Ralph H. Higby . . . in
    consultation with the author. 2d ed. New York, The
    Spice Mill Publishing Co., 1927. 126p. Illus.
    1st edition 1912 (Kessler alone)
Kesterson, J.W. and Mc Duff, O.R.
    Florida citrus oils. Commercial production methods and
    properties of essential oils. Technical bulletin. no.452.
    (1947-48 season). Gainesville, Florida, Univ. of
    Florida Agri. Experiment Station, 1948. 44p. Illus.
    Literature cited.
Keverne, Richard
    Tales of old inns. London, Collins, 1939. 192p.
    Illus. 2nd ed. 1947, 160p. Illus.

Kilner, Walter R.
A compendium of Modern Pharmacy and Druggists'
Formulary. Springfield, Ill., O.C. St. Clair, 1882.
686p.

King, Albion Rey
The psychology of drunkenness, Mt. Vernon, Ia.,
1931. 72p.   NYPL

King, Frank Alfred
Beer has a history. London, New York, Hutchinson's
Scientific and Technical Publications, 1947. 180p.
Illus.

King, William
Observations on the artificial mineral waters of Dr.
Struve. Brighton, 1826. 53p.   BM

Kingsford, Arthur Charles
Report on the tea industries of Java, Formosa and
Japan, after a special visit to these countries in 1904.
Colombo, Times of Ceylon Press, 1907. Irregular
pagination, Illus.

Kinross, Lord
The kindred spirit. A history of gin and the house of
Booth. London, Newman Neame, Ltd., 1959. 99p.
Illus.

Kinsley, Charles
The circle of useful knowledge. Clinton, Iowa,
Published by author, 1891. 255p.

Kirby, Jeremiah
Essays and poems (domestic brewing). Edinburgh,
1822.   BM

Kirby, Mary and Elizabeth
Aunt Martha's Corner cupboard, or stories about tea,
coffee, etc. London, T. Nelson and Sons, 1893.
144p. Illus.

Kirk, Alexander
Grape culture up-to-date. Sheffield-Pawson and
Brailsford; London, Simpkin, Marshall, Hamilton,
Kent; The Country Gentlemen's Assoc., 1909. 75p.
Illus.

Kirk, Mrs. Alice Gitchell
The People's home recipe book. Book II of the
People's Home Library. Cleveland, R.C. Barnum Co.,
1920. 238p.

Kirk, Mrs. E.W.
Tried favorites cookery book. 23rd and enl. edition.
Edinburgh, J.B. Fairgrieve and Co., 1934.   314p.
24th edition. A.D. Johnston, 314p. 1942.

Kirkby, William
See Kelynack, T. N. and Kirkby, William.
Arsenical poisoning in beer drinkers.

_____.
The evolution of artificial mineral waters. Manchester,
Jewsbury and Brown, 1902. 155p. Illus. Biblio-
graphy.
Kirschbaum, Emil
Distillation and rectification. Brooklyn, Chemical
Publishing Co., 1948. 426p.
Kirshenbauer, H. G.
Fats and oils. An outline of their chemistry and
technology. New York, Reinhold Publishing Corp.,
1944. 154p. Illus. Bibliography.
Kirton, John William
Intoxicating drinks, their history and mystery.
London, Ward, Lock and Co., 1879. 144p.
Kirwan, Andrew Valentine
Host and guest. A book about dinners, dinner-giving,
wines, and desserts. London, Bell and Daldy, 1864.
410p.
Kirwan, Richard
An essay on analysis of mineral waters. London, D.
Bremner, 1799. 279p.
Kitchener, William
Apicius Redivivus or cook's oracle. London, Samuel
Bagster, 1817. unpaged.

_____.
The art of invigorating and prolonging life by food,
clothes, air, exercise, wine, etc. London, Geo. B.
Whittaker (1828). 6th edition, 337p.
Klaunberg, Henry J.
Tea; a symposium on the pharmacology and the
physiologic effects of tea. Washington, Biological
Sciences Foundation, 1955. 64p. Illus.   LC
Klein, Carl H. von
The old Egyptian use of beer, as a food, as a
beverage and as a mendicant. Chicago, Fred Klein
Co., 1911. 15p. Illus.   LC
Klerk, W. A. de
The white wines of South Africa. Cape Town, A. A.
Balkema, 1967. 110p. Illus-photos, drawings.
Kloss, C. A.
The art and science of brewing. London, Stuart and
Richards, 1949. 121p. Illus. Bibliography.

Knaggs, H. Valentine
The healthy life beverage book.   London, C.W. Daniel,
1911.   128p.

————————.
The romance of sugar.   London, C.W. Daniel Co.,
1931.   46p.
Knapp, Arthur William
. . . The cocoa and chocolate industry; the tree, the
beau, the beverage.   London, Sir I. Pitman and Sons,
Ltd., 1923.   147p.   Illus.   Bibliography.

————————.
Cocoa and chocolate, their history from plantation to
consumer.   London, Chapman and Hall, Ltd., 1920.
210p.   Illus.   Bibliography.

————————.
Cacao fermentation.   London, Bale Sons and Danell,
1937.   171p.   LC

————————.
Scientific aspects of cacao fermentation.   In six parts
reprinted from Bulletins of Imperial Institute.   London,
1935 and 1936.   106p.
Knapp, H.B.
See Auchter, E.C. and Knapp, H.B.
Orchard and small fruit culture.
Knight, Richard Payne
An analytical inquiry into the principles of taste.   2nd
edition.   London, T. Payne and J. White, 1805.
470p.
Knight, Thomas Andrew
A treatise on the culture of the apple and pear and the
manufacture of cider and perry.   3rd edition.   Ludlow,
Printed by H. Procter, 1809.   156p.   1818   5th edition.
Longman, Hurst, Rees, Orme and Brown, 177p.
Knittel, John
Cyprus wine from my cellar.   London, John Long Ltd.,
1933.   288p.
Knorr, W.L.
Knorr's catalogue of ice cream machinery.   Pittsburgh,
1895.   48p.   Illus.
Knott, Henry
The Destroyer.   Chicago, W.R. Vansant and Co.,
1908.   222p.   Illus.
Knox, Thomas W.
Teetotaler Dick: his adventures, temptations and
triumphs.   New York, Ward and Drummond, 1890.
418p.

Koch, Albin A.
Official mixing guide, how to make fancy and mixed
drinks. Chicago, Mode Art Studio Inc., 1933. 36p.
LC

Koehler, Franz A.
Coffee for the armed forces. Washington, Historical
Branch, Office Quartermaster General, 1958. 134p.
Illus.

Koenen, Anton
From vineyard to table. London, Published by author,
1930. 32p. NYPL

Koken, John M.
Here's to it! (toasts). New York, A. S. Barnes,
1960. 146p. WI

Koonin, Dr. Paul M.
Health cocktails (from fruit and vegetables) 3rd edition.
Sydney, Published by author, 1941. 121p. Illus-
drawings.

Ko-operatieve Wijnbouwers Vereniging
Zuid-Afrika Beperkt
See K. W. V. Public Relations Department

——————
Cooking with Cape wine. Paarl (South Africa), n d.
32p. PLOSA

——————
Wine handbook for hoteliers. Paarl, K. W. V., 1961.
24p. PLOSA

Korab, Harry E.
See American Bottlers' of Carbonated Beverages.
Dissolving caustic before addition to bottle washer
(schemes for).

——————
Microbiological aspects of one-trip glass bottles as
used by the carbonated beverage industry. Reprinted
from Food technology, 1963. Published by American
Bottlers' Carbonated Beverages, Washington, D. C.
1963. 2p.

Koren, John
Alcohol and society. New York, Henry Holt and Co.,
1916. 271p.

——————
Economic aspects of the liquor problem. Boston and
New York. Houghton, Mifflin and Co., 1899. 327p.
Bibliography.

Krafft, Michael August
American distiller (The). Philadelphia, Printed for
Thomas Dobson, 1804. 219p.   LC
Kramer, Albert J.
Inventions at your service. Important patents available
to the public free of charge. Washington, D.C.,
Progress Press, 1946. 139p.
Krause, Marie V.
Food, nutrition and diet theraphy. 2nd edition.
Philadelphia - London, W.B. Saunders, 1960. 621p.
Illus.
Krebs, Roland
Making friends is our business. 100 years of
Anheuser-Busch, 1953. St. Louis Anheuser-Busch, Inc.,
(in collaboration with Percy J. Orthwein.) 445p.
Illus.
Kressman, Edouard
The wonder of wine. New York, Hastings House, 1968.
227p.
Krickauff, Freidrich E.H.W.
The future of our wine industry and the results of
manuring vineyards in Europe and Australia. Adelaide,
Basedow, Eimer and Co., Printers, 1899. 36p.
                              (National Agricultural Library)
Kronlein, Hans
Handbuch fur mixer. Dresden, 1925. (In German).
Hauptverwaltung des Genfer Verbandes der hotel-und
restaurant-Angestellton Deutschlands. 358p. Illus.
Krout, John Allen
The origin of prohibition. New York, A.A. Knopf,
1925. 339p. Bibliography   NYPL

Labarge, Margeret Wade
A baronial household of the thirtenth century. London,
Eyre and Spottiswoode, 1965. 235p. Illus. Biblio-
graphy.
Laborie, Pierre Joseph
Abridgement of "The coffee planter of St. Domingo."
By W.G. McIvor, Madras. J. Higginbotham, 1863.
82p.   LC

The coffee planter of Santo Domingo,   London, T.
Cadell and W. Davies, 1798. 145p.   NYPL

Lacour, Pierre
The manufacture of liquors, wines, and cordials without
the aid of distillation. New York, Dick and Fitzgerald,
1853. 312p. Entered 1863. Same
Ladd, E. F.
Foods and food products, Bulletin no. 69. Whiskey and
other beverages, drugs and medicines. North Dakota
Agricultural College. Government Agricultural Exper-
iment Station of North Dakota. Fargo N.D. June 1906.
48p.
Ladies Home Journal
Women's buying habits and attitudes toward soft drinks.
Philadelphia, Reader Reaction Bureau, 1961. paged
by sections.
Ladies of the Mission
The old brewery and the new Mission House at the
five points. New York, Stringer and Townsend, 1854.
304p.
Lady (A)
Art of cookery made plain and easy. New edition,
London, W. Strahan J. Livington and Sons, etc.,
1778. 397p.

_____.
See Rundell, Mrs.
Domestic Cookery for the use of private families.

_____.
New system of domestic cookery, etc., (by a lady).
London, T. Allman Holborn Hall, 1839. 419p.
Laerne, C.F. Van Delden
Brazil and Java. Report on coffee-culture in America,
Asia and Africa. London, W.H. Allen and Co., 1885.
637p. Illus.
Laird, W.H.
American Bartender or the art and mystery of mixing
drinks. St. Johns, New Brunswick, Published for the
proprietor, 1886. 65p. (McGill Univ.)
Laffer, H. E.
The wine industry of Australia. Adelaide, Australian
Wine Board, 1949. 136p. Illus.
Lake, Max
Classic wines of Australia. Brisbane, The Jacaranda
Press, 1967. 134p. Illus-drawings. Glossary.

_____.
Hunter wine. Brisbane, Jacaranda Press, 1964. 94p.
Illus.

———. Vine and scalpel. Brisbane, Australia, Jacaranda
Press, 1967. 72p. Illus-engravings.
Lake Roland Garden Club
Wine and dine with the Lake Roland garden club.
Ruxton, Md., 1935. 236p. Illus.   LC
Lamb, Douglas L.
Guide to Bordeaux wines and cognac. Sydney, J.
Sands, 1948. 34p.   NYPL
Lamb, Ruth de Forest
American chamber of horrors. The truth about food
and drugs. New York, Farrer and Rinehart Inc.,
1936. 418p. Bibliography.
Lambert, Edward
Art of confectionery (The). London, F. Newbury, 1750.
66p.   BM
La Montagne and Sons
The wines of Bordeaux. New York, 1911. 53p. NYPL
Lamore, Harry
The bartender. New York, R.K. Fox, 1896. 90p.
                                                 BM
Lampray, J.H.
Brewer's and distiller's diary and text-book. London,
1882. 24p.   Stopes
Lamson-Scribner, F.
Fungus diseases of the grape and other plants and
their treatment. Little Silver, N.J., J.T. Lovett Co.,
1890. 134p. Illus.
Lancaster, H.M.
The maltster's materials and methods. London,
Published by The Institute of Brewing, 1936. 208p.
Illus.
Lancaster, Hugh
Practical floor malting. London, The Brewing Trade
Review, 1908. 211p. Illus. Works referred to.
Lancaster, Osbert.
Story of tea (The). London, Ceylon Tea Centre,
4th Edition, 1967. 24p. Illus-photos.
Lance, E.J.
The hop farmer--hop culture--embracing its history,
laws and uses, etc. London, James Ridgeway and
Sons, 1838. 212p. Illus.
Landauer, Bella C.
Some alcoholic Americana. New York. Privately
printed at the Harbor Press, 1932. unpaged (36).
Illus-photos of engravings.

Landfield, Jerome
  California, America's vineyard. San Francisco.
  Verdier Cellars, 1945. 36p. (Berkeley)
Lane, Betty
  A.B.C. of spice cookery. (The). New York,
  Published by American Spice Trade Association, 1950.
  48p.
Lane, Jane
  Gin and bitters. (A novel about gin trade 1700's)
  London, Andrew Dakers Ltd., 1945. 331p.
Lane-Clayton, Janet E.
  Milk and its hygenic relations. London, Longmans,
  Green and Co., 1916. 348p. Illus. References.
Lanford, C.S.
  See Sherman, Henry C. and Lanford, Caroline Sherman
  Essentials of nutrition.
Langden, Amelie
  Dainty drinks and sherbets. Minneapolis, Great Western
  Printing Co., 1906. 72p. (Brown Univ.)
Langdon, David
  See Clayton, David and Langdon, David
  Wake up and die!
Langenbach, Alfred
  German wines and vines. London, Vista Books, 1962.
  190p. Illus. Bibliography.
Langford, T.
  Plain and full instructions to raise all sorts of fruit
  trees. London, J.M. for Rich Chiswell, 1699. 148p.
                                                      BM
Langmead, Frederick and Hunt, T.C.
  Review of the effects of alcohol on man. London,
  Medical Committee on the alcohol problem in Great
  Britain. Various contributors, V. Gollanz, 1931.
  300p. NYPL
Langseth-Christensen, Lillian and Smith, Carol Sturm
  The chocolate and coffee cookbook. New York, Walker
  and Co., 1967. 96p. Illus-drawings.
Langwill, K.E.
  See Jordan, Stroud and Langwill, Katheryn E.
  Confectionery analysis and composition.

_____.

  See Jordon, Stroud
  Chocolate evaluation. Assisted by Katheryn E. Langwill.

Lanham, Herbert
   Brewers and bottlers accounts. London, 1906. 191p.
Lansdell, J.
   Grapes: and how to grow them. Third Edition.
   London, W.H. and L. Collingridge, 1919. 114p.
   Illus.
Lansdell, J. (Revised and modernised by A.J. Macself)
   Grapes, peaches, nectarines and melons. London,
   W.H. and L. Collingridge, Ltd., 1946. 144p.

———.
   See Sanders, T.W. and Lansdell, J.
   Grapes: peaches, peaches, melons, and how to grow
   them. London, W.H. and L. Collingridge, 1924.
   150p. Illus.
Lariar, Lawrence, Ed.
   You've got me on the rocks. New York, Dodd, Mead
   and Co., 1956. unpaged. Illus.
Laroque, Jean de.
   A voyage to Arabia the Happy, by the way of the
   Eastern ocean, and the streights of the Red-sea:
   perform'd by the French for the first time, A.D.
   1708, 1709, 1710. Together with a particular relation of a journey from the port of Moka to the court
   of the king of Yemen. Also, an account of the coffee-
   tree, and its fruit . . . Likewise an historical
   treatise of the first use of coffee, and the progress
   it afterwards made both in Asia and Europe; how it
   was introduced into France. London, G. Strahan,
   1726. 312p.
Larsen, N.
   156 recettes de boissons Americaines. Paris,
   Librairie Bernardin-Bechet, 1932. (In French).
   94p.
Larson, C.R.
   Fountain operator's manual. n p. Syndicate Store
   Merchandising Co., 1940.   (Seattle Public)
Lascelles, Arthur Rowley William
   A treatise on the nature and cultivation of coffee; with
   some remarks on the management and purchase of coffee
   estates. London, S. Low, Son, and Marston, 1865.
   71p.   LC
Latchford-Marble Glass Co.
   The history of glass containers. Los Angeles, n d,
   ca1954. 24p. Illus.

Lathrop, Elise
    Early American Inns and taverns. New York, Robert
    M. McBride, 1926. 365p. Illus. Bibliography.
Laufer, Stephen
    Standardizing methods of analysis (brewing) New York,
    Reprint of articles in American Brewer, 1934. 19p.
                                                        NYPL
Laumer, William F. Jr.
    About wines. Some curiosities, odds and ends, facts
    and fancies. St. Petersburg, Fla. National Rating
    Bureau, 1961. 154p.
Launay, Andre
    The Merrydown book of country wines. London, The
    New English Library, 1968. 125p.
Laureat, John Skelton
    The Tunning of Elynour Rumming. London, The
    Fanfrolico Press, 1928. 47p. Illus.
Laurence, John
    Fruit Garden Kalendar (Mr. Laurence's). London,
    Bernard Lintot, 1718. 150p.
Laurent, A.
    A dictionary of the art of brewing, malting and vinegar
    making. Reprinted from Country Brewers' Gazette
    by Rockliffe Bros., Liverpool, 1881. 160p.
    Dictionary.
La Wall, Charles H.
    The curious lore of drugs and medicines. (four
    thousand years of pharmacy). Garden City, New
    York, Garden City Publishing Co., 1927. 665p.
    Bibliographical notes.

    _____.
    Four thousand years of pharmacy. Philadelphia and
    London, J.B. Lippincott Co., 1927. 665p.
Laver, James
    Drinking in England. Published in Gilbey's Compleat
    Imbiber issue as a catalogue of the centenary exhibition
    of drinking through the centuries. London, 1957.
    29p.

    _____.
    The House of Haig, Markinch, John Haig and Co., Ltd.,
    1958. 73p. Illus.

    _____.
    Victorian vista. (Wine-an anthology). London, Hulton
    Press, 1955. 256p.   LC

La-Vogue, Bruno (Massard, Secondin)
   . . . The art and secrets in the manufacture of wines
   and liquors according to ancient and modern inter-
   national methods--requiring no machinery . . . . New
   York, La-Vogue, 1934. 63p.
Law, Ernest
   King Henry VIII's newe wyne seller at Hampton Court.
   Historically described. London, G. Bell and Sons,
   1927. 29p. Illus-photos.
Law, William
   Hints on the cooking of coffee,   BM

──────── .
   The history of coffee, etc. London, 1850. 45p.
                                                        GBPOL
Lawlor, C. F.
   The Mixicologist; or how to mix all kinds of fancy
   drinks. Cincinnati, Published by Lawlor and Co.,
   1895. 169p.
Lawlor, Pat
   The Froth-Blowers Manual. A joyful history. Beer
   ballads and stories. A beer encyclopaedia to settle
   all arguments. Wellington, Published by author, 1965.
   131p. Illus.

──────── .
   Wholesale wine and spirit trade. A Wellington history.
   Wellington, The Wellington District Wholesale Wine and
   Spirit Merchant's Association. 1966. 31p.
Lawrence, John
   See Moubray, Bonington, Esq. (pseud).
   A practical treatise on breeding.

──────── .
   A practical treatise on brewing. London, 1819. (Scho)
Lawson, Arthur
   See Breen, Mary and Arthur Lawson. The weekend
   companion.
Layton, Thomas Arthur
   Choose your wine. London, Duckworth, 1940. 168p.

──────── .
   Cognac and other brandies. London, Harper Trade
   Journals Ltd., 1968. 153p. Illus-photos.

──────── .
   Dining 'round London. London, Transatlantic Arts Ltd.,
   1945. 57p.

_____. Five to a feast. London, Gerald Duckworth and Co., Ltd., 1948. 219p.

_____. Modern wines. London, William Heinemann, Ltd., 1964. 190p.

_____. Restaurant roundabout. London, Duckworth, 1944. 252p.

_____. Table for two. London, Duckworth, Gerald and Co., 1942. 232p.

_____. Winecraft. The encyclopedia of wines and spirits. New edition. London, Harper and Co., 1961. 295p. Glossary in four (4) languages.

_____. Wine's my line. London, Duckworth, 1955. 256p. Illus.

_____. Wines and castles of Spain. New York, Taplinger Publishing Co., 1959. 246p.

_____. Wines and Chateaux of the Loire. London, Cassell and Co., Ltd., 1967. 225p. Illus-photos.

_____. Wines of Italy. London, Harper Trade Journals Ltd., 1961. 221p. Illus. Glossary.

_____. A year at the Peacock. London, Cassell and Co., Ltd., 1964. 216p. Illus.

Leacock, Stephen
Wet wit and dry humor. New York, Dodd Mead and Co., 1931. 260p.

Leadbetter, Charles
Royal guager. London, J. and F. Rivington, 1766. 493p.   (Jordan Winery Library)

Leake, Chauncey (Dr.) and Silverman, Milton (Dr.)
Alcoholic beverages in clinical medicine. Cleveland. World Publishing Co., 1966. 160p. Bibliography.

Leake, John MD
Dissertation on the properties and efficacy of the Lisbon diet drink etc., 8th edition. London, R. Baldwin, (1783). 152p.

Le Brocq, Philip
    Description with notes of certain methods of planting
    (Grapes), etc. London, 1786. 43p.   BM
Lee, Edwin
    The baths of Germany. London, 1839. 268p.   BM

————·
    Mineral springs of England. London, 1841. 124p. BM

————·
    The watering places of England, considered with
    reference to their medical topography. 3rd edition.
    London, J. Churchill, 1854. 280p.
Leedom, William S.
    The vintage wine book. New York, Vintage Books.
    1963. 264p. Bibliography.
Lees, F.R. (Dr.)
    Argument legal and historical for the legislative
    prohibition of the liquor traffic. London, William
    Tweedle, 1856. 317p.

————·
    First prize essay on sacramental wine.
    Liverpool, Williams and Co. printer, n d, ca1861, 16p.

————·
    Text-book of temperance. Rockland, Maine and New
    York. Z. Pope Vose and Co., and J.N. Stearns, n d,
    entered 1869. 312p.

————·
    The text-book of true temperance. London, Trubner
    and Co., 1871. 282p.
Lees, William Nassau
    A memorandum written after a tour through the tea
    districts of eastern Bengal in 1864-1865. Calcutta,
    Printed at the Bengal Secretariat Press, 1866. 112p.
                                         LC

————·
    Tea culture in India. London, W.H. Allen and Co.,
    1863. 395p.   BM
Lefevre, Nicholas
    Discourse of Sir Rawleigh's Great Cordial. London,
    1664. 110p.   BM
Leffman, Henry and Beam, William
    Select methods in food analysis. Philadelphia P.
    Blakiston's Son and Co., 1901. 383p. References.
    1906, 2nd edition, 396p.
Le Gallienne, Richard
    The romance of perfume. New York, Paris, R. Hudnut,
    1928. 46p. Illus.

Leggett, Herbert D.
  ✓ Early history of wine production in California. San
  Francisco, (Thesis), 1941. 124p. Bibliography   WI
Legrand, N. E.
  Champagne, 2nd edition. Rheims, 1899.   BV
Lehrian, Paul
  The Restaurant. London, Practical Press Ltd., 1953.
  149p. Illus.
Leifchild, J.
  Complete directions for brewing fine, rich and whole-
  some ale and beer, etc. London, Published by author,
  1802. 36p.
Leigh, Olga de Leslie
  Five hundred and one easy cocktail canapes. New York,
  Crowell Publishing Co., 1953. 151p.
                                    (Cincinnati Public)
Leipoldt, C. Louis
  300 years of Cape wine. Cape Town, Stewart, 1952.
  230p.
Leitch, Mary and Margeret
  See Crafts, Dr. and Mrs. Wilbur F. and Misses
  Mary and Margeret W. Leitch
  Intoxicants and opium. In all lands and times.
Lelong, B. M.
  A treatise on citrus culture in California, etc.
  Sacramento, Published by State Board of Horticulture
  of the State of California, 1888. 96p. Illus. Books
  recommended.
Lemery, Louis
  New curiosities in art and nature. London, 1711.
  354p.   BM
Lemery, M. L.
  Treatise of all sorts of foods. Both animal and
  vegetable: also of drinkables. London, Printed for T.
  Osborne in Gray's Inn., 1745. 372p.
Lemp, Wm. J. Brewing Co.
  Toasts. St. Louis, 1901. 40p. Illus.
Leon, Simon I.
  An encyclopedia of candy and ice cream making. New
  York, Chemical Publishing Co., 1959. 454p. Illus.
Leroux and Co., Inc.
  Manual on cordials. Philadelphia, 1947. 64p. Illus.
Lesparre, Jean N.
  Herbs, spices and seasonings. Middletown, New York,
  The Dahls, 1946. 73p.

Letheby, H.
 On food: its varieties, etc. London, Longmans, Green
 and Co., 1870. (Lectures on food). 277p.
Lettsom, John Coakley
 History of some effects of hard drinking. London, 1789.
 12p.   BM

_____
 The natural history of the tea-tree with observations
 on the medical qualities of tea and effects of tea
 drinking. London, Edward and Charles Dilly, 1772.
 64p.
Levett, Jack
 Making wines at home. London, Foyle, 1957. 87p.
Levesque, John
 The art of brewing and fermenting and making malt,
 etc. Third edition, London, J. Leath, 1845.
 129p. 5th edition, 1853. 131p. Illus-drawings.
 6th edition, ca1854. 129p. Illus-drawings.
Levine, Max
 See Buchanan, J.H. and Levine, Max
 Bottle washing and its control in the carbonated
 beverage industry.

_____
 See American Bottlers of Carbonated Beverages.
 Memorandum on sweetening agents for carbonated
 beverages.

_____
 See Toulouse, J.H. and Levine, Max
 Suggestions for maintaining quality and uniformity of
 bottled carbonated beverages.
Levine, Max and Toulouse, J.H.
 Suggestions on elimination of spoilage in the carbonated
 beverage industry. ABCB Educational Bulletin no. 7.
 Washington, Publ. by ABCB, 1934. 15p.

_____
 Buchanan, J.H. and Levine, Max (See)
 The testing of washing solutions.
Levy, Hermann
 Drink. An economic and social study. London,
 Routledge and Regan Paul Ltd., 1951. 256p.
Lewis, George C.
 Coffee planting in Ceylon, past and present. Colombo,
 1855.   (Money)
Lewis, J. Sydney
 Old glass and how to collect it. 5th edition.
 Edinburgh, T. Werner Laurie, 1939. 279p. Illus.

Lewis, Robert A.
   The wines of Madeira. Tring, Herts. England, Shire
   Publications, (1968). 40p. Illus-photos.
Lewis, V.B.
   The complete buffet guide or how to mix all kinds of
   drinks. Chicago, M. A. Donahue, 1902. 180p.
Ley, S. Henry
   Merry mixer (The). New York, Jos. S. Finch and Co.,
   Inc., 1935. 21p. Illus-drawings.
Leyel, Mrs. C.F.
   Elixirs of Life. London, Faber and Faber, 1948.
   221p. Illus.

————— .
   Herbal delights. London, Faber and Faber, 1937.
   429p. Illus.

————— .
   The magic of herbs. New York, Harcourt Brace and
   Co., 1926. 320p. Bibliography.

————— .
   Summer drinks and winter cordials. London, George
   Routledge and Sons Ltd., n d, (1925). 88p.
Libby Glass Manufacturing Co., (The).
   Notes for an epicure. A handbook on the traditions and
   service of wine and other beverages. Toledo, 1933.
   44p. Illus.
Licensed Beverage Industries, Inc.
   The A B C's of alcoholic beverages. A glossary of
   terms. New York, n d. 16p. Illus.

————— .
   Facts about the licensed beverage industries. Their
   role in the American economy. Their contributions to
   the social welfare. New York, 1962. 71p. List of
   available materials.

————— .
   That great American Spirit. New York, n d, ca1960.
   15p. Illus.

————— .
   Time for hospitality. New York, 1957. 24p. Illus.
Lichine, Alexis
   Alexis Lichine's encyclopedia of wines and spirits.
   London, Cassall and Co., Ltd., 1967. 695p.
   Bibliography.

Wines of France, by Alexis Lichine in collaboration
with William E. Massee. New York, Alfred Knopf,
1958. 326p. Illus. London, Cassell, 1961.
4th edition, New York, Knopf, 1963. 328p. Illus.

Lieber, Hugo
The use of coal tar colors in food products. New
York, H. Lieber and Co., 1904. 150p.

Liebig, Justus
Chemistry in its application to agriculture and
physiology. 2nd edition. London, Taylor and Walton,
1842. 409p.

Liebowitz, Daniel and Brown, W. Jann and Olness, Marlene
Cook to your heart's content on a low fat, low-salt
diet. Menlo Park, California. Pacific Coast Publishers
1969. 150p. Illus-drawings.

Lightbody, James
Art of brewing beer or (Every man his own guager).
London, Hugh Newman, 1695. 68 leaves.   BM

Lillard, Benj.
Practical hints and formulas for busy druggists.
New York, J.H. Vail Co., 1884. 80p.

Lille, Charles
British perfumer. 2nd edition. London, J. Soutar,
1822. 372p.   BM

Lillywhite, Bryant
London coffee houses. A reference book of coffee
houses of the 17th, 18th and 19th centuries. London,
George Allen and Unwin Ltd., 1963. 858p. Illus.

Lima, Jose Joaquim da Costa
Port wine. The Office International du Vin has awarded a first prize to this treatise on Port Wine.
(English version). Portugal, Lito Nacional, 1939.
31p.

Lincoln, Mrs. D. A.
Frozen dainties. Nashua, N.H. Published by White
Mountain Freezer Co., 1894. 31p.

Lincoln, Waldo
American Cookery Books 1742-1860. Revised and
enlarged by Eleanor Lowenstein. Published by American
Antiquarian Society, Worcester, Mass. 136p. 500
copies printed no. 3 96. Bibliography.

Linde, F.
Tea in India, 1879.   (Listed in Peddie)

Linden, Dietrich
    Treatise on origins, natures and virtues of Chalybeate
    waters and hot baths.   London, Printed for D. Brown
    and J. Ward, 1755.   341p.   (University Missouri)
Lindegaard, P.
    New method of forcing grapes and keeping them in
    winter, 1817.   (Listed in Peddie)
Lindemann, E. H.
    The practical guide and receipt book for distillers,
    wine-growers, druggists, manufacturers of wines,
    liquors, cordials, etc.   San Francisco, M. Weiss,
    1875.   41p.   Illus.   LC
Lindinger, Fritz
    Manual for the liquor trade.   New York, Published
    by author, 1904.   164p.
Lindlahr, Anna
    The nature cure cook book and A B C of natural
    dietetics, by Mrs. Anna Lindlahr and Henry Linlahr.
    5th edition.   Chicago, Nature Cure Publishing Co.,
    1917.   469p.
Lindley, George
    A guide to the orchard and kitchen garden, etc.
    London, Longman, Rees, Orme, Brown and Green,
    1831.   597p.   List of books quoted.
Ling, Arthur R.
    See Anon.
    Journal of The Institute of Brewing.   Containing the
    transactions of the various sections together with
    abstracts of papers published in other journals, etc.
    Edited by Arthur R. Ling.

_____.
    Malting.   London, Harrison and Sons, 1908.   27p.
                            (Nowak, Modern brewing)

_____.
    See Sykes, Walter John
    The principles and practice of brewing, by Walter
    J. Sykes.
Linnaeus, Charles
    Voyages and travels in the Levant; in the years 1749,
    50, 51, 52.   London, Printed for L. Davis and
    C. Reymers, 1766.   456p.
Lippincott, Charles and Co.
    Advance circular, Soda Fountains, Philadelphia, 1890.
    16p.   Illus.

————. Catalogue and price list soda water apparatus. Philadelphia, 1873. 52p. Illus.

————. Catalogue of apparatus for making and bottling soda water. Philadelphia. Bound with catalogue of apparatus for making and dispensing soda water, mineral waters, etc. n d, ca1886. 112p. Illus.

————. Instructions and sundry catalogue. Information regarding setting up and operating machinery employed in manufacturing, dispensing and bottling carbonated beverages. Philadelphia, n d, (between 1894 and 1900). 289p. Illus.

————. Soda water apparatus. Philadelphia, Chas. Lippincott n d. 52p. Illus-engravings.

Lipton, Sir Thomas
    Lipton's autobiography. New York, Duffield and Green, 1932. 278p. Illus-photos.

Lipton and Co.
    All about tea. London, 1903. 31p.   BM

Liquid Carbonic Acid Manufacturing Co.
    Catalog no. 37. Carbonating machinery and supplies. Chicago, 1904. 111p. Illus.

————. Catalogue, gas, machinery, flavors. Chicago, 1896. 48p. Illus.

Liquid Carbonic Co.
    ABC of fountain profits. Chicago, n d.
                                (St. Louis Public)

————. Catalog no. 36. (Soda fountain products). Chicago, 1903. 148p.   NYPL

————. Dispenser's catalog no. 532. Chicago, n d. ca1925. 108p.

————. Its history, organization, production and markets--also 50th anniversary. Chicago, 1938. 80p.
                            (Massachusetts Institute Tech.)

————. 1910 soda water guide and book of recipes. Rev. ed. Chicago, 1909. 192p. Illus.

———— .
Sales manual. Chicago, 1934. (Chapman, author).
148p. (Cleveland Public)

———— .
Soda water, how to make it and how to serve it with
profit. Chicago, 1905. 84p. LC
Liquid Carbonic Co., Ltd.
Study of effect of air on carbonation (A). London,
n d. unpaged (12).
Liquid Carbonic Corporation
"Goin' to Town." A resume of the sound film by the
same name, pointing out a goal of achievement for the
bottling industry. Chicago, 1936. 64p. Illus.

———————— .
Price list, syrup tables, directions. Red Diamond
Extracts. Chicago, n d, (1952), 36p. Illus.

———————— .
Sanitation Program for carbonated beverage plants.
Chicago, n d, ca1950. 8p.
Liquor Store Magazine
Practical encyclopedia of alcoholic beverages. Frank
Haring, editor. New York, 1959. unpaged (48).
Illus.
Little, A. C.
See MacKinney Gordon and Little, Angela C.
Color of foods. Technical references to
beverages
Little, Arthur D. Inc. (Sponsored by)
Flavor research and food acceptance. New York,
Reinhold Publishing Co., 1958.
A survey of the scope of flavor and associated re-
search, compiled from papers presented in a series
of symposia given in 1956 and 1957. 391p. Illus.
References.
Littlejohn, Robert M.
Tea. n p. The Quartermaster Corps Subsistance
School Bulletin no. 15 series X, 1930. 42p.
Liverseege, J. F.
Adulteration and analysis of food and drugs. London,
J. and A. Churchill, 1932. 599p.
Livesay, Joseph
New lectures on malt liquors. Preston, Norwich
Temperance Depot, 1870. 16p. NYPL

258

Lloyd, F. C.
   The art and technique of wine. Edited by Stephen
   Gwynn. London, Constable and Co., 1936. 254p.
   Illus.
Lloyd, Frederick J.
   Report on investigations in cider making. London,
   His Majesty's Stationary Office, 1903. 145p.   LC
Lloyd, J. U. (Prof.)
   Elixirs and flavoring extracts. Their history, formulae
   and methods of prep. New York, William Wood
   and Co., 1892. 191p.
Lock, Charles George Warnford
   Coffee: its culture and commerce in all countries.
   London, New York, E. and F. N. Spon, 1888. 264p.
   Illus. Bibliography.
Locke, Edwin A.
   Food values. New York, Appleton and Co., 1911.
   110p.
Locke, John
   Observations on growth and culture of wines and
   olives. London, 1679. 73p.   BM
Lockhart, Ernest E. and Bloomhardt, Fred B.
   A survey of world literature on coffee. New York,
   The Coffee Brewing Institute, Inc. Publication no. 7
   March 1956, 23p. Publication no. 13 June 1956, 35p.
   Publication no. 23 June 1957, 32p.
Lockhart, Sir Robert Bruce
   Scotch. The whisky of Scotland in fact and story.
   London, Putnam, 1952. 184p.
Lodge, E. A.
   Art of manufacture of perfumery. Cincinnati, E.
   Shepard, 1849. 124p.   (New York State Library)
Lodge, James Lee
   Coffee, its history, preparation, etc. Birmingham,
   Midland Educational Co., 1894. 14p.   BM
Loeb, Robert H. Jr.
   How to wine friends and affluent people. A step-by-
   step cook book. Chicago, Follett Publishing Co., 1965.
   131p. Illus-drawings.

———————— .
   Nip ahoy; the picture bar guide. Chicago, Wilcox and
   Follett Co., 1954. 96p. Illus.

———————— .
   Wolf in Chef's clothing. Chicago, Wilcox and Follett,
   1950. 103p.

(Von) Loesecke, Harry W.
Bananas. Chemistry, physiology, technology. Second revised edition. New York, Interscience Publishers, Economic Crops Volume 1. 1950. 189p. Illus. References.

———— .
See Chace, E.M.; H.W. Von Loesecke and J.L. Heid.
Citrus fruit products. Circular no. 577, U.S. Dept. Agriculture.

———— .
Drying and dehydration of foods. New York, Reinhold Publishing Co., 1943. 302p. Suggested reading.

———— .
Outlines of food technology. Second edition. New York, Reinhold Publishing Corp., 1949. 585p. Illus. Suggested reading.

Loftus, William R.
Brewer (The). A familiar treatise on the art of brewing with directions for selection of malt and hops . . . instructions for making cider and British wines. London, Loftus. 1856. 192p. New edition, 1857, 192p. New sterotyped edition, 1863, 140p.

———— .
Brewing saccharometer (Description of the new and improved) with full instructions for its use. London, W.R. Loftus, 1872. 31p.

———— .
Loftus's new mixing and reducing book. London, Published by William R. Loftus, n d, ca1869. 96p.

———— .
The maltster, etc. New and revised edition. London, Published by author, 1876. 186p.

Loftus (publisher)
The spirit merchant. London, 1866. 118p.
(Bourbon Institute Library)

Lolli, Giorgio and others.
Alcohol in Italian culture. New Haven, Yale Center of Alcohol Studies, 1958. 140p. Bibliography.

———— .
See Sadoun, R. Giorgio Lolli, Milton Silverman. Drinking in French culture.

———— .
Social drinking. How to enjoy drinking without being hurt by it. Cleveland, World Publishing Co., 1960. 317p.

London, Jack
    John Barleycorn.   Toronto, Bell and Cockburn, 1913.
    343p. Illus.
London, Robert and Anne
    See Gordon, Robert I.
    Cocktails and snacks.
London College
    Essentials of pharmacy for students.   9th edition.
    London, London College of Chemistry and Pharmacy,
    n d, ca1926. 178p.
London Genuine Tea Co.
    The history of the tea plant; from the sowing of the
    seed, to its package for the European market.   London,
    Published by Lackington, Hughes, et al, 1819.   60p.
                                                           LC
Long, Joseph
    Directions for using the new patent saccharometer for
    brewing ale and beer, etc.   (Blake's) London,
    Published by author, 1824.   20p.   GBPOL

    Tables for ascertaining the strength of spirits with
    Sykes hydrometer. London, Published by author, 1830.
    143p.   BM

    Tables of specific gravity of wash, worts, etc.
    London, Published by author, 1830. 1p.   BM
Long, Lucy
    Tressler, Donald D. Evers, Clifford F. and Long, Lucy
    (See)
    Into the freezer and out.
Longwood, William
    The poisons in your food.   New York, Simon and
    Schuster, 1960. 277p. Bibliography.
Longworth, Nicholas
    See Buchanan, Robert
    The culture of the grape, and winemaking.   Appendix
    containing directions for the cultivation of the strawberry
    by N. Longworth.
Loos, Mary and Duranty, Walter
    Return to the vineyard.   (A novel).   New York, Double-
    day, Doran and Co., 1945.   243p.
                        (Brady Library-Fresno State College)
Lo Pinto, Maria
    Art of making Italian desserts.   (Liquor).   New York,
    Doubleday, 1952. 223p.   LC

Lorenz, E. S.
New Anti-Saloon songs. (Words and music). Dayton,
Ohio, Lorenz Publishing Co., 1905. 139p.

Lott, F. E.
See Mathews, Charles George and Lott, Francis
Edward.
The microscope in the brewery and malt house.

Loubat, Alphonse
The American vine-dresser's guide. New York, D.
Appleton, 1872. (English and French texts on facing
pages) 123p.

Loughlin, James E.
Rainbows in deserts. Reprint of article from
DYESTUFFS September 1955 Vol. 41, no. 3. New
York National Analine Div. Allied Chemical and Dye
Corp. unpaged (12).

Loureiro, P.
Tables showing the approx. cost of tea--laid down in
New York, etc. New York, George F. Nesbitt and
Co., 1858. 51p.

Loveless, Richard Downe
Everyday wrinkles for brewers. Second title-New
handbook on brewing. Birmingham, Published by
author, 1881. 55p.

————————.
Every man his own brewer, or the A B C of brewing
clearly explained for the amateur and the household.
Birmingham (England), 1881. 36p.   (Stopes)

Lovell, Robert
Compleat herbal. Oxford, W. Hall for R. Davis,
1659. 641p.   BM

Lovibond, Thos. Watson
Brewing with raw grain: a practical treatise.
London, E. and F. N. Spon, 1883. 75p.

Lowe, A. E.
See Bolte, Arthur H. and Low, Arthur E.
Management and cost control in the carbonated
beverage industry.

Lowe, Belle
Experimental cookery from the chemical and physical
viewpoint. Third edition. New York, John Wiley
and Sons, Inc., 1944. 611p. Illus. Literature cited.

Lowe, Paul E.
Bartender's quick reference manual. Philadelphia,
Mc Kay, 1908. CBI

_____ .
Drinks. How to mix and how to serve. London,
Stanley Paul and Co., Ltd., n d, ca1924. 160p.

_____ .
Drinks as they are mixed. Chicago, Frederick Drake
and Co., 1904. 135p. Illus. 1900, 160p.

_____ .
The twentieth century book of toasts. Philadelphia,
David McKay, n d. 180p.
Lowe, T.A.
Fruit farm in England. London, Rockliff, 1946.
121p. Illus.
Lowenstein, Eleanor
See Lincoln, Waldo
American Cookery Books 1742-1860. Revised and
enlarged by Eleanor Lowenstein.
Loyd, Rev. J.F.
Wine as a beverage. (Teaching of the Scriptures -
those of fermented drinks.) New York, Hitchcock
and Stevens, 1874. 52p. NYPL
Lucas, Charles
Analysis of Dr. Rutty's methodical synopsis of mineral
waters. London, 1757. 200p. BM

_____ .
Cursary examination of the methodical synopsis of
mineral waters, etc. Dublin, 1763. 87p. BM

_____ .
An essay on waters. Of simple waters; of cold
medicated waters; of natural baths. London, Printed
for A. Millar, 1756. 3 vol. LC
Lucas, Edwin W. and Stevens, Harold B.
Book of pharmacopoaes and unofficial formularies.
London, Churchill, 1915. 524p. NYPL

_____ .
Book of prescriptions. 11th edition. London, J. and
A. Churchill, 1926. 382p. (Cincinnati Public)

_____ .
The book of receipts. 12th edition. Philadelphia,
Blakiston, 1924. 473p. (Cincinnati Public)
Lucia, Salvatore Pablo
Alcohol and civilization. New York, San Francisco
Toronto, London, McGraw-Hill Book Co., 1963. 416p.
References.

_____ A history of wine as theraphy. Philadelphia, J. B.
Lippincott and Co., 1963. 234p. Illus-photos.
Bibliography.

_____ Wine and health. Menlo Park, California. Pacific
Coast Publishers, 1969. 86p. Selected References.

_____ Wine as food and medicine. New York, Blakiston Co.,
1954. 149p. References.

Luck, Mrs. Brian
The Belgian cookbook. London, William Heinemann,
1915. 176p.

Luckwill, L.C. and Pollard, A. Editors
Perry Pears. Bristol, Published for The National
Fruit and Cider Institute by the University of Bristol,
1963. 216p. Illus. Bibliography.

Luhmann, Dr. E.
Die Industrie der Alkoholfreien Getranke, Wien and
Leipzig. A Hartleben's Verlag, 1905. (In German).
364p. Illus.

Lukas, Jan
The book of wine. No place. Printed in Czechoslavakia.
Artia, 1964. 73p. Illus-photos.
                    (Brady Library-Fresno State College)

Luke, Sir Harry
The Tenth Muse. 2nd and enlarged edition. With the
collaboration of Elizabeth Godfrey. Recipes for food
and drinks. London, Putnam, 1962. 288p. Illus.

Luke, Thomas D.
Spas and health resorts of British Isles. London, A.
and C. Black, 1919. 318p.   NYPL

Luker, Henry and Co., Ltd., (Wines, etc.)
Price list. Southend on sea, n d.
4 p.

Lund, John and Richardson, George B.
Mineral water manufacturer's accounts. London,
The Accountant, 1902. 72p.   (Brisbane Public)

Lund, V. Harriron
"Magic of the grape." Erie, Pa. The E. Agresti Co.
n d, ca1930. 75p. Illus.

Lunge, George
Treatise on the distillation of coal-tar and ammoniacal
liquor, etc. and the separation from them of valuable
products. London, John Van Voorst, 1882. 382p.

Lupoiu, Jean
Cocktails. Paris, Les Oeuvres Francaises. 1938.
(In French). 181p.

Lurie, George A.
Here's how . . . a book of recipes for the mixing
of beverages. Milwaukee, Wisc., G.A. Lurie, 1938.
175p.

Lutz, H. F.
Viticulture and brewing in the ancient Orient.
Leipzig, J.C. Hinrich'ssche Buchhandlung, 1922.
166p. Illus-photos, drawings. Notes.

Lyle, Oliver
Technology for sugar refinery workers. 2nd edition.
London, Chapman and Hall Ltd., 1950. 525p. Illus.

Lynch, Patrick and Vaizey, John
Guinness's Brewery in the Irish economy. 1759-1876.
Cambridge, University Press, 1960. 278p. Illus.
Glossary-References.

Lynch, S. John and Mustard, Margeret J.
Mangos in Florida. State of Florida Dept. of Agri-
Bull. no. 20, Tallahassee, March 1955. 83p.
Illus-photos. Literature cited.

Lynn, French
The beer bust songbook, or, pictures to look at while
others are singing. San Francisco, Pearon, 1963.
64p. Illus.

(M., J.B.)
Spices. Jamaica pepper to Zedoary. Published in
The Mineral Water Trade Review and Guardian
London from October 1951 to January 1953. Chapter
CLXIV through CLXXVII prior chapters missing.

M.A.L.T.
What is beer? London, 1886. 34p.   GBPOL

Maanen-Helmer, Elizabeth van
. . . What to do about wines. New York, H. Smith
and R. Haas, 1934. 184p.

Mabon, Mary Frost
A B C of America's wines. New York, A.A. Knopf,
1942. 233p.

Mabson, Richard R.
Forty five years history of the tea trade. London,
Sellar and Co., 1881. folio   BM

McAdoo, William Gibbs
  The Challenge. Liquor and lawlessness versus
  constitutional government. New York, The Century
  Co., 1928. 305p.
Mac Arthur, Sir W.
  Letters on the culture of the vine. Sydney, Maro,
  1844. 153p. NYPL
McAuley, Jerry
  His life and work. New York, Published by Mrs.
  Jerry McAuley and Ward Drummond, 1885.
  227p. same publ. by N.Y. Weekly Witness.
Macauley, Thurston
  The festive board. (a literary feast prepared by).
  London, Methuen and Co., Ltd., 1931. 142p.
Mc Bride, David
  Experimental essays on medical and philosophical
  subjects. The fermentation of elementary mixtures,
  nature, etc., of fixed air. London, 1764. 296p.
                                          GBPOL
Mc Bride, Duncan
  General instructions for the choice of wines and
  spiritous liquors. London, J. Richardson, 1793.
  102p. (Crerar)
Mc Bride, T.M.
  See Townsend, Jack
  The bartender's book; being a history of sundry
  alcoholic potations, libations, and mixtures . . ..
Mc Bride, Mary Margeret
  See Josephy, Helen and Mc Bride, Mary Margeret
  Beer and skittles. A friendly guide to modern Germany
Mc Calman, Godfrey
  A natural, commercial and medicinal treatise on tea.
  1787. (Listed in Peddie)
McCance, R.A. and Widdowson, E.M.
  The chemical composition of foods. Brooklyn, N.Y.,
  Chemical Publishing Co., 1947. 156p. References.
Mc Carthy, Raymond G. and Douglass, Edgar M.
  Alcohol and social responsibility. New educational
  approach. New York, Thomas Y. Crowell Co., 1951.
  304p. Bibliography.
  _____.
  Drinking and intoxication. Selected readings in social
  attitudes and controls. New Haven, College and
  University Press, 1959. 455p.

Mac Cartie, J.C.
Handbook for Australian brewers. Melbourne, Lawrence and O'Farrell, 1884. 88p. (Mitchell Library-Sydney)
McClellan, Walter S.
The utilization of ingested carbon dioxide, and Bibliography; physiological values of carbon dioxide and carbonation of liquids. Washington, American Bottlers of Carbonated Beverages, 1955. 231p. Bibliography.
Mc Clelland, John
Report on physical condition of Assam tea plant. Calcutta, Transactions of Agriculture and Horticultural Society of India, 1837. 58p. BM
Mac Clure, Victor
Good appetite my companion. London, Odhams Press Ltd., 1955. 240p. Illus.

_____.
Party fare. London, Putnam, 1957. 262p.
(Brisbane Public)
Mac Collom, William
Vines and how to grow them. London, The Garden Library, 1911. 315p. BM
Mc Caig, E.
See Tolson, Berneita and McCaig, Edith
The beer cookbook.
Mc Cauley, W.F.
Anti-saloon songs. New York. The Lorenz Publishing Co., 1899. 64p.
Mc Cook, Henry Christopher
The Latimers. A tale of the Western insurrection (whiskey insurrection) of 1794. Philadelphia, George W. Jacobs and Co., 1898. 593p.
Mc Cord, William and Mc Cord, Joan with Gudeman, Jon
Origins of alcoholism. London, Tavistock Publications Board of trustees of Leland Stanford Junior University, 1960. 193p. Notes.
Mc Cormick, Katherine Reynolds
Tea; its part in peace and war. Baltimore, 1917. 34p. Illus. (Cincinnati Public)
Mc Cormick and Co.
The charm of tea. Baltimore, 1928. 8p.
(Cincinnati Public)

_____.
Spices, their nature and growth and the vanilla bean. Baltimore, 1926. 32p. LC

——————.

    Story of extracts. Baltimore, 1919. 14p.
1928, 12p. Illus.

——————.

    Tea; its cultivation, manufacture and packing.
Baltimore, 1926. 12p. Illus.   (Cincinnati Public)

McCulloch, John
    Distillation, brewing and malting. San Francisco,
A. Roman and Co., 1867. 84p.   LC

Macculloch, John
    Remarks of the art of making wine, etc., London,
Longman, Hurst, Rees, Orme and Brown, 1821. 263p.
1829, 280p. Published by Longman, Rees, Orme,
Brown and Green.

Mc Cullouch, John Jr.,
    Observations on the manufacture of rum. London, John
Nichols, 1847. 15p.

Mc Culloch-Williams, Martha
    Dishes and beverages of the old South. New York,
McBride Nast and Co., 1913. 318p.

Mc Cully, Helen
    Nobody ever tells you these things. (About food and
wine). London, Angus and Robertson, 1968. 308p.

Mac Donald, Aeneas
    Whisky. New York, Duffield and Green, 1934. 135p.

Mac Donald, Duncan
    New London family cook. London, 1808. 634p. NYPL

Mac Donald, George B.
    Apology for disuse of alcoholic drinks. London, 1841.
36p.   BM

Mc Donald, John
    The Maltster, distiller and spirit dealers' companion.
Elgin, 1828. 190p.   BM

Mc Donald, John General
    Secrets of the great whiskey ring. St. Louis, W. S.
Bryan, 1880. 346p.

Mcdonald, Ian
    Smuggling in the Highlands. An account of Highland
whisky, etc. Stirling, Eneas Mackey, 1914. 124p.

Mc Donald, J. H.
    Coffee growing: with special reference to East Africa.
London, Published by East Africa (Newspaper), 1930.
205p. Illus.

Mac Donell, Anne
    See Digby, Sir Kenelm
    The closet of Sir Kenelm Digby, knight, opened.
Mc Donough, Everett Goodrich
    Investigations in the autoxidation of aldehydes used
    in perfumery. New York (Thesis), 1932. 49p.
    Bibliography.   LC
Mc Donough, Patrick
    Mc Donough's bar-keepers' guide and gentlemen's
    sideboard companion. Rochester, N.Y., Post
    Express Print., 1883. 50p.   LC
Mc Douall, Robin
    Cooking with wine. London, Allen Lane, The Penguin
    Press, 1968. 144p.
MacDougall, Alice Foote
    Coffee and waffles. Garden City, New York, Doubleday
    Page and Co., 1926. 115p.
Mc Dowall, R.J.S.
    The whiskies of Scotland. London, John Murray, 1967.
    164p. Illus-drawings. Bibliography.
Macduff, Ian Malcolm
    Home-brewing for beginners. Nelson, 1958. 8p.
                   (National Library-Wellington, N. Z.)
McDuff, O.R.
    See Kesterson, J.W. and Mc Duff, O.R.
    Florida citrus oils. Commercial production methods
    and properties of essential oils.
Mc Elhone, Harry
    Barflies and cocktails. Over 300 cocktail recipes by
    Harry and Wynn. Paris, Lecram Press, 1927.
    110p. Illus-drawings.

——————.
    "Harry" of Ciro's. (Harry Mc Elhone) (See)
    A B C of mixing cocktails. London, Odhams Press,
    Ltd., n d. 110p.
Mc Evoy, J.P.
    The sweet dry and dry or see America thirst.
    Chicago, P. F. Volland Co., 1919. unpaged (24).
    Illus-drawings.
Mc Ewan J.
    See Chandler, S. E. and Mc Ewan, J.
    Tea, its culture, manufacture and commerce.
Mc Ewan, John
    Commerce in tea. London, Seventh Inter-geographical
    Congress, 1899. 19p.   BM

MacEwan, Peter
The art of dispensing. 9th edition. London, The
Chemist and Druggist, 1915. 596p.

―――――. Pharmaceutical formulas. 'P. F.' being the Chemist
and Druggists Book of useful recipes for the drug
trade. London, The Chemist and Druggist, 1919.
1062p.

M'Ewen, George
The culture of the peach and nectarine. Edited and
enlarged by John Cox. London, Groombridge and
Sons, 1859. 52p.

Mc Ewin, George
The South Australian Vigneron and gardener's manual,
etc. Adelaide, James Allen, 1843. 124p. Facsimile
edition by Public Library of South Australia, Adelaide
1962.

Mc Gee, W.
From vineyard to decanter, 1876.
            (Massel-Applied Wine Chemistry and Technology)

Mc Gill, Angus, Ed.
PUB. A celebration. London, Longmans, Green and
Co., Ltd., 1969. 242p. Illus-drawings.

Mc Gowan, Alexander T.
Tea planting in the outer Himalayah. London, 1861.
73p.   BM

Mc Greal Bros. Co.
Mc Greal's Blue book. (Cocktails). Rochester, N.Y.,
1916. 43p. Illus.   LC

Macgregor, James
Beer making for all. London, Faber and Faber Ltd.,
1967. 126p.

―――――. Wine making for all. London, Faber and Faber, 1966.
144p.

M' Harry, Samuel
The practical distiller; or an introduction to making
whiskey, gin, brandy, spirits, etc., sundry extracts--
for making cider, domestic wines and beer. Harris-
burgh, Penna., John Wyeth, 1809. 184p.

Machet, J.J.
Receipts for homemade wines, cordials, etc. London,
1815. 286p.   GBPOL

McHugh, Stuart
    See Cox, Helen
    The food, flowers and wine cookbook. (Flowers, Stuart
    Mc Hugh. Wines, George Dowglass).

Mc Indoe, David
    Chapman's New Zealand grape manual or plain directions
    for planting cultivating vineyards and for making wine.
    Auckland, G. T. Chapman, 1862. 111p.
                                (National Library- Wellington)

McIntyre, William
    See Partch, Virgil and McIntyre, William
    VIP tosses a party.

Mackay, Ian
    Puborama. Auckland, Oswald-Sealy (N. Z.) Ltd., 1961.
    103p. Illus.

Mackay, Margeret
    The Wine Princes (a novel). New York, John Day
    Co., 1958. 374p.

Mackaye, Payson
    Coffee man's manual. New York, Spice Mill Publ.
    Co., 1942. 77p.   (St. Louis Publ.)

Mackenzie, Colin
    One thousand experiments in chemistry with illustrations
    of natural phenomena; and practical observations on the
    manufacturing and chemical processes persued in the
    successful cultivation of the useful arts. London, Sir
    Richard Phillips and Co., 1821. 528p. Illus.

Mackenzie, Compton
    Whisky galore. London, Chatto and Windus, 1954.
    264p.

MacKenzie, Dan
    Aromatics and the soul; a study of smells. London,
    W. Heinemann, 1923. 164p.

Mackenzie, Edward L.
    The whole art of confectionary. Otley, W. Walker
    and Sons, 1860. 63p.   BM

Mc Kenzie, F. A.
    "Pussyfoot" Johnson. London, Hodder and Stoughton,
    n d, ca1921. 178p. Illus.

Mackenzie, John E.
    The sugars and their simple derivatives. London,
    Gurney and Jackson, 1913. 242p. Illus.

McKenzie, W. F.
    Fruit culture for the amateur. London, Garden
    Publications Ltd., 1947. 174p. Illus- drawings.

Mackinney, Gordon and Little Angela C.
Color of foods. Westport, Conn. Avi Publishing Co.,
Inc., 1962. 308p. Illus-photos-drawings.
MacLaren, Hale
Be your own guest. Section on wines by Emerson Wirt
Axe. Boston, Houghton Mifflin Co., 1952. 178p.
Mc Laren, Moray
Pure wine or in vino veritas. Edinburgh, Alastair
Campbell, 1965. 60p. Illus.
MacLaren, W. A.
Rubber, tea and cocoa. London, Ernest Benn, 1924.
334p. Bibliography. (Berkeley)
Mc Laughlin, Laura I.
See Chatfield, Charlotte and McLaughlin, Laura I.
Proximate composition of fresh fruits.
Mc Lean, James M.
Book of wine. Philadelphia, Dorrance and Co., 1934.
53p. LC
MacMahon, Albert C.
MacMahan's latest recipes and American Soda Water
Dispensers' Guide. Chicago, Goodall and Loveless,
1893. 95p.
Mc Minn, J. M.
See Saunders, Wm.
An essay on the culture of the native and exotic grape
ale both sides of the grape question. (A contribution to
the classification of the species of the grape vine,
with hints on culture by J. M. McMinn.)
McMullen, Thomas
Handbook of wines, practical, theoretical, and
historical; with a description of foreign spirits and
liqueurs. New York, D. Appleton and Co., 1852.
327p.
Macnab, Shirley
Under the black tiles (Liquor). Hitchin, England,
Eric Anderson and Associates, n d. 52p.
Bibliography.
McNair, James B.
Citrus products. Part 1. Field Museum Natural
History. Publication 238 Botanical Series. Vol. VI,
No. 1, Chicago, 1926. 212p.

————————
Citrus Products. Part 2. Field Museum Natural History. Publication no. 245 Botanical series. Vol. VI,
no. 2 Chicago, 1927. pgs. 213 to 391.

272

————— .
Spices and condiments. Botany Leaflet no. 15.
Chicago, Field Museum of Natural History, 1930. 64p.
Illus-drawings.
M' Neil, Duncan
The reformed drunkard. With other poems and songs.
Glasgow. Printed by the Scottish Cooperative Whole-
sale Society Ltd., 1899. 120p.
MacNiel, Stanley S.
Zodiac cocktails; cocktails for all birthdays. New
York, Mayfair Publishing Co., 1940. 55p. Illus.
McNeill, Florence Marian.
The Scots cellar, its traditions and lore. Edinburgh,
R. Paterson, 1958. 290p. Illus.

————— .
The Scots Kitchen. London and Glasgow, Blackie and
Sons Ltd., 1930. 259p.
Mc Neish, James
Tavern in the town. Wellington (N. Z.), A. H. and A.
W. Reed, 1957. 269p. Illus.
Mc Nish, Robert
The anatomy of drunkenness. 3rd edition. Glasgow,
W. R. M'Phun, 1829. 210p. 1828, 2nd edition, 195p.
McPhee, John
Oranges. New York, Farrar, Straus and Giraux,
1967. 149p.
Macpherson, John, MD
The baths and wells of Europe. 3rd edition, revised.
London, Edward Stanford, 1888. 379p.

————— .
Our baths and wells. The mineral waters of the
British Islands with a list of sea bathing places.
London and New York, Macmillan and Co., 1871.
198p.
Macself, A. J.
See Sanders, T. W.
Fruit and its cultivation in garden and orchard.

————— .
See Lansdell, J. (Revised and modernised by A. J.
Macself)
Grapes, peaches, nectarines and melons.
MacSwiney, E.
The mineral water maker's Vade Mecum. London,
J. Gilbert Smith and Co., 1891. 70p. Glossary.

McWilliam, D. M.
    The wine merchants book of recipes. Glasgow,
    William Gilmour, n d. 108p.
    1947, Second edition (Revised). London, Food Trade
    Press, 1947. 126p.
Madden, John
    Shall we drink wine? Milwaukee, Owen and Weirbrecht,
    1891. 220p.   LC
Madden, Joe (The Markee)
    Set 'em up! New York, Published by a "Punch-drunk
    author." 1939. 136p. Illus.

———— What'll you have boys? New York, Farrar and Rine-
    hart, 1934. 138p. Illus. Glossary.
Madden, Thomas More
    The principal health-resorts of Europe and Africa for
    the treatment of chronic diseases. Philadelphia,
    Lindsay and Blakiston, 1876. 276p.
Magalhaes, Jose Jacinto de.
    Description of a glass-apparatus for making in a few
    minutes, and at a very small expense, the best mineral
    waters of Pyrmont, Spa, Seltzer, Seydschutz, Aix-la-
    Chapelle, etc. London, Published by author, 1783.
    80p.   LC
Maggs Bros., London
    Food and drink through the ages, 2500 B.C. to 1937 A.D.
    a catalogue of antiquities, manuscripts, books, and
    engravings treating of cookery, eating and drinking.
    London, 1937. 191p. Illus.
Mahoney, Charles S.
    The Hoffman house bartender's guide; how to open a
    saloon and make it pay. New York, R.K. Fox, 1905.
    233p. Illus.
Maignen, P.A.
    Water, preventable disease and filtration. London,
    Published by author, 1886. 70p.
Maior, Julio, M. de O.P. Viscount Villa
    Viniculture of claret. San Francisco, Payet,
    Upham and Co., 1884 148p.   (Davis)
Mairet, Ethel
    A book of vegetable dyes. Hammersmith W. London,
    Douglas Pepler, 1916. 153p. Bibliography.
Maison Glass
    See Anon.
    Wine Manual. Edited and published by Maison E.H.
    Glass, Inc.,

Makus, Edwin W.
Standard blue book of mixed drinks. Milwaukee,
Published by author, 1933. 109p.   NYPL
Malepegne, M. F.
See Prestoe, H. and Malepegne, M. F.
Report on coffee cultivation in Dominica.
Malepeyre, M. F.
See Pradel, P. and Malepeyre, M. F.
A complete treatise on perfumery containing notices of
the materials used in the art.
Malet, William E.
The Australian winegrowers' manual. Sydney, Belder
and Foster, printers, 1876. 256p.   ANL
Malins, Joseph
Professor Alcoholico. A temperance poem.
Birmingham, G. H. Bernarsconi, 1876. 22p.
Mallet, P.
A narrative of circumstances relating to the excise
bill on wine. London, F. G. and J. Robinson, 1795.
44p.   (Yale Univ.)
Malone, Dorothy
How Mama could cook! New York, A. A. Wyn, Inc.,
1946. 178p.
Maloney, James C.
Maloney's Twentieth century guide. How to mix
drinks. 11th edition enlarged. Chicago, Published
by author, Distributed by Albert Pick and Co., 1913.
110p.
Maloney, Ralph
The 24 hour drink book. A guide to executive survival.
New York, Ivan Obelensky, Inc., 1962. 137p. Illus.
Manbre and Garten Ltd.
One hundred years of progress. (Brewing). London,
Private edition, 1955. 32p.   BM
deManio, Jack
Jack De Manio's drinkards. Cocktails. London,
Card Publications Ltd., 1968. 15 cards Illus-photos.

————————.
Jack De Manio's drinkards. Non-alcoholic drinks.
London, Card Publications Ltd., 1968. 16 cards,
Illus-photos.
Mankey, J. Compiler
Why be teetotal? Scientific evidence regarding alcoholic
beverages and their effects . . . on life. Melbourne,
Spectator Publishing Co., 1940. 209p.

Manley, R.O.B.
Honey production in the British Isles. London, Faber
and Faber, 1936. 328p.

Mann, Harold H.
The factor which determines the quality of tea.
Calcutta, India Tea Ass'n Publication no. 4, 1907.
29p. (National Agricultural Library)

_____ .
Green manuring in tea industry in India. Calcutta,
India Tea Ass'n., 1906. 43p.
(National Agricultural Library)

_____ .
The tea soils of Cachar and Sylhet. Calcutta, India
Tea Ass'n, no. 1., 1903. 89p.
(National Agricultural Library)

_____ .
Treatment of deteriorated tea. Calcutta, India Tea
Ass'n, no. 4., 1906. 24p.
(National Agricultural Library)

Mann, J.A.
Cocoa, its culture, manufacture and uses, 1860.
(Listed in Peddie)

Mann, Marty
New primer on alcoholism. How people drink, how
to recognize alcoholics and what to do about them.
New York, Holt, Rinehart and Winston, Inc., 1962.
238p. Bibliography.

_____ .
Primer on alcoholism. New York, Rinehard and Co.,
Inc., 1950. 216p. Bibliography.

Manning, Robert
Book of fruits: being a descriptive catalogue of the
most valuable varieties of the pear, apple, peach,
plum and cherry for New England culture. Salem,
Ives and Jewett, 1838. 118p. Illus.

Manning, Sydney, A.
A handbook of the wine and spirit trade. London, I.
Pitman, 1947. 170p. Illus. Bibliography.
1950, same.

Manoha, G. Ed.
Cooking with wine. New York, Lumen Publishers, 1957.
105p. Illus.

Mansur, Caroline E. Comp.
The Virginia Hostess 17th and 18th century, Vol. I.
Pohick, Published by Ann Mason Guild of Pohick Church,
1960. 99p. Bibliography.

Mant, J. B.
The pocket book of mensuration and guaging. London
Crosby, Lockwood and Son, 1891. 249p. BM
Manton, A. J.
See Nithsdale, W. H. and Manton, A. J.
Practical brewing and the management of British beers.
Manufacturing Chemists' Association, Inc.
The chemical industry facts book. 5th edition.
Washington, Published by The Association, 1962. 183p.

Food additives. What they are. How they are used.
Washington, 1961. 63p. References.
Manville, Bill
Saloon Society. New York, Duell, Sloan and Pearce,
1960. 124p. Illus.
Manville, C. H.
Carbonated Bottled Beverages. Jefferson City, Mo.
Published by the Food and Drug Department of State
of Missouri, n d. 12p.
Marah, W. H.
An essay on the cultivation and manufacture of coffee
for which the prize offered by the Royal agricultural
society (Jamaica) was awarded to W. H. Marah.
Colombo, Printed at the Observer Press, 1849. 64p.
LC
Marchant, W. T.
In praise of ale; or, Songs, ballads, epigrams, and
anecdotes relating to beer, malt, and hops, with
some curious particulars concerning ale-wives and
brewers, drinking-clubs and customs. London, G.
Redway, 1888. 632p.
Marco, G. F.
See Gale Hyman
The how and when, published and edited by Hyman
Gale and Gerald F. Marco.
Marcus, Irving H.
Dictionary of wine terms. San Francisco, Wine and
Vines, 1964. 64p. Illus.
Mariani, Angelo
Coca and its therapeutic application. 2nd edition.
New York, J. N. Jaros, 1892. 78p. 3rd edition,
1896, 76p.
Mariani and Co.
Coca Erythroxylon. Its uses in the treatment of
disease. 4th edition. Paris and New York, 1896.
52p.

Maril, Lee
 Savor and Flavor. Berries in fact and fancy. New
 York, Coward-McCann, 1944. 63p.
Mario, Thomas
 The Playboy gourmet, a food and drink handbook for the
 host at home. New York, Crown Publishers, 1961.
 320p. Illus.
Maritzen, August
 Illustrated catalogue of architectural and engineering
 work designed by August Maritzen. (Breweries).
 Chicago, Published by the author, 1892. unpaged (44).
 Illus-engravings.
Mark, George
 The tea plant, its history and properties. Dublin,
 Published by author, 1848. 24p.
Markham, E. A.
 See Frandsen, J. H. and E. A. Markham
 The manufacture of ice creams and ices.
Markham, Gervaise (G. M.)
 Country contentments or the English housewife. London,
 John Harison, 1631. 252p.   LC
 _____.
 Maison Rustique, or the Country Farme. Estienne, 1616.
 468p.   BM
Markkanen, T.
 See Takala, Martti, Toivo A. Pihkanen; Touko
 Markkanen
 The effects of distilled and brewed beverages.
 _____.
 See Allardt, Erik; Toiko Markkanen; Martti, Takala
 Drinking and drinkers. Alcohol research in Northern
 countries.
Marks, Robert
 Wines; how, when, and what to serve. New York,
 Schenley Import Corp., 1934. 63p. Illus. Glossary.
Marlowe, Dave
 Coming, Sir! The autobiography of a waiter. London,
 George G. Harrap and Co., Ltd., 1937. 267p.
Marquis, Don
 Her foot is on the brass rail. New York, The March-
 banks Press, 1935. 23p.   NYPL
 _____.
 The old soak and hail and farewell. Garden City, N. Y.,
 Doubleday Page and Co., 1927. 141p. Illus.

———— .
The old soak's history of the world. Garden City,
N.Y., Doubleday Page and Co., 1924. 144p. Illus.
Marr, E.
See Crane, E.J.; Austin M. Paterson and Eleanor
B. Marr.
A guide to the literature of chemistry.
Marrill, Annabel and Watt, Bernice K.
Energy value of foods . . . basis and derivation.
USDA Agriculture Handbook no. 74. Washington,
March 1955. 105p.
Marrison, L. W.
Wines and spirits. Baltimore, Penguin Books, 1957.
320p. Bibliography.
Marsh, D.B.
See Institute (The)
Good Housekeepings book of cool drinks.
Marsh, G.L.
See Amerine Maynard and George Marsh
Wine making at home.

———— .
See Joslyn, M.A. and Marsh, G.L.
Utilization of fruit in commercial production of fruit
juices.
Marshall, Mrs. A.B.
The book of ices. Revised and enl. London, Ward,
Lock and Co., Ltd., n d. 67p.

———— .
Fancy Ices. London, Simpkin, Marshall, Hamilton,
Kent and Co., Ltd., n d, ca1890. 238p.
Marshall, James
Elbridge A. Stuart. Founder of the Carnation Company.
Los Angeles, The Carnation Co., 1949. 238p.
Marshall, Wm.
Rural economy in Gloucestershire. (cider). London,
Printed for G. Nicol, 1796. 2 vol. (Davis)
Martin, Benjamin
Sure guide for distillers. London, 1759. 36p. GBPOL
Martin, Edith, Comp.
Cornish recipes. Ancient and modern. 2nd edition
rev., Truro, Cornwall. A.W. Jordan. Issued by
Cornwall Federation of Women's Institutes, 1929.
63p. 1950, 73p.
Martin, E.J.
See Anon.
The Cider Factory, plant and layout.
279

Martin, Geoffrey
. . . Perfumes, essential oils and fruit essences, etc.
London, C. Lockwood and Son, 1921. 188p. Illus.
Literature.

Martin, Milward W.
Twelve full ounces. New York, Holt, Rinehart and
Winston, 1962. 136p. Illus.

Martin, Remy
See de Vilmorin, Louise
Cognac. Remy Martin.

Martin, Robert Montgomery
The past and present state of the tea trade of England,
and of the continents of Europe and America. London,
Parbury, Allen and Co., 1832. 222p.   LC

Martin, William
Rough sketch of renewal system, pruning grape wines.
Pittsburg, 1854.   (Location Unknown)

Martindale, William
Coca and cocaine. 2nd edition. London, H.K. Lewis,
1892. 76p.

Martindale, W. Harrison (Revisor)
The Extra Pharmacopoeia of Martindale and Westcott.
19th Edition, 2 vol. London, H.K. Lewis and Co.,
Ltd., 1928-1929. 1207, 758p.

Martyn, Charles, Comp.
Foods and culinary utensils of the ancients. New York,
Caterer Publishing Co., n d, ca1900. 72p. Illus.

————————.
The wine steward's manual. New York, The Caterer
Publishing Co., 1903. 120p. Illus.

Marvel, Tom
A pocket dictionary of wines. New York, Multi-
merchandising Service Inc., n d. 47p.

Maryland Wine and Liquor Co.,
Here's How. Chicago, 1939. 56p. Illus.

Mascall, Leonard
A boke of the arte and manor how to plant and graffe
all sort of trees, etc. London, Thomas Wight, 1590.
84p.

Maskell, Henry Parr
The taverns of old England. London, Philip, Allen and
Co., Ltd., 1927. 235p. Illus.

Maschal, H.T.
See Brodner, Joseph Carlson, Howard M. and Maschal,
Henry T. Editors.
Profitable food and beverage operation.

Mason, Dexter
The art of drinking; or, What to make with what you
have, together with divers succulent canapés suitable to
each occasion. New York, Farrar and Rinehart, 1930.
76p.

_____ .
Tipple and snack, good things to eat and better things
to drink. New York, Farrar and Rinehart Inc., 1931.
83p.
Mason, Simon
The good and bad effects of tea considered. London,
1745. 52p.   BM
Mass-observation
The pub and the people; a Worktown study. London, V.
Gollancz, Ltd., 1943. 350p. Illus. List of relevant
references.
Massee, William Edman
Massee's guide to eating and drinking in Europe.
New York, McGraw-Hill Book Co., 1963. 219p.

_____ .
Massee's wine-food index. New York, McGraw-Hill,
1962. 203p. Illus-drawings.

_____ .
Wine handbook. Garden City, N.Y., Doubleday, 1961.
217p. Illus-drawings.

_____ .
Wines and spirits; a complete buying guide. New York,
McGraw-Hill, 1961. 427p. Illus-drawings. Biblio-
graphy. Pronunciation guide.
Massel, A.
Applied wine chemistry and technology. London,
Heidelberg Publishers, Inc. 1969. 288p. Illus-drawings.
Advertising Bibliography and Glossary.

_____ .
Dicta technica. Modern techniques in the beverage
industry. 2nd edition. London, Oenological Research
Labs, 1967. 95p. Technical Terms.
Masson, Paul
See Reeve, Lloyd Eric.
Gift of the grape;
Massingham, H. J.
The English countryman; a study of the English tradi-
tion. London, Batsford, 1942. 148p. Illus.

281

Master Brewers Ass'n of America
    See Vogel, Edward H.
    The practical brewer, a manual for the brewing
    industry.

_____ .
    Proceedings annual convention.
    1935 Cincinnati Illus-photos 115p.
    1937 Milwaukee Illus-photos 95p.
    1938 Buffalo Illus-photos 152p.
    1941 Baltimore Illus-photos 120p.

_____ .
    Technical proceedings.
    1955 San Francisco 100p. 48th annual conv.
    1961 Montreal 103p. 74th anniversary. Illus.
Masters, James E.
    Old English wines and cordials. Rules and receipts for
    making, etc. Original 1737. Reprint Bristol, Light-
    house Press, 1938. 31p.   (Harvard Univ.)
Masters, J.W.
    Run through Assam tea gardens, 1863.   BM
Masters, T.
    Short treatise concerning some patent inventions
    applicable to ice, artificial cold, soda water, etc.
    London, Masters and Co., 1850. 112p.   NYPL

_____ .
    The ice book. London, Simpkin, Marshall and Co.,
    1844. 198p.

_____ .
    Patent inventions and apparatus for production of ice
    and artificial cold, soda water, lemonade and all
    aerated beverages, etc. London, Published by author,
    1850. 120p. Illus.
Masurovsky, B. I.
    Sherbets, water ices, and modern soda fountain
    operation. Milwaukee, The Olsen Publ. Co., 1933.
    188p. Bibliography.
Mathias, Peter
    The brewing industry in England, 1700-1830.
    Cambridge, University Press, 1959. 595p. Illus.
    Bibliography.
Matthews, Charles George
    Manual of alcoholic fermentation and the allied indus-
    tries. London, E. Arnold, 1902. 295p. Illus.

The microscope in the brewery and malt-house, by
Chas. Geo. Matthews and Francis Edw. Lott. London,
Bemrose, 1889. 198p. Illus. Glossary. 2nd edition,
1899. 252p. Illus.
Matthews, John
   Aerated beverages. Instructions to operators, etc.,
   Containing Catalogue no. 1 and catalogue no. 2. New
   York, 1876. 64, 112, 80p. Illus-engravings.

   See Chester, Thomas
   Carbonated beverages. The art of making, dispensing,
   and bottling soda-water, mineral-waters, ginger-ale and
   sparkling liquors.

   See Carbonated Drinks. An illustrated quarterly gazette.
   New York, 1877-1881. Volumes I, II, III, IV, V. Illus.

   Catalogue of soda water apparatus. New York, 1868.
   64p. Illus-engravings.

   Directions for using Matthew's machines for making
   soda water, etc. New York, 1866. 18p.

   Instructions for operators of Matthews' apparatus for
   manufacturing, dispensing and bottling soda water.
   New York, E. D. Slater, printer, 1874. 64p. Illus.
                                                           LC

   Matthrews' illustrated catalogue and price list no. 1.
   of apparatus for making, cooling and dispensing soda
   water and other aerated beverages. New York, 1873.
   unpaged Illus. 1891, 223p. Illus.

   The Matthews' syrup book; instructions for making
   sirups and beverages for bottling and dispensing. New
   York, Lehmaier and Bro., printers, 1890. 26p.
   Illus.   LC

   Soda water. Is it a wholesome beverage? New
   York, 1871. 10p.   LC
Matthews, John Apparatus Co.
   Book of directions for carbonated beverages. New
   York, January 1895. 126p. Illus.

_____.
Catalogue and price list of apparatus, machinery and materials for making and serving carbonated beverages. New York, n d, (1894). 245p. Illus.

_____.
Soda water apparatus and machinery. New York, n d, ca1890. unpaged (16).

Mattice, Marjorie
See Bridges, Milton Arlanden
Food and beverage analyses. 3rd edition, thoroughly rev. by Marjorie R. Mattice.

Matz, B. W.
Dickensian inns and taverns. 2nd edition. London, Cecil Palmer, 1923. 280p. Illus.

_____.
The inns and taverns of "Pickwick". 2nd edition. London, Cecil Palmer, 1922. 251p. Illus.

Maupin, Mr.
L'Art de la vigne. Paris, Chez Musier, 1780. (In French). 136p. 1779, 100p. (contains Moyen certain et Fonde Parms, 1781. 72p.)

Maurer, Edward S.
Perfumes and their production. London, United Trade Press, 1958. 320p.   LC

Maurice, Arthur Bartlett, Ed.
How they draw prohibition. New York. The Association Against the Prohibition Amendment, 1930. unpaged - cartoons.

Maveroff, Piaggio Achilles
Enologia, Mendoza, 1949. 511p.
                                    (National Agricultural Library)

Max Henius Memoir Committee
Max Henius. A Biography. (Beer brewing). Chicago, 1936. (400 copies - copy no. 200). 221p. Illus.

Maxwell, George A.
Winery accounting and cost control. New York, Prentice Hall Inc., 1946. 137p.   LC

Maxwell, Sir Herbert
Half-A-Century of Successful Trade. (W. and A. Gilbey)., 1857-1907. Director's edition. London, Published by W. and A. Gilbey Ltd., 1907. 85p. Illus.

_____.
Three fourths of a century of successful trade. (Liquor). London, W. and A. Gilbey, 1929. 112p.
                                                        (Davis)

284

Maxwell, John, Ed.
   The Gold Coast handbook 1928. Westminster.
   Published for the government of the Gold Coast
   by the Crown Agents for the Colonies, 1928.
   528p. Illus.
Maxwell, Kenneth
   Fairest vineyards. (Description of the products of the
   Cape of Good Hope.) Johannesburg, Hugh Keartland
   Publishers, Ltd., 1966. 84p. Illus.
May, Earl Chapin
   The canning clan. New York, The Macmillan Co.,
   1937. 487p. Bibliography.
May, Richard, the brewer
   Brewer and victualler guide. London, Printed for
   author, 1780. 83p.   BM
May, W. J.
   Vine culture for amateurs by a practical hand. London,
   1875.   BM
Mayabb, James E.
   International cocktail specialties, from Madison
   Avenue to Malaya. New York, Hearthside Press,
   1962. 125p. Illus.
Maynard, S. T.
   The practical fruit grower. New York, Orange-Judd Co.
   1904. 124p. Illus-engravings.
Maynard, Theodore
   A tankard of ale; an anthology of drinking songs.
   New York, McBride, 1920. 205p.
Mazade, Marcel
   First steps in Ampelography. A guide to facilitate the
   recognition of vines. Published in Melbourne by
   authority of Dept. of Agriculture-Vitacultural Station,
   Rutherglen, Victoria. Translated by Raymond Dubois
   and W. Percy Wilkinson, 1900. 95p. Illus-drawings.
Mead, Peter B.
   An elementary treatise on American grape culture and
   wine making. New York, Harper and Brothers, 1867.
   483p. Illus-engravings.
Mead, William E.
   English medieval feast. London, G. Allen; M. Unwin,
   1931. 272p.   BM
Meade, G. P.
   See Spencer, Guilford L. and Meade, George P.
   Cane sugar handbook. A manual for cane sugar
   manufacturers and their chemists.

Meadowcroft, W. and Son Ltd.
Instructions for the manufacture of aerated beverages,
mineral waters, fruit syrups, (or wines) and cordials.
Blackburn, Lancs, January 1924. 70p.

_____ .
Modern aerated water machinery and appliances.
Catalogue no. 72, Blackburn, England, 1922. 156p.
Illus-photos.
Mearns, John
Treatise of the pot culture of the grape. London, 1843.
BM
Medbury, Henry E. Ed.
The manufacture of bottled carbonated beverages.
Washington, American Bottlers of Carbonated
Beverages, 1945. 17p. Illus- Selected Bibliography.
Medlock, Addison
Eat, drink and be healthy---and tomorrow you live.
Salt Lake City, 1933. 98p. LC
Meech, W. W.
Quince culture. New York, Orange-Judd Co., 1896.
180p. Illus-engravings.
Meehan, Thomas, Ed.
The gardner's monthly. (Fruit). Volume X.
Philadelphia Brinckloe and Maret, 1868. 378p.
Meighn, Moira
A little booke of conceited secrets and delightes for
ladies. (Formulary). London and Boston, The
Medici Society. Printed in England, 1928. 79p.
Meier, Frank
The artistry of mixing drinks. Paris, Fryam Press,
1936. 182p. Illus.
Melick, Henry C. W.
The sale of food and drink at common law and under
the uniform sales act. New York, Prentice Hall, Inc.,
1936. 346p. LC
Mellon, M. G.
Colorimetry for chemists. Columbus, Ohio. The G.
Frederick Smith Chemical Co., 1945. 131p. Illus.
Bibliography.
Melville, John
Guide to California wines. Garden City, N. Y.,
Doubleday, 1955. 270p. Bibliography.

_____ .
Guide to California wines. A new and revised edition
by Jefferson Morgan. San Carlos, Calif. Nourse
Publishing Co., 1968. 234p.

Mendelsohn, Oscar A.
  The dictionary of drink and drinking. London, The
  Macmillan Co., 1965. 382p. Dictionary.

_____.
  Drinking with Pepys. London, Macmillan and Co.,
  Ltd., 1963. 125p. Illus.

_____.
  The earnest drinker. A short and simple account of
  alcoholic beverages. London, George Allen and Unwin,
  1951. 241p. Glossary.

_____.
  The earnest drinker's digest. Sydney, Consolidated
  Press Ltd., 1946. 229p. Illus. Glossary.
Mennell, Robert O.
  Tea. An historical sketch. London, Effingham Wilson,
  1926. 63p. Illus.
Menon, A. K.
  Indian essential oils; a review. New Delhi, Council of
  Scientific and Industrial Research, 1960. 89p.
  Bibliography.   LC
Menzies, James
  Common things made plain. London, Groomsbridge,
  1857. 186p.   LC
Meredith, Joseph
  Treatise on the grape wine. London, George Philip
  and Son, 1876. 96p. 1881, J. C. Nimmo and Bain,
Meriton, George
  In praise of Yorkshire ale. New York, Francis
  Hillgard, 1685. 113p.   BM
Merory, Joseph
  Food flavorings; composition, manufacture, and use.
  Westport, Conn., Avi Publishing Co., 1960. 381p.
  Illus. Bibliography. 2nd edition, 1968,   478p.
Merrill, Annabel L. and Watt, Bernice K.
  Energy value of foods. Basis and derivation. USDA
  handbook no. 74, Washington, 1955. 105p.

_____.
  See Watt, Bernice K. and Merrill, Annabel L.
  Composition of foods, how, processed, prepared.
Merry, Tom
  Where to drink? (Irish bars). Dublin, 1949. 195p.
                                                           NYPL
Merrydown Wine Co.
  Merrydown, Wine of Sussex, Published by Merrydown
  Wine Co., Ltd., Horam, Sussex, 1966. 24p. Illus-
  photos.

Merz, Charles
   The dry decade. Garden City, Doubleday, Doran and
   Co., Inc., 1937. 343p.

   _____.
   The great American band wagon. New York, The John
   Day Co., 1928. 263p.
Meserole, H. H. H. and Johnson, O'Neal
   Ice cream at the drug store soda fountain. Harrisburg,
   Pa., International Ice Cream Mfgrs. Ass'n., 1933.
   2 vol.   LC
Methodist Church
   Doctrine and discipline of the Methodist church. Reprint
   from Beverage Alcohol, etc., Washington, 1957. 15p.
Mew, James
   Drinks of the world by James Mew and John Ashton
   London, The Leadenhall Press, New York, Scribner
   and Welford, 1892. 362p. Illus.
Meyden, Theodoro A.
   Trattato della natvra de Vino, etc. (Wine).
   Roma, Appresso Giacomo Mascardi, 1608. (In Italian).
   127p.
Meyer, Elise Landauer
   The art of cooking with spirits. Garden City, Double-
   day and Co., Inc., 1964. 325p. Illus.
Meyer, George J. Mfgr. Co.
   Bottle scuffing and its prevention. Bulletin no. 150,
   Cudahy, Wisc, 1950. 22p. Illus-photos.
Meyer, Jean Robert
   "Bottoms up" . . . Brooklyn, N.Y., The Jean' Robert
   Meyer-Studio, 1934. 34p. Illus.
Michael, P.
   Ices and soda fountain drinks. A treatise on the
   subject of ices, sundaes, wholesale ice cream, cordials
   and soda fountain drinks. London, Maclaren and Sons,
   Ltd., nd, ca1923. 184p. Illus.
Mida, Lee W.
   Mida's, Lee W. Continuous Directory and Merchandiser
   for the spirits and vinous industries. Chicago,
   Published by Mida's Services Inc., 1934. paged by
   sections.
Mida, William
   Wm. Mida's hand-book for wholesale liquor dealers.
   Chicago, Published by Wm. Mida. Second and
   enlarged edition, 1884. 93p.

Middleton, Scudder
  Dining, wining and dancing in New York . . . .
  New York, Dodge, 1938. 165p.
Middleton, W. H.
  Manual of coffee planting in Natal. Durban, 1866.
                                              (Money)
Milbourn, Thomas
  The Vintners' Company, their muniments, plate, and
  eminent members; with some account of the Ward
  of Vintry. Westminster, Vintners' Company, 1888.
  130p. Illus.
Miller Brewing Co.
  Heritage born and pledged anew. Milwaukee, 1955.
  31p.   (Milwaukee Public)

———.
  Miller High-Life centennial edition. 1855-1955.
  Milwaukee, 1955. 80p.   (Milwaukee Public)

———.
  Quality since 1855. Milwaukee, n d, ca1955. 24p.
                                   (Milwaukee Public)
Miller, Carey D. and Bazore, Katherine
  Fruits of Hawaii. Honolulu. Univ. Hawaii
  Agricultural Experiment Station Bulletin no. 96.
  October, 1945. 127p.
Miller, Carey D.; Bazore, Katharine and Bartow, Mary
  Fruits of Hawaii. Description, nutritive value and
  recipes. Honolulu, University of Hawaii Press,
  1965. 229p. Illus-photos. Bibliography.
Miller, Francis Justin
  Carbon dioxide in water, in wine, in beer, and in other
  beverages. Oakland, California, 1958. 49p. Illus.
  Literature cited.
Miller, James
  Alcohol: its place and power. Philadelphia, Lindsay
  and Blakiston, 1870. 179p.
Miller, Val
  Standard recipes for ice cream makers. Chicago,
  Laird and Lee, 1909. 138p.
Millis Advertising Company
  What is wrong with the bottled carbonated beverage
  industry. Indianapolis, 1928. 34p. Illus.

Mills, Frederick C.
  The wine guide; being practical hints on the purchase
  and management of foreign wines; their history, and a
  complete catalogue of all those in present use. To-
  gether with remarks upon the treatment of spirits,
  bottled beer, and cider . . . . London, Groombridge,
  and Sons, 1861. 64p.
Mills, John
  Christmas in the olden times or the Wassail Bowl.
  London, H. Hurst, 1846. 141p.   NYPL
Mills, Samuel A. Comp.
  The wine story of Australia. (Penfold and Co.,
  Winery). Sydney, Printed by Attkins, Mc Guitty, Ltd.,
  1908. 32p. Illus.
Milner, Duncan C.
  Lincoln and liquor. 2nd edition with supplement.
  Chicago, W. P. Blessing and Co., n d, ca1910.
  185p.
Miloradovich, Milo
  The art of cooking with herbs and spices. Garden
  City, N.Y., Doubleday and Co., 1951. 304p.
Ministry of Agriculture, Fisheries and Food. Great
  Britain.
  Cider apple production. Bulletin no. 104. 4th
  edition. London, HMSO, 1963. 45p. Illus.
Ministry of Food
  The advertising, labelling and composition of food.
  London, His Majesty's Stationary Office, 1949.
  81p.
Minrath, William R. Ed.
  Van Nostrand practical formulary. Princeton, N.J.,
  D. Van Nostrand Co., Inc., 1957. 336p.
Mirrlees, Emily Lina and Coker, Margeret Rosalys
  Wishful cooking. London, Faber and Faber, 1949.
  228p.
Misch, Robert Jay
  Quick guide to wine. A compact primer. New York,
  Doubleday and Co., 1966. 98p. Illus-drawings.
  PRONUNCIATION OF WINE TERMS
Misiatrus, Philander (pseud)
  Honour of the gout. (Wine). London, 1699. 42p.
                                                  GBPOL
Mitchell, C. Ainsworth
  Edible oils and fats. London, Longmans, Green and
  Co., 1918. 159p. Bibliography.

290

————. Mineral and aerated waters. London, Constable and Co., Ltd., 1913. 227p. Illus, Bibliography.

————. Oils, animal, vegetable, essential and mineral. 2nd edition. London, Sir Isaac Pitman and Sons Ltd., 1916. 138p.

————. Vinegar: its manufacture and examination. London, Charles Griffin and Co., 1916. 201p.

Mitchell, Clara G. Comp.
The way to a man's heart. Choice recipes. 4th edition. Denver, Colo. The Smith-Brooks Printing Co., 1916. 242p.

Mitchell, Donald G.
The Chocolate Industry. No. 17 in the series of American Industries. Boston, Bellman Publishing Co. 1951. 47p. Illus. Bibliography.

Mitchell, John
Treatise on the falsifications of food, etc. London, Hippolyte, Balliere, 1848. 341p.

Mitchell, J.R.
Scientific winemaking, made easy. Andover, Hampshire, Amateur Winemaker, 1969. 246p. Illus-drawings.

Mitchell, S. Weir
A Madeira party. (contains also "A little more Burgundy". New York, The Century Co., 1910. 165p.

Mitchell, Sir Thomas L.
Notes on the culture of the vine and the olive and methods of making wine and oil in Southern parts of Spain. Sydney, D. L. Welch, 1849. 28p.   ANL

Mitchells and Butlers Ltd.
Fifty years of brewing. 1879-1929. Cape Hill, 1929. 120p. Illus.

Mitzky and Co., C.
Our native grape. Rochester, N.Y., 1893. 218p.
                                                            (Davis)

"Mixer" (pseud)
See Brown, Florence Isabella
The bartender's friend.

Mittelstaedt, Otto
Technical calculations for sugar works. New York, John Wiley and Sons, 1910. 117p.

Mlle. Mixer (pseud)
> Two hundred toasts. New York, No publisher, 1906.
> unpaged (40).

Mock and Blum
> List of United States, British and German patents cover-
> ing the manufacture of non- alcoholic beers and similar
> malt beverages, including malt extracts. New York,
> 1918. 141p.   LC

Moehlman, Conrad Henry
> When all drank and thereafter. A study in prohibition
> perspective. New York, Alcohol Information Com-
> mittee, 1930. 149p.

Mogen David Wine Co.
> Food, fun and festivity with Mogen David wines and
> champagnes. Chicago, n d, (1967). 32p. Illus-
> drawings.

Mohr, Frederick
> The grape vine. Practical scientific treatise on its
> management. New York, Judd, 1867. 129p. (Davis)

Moir, William
> Brewing made easy. London, 1802. 40p.   BM

Molson, Brewery
> See Denison, Merrill
> The Barley and the Stream. The Molsom Story.

Molyneaux, E.
> Grape growing for amateurs. London, L. U. Gill,
> 1891. 124p.   BM

Molyneux, William
> Burton- on- Trent: its history, its waters, and its
> breweries. London, Trubner and Co., 1869.
> 264p. Illus.

Monahan, Michael
> Dry America. New York, Nicholas Brown, 1921.
> 174p. 1929, Same.

_____.
> A text- book of true temperance. New York, United
> States Brewers Ass'n, 1909. 216p. 1911, 323p.

Monckton, H. A.
> A history of English ale and beer. London, The
> Bodley Head, 1966. 238p. Bibliography.

_____.
> History of the English public house (A). London, The
> Bodley Head, 1969. 175p. Illus-photos.

Moncreiff, John
Inquiry into the medicinal qualities and effects of the
aerated alkaline water. Baltimore, Edward J. Coale,
1810. 102p. LC

Moncrieff, R.W.
The Chemical Senses. New York, Reprinted 1946.,
John Wiley and Sons, Inc., 424p. Glossary.

_____ .
The chemistry of perfumery materials. London,
United Trade Press Ltd., 1949. 344p. References.

_____ .
Odour preferences. London, Leonard Hill, 1966.
357p. References.

Moncure, W.A.P.
Alwood, Wm. B. and Davidson, R. J. and Moncure,
W.A.P.
The chemical composition of apples and cider.

Money, Edward
The cultivation and manufacture of tea. London, W. B.
Whittingham and Co., Calcutta, Thacker and Co.,
1878. 189p.

Monier-Williams, G. W.
Trace elements in food. New York, John Wiley and
Sons, Inc., 1949. 511p. References.

Monro, Donald
A treatise on mineral waters. London, 1770. 2 vol.
(Kirkby)

Monroe, Margaret E. and Stewart Jean
Alcohol education for the layman. A bibliography.
New Brunswick, N.J., Rutgers University Press, 1959.
166p. Recommended titles.

Monson-Fitzjohn, G.J.
Drinking vessels of bygone days. London, Herbert
Jenkins Ltd., 1927. 144p. Illus.

Montagne, Prosper with collaboration of Dr. Gottschalk.
Larousse Gastronomique. Prefaces by Auguste
Escoffier and Phileas Gilbert. Edited by Nina Froud
and Charlotte Turgeon. London, Paul Hamlyn Ltd.,
First English edition, 1963. 1098p.

Montagne, Harry
Bartender's Guide. How to mix drinks. "2 books
in one." n p, by Royal Publ. Co., 1914. Contains
Montague, Harry. The Up-to-date bartender's guide.
I. and M. Ottenheimer, 1963. 62, 64.

——————. New Bartender's Guide. Telling how to mix all the standard and popular drinks called for everyday. Baltimore, I and M Ottenheimer, 1914. Volume contains also Montague, Harry, The Up-to-date bartenderls guide. Same publisher, 1913. 62, 64.

——————. New Bartender's guide. How to mix drinks. Cover- "2 books in one." New York, Padell Book and Magazine Co., 1957. Contains Montague, Harry - The up to-date bartender's guide. I. and M. Otten- heimer, 1913. 62, 64.

Montague, J. R.
See Spalding, W. B. and Montague, J. R.
Alcohol and human affairs.

Montgomery, Edward Gerrard and Taylor, Alice M.
World trade in cocoa. Washington, Government
Printing Office, 1947. 175p. Illus.   LC

Monzert, Leonard
The independent liquorist; or The art of manufacturing
and preparing all kinds of cordials, syrups, bitters,
wines, champagne, beer, punches, tincture, extracts,
essences, flavorings, colorings. New York, John
F. Trow and Co., 1866. 193p.

——————. The licensed victualler, or the art of manufacture of all
kinds of syrups, etc. London, International Publishing
Co., n d, ca1880.   (Location Unknown)

——————. Monzert's practical distiller; an exhaustive treatise on
the art of distilling and rectifying spirituous liquors
and alcohol . . . Danbury, Conn., Behrens
Publishing Co., 193- ? 156p. Illus.

Moodie-Heddle, Enid (E. M. Heddle)
Story of vineyard. Melbourne, Cheshire, 1960. 32p.
                                                          ANL

Moody, B. E.
The origin of the 'reputed quart' and other measures.
Reprinted from Glass Technology, 1960. 28p. Illus.

——————. Packaging in glass. London, Hutchinson and Co., by
United Glass Co., 1963. 304p. Illus. Glossary.

Moon, D. J.
See Turner, B.C.A. and Moon, D. J.
Simple guide to home-made beer.

Moonen, L.
    Australian wines. Melbourne, Victoria Chamber of
    Commerce, 1883. 20p.   PLOSA
Moor, C.G. and Partridge, William
    Aids to the analysis of food and drugs. 4th edition.
    London, Bailliere, Tindall and Cox, 1918. 268p.
Moor, S.
    Publican's friend and sure guide to do well. London,
    1812. 236p.   GBPOL
Moore, Helen Watkeys
    On Uncle Sam's water wagon: 500 recipes for delicious
    drinks, which can be made at home. New York and
    London, G. P. Putnam's Sons, 1919. 222p.
Moore, John
    England's interest or the gentlemen and farmer's
    guide. London, Bettesworth, 1707. 166p. (Crerar)
Moore, John, ed.
    Whitbread Craftsman. Whitbread Library No. 5.
    London, Whitbread and Co., Ltd., 1948. 40p. Illus.
Moore, Lew Comp.
    Dictionary of foreign dining terms. A concise guide
    to the food and wines of 15 nations. London, W. H.
    Allen, 1958. 133p.

———·
    Diners' dictionary of foreign terms. New York,
    Sterling Publishing Co., 1958. 127p.
Moore, Philip
    The hope of health. London, J. Kingston, 1565.
    64p.   BM
Moore, R.
    The Artizans' guide and everybody's assistant.
    Montreal, John Lovell, 1873. 284p.

———·
    Everybody's guide; or, things worth knowing. New
    York, The World, 1884. 410p.

———·
    The Universal assistant, etc. New York, J. S.
    Ogilvie, (1905). 1016p.
Moore, Roy W.
    Down from Canada came tales of a wonderful beverage.
    New York, Published by The Newcomen Society in
    North America, 1961. 28p.
Moorman, John Jennings
    Mineral springs of North America; how to reach, and
    how to use them. Philadelphia Lippincott, 1873.
    294p. Illus.

——————.
The mineral waters of the United States and Canada,
with a map and plates, and general directions for
reaching mineral springs. Baltimore, Kelly and Piet,
1867. 507p.

Moppett, H. J.
Tea manufacture. Its theory and practice in Ceylon.
Second edition. Colombo, The Times of Ceylon
Co., Ltd., 1931. 108p. Illus.

More, Jonas
Cyder book. (Compleat cyderman).
(Warner- Liquor cult and its culture)

Moreira, Nicolau J.
Brazilian coffee. "O Novo Mundo". New York, n d,
ca1875. 11p.

Morel, Julian J.
Progressive catering. A comprehensive treatment of
food, cookery, drink, catering services and management.
Edited by W. Bently Capper. London, The Caxton
Publishing Co., Ltd., 1952. 4 vol. 318, 353, 378,
406. Illus- photos drawings.

Morewood, Samuel
An essay on the inventions and customs of both ancient
and moderns in the use of inebriating liquors, etc.
London, Longman, Hurst, Rees, Orme, Brown and
Green, 1824. 375p. Illus.

——————.
A philosophical and statistical history of the inventions
and customs of ancient and modern nations in the manufacture and use of inebriating liquors; with the present
practice of distillation in all its varieties. Dublin,
W. Curry, Jr., and W. Carson, 1838. 745p. Illus.

Morfit, Campbell
Perfumery: its manufacture and use . . . Philadelphia,
Carey and Hart, 1847. 285p. Illus.

Morgan, Agnes Fay and Hall, Irene Sanborn
Experimental Food study. New York, Farrar and Rinehart, 1938. 414p.

Morgan, Dan (pseud)
The complete bartender's joke book. New York,
Stravon Publishers, 1952. 128p. Illus.

Morgan, J.
See Melville, John.
Guide to California wines.

Morgan, Louise
    Home-made wines. London, Hutchinson, 1959.
    167p. Illus.
Morgan, P.C.
    Handbook of statistics and information relating to the
    trade in alcoholic liquors. London, J. S. Phillips,
    1892. 71p.   BM
Morgan, R. Harold
    Beverage manufacture (non-alcoholic). London, Att-
    wood and Co., Ltd., 1938. 240p.

_____ .
    Hygiene in soft drinks manufacture. London, National
    Association of Soft Drinks Manufacturers, 1947. 15p.
Moritz, Edward R.
    Technology of brewing. London, 1894. 20p.   GBPOL
Moritz, Edward Ralph and Morris, George Harris
    A text-book on the science of brewing. London, E. and
    F. N. Spon, 1891. 534p. Illus.
Moroney, James
    Price List of finest old wines and spirits. Philadelphia,
    n d, ca1899. 48p.
Morrice, Alexander
    A practical treatise on brewing. Also Summary of laws
    relating to brewers. 7th edition. London, Sherwood,
    Gilbert and Piper, 1827. 262p.

_____ .
    A practical treatise on brewing the various sorts of
    malt liquors, etc. 6th edition. London, Sherwood,
    Noely and Jones, 1819. 224p. Illus.
Morris, Sir Daniel
    Cocoa, how to grow and how to cure. Kingston, A. W.
    Gardner, 1887. 42p.   NYPL
Morris, Denis
    The French vineyards. London, Eyre and Spottiswoods,
    1958. 223p. Illus. Bibliography.
Morris, G. H.
    See Moritz, Edward Ralph and Morris, George Harris
    A text-book on the science of brewing.
Morris, George Simpson
    The bottlers' formulary; practical recipes, formulas
    and processes for making the soluble flavors used in
    the manufacture of carbonated beverages. Kansas
    City, Kan. The Morris Chemical Co., 1910. 88p.
    Advertising matter.   LC

Morris, Thomas
Principles of food preservation. New York, D. Van
Nostrand, 1933. 239p. LC

Morris, William
Praise of wine. Los Angeles, Ward Ritchie Press,
1958. 11p. (Napa)

Morrison, John
Beer duty tables for use of members of excise branch.
Preston, Snape and Co., 1882. 197p. BM

Morrison, R. D.
Tea, its production and marketing. London, Tea
Centre, 1946. 24p. (National Agricultural Library

_____.
Tea: memorandum relating to the industry and tea
trade of the world. London, International Tea Committee, 1943. 90p. LC

Morrison, Plummer and Co.
The druggists ready reference. Description and prices
all druggists sundries and materials. Published by
Morrison, Plummer. Chicago, 1882. 554p.

Morrissey, Charles T. and Co.
Morrissey's catalogue and net wholesale price list.
Preparations for making delicious drinks. Chicago,
n d, ca1916. 16p. Illus-photos.

Morrow, Honore W.
Tiger! Tiger! The life story of Henry B. Gough.
New York, William Morrow and Co., 1930. 296p.

Mortimer, W. Golden
Peru. History of Coca. New York, J. H. Vail and C
1901. 576p. Bibliography.

Mortlock, Geoffrey, Comp.
The flowing bowl, a book of blithe spirits and blue
devils; by Geoffrey Mortlock and Stephen Williams.
London, New York, Hutchinson, 1947. 259p.

Morton, Alexander
Just what you want to know about wine. New York, T.
McMullen and Co., 1890. 16p. LC

Morton, Dorothy
Catering for the young. London, T. Werner Laurie
Ltd., 1930. 189p.

Morwyng, Peter
A new booke of distillatyen of waters, etc. Treasure
of Euonymus, 1559. 408p. GBPO

Moseley, Benjamin
  A treatise concerning the properties and effects of
  coffee. 5th edition. London, J. Sewall, 1792. 80p.
Mott, Edward Spencer
  Cakes and ale; a dissertation on banquets interspersed
  with various recipes, more or less original, and
  anecdotes, mainly veracious, 4th edition. New York,
  Duffield, 1897. 282p.

————————.
  The flowing bowl; a treatise on drinks of all kinds and of
  all periods, interspersed with sundry anecdotes and
  reminiscences. London, G. Richards, 1903. 243p.
  1899, New York, Duffield
Mottram, V. H. and Graham, George
  Hutchison's food and the principles of dietetics.
  10th edition. London, Edward Arnold and Co., 1948.
  727p.
Moubray, Bonington (pseud). (John Lawrence)
  Practical instructions in brewing ale and table beer
  for the use of private families. Second title - Every
  Man his Own Brewer. London, Sherwood, Jones
  and Co., 1824. 59p.

————————.
  A practical treatise on breeding, rearing and fattening
  all kinds of domestic poultry, pheasants, pigeons
  and rabbits; etc., with instructions for the private
  brewery on cider, perry and British wine making. 7th
  edition. London, Sherwood, Gilbert, and Piper, 1834.
  467p. Illus.
Moufet, Thomas
  Healths improvement or rules, etc. London, 1655.
  296p.   BM
Moulton, Thomas
  This is the Myrrour of Glasse of health necessary.
  (Food and drink). London, Robert Wyer, 1539.
  no pagination   BM
Mouquin, Incorporated
  The Mouquin Epicure. An unusual recipe book.
  Brooklyn, 1933. unpaged (32).
Mouraille, L. P.
  Practical guide to treatment of wine in English cellars.
  London, Simpkin, Marshall and Co., 1889-90. 124p.
                                                   NYPL

Mournetas, Andre and Pelisier, Henry
    The vade-mecum of the wine lover. Paris, Edited
    by La Conception Publicitaire, 1953. 64p. Illus.
Mowat, Jean, Ed.
    Anthology of wine. Essex, Houldershaw, n d. 78p.
    Illus.
Mowbray, E. G. B. de.
    Notes on tea manufacture. Colombo, The Times of
    Ceylon, 1934. 68p. Illus.
Moxon, Elizabeth
    English housewifery. Leeds, Griffith and Wright,
    1764. 203p.   GBPOL
Moyen - Certain et Fonde
    See Maupin, Mr.
    L'Art de la vigne.
Moyls, A. W.
    See Atkinson, F. E. Britton, Dorothy and Moyls, A.W.
    Fruit juices, cider and wines.
Muckensturm, Louis Jaques
    Louis' mixed drinks, with hints for the care and serving
    of wines. Boston, New York, H. M. Caldwell Co.,
    1906. 113p.
Mueller, Charles Christopher
    Experts home complete American drink mixers' guide.
    New York, National Alcoholic Drinks Publications, 1937.
    107p.   NYPL

_____.
    Pioneers of mixing at elite bars. Assisted by Albert
    Hoppe, A.V. Guzman and James Cunningham. New
    York, Published by Trinity Press, 1934. volumes,
    Illus.
Mueller, C.C. and Hoppe, A.L.
    Pioneers of mixing cognac, etc. New York, National
    Alcoholic Drinks Publication, 1936. 56p.   NYPL

_____.
    Pioneers of mixing gin, etc. New York, 1936.
    National Alcoholic Drinks Publication. 63p.   NYPL

_____.
    Pioneers of mixing Irish and Scotch whiskeys. New
    York, National Alcoholic Drinks Publication, 1936.
    58p.   NYPL

_____.
    Pioneers of mixing liqueurs and cordials. National
    Alcoholic Drinks Publication, New York, 1934. 63p.
                                                    NYPL

_____.
Pioneers of mixing rums. New York, National
Alcoholic Drinks Publication, 1936. 64p.   NYPL

_____.
Pioneers of mixing whiskeys, ryes and bourbons.
New York, National Alcoholic Drinks Publication,
1934. 107p.   NYPL

_____.
Pioneers of mixing wines. New York, National
Alcoholic Drinks Publication, 1934. 111p.   NYPL

Mueller, Wolf
    Bibliographie des Kaffee, des Kakao, des Schokolade,
    des Tee, etc. from 1900. Bad Boklet, Austria
    Walter Krieg Verlag, 1960. 225p. Illus.

_____.
    Bibliographie des Kakao, etc. 1500 to 1950. Hamburg,
    Verlag Gordian-Max Rieck, 1951. 146p.

Muir, Augustus
    How to choose and enjoy wine. London, Odhams
    Press, 1953. 160p. Illus. Dictionary of Wine.

Mulder, Gerardus Johannes
    The chemistry of wine. London, J. Churchill, 1857.
    390p.

Muldoon, Hugh C.
    Lessons in pharmaceutical latin, etc. 4th edition.
    New York, John Wiley and Sons, 1946. 256p.
    Dictionary.

Muller, Arno
    Internationaler Riechstoff-Kodex. International
    compendium of aromatic materials. Heidelberg,
    Dr. Alfred Huthig Verlag, 1942. (In German).
    318p.

Mulqueen, J. T. Ed.
    The Revenue Review. (Periodical). Bound volumes
    III and IV. Falkirk. George Inglis. Publ. 1904 and
    1905. 894, 864 ps.

Mumford, P. M.
    See Anon
    The cider factory, plant and layout.

Munson, T. V.
    Foundations of American grape culture. Denison,
    Texas. T. V. Munson and Son, 1909. 252p. Illus.

Murneek, A. E.
    See Talbert, T.J. and Murneek, A.E.
    Fruit crops principles and practices of orchard and
    small fruit culture.

301

Murphy, D. F.
   The Australian wine guide. Melbourne, Sun Books, 1968
   215p. Illus-photos, Bibliography.
Murray, J. A.
   Beverages. (Soft drinks). London, Constable and Co.,
   1912. 84p.   LC
Murray, John, MD
   A system of materica medica and pharmacy. 4th
   edition. Volume II. Edinburgh, Adam Black, 1822.
   568p.
Murray, John A.
   Report by Thomas Tucker upon the settlement of
   revenues of excise and customs in Scotland, 1656.
   Edinburgh, Printed for The Bannatyne Club, 1825.
   68p.
Murray, Marr
   Drink and the war from patriotic point of view.
   London, Chapman and Hall, 1915. 156p.
                          (Institute Brewing Library)
Mulder, Gerardus
   Chemistry of animal and vegetable physiology.
   Edinburgh and London, W. Blackwood and Sons, 1845.
   827p.   LC
Munch, Frederick
   School for American grape culture. St. Louis, C.
   Witter, 1865. 139p.   LC
Munro, Norman L.
   How to carve and how to serve a dinner; also how to
   brew; from a barrel of beer to a bowl of bishop.
   New York, Published by author, 19--. 56p. Illus.
                                                           LC
Murray, Samuel W.
   Wines of the U.S.A., how to know and choose them.
   Concord, Mass., Wine Press, 1957. 31p. Illus.
Muspratt, Dr. Sheridan
   Chemistry, theoretical, practical and analytical as
   applied to and relating to the arts and manufactures.
   Glasgow, William Mackenzie, 1803. 2 vol. (836,
   1136), Illus.
Mustard, M. J.
   See Lynch, S. John and Mustard, M. J.
   Mangos in Florida
Myers, Fred L. and Son
   Jamaica rum cocktails. Kingston, n d. 8p.

302

_____ Myers' Jamaica rum cocktails, etc. Kingston, n d.
24p. Illus.

_____ Myers' Jamaica rum recipes. (Kingston), n d. 16p.
Myrick, Herbert
    The hop. Springfield, Mass. Orange Judd Publishing
    Co., 1899. 300p.   NYPL
Myrtle, Andrew Scott
    Practical observations on Harrogate waters. London,
    John Churchill and Sons, 1867. 98p.

Naironus, A. F.
    Discourse on coffee, its description and virtues.
    London, Abel Roper, 1710. 33p.   BM
Nash, Dr. Elwin H. T.
    Dr. Nash's Cookery Book. London, Simpkin,
    Marshall Ltd., n d, ca1937. 183p.
Nash, Harvey
    Alcohol and caffeine. A study of their psychological
    effects. Springfield, Ill., Charles C. Thomas, 1962.
    169p. References.
Nash, John
    Brewer's license, its history, etc., London, 1873.
    11p.   BM

_____ Facts and falacies regarding brewer's license tax.
    London, 1874. 25p.   BM
National Aniline and Chemical Company, Inc.
    National Certified food colors. New York, 1922.
    5p. and 2 color cards. ca1930, 18p. Illus.
National Analine Division. Allied Chemical and Dye Corp.
    National Certified Colors. New York, 1952. 24p.
    Illus.

_____ National certified food-drug and cosmetic colors. Card
    no. 242. New York, n d. Color cards unpaged (6p
    plus 8 cards).
National Association of Soft Drinks Manufacturers, Ltd.
    The rules, 1946. List of members, 1951. London.

_____ Simple costings in the soft drinks industry. London,
    1953. 33p. fold-out forms.

——————.

See Craig, Elizabeth

Sip softly.

——————.

See Curtis, Kenneth, J.

The soft drinks industry legal handbook.

——————.

See Penn, Kenneth, Ed.

The soft drinks trade manual.

——————.

See Anon.

What's in a soft drink!

National Automatic Merchandising Ass'n.

Blue book of automatic merchandising.   Published by
The Association.   Chicago, 1962.   200p.

National Book League

Food and wine.   An exhibition of rare printed books
assembled and annotated by Andre L. Simon.   London,
1961.   60p.   Bibliography.

National Bottlers' Gazette

Bottler's Sales Manual.   New York, 1947.   143p.
Illus-photos.

National Brewers' Academy and Consulting Bureau

Practical points for brewers, a reference book for all
interested in the arts of brewing and malting, compiled
by the staff of the National Brewers' Academy, editors:
Emil Schlichting and H. Winther.   New York, 1938.
174p.   Advertising matter.

——————.

Practical points for practical brewers.   A reference
book for all interested in the arts of brewing and
malting.   Editors, Francis Wyatt and Emil Schlicting.
New York, 1909.   176p.

National Brewing Co.

See Anon.

Brew in your stew.

National Canners Ass'n.

See Anon.

Canner's Directory.

——————.

See Anon.

Dietetic Canned Foods.

National Coffee Department of Brazil

Coffee facts and fancies.   New York, Originally
published by Pan-American Coffee Bureau, n d.   16p.

National Council of Applied Economic Research
Economically weak tea gardens in North-East India.
New Delhi, 1961. 83p.
National Distiller Products Corp.
The Host's handbook. 4th edition. New York, 1940.
56p. Illus.

—————— .
Mine Host's Handbook. New York, 1936. 51p. Illus.
National Federation of Coffee Growers of Columbia
Columbia, land of coffee. Bogota and New York.
Reprinted 1949. (Courtesy of American Can Co.)
32p. Illus.

—————— .
The land of coffee. New York, 1932. 24p. Illus.
National Federation of Women's Institutes
Home made wines, syrups, and cordials; recipes of
Women's Institute members, edited by F. W. Beech.
London, 1954. 117p. Illus.
National Food and Nutrition Institute
Proceedings. U.S. Dept. Agri. Handbook no. 56,
1953. Washington. 161p.
National Fruit and Cider Institute
Annual reports. 1917, 1947, 1949. Long Ashton,
Bristol. 1917, 92p; 1947, 241p; 1949, 174p.
Illus-photos. List of publications.
National Mineral Water Trade Guild
See National Union of Mineral Water Mfgrs. Ass'ns Ltd.
The organization of the mineral water industry and The
National Mineral Water Trade Guild.
National Temperance Society
Bible wines. A series of 8 pamphlets. New York,
1869-1894.   LC
National Trade Development Ass'n.
Innkeeping. A manual for licensed victuallers.
Edited by Brian Spiller, London, Barrie and Rockliff,
1964. 243p. Illus.
National Training School for Cookery
See Anon.
Official handbook for the National Training School for
Cookery.

—————— .
See Clarke, Mrs. Edith
Plain cookery recipes.

National Union of Mineral Water Mfgs. Ass'ns Ltd.
The organization of the mineral water industry and The National Mineral Water Trade Guild. (Organization Birmingham, 1936-1937), (National Mineral, etc. Leeds, 1925). 8p. and 20p.

National Wine Boards of Portugal
Wines of Portugal. Lisbon, Junta Nacional do Vinho, 1948. Unpaged. Illus.

de Navarre, M. G.
Emulsions. Bulletin no. 7. New York, The American Perfumer, September 1938. 26p. Illus.

Naves, Y. R.
Natural perfume materials; a study of concretes, resinoids, floral oils and pomades, by Dr. Y. R. Naves and G. Mazuyer. New York, Reinhold Publishing Corp., 1947. 338p. Illus. Bibliographical references.

Neave, G. B. and Heilbron, I. M.
The identification of organic compounds. London, Constable and Co., 1911. 103p.

Necker, Walter L. and Wynn, Elizabeth, Compilers
List of periodicals currently received in the library branch of the Institute. Chicago, Quartermaster Food and Container Institute. September, 1961. 34p.

Needham, J.
Directions for brewing with Needham-Rawlings Co., patent machine. London, 1813. 14p.   GBPOL

Neergaard, William
Formula book of elixirs, syrups, wines, etc. New York, Sidney H. Neergaard, n d. 12p.

Neil, Marion H.
Canning, preserving and pickling. Philadelphia, David McKay, 1914. 284p.

Nelson, Charles B.
The instructor. Recipes, how to mix, handle and serve . . . contains over 500 drinks. Kansas City, Mo. Nease Printing Co., 1933. 25p.   LC

Nelson, John H.
The Druggist's hand-book of private formulas. Revised Edition. New York, J. H. Vail and Co., 1882. 338p.

Nesbit, W. B.
Drink, Chicago, Volland and Co., 1911. 48p.   LC

Nesbit, Wilbur D.
After dinner speeches, and how to make them. Chicago, The Reilly and Lee Co., 1927. 238p.

Nessel, Mathieu
Treatise concerning the medicinal Spaw waters, etc.
London, 1715. 56p. GBPOL
Nestlé Company
Perfect endings; chocolate dessert and beverage cookbook. New York, 1962. 192p. Illus-photos.
Nettleton, Joseph A.
Adulteration of beer by publicans. London, Published
by author, 1887. 29p. NYPL

——————. Condensing and cooling in distillation, 1897.
(Nettleton- Mfg. whisky 1913)

——————. Every brewer his own analyst. London, Ford Shapland
and Co., 1884. 61p. BM

——————. Flavour of whisky, 1894.
(Nettleton- Mfg. whisky 1913)

——————. Manufacture of spirit as conducted at various distilleries
of the United Kingdom. London, M. Ward and Co.,
1893. 431p. NYPL

——————. The preservation of hops, 1891.
(Nettleton- Mfg. of whisky 1913)

——————. Study of history and meaning of expression "Original
Gravity". London, A. Lampray, 1881. 72p. GBPOL

——————. A study of the lost art of brewing, etc. London, 1883.
BM

——————. The manufacture of whisky and plain spirit. Successor
to Mfg. of spirit in United Kingdom 1893. Aberdeen,
G. Cornwall and Sons, 1913. 606p. Illus.

——————. A study of the history and of the art of brewing. London
Ford, Shapland and Co., 1883. 61p.
Neubert, A. M.
See Smock, R. M. and Neubert, A. M.
Apples and apple products.
Neumann, Ruth Vendley
Cooking with spirits. Chicago, Reilly and Lee, 1961.
249p.

Neumann, Ruth Vendley
Cooking with spirits. Chicago, Reilly and Lee, 1961.
249p.
Nevile, Sir Sydney Oswald
Seventy rolling years. (Beer and brewing). London,
Faber and Faber, 1958. 288p. Illus.
New York Agricultural Experiment Station
Annual report. (14th), for year 1895. Albany and
New York, 1896. 666p.

_____.
Grape varieties . . . introduced by the New York
State Agricultural Experiment Station, 1928-1961.
Bulletin No. 794. Geneva, New York, 1962. 47p.
Illus.
New Zealand, Dept. of Agriculture
Grape growing in the home garden, by F. Berry-
Smith. Bulletin no. 291. Auckland. 1957. 15p. Illus.
Newcombe, F.
The dairyman's guide to Orange drink production.
Bradford, Yorkshire, ESSONIA, W. Ryder and Co.,
1955. 33p.

_____.
The 'Know-how of lollie ice manufacture. Bradford,
Yorkshire, ESSONIA, W. Ryder and Co., 1956.
35p. Illus.
Newcombe, Frederick N.
The licensing question, its history, its laws, etc.
London, Pewtress and Co., 1883. 126p.
Newell, Robert C.
Gin and bear it! New London, Ct. Arthur C. Croft
Publications, 1954. 48p. Illus.
Newhall, Charles S.
The vines of northeastern America. New York, G.P.
Putnam's Sons, 1897. 207p. Illus. Glossary.
Newland, H. Osman
Planting, expression and culture of coconuts. London,
Charles Griffin and Co., 1919. 111p.   (Crerar)
Newlands, John A. R. and E. R. Benjamin
Sugar. A handbook for planters and refiners. London,
E. and F. Spon Ltd., 1909. 876p.
Newman, Henry W.
Acute alcoholic intoxication. Stanford University,
California, Stanford University Press, 1941. 207p.
References.

Newman, Lewis F.
Newman's book on scientific barkeeping containing a full
and complete list of standard and fancy drinks and
syrups, and the way to make and serve them.
Fayetteville, N. C. Fayetteville Printing and Publishing
Co., 1891.   72p.   LC
Newmark, A.
Tannin and its uses in wine.   Fairfield, Australia.
The Newmark Chemical Lab., 1935.   31p.
Newnham, William
Some observations on the medical and dietary properties
of green tea.   London, 1827.   32p.   GBPOL
Newton, E. E.
A short account of Twinings in the Strand.   London,
R. Twining and Co., Ltd., 1922.   20p.
Newton, J. Challender
Homemade wines.   London, Chiswick Polytechnic
School of Art, 1935.   22p.   BM
Newton, William of Truro
Teetotalism.   An essay on the impropriety of making
and using intoxicating liquors.   Falmouth, Published by
author, 1839.   23p.
Nicholls, Henry A.
On cultivation of Liberian coffee in West Indies.   London
Silver and Co., 1881.   31p.   BM

_____.
Textbook of tropical agriculture.   London, Macmillan
1929.   629p.   BM
Nicholls, John Ralph
Aids to the analysis of food and drugs.   7th edition.
London, Bailliere, Tindall and Cox, 1952.   516p.
Nichols, William B. and Co.
The brewing industry; a brief survey of markets,
distribution methods, etc.   New York, 1933.   20p.

                                                        LC
Nicol (R).
Treatise on coffee.   London, Baldwin and Cradock,
1831.   33p.   BM
Niehaus, G.
See Theron, Christian J. and Niehaus, Charles G.
Wine making.
van Niekerk, J.A.H.
A survey of the control of alcoholic beverages in other
countries.   Johannesburg, Brewer's Institute of South
Africa, 1958.   265p.   Bibliography.

"Nirvana"
Chocolate making. A comprehensive treatise on the
making of chocolate goods. London, The British Baker-
(Maclaren and Sons), n d, ca1920. 181p. Illus.
Nisbet, William MD
A practical treatise on diet, etc. London, R. Phillips,
1801. 434p.
Nithsdale, William Henry
Practical brewing, by W. H. Nithsdale and A. J.
Manton. 3rd edition. rev. London, Food Trade Press,
1947. 244p. Illus.

——— Practical brewing and the management of British
beers. Glasgow, John Smith and Son (Glasgow), Ltd.,
1924. 152p. Glossary.
Noback, G.
Tables of results of brewing, 1881.   (Scho)
Noling, A. W.
Aromatic Chemicals. Indianapolis, Hurty- Peck and Co.,
1965. 59p.

——— Beverage base inventory control. Helpful service
bulletin no. 14. Indianapolis, Hurty- Peck and Co.,
n d, (1960). 7p. Illus.

——— Beverage bases. Indianapolis. Published by Hurty- Peck
and Co., for internal distribution only, 1961. 142p.

——— Beverage flavoring materials in the bottled carbonated
beverage industry. Washington, D. C. Published by
ABCB, 1954. 29p.

——— Beverage flavors. Indianapolis, Published by Hurty-
Peck and Co., 1946. 64p. Illus. Dictionary.

——— See Hurty- Peck and Co.
A bibliography of books and booklets on beverages,
their history and manufacture.

——— Brewing, bottling and allied trades exhibition, 1964.,
Orange, California, Published by author, 1966. 12p.
Illus.

——— Cloudy beverages. What they are and how to handle
them. Helpful Service Bulletin no. 4. Indianapolis,
Hurty- Peck and Co. nd, 1947. 8p. Illus.
310

——————.
History of Hurty-Peck and Company. Its first fifty
years. Abridged edition. Indianapolis, Hurty-Peck
and Co., 1969. 40p. Illus-photos.

——————.
History of Hurty-Peck and Company. Its first 50
years. 1903-1953. Indianapolis, Hurty-Peck and Co.,
1965. 175p. Illus-photos of plants.

——————.
See Hurty-Peck and Co.
Ice and ice-cold Tall-One.

——————.
Lemon. Notes from various trade references on lemon
and its uses. Orange, California, 1958. unpaged.

——————.
Measuring sugar content of syrup and beverages.
Indianapolis, Hurty-Peck and Co., 1961. 12p. Illus.

——————.
Measuring the acid content of soft drinks. Indianapolis,
Published by Hurty-Peck and Co., 1963. 16p. Illus.

——————.
Proposal showing profit possibilities in the development
of an organization to establish and operate a number
of bottling plants. Dayton, Ohio, September 20, 1927.
21p. includes The Tall-One Merchandising Plan 16p.

——————.
Soda water flavors. A description of what they are
and instructions in their care and use. Indianapolis,
1945. 23p.

——————.
See Tall-One (The).
Merchandising Plan.

——————.
See Tall-One Company (The).
75,000 case bottling plants. Costs and organization.
Dayton, Ohio, n d, (1928). 12p.
Noling, A. W. and Towey, J. M.
Sunstruck off-flavor in soft drinks. Helpful service
bulletin no. 13. Indianapolis, Hurty-Peck and Co.,
1958. 23p. Illus. Bibliography.
Noling, L. J.
Grape. Information about grapes, history, uses, etc.
Indianapolis, Hurty-Peck and Co., 1956. 26p.
Illus-photos, drawings.

_____.

Lemon.   Information about lemons and lemon processing.
A discussion of lemon beverage flavors and the different
types of lemon soft drinks.   Indianapolis, Hurty Peck
and Co., 1958.   27p.   Illus.   Bibliography-References.
Noolas, Rab.
    Merry-go-down.   A gallery of georgeous drunkards
    through the ages.   Limited edition 600 copies copy
    no. 68.   London, The Mandrake Press, 1930.   231p.
    Illus.
Nooth, Dr.
    See Elliot, John
    An account of the nature and medicinal values of the
    principal mineral waters of Great Britain and Ireland.
Norris, Sheila
    Your life is more pleasant with wine.   n p, Australia,
    The Australian Wine Board, n d.   unpaged (16),
    Illus-drawings-color.
North, Sterling, Ed.
    So red the nose; or, Breath in the afternoon, edited,
    by Sterling North and Carl Kroch.   New York, Farrar
    and Rinehart, 1935.   72p.   Illus.
North Dakota
    See State Laboratories Department
    Food and drug bulletins.   Bismark, N. D. From June
    1942 Annually to May 1967.   Bulletin numbers from 67
    to 150.
North Dakota Regulatory Department
    Analyses of foods and drugs also beverages, etc.
    Bulletin no. 52, Bismarck, N. D. December 1937.
    159p.
Northwestern Extract Co.
    The Norwesco Hand Book.   Milwaukee, 1923.
    126p.   Illus.

_____.

Norwesco 1947 Catalog, Reference tables.   Handbook.
Milwaukee.   52p.   Illus.
Norton, Charles
    Modern Blending and rectification, containing recipes
    and directions for producing gins, cordials, all types of
    bitters, drinking specials, and all kinds of punches, etc.
    Chicago, 1911.   106p.   Illus.

312

_____. Modern manual for rectifiers, compounders, and all
dealers in whiskies, wines and liquors. Chicago,
Foote and Salomon, 1900. 88p.   LC

_____. Modern yeasting and distillation; a work on the
manufacture of whiskey and alcohol. Chicago. Mitchell,
Larimer and Titus, printers, 1911. 68p. Illus.   LC
Nott, John
Cook's and confectioner's dictionary. London, Charles
Rivington, 1724. unpaged.   GBPOL
Notter, J. Lane and Firth, R. H.
Practical domestic hygiene. 4th edition. London,
Longmans, Green and Co., 1905. 320p. Illus.
Nowak, Carl Alfred
Modern brewing; a comprehensive reference book
dealing especially with cereal beverage manufacture in
the United States since prohibition. St. Louis, Mo.,
C. A. Nowak, 1931. 350p. Illus.

_____. Modern brewing (2nd edition). a practical hand book of
contemporary brewing practice. St. Louis, Published
by author, 1934. 318p. Illus.

_____. New fields for brewers and others active in the
fermentation and allied industries. a complete and
comprehensive reference book for beverage manufacturers
bottlers, brewers, brewing chemists, distillers, food
chemists, maltsters, students. St. Louis, Mo., C. A.
Nowak, 1917. 317p. Illus. Bibliography of related
literature and patents.

_____. Non-intoxicants; a practical manual on the manufacture
of soft drink extracts and cereal beverages. St. Louis,
Mo., C. A. Nowak, 1922. 295p. Illus. Bibliography
of related literature.

_____. Selected practical methods of manufacturing low
alcoholic malt and maltless beverages and beers, St.
Louis, Published by author, 1918.   (Scho)
Noyes, W. A.
Organic chemistry for the laboratory. Easton, Penna.
Chemical Publishing Co., 1897. 257p.

Nugey, Anthony L.
    Brewing formulas practically considered. Bayonne,
    N.J., Printed by Jersey Printing Co., Inc., 1937.
    59p. Illus. Advertising matter.
Nunn, F.J.R.
    Raw grain in brewing, 1881.   (Scho)
Nurnberg, John J.
    Crowns-the complete story. Third edition. Wilmington,
    Delaware. Published by the author, 1961. 355p.
    Illus.
Nutt, Frederic
    Receipts for homemade wines, cordials, etc. London,
    1815. 261p.   GBPOL

————————— .
    The Complete Confectioner. 6th edition. London,
    Mathews and Leigh, 1809. 261p.
N. V. Sluys Boechout
    Vade-mecum for the user of Sluys' flavours, perfume
    oils, raw materials and specialties. Boechout,
    Belgium, 1963. 113p. Illus.
Nye, Gideon, Jr.
    Tea; and the tea trade. New York, Printed by G. W.
    Wood, 1850. 56p.
Nye, Noel
    What shall we drink? London, The Temperance Council
    of Christian Churches, 1933. 60p.   NYPL

Oaks, Lewis Weston
    Medical aspects of the Latter-day saint word of
    wisdom. Provo. Brigham Young University, 1929.
    126p. Bibliography.   LC
Obsopaeo, Vincentio
    De arte bihendi. Libri tres, Avtore Francoforti ad
    Moenum, 1582. (In Latin). unpaged.
O'Connor, J. B.
    Vanilla, its cultivation in India. Calcutta, Office of
    Superintendent of Printing, 1881. 25p.   BM
Odell, George Talbot
    Beverages. A manual for mixing cocktails, etc.
    Washington, D. C. Newspaper Information Service, Inc.
    1936. 24p. Illus.

314

Oechs, Anthony and Co., Inc.
Commentary on wines. Text by Blake Ozias. New
York, 1934. 59p. Illus.
Oesterreicher and Co.
The rational manufacture of American wines. St.
Louis, 1872. 144p.   LC
Oinophilis, Boniface
See (Sallengre, Albert Hendrick de)
Ebrietatas enconium: or The praise of drunkenness,
etc.
Okakura, Kakuzo
See Kakuzo, Okakura
Okakura, Kakuzo
The book of tea. New York, Fox Duffield, 1906.
160p.
1906, London and New York, Putnam's.
1931, 15th edition, New York, Duffield
n d, Tokyo, Kenkyusha.
Olcott, Henry S.
Sorgo and imphee. The Chinese and African sugar
canes. New York, A. Moore, 1857. 350p. Illus-
engravings, drawings.
Old Bohemian (an)
Philosophy in the kitchen. General hints on food and
drink. London, Ward and Downey, 1885. 232p.
Oldham, Chas F.
California wines. A paper read before The Society
of Arts. London, No Publisher, 1894. 15p. Illus.
Oldham, Chas. H.
The cultivation of berried fruits in Great Britain.
London, Crosby Lockwood and Son, Inc., 1946.
374p. Bibliographies.
O'Leary, A. MD
Ingesta: eating and drinking, as an art instead of mere
animal indulgence. Boston, Published by author, 1866.
128p.
Oliver, Basil
The renaissance of the English public house. London,
Faber and Faber, 1947. 181p. Illus.
Oliver, William
Practical dissertation on Bathe waters. London,
Printed by J. D., 1707.   BM
Olivier, Stuart
Wine journeys. New York, Duell, Sloan and Pearce,
1949. 312p.

Olivieri, F. Emanual
Cocoa planting and its cultivation. Port of Spain,
Fair Play Types, 1897. 28p.   BM
_____.
Treatise on cocoa. 3rd edition. Trinidad, Mole
Bros., 1903. 101p.   LC
Olness, Marlene
See Liebowitz, Daniel and Brown, W. Jann and
Olness, Marlene
Cook to your heart's content on a low-fat, low-salt
diet.
Olsen, John C.
Pure foods, their adulteration. New York, Ginn and
Co., 1911. 210p.   LC
"One of the old school"
See Anon.
Wine and spirit adulterators unmasked.
One Who Knows.
"Drinks". Formulas for making "Ozonated non-
alcoholic drinks to resemble alcoholic cocktails and
mixed drinks. New York, Namreh Publishers, 1921.
96p.
O'Neill, Gil and Mercia
Cooking in wine (a bachelor's guide to), n p
Australia, J. B., Studia Productions, n d. unpaged
(334 recipes).
Oppenheim, A. L.
See Hartman, Louis Francis and Oppenheim, A. L.
On beer and brewing techniques in ancient
Mesopatamia.
Opperman, D. J. Ed.
Spirit of the vine: Republic of South Africa. Cape
Town, Human and Rousseau Publ., (Pty), Ltd., 1968.
360p. Illus-photos.
Ordish, George
Wine growing in England. London, Rupert Hart-
Davis, 1953. 128p. Illus. Bibliography.
Ordish, Olive
Aylett, Mary and Ordish, Olive
First catch your hare. A history of the recipe makers.
Organization for European Economic Cooperation
The main products of the overseas territories: cocoa,
Paris, 1956. 164p.   LC

Oriental Tea Company
    The cup that cheers but not inebriates. Story of
    Boston Tea Party, 1773. Vol. VI No. 12, December
    1873. Boston. 4p.
Orton, Vrest
    Proceedings of the company of Amateur brewers. n p.
    Privately printed, 1932 for the members of the society.
    159p. Illus.-etchings.-glossary.
Osborn, John
    Vineyards in America: with remarks on temperance--
    culture of grape vine in the United States, New York,
    Published by author, 1855. 24p.   LC
Osgood, G.
    Sterile filling. Reprinted from Brewer's Guild
    Journal, Ashton-under-Lyne, Lancs., John C.
    Carlson, Ltd., 1950. 23p. Illus.
O'Sullivan, H. D.
    The life and work of Cornelius O'Sullivan Guernsey.
    Guernsey Star and Gazette Co., Ltd., n d, ca1920.
    235p.
Oswald, Felix L.
    The poison problem or the cause and cure of in-
    temperance. New York, D. Appleton and Co., 1887.
    138p.
Other, A. N.
    Pick-me-up! London, The Centaur Press, 1933.
    unpaged (14 on one side), Illus-drawings.
Ott, Edward
    From barrel to bottle (notes on the home bottling of
    wine). London, Dennis Dobson, 1953. 61p.
    Vineyard glossary.
Otter-Swain Corporation
    Beverages-manufacture and sale. Lesson 8.
    Fruit Juices. The ninth of a series of training
    instruction in a Commercial Co-operative Service
    System. Chicago, n d. 24p.
Ough, C. S. and Amerine, M. A.
    Effects of temperature on wine making. California
    Agricultural Experiment Station Bulletin 827 Division
    of Agricultural Sciences. Univ. of California, n p,
    Berkeley or Davis, October 1966. 36p. Illus.-photos.
    Literature cited.

Ovington, J.
　　An essay upon the nature and qualities of tea.　London,
　　R. Roberts, 1699.　Facsimile 1928 with preface by
　　Augustine Birrell.　Published by the Institute of
　　Grocers, London.　39p.
Owen, Jeanne
　　The Lejon Cookbook.　Published by National Distiller
　　Products Corp., 1947.　64p.

—————·
　　A wine lover's cook book.　New York, M. Barrows
　　and Co., Inc., 1940.　197p.
Owen, R. Jonas
　　Practice of perfumery.　London, Houlston and Sons,
　　1870.　85p.　　　　　　　　　　　　　　　　　　　BM
Owen, Theodore C.
　　First years work on a coffee plantation.　Colombo,
　　A. M. and J. Ferguson, 1877.　55p.

—————·
　　Tea planter's manual.　Colombo, Allen.　London,
　　1886.　162p.　　　　　　　　　　　　　　　　　　BM
Owen, W.
　　Account of the nature, properties and uses of all
　　remarkable mineral waters in Great Britain.　London,
　　1769.　　　　　　　　　　　　　　　　　　　　　(Kirkby)
Owens-Illinois
　　See Anon.
　　Handling empty deposit bottles.
Oxford, Arnold Whitaker
　　English cookery books to the year 1850.　London,
　　Henry Froude, 1913.　192p.
Ozias, Blake
　　All about wine.　New York, Thomas Y. Crowell, 1967.
　　144p.　Illus-photos, drawings.

—————·
　　See Oechs, Anthony and Co., Inc.
　　Commentary on wines.

—————·
　　How the modern hostess serves wine.　New York,　The
　　Epicurean Press, Inc., 1934.　27p.　Illus.　　　　LC

Pabst Brewing Co.
　　A pamphlet.　(No title).　Milwaukee, 1893.　60p.
　　　　　　　　　　　　　　　　　　(Cornell University)
318

Packer, Joy
Valley of the vines. A novel about South Africa.
Philadelphia and New York, J. B. Lippincott, 1955.
278p.
Packman, W. Vance
Gentlemen's own guide to wines and spirits. London,
Published by author, 1902. 91p. BM

_____ .
Wine and spirit manual and Packman's handy agency
list. London, 1903. 264p. BM
Pacottet, Paul
Vinification. Vin, eau-de-vie, vinaigre. Paris,
Librairie J -B Bailliere et Fils., 1904. 448p.
Illus- In French.
Paddleford, Clementine
New easy ways to cook with rum. New York,
Bacardi Imports, Inc., n d. unpaged (16).
Paddock, Wendell and Orville B. Whipple
Fruit-growing in arid regions. New York, The
Macmillan Co., 1912. 395p.
Page-Croft, J.
A talk on tea. London, 1928. (Ukers-All about tea)
Paguierre, M.
Classification and description of the wines of
Bordeaux. Edinburgh, William Blackwood, 1828.
164p.
Paige, William Victor
Is this your wine? London, C. Johnson, New York,
McBride, 1957. 76p. Illus.
Painter, Orrin C.
William Painter and his father. Crowns, Baltimore,
The Arundel Press, 1914. 152p.
                                (State Library - Michigan)
Palmer, Arthur E.
Brewer's pocket companion. Wolverhampton, 1901.
128p. BM
Palmer, Carl J.
History of soda fountain industry. Chicago, Soda
Fountain Manufacturers Ass'n, 1947. 87p. LC
Palmer, J. S.
Palmer's popular receipts, proper guide for making
wines. London, 1850. 36p. GBPOL
Pan American Coffee Bureau
Annual coffee statistics. No. 25. New York, 1961.
99p.

_____. Annual coffee statistics. 30th edition. n p New York, 1966. 184p. and 198p. (tables). Illus-maps, charts.

_____. Coffee. The story of a good neighbor product. New York, 1949. 18p. Illus.

_____. Fun with coffee. New York, 1956. 32p. Illus.

_____. Impact of coffee on the U.S. economy. New York, 1962. 72p. Illus.

Papin, Denys MD
A new digester or engine for softening bones . . . cookery, voyages at sea, confectionery, making of drinks, chymistry and dying. London, Henry Bourriche, 1681. Vol. III from the Mallinkrodt Collection of Food Classics. 54p.

Park and Tilford
Wholesale price list. New York, 1894. 6p.

Parke, Gertrude
The big chocolate cookbook. New York, Funk and Wagnalls, 1968. 325p.

Parker, Cecil J.
Background to the crown. London, Published by The Crown Cork Co., Ltd., n d, ca1941. unpaged (32), Illus.

Parker, Henry
The vintner's answer to some scandulous pamphlets. London, 1642. 32p.   (Yale Univ.)

Parker, Hubert H.
The hop industry. London, P. S. King and Son Ltd., 1934. 327p. Illus. Bibliography.

✓ Parker, Milton E.
Food-plant sanitation. McGraw-Hill Book Co., 1948. 447p.

Parker, Milton E. and Harvey, E. S. and Stateler, E. S.
Elements of food engineering. Vol. 1. New York, Reinhold Publishing Co., 1952. 386p. Illus.

Parker, Robert H.
In praise of wine. (A poll of the poets). New York, Dial Press Ltd., 1933. 11p.   WI

Parkes, B.
The domestic brewer and family wine maker. London, Wetton and Jarvis, 1821. 127p. Illus.

Parkinson
See Cook and Confectioner
The Complete Confectioner by Parkinson. 154p.
Parkinson Renown
Perfect cooking with Parkinson Renown gas cookers.
Green edition. n p. Printed in Birmingham, England,
n d. 287p.
Parks, Mal, Ed.
First annual soda fountain handbook. New York,
Hearst Magazines Inc., 1942. 184p. Illus.
Parloa, Maria
Chocolate and cocoa recipes, by Miss Parloa, and
home made candy recipes, by Mrs. Janet McKenzie
Hill. Dorchester, Mass., W. Baker and Co., Ltd.,
1909. 63p. Illus.

————————.
See Baker, Walter and Co.
Choice recipes by Miss Maria Parloa.

————————.
Chocolate and cocoa recipes. Dorchester, Mass.
Walter Baker and Co., Ltd., 1922. 64p. Illus-photos.

————————.
See Baker, Walter and Co., Ltd.
Chocolate and cocoa recipes by Miss Parloa.

————————.
Choice recipes. Dorchester, Mass. Walter Baker
and Co., Ltd., 1906. 64p. Illus-photos.
Parrish, Edward
A treatise on pharmacy. 4th edition enlarged and
thoroughly revised by Thos. S. Weigand. Philadelphia,
Henry C. Lea, 1874. 977p.
Parry, Ernest John
The chemistry of essential oils and artificial perfumes.
London, Scott, Greenwood and Co., 1899. 411p. Illus.
2nd edition, 1908, 546p.
4th edition, 2 vol. 1921-1922. 549, 357p. Illus-
photos.

————————.
Food and drugs. Volume 1. The analysis of food and
drugs. Vol. II. The sale of food and drug acts, 1875-
1907. London, Scott Greenwood and Son, 1911.
Vol. 1-744p. Vol. 2-181p.

————————.
Parry's cyclopaedia of perfumery; a handbook on the
raw materials used by the perfumer. London, J. and
A. Churchill, 1925. 2 v.

―――― See Durvelle, J. P.
The preparation of perfumes and cosmetics by J. P.
Durvelle, tr. from the fourth French ed. by Ernest J.
Parry.

―――― Raw materials of perfumery (The). Their nature,
occurance and employment. London, Sir Isaac
Pitman and Sons Ltd., n d, ca1912. 112p. Illus-
photos.

Parry, J.W.
The spice handbook; spices, aromatic seeds and
herbs. Brooklyn, Chemical Publishing Co., 1945.
254p. Illus. Glossary.

Parsons, the Rev. B.
Anti-bacchus: an essay on the crimes, diseases and
other evils connected with the use of intoxicating
drinks. London, John Snow, 1843. 136p.

Parsons, H.
Grapes under glass. London, W. H. and L.
Collingridge Ltd., 1955. 64p. Illus.

Part, Alexander Francis
The art and practice of innkeeping. London, William
Heinemann, 1922. 308p. Illus-photos.

Partch, V. I.
See Armstrong, J. and Partch, Virgil I.
VIP's new bar guide.

Partch, Virgil and McIntyre, William
VIP tossed a party. New York, Simon and Schuster,
1959. 112p. Illus.

Partridge, Burgo
A history of orgies. New York, Bonanza Books,
1960. 247p.

Partridge, William
See Moor, C. G. and Partridge, William
Aids to the analysis of food and drugs.

Pascall, Frank
Old-time recipes, AD 1720 to 1780. Wines,
bitters, preserves, confections of two hundred years
ago. London, F. Pascall, n d, ca1913. 38p.

Pasteur, Louis
Studies on fermentation. The diseases of beer, their
causes, and the means of preventing them. A
translation made with the author's sanction, of
"Etudes sur la bière". London, Macmillan and Co.,
1879. 418p. Illus. 1945, New York, American
Library Service.

Patent Office Great Britain
Subject list of works on domestic economy. Library
series no. 9 biographical series no. 6. London, 1902.
136p.   NYPL

Patrick, C. H.
Alcohol, culture and society. Durham, Duke
University Press, 1952. 176p.   LC

Patrick, George T. W.
The psychology of relaxation. Boston, New York,
Houghton, Miffling, 1916. 280p.   NYPL

Patten, Marguerite
500 recipes for home-made wines and drinks.
London, Paul Hamyln, 1963. 96p.

——————.
Invalid cookery book; with a section on feeding
children . . . . London, Phoenix House, 1953. 160p.
Illus.

Patents for inventions
See Commissioner of Patents. Abridgements of
specifications, etc.

Patterson, A. M.
See Crane, E. J.; Austin M. Patterson and Eleanor
B. Marr.
A guide to the literature of chemistry.

Patton, Rev. William
The laws of fermentation and the wines of the
ancients. New York, National Temperance Society
and Publication House, 1872. 133p.

Paul, Charlie
American and other iced drinks. Recipes. London,
Printed by McCorquedale. 1912. 71p. Illus.

Paul, Elliot and Quintanilla, Luis
Intoxication made easy. New York, Modern Age
Books, 1941. 146p. Illus.

Paulli, Simon
A treatise on tobacco, tea, coffee and chocolate, etc.
London Printed for T. Osborne, 1746. 171p.   LC

Pauls and White Ltd. (Publishers)
The brewing room diary and yearbook. 71st issue.
Ipswich, Suffolk, 1969. 193p. Advertising
Payne, Brigham
The story of Bacchus and centennial souvenir.
Hartford, Conn., A. E. Brooks, 1876. 111p. Illus.
Peabody, Richard R.
The commonsense of drinking. Boston, Little
Brown and Co., 1931. 191p. Bibliography.
Peale, Albert Charles
Lists and analyses of the mineral springs of the
United States, Washington, Government Printing Office,
1886. 235p.   LC
Pearks, Gillian
Complete home wine-making. London, Herbert
Jenkins, 1962. 143p. Illus.
Pearkes, Gillian
Growing grapes in Britain. A handbook for winemakers.
Andover, Hampshire, Amateur Winemaker, 1969.
156p. Illus-drawings.
Pearl, Raymond
Alcohol and longevity. New York, Alfred A. Knopf,
1926. 273p. Literature cited.
Pearson, David
See Cox, H. E. and Pearson, David
The chemical analysis of foods.
Pearson, J. R.
Vine culture under glass. 3rd edition. London,
Journal of Horticulture and Cottage Gardener, 1873.
40p.
Peattie, Donald Culross
Cargoes and harvests. New York, London, D.
Appleton and Co., 1926. 311p. Bibliography.
Peck, A. M.
Coffee, tea and chocolate. New York, W.P.A.
Report, 1938. 58p.   NYPL
Peck, J. E.
Fancy drinks and how to mix them. New York,
Excelsior Publishing House, 1891. 106p.   LC
Peddie, Alexander
Hotel, innkeeper, vintner and spirit dealer's assistant,
1823.   (Listed in Peddie-New Series)
Peddie, James
Dictionary of confectionery. London, Smith and
Ainslie, 1894. 19p.   BM

Peedle, Thomas and Coxbie, Thomas
Fallacy of water drinking. A. Alsop, publisher, 1650.
(Wine and Food Society)
Peeke, Hewson Lindsley
Americana ebrietatis; the favorite tipple of our fore-
fathers and the laws and customs relating thereto. New
York, Privately printed, 1917. 154p.
Peile, C. C.
Handybook of law relating to brewers, London, 1881.
136p. (Bird)
Peixotto, Ernest Clifford
A bacchic pilgrimage; French wines. New York,
London, C. Scribner's Sons, 1932. 201p. Illus.
Pelisier, H.
See Mournetas, Andre and Pelisier, Henry
The vade-mecum of the wine lover.
Pellegrini, Angelo M.
The unprejudiced palate. New York, The Macmillan
Co., 1948. 235p.

_____.
Wine and the good life. New York, Alfred A. Knopf,
1965. 307p.
Pellicot, Andre
The vine and winemaking in southern France.
Melbourne, Walker, May and Co., 1868. 76p. ANL
Peninou, Ernest P. and Greenleaf, Sidney S.
A directory of California wine growers and wine
makers in 1860. Berkeley, Tamalpais Press, 1967.
84p. Illus.

_____.
Winemaking in California. San Francisco, Peregrine
Press, 1954. 2 vol. Illus. LC
Penn, Kenneth
See Anon.
S.D.I. Being an account of the soft drinks industry
in Britain during the emergency years 1942-1948.
Penn, Kenneth Ed.
The Soft Drinks Trade Manual. London, Published by
The National Association of Soft Drinks Manufacturers,
1948. 127p.
Pennell, Elizabeth Robins
My cookery books. Boston and New York, Houghton
Mifflin and Co., 1903. 170p. Illus. Bibliography.

Penney, Miss L. Ed.
Readings and recitations. no. 7. Milwaukee,
Right Worthy Grand Lodge, Independent Order of Good
Templars, 1888. 119p.

Penning-Rowsell, Edmund
✓ The wines of Bordeaux. London, The International Wine
and Food Society-Michael Joseph, 1969. 320p.
Bibliography.

Pennington, Mrs.
The Royal cookbook. London, R. Snagg, 1787. 142p.
LC

Pennington, Blanch
Teas of the U.S.A. Evanston, Ill., Signal Press, 1943.
31p. (National Agricultural Library)

Penny, Mrs. Fanny Emily
Fickle fortune in Ceylon. (Tea). Madras. Addison
and Co., 1887. 69p. LC

Penrith, Akers Mfg. Co.
Information for bottlers. Minneapolis, 1951. 38p.

✓ Penzer, Norman Mosley
The book of the wine label. London, Home and
Van Thal, 1947. 148p. Illus-photos. Bibliography.

Pepsi-Cola Co.
Hospitality recipes out of a Pepsi-Cola bottle. Long
Island City, N.Y., 1940. unpaged (20).

_____.
See Martin, Milward W.
Twelve full ounces.

Percival, MacIver
The glass collector. 2nd edition. London, Herbert
Jenkins, n d, ca1917. 331p. Bibliography.
3rd edition, n d, 331p.

Perdix, Elizabeth
Wine for the vintage. New York, L. Raley, 1939.
256p. (Ohio State University)

Pereira, Jonathon
A treatise on food and diet. New York, Fowler and
Wells, 1843. 320p.

Perfecto
Notes on American confectionery with methods of
working different branches of candy making, ice cream
and soda water. Philadelphia, Published by author,
1891. 87p.

326

Perfumery and Essential Oil Record
    Annual directory and buyers guide.   Published by G.
    and M. Press Ltd., 1956 edition.   222p.   1957, 240p.

_____.
    Golden Jubilee Special Number.   Published by G. and
    M. Press Ltd., 1959.   161p.   Illus.
Perkin, Arthur G. and Everest, Arthur E.
    Natural organic colouring matters.   London, Monograph
    on Industrial Chemistry, 1918.   55p.   GBPOL
Perkins, Arthur J.
    Vine-pruning: its theory and practice.   Adelaide, Vardon
    and Pritchard, 1895.   74p.   Illus-Photos, drawings.
Perold, A. I.
    A treatise on vitaculture.   London, Macmillan and Co.,
    1927.   696p.   Illus.   Bibliography.
Perry, Martin H.
    And to drink, sir!   London, The St. Giles Publishing
    Co., Ltd., 1947.   72p.   Illus-Glossary.
Perry, Thomas
    The method of brewing English dry lager beer, by the
    top fermentation system, etc.   Torquay, Published
    by author, 1883.   29p.   (Davis)
Persons, Warren Milton
    Beer and brewing in America; an economic study.
    New York, United Brewers Industrial Foundation, 1941.
    48p.   Illus.   1937, revised by Standard Statistics.
Persoz, Juan F.
    New process of the culture of the vine.   New York,
    C. M. Saxton and Co., 1857.   58p.   NYPL
Peter, Lord Bishop of Cork and Rosse
    A discourse of drinking healths.   Dublin, John Hyde,
    1716.   217p.
Peters, Lulu Hunt
    Diet and health with key to the calories.   Chicago,
    Reilly and Lee, 1921.   127p.
Peterson, J.
    Intoxicating liquor licensing acts.   Various dates.
                                                        (Bird)
Peterson, Mrs. M. E.
    Peterson's preserving, pickling, etc.   Philadelphia,
    1869.   72p.   LC
Peterson, Maude Cridley
    How to know wild fruits.   A guide to plants when not
    in flower by means of fruit and leaf.   New York, The
    Macmillan Co., 1905.   340p.   Illus-drawings.

Petrar, M. Francesco
Chronica delle viti de Pontefici. From beginning to
anno domini MDXXIIII. Venizia, 1526. (In Italian).
(Unpaged).

Petty, Florence
The pudding Lady's Recipe Book. London, G. Bell
and Sons, 1939. 120p.

Petulengro, Gipsy
Romany remedies and recipes. 9th edition. Methuen
and Co., Ltd., 1947. 47p.

Pfafflin, Henry G.
Suggested bottlers syrup formulas using other than
cane or beet sugar. Indianapolis, Hurty-Peck and Co.,
n d, (1941). 8p.

Pfizer Chas. and Co., Inc.
Food preservatives. New York, 1966. 36p. Illus.

_____ .
Our smallest servants. The story of fermentation.
Brooklyn, N.Y. Printed in Holland, 1955. 32p.
Illus. Bibliography.

Pfizer, Charles and Co., Inc., Chemical Sales Division
See Anon.
Pfizer products for the food industry-products for the
beverage industry.

Phelan, Thomas A.
The book of tea secrets; being a little treatise on
"the cup that cheers". New York, Ajax Publishing Co.
1910. 32p. Illus.   LC

Phelps, Idelle Compiler
Your health! Philadelphia, George W. Jacobs Co.,
(Toasts), 1906. (Unpaged). Illus.

Phelps, Richard Harvey
The vine: its culture in the United States. Wine
making from grapes and other fruit; useful recipes,
etc., Hartford, Press of Case, Tiffany and Co.,
1855. 83p. Illus.

Phillips, John
Cyder, a poem. London, H. Hills, 1709, 48p.

Phin, John
Open air grape culture . . . and manufacture of
domestic wine, etc. New York, C. H. Saxton, 1862.
375p. Illus. Bibliography.

328

Piaz, Antonio dal
    Brandy distillation. (Part I). Cognac distillation
    and manufacture (Part II). Sacramento, 1892. 125p.
    total. Illus-engravings
                        (Brady library-Fresno State College)
Pick, Barth and Co.
    Soda fountain and luncheonette supplies. Chicago,
    Various dates.   POSL
Pickett, Deets, Ed.
    The cyclopedia of temperance, prohibition and public
    morals. New York-Cincinnati, The Methodist Book
    Concern, 1917. 406p.

_____ .
    Temperance and the changing liquor situation. New
    York, The Methodist Book Concern, 1934. 176p.
    Bibliography.
Pickett, Elbert Deets
    The wooden horse; or, America menaced by a
    Prussianized trade. (Beer and Brewing). New York,
    The Abington Press, 1918. 88p.   LC
Pierce, Daren
    See Erlanger, Beta and Pierce, Daren
    Compleat Martini cook book.

_____ .
    See Trahey, Jane and Pierce, Daren
    Son of the martini cookbook.
Pierce, Newton B.
    The California vine disease. Washington, U. S.
    Dept. Agri. Bulletin No. 2, 1892. 215p. Illus-color
    plates.
Pierce, S. S. Co.
    The Epicure (periodical). Vol. VIII, No. 3. Boston,
    June 1894. 42p.
Piesse, Charles H.
    Chemistry in the brewing-room. London, Trubner and
    Co., 1877. 62p. Illus.
Piesse, G. W. Septimus
    The art of perfumery. and the methods of obtaining
    odours of plants. London, Longman, Brown, Green,
    and Longmans, 1855. 287p.
Pihkanen, T. A.
    See Takala, Martti, Toivo A. Pihkanen, Touko
    Markkanen
    The effects of distilled and brewed beverages.

Pitt, John
How to brew good beer. A complete guide to the art
of brewing ale, bitter ale, table ale, brown stout,
porter, and table beer. London, Longman, Green,
Longman, and Roberts, 1864. 2nd edition. 148p.
Illus.
Pittman, David J. and Snyder, Charles R. Editors.
Society, culture and drinking patterns. New York,
London, John Wiley and Sons, 1962. 615p.
Plaisted, Arthur H.
Ale feasts and country taverns. Medmenham, Bucks
Village Bookshop, 1962. 64p. Illus.
Plat, Sir Hugh
Divers chemical conclusions concerning the art of
distillation, also known as "Jewel house of art and
nature". London, Bernard Alsop, 1594.
(Facsimile ed. publ. at Milford, Conn. 1941, by
P. Short). 232p.   GBPOL
                    .
_____
Jewel House of art and nature. See Divers chemical
conclusions concerning the art of distillation. London,
1594. 232p.   GBPOL
Platina (i.e. Bartoloweo de Sacchi di Piadena)
De Honesta Voluptate. (Indulgence and Good Health).
Reprint 1967, St. Louis, of original dated 1475 at
Venice. Has English translation on opposite pages.
Unpaged. (The first dated cookery book). Published
by Mallinckrodt Chemical Wks from the M-collection
of food classics Volume V.
Playfair, Lyon
See Liebig, Justus
Chemistry in its application to agriculture and
physiology.
Pleasants, H. R.
See White, P. S. and Pleasants, H. R.
The war of four thousand years.
Plimmer, R. H. Aders
Analyses and energy value of foods. London, His
Majesty's Stationary Office, n d, ca1920. 255p.
                    .
_____
The chemical changes and products resulting from
fermentations. London, Longmans, Green, 1903.
184p.

Pliny Moore Papers - IV
   "Journal of Drink", 1774. Champlain 1929. (86
   copies printed no. 24). Privately printed. 12p.
Ploughman, William
   Economy in brewing also complete family brewer.
   Romsey, Printed for author, 1803. (also known as
   "concise instructions for brewing in private families.)
   46p.   BM
Pocock, J.
   The brewing of non-excisable beers. Bangor, Published
   by author, 1895. 64p. Illus.
   1900, London, W. J. Bush and Co., 71p.

_____.
   Practical aerated water maker and book of English
   recipes. London, Stevenson and Howell, 1897. 193p.
                                   (State Library-Victoria)
Poffenberger, A. T. Jr.
   See Hollingsworth, H. L. and Poffenberger, Jr., A. T.
   The sense of taste.
Poling, Daniel A.
   John Barleycorn. His life and letters. Philadelphia,
   The John C. Winston Co., 1933. 245p. Illus.
Pollard, Alfred
   See Luckwill, L. C. and Pollard, A.
   Perry pears.

_____.
   See Beech, Frederick Walter
   Wines and juices.
Pollard, Alfred and Beech, Frederick Walter
   Cider-making. London, Rupert Hart-Davis, The
   Countryman Library, 1957. 96p. Illus-Bibliography.
Pollock, Allan
   A botanical index to all the medicinal plants. New
   York, Published by author, 1872. 137p.
Poole, Mrs. Hester M.
   Fruits and how to use them. New York, Fowler and
   Wells, 1890. 242p.
Poole, T. (Butler to Sir W. Aston)
   The family brewer. London, 1791. 91p.   USBA

_____.
   Treatise on strong beer and ale fully explaining the art
   of brewing. London, Published by author, 1783. 91p.
                                             (Yale Univ.)

Poore, George Vivian
Coffee and tea. London, H. K. Lewis, 1883. 44p. LC
Popham, H. E.
The taverns in the town . . . . London, Robert Hale,
Ltd., 1937. 221p. Illus-drawings.
Popp, Charles W.
Modern confectioner. London, Robert Banks and Son,
1910. 131p. BM
Porter, Ebenezer
The fatal effects of ardent spirits. Hartford, Peter
B. Gleason and Co., 1811. 22p.
Porter, George
The tropical agriculturalist. London, Smith Elder
and Co., 1833. 429p. LC
Portman, Harry
Harry's A B C of mixing cocktails. Kansas City,
Printing Service Inc., 1933. 91p.
"Portuguese"
The wine question considered. Observations on
pamphlets of James Warre and Fleetwood Williams,
London, 1824. 65p. BM
Postgate, Raymond William
An alphabet of choosing and serving wine. London,
Herbert Jenkins, 1961. 94p.

_____.
The home wine cellar with chapters on home bottling
and other advice on the care of wine. London, Herbert
Jenkins, 1960. 94p. Illus.

_____.
The plain man's guide to wine. New York,
Eriksson-Taplinger Co., 1960. 136p. Illus.
1962, London, Michael Joseph, 136p. Illus.
1965, London, Michael Joseph, 164p. Illus.

_____.
Portuguese wine. London, J. M. Dent and Sons, Ltd.,
1969. 102p. Illus-drawings.
Potter, Alonzo
Addresses by himself and others. Boston,
Massachusetts Temperance Society, 1861. (Cover title
Drinking usages of Society.) 98p.
Potter, John G. Comp.
Brewery Manual (The). London, 1961-62, Norlands
Publishing Co., 418p. 1964, Attwood and Co., Ltd.,
398p.

Potter and Clarke Ltd.
  Botanic brewers' guide (The). London, 1899. 36p.
  3rd edition, 1909, 42p. 6th edition, 1926, 43p.
Poucher, William Arthur
  Perfumes, cosmetics, and soaps: with special
  reference to synthetics. 3rd edition. Princeton,
  N.J., Van Nostrand, 1929-30; 3 v. Illus.
Poupon, Pierre and Forgeot, Pierre
  A book of Burgundy. London, Lund Humphries, 1958.
  78p. Illus.
Powell, Aaron Macy
  The beer question. New York, National Temperance
  Society and Publication House, 1881. 55p.   LC
Powell, E. P.
  The orchard and fruit garden. New York, Doubleday
  Page and Co., 1914. 322p. Illus-photos.
Powell, Frederick
  Bacchus dethroned. Prize essay. New York, National
  Temperance Society and Publication House, 1879.
  268p.
Powell, John
  Powell's complete book of cookery or guide to
  preferment. London, 1687. 128p.   LC
Powell, Mrs. Milton Powell
  Eating for perfect health . . . . London, Butterworth's
  Ltd., 1927. 165p.
Powley, R. and Sons Ltd.
  Bottlers' requisites. (catalogue). Sunderland,
  England, n d, ca1925. 111p. Illus-photos.
Powner, Willard Earle
  Bartender's guide. How to mix drinks. For home
  and professional use. Chicago, Publ. by Stein
  Publishing House, 1943. 64p. 1955 edition, 128p.
  1957 edition, 128p.

_____.
  The complete bartender's guide, how to mix drinks;
  a manual of quick reference. Chicago, The Charles
  T. Powner Co., 1934. 128p.

_____.
  The complete bartender's guide. Chicago, The
  Charles T. Powner Co., 1948. (Cover title- Tom and
  Jerry's Bartender's guide.) 128p.
Pozen, Morris A.
  Successful brewing. Chicago, New York, Brewery Age
  Publishing Co., 1936. 243p. References and notes.
  1935 Same.

Practical Brewer (A)
The publican, innkeeper and brewer's guide. London,
C. Goodman, n d, ca1840. 152p.
Practical Man (A)
The butler, the wine-dealer and private brewer.
London, G. Biggs, n d, ca1840. 134p.

_____.
The innkeeper and public brewer. London, G. Biggs,
n d, ca1840. (Back cover title The Butler Wine
dealer.) 152p.
Pradel, P. and Malepeyre, M. F.
A complete treatise on perfumery: containing notices
of the materials used in the art. Philadelphia, H.C.
Baird, 1864. 534p. Illus.   LC
Pratt, E.
Metallic and mineral waters. London, 1684.   (Kirkby)

_____.
The licensed trade. An independent survey. London,
John Murray, 1907. 329p.
Pratt, J. T.
Food adulteration. Chicago, P.W. Barclay and Co.,
1880. 137p.
Preece, I. A.
The biochem stry of brewing. Edinburgh, Oliver and
Boyd, 1954. 393p. Illus. References.

_____.
Malting, brewing and allied processes. A literature
survey, prepared for the Institute of Brewing, London,
1957, 32p. 1958, 31p. 1960, 31p. 1961, 32p.
1963, 32p. 1959, 31p.
Prescott, Albert B.
Chemical examination of alcoholic liquors. A manual
of the constituents of the distilled spirits and fermented
liquors of commerce, and their qualitative and
quantitative determination. New York, D. Van
Nostrand, 1875. 108p.
Prescott, Henry Paul
Strong drink and tobacco smoke; the structure, growth,
and uses of malt, hops, yeast, and tobacco. London,
Macmillan, 1869. 71p. Illus.
Prescott, Samuel Cate and Winslow, Charles-Edward Amory.
Elements of water bacteriology. New York, John
Wiley and Sons, 1904. 162p. References.

Prestoe, H. and Malepegne, M. F.
Report on coffee cultivation in Dominica. Trinidad,
1875. 35p.   BM
Pretyman, Mrs. Hannah
Recipes for homemade wines. London, Wren Booms,
1946. 30p.   BM

——————·
Thirty three recipes for homemade wines. London,
1947. 81p.   (Univ. Chicago)
Preyer, Edgar R.
Preyer's information and guide for the liquor business.
New York, Published by the author, 1901. 143p.
Illus.
Price, Elizabeth
The new universal and complete confectioner. London,
Alex Hogg, n d, ca1780. 94p.   LC
Price, Pamela Vandyke
Cooking with wine, spirits, beer and cider. London,
Jenkins, 1959. 94p.

——————·
France, a food and wine guide. London, B. T.
Batsford Ltd., 1966. 328p. Illus.

——————·
Winelovers' handbook. London, Conde Nast Publications
Ltd., 1969. 80p. plus. Illus-drawings.
Priscilla Publishing Co.
Sandwiches and beverages. Boston, 1928. 20p.   LC
Priestly, Joseph
Directions for impregnating water with fixed air in
order to communicate to it the peculiar spirit and
virtues of Pyrmont water. A reprint of the original
pamphlet by Dr. Priestley on carbonation of water,
with supplemental data concerning early studies of
carbon dioxide, effervescent mineral waters, and the
origin of carbonated flavored beverages. Washington,
D. C. American Bottlers' of Carbonated Beverages,
1945. 18p. Illus.

——————·
Experiments and observations relating to different kinds
of air and other branches of natural philosophy.
Birmingham (England), 1779-1781. 2 vol.   GBPOL

——————·
Experiments and observations on different kinds of air.
London, J. Johnson, 1774. 324p. Also directions for
impregnating water with fixed air. London, J. Johnson
1772. 22p.

———— Experiments and observations relating to the analysis
of atmospherical air. London, Reprinted for J.
Johnson, 1796. 89p.   BM

———— Lectures on experimental philosophy. Dublin, William
Jones, 1794. 208p.

Prince, Guy
Current books about wine. London, National Book
League, 1955. 13p.

Prince, William R.
A treatise on the vine: embracing its history from
earliest ages to present day. New York, T. and J.
Swords, 1830. 355p.   LC

Pringle, Sir John
Discourse on different kinds of air. London, 1774.
31p.   BM

Pringle, William
Science and coffee. Madras, Addison and Co., Reprinted from Madras Mail, 1897. 66p.   BM

Prynne, William
Healthes; Sicknesse . . . . London, no Publisher,
1628. 95p.   NYPL

Prochaska, Joseph
See Willkie, Herman Frederick
Fundamentals of distillery practice; a handbook on the
manufacture of ethyl alcohol and distillers' feed
products from cereals. By Herman F. Willkie and
Joseph A. Prochaska.

Proskauer, Julien J.
Fun at cocktail time, provided by Seagram's. New
York, Seagram-Distillers Corp., 1934. 38p. Illus.

———— What'll you have? A not too dry text book about
cocktails. Almost 200 of them, and what to serve
with them, wines, liqueurs, cordials, how, when and
where to serve them. New York, Chicago, A. L.
Burt Co., 1933. 128p. Illus-drawings.

Prosser, James
See Tichborne, C.R.C. and Prosser, James
The Mineral Waters of Europe including a short
description of artificial mineral waters.

Prudden, T. Mitchell
Drinking-water and ice supplies. New York, G.P.
Putnam's Sons, 1891. 148p. Illus.

Public Library of South Australia
Research Service Bibliographies Series Four. No. 82.
Wine and vitaculture. Adelaide, 1967. 69p.
Bibliography.

Puffer, A. D. and Sons Mfg. Co.
Catalogue of Puffer's Frigid Soda and Mineral Water
Apparatus. Boston, 1881. 167p. Illus. 1878,
92p. Illus.

Directions, suggestions and rules for setting up and
operating the various machinery for manufacturing,
dispensing and bottling carbonated beverages. Boston,
n d, ca1882. 138p. Illus.

Frigid Soda Water Apparatus (Catalogue of) Boston,
1889. 326p. Illus.

"PYRAMID" (George B. Beattie)
The mechanical side of mineral water manufacture.
London, Published by The Mineral Water Trade Re-
view, n d, (1934). 350p. Illus.

Mineral water spoilage prevention. London, Published
by The Mineral Water Trade Review, 1937. 218p.
Illus.

Quartermaster Food and Container Institute for the
armed forces
Chemistry of natural food flavors--a symposium.
Washington, May 1957. 200p. Illus. Literature cited.

Flavors, Beverages and condiments. Volume IX.
15 October 1946. n p.
4 parts flavoring agents, Part 1 16p. Spices,
condiments, salt. Part 2, 46p. Sugars, syrups,
candies and starches. Part 3, 33p. Coffee, tea and
cocoa, Part 4, 51p. Bibliography.

Horsford's THE ARMY RATION of 1864. Library
Bulletin, Supplement no. 1. July 1961. Chicago,
Published originally by D. Van Nostrand, New York,
1864. 43p.

Quelch, Mary Thorne
 Herbal remedies and recipes and some others. London,
 Faber and Faber, 1945. 272p.

――――――. Herbs for daily use. London, Faber and Faber, 1941.
 328p.
Quinby, Winfield, S.
 How to make perfect coffee. Boston, and Chicago.
 The W. S. Quinby Co., 1922. 27p.   LC
Quinn, Elton L. and Jones, Charles
 Carbon dioxide. New York, Reinhold Publishing Co.,
 1936. 294p.   (Crerar)
Quinn, George
 Fruit tree and grape vine pruning. Prepared by
 direction of the Hon. Minister of Agriculture. 5th
 edition. Adelaide, South Australian Government, 1915.
 277p. Illus.
Quinn, James P.
 Scientific marketing of coffee. New York, Tea and
 Coffee Trade Journal, 1960. 245p.
Quintanilla, Luis
 See Paul, Elliot and Quintanilla, Luis
 Intoxication made easy.
Quintus, R. A.
 The cultivation of sugar-cane in Java. London, Norman
 Rodger, 1923. 164p.
Quarterly Journal of Studies on Alcohol
 Cross-cultural study of drinking (A). Supplement
 no. 3. New Brunswick, N.J., Center Alcohol Studies,
 Rutgers University, April 1965. 114p.

Rack, John
 The French wine and liquor manufacturer. A practical
 guide and receipt book for the liquor merchant. New
 York, Dick and Fitzgerald, 1865. 268p. Illus.
 4th edition, 1868, 273p. Illus.
Rafinesque, Constantine Samuel
 American manual of the grape vine and the art of
 making wine. Philadelphia. Printed for author, 1830.
 64p.   LC

338

Rahr Malting Co.
    See Kent, Rockwell
    To thee! a toast in celebration of a century of
    opportunity and accomplishment in America; 1847-1947.
Rainbird, George M.
    Inns of Kent. 2nd edition. London, Published for
    Whitbread and Co., by The Naldrett Press Ltd., 1949.
    66p. Illus.

——————.
    The pocket book of wine. London, Evans Brothers
    Ltd., 1963. 157p. Glossary-Bibliography.

——————.
    Sherry and the wines of Spain. London, Michael
    Joseph, 1966. 224p. Illus-photos. Bibliography-
    glossary.
Rainford, Bentham
    Sicily and its wine. London, n d,   BV
Ramsay, William
    A book of toasts. New York, Dodge, 1906.
    (unpaged).
Ramsden, A. R.
    Assam Planter. Tea planting and hunting in the
    Assam jungle. London, John Gifford, 1945. 159p.
    Glossary of native words.
Ramsden, Jesse
    Account of experiments to determine specific gravity
    of fluids thereby to obtain the strength of spiritous
    liquors. London, 1792. 33p.   BM
Ramsey, Edward B.
    Old Scottish conviviality. Edinburgh, T. N. Foulis
    Ltd., 1922. 54p.   NYPL
Raper, Elizabeth
    Receipt book of Elizabeth Raper. Soho, Nonesuch
    Press, 1924. 95p.
Rathbone, W. and Fanshowe, E. L.
    Liquor legislation in U. S. and Canada. London,
    Cassell and Co., 1892. 432p.
                            (Brady Library-Fresno State College)
Rattray, Brenda
    Giving a party. Recipes by Kathleen Thomas. London,
    Longacre Press, 1960. 175p. Illus-drawings.
Ravaz, L.
    See Viala, P. and Ravaz, L.
    American vines, their adaptation, culture, grafting and
    propagation.

339

Rawling, Ernest P.
Rawling's book of mixed drinks. San Francisco, Guild
Press, 1914. 100p.   LC
Rawlings, H. D.
Sparkling draughts, their introduction, manufacture and
consumption. London, No Publisher, n d, ca1870.
24p. Illus-engravings.
Rawlingson, J.
A new method of brewing malt liquor in small quantities
for domestic use. 2nd edition. London, J. Johnson,
1807. 32p.
Rawnsley, Kenneth
Health giving brews. London, Thorsons Publishers,
1955. 79p.

————————.
Homemade wines, how to go about it. Originally
published as Health Giving Brews (title page). London,
Thorson's Publishers, Inc., 1955. 79p.
Ray, Cyril, Ed.
The Compleat Imbiber. Volume 1. London, Putnam
and Co., Ltd., 1956. 256p. Illus-drawings.
Vol. 2, New York, Finehart and Co., 1957, 256p.
Illus-drawings.
Vol. 3, London, Putnam, 1960, 175p. Illus-drawings.
Vol. 4, London, Vista Books, 1961, 208p. Illus-photos,
drawings.
Vol. 5, London, Vista Books, 1962, 208p. Illus-photos,
drawings.
Vol. 6, London, Vista Books, 1963, 224p. Illus-photos,
drawings.
Vol. 7, London, Studio Vista Ltd., 1964, 224p. Illus-
photos, drawings.
Vol. 8, London, Collins, 1965, 224p. Illus-photos-
drawings.
Vol. 9, London, Collins, 1967, 224p. Illus-photos-
drawings.
Vol. 10, London, Collins, 1968, 224p. Illus-photos-
drawings.

————————.
The Gourmet's companion. London, Eyre and
Spottiswoode, 1963. 503p. Illus.

————————.
Introduction to wines. Leeds, The Observer, 1960.
35p. Illus.

Ray, Cyril
Lafite. The story of Chateau Lafite-Rothschild.
London, Peter Davies, 1969. 162p. Illus-photos, etc.
Bibliography.

———— .
The wines of Italy. London, George Rainbird for
McGraw-Hill Publ. Co., 1966. 192p. Illus.
Bibliography-Glossary.
Ray, Georges
The French Wines. New York, Walker and Co.,
First published in Paris in French 1946., 1965.
152p.
Raymond, Irving Woodworth
The teaching of the early church on the use of wine
and strong drink. New York, Columbia University
Press, 1927. 170p.
Rea, Frederick B.
Alcoholism, its psychology and cure. London,
Epworth Press, 1956. 143p.   NYPL
Reach, Angus B.
Claret and olives from the Garonne to the Rhone.
New York, George P. Putnam, 1853. 235p. Illus.
Read, George
The Confectioner. London, Charles Knight and Co.,
1842. 148p.
Read Brothers
A bottle of beer. New York, H.P. Finlay and Co.,
1890. 15p.   LC
Reade, A. Arthur
Study and stimulants: or, the use of intoxicants and
narcotics in relation to intellectual life. 2nd edition.
London, Simpkin, Marshall and Co., 1883. 233p.

———— .
Tea and tea drinking. London, Sampson, Low, Marston,
Searle and Rivington, 1884. 154p. Illus.
Reboux, Paul
Food for the rich. London, Anthony Blond Ltd., 1958.
214p. Illus.
Rector, T. M.
Scientific preservation of food. New York, John Wiley
and Son, 1925. 213p.   LC
Redding, Cyrus
Every man his own butler. London, Whittaker and Co.,
1839. 200p.

_____.
French wines and vineyards; and the way to find them.
London, Houlston and Wright, 1860. 240p.

_____.
A history and description of modern wines. London,
Publisher ? (title page missing), 1833. 407p. Illus.
2nd edition, Whittaker and Co., 1836. 423p.
3rd edition, London, Henry G. Bohn, 1851. 440p.
Reddington, William
A practical treatise on brewing, etc. London, John
Clarke, 1760. 183p.
Reddish Chemical Co., Ltd.
Detergents and sterilizers for the brewing industry.
Cheadle, Cheshire, 1966. 28p.
Redgrove, Herbert Stanley
Scent and all about it; a popular account of the sciences
and art of perfumery. London, W. Heinemann, 1928.
99p. Bibliography.

_____.
Spices and condiments. London, Sir Isaac Pittman and
Sons, 1933. 361p. Bibliography. (Los Angeles Public)
Redmayne, Paul
. . . Cocoa and chocolate, by Paul Redmayne . . .
and Thomas Insull. London, New York, etc.,
Oxford University Press, 1939. 57p. Illus.
Reed, Adele
Old bottles and ghost towns. Bishop, California,
Published by author, 1961. 55p. Illus.
Reed, William
The history of sugar. London, Longmans, Green, and
Co., 1866. 206p.
Reemelin, Charles
The vine-dresser's manual, an illustrated treatise on
vineyards and wine-making. G. M. Saxton, 1855.
103p. Illus.

_____.
The wine-maker's manual. Cincinnati, R. Clarke and
Co., Printers, 1868. 123p. Illus.
Reeve, Lloyd Eric.
Gift of the grape; based on Paul Masson Vineyards,
by Lloyd Eric Reeve and Alice Means Reeve. San
Francisco, Filmer Publishing Co., 1959. 314p.
Illus-photos.

Reeve-Jones, Alan
    London pubs. Research and spirited inquiry by Betty
    James. London, Batsford, 1962. 200p. Illus.
Refined Syrups and Sugars Inc.
    This is liquid sugar. Yonkers, N.Y., 1955. 205p.
    Glossary.
Reibstein, August
    "Mixology" recipes for old and new mixed drinks.
    Published by author, 1933. 76p.   LC
Reid, Charles
    The planting engineer (tea). Colombo, Times of
    Ceylon, 1920. 371p.   (National Agricultural Library)
Reid, T. W.
    Book of the Cheese (The). Traits and tales of a
    Johnsonian Haunt. Compiled by T. W. Reid and
    edited by R. R. D. Adams. 4th edition, London, T.
    Fisher Unqin, 1901. 200p. Illus.

_____.
    See Anon.
    Book of the Cheese, etc.

_____.
    Traits and stories of Ye Olde Cheshire Cheese.
    Originally edited by Thomas Wilson Reid. London,
    Beaufoy A. Moore, 1886. 133p. Illus.
Reilly, Hugh
    Easy does it. The story of Mac. (Temperance). New
    York, P. J. Kenedy and Sons, 1950. 277p.
Reilly, Joseph
    Distillation. London, Methuen and Co., 1936. 136p.
Reimund, Donn A.
    Bibliography of tree nut production and marketing re-
    search. 1945-1960. U.S.D.A. Misc. Publ. no. 862.
    (Compiled by A. D. Reimund,) Washington, 1961.
    46p.
Reinhardt, Charles MD
    120 years of life and how to obtain them. (A treatise
    upon the use of lactic ferments for the prevention and
    cure of disease and the prolongation of life.)
    London, The London, Publicity Co., Ltd., 1909.
    50p.
Reinhardt, Charles Nicholas
    "Cheerio!" A book of punches and cocktails. How to
    mix them, and other rare, exquisite and delicate drinks.
    By Charles, formerly of Delmonicos. New York, The
    Elf, 1930. 53p.

_____.
See Charles formerly of Delmonicos.
Punches and cocktails (Book of).

Rembaugh, Dr. A. C.
Alcohol. Philadelphia. Published by Philadelphia
Social Science Association. Read at a meeting May
26th, 1885. 20p.

Remington, Joseph P.
The practice of pharmacy. Philadelphia, J. B.
Lippincott Co., 1886. 1080p. Illus. 5th edition,
1907. 1541p. Illus.

Rendle, William Edgcombe
England a wine-producing country: being a treatise
on the new patent fruit-tree and plant protectors.
London, Allan, 1868. 71p. Illus.

Renner, H. D.
The origin of food habits. London, Faber and Faber,
1944. 261p.

Renner, Hans Deutch
Pocket guide to wine. London, The Citizen Press
Ltd., n d, ca1945. 16p.   WI

Repplier, Agnes
To think of tea! Boston and New York, Houghton
Mifflin, 1932. 207p. Illus.

Resuggan, J. C. L.
The cleaning and sterilization of bottles and other glass
containers. London, United Trade Press Ltd., 1957.
224p. Illus.

_____.
Quaternary ammonium compounds. In chemical
sterilization. London, United Trade Press Ltd.,
1951. 119p. References.

Reynolds, Bruce
A cocktail Continentale. New York, George Sully and
Co., 1929. 290p. Illus.

Reynolds, Philip Keep
The Banana. Its history, cultivation and place among
staple foods. Boston, Houghton Mifflin Co., 1927.
181p. Bibliography.

Reynoldson, John
Practical and philosophical principles of making malt.
Newark, M. Hage, 1808. 293p.

Rhoads, W. M.
Poker, smoke, and other things, mixed drinks by the
bar-fan. Chicago, The Reilly and Britton Co., 1907.
69p. Illus.

——————.
Toasts. Philadelphia, 1904. The Penn Publishing Co.,
30 l. Illus.
Rhodes, James B.
Publican's handbook and general spirit calculator.
Manchester, A. Heywood and Son, 1899. 137p.   BM
Rice, Wallace
Toasts and tipple; a book of conviviality. Compiled
by Wallace Rice and Frances Rice. n p, M. A.
Donahue and Co., n d, unpaged. Illus.
Rich, H. S. and Co., Publishers
The Beverage Blue Book for 1923. Chicago,
Directory. 324p. Advertising. 1925, 336p.
Advertising.
Richards, Ellen H.
Food materials and their adulterations. Household
Manuals, II Boston, Estes and Lauriat, 1886. 183p.
Bibliography.
Richards, Lenore and Treat, Nola
Tea-room recipes. Boston, Little Brown and Co.,
1927. 147p.
Richards Rosen Associates, Inc.
A guide to pink elephants. 200 most requested mixed
drinks. New York, n d. 200p.
Richardson, A. E.
The old inns of England . . . . London, Batsford, 1934.
118p. Illus.
Richardson, A. E. and Eberlein, Donaldson, H.
The English inn, past and present. London, B. T.
Batsford Ltd., 1925. 208p. Illus.
Richardson, Benjamin Ward
Brief notes for temperance teachers. Milwaukee,
Right Worthy Grand Lodge, Independent Order Good
Templars, (1883). 127p.

——————.
Dialogues on drink. New York, National Temperance
Society and Publication House, 1886. 155p.

——————.
The temperance lesson book. Alcohol and its action
on the body. New York, National Temperance Society
and Publication House, 1884. 220p.
Richardson, George B.
See Lund, John and Richardson, George B.
Mineral water manufacturer's accounts.

Richardson, John
Philosophical principles of the science of brewing, etc.
York, Printed by A. Ward for G. G. and J. Robinson,
1788. 347p. LC

_____.
Remarks on Baverstock's hydrometical observations
and experiments in the brewery. Hull, G. G. and J.
Robinson, 1785. 95p. USBA

_____.
Statical estimates of the materials of brewing, or a
treatise on the application and use of the saccharameter.
London, G. Robinson, 1784. 243p. Illus-drawing.

_____.
Theoretic hints on improved practice of brewing malt-
liquors, etc. 2nd corrected edition. London, G.
Robinson, 1777. 74p.
Richmond, A. B.
Leaves from the diary of an old lawyer. Intemperance
the great source of crime. New York, American Book
Exchange, 1880. 387p.
Ricket, E. and Thomas, C.
The gentlemen's table guide. Recipes wine cups,
American drinks, etc. London, Published by authors,
1871. 53p. plus menus (20p.).
Ricketts, R. W.
Cleaning in the brewery bottling store and licensed
house. Cheadle, Cheshire, Reddish Chemical Co.,
Ltd., n d, ca1960. 21p.
Riddell, Patrick
I was an alcoholic. The story of a cure. London,
Victor Gollancz, 1955. 222p.
Rideal, Samuel
Carbohydrates and alcohol. New York, Industrial
Chemistry, 1920. 219p. (Crerar)
Ridgeway, James
A practical treatise explaining the art and mystery of
brewing porter, ale, two-penny and table beer.
London, 1860. BG
Ridley, Henry N.
Spices. London, Macmillan and Co., Ltd., 1912.
449p. Illus.
Rieck, Max
Gordian essays on cocoa. Hamburg, 1936. (In German).
86p. LC

Riesenberg, Emily
Preserving and canning. Chicago, Rand McNally and
Co., 1914. 104p.
Rigby, W. O. and Rigby, Fred
Rigby's Reliable Candy Teacher. 15th edition.
Topeka, Kansas. Rigby Publishing Co., 1923. 268p.
Riker, Douglas H.
The Wine book of knowledge. Los Angeles, The
Ascot Press, 1934. 71p. Illus.
Riley, John J.
A history of the American soft drink industry; bottled
carbonated beverages, 1807-1957. Washington,
American Bottlers Carbonated Beverages, 1958.
302p. Illus.

———————.
Organization in the soft drink industry; a history of the
American Bottlers of Carbonated Beverages.
Washington, D.C. American Bottlers of Carbonated
Beverages, 1946. 357p. Illus.

———————.
Scientific and medical origin of carbonated waters.
American Bottlers of Carbonated beverages, 1948
edition. Washington. 35p. List of references.
1959, 38p.

———————.
The twentieth century in the bottled carbonated beverage
industry. 1958. Preliminary draft. Washington.
52p.
Riley, Walter A. J.
Brewery by products. London, The Brewing Trade
Review, 1913. 162p. Illus- Bibliography.
Rimmel, Eugene
The book of perfumes. 4th edition. London, Chapman
and Hall, 1865. 266p. Illus.
Also Philadelphia, 1864. 266p.
Ripperger, Helmut Lothar
Coffee cookery. New York, Stewart, 1940. 94p.

———————.
Spice Cookery. New York, George W. Stewart, 1942.
95p.
Rittich, Virgil J. and Eugene A.
European grape growing in cooler districts where
protection is necessary. Minneapolis, Burgess
Publishing Co., 1941. 93p.   (Crerar)

347

Rivers, William H. R.
   The influence of alcohol and other drugs on fatigue.
   London, W. W. Arnold, 1908. 136p.   LC
✓ Rixford, Emmet H.
   The wine press and the cellar. A manual for the wine-
   maker and the cellar-man. San Francisco, Payot,
   Upham and Co., New York, D. Van Nostrand, 1883.
   240p. Illus. Bibliography.
✓ Roate, Mettja C.
   How to make wine in your own kitchen. New York,
   Mc Fadden-Bartell Corp., 1963. 175p.
Robb, Marshall J.
   Scotch whiskey. New York, Dutton, 1951. 127p.
   Illus.
"Robert"
   Cocktails. How to mix them. London, Herbert
   Jenkins.
   2nd printing 1922 112p. (Embassy Club).
   3rd printing 1922 112p. (Embassy Club).
   5th printing n d 112p. (Embassy Club).
   6th printing n d 112p. (American BarNice).
   8th printing n d 112p. (American BarNice)
   12th printing n d 112p. (American BarNice)
   7th printing nd
Roberts, A. Boake and Co., Ltd.
   Diary for the brewing and syrup rooms. London,
   59th year of publication, 1950. 115p. 1947, 84p.
   1948, 72p. 1949, 72p. 1951, 115p. 1952, 111p.
   1953, 111p.

_____.
   Handbook of chocolate and confectionary. London,
   1932. 80p.   (Confectionery Production Manual)

_____.
   Technical materials for brewing. London, n d. 44p.
Roberts, George Edwin
   Cups and their customs. London, J. Van Voorst,
   1869. 62p. Illus.
Roberts, Harry
   See Roundell, Julia Anne Elizabeth (Tollemache).
   The still-room, by Mrs. Charles Roundell and
   Harry Roberts.
Roberts, John
   A comprehensive view of the culture of the vine under
   glass. London, Longman and Co., 1842. 83p.

Roberts, William Henry
    The British wine maker and domestic brewer.
    Edinburgh. 5th edition, A and C Black, 1849.
    384p. Illus.

——————— .
    The Scottish ale-brewer; a practical treatise on the art
    of brewing ales according to the system practised in
    Scotland. Edinburgh, Oliver and Boyd, 1837. 160p.
    Illus.

——————— .
    The Scottish-ale brewer and practical maltster (with
    supplement on the relative value of malt and sugar).
    3rd edition. Edinburgh, A and C Black, 1847. 251p.
Robertson, Mrs. Hannah
    The young ladies school of arts. Edinburgh, R.
    Spence, 1777. 206p.   GBPOL
Robertson, Jean and Andrew
    Food and wine of the French provinces. London-
    Glasgow, Collins, 1968. 218p. Illus-drawings.
Robinson, Edward F.
    Early history of coffee houses in England. London,
    Kegan, Paul and Co., 1893. 240p.   (Cornell Univ.)
Robinson, Henry Morton
    Water of life. A novel. New York, Simon and
    Schuster, 1960. 621p.
Robinson, James
    The whole art of making British wines, liqueurs,
    brewing fine and strong Welsh ales. London, Longman,
    Brown, Green and Longmans, 1848. 275p.
Robinson, Jonathon
    Great evil of health drinking. London, 1784. 128p. BG
Robson, Edgar Iliff
    A guide to French Fetes. London, Methuen and Co.,
    Ltd., 1930. 238p. Illus.

——————— .
    A wayfarer in French vineyards. Boston, and New
    York, Houghton Mifflin, 1928. 212p. Illus-etchings.
Rodale, J. I. and staff
    The complete book of food and nutrition. Emmaus,
    Pa. Rodale Books, Inc., 1961. 1054p.
Rodriguez, D. W.
    Coffee. A short economic history with special reference
    to Jamaica. Kingston, Commodity Bulletin no. 2 Ministry
    ot Agriculture and lands, 1961. 77p. Illus-Bibliography.

Roe, Charlie and Jim Schwenck
The home bartender's guide and song book. New York, Experimenter Publishing Inc., 1930. 94p. Illus.

Roe, Edward P.
Success with small fruits. New York, Dodd, Mead and Co., 1886. 388p.

Roessler, E. B.
See Amerine, M. A. and Roessler, E. B.
Sensory evaluation of wines.

Roger, J. R.
The wines of Bordeaux. London, Andre Deutsch, 1960. 166p. Bibliography.

Rogers, Cameron, Ed.
Full and By-being a collection of verses by persons of quality in praise of drinking. London, William Heinemann Ltd., 1925. 153p. Illus.

Rogers, Kenneth
The Mermaid and Mitre taverns of old London. London, The Homeland Association Ltd., 1928. 204p. Illus.

Rogers, R. Vashon, Jr.
Drinks, drinkers and drinking; or the law and history of intoxicating liquors. Albany, Weed Parsons and Co., 1881. 241p.

Rohan, T. A.
Processing of raw cocoa for the market. Rome. Food and Agriculture Organization of the United Nations. Study no. 60, 1963. 207p. Illus-photos. References.
GBPOL

Rohde, Eleanour Sinclair
A garden of herbs. London, Philip Lee Werner; publisher to the Medici Society Ltd., 1921. 232p. Authorities quoted.

———.
Rose recipes. London, Routledge, 1939. 94p. Illus.

———.
The scented garden. Boston, Hale, Cushman and Flint, Inc., 1936. 311p. Illus.

Rollat, Edouard
Wine guide and cocktail book. New York, Vendome Liquor Co., 1934. 60p.   (St. Louis Public)

Rolleston, Samuel
Dissertation on barley wine (A). Origin and antiquity, Oxford James Fletcher, 1750. 38p.

Rolli, Otto Christian
Wine for home and medicinal use. Canton, Ohio,
1933. 30p.   LC

_____.
Wines and cordials for home and medicinal use.
Canton, Ohio, 1934.   LC
Rollin, Betty
The Non-Drinker's Drink Book. Recipes by Lucy
Rosenfeld. London, Frederick Muller, 1967.
192p. Illus-drawings.
Rolph, George M.
Something about sugar. Its history, growth, manufacture
and distribution. San Francisco, John J. Newbegin,
1917. 341p.
Romanne, Mrs. James C.
Herb-lore for housewives. (Wine and other beverage
recipes). London, Herbert Jenkins Ltd., 1938. 264p.
Illus-photos.
Romer, Frank
Reviewing American brewing. Baltimore, Crown Cork
and Seal Co., 1942. 48p. Illus.   LC
Romero, Matias
Coffee and India rubber culture in Mexico. New York,
G. P. Putnam's Sons, 1898. 417p.
Ronay, Egon
Egon Ronay's 1965 guide to 1000 pubs and inns in
England and Wales, etc. London, Gastronomes Limited
in association with Hutchinson, 1965. 442p. Illus.
Rooker, William A.
Fruit Pectin. Its commercial manufacture and uses.
New York, Avi Publishing Co., 1928. 170p.
Roos, Henry
New and standard mixed drinks. New York Caterer
Publishing Co., 1906. 100p. (U. S. Catalog)
Roos, L.
. . . Wine-making in hot climates. Translated by
Raymond Dubois . . . and W. Percy Wilkinson . . .
Melbourne, R. S. Brain, Government Printer, 1900.
273p. Illus.
Roose, Samuel
New and complete treatise on ullaging. London, 1832.
23p.   BM

_____.
Wine and spirit dealer's guide. London, 1835. 124p.
                                              BM

Root, J.
The horrors of delerium tremens. New York,
Josiah Adams, 1844. 483p.

Root, Waverley Lewis
The food of France. New York, Knopf, 1958. 486p.
Illus.

Rorer, Mrs. S. T.
Canning and preserving. Revised and enlarged edition.
Philadelphia, Arnold and Co., 1912. 107p.

_____.
Ice creams, water ices, frozen puddings. Philadelphia,
Arnold and Co., 1913. 165p.

Rosatti, G.
The wine industry of Italy. London, 1888.   BV

Rose, Achilles
Carbonic acid in medicine. New York, Funk, Wagnalls
and Co., 1905. 259p.   LC

Rose, Arthur and E.
Bibliography of distillation literature. State College,
Pa., Published by authors, 1948-1955 (covers years
of 1941 to 1954). 3 vol.   LC

Rose, John
The English vineyard vindicated. London, J. M. and
John Crook, 1669. 48p.

_____.
The English vineyard vindicated. London, 1675. Falls
Village, Connecticut, Herb Grower Press, 1966 (Re-
print). Pages various by sections.

Rose, Robert Hugh, MD
Eat your way to health. A scientific system of weight
control. New edition. New York and London, Funk
and Wagnalls Co., 1924. 230p.

Rose, Robert Selden
Wine making for the amateur. New Haven, Printed
for members of the Bacchus club, 1930. "Five
hundred and fifteen copies . . . no. 333. 100p.
Illus.

Rose, S.
The spirit merchant's and excise officer's assistant.
Tables about strength of liquors. London, Published
by author, 1827. 40p.

Rose and Company
The aerated water makers guide. Dewsbury,
Published by the company, n d, (England). 43p.

Rosen, Ruth Chier
POP, Monsieur. Champagne recipes for everyday food and drink. New York, Richards Rosen Associates, Inc., 1956. 140p. Illus.
Rosenbaum, Elizabeth
See Flower, Barbara and Rosenbaum, Elisabeth
The art of cooking by Apicius.
Rosenbloom, Morris Victor Ed.
Bottling for profit; a treatise on liquor and allied industries. By Morris Victor Rosenbloom and A. B. Greenleaf. New York, American Industries Surveys, Inc., 1940. 192p. Illus. Bibliography.

———. The liquor industry. A survey of its history, manufacture, problems of control and importance. Braddock, Pa., Ruffsdale Distilling Co., 1937. 105p. Bibliography.
Rosenthal, Eric
Tankards and Traditions. Cape Town, Howard Timmons, 1961. 209p. Illus.
Ross, W.
The present state of the distilleries of Scotland. Edinburgh, 1786.   BV
Ross Mackenzie, John
Brewing and malting. London, Sir Isaac Pitman and Sons Ltd., 1921. 143p. Illus. 3rd edition, New York, Pitman Publishing Co., 1934. 182p. Illus.

———. Brewing and malting and laboratory companion (A standard manual of) London, Crosby Lockwood and Son, 1927. 412p. Illus.

———. Brewing and malting waters. 1900.   (Bird)
Rossi, P. H.
See Gottlieb, David and Peter H. Rossi
A bibliography and bibliographic review of food and food habit research.
Roth, Rodris
Tea drinking in 18th century America: its etiquette and equipage. Washington, U. S. National Museum Bull. 225 Smithsonian Institution, 1961. pages 61 to 91 Illus.
Roueche, Berton
Alcohol. Its history, folklore, effect on the human body. New York, Grove Press, Inc., 1962. 151p.

Roundell, Julia Anne Elizabeth (Tollemache)
    The still-room by Mrs. Charles Roundell and Harry
    Roberts. London and New York, J. Lane, The Bodley
    Head, 1903. 155p. Illus.
Rous, Thomas Bates
    Observations on the commutation project with a
    supplement. London, J. Debbrett, 1786. 39p.
Rouse, Lewis
    Tunbridge Wells, or a directory for drinking those
    waters. London, 1725. 50p.   BM
Routh, Jonathan
    The Good Cuppa Guide. Where to have tea in London.
    London, Wolfe Publishing Co., 1966. 64p. Illus.
    _____.
    The Hangover Book. Prevention, preparation,
    treatment and cure. London, Wolfe Publishing Co.,
    Ltd., 1967. 32p. Illus-drawings.
Rowe, J.W.F.
    The World's Coffee. A study of the economics and
    politics of the coffee industries of certain countries and
    of the international problem. London, HMSO, 1963.
    200p.
Rowntree, Joseph and Sherwell, Arthur
    Public control of the liquor traffic: being a review
    of Scandanavian experiments. London, Grant Richards,
    1903. 296p.
Rowntree, Joshua
    The Imperial Drug Trade. London, Methuen and Co.,
    1905. 304p.
Rowsell (Penning), Edmund
    Red, white and rose'. A guide to wines and spirits.
    London, Pan Books, Ltd., 1967. 129p. Illus-
    photos, drawings.
Roy, K. K.
    The Marketing of tea. Calcutta, K. K. Roy (Private)
    Ltd., 1962. Obtainable from publisher
Royal Oporto Wine Co.
    A Portuguese. London 1824. 15p.
                        (Rosenthal-Booksellers, Oxford)
Roycroft, E. A.
    See Turner, B.C.A. and Roycroft, E.A.
    AB-Z of wine making. London, Pelham Books, 1966.
    203p. Illus-photos.
Royle, John Forbes
    On cultivation of tea in northwest provinces of India,
    1834.   (Listed in Peddie)

354

Ruck, J. A. Comp.
Chemical methods for analysis of fruit and vegetable products. Summerland, B.C. Publication 1154 of Canada Dept. Agri. Contribution no. B7, Research Station, Revised 1963. 47p. Illus.

Rudd, Hugh R
Hocks and Moselles. London, Constable, 1935. 165p. map.

Rudkin, William
Hints to liquor merchants. New York, Thitchener and Glastaeter, n d, ca1890. 16p.

Rudy, Preston O.
The marketing of coffee. Chicago, 1918. 98p. Bibliography   NYPL

Ruff, Donald G.
Bottling and canning of beer, by Donald G. Ruff and Kurt Becker. Chicago, Published for Siebel Institute of Technology., 1955. 209p. Illus. References.

Ruiz, Ing. Juan Zapata
Beverages. Soft drink bottlers handbook. Chicago and Mexico, All-American Publishers Service, Inc., 1966. 112p. Illus-photos, Advertising.

Rundell, Mrs.
Domestic Cookery for the use of private families. London, Milner and Co., n d. Second title page, A new system of Domestic cookery by A Lady. A new edition. London Milner and Co., n d, ca1850. 350p. 1866, Halifax Milner and Sowerby, 350p.

Ruppert, Jacob, brewer, sponsor.
Beer in the home. New York, 1933. unpaged (16). Illus.

Rush, Benjamin
The effects of ardent spirits upon the human mind and body. no. 25. n p. No Publisher, n d. 8p.

Russell, J. Vance
Outlawing the Almighty. Springfield, Mass. John J. Mc Carthy, 1923. 120p.

Russell, Richard
Dissertation on the use of sea-water, etc., also an account of the nature and properties of all the remarkable mineral waters of Great Britain, etc. 1760-1762.   GBPOL

Rust, L.O.
See Justin, Margaret M.; Rust, Lucile Osborn and Vail, Gladys E.
Foods. An introductory college course.

Rusticus, (pseud)
> How to settle in Victoria. (wine). Melbourne. Slater,
> Williams and Hodgson, 1855. 118p.   ANL

Ruswel, O. F.
> Practical guide to malting. London, 1905. 74p.
>   (Bird)

Rutherford, H. K.
> Ceylong tea planter's notebook. 9th edition. Colombo.
> Times of Ceylon, 1931. (Forrest-100 years Ceylon tea)

Ruthven, Lord Patrick
> The ladies cabinet enlarged and opened. London, 1655.
> 252p.   GBPOL

Rutty, John
> A methodical synopsis of mineral waters comprehending
> the most celebrated medicinal waters of Great Britain,
> Ireland, France, Germany and Italy. London, 1757.
> 660p.   BM

Ryan's Liquor Shop
> BOTTOMS UP. Ryan's guide to pleasant drinking.
> New York, Leonard Wolf Associates, n d. 46p. Illus.

Rylands, Dan
> Complete catalogue of all accessories for making aerated
> waters, cordials, ices, etc. Barnsley, England, 1888.
> unpaged.

Sabin, A.
> Wine and spirit merchants accounts. London, Mc Gee
> and Co., 1904. 176p.   LC

Sabin, Mrs. Belle Carpenter
> Wines and fresh fruit beverages. Chicago, American
> Publishing Co., 1919. 75p.   LC

Sabine, H.
> Complete cellarman or innkeeper and publican's sure
> guide. London, Published by author, 1818. 48p.
>   NYPL

Sabonadiere, William
> The coffee planter in Ceylon, 2nd edition. London,
> E. and F. Spon, 1870. 168p.   NYPL

Saddington, Thomas
> Plain directions for family brewers. London, J.
> Fairburn, 1823. 28p.   (Scho)

Sadler, E. and Fletcher, C. R. L.
    Wine ghosts of Bremen. Oxford, W. Hauff, 1939.
    64p.   (Wine and Food Society Library)
Sadoun, R. and Lolli, Giorgio and Silverman, Milton
    Drinking in French culture. New Brunswick, N. J.,
    Rutgers Center of Alcohol Studies, 1965. 133p.
    Bibliography.
Sagarin, Edward
    The science and art of perfumery. New York,
    London, McGraw-Hill Book Co., Inc., 1945.
    268p. Illus. Literature of perfumery.
Saint-Arroman, A.
    Coffee, tea, and chocolate: their influence upon the
    health, the intellect, and the moral nature of man.
    Philadelphia, T. Ward, 1846. 90p.   LC
St. Pierre, Louis de
    Art of planting and cultivating the vine and also of
    making, fining and preserving wines. London, 1772.
    344p.   BM
St. Sure, Savarin (Pseud)
    Bohemian Life. Monthly publication. no. 44 - April
    1943 to no. 101 - January 1948 (not consecutive).
    Bohemian Distributing Co., Los Angeles. 44 issues
    4 pages each, loose.
Saintsbury, George
    Notes on a cellar-book. London, Macmillan and Co.,
    1920. 227p. 1933. 172p. 1939. same. 1963. same.
Sala, G. A.
    In a wine cellar in Store Street. London, Tobert
    James and Co., 1881. 16p. Illus-engravings.
Salada Tea Co.
    The story of the tea plant. Published in Canada.
    Published by the Company, (1946). unpaged (20).
    Illus-drawings.

_____.
    Teamwork. Bound volume of employee publication
    April 1929 to February 1934. Boston. paged by
    volume (year) Typed table of contents and index, Illus-
    photos-drawings.
Salem, Frederick William
    Beer, its history and its economic value as a national
    beverage. Hartford, Conn., F.W. Salem and Co.,
    1880. (List of brewers in U.S.) 275p.

Salis, Mrs. de
Drinks ala mode. Cups and drinks of every kind for every season. London, Longmans, Green and Co., 1891. 100p. 4th impresson, 1913.

_____.
The housewife's referee. London, Hutchinson and Co., 1898. 276p.
(Sallengre, Albert Hendrick de)
Ebrietatas enconium; or The praise of drunkenness, etc. by Boniface Oinophilis, de Monte Fiascone (pseud). London, Orig. 1723. Reprint London, F. Pitman, 1873. 96p.
Salmon, William
The family dictionary; or household companion. 3rd edition. London, Printed for Rhodes at the Star, 1705. 380p.

_____.
SEPLASIUM. The compleat English physician. London, 1693. 1207p.   BM
Saltus, Francis S.
Flasks and flagons. (Poetry). Buffalo, Charles Wells Moulton, 1892. 177p.
Salzman, Louis F.
English industries in the middle ages. Oxford, Clarenden Press, 1923. 360p.   (Indiana Univ.)
Samson, George Whitefield
The divine law as to wines . . . . Philadelphia, Lippincott, 1885. 613p. 1881. 467p. 1879. same.
Samuelson, J.
Drink, past, present and possible future. Liverpool, Philip Son and Nephew, 1916. 43p.   NYPL
Samuelson, James
The history of drink. A review, social scientific and political. 2nd edition. London, Trubner and Co., 1880. 288p.
Sanborn, Helen J.
A winter in Central America and Mexico. Boston, Lea and Shepard, 1886. 321p.
Sandeman, F.
History of cognac, brandy. Carlisle, Hudson, Scott and Co., 1905. 41p.   BM
Sandeman, Patrick W.
Port and sherry; the story of two fine wines. London, Sandeman, 1955. 63p. Illus.

Sandeman, Geo. G. Sons and Co.
  Jerez and its wine, sherry. London, Sandeman, 1953.
  8p.
Sanders, John
  Practical treatise on the cultivation of the vine under
  glass as well as in the open air. London, 1862. 31p.
                                                    NYPL
Sanders, T. W.
  Fruit and its cultivation. 4th edition. London, W. H.
  and L. Collingridge, 1926. 97p. Illus.

_____.
  Fruit and its cultivation in garden and orchard. 5th
  revised edition by A. J. Macself. London,
  W. H. and L. Collingridge, n d, ca1943. 288p. Illus.
Sanders, T. W. and Lansdell, J.
  Grapes: peaches, melons, and how to grow them.
  London, (1924), W. H. and L. Collingridge.
  150p. Illus.
Sanderson, J. M.
  See Cook and Confectioner.
  The Complete Cook J. M. Sanderson, Philadelphia,
  Leary and Getz. Entered 1849. 196p.
Sandford, William
  A few practical remarks on the medicinal effects of
  wine and spirits, etc., Worchester, Published by
  author, 1799. 151p.
Sanitas (pseud)
  What to drink. London, Swan, Sonneheim and Co.,
  1896. 126p.   BM
Sargent, John William
  Toasts for the times. Pictures and rhymes. New
  York, Consolidated Retail Booksellers, 1904. unpaged
  Illus-drawings.
Sasena, Joseph P.
  Fine beverages and recipes for mixed drinks.
  Cleveland, 1933. 66p.   LC
Satterly, John and Elworthy Reginald T.
  Mineral springs of Canada, Ottawa, Bureau of Mines
  Bulletin no. 16, 1917-1918. 222p.   (Toronto Public)
Saucier, Ted
  Bottoms up. New York, Greystone Press, 1951.
  270p. Illus.

Saunders, Wm.
An essay on the culture of the native and exotic grape
and both sides of the grape question. 1. An essay----.
2. Physiography in its application to grape culture
by F. J. Cope. 3. A contribution to the classification of the species of the grape vine, with hints on
culture by J.M. McMinn. Philadelphia, A. M.
Spangler, New York, C. M. Saxton, 1860. 96p.   LC
Saunders, William
Tea culture as a probable American industry.
Washington, Report no. 18., G.P.O. 1879.   21p.
                                                      NYPL

Saunders, William
A treatise on the chemical history and medical powers
of some of the most celebrated mineral waters; with
practical remarks on the aqueous regimen. London,
W. Phillips, 1800.   483p.
Savage, John
See Coffin, Robert Barry
Ale in prose and verse, by Barry Gray (pseud),
and John Savage.
Savage, William G.
Canned Foods in relation to health. (Milroy lectures
1923). Cambridge, University Press, 1923.   146p.
Bibliography.

_____ .
Food and the public health. London, Cassell and
Company, Ltd., 1919.   155p.
Sawer, John Charles
Odorographia, a natural history of raw materials and
drugs used in the perfume industry. Intended to serve
growers, manufacturers; and consumers. London,
Gurney and Jackson, 1892-94.   2 v.   Illus.
Sawyer, George F.
Bottlers' extracts: how to make them. Livingston,
Texas. Sawyer Bros., 1904.   56p.   LC
Saxe, De Forest W.
Saxe's guide, or, Hints to soda water dispensers.
Complete and modern formulae for the manufacture and
dispensing of all carbonated drinks. Omaha, Neb.,
The Phospho-Guarano Co., 1890.   79p.   Illus.
Advertising. 2nd ed., New Guide, 1893, Saxe Publ Co.,
Chicago., 94p. Illus. 3rd ed., New Guide, 1894,
Saxe Publ Co., Chicago, 110p. Illus. 4th ed., New
Guide, 1897, Saxe Publ Co., Chicago 148p. Illus.

Saxon, Edgar J.
  Sensible food for all in Britain and the temperate
  zones. Ashingdon, Rochford, Essex, The C.W.
  Daniel Co., 1949. 128p.
Saywell, Lawrence George
  See Cruess, William Vere
  Laboratory examination of wines and other fermented
  fruit products, by W. V. Cruess . . . M. A. Joslyn
  . . . and L. G. Saywell.
Scamell, George
  Breweries and maltings: their arrangement,
  construction, and machinery. London and Edinburgh,
  A. Fullarton, 1871. 134p. 2nd edition. London,
  E and F. N. Spon, 1880. 178p.
Scarborough, N. F.
  Sweet manufacture. A practical handbook on the manufac-
  ture of sugar confectionery. 3rd edition. London,
  Leonard Hill Ltd., 1941. 122p.
Scarisbrick, Joseph (of the Inland Revenue.)
  Beer manual: historical and technical. Revenue
  Series no. 1. 2nd edition revised and improved.
  Wolverhampton, 1892. 106p.

_____ .
  Beer taxation. Wolverhampton, 1908.   (Bird)

_____ .
  Spirit manual, historical and technical. London, 1894.
  147p. (Jordan Wine Co.)
Schaefer, The F. M. Brewing Co.
  Our one hundredth year, 1842-1942. New York, 1942.
  unpaged (22). Illus.
Schell, J. Henry
  Mixed drinks up to date. Milwaukee, Caspar.
  (U.S. Catalog, 1902).
Schenk, Henry A
  The new medical wine book. San Francisco, 1922.
  24p.   LC
Schenley Import Corporation
  An introduction to wines, by Oscar Wile. New York,
  1934. 56p.   LC

_____ .
  Wine without frills; everyday enjoyment of imported
  wines and spirits. New York, Schenley, 1939. 61p.
  Illus.

_____.
Wines; how, when, and what to serve. New York,
Schenley, 1936. 62p. Illus. Glossary
Schenley Products Co.
Merry Mixer. A booklet of mixtures and mulches,
fizzes and whizzes. New York, 1936. 34p. Illus.
1936 (August) same.

_____.
Merry mixer (The). New York, 1938. unpaged (20).
Illus.
Scherer, P. and Co.
Complete list of mineral waters, foreign and domestic
with their analyses, uses and sources. New York,
F. A. Ringler and Co., 1882. 59p.   LC
Schimmel and Co.
Praktische Vorschriften (Lkquor). Leipzig, 1898.
(In German.) 99p.

_____.
Annual report on essential oils, aromatic chemicals
and related materials. New York, 1945. 127p.
Illus. Bibliography.

_____.
Schimmel Briefs. Volume I No.'s 1-189 from April
1935 to December 1950. New York. paged by
sections.
Schlicting, E.
See Wyatt, Francis and Schlicting, Emil
Practical points for practical brewers.
Schlicting, Emil and Winther, H. Editors
Practical points for brewers. Compiled by the staff
of the National Brewers' Academy. New York,
National Brewers' Academy and Consulting Bureau,
1933. 174p.
Schlink, F. J.
Eat, drink and be wary. Washington, N. J. Consumers'
Research, Inc., 1935. 322p. References.
Schlittler, E. and B. Frères
Schweizerische Korkenfabrik, (Catalog of corks and
corking machinery. (In German). Naefels, Switzerland,
n d, ca1927. 20p.
Schlüter, Hermann
The brewing industry and the brewery workers' move-
ment in America. Cincinnati, O., International Union
of United Brewery Workmen of America, 1910, 331p.

Schmeiser, Alan
Have bottles . . . will "Pop". Dixon, California,
Michalan Press, 1968. 194p. Illus-photos.
Schmidt, A. William
Fancy drinks and popular beverages, how to prepare
and serve them. By the only William. New York, .
Dick and Fitzgerald, 1896. 155p.

_____.
The flowing bowl when and what to drink. By the
only William (William Schmidt). Full instructions how
to prepare, mix and serve beverages. New York,
C. L. Webster and Co., 1892. 294p.
Schmidt, E.
Brewery architects and engineers handbook. Chicago,
Published by author, 1898. 85p.   LC
Schmidt, J. A.
Diseases of the vine, how to prevent and cure them,
according to doctrines of M. Pasteur. New York, 1868.
47p.   (Univ. Illinois)
Schoellhorn, Fritz
Bibliographie des Brauwesens. (Beer and brewing).
Berlin, 1928. (In German and English). double
pages total number - 438.
Schoengold, Morris D. Ed.
Encyclopedia of substitutes and synthetics. New York,
Philosophical Library, 1943. 282p.
Schoffer, C. H.
The coffee trade. New York, E. Sauer, etc., 1869.
58p.   LC
Scholefield, A. J. B.
The treatment of brewing water. Liverpool,
Published by the author, n d, ca1950. 56p.
School of Hotel Administration
Hotel Management and related subjects. A selected
list of books, pamphlets and periodical articles.
No. 11, July 1952 for 1951.   19p.
No. 12, June 1953 for 1952.   48p.
No. 13, June 1954 for 1953.   80p.
No. 14, June 1955 for 1954.   114p.
No. 16, June 1956 for 1965.   157p.
No. 17, June 1958 for 1957.   165p.
No. 19, August 1960.   64p.
No. 20, August 1961.   60p.
                (Cornell University, Ithaca, N.Y.)

Schoonmaker, Frank
　✓ American wines, by Frank Schoonmaker and Tom Marvel,
　New York, Duell, Sloan and Pearce, 1941. 312p. Illus.

　The complete wine book, by Frank Schoonmaker and Tom
　Marvel. New York, Simon and Schuster, 315p. Illus.
　Bibliography.

　✓ Dictionary of wines; edited by Tom Marvel. New York,
　Hastings House, 1951. 120p. Illus.

　✓ Encyclopedia of wine (Frank Schoonmaker's). New York,
　Hastings House, 1964. 410p. Illus.

　Vintage chart, 1945-1954. New York, Sherry Wine
　and Spirits Co., 1955. 19p.

　✓ The wines of Germany. New York, Hastings House,
　1956. 152p. Illus. 1966, 156p. Illus.
Schoppfer, Theodore
　Philosophy of beer, 1733.　　　　　　　　　(Scho)
Schreiber, G. R.
　A concise history of vending in the U. S. A. Chicago,
　Published by Vend., 1961. 46p.
Schroeter, Louis C.
　Sulphur dioxide. Applications in foods beverages and
　pharmaceuticals. Oxford and other cities, Pergamon
　Press, 1966. 342p. Illus. References.
Schultz, Carl H.
　Carl Schultz's mineral spring waters, their chemical
　composition, physiological action, therapeutic and
　general use. New York, W. Wallach, Printer, 1880.
　36p.　　　　　　　　　　　　　　　　　　　LC

　Schultz and Warker's mineral spring waters, their
　chemical composition, physiological action and therapeu-
　tical use; with a short review of the history of mineral
　waters. New York, Baker and Godwin, Printers, 1865.
　70p. Illus.
Schultz, Christian
　See Thomas, Jerry
　How to mix drinks, or, Bon-Vivant's companion.

_____.
A manual for the manufacture of cordials, liquors,
fancy syrups, etc. New York, Dick and Fitzgerald,
1862. Bound with Thomas, Jerry. How to mix drinks,
copy in cocktails. pgs 92 to 233. Illus.
Schultz, H. W.; Day, E. A. and Libbey, L. M. Editors.
Symposium on food: the chemistry and physiology of
flavors. Westport, Conn., The Avi Publishing Co.,
1967. 552p. Illus-photos, drawings. Bibliographies.
Schwaab, E. F.
Secrets of canning. New York, John Murphy Co.,
1890. 142p.   LC
Schwartz, Robert J. Compiler and Editor
The dictionary of business and industry. New York,
B. C. Forbes and Sons Publishing Co., 1954. 561p.
Schwarz, Anton
Bibliography of the writings of Anton Schwarz.
Contained in Arnold - History of the Brewing Industry
and Brewing Science in America, pages 25-27.
Chicago, 1933. 2p. Bibliography.
Schwarz, Anton
See Thausing, Julius E.
The theory and practice of the preparation of malt and
the fabrication of beer, with especial reference to the
Vienna process of brewing.
Schwarz Laboratories
See Hackstaff, B.W. and Brenner, M.W.
An analysis of packaging costs in the brewing industry.
_____.
Comparative analysis of bottled and canned beers.
New York, 1936. 75p. References.
_____.
Extract and alcohol tables. New York, n d, 1950. 47p.
Schwenck, Jim
See Roe, Charlie and Schwenck, Jim
The home bartender's guide and song book.
Scotch Whisky Ass'n.
Scotch whisky. Edinburgh, n d. 12p. Illus.
London, n d. 16p. Illus.
Scott, Albert L.
See Fosdick, Raymond B. and Scott, Albert L.
Toward liquor control.
Scott, Dick
Winemakers of New Zealand. Auckland, Southern Cross
Books, 1964. Part 1 79p. Part 2 unpaged (20p.)
Illus.

Scott, George E.
Wine. Chicago, Published by author, (1936). 103p.
Scott, J. M.
The Great Tea Venture. New York, E. P. Dutton and
Co., Inc., 1965. (Same as The Tea Story published
in London 1964.) 204p. Illus-photos.

————— The tea story. London, William Heinemann, Ltd.,
1964. 204p. Illus. Bibliography.
Scott, James Maurice
The man who made wine. New York, Dutton, 1954.
124p. Illus.

————— Vineyards of France. London, Hodder and Stoughton,
1950. 163p. Illus-drawings.
Scottish Licensed Trade Ass'n.
Handbook, 1968-1969. Edinburgh. 224p. Advertising.
Scoville, Wilbur L.
The art of compounding. 2nd edition. Philadelphia,
P. Blakiston Son and Co., 1897. 271p.

————— Extracts and perfumes. Boston, The Spatula Publishing
Co., n d. 101p. n d, ca1910, 112p. 3rd edition,
n d, 112p.
Scrivener, Mathew
Treatise against drunkenness (by Charles Brown).
London, St. Augustines de Tempore, 1685. 193p.   BM
Scudamore, Sir Charles
A treatise on the composition and medical properties
of the mineral waters of -- (12 different springs).
2nd edition. London, Longman, Rees, Orme, Brown,
Green and Longmans, 1833. 215p.
Seabrook, W. P.
Modern fruit growing. 6th edition. completely revised.
London, Ernest Benn Limited. 1944. 307p. 8th
edition, 1947. 313p.
Seager, Robert
Practical treatise on manufacture of cheap non-alcoholic
beverages. Edinburgh, National Temperance Publication
Depot, 1888. 96p.   BM
Seagram-Distillers Co.
Seagram's vacation-time food and drink guide. New
York, n d. 32p. Illus.

_____.
Seagram's weekend bar and barbecue book. New York,
n d. 34p. Illus- drawings.
Seagram, Joseph E. and Sons Inc.
See Willkie, Robert T.
Distillers' grain manual compiled by Robert T. Willkie
and Rolland S, Mather.

_____.
Welcome to house of Seagram. Louisville, 1943.
unpaged   (Louisville Public)
Seaman, Valentine
Dissertation on the mineral waters of Saratoga, etc.
New York, Printed by Samuel Campbell, 1795. 40p.
                                          NYPL
Sears, Fred C.
Productive small fruit culture. Philadelphia, J. B.
Lippincott, 1920. 368p.   (Davis)
Sedgwick, James
A new treatise on liquors wherein the use and abuse
of wine, malt drinks, water, etc. are particularly
considered in many diseases, etc. London, Charles
Rivington, 1725. 407p.
Seguin, A. Cloud
The odoriferous formulary. How to prepare flavoring
extracts, cordials, syrups, etc. Baltimore, W. R.
Mc Kenley Jr., 1885. 30p.   LC
Seibel, J. E. II
Beer and health. Chicago, Seibel Publishing Co.,
1934. 24p.   LC
Seldes, Gilbert Vivian
The future of drinking. Boston, Little Brown, and Co.,
1930. 173p. Illus.
Seliger, Robert V.
Alcoholics are sick people. Baltimore, Alcoholism
Publications, February, 1945. 80p.
Selivanova, Nina Nikolaevna
Dining and wining in old Russia. New York, Dutton,
1933. 154p.
Sellers, Charles
Oporto, old and new; being a historical record of the
port wine trade, and a tribute to British commercial
enterprise in the north of Portugal. London, Harper
1899. 314p. Illus.

Selley, Ernest
      The English Public House as it is. London, Longman's
      Green and Co., Ltd., 1927. 184p.
✓ Seltman, Charles Theodore
      Wine in the ancient world. London, Routledge and
      Paul, 1957. 196p. Illus. Bibliography.
Seltzer, R. E.
      See Hoos, Sidney and Seltzer, R.E.
      Lemon and lemon products. Changing economic relation-
      ships.
Senn, Charles Herman
      Cookery for invalids and the convalescent. 7th edition.
      London, Food and Cookery Publishing Agency, 1916.
      123p.

_____ .
      A dictionary of foods and culinary encyclopedia. 4th
      edition. London, The Food and Cookery Publishing Co.,
      1920. 166p. 5th edition, Melbourne, Ward Lock and
      Co., Ltd., n d, 188p.

_____ .
      See Steedman, M. E. and Senn, Charles Herman
      Homemade summer and winter drinks. Cups, liqueurs,
      cocktails and invalid drinks.

_____ .
      Ices and how to make them. London, Universal Food
      and Cookery Ass'n, 1900. 77p.
Serjeant, Richard
      A man may drink. Aspects of a pleasure. London,
      Putnam and Co., Ltd., 1964. 191p. Bibliography.
Serocold, Walter Pearce, Ed.
      The Story of Watneys. (Beer and brewing). St. Albans,
      Herts, Watney, Combe, Reid and Co., 1959. 130p.
      Illus.
Sethness, Charles O. et al
      Modern, simple and practical formulae pertaining to
      manufacture of cordials, bitters, gins, whiskies,
      brandies, and liquors of all kinds. Chicago, Sethness
      Co., 1905. 164p.   LC
Seymour, William
      A practical treatise on brewing and after-management
      of malt liquors. London, R. Boyd, upper St. Islington
      printer, 1846. 72p.
Shales, Ken
      Brewing better beers. Andover, Hampshire. Amateur
      Winemaker, 1969. 76p. Illus-drawings. Glossary.

_____. A short guide to home brewing. Liverpool, Leigh
Williams and Sons, n d. 4p.

Shand, Phillip Morton
Bacchus; or, Wine today and tomorrow. London, K.
Paul, Trench, Trubner and Co., Ltd., New York, E.
P. Dutton and Co., 1927. 96p.

_____. A book of food. London, Jonathan Cape, 1927. 319p.

_____. A book of French wines. Rev. and enl. ed., London,
J. Cape, 1960. 415p. Glossary. Same. London,
Alfred A. Knopf, 1928. 3rd rev. ed., London, 1964.
301p.

_____. A book of other wines than French. New York, A. A.
Knopf Ltd., 1929. 185p. Bibliography.

_____. A book of wine. London, Guy Chapman, 1926. 320p.
Bibliography- Glossary.

Shane Na Gael
Irish toasts. 1908. New York, Dodge Publishing Co.,
111p.

Shane, Ted
Bar guide. Cartoons by Vip, (pseud). Published by
True, the man's magazine. New York, Fawcett
Publication, 1950. 179p. Illus- drawings.

_____. Funny bar book and guide to mixed drinks. Cartoons
by Vip (pseud). Rev. and enl. ed. of Bar guide.
Greenwich, Conn., Fawcett Publications, 1955.
144p. Illus- drawings.

Shannon, R. MD
Practical treatise on brewing, distilling and rectification.
London, Robert Scholey, 1805. Paged by sections
(873). Illus- engravings.

Shaver, Gordon O.
Wines and liquors from the days of Noah. A safe
guide to sane drinking. n p, Published by author, 1939.
19p.

Shaw, Charles G.
Nightlife. Vanity Fair's intimate guide to New York
after dark. New York, The John Day Co., 1931. 182p.
Illus.

Shaw, Daphne Comp.
A catalogue of British scientific and technical books.
3rd edition. London, British Science Guild, 1930.
754p.
Shaw, Henry
The vine and civilization. St. Louis, 1884. 71p.
(Brady Library- Fresno State College)
Shaw, Peter
Juice of the grape or wine preferable to water. London,
W. Lewis, 1724. 56p. NYPL

_____.
Three essays in artificial philosophy or unusual
chemistry. An essay for the improvement of distillation,
etc., London, 1731. 192p. BM
Shaw, Thomas George
The wine trade and its history. London, P. Richardson,
1851. 16p. BM

_____.
Wine, the vine, and the cellar. London, Longman,
Green, Longman, Roberts and Green, 1863. 505p.
Illus.
Shaw, Alex D., and Co., Inc.
Simple facts about wines, spirits, ale and stout . . . .
New York, 1934. 64p.
Shaw Publishing Co.
Manufacturers' practical recipes. London, 1948. 424p.
Shay, Frank, Comp.
Drawn from the wood; consolations in words and music
for pious friends and drunken companions. New York,
The Macaulay Co., 1929. 186p. Illus.

_____.
More pious friends and drunken companions . . . . New
York, Macaulay Co., 1928. 190p. Illus.

_____.
My pious friends and drunken companions; songs and
ballads of conviviality. New York, Macaulay, 1927.
192p. Illus.

_____.
My pious friends and drunken companions and more
pious friends and drunken companions . . . New York,
Dover, 1961. 235p. Illus.
Shear, S. W. and Blair, R. E.
California fruit statistics and related data. Berkeley,
California Agricultural Experiment Station. Bulletin
763. June 1958. 269p.

Sheen, James Richmond
Wines and other fermented liquors; from the earliest ages to the present time . . . London, R. Hardwicke, 1865. 292p. Illus.

Shelley, Henry C.
Inns and taverns of old London. Historical and literary associations, etc. Boston, L. C. Page and Co., New edition, 1928. 366p. Illus.

Shepherd, Cecil William
Wine you can make; a practical handbook on how to make these cheap and delicious wines in one's own home. London and Melbourne, Ward, Lock and Co., Ltd., 1954. 128p. Illus. Same, 1958.

_____.
Wines, spirits, and liqueurs. New York, Abelard-Schuman, 1959. 160p. Illus-drawings.

Sheridan, J. E.
The complete buffet manual; or, How to mix fancy drinks. making all kinds of domestic wines, liquors, brandies, beers, cordials, extracts, syrups, etc. Chicago and New York, The Henneberry, 1901. 145p. Illus.

Sheridan, John
A complete treatise of the art of distillation, also the whole art of rectification. From the French of A. P. Dubrunfaut. London, Sherwood, Gilbert and Piper, 1830. 283p. Illus-drawings.

Sherman, Henry C.
Chemistry of food and nutrition. New York, The Macmillan Co., 1913. 355p. References-Suggested reading. 2nd edition, 1919. 454p. 6th edition, 1941. 611p. References.

_____.
Food products. 4th edition. New York, The Macmillan Co., 1948. 428p. References- Suggested Reading.

Sherman, Henry C. and Lanford, Caroline Sherman
Essentials of nutrition. New York, The Macmillan Co., 1940. 418p. Glossary.

Sherrard-Smith, W.
Make mine wine. Chatham, W. and J. Mackay, 1959. 173p. Illus.

_____.
Make your own wine. London, Phoenix House, 1964. 120p. Illus.

371

———— 222 Reputed Wine Recipes. Herne Bay, Published by
author, n d, ca1964. 8p.

———— Winebook for beginners. n p. No Publisher, n d.
62p. Illus.

———— Winemaking in earnest. London, 1962. 95p.
(Brady Library- Fresno State College)
Sherwell, Arthur
See Rowntree, Joseph and Sherwell, Arthur
Public control of liquor traffic.
Shevlin, James and Hetherington, Thomas
Alcoholic spirit testing. Being a treatise on the true
effects which are produced on "obscured" spirits, either
by "evaporation" or by the addition of water. Gravity
tables. London, Eyre and Spottiswoode, 1899. 142p.
Shih, Ko Ching and Shih, C. Y.
American brewing industry and the beer market.
Milwaukee, Published by authors, 1958. 126p.
Bibliography.
Shillington, D. F. and Bunting, John J. Compilers
Bunting's book on breakfast beverages. London, Bunting
and Co., Ltd., 1920. 99p. Illus.
Shirley, Cecil
Fetters on freedom. The story of prohibition in
America. London, Mills and Boon, 1920. 53p.
Shirley, John
Accomplished ladies rich closet of rarities (Art of
distilling and making wines). London, N. Bodington
and J. Blare, 1687. 214p.   BM
Shirley, Thomas
Curious distillatory or the art of distilling coloured
spirits, liquors, cyder, etc., from vegetables. London,
1677. 111p.   GBPOL
Shoemaker, James Sheldon
Small fruit culture. A text for instruction and reference
work and a guide for field practice. 2nd edition.
Philadelphia, The Blakiston Co., 1948. 433p. Illus.
Shore, A.
A practical treatise on brewing, etc., London,
Published by author, 1804. 103p.
Shore, William
Cups; how to make, why to take. Perth, H. Cleeg and
Son, 1924. 15p.   BM

Short, Richard of Bury
Peri Phychopsoias of drinking water, etc. London, John
Crook, 1656. 173p.
Short, Thomas
Discourses on tea, wines, spirits with rules for gouty
people. London, T. Longman, 1750. 424p.

—————— Dissertation on tea. London, Fletcher Gyles, 1730. 119p. BM

—————— An essay toward a natural and medicinal history of principal
mineral waters of Cumberland, Northumberland and Sheffield. Printed by John Garnet for author. 1740. 230p.
(Bodleian Library, Oxford)

—————— General treatise on different sorts of cold mineral
waters of England. London, 1765. 248p.   BM

—————— The natural, experimental and medicinal history of
the mineral waters of Derbyshire, Lincolnshire and
Yorkshire particularly those of Scarborough. London,
Published by the author, 1734. 359p.

—————— A rational discourse on the inward uses of water, etc.
London, Samuel Chandler, 1725. 70p.

—————— A view of the prejudice arising both to the country and
the revenue from imposition on ale, beer, etc. Edin-
burgh, 1748. 11p.   Walford- book dealer)
Shortt, John
Handbook to coffee planting in Southern India. Madras,
1864. 200p.   GBPOL
Shreve, Franklin
10000 secrets of the rich and wise. Sioux Falls,
S. D., Published by author, 1900. 128p. Illus.   LC
Sibson, Alfred
Agricultural chemistry. New edition. London,
Routledge, Warne and Routledge, 1862. (Cover title-
Agricultural Chemistry. Sibson and Voelcker). 239p.
Sichel, Allan
A guide to good wine. London, Chambers, 1952.
200p. Illus.

—————— The Penguin book of wines. Harmondsworth, Middx.
Penguin Books, 1965. 297p.
Siebel, John E., Dr.
List of the writings of Dr. Siebel. On pages 16- 21 in

373

Arnold History of the Brewing Industry and brewing-science in America. Chicago, 1933. 4p. Bibliography.

Sievers, Arthur F.
Methods of extracting volatile oils from plant material etc. Technical Bulletin no. 16. Washington, Dept. of Agri., 1928. 35p. Illus.

Sigmond, George Gabriel
Tea; its effects, medicinal and moral. London, Longman, Orme, Brown, Green and Longmans, 1839. 144p.

Sigsworth, E. M
The brewing trade during the industrial revolution. The case of Yorkshire. York, St. Anthony's Press, University of York, Borthwick Institute of Historical Research, Borthwick papers no. 31., 1967. 36p.

Silent Partner
See Anon.
Liquor dealer's silent partner. Containing tables of valuable information for liquor dealers and proprietors of hotels and saloons. Instructions for amount of water to add to reduce proof of liquor.

Sillett, S. W.
Illicit scotch. Aberdeen, Beaver Books, 1965. 121p. Illus. Bibliography and Glossary

Silverman, Milton
See Leake, Chauncey (Dr.), and Silverman, Milton (Dr.) Alcoholic beverages in clinical medicine.

——— See Sadoun, R. and Lolli, Giorgio and Silverman, Milton. Drinking in French culture.

——— Magic in a bottle. New York, The Macmillan Co., 1942. 332p. Bibliography.

Simmonds, Charles
Alcohol. Its production, properties, chemistry and industrial applications. London, Macmillan and Co., 1919. 574p. Illus. Bibliography.

——— Alcohol in commerce and industry. London, Pittman's Common Commodities and Industries, 1922. 119p.
(Crerar)

Simmonds, N. W.
Bananas. Tropical Agriculture Series. 2nd edition. London, Longmans, Green and Co., Ltd., 1966. 512p. Illus. References.

374

Simmonds, Peter Lund
   Coffee and chicory: their culture, chemical composition,
   preparation for market, and consumption, with simple
   tests for detecting adulteration, and practical hints for
   the producer and consumer. London, E. and F. N.
   Spon, 1864. 102p.

———— Hops: their cultivation, commerce, and uses in various
   countries. A manual of reference for the grower,
   dealer, and brewer. London, E. and F. N. Spon,
   1877. 135p.

———— The popular beverages of various countries natural and
   artificial, fermented, distilled, aerated and infused
   history, production, consumption. London, J. Gilbert
   Smith, 1888. 255p.

———— Tropical Agriculture. London, E. and F. N. Spon,
   1877. 515p. Bibliography.
Simon, André Louis
   The art of good living: a contribution to the better
   understanding of food and drink together with a
   gastronomic vocabulary and a wine dictionary. London,
   Constable, 1929. 201p.

———— Bibliotheca Bacchica. Bibliographie Raisonnee Tome I
   Incunables. London and Paris, Maggs Brothers, 1927.
   (In French). 238p. Illus.

———— Bibliotheca Gastronomica. A catalogue of books and
   documents on gastronomy. London, The Wine and Food
   Society, 1953. 196p. Illus.

———— Bibliotheca vinaria; a bibliography of books and pamphlets
   dealing with viticulture, wine-making, distillation, the
   management, sale, taxation, use and abuse of wines and
   spirits. London, G. Richards, Ltd., 1913. 339p.

———— The blood of the grape; the wine trade text book.
   London, Duckworth, 1920. 302p.

———— Bottlescrew days; wine drinking in England during the
   eighteenth century. Boston, Small Maynard, 1927.
   273p. Illus.

By request; an autobiography. London, The Wine and
Food Society, 1957. 180p. Illus.

Champagne. New York and London, McGraw-Hill and
Co., Inc., 1962. 224p. Illus. Bibliography.

Champagne. London, Wine and Food Society, 1949.
15p.

Champagne. The elixir of youth. London, Pommery
and Greno, Ltd., 1930. 31p. Illus.

Champagne; with appendices on corks; methods of keeping
and serving champagne vintages; brands, shippers.
London, Constable, 1934. 140p.

The commonsense of wine. London, Published by the
Wine and Food Society and Michael Joseph, 1966.
192p.

A concise encyclopedia of gastronomy. Section VIII.
Wine, beer, cider, spirits. London, The Wine and
Food Society, 1948. 178p.

A dictionary of wine. London, Toronto, etc. Cassell,
and Co., Ltd., 1935. 266p. Illus.
Same. New York, Longmans, Green, 1936.

A dictionary of wines, spirits and liqueurs. London,
H. Jenkins, 1958. 167p.

A dictionary of wines, spirits and liqueurs. New York,
The Citadel Press, 1963. 190p. Illus-drawings.

Drink. London, Burke, 1948. 272p. Illus.

Elixir of Youth. London, Wine Trade Club, 1924.
(Simon's In the Twilight)

English fare and French wines; being notes toward the
furtherance of the entente cordiale gastronomique.
London, N. Neame, 1955. 78p. Illus.

English wines and cordials. London, and Chesham, Gramol, 1946. 144p.

German wines. London, Wine and Food Society, n d, (1939). (Simon's In the Twilight)

The gourmet's week-end book. London, Seeley Service, 1952. 347p. Illus.

The great wines of Germany and its famed vineyards, by Andre L. Simon and S. F. Hallgarten. New York, McGraw-Hill, 1963. 191p. Illus-photos. Glossary and Bibliography.

Guide to good food and wines; a concise encyclopedia of gastronomy, complete and unabridged. London and Glasgow, Collins, 1956. 816p. List of Sources. Same, 1960.

The History of Champagne. London, George Rainbird Ltd., Ebury Press, 1962. 192p. Illus. Bibliography.

History of the champagne trade in England. London, Wyman, 1905. 193p.

The history of the wine trade in England. Originally published in 3 volumes 1906-07. London, The Holland Press, 1964. 3 volumes, 387, 339, 423 pgs. List of authorities.

The history of the wine trade in England. London, Wyman, 1906. 3 volumes, Illus.
HP Library has: vol. 1, 1906. 387p.
               vol. 2, 1907. 339p.

How to enjoy wine in the home. London, Newman Neame, 1953. 32p. Illus.

How to serve wine in hotels. London, 1952.
(Location Unknown)

In praise of good living. An Anthology. London, Frederick Mueller, 1949. 63p.   BM

—— In the twilight. London, Michael Joseph, 1969. 182p. Bibliography of his works.

—— In vino veritas, a book about wine. London, G. Richards, Ltd., 1913. 202p.

—. Know your wines. London, Coram Publishers, 1956. 115p. Illus.

—— Let mine be wine; the philosophy of wine. The anatomy of wine. The geography of wine. The choice of wine. The service of wine. London, Wine and Food Society, 1958. 24p.

—— Madeira and its wines. Funchal. Issued by Madeira Wine Ass'n, 1947.   (Simon's In the Twilight)

—— Madeira; wine, cakes and sauce, by Andre L. Simon and Elizabeth Craig. London, Constable, 1933. 153p.

—— Menus for gourmets. London, Herbert Jenkins, 1961. 96p.

—— The noble grapes and the great wines of France. New York, McGraw-Hill, 1957. 180p. Illus. Bibliographies.

—— Notes on the late J. Pierpont Morgan's Cellar book, 1906. London, Privately printed for the author at the Curwen Press, 1944. 37p.

√ Partners. A guide to the game of wine and food matching. London, Wine and Food Society, n d. 20p.

—— Port. London, Constable, 1934. 130p.

—— Rum. London, The Wine and Food Society, 1950. 16p.

—— The supply, the care and the sale of wine. A book of reference for wine-merchants. London, Duckworth, 1923. 208p.

—— Tables of content; leaves from my diary. London, Constable, 1933. 279p.

———— Vintagewise, a postscript to Saintsbury's Notes on a cellar book. London, M. Joseph, Ltd., 1946. 174p. Same. 5th revised impression, 1950.

———— See Golding, Louis and Simon, Andre L. Editors. We shall eat and drink again. A wine and food anthology.

———— What about wine! All the answers. London, Newman Neame, 1953. 56p. Illus-engravings.

———— The wine and food menu book. London, Mueller, 1956. 377p.

———— Wine and spirits; the connoisseur's textbook. London, Duckworth, 1919. 272p.

———— Wine and the wine trade. London, Sir Isaac Pitman and Sons, Ltd., (1921), 110p. Illus-photos, engravings. Bibliography. 2nd edition, London, Pitman, 1934. 128p.

———— The wine connoisseur. London, The Wine Trade Club Ltd., 1923. 32p.

———— The wine connoisseur's catechism. London, The Wine and Food Society, 1934. 40p.

———— Wine in Shakespeare's days and Shakespeare's plays. London, Imprinted at the Curwen Press, 1931. Reprinted by Wine and Food Society Co., 1964. 35p. Illus.

———— Wine maketh the heart glad and gladdens the heart of man. London, E. J. Burrow and Co., 1931. 25p.
                                                            BM

———— A wine primer. Revised edition. New York, Erilsson-Taplinger, 1960. 152p.

———— Wines and liqueurs from A to Z; a glossary. London, The Wine and Food Society, 1935. 59p. Same, 1952. Glossary.

————— Wines and spirits; the connoisseur's textbook. London,
Skilton, 1961. 194p. Illus.

————— The wines of France. New York, The Wine and Food
Society, 1935. 64p.

————— The wines of France. Printed in France by French
Government, 1939. 32p.

————— Wines of the world. London, McGraw-Hill Publishing
Co., Ltd., 1967. 719p. Illus-coloured photos.
Bibliography-Glossary.

————— The 'Wines of the world' pocket library. London,
The Wine and Food Society, 1951. 16 volumes about
15p. each.

————— ✓ The Wines, Vineyards and Vignerons of Australia.
Melbourne, Lansdowne Press, 1966. 194p. Illus-
photos. Bibliography and Glossary Wine Tasting Terms.
Simon, S.P.E.
See Anon.
Liqueurograph Chart (The). Devised by Peter Hall-
garten and S.P.E. Simon.
Simon, S.P.E. and Hallgarten, Peter
The Wineograph Chart. 4th revised edition. London,
Wineographs, nd, ca1964.
Simons, Simon
Alcoholic drinks: easy way to make them, cordials,
liquors, cocktails, etc. Providence, R.I., Acton
Press, 1934. 16p.   LC
Simpson, G.
See Anon.
Ash's Patent Piston Freezing Machine, and wine cooler.
Simpson, John
The grape wine, its preparation and cultivation. London,
1883.   BM
Simpson, W.
Philosophical discussion of fermentation, W. Cooper,
1675. 149p.   GBPOL
Sinclair, Sir John, Bart
The code of health and longevity, etc. 4th edition.
London, Published by the author, 1818. 566p.

Sinclair, Robert
Essential oils. The basis of nature's perfume. London,
Unilever Limited, 1957. 36p. Illus.
Sinclair, Upton
The Cup of Fury. Great Neck, N.Y., Channel Press,
Inc., 1956. 190p. Bibliography.
Sinclair, W. J. (Sir William Japp)
Beverages: water, tea, cocoa, etc. 1881. 24p.   BM
Sinclair, Walton B.
See Bartholomew, Elbert T. and Sinclair, Walton B.
The Lemon Fruit.

_____.
The Orange. Its biochemistry and physiology.
(Berkeley). University of California Division of
Agricultural Sciences, 1961. 475p. Literature cited.
Singleton, V. L.
See Amerine, M. A. and Singleton, V. L.
Wine, an introduction for Americans.
Sivitz, Michael and Foote, Elliott H.
Coffee processing technology. Westport, Conn.,
Avi Publishing Co., 1963. 2 vol. 598, 379. Illus.
Skinner, Charles M.
Myths and legends of flowers, trees, fruits, and plants.
In all ages and in all climes. Philadelphia and London
J. B. Lippincott Co., 1925. 302p. Illus.
Skinner, H. Burchstead, MD
The American Prize-Book. Boston, Published by
author, 1853. 194p.
Skinner, William Woolford
American mineral waters: the New England States.
Washington, Government Printing Office, 1911. 111p.
                                                        LC
Skrimshire, Fenwick
A series of popular Chymical Essays. In 2 volumes,
London, John White, 1802. Vol. 1. 192p. Vol. 2.
150p.
Skrine, Edward H. and Brownen, George
The tea we drink. London, Simpkin Marshall, 1901.
26p.   BM
Skuse, E.
The confectioners' hand-book and practical guide to the
art of sugar boiling in all its branches . . . 3rd edition.
London, 1881. 182p. Illus. 11th edition. London,
Bush, 1921. 13th edition. London, Bush, 1957. 344p.
Illus.

Slater, Leslie G.
>The secrets of making wine from fruits and berries.
>Lilliwaup, Washington, Terry Publishing Co., 1965.
>90p. Illus.

Sleigh, G.
>Brewer's assistant. Bath, 1815. 338p. USBA

Slessor, Kenneth
>The grapes are growing; the story of Australian wine.
>Sydney, The Australian Wine Board, 1958. unpaged
>n d, Illus.

Sloane, T. O'Conor
>Liquid air of the liquidation of gases. London,
>Sampson, Low, Marston and Co., 1899. 365p.

Smedley, Jack and Jill
>The hangover cookbook. New York Essandess Special
>Publication, 1968. 96p. Illus-drawings.

Smeed, T.
>The wine merchant's manual. A treatise on the
>fining, preparation of finings, and general management
>of wine. London, Smith, Elder and Co., 1845, 81p.

Smith?
>The school of arts, London, 1799. BM

——————
>Tsiology: a discourse on tea. (By a dealer). London,
>W. Walker, 1827. 147p. LC

Smith, Albert
>A bowl of punch. London, D. Bogue, 1848. 125p. LC

Smith, Brooke
>Prohibition and the bible. Brownwood, (Texas?)
>Published by the author, 1932. 207p.

Smith, C. S.
>See Langseth-Christensen, Lillian and Carol Sturm Smith
>The chocolate and coffee cookbook.

Smith, Charles
>Smacks and smiles. Fancy drinks and how they are
>mixed. New York, Popular Publishing Co., 1904. 128p.
>(U.S. Catalog)

Smith, David
>Carbonated waters: a guide to their manufacture with a
>treatise on the purification of the water, clarification
>and manipulation of syrups, and preservation of
>carbonated beverages. New York, W. B. Keller, 1882.
>63p. LC

(Smith, E.)
　Compleat housewife or accomplished gentlewoman's
　companion. By E----- S-----. 3rd edition. London,
　J. Pemberton, 1729. 332p.
Smith, Edward, MD
　Foods. 4th edition. London, Henry S. King and Co.,
　1876. 485p.
Smith, George
　A complete body of distilling, explaining the mysteries
　of that science, in a most easy and familiar manner;
　containing an exact and accurate method of making all
　the compound cordial-waters now in use. The 2nd
　edition. London, Printed for H. Lintot, 1731. 152p.
　1749. 150p.

_____.
　The nature of fermentation explained. By way of
　appendix to the Compleat Body of Distilling. London,
　Printed for B. Lintot, 1729. 56p.　　　　　　　　LC

_____.
　The practical distiller and a treatise on making artificial
　wines. London, B. Lintot, 1734. 57p.
　　　　　　　　　　　　　　　　　　(Harvard University)
Smith, Harold Hamel
　Fermentation of cacoa. London, John Baxe and Sons
　and Danielson, 1913. 318p.　　　　　　　　　　　LC

_____.
　The future of cacao planting. London, John Baxe and
　Co., 1908. 95p.　　　　　　　　　　　　　　　　BM
Smith, Hugh
　An essay on foreign teas with observations on mineral
　waters, coffee, chocolate, etc. London, G.G. and J.
　Robinson, 1780. 80p.　　　　　　　　　　　　　BM
Smith, J. Gilbert, Ed
　The aerator's and bottler's cyclopaedia. Compiled
　by Theodore F. Garrett. London, Published by J.
　Gilbert Smith, n d, ca1907. 105p. Illus.

_____.
　Mineral Water Maker's Manual for 1887. London,
　Published by J. Gilbert Smith, 1887. 135p.
　Advertising. for 1888. 139p. Advertising. For
　1892. 95p. Advertising.

_____.
　See Mac Swinney, E.
　The mineral water maker's Vade Mecum. London, J.
　Gilbert Smith and Co., 1891. 70p.

_____ .
See Simmonds, P. L.
The popular beverages of various countries natural and
artificial, fermented, distilled, aerated and infused
history, production, consumption.

_____ .
St. Paul's Bottling Co. book of reference.   London,
1890.   (Location Unknown)
Smith, Jacqueline Harrison and Halsey, Sue Mason
Maury, Compilers
Famous old recipes.   Philadelphia, John H. Winston
Co., 1906.   331p.
Smith, John
Fruits and farinacea.   The proper food of man, etc.
London, John Churchill, 1845.   422p.

_____ .
Vegetable Cookery.   London, Frederick Pitman, 1866.
241p.
Smith, John W.
So mixe ich fur meine Freunde.   Ein Cocktail-Buch.
Weisbaden, Verlag der Greif, n d.   (In German).
173p.
Smith, Karl L.
Growing and preparing guavas.   State of Florida Dept.
of Agri.   Tallahassee, August 1952.   48p.   Illus-
photos.
Smith, Randolph Wellford
The sober world.   Boston, Marshall Jones Co., 1919.
291p.
Smith, Samuel Hanbury
Some remarks on medicinal mineral waters, natural
and artificial.   Hamilton, Ohio, 1855.   40p.   LC
Smith, W. B.
Bleasdale 1850-1950.   Adelaide, Pott's Bleasdale
Vineyards, 1950.   21p.   PLOSA
Smith, W. Stanley
Extracts and how to increase them.   Wrexham.   Publish-
ed by author, 1910.   58p.   (Institute of Brewing)
Smith, Walton Hall and Helwig, Ferdinand C.
Liquor.   The servant of man.   Boston, Litte Brown
and Co., 1940.   273p.   Bibliography.
Smith, A. J. and Co., Ltd.
Wine List.   London, Summer 1963.   46p.   Illus-
drawings.

Smith, S. and Son Ltd.
    One hundred years of good earth. (wine). Angoston,
    South Australia, 1949. Unpaged (42). Illus-photos,
    drawings.
Smock, R. M. and Neubert, A. M.
    Apples and apple products. New York, Inter-Science
    Publishers, Inc., 1950. 486p. Illus.
Smyth, William Augustus
    The publican's guide or key to the distill-house. A
    new edition with additions. London, Published by
    author, 1781. 104p.
Snell, Foster D., Inc., Chemists-Engineers
    Report to The Aromanilla Company, Inc., on
    comparative evaluation by the flavor profile method
    of Aromanilla, Pure vanilla extract and a vanilla-
    coumarin blend as flavoring agents in plain pound cake.
    New York, Published by Aromanilla, 1950. 19p. Illus.
Snively, John H.
    Soda water, what it is and how it is made. Published
    in Harper's New Monthly Magazine, 1872. Pages 341
    to 346.

_____.
    A treatise on the manufacture of perfumes and kindred
    toilet articles. Nashville, C. W. Smith, 1877.
    243p. Illus.
Snowden, Philip
    Socialism and the drink question. London, Published
    by Independent Labour Party, 1908. 205p.
Snyder, Charles R.
    Alcohol and the jews. Glencoe, Illinois and New Haven.
    Free Press, 1958. 227p.   LC

_____.
    See Pitman, David J. and Snyder, Charles R.
    Society, culture and drinking patterns.
Snyder, Mrs. S. P.
    Treatise on food conservation. Binghampton, Health
    Publishing Co., 1917. 205p.   LC
Soames, Peter
    Treatise on manufacture of sugar from sugar cane.
    London, E. and F. N. Spon, 1872. 136p.   BM
Soap, Perfumery and Cosmetics
    SPC Year Book, 19th edition. London, United Trade
    Press, Ltd., 1961. 314p. Illus.

Societe Hellenique de Vins et Spiritueux
Booklet describing the producing of wines and spirits
in Greece. (by this company).
Athenes-Grece (Athens). Printed in Switzerland, n d.
(In French and German only). 32p. Illus-photos of
wine and spirit producing and of Greece.
Society of Soft Drink Technologists
Your key to quality. Washington. Published by the
Society, 1960. 43p. Bibliography.
The Soda Fountain
The dispenser's formulary; or, Soda water guide; a
practical handbook for soda fountain operators, con-
sisting of over 2,000 tested formulas for soda fountain
products, etc., 3rd edition, rev. and enl. New
York, D.O. Haynes and Co., 1915. 274p. Illus.
4th edition, Soda Fountain Publ. 1925. 253p.

_____.
Dispenser Soda Water Guide (The). A collection of
over 1300 formulas for soda fountain, etc. Compiled
by The Soda Fountain. 2nd edition. revised and
enlarged. New York, D. O. Haynes and Co., 1909.
139p.

_____.
Dispenser Soda Water Guide (The). A compilation of
trade winning beverages from "The Soda Fountain".
Chicago, Entered 1905. Dispenser Publishing Co., 116p.
Soft Drinks Industry Ass'n.
S.D.I. Being an account of the soft drinks industry in
Britain during the emergency years 1942-1948. Compiled
from the records of the Association and edited by Kenneth
Penn. Issued by the Soft Drinks Industry (Wartime)
Ass'n, Ltd., London, n d, ca1949. 106p. Illus.
Soglow, O.
See Anthony, Norman and Soglow, O.
The drunk's blue book.
Sohn, Charles E.
Nutrition. London, Henry Kimpton, 1914. 256p.   BM
Solis, Virgil
Drinking cups, ewers, vases, etc. London, James
Russell, 1862. 23p.   LC
Solvay Sales Corporation
The Solvay Sales Blue Book. New York, 1943. 76p.
Sommer, Hugo H.
Market milk and related products. 2nd edition.
Madison, Wisc., Published by author, 1946. 745p.
Illus.

—————— .
The theory and practice of ice cream making. 4th
edition. Madison, Wisc., Published by author, 1944.
666p. Bibliography. 5th edition, 1946. 679p. Illus.
Somerville, O. E.
In the vine country, by E. OE. Somerville and Martin
Ross . . . . Allen, 1893. 237p. Illus.
Soothill, Jay H.
See Kepner, Charles David and Soothill, Jay Henry
The Banana Empire. A case study in American
imperialism.
Southby, E. R.
Brewing: practically and scientifically considered.
London, Printed by Unwin Brothers, 1877. 150p.

—————— .
A systematic handbook of practical brewing, etc.
3rd edition. London, The Brewing Trade Review,
1895. 391p. 2nd edition, 1885. 301p.
Southern Comfort Corp.
The art of gracious tippling since 800 BC. St. Louis
1943. unpaged (32). Illus.

—————— .
How to make 44 favorite party drinks. St. Louis,
n d. 12p. Illus.
Southworth, May E. Comp.
One hundred and one beverages. San Francisco,
P. Elder and Co., 1904. 87p.
Souttar, Robinson
Alcohol: its place and power in legislation. London,
Hodder and Stoughton. 1904. 259p. Bibliography.
Spalding, W. B. and Montague, J. R.
Alcohol and human affairs. Yonkers, World Book Co.,
1949. 248p.   BM
Speechly, William
A treatise on the culture of the vine, etc. 3rd edition.
London, Longman, Hurst, Rees, Orme and Brown, 1821.
232p. Illus- drawings.
Spencer, Edward
The flowing bowl. A treatise on drinks of all kinds
and of all periods, etc. London, Stanley Paul and Co.,
Ltd., 1925 (reprinted). 242p.
Spencer, Guilford L. and Meade, George P.
Cane Sugar Handbook. A manual for cane sugar manufac-
turers and their chemists. 8th edition. New York,
John Wiley and Sons Inc., 1945. 834p. Illus.

387

Spencer, S.
See Gillman, A. W. and Spencer, S.
Brewer's materials.
Spender, John Kent, MD
The Bath Thermal Waters, historical, social and
medical. London, J. and A. Churchill, 1877. 292p.
Spiller, Brian
See National Trade Development Ass'n.
Innkeeping. A manual for licensed victuallers, edited
by Brian Spiller.
Spinola, Oberto
The Martini museum. Turin, Martini and Rossi,
S. P. A. nd, 52p.
Springett, Leslie E.
Quality of coffee. New York, Published by author,
1935. 137p.   NYPL
Springwater, Dr. (pseud)
See Anon.
Cold water man (The), or a pocket companion for the
temperate.
Spooner, Alden
The cultivation of American grape vines and the making
of wine. Brooklyn, Published by author, 1846. 96p.
Illus- drawings. °
Stables, W. Gordon
Tea, the drink of pleasure and health. London, Field
and Tuer and others, n d, (1882). 111p.
Stainbank, H. E.
Coffee in Natal: its culture and preparation. London,
Edward Stanford, 1874. 78p. Illus.
Stafford, Hugh
A treatise on cyder- making. London, Printed for E.
Cave at St. John's Gate, 1753. 68p. Illus.
Stambaugh, Scott U.
The Papaya. A fruit suitable to South Florida. State
of Florida, Dept. of Agri. Tallahassee, New series
no. 90, Sept. 1955. 56p. Illus- photos.
Stamp (Lord)
The National Capital. And other statistical studies.
(Chapter on Alcohol as an economic factor). London,
Staples Press, Ltd., 1937. 299p.
Standage, H. C.
Temperance and light drinks. London, J. S. Virtue,
1893. 88p.   BM

Standard Bottling and Extract Co., O. A. Atkins, President
The Standard Soda Water Flavors. Boston, n d,
ca1900. 16p. Illus.
Stanley, Louis T.
The old inns of London. London, B. T. Batsford Ltd.,
1957. 124p. Illus.
Stanley-Wrench, Mollie
Cocktail snacks and canapes. London, Herbert Jenkins
Ltd., 1959. 91p.
Stansfield and Co.,
How good beer is served. London, Fulham, 1908.
32p.   BM
Stanton, Arthur G.
Report on British grown tea. London, Clowes and
Son, 1887. 22p.   BM
⸻ .
Tea, 1910.   (Torgesheff-China as tea producer)
Star Liquid Machinery Corp. (The).
Manufacturers of machinery for beverage, food and
chemical industries. (Catalog). (no title). New
York, n d, ca1949. unpaged. (48).
Starke, J. Dr.
Alcohol. The sanction for its use. Scientifically
established and popularily expounded by a physiologist.
Trans. from German. New York, G. P. Putnam
and Sons, 1907. 317p. Bibliography. Same 1910.
Stark, William P.
Inside facts of profitable fruit growing. Stark City,
Mo. Published by author, 1916. 88p. Illus-photos.
Starling, Ernest H.
The action of alcohol on man. London, Longmans,
Green and Co., 1923. 291p. Illus-Literature.
State Laboratories Department
Food and Drug Bulletins. Bismarck, North Dakota.

June 1942.	190p.	# 67	July 1951.	179p.	#93.
July 1943.	141p.	# 69	July 1952.	148p.	# 97.
July 1944.	141p.	# 71.	July 1953.	139p.	# 99.
July 1945.	100p.	# 73	July 1954.	149p.	# 104.
July 1946.	128p.	# 77	July 1955	212p.	# 109.
July 1947.	121p.	# 83.	June 1956.	127p.	# 111.
July 1948.	134p.	# 85	June 1957.	122p.	# 114
July 1949.	166p.	# 87	May 1958.	124p.	# 118.
July 1950.	124p.	# 90	May 1959.	111p.	# 122.

State Laboratories Department Card 2
    July 1960. 112p. # 125.
    June 1961. 109p. # 128.
    June 1962. 140p. # 131.
    June 1963. 110p. # 134.
    June 1964. 74p. # 138.
    June 1965. 95p. # 141.
    May 1966. 100p. # 144.
    May 1967. 100p. # 150.
Stateler, E. S.
    See Parker, Milton E. , Harvey, E. S. and Stateler,
    E. S.
    Elements of food engineering.
Statist (The)
    All about beer. Portraits of a traditional industry.
    E. J. Hickey, editor, London, (1952). 104p. Illus.
Staveacre, Frederick William F.
    Tea and tea dealing. London, I. Pitman, 1929. 139p. Illus.
Stavely, S. W.
    The new whole art of confectionery. Derby, Sutton
    and Son, 1827. 80p.   BM
Stebbins, J. E.
    Fifty years history of the temperance cause. In-
    temperance, its aspect and its remedy. Hartford,
    Conn., J. P. Fitch, 1876. 500p.
Steedman, M. E.
    Homemade beverages and American drinks. London,
    The Food and Cookery Publ. Agency. 1917. 87p.
Steedman, M. E. and Senn, Herman C
    Homemade summer and winter drinks. Cups,
    liqueurs, cocktails and invalid drinks. London, Ward
    Lock and Co. , 1924. 160p.
Steel, Anthony
    The custom of the room or early winebooks of Christ's
    College, Cambridge. Cambridge, Heffer, (1949). 123p.
    Illus.
Steel, F. A. and G. Gardiner
    The complete Indian housekeeper and cook. New and
    rev. ed. London, William Heinemann, 1904. 390p.
Steel, James
    Selection of the practical points of malting and brewing,
    with strictures thereon for the use of brewery proprie-
    tors. Glasgow, Robert Anderson, 1878. 130p. Illus.

    Supplement to Steel on malting and brewing. Glasgow,
    Robert Anderson printer, 1887. 100p.

Steel, John H. MD
An analysis of the Congress spring with practical re-
marks on its medical properties. Saratoga Spring, G.
M. Davidson, 1847. 35p.

———————.
An analysis of the mineral waters of Saratoga and
Ballston. 2nd edition. Albany, D. Steele, 1819.
118p.
Steele, G. F.
My new cocktail book. 2nd edition, New York, The
Charles Watson Russell Press, August 1934. 190p.
Stegner, Mabel
Electric blender recipes. New York, M. Barrows,
1952. 225p.   LC
Steineberg, L.
Dominion compounder's guide (or the secret of the
liquor trade). Montreal, Ensabe Senecal, 1870. 112p.
(Toronto Public)
Steiner, Paul
Bottoms Up! New York, Dell Publishing Co., 1957.
Unpaged.   NYPL
Stennis, Mary A.
Florida fruits and vegetables in the commercial menu.
Reprint Bulletin no. 50 new series. State of Florida,
Dept. of Agriculture. Tallahassee, April 1933.
164p.
Stephan, John
See Anon.
A treatise on the manufacture, imitation, adulteration,
and reduction of foreign wines, brandies, gins, rums,
etc.
Stern, Gladys Bronwyn
Bouquet. New York, A. A. Knopf, 1927. 263p. Illus.
Sterne, Francis
See Weil, B. H. and Sterne, Frances
Literature search on the preservation of food by
freezing.
Steuart, Mary E.
Everyday life on a Ceylon cocoa estate. London, Henry
J. Drane, 1905. 256p.   BM
Stevens, H. B.
See Lucas, Edwin W. and Stevens, Harold B.
Book of prescriptions.

———— See Lucas, Edwin W. and Stevens, Harold B.
Book of Pharmacopoaes and unofficial formularies.
Stevenson, J.
Advice, medical and economical relative to the purchase and consumption of tea, coffee, chocolate, wines and malt liquors. London, F. C. Westley, 1830. 204p. Authorities quoted.

———— Treatise on tobacco, tea, coffee, and chocolate.
London, 1758.   (Ukers- All about tea)
Stevenson, P.
Explanation of the partial process of evaporation.
Edinburgh, 1841. 10p.   GBPOL
Stevenson, Thomas
Treatise on alcohol, etc. London, Gurney and Jackson, 1888. 73p.   (Yale Univ.)
Stevenson, Wm and Howell, Reginald
S and H gallonage table. London, 1916. folio   BM
Stevenson, Thomas MD
Spirit-gravities with tables. London, John Van Voorst, 1880. 73p.
Stevenson and Howell Limited
Label booklet, price list and formulas. London, n d ca1897. 63p. Label paste-ins.

———— The manufacture of aerated beverages, cordials, etc.
3rd edition. London, 1891. 92p. 5th edition, 1906, 122p. 7th edition, 1926, 208p. 8th edition, 1956. 92p.

———— The mineral water trade and the food and drugs act.
London, n d, ca1911. 12p.

———— Non-alcoholic fruit wines and cordials, revised issue
London, October 1932. 15p.

———— Non-excisable fruit wines and cordials. London, n d.
25p.
Stewart, D. A.
Drinking patterns. Campbelltown, N. B., Canada, Tribune Publishers, 1951. 174p.   (Toronto Public)
Stewart, F. L.
Sorgham and its products. Philadelphia, J. B. Lippincott Co., 1867. 240p.

_____ .
Sugar made from maize and sorgham, a new discovery.
Washington, The Republic Co., 1882. 102p.   (Crerar)
Stewart, George R.
    American ways of life. (Drinks and drinking).   Garden
    City, N.Y., Doubleday, 1954.   310p.   (Bourbon Institute)
Stewart, Oliver W.
    See Hanly, J. Frank and Stewart, Oliver Wayne, Eds.
    Speeches of the flying squadron.
Stewart, William
    Practical instructions for brewing porter and ales
    according to English and Scottish methods.   Edinburgh,
    Adam and Charles Black, 1849.   (Bound in and part of
    Thomson, Thomas-Brewing and distillation.)
    pgs. 325 to 378.
Stieff, Frederick Philip
    Eat, drink and be merry in Maryland.   New York,
    G. P. Putnam's Sons, 1932.   326p.   Illus.
Stiles, Harry W. Comp.
    The Chapin and Gore manual.   A complete guide to
    the popular system of barkeeping in use by Chapin and
    Gore.   Chicago, Stromberg, Allen and Co., Printers,
    1896.   76p.   Advertising.   LC
Stockbridge, Mrs. Bertha Edson (Lay)
    What to drink; the blue book of beverages; recipes and
    directions for making and serving non-alcoholic drinks
    for all occasions.   New York, London, D. Appleton
    and Co., 1920.   177p.   Illus.
Stoddard, Cora Francis
    Handbook of modern facts about alcohol.   Westerville,
    Ohio, The American Issue Publishing Co., 1914.
    105p.   References.
Stoker, T. G.
    Notes on the management of the tea plant.   Calcutta,
    Thacker, Spink and Co., 1874.   20p.   LC
Stoll, Horatio Francis
    The grape districts of California, San Francisco, 1931.
                        (Schoonmaker-Complete Wine Book)
_____ .
What wine to serve.   New York, Reprinted from New
York World Telegram, 1933.   8 leaves.   NYPL
_____ .
Wine-wise, a popular handbook on how to correctly judge,
keep, serve and enjoy wines.   San Francisco, H. S.
Crocker Press, 1933.   124p.   Illus.

Stone, J. William
   Brief history of beverage alcohol and of Kentucky
   Bourbon whiskey. Compiled for Brown and Forman,
   Louisville, 1921. 23p. Typescript. Bibliography.
                              (Filson Club, Louisville)
Stone, Marion Edward
   American liquor control, Boston, The Christopher
   Publishing House, 1943. 177p.
Stone, Samuel, L. E.
   Liquor buyers guide. The professional book for the
   amateur. Los Angeles, 1968. 123p.
Stone, William L.
   Reminiscences of Saratoga and Ballston. New York,
   Virtue and Yorsten, 1875. 451p. Illus.
Stong, Philip D.
   See Elliott, Virginia
   Shake 'em up! A practical handbook of polite drinking,
   by Virginia Elliott and Phil D. Stong.
Stopes, Henry
   Barley and the beer duty. A short, practical treatise
   on a matter of national interest affecting consumers
   of beer, growers of barley, brewers, maltsters, and
   divers others. London, W. A. May, 1901. 131p.
   Illus.   LC

   _____
   Brewing and malting machinery and appliances.
   London, 1881. 76p.   GBPOL

   _____
   Cider, its history manufacture and properties. London,
   1888. 26p.   BM

   _____
   Drying malt; practically considered. London, 1882.
                                                    GBPOL

   _____
   Engineering of malting. London, Paper read before
   the Society of Engineers, Westminster Town Hall,
   May 5, 1884. 31p.

   _____
   Malt and malting. London, F. W. Lyon, 1885. 662p.
   Illus. Bibliography.
✓ Storm, John
   An invitation to wines; an informal guide to the selection
   care, and enjoyment of domestic and European wines.
   New York, Simon and Schuster, 1955. 201p. Illus-
   drawings. Bibliography.

Story, Dr. Charles A.
  Alcohol: its nature and effects. New York, The
  National Temperance Society and Publication House,
  1874. 392p.
Stouffer Foods Corporation
  Here's how, by Stouffer's. Cleveland, 1962. 87p.
  Illus.
Stouffer's Restaurants
  Nectars, Stouffer's. New York, Pickwick Ltd., 1939.
  127p. Illus.
Stratton, Rev. J. Y.
  Hops and hop-pickers. London, The People's Library.
  Society for promoting Christian knowledge, 1883. 191p.
  Illus.
Straub, Jacques
  A complete manual of mixed drinks. Chicago, R.
  Francis Welsh Publishing Co., 1918. 159p.

————— Drinks. Contains about seven hundred accurate
  directions for mixing various kinds of popular and
  fancy drinks. Chicago, The Hotel Monthly, 1914. 96p.
Strauss, Robert and Bacon, Selden D.
  Drinking in college. New Haven, Yale University
  Press, 1953. 221p.
Strecker, Edward A., and Chambers, Jr., Francis T.
  Alcohol, one man's meat. New York, Macmillan Co.,
  1938. 230p.
Street, Julian Leonard
  Civilized drinking. Redbook Magazine, 1933. 33p.

————— Table topics. Edited, and with additions, by A. I. M. S.
  Street. New York, Knopf, 1959. 289p. Illus.
  Acknowledgements.

————— Where Paris dines, with information about restaurants
  of all kinds, costly and cheap, dignified and gay,
  known and little known: and how to enjoy them; to-
  gather with a discussion of French wines and a table
  of vintages by a distinguished amateur. Garden City,
  N. Y., Doubleday, Doran and Co., 1924. 322p. Illus.

————— Wines, their selection, care and service. New York,
  Knopf, 1933. 194p. Second printing, December, 1933.
  Third printing, February, 1934. Revised 1948, 288p.

Stringer, Carlton
Wines; what to serve, when to serve, how to serve.
Scarborough, N.Y., Canapé Parade, 1933. 63p.
Illus.

Strom, S. Alice Edith
And so to dine. A brief account of the food and
drink of Mr. Pepys, based on his diary. London,
Frederick Books, George Allen and Unwin, Ltd., 1955.
99p. Illus.

Strong, L. A. G.
A brewer's Progress, 1757-1957. A survey of
Charrington's Brewery on the occasion of its
bicentenary. London, Privately printed, 1957.
88p. Illus.

Strong, Stanley
The romance of brewing. London, Published by
Review Press Ltd., for The Crown Cork Co., Ltd.,
Southall, Middlesex, Privately circulated, 1951.
120p. Illus.

Strong, W. C.
Culture of the grape. Boston, J. E. Tilton and Co.,
1867. 355p. Illus.

Stuart, George R.
The saloon under the searchlight. New York, Fleming
H. Revell Co., 1908. 64p.

Stuart, M.
Scriptural view of the wine question. In a letter to
the Rev. Dr. Nott. New York, Leavitt, Trow and
Co., Printers, 1848. 64p.

Stuart, Thomas
Stuart's fancy drinks and how to mix them. New York,
Excelsior Publishing House, 1904. 134p.

Stubbs (Stubbe), Henry
Indian Nectar or a discourse concerning chocolate,
etc. London, J. C. and M. A. Crook, 1662. 184p.
NYPL

Sturge, Mary D.
See Horsley, Sir Victor and Sturge, Mary D.
Alcohol and the human body.

Sugar Information, Inc.
Sugar as a food. New York, January 1955. 31p.
References.

Sullivan, Jere
The drinks of yesteryear. A mixology. Published by
author, n p, ca1930. 52p.

Sullivan, W. C.
    Alcoholism. A chapter in social pathology. London,
    James Nisbet and Co., 1906. 214p.
Sulz, Charles Herman
    Sulz's Compendium of flavoring. New York, Dick
    and Fitzgerald Publishers, 1888. 140p. Illus.

_____.
    A treatise on beverages; or, The complete practical
    bottler. Full instructions for laboratory work, with
    original practical recipes for all kinds of carbonated
    drinks, mineral waters, flavorings, extracts, syrups,
    etc. New York, Dick and Fitzgerald, 1888. 818p.
    Illus.
Sumner, John
    A popular treatise on tea, its qualities and effects.
    Birmingham, Printed by Wm. Hodgetts, 1863. 44p. BM
Sunderland, Septimus
    Old London's Spas, Baths and Wells. London, John
    Bale and Sons and Daniellsson Ltd., 1915. 169p.
    Illus. Bibliography.
Sundin, Knut W.
    Two hundred selected drinks. Goteborg, Ragner
    Orstadius Boktryckeri, 1930. 87p.   LC
Sunkist Growers Products Department
(California Fruit Growers Exchange)
    Exchange Citrus Pectin. Ontario, California.
    2nd edition, 1934.   63p.
    3rd edition, 1936.   117p.
    4th edition, 1941.   117p.
    5th edition, 1949.   117p.
    6th edition, 1954.   146p.
Sutherland, Douglas
    Raise your glasses. A light-hearted history of
    drinking, London, Macdonald and Co., 1969. 200p.
    Illus-photos. Bibliography.
Sutherland, George
    South Australia wine-growers manual. Adelaide,
    Department of Agriculture, 1892. 70p.   ANL
Suttor, George
    The culture of the grape vine and the orange in
    Australia and New Zealand. London, Smith, Elder
    and Co., 1843. 184p.
Suydam, James
    A treatise on the culture and management of grape
    vines. Brooklyn, 1856.   (Fuller)

Suzanne, Alfred
La Cuisine Anglaise et la Patisserie. London,
Librairie Francaise, 1894. (In French some English
words.) 455p. Illus.
Swan, Fred W.
Drink and service manual. Chicago, The Reilly and
Lee Co., 1933. 89p.   LC
Swartout, J. M.
Small fruits. (by R.E. Barker, i.e., J. M. S.)
New York, Rinehart, 1954. 90p.   PLOSA
Swiss Exporter Ltd.
Swiss spas, Zurich, 1921. 318p.
                              (Riley Memorial Library)
Swiss Wine Growers Ass'n.
The bright and fragrant wines of Switzlerland.
Lausanne, n d. 23p. Illus.
Switzer, Maurice
Who was the first toper? Being a dry discourse on
a wet subject. Reprinted from Kant-slip. New York,
Kelly-Springfield Tire Co., 1919. 19p. Illus.
Syers, R.
The coffee guide. Liverpool. D. Marples and R.
Taylor, 1832. 84p.   (Davis)
Sykes, Walter J.
Principles and practice of brewing (The). London,
Charles Griffin and Co., Ltd., 1897. 511p. Illus.
List of books consulted. London, with Arthur R. Ling,
1907, 588p. Illus.
Symington, J. D.
Notes on port wine, 1948.
(Massel - Applied Wine Chemistry and technology)
Symonds, John Addington
Wine, women and song. Medieval latin students' songs
now first translated into English verse with an essay
by--. New York and London. The Mc Clure Co., Chatto
and Windus, 1907. 180p.
Symons, William
The practical Gager; or the young gager's assistant.
London, Wingrave and Collingwood, 1815. 384p.
Syrett, Iris
Rum in the kitchen. London, Rum Merchants Ltd.,
n d. 19p. Illus.

T., H.
    Dreadful character of drink, 1682.
                                    (Food and Wine Exhibition)
Tait, Geoffrey Murat
    Port. From the vine to the glass. London, Harper
    and Co., 1936. 174p. Illus.

————— .
    Practical handbook on port wine. London, Harper and
    Co., 1925. 60p. Illus.
Takala, Martti
    See Allarde, Erik, Touko, Markkanen, Martti, Takala
    Drinking and drinkers.

————— .
    The effects of distilled and brewed beverages.
    Helsinki, The Finnish Foundation for Alcohol Studies,
    1957. 195p. Bibliography.
Talbert, T. J. and Murneek, A. E.
    Fruit crops. Principles and practices of orchard and
    small fruit culture. Philadelphia, Lea and Febiger,
    1939. 345p. Illus. Selected references.
Tall-One Co., (The)
    Merchandising plan. (By A. W. Noling). Dayton,
    Ohio, n d, (1928), 16p.

————— .
    75,000 case bottling plants, costs and organization. (by
    A. W. Noling). Dayton, Ohio, n d, (1928), 12p.
    forms; illustrations of equipment.
Tarling, W. J.
    Cafe Royal Cocktail Book. London, Coronation edition,
    Pall Mall Ltd., 1937. unpaged. Illus- Glossary.
Tassigny de and Gauthier Ltd.
    Wines, whys and wherefores. London, 1951. 24p. BM
Tate, Francis G. H.
    Alcoholometry. An account of the British method of
    alcohol strength determination. London, H.M.S.O.
    1930. 92p. References.
Taussig, Charles William
    Rum, Romance, Rebellion. London, Jarrolds, n d.
    ca1928. 286p. Illus. Bibliography.
Taylor, Adam
    Treatise on the ananas or pineapple. Devizes.
    Printed by T. Burrough, 1769. 62p.   BM
Taylor, Alice M.
    See Montgomery, Edward Gerrard and Taylor, Alice M.
    World trade in cocoa. Washington, Govt. Printing Office,
    1947. 175p. Illus.   LC

Taylor, Allen
What everybody wants to know about wine. New York,
A. A. Knopf, 1934. 312p. Illus. LC
Taylor, Bert L. and W. C. Gibson
The log of the water wagon. Boston, H. M. Caldwell
and Co., 1905. 128p. NYPL
Taylor, D. D. Cottington
Jams, jellies and fruit bottling. London, Good House-
keeping Magazine, n d. 107p.

See Heath, Ambrose and Taylor, D. D. Cottington,
Compilers.
National Mark Calendar of Cooking. Compiled for The
Ministry of Agriculture. London, 1936. 128p.
Taylor, E. of Berwick
The lady's housewife's and cook aids' assistant.
Berwick upon Tweed, R. Taylor, 1769. 276p. BM
Taylor, F.
Hops and the hop trade, 1909. (Bird)
Taylor, Frederick
Nebraska State Horticultural Society for year 1895
(annual report). The grape, cherry, plum, Lincoln.
299p. Illus-photos. (Brady Library-Fresno State Col.)
Taylor, Greyton H.
Treasury of wine and wine cookery. New York,
Harper and Row, 1963. 278p. Illus.
Taylor, H. V.
The plums of England. London, Crosby Lockwood and
Son, 1949. 151p. Illus.-colored plates. Bibliography.
Taylor, Howard E.
Handbook of wines and liquors. Stamford, Conn., J.O.
Dahl, 1933. 56p. LC
Taylor, J.
Tables for calculating wine, beer, cider, etc.
(Excise duties), 1820. (John Lyle--Book dealer)
Taylor, John
Drinks and welcome; or the famous history of the most
part of drinks, in use now in the kingdomes of Great
Britaine and Ireland, etc. London, Printed by Anne
Griffin, 1637. 26p. NYPL
Taylor, J. P.
Coffee growing in Mexico. Mexico, F. P. Hoeck,
1893. 80p. NYPL
Taylor, Norman
Cinchona in Java. The story of quinine. New York,
Greenberg, Publisher, 1945. 87p. Illus. Bibliography.

Color in the garden. New York, Van Nostrand, 1953. 110p. Illus. Bibliography.

Fragrance in the garden. New York, Van Nostrand, 1953. 110p. Illus. Bibliography.

Fruit in the garden. New York, Van Nostrand, 1954. 134p. Bibliography.

Taylor, Sidney B. Ed.
Wine, wisdom and whimsy. Portland, Oregon. Winepress Publishing Co., 1969. 159p. Illus-drawings.

Taylor, W. A. and Co.
Fine art of wine drinking. New York, 1903.

Taylor Wine Co.
Wines for everyday enjoyment. Hammondsport, N.Y., n d. 23p. Illus.

Tea Association of U.S.A.
Tea. New York, 1930. 24p. Illus.

Tea Bureau
The cup that cheers. A handbook of tea. New York, n d, ca1920. 40p. Illus.

Memorandum on tea. New York, 1945. 21p.
(National Agricultural Library)

The story of tea. Toronto, n d, ca1940. 24p. Illus-photos-drawings.

Tebb, William
Tea and effects of tea drinking. London, T. Cornell and Sons, 1905. 26p.   BM

Teetgen, Ada B.
Profitable herb growing and collecting. London, George Newnes Ltd., 1916. 180p. Illus.

Tennent, Sir James E.
Wine, its use and taxation. London, James Madison, 1855. 178p.   NYPL

Terrington, William
Cooling cups and dainty drinks. A collection of recipes for "cups" and other compounded drinks, and of general information on beverages of all kinds. London and New York, G. Routledge and Sons, 1869. 223p.

Terry-Thomas
Festive guide to wine. Pages 17-28 in ILLUSTRATED, December 7, 1957. London, (Periodical). Illus-photos.

Thacher, James
 American orchardist (The). 2nd edition. Plymouth,
 Mass., J. W. Ingraham, 1825. 236p. (Crerar)
Thatcher, Frank
 Brewing and malting practically considered. London,
 Printed and published by the Country Brewers' Gazette,
 Ltd., 1898. 117p.

_____.
 A treatise of practical brewing and malting. London,
 The Country Brewers' Gazette Ltd., 1905. 560p.
Thausing, Julius E.
 The theory and practice of the preparation of malt and
 the fabrication of beer, with especial reference to the
 Vienna process of brewing. Philadelphia, H. C. Baird
 and Co., 1882. 815p. Illus.
Thayer, and Co.
 Fluid and solid extracts with formulas and receipts.
 (Descriptive catalogue). Cambridgeport, Mass., 1885.
 270p.
Thenard, Lewis J.
 Memoir on vinous fermentation, 1804. (Scho)
Theron, Christian J. and Niehaus, Charles G.
 Wine making. Pietermaritzburg, South African
 Bulletin no. 98, 1947-48. 98p. BM
Thiébaut de Berneaud, Arsène
 The vine-dresser's theoretical and practical manual,
 or The art of cultivating the vine: and making wine,
 brandy, and vinegar. New York, P. Cranfield, 1829.
 158p.
Thomann, Gallus
 Alleged adulterations of malt liquors. The whole truth
 about them. New York, United States Brewers Ass'n.,
 1886. 30p.

_____.
 American beer; glimpses of its history and description
 of its manufacture. New York, United States Brewers'
 Association, 1969. 104p.

_____.
 Documentary history of the United States Brewers'
 Association. 2 parts. Part 1. 1896, part 2. 1898.
 U. S. Brewers' Ass'n. 2 vol. paged consecutively
 (277p).

_____.
 Effects of beer on those who make it and drink it. New
 York, United States Brewing Ass'n., 1886. 46p. LC

402

—————. Liquor laws of the United States. Their spirit and effect. New York, United States Brewers' Ass'n., 1885. 256p.

—————. Real and imaginery effects of intemperance. New York, Published by United States Brewers Ass'n, 1884. 167p.

Thomas, Albert
(Butler to principal of Brasenose College)
Wait and see. London, Michael Joseph, Ltd., 1944. 186p.

Thomas, C.
See Ricket, E. and Thomas, C.
The gentlemen's table guide. Recipes wine cups, American drinks, etc.

Thomas, Frank A. (pseud)
Wines, cocktails and other drinks. New York, Harcourt, Brace and Co., 1936. 228p. Dictionary.

Thomas, Jerry
The bartender's guide; or, How to mix all kinds of plain and fancy drinks, embracing punches, juleps, cobblers, etc. Danbury, Ct. Behrene Publishing Co., 1887. 130p.

—————. The Bon-Vivant's Companion: or, How to mix drinks. 4th printing. Edited by Herbert Asbury, New York, Alfred A. Knopf, Inc., 169p. Illus-etchings. 5th printing, 1929. Seventh printing, 1934, Grosset and Dunlop.

—————. How to mix drinks, or, Bon-Vivant's companion. New York, Dick and Fitzgerald, Entered 1862. Bound with Christian Schultz. A manual for manufacture of cordials, liquors, fancy syrups, etc., 87p. (Thomas) 89 to 244ps. (Schultz).

Thomas, H.H.
The book of the apple. London, John Lane Bodley Head Ltd., 1923. 112p. Illus.

Thomas, John J.
The American fruit culturist, etc., 8th edition. New York, William Wood and Co., 1875. 576p. Illus-drawings.

—————. The fruit culturist. Auburn and Geneva, New York, J.C. Derry and Co., 1846. 220p. Illus-engravings.

Thomas, Owen
See Bunyard, George and Thomas, Owen
The Fruit Garden.
Thompson, Charles John Samuel
The mystery and lure of perfume. Philadelphia, Lipp-
incott, 1927. 247p. Illus.
Thompson, Edward E.
Long's portable soda fountain. Rochester, Published
by author, 1870. 20p.   LC
Thompson, Harry
Australian milk bar and soda fountain practice.
Sydney, 1940. 64p.   (Brisbane Public)
Thompson, Sir Henry
Food and feeding. 8th edition. London, Frederick
Warne and Co., 1894. 222p.
Thompson, Vance
Drink. A revised and enlarged edition of drink and
be sober. New York, E. P. Dutton and Co., 1918.
231p.
———————.
Drink and be sober. New York, Moffat, Yard and Co.,
1915. 231p.
Thompson, Walter
Control of liquor in Sweden. New York, Columbia
Univ. Press, 1935. 244p.   NYPL
Thomson, David
A practical treatise on the culture of the pine-apple.
Edinburgh and London, William Blackwood and Sons,
1866. 53p.
Thomson, Thomas
Brewing and distillation. With practical instructions
for brewing porter and ales according to the English
and Scottish methods, by William Stewart. Edinburgh,
A. and C. Black, 1849. 324p.
Thomson, William
A practical treatise on the cultivation of the grape
vine. 3rd edition. Edinburgh and London, William
Blackwood and Sons. 74p. Illus-engravings.
6th edition, 1869. illus-engravings.
7th edition, 1871. Illus-engravings.
9th edition, 1879. Illus-engravings.
10th edition, Reprint 1903. 105p. Illus-engravings.
Thorne, Guy
The great acceptance. The life story of F.N. Charrington. (of brewing family). 5th edition. London, Hodder
and Stoughton, 1913. 272p.

Thornton, F. W.
Brewery accounts. New York, Ronald Press, 1913.
102p. LC
Thornton, William W.
See Woolen, William W. and Thornton, William W.
Intoxicating liquors: the law relating to drunkenness.
Thorpe, Edward and Brown, Harold T.
Report on determination of original gravity beers
by distillation process. London, Harrison and Sons,
1915. 143p. (Scho)
Thorpe, Thomas Edward
Joseph Priestley. London. J.M. Dent, 1906.
228p. BM
Threale, Thomas
Compleat family brewer, London, 1802. 35p. GBPOL
Three Feathers Distillers, Inc.
Life of the party. New York, n d. 69p. Illus-
drawings.
Three Millers Co., (The).
Supplies for the soda fountain, ice cream and
confectionery mfgrs. Boston, 1924. (with separate
price list). 75p. Illus. (Price list 18p.)
Thudichum, John Louis William
On wines, their production, treatment and use. Six
lectures. London, Royal Society for encouragement of
arts, manufactures and commerce, 1873. BM

A treatise on the origin, nature, and varieties of
wine; being a complete manual of viticulture and
oenology. By J.L.W. Thudichum, M.D., and August
Dupré. London, and New York, Macmillan Co., 1872.
760p. Illus.

A treatise on wines, their origin, nature and varieties,
with practical directions for viticulture and vinification,
London, G. Bell and Sons, 1896. 387p. Illus.
Thurber, Francis B.
Coffee: from plantation to cup. (A brief history of
coffee production and consumption). New York,
American Grocer Publ. Association, 1881. 416p.
Illus. 9th edition, 1884.
Thurston, Azor
Pharmaceutical and food analysis. New York, D.
Van Nostrand Co., 1922. 416p.
Thurston, Charles S.
Beer gravity tables and ready reckoner. Ipswich,
Published by author, 1891. 35p. BM

Thurston and Braidich
Water soluble and bulking gums. New York, n d,
ca1944. 22p. Bibliography. 1950 revised, 28p.
Tibbles, William
Food and hygiene. London, Rebman and Co., 1907.
762p.   LC

_____.
Foods. Their origin, composition and manufacture.
London, Bailliere, Tindall and Cox, 1912. 950p.
Tichborne, C. R. C. and Prosser James
The mineral waters of Europe including a short
description of artificial mineral waters. London,
Bailliere, Tindall and Cox, 1883. 234p.
Tickner, John
Tickner's Pub. London, Putnam and Co., 1965.
86p. Illus.
Tidbury, G. E.
The Clove Tree. London, Crosby Lockwood and Son,
1949. 212p.
Tilden, J. H. MD
Food, its composition, preparation, combination, and
effects with appendix on cooking. Denver, 1921.
306p.

_____.
Food. Its influence as a factor in disease and
health. 3rd edition, revised. Denver, 1914. 262p.
5th edition, 1921, 254p.
Tilden and Co.,
Formulae for making tinctures, infusions, syrups,
wines, mixtures, pills, etc. New Lebanon, N. Y.,
1858. 162p. New York, 1874. 230p.
Tilley, Frank
Teapots and tea. Newport, Mon., England, Ceramic
Book Co., 1957. 135p. Illus.   LC
Timbs, John
Clubs and club life in London, from 17th century to
present time. London, John Camden Hotten, 1872.
544p. Illus.
The Times. London
Beer in Britain. Compiled from a special supplement
of The Times, April 1958. London, Times, 1960.
124p. Illus.
Timm, H.
Limonaden und alkoholfreie getranke. Wien and
Leipzig, A. Hartleben's Verlag, 1909. 184p. Illus.
(In German).

Titterton, W. R.
Drinking songs and other songs. London, Cecil
Palmer, 1928. 64p. Illus.
Tizard, William Littell
The rationale of malting, etc. London, Gilbert
and Rivington, 185-. 110p. Illus.   LC

———— .
The theory and practice of brewing. 4th edition.
London, Published by author, 1857. 520p.
Brewer's lexicon.

———— .
Voice from mash-tun. London, Sold by the author,
1845. 71p.
Tobe, John H. Comp.
How to make your own wines and beers. St.
Catherines, Ont., Modern Publications, Reg'd., 1962.
52p.
Tod, H. M.
Vine growing in England, London, Chatto and Windus,
1911. 113p.   BM
Todd, F. Dundas
Little red guide to home brewed wines. Victoria, B.C.
Victoria Printing and Publishing Co., 1922. 32p.   BM
Todd, Serano Edwards
The apple culturist. New York, Harper and Brothers,
1871. 334p.
Todd, William John
A handbook of wine; how to buy, serve, store, and
drink it. London, J. Cape, 1922. 103p. Illus.
Glossary of terms.

———— .
Port: how to buy, serve, store and drink it. London,
Jonathan Cape, 1936. 95p. Illus.
Toledo Blade
Beer and the body. New York, The National
Temperance Society and Publication House, 1884. 24p.
Tolkowsky, T.
Hesperides. A history of the culture and use of citrus
fruits. London, John Bale, Sons and Curnew, Ltd.,
1938. 324p. Illus. Bibliography. (Univ. of Florida)
Tolles, Delight
Banquet libations of the Greeks. Ann Arbor, (Thesis),
1943. 114p.   (Berkeley)
Tolman, L.M.
Study of American beers and ales. Washington, Dept.
Agri. Bulletin no. 473, 1919. 23p. (St. Louis Public)

Tolson, Berneita and McCaig, Edith
The beer cookbook. New York, Hawthorn Books, Inc.,
1968. 208p. Illus-drawings.
Tomes, Robert
The champagne country. London, Routledge, 1867.
231p.
Tooth and Co.
Over a century of brewing tradition. The story of
Tooth and Co., Limited. Sydney, Published by Kent
and Waverley Breweries, 1953. 78p. Illus.
Tooze's Minneapolis
How? When? Where? (Cocktails). Minneapolis, n d,
ca1915. 40p.
Torelli, A.
900 recettes de cocktails et boissons Americaines.
Paris, S. Bornemann, 1927. (In French). 192p.
Torgasheff, Boris P.
China as a tea producer. Shanghai, China, The
Commercial Press Limited, 1926. 252p. Illus-
Bibliography.
Toulouse, J. H. and Levine, Max
Suggestions for maintaining quality and uniformity of
bottled carbonated beverages. Washington, ABCB
Educational Bulletin no. 8. Published by ABCB.,
1935. 20p. Illus-drawings.

———— See Levine, Max and Toulouse, J. H.
Suggestions on elimination of spoilage in the carbonated
beverage industry.
Tournefort, Joseph P.
Compleat herbal. London, R. Bonwicke, etc., 1719.
626p.   GBPOL
Tovey, Charles
British and foreign spirits. Their history, manufacture,
properties, etc., London, Whittaker and Co., 1864.
376p.

———— Champagne: its history, manufacture, properties, etc.,
with some remarks upon wine and wine merchants.
London, John Camden Hotten, 1870. 140p. Illus.

———— Wine and wine countries: a record and manual for
wine merchants and wine consumers. New edition.
London, Whittaker, 1877. 519p. Illus.

———— Wine revelations. London, Whittaker and Co., 1883.
82p.   BM

Wit, wisdom and morals. Distilled from Bacchus.
London, Whittaker and Co., 1878. 295p.

Tovey, John M.
Cherry. Information about industry and flavors.
Indianapolis, Hurty-Peck and Co., 1952. 10p. Illus-
drawings.

_____.
Orange. Information about different varieties, etc.
Indianapolis, Hurty-Peck and Co., 1952. 14p. Illus-
drawings.

_____.
See Noling, A. W. and Towey, John M.
Sunstruck off-flavor in soft drinks. (Helpful service
bulletin no. 13). 23p. Illus. Bibliography.

Townsend, Jack
The Bartender's book; being a history of sundry
alcoholic potations, libations, and mixtures, together
with charts, recipes and tables, by Jack Townsend and
Tom Moore McBride. New York, Viking Press, 1951.
148p. Illus.-drawings.

Townsend, William H.
Lincoln and liquor. New York, The Press of the
Pioneers, Inc., 1934. 152p. Illus. Bibliography.

Toye, Nina
Drinks, long and short, by Nina Toye and A. H.
Adair; London, W. Heinemann, Ltd., 1925.
67p.

Toye, Nina and Adair, A. H.
Petits and grands verres choix des meilleurs cocktails.
Paris, Au Sans Pareil, n d, ca1900. (In French).
132p.

Tozier, Josephine
Among English Inns (Little pilgrimages). The story
of a pilgrimage to characteristic spots of rural
England. Boston, L. C. Page and Co., 1904. 250p.
Illus.

Trade Recipes
How to make 300 secret trade recipes. Success
Publishing Co., 1916. 32p.   BM

_____.
One hundred secret trade and family recipes for
summer and winter drinks. London, Success Publ. Co.
1923. 16p.   BM

Trader Vic
See Bergeron, Victor Jules
Trader Vic's Book of food and drink.
Trahey, Jane and Pierce, Daren
Son of the Martini cookbook. New York, Clovis Press,
1967. unpaged. Illus-drawings.
Traveller, A.
See Anon.
One hundred ways, especially prepared for connoisseurs
as well as the novitiate. (cocktails).
Travers, G. W.
A century of brewing Hudson ales and the Evans
brewery. New York, Moss Engraving Co., 1866.
56p.   NYPL
Travers, Joseph and Sons Ltd.,
Past and present in an old firm. (Tea). London,
Hazell, Watson and Viney, Ltd., 1907. 55p. Illus.
Tremlett, Rex
Homemade wine. Norwich (Great Britain). Fletcher
and Son, Ltd., 1968. 125p.
Tressler, Donald K. and Evers, Clifford F.
The freezing preservation of foods. New York, Avi
Publishing Co., 1943. 789p. Bibliography.
Tressler, Donald E., Evers, Clifford F. and Long, Lucy
Into the freezer-and out. New York, Avi Publishing
Co., Inc., 1946. 223p.
Triebold, Howard O. and Aurand, Leonard W.
Food composition and analysis. Princeton, N.J.,
D. Van Nostrand Co., Inc., 1963. 497p. References.
Tripp, C. Howard
Brewery management. London, F. W. Lyon, 1892.
234p.

_____.
Licensing acts of 1902. London and Derby, Bemrose
and Sons, 1903. 30p.   BM
Tritton, Suzanne, M.
Amateur wine making; an introduction and complete guide
to wine, cider, perry, mead and beer making, and to
the cultivation of the vine. London, Faber, and Faber,
1957. 239p. Illus.

_____.
Grape growing and wine making including the Vintner's
calendar. Almondsbury, Glos., Grey Owl Research
Laboratories, 1949. 32p. Illus. n d, ca1950.
41p. Illus.

410

—— Successful wine and beer making. Revised edition.
Almondsbury, Glos., Grey Owl Laboratories, 1962.
68p.

—— Successful wine making. Mead, perry, cider, fruit
wines, sparkling wines, vegetable wine, wine recipes.
Almondsbury, Glos., Grey Owl Research Laboratories,
1956. 40p.

—— Successful winemaking. Including mead, vermouth
and liqueurs. Almondsbury, Glos. 1959, Grey Owl
Laboratories, 51p.

—— Tritton's guide to better wine and beer making for
beginners. London, Faber and Faber, 1965. 157p.
Illus- photos.

—— Wine making from fruit pulps and concentrates. First
edition, 1962. Almondsbury, Glos., Grey Owl Research
Laboratories, 1962. 18p. Revised edition, 1963. 22p.
Tritton's Wine Making, etc.

Trowbridge, J. M.
The cider makers' hand book. A complete guide for
making and keeping pure cider. New York, Orange
Judd Co., 1911. 119p. Illus.

Truman, Benjamin Cummings
See how it sparkles. Los Angeles, G. Rice and
Sons 1896. 63p.   LC

Truman, Buxton, Hanbury and Co.
See Birch, Lionel
The story of beer.

Tryon, J. H.
A practical treatise on grape culture. Willoughby,
Ohio, 1887.   (Hedrick- Grapes of New York)

Tryon, Thomas
Health's grand preservative or the woman's best
doctor. Nature of brandy, rum, and other distilled
spirits. London, 1682. 22p.   BM

—— New art of brewing beer, ale and preparing all sorts
of liquors. London, Wm. Robesha, 1690. 142p.   BM

—— Treatise on cleanness of meats and drinks. London,
Published by author, 1682. 21p.   BM

_____.
Way to get health. London, G. Conyers, 1702.   LC

_____.
Way to health, long life and happiness. London,
R. Baldwin, 1691. 669p.   BM

_____.
Way to get wealth. Directing how to make 23 sorts
of English wine, equal to French, etc. London, G.
Conyers, 1702. 3 vol. in one.   LC

Tubbs, D. B.
Kent pubs. London, B. T. Batsford, Ltd., 1966.
144p. Illus.

Tuck, Charles A.
Cocktails and mixed drinks. London, K aye and Ward,
1967. 91p. Illus- drawings.

Tuck, John
Guide to young brewers particularly adapted to the
families of the nobility and gentry, farmers and
private brewers. London, Francis Westley, 1820.
184p.   GBPOL

_____.
The private brewer's guide to the art of brewing ale
and porter. London, W. Simpkin and R. Marshall,
1822. 262p.

Tucker, J. H. Ph. D.
Manual of sugar analysis. New York, D. Van
Nostrand, 1 883. 353p.

Tucker, Josiah
An impartial inquiry into the benefits arising to the
nationa f rom the present great use of low priced
spirits, etc. London, T. Trye, 1751. 33p.
                        (New York State Library)

Tucker, Stephen Allen
A practical and scientific treatise on the manufacture
of pure high class, carbonated beverages and bottler's
soluble extracts, etc. Philadelphia, 1919. 63p.   LC

Tudor, Alice M.
A little book of healing herbs. London and Boston,
The Medici Soci ety, 1927. 74p.

✓ Tudor, Emma
October dawn; a short and practical treatise on the
manufacture of home made wines from the native
grapes of New England. Cambridge, Printed privately
at the Riverside Press, 1926. 63p.

Tuffin, Hensley R.
Grapes, peaches, nectarine. London, Collingridge, 1957.
92p.   LC

Tufts, James W.
Advertising folder (16 pages) with illustrations of fountains shown at Columbian Exposition, Boston, n d, ca1893.

———— .
Arctic Soda Water apparatus. Boston, 1873. 48p. Illus- advertising. 1885. 16p. 1888. 220p. Illus- advertising.

———— .
Arctic Soda Water Apparatus, Book of Directions. Boston, (1889). 276p. Illus- advertising.

———— .
Book of directions Arctic Soda water Apparatus. Boston, n d, ca1896. 184p. Illus- advertising.

———— .
Book of directions for setting and operating soda water apparatus. Boston, 1895. 220p. Illus. n d, ca1900, 243p.

———— .
Descriptive catalogue of Arctic Soda-Water Apparatus. Boston, 1874. 64p. Illus.

———— .
Descriptive catalogue of James W. Tufts Arctic Soda-Water Apparatus. Boston, 1876. 176p. Illus- advertising. 1890. 304p. Illus- advertising.

———— .
Illustrations of James W. Tuft's Soda-Water Apparatus. Boston, 1875. 80p. Illus.
Turnbow, Grover D. et al.
Ice cream industry. New York, Wiley, 1947. 654p.
(General Foods Research Lib.)
Turnbull, Grace H.
Fruit of the vine as seen by many witnesses of all times. Third printing. Baltimore, Published by author, 1952. Cover title - A symposium of social drinking. 178p. Illus.
Turnbull, William W.
Law and liquor. London, 1877. (Stopes)
Turner, Bernard C. A.
Enjoy your own wine; a beginner's guide to making wine at home. London, Mills and Boon, Ltd., 1959. 94p. Illus- drawings.

———— .
Improve your winemaking. London, Pelham Books, 1964. 143p.

——— .
The Pan book of winemaking. London, Pan Books, 1964. 173p. Illus.

——— .
A practical guide to winemaking. London, Hutchinson, 1966. 144p. Illus.

——— .
The winemaker's companion; a handbook for those who make wine at home, by B. C. A. Turner, and C. J. J. Berry. 2nd edition. London, Mills and Boon, 1963. 228p. Illus.

Turner, Bernard C. A. and Down, Peter
Behind the wine list. London, Mills and Boon, 1968. 124p. Illus- photos, drawings.

——— .
Simple guide to home- made beer. London, Mills and Boon Ltd., 1968. 89p. Illus- photos.

Turner, Bernard C. A. and Roycroft, E. A.
AB- Z of wine- making. London, Pelham Books, 1966. 203p. Illus- photos. Dictionary.

Turner, Frank Grant
Negligence with food, drink, drugs. Miami, Fla. Portia T. Mc Leland, 1933. 275p.   LC

Turner, C.
Brief account of the mineral waters of Spa. London, 1733.   (Kirkby)

——— .
Full and distinct account of the mineral waters of Spa and Pyrmont. London, 1733.   (Kirkby)

Turner, Henry A.
Treatise on tea. London, 1880.

(Ukers- All about tea)

Turner, William
Booke of the natures and properties as well as the bathes in England as of other bathes in Germany, Italy, etc. Collen. Printed by A. Birchman, 1562. 4p.   BM

——— .
A book of wines, by William Turner, (1568), together with a modern English version of the text by the editors and a general introduction by Sanford V. Larkey, and an oenological note by Philip M. Wagner. New York, Scholars' Facsimiles and Reprints, 1941. facsim. (95p.) 79p.

—————— .
A new boke of natures and properties of all wines
that are commonlye used in England.   London,
Imprinted by W. Seres, 1568.   95p.   LC

—————— .
Pure treasure of the English Bathes.   J. Winder for
J. Perin, 1596.   GBPOL
Turner, William
See Bird, A. E. P. and Turner, William
Cocktails, their kicks and sidekicks.
Turnstall, Arthur C.
Tea roots.   Calcutta, India Tea Ass'n, 1916-1918.
2 vol.   (National Agricultural Library)
Tuson, Richard V.
Cooley's cyclopedia of practical receipts.   5th edition.
London, J. and A. Churchill, 1872.   1201p.
1897, 6th edition.   2 vols.
Tutuola, Amos
The palm-wine drinkard and his dead palm-wine
tapster in the Dead's Town.   New York, Grove,
1953.   130p.
Tweed, E. J.
The economics of brewing, remarks on distillation and
rectifying.   London, Groombridge and Sons, 1861.
96p.
Twining, Stephen H.
The House of Twining, 1706-1956.   Being a short
history of the firm of R. Twining and Co., Ltd.,
London, Publishing by Twining, 1956.   Cover title-
Two Hundred and fifty years of tea and coffee.
115p.   Illus.
Tysser, H. F. Ed.
The Fruit Annual, 1954-1955. Year book and directory
of the World Fruit Trade.   London, British-Continental
Trade Press, Ltd., 503p.

—————— .
See Anon.
Fruit Annual and Directory. H. F. Tysser, Ed.
1937-1938.   First Year-Book and directory of the
World's Fruit Trade.   London, British-Continental
Press Ltd., 1937.   355p.   Dictionary of fruit
terms in English-French-Spanish-German.
1948-1949.   348p.   Dictionary.

Ugarte, José P.
The cultivation and preparation of coffee for the market. 2nd edition. 1916. 101p. Illus.

Ukers, William Harrison
All about coffee. 2nd edition. New York, The Tea and Coffee Trade Journal Co., 1935. 818p. Illus. Bibliography.

_____ . All about tea. New York, The Tea and Coffee Trade Journal Co., 1935. 2 v. Illus. Bibliography of tea.

_____ . Coffee facts; elementary facts about the product and a statistical presentation of its production and consumption. New York, Tea and Coffee Trade Journal Co., 1951. 120p. Illus.

_____ . Coffee merchandising; a handbook to the coffee business giving elementary and essential facts pertaining to the history, cultivation, preparation, and marketing of coffee. New York, The Tea and Coffee Trade Journal Co., 1924. 245p. Illus.

_____ . Japan and Formosa (tea). New York, Tea and Coffee Trade Journal, 1925. 58p. (National Agri. Library).

_____ . Java and Sumatra. (tea). New York, Tea and Coffee Trade Journal, 1926. 63p. (National Agri. Library)

_____ . The romance of coffee. An outline history of coffee and coffee drinking through a thousand years. New York, The Tea and Coffee Trade Journal Co., 1948. 280p. Illus.

_____ . The romance of tea; an outline history of tea and tea-drinking through sixteen hundred years. New York, London, A. A. Knopf, 1936. 276p. Illus.

_____ . Tea in a nutshell. New York, 1926. (Ukers-All about Tea).

_____ . Ten years of coffee progress 1935-1944. New York, Pan American Coffee Bureau, 1945. 31p.   NYPL

_____ . A trip to Brazil (coffee). New York, Tea and Coffee Trade Journal, 1935. 37p.   NYPL

416

———.
Trip to Ceylon. (tea). New York, Tea and Coffee
Trade Journal, 1925. 92p. NYPL

———.
Trip to China (tea). New York, Tea and Coffee Trade
Journal, 1926. 43p. (National Agricultural Library)

———.
Trip to India (tea). New York, Tea and Coffee Trade
Journal, 1925. 38p. (National Agricultural Library)

———.
What everyone should know about tea. New York,
1926. (Ukers-All about tea).
United American Soda Fountain Co.,
Favorite fountain formulas. Watertown, N.Y., 194?
63p. POSL
United Brewers Industrial Foundation
American beer and ale; a handbook of facts and figures.
New York, 1937. 30p. LC

———.
See Davison, Eloise
Beer in the American home.

———.
Clean-up or close-up. A self-regulation program unique
in industry. New York, n d, ca1940. 20p.

———.
Scientific moderation in drinking. New York, Published
by the Foundation, n d, ca1939. 24p.

———.
What are the facts about beer. New York, n d, ca1941.
unpaged (12).
United Fresh Fruit and Vegetable Ass'n.
Bananas. Washington, D. C. 1969. 37p. Illus-
photos.
United Fruit Co.
See Bogert, L. Jean
Dietary uses of the banana in health and disease.
United Interest Soda Generator and Fountain Co.
A. D. Puffer's improved and simplified carbonic acid
generator. Boston, May 11, 1855. 4p. Illus.
United Kingdom Bartender's Guild
Approved cocktails. n d, London, Pall Mall Ltd.,
(1953). unpaged. Glossary.

———.
The U. K. B. G. guide to drinks. 2nd edition,
revised. London, 1955. 295p. Illus.

United States Bottlers Machinery Co.
Bottling and packaging engineer. Chicago, May 1921
issue. 12p. Illus.

_____.
Bottling engineer handbook. Chicago, 1940. 192p.
Illus. 1946. 96p. Illus.
United States Brewers Foundation, Inc.,
Barley, hops and history. New York, n d. unpaged
(28). Illus.

_____.
A beer dispensing handbook. New York, 1952. 50p.

_____.
Brewers Almanac. The Brewing Industry in the
United States. New York.
1949. 125p. 1956. 116p.
1950. 112p. 1959. 118p.
1951. 116p. 1960. 118p.
1955. 116p. (centennial issue)

_____.
Questions and answers on beer. New York, n d,
ca1953. unpaged (20). Illus.
United States Brewers' Ass'n.
See Thomann, Gallus
Alleged adulterations of malt liquors. The whole truth
about them.

_____.
Brewers' Convention (26th) held at Niagara Falls.
September 1886. Published in New York, 1886. 99p.

_____.
Brewers' Convention (34th) held at Syracuse, New York.
New York, 1894. 104p. Illus-photos.

_____.
The Brewing Industry of the United States (Brewers'
Almanac), New York. H-P Library has copies for the
years 1962-1963.

_____.
See Henius, Max
Danish beer and continental beer gardens.

_____.
See Thomann, Gallus
Documentary history of the United States Brewers'
Association. 2 parts. Part 1. 1896, part 2. 1898.

_____.
History of brewing and the growth of the United States
Brewers' Ass'n. New York, 1937. 24p.   LC

418

———————.
Proceedings of the one hundredth anniversary convention,
Bal Harbour, Florida, 1962. 185p. Illus.

———————.
See Clausen, Henry Jr.
Souvenir of 25th convention of United States Brewers'
Association. Address by Clausen, New York, 1885.
40p. Illus.

———————.
See Monahan, M. (Michael), Editor and Compiler
A text-book of true temperance.

———————.
The Year Book. New York.
1909. 204p. 1913. 311p.
1910. 302p. 1914. 353p.
1911. 330p. 1915. 360p.
1912. 299p. 1916. 332p.
1918. 146p. wrapper
1919. 200p. wrapper

United States Cuban Sugar Council
Sugar. Facts and figures. Washington, 1952. 176p.
Glossary.

United States Industrial Chemicals Co.
Ethyl alcohol handbook. New York, 1962. 131p. Illus-
photos.

U.S. Bureau of the Census
Statistical Abstract of the United States. 72nd edition.
Washington, U.S. Department of Commerce, 1951.
1047p.

U.S. Dept. of Agriculture
Competitive relationships between sugar and corn
sweeteners. Washington, U.S. Dept. of Agriculture,
June 1951. 245p.

———————.
Foods and food adulterants. Bulletin no. 13. U. S.
Dept. of Agriculture. Washington, 1887. (5 parts).
627p.

———————.
Fruits - non-citrus - by States, 1960 and 1961.
Washington. Part 1. May 1962. Part 2. July 1962.
Part 1. 24p. Part 2. 16p. paper covers.

———————.
Sensory methods for measuring differences in food
quality. Bulletin no. 34. Agriculture Information, 1951.
134p. Literature cited.

‾‾‾‾‾‾‾‾•
Special report on the beet-sugar industry in the United
States. (by Harvey W. Wiley). Washington, Government
Printing Office, 1898. 240p.

‾‾‾‾‾‾‾‾•
Yearbook of U.S. Dept. of Agriculture for 1895.
Washington, 1896. 656p.
1908. 822p. 1918. 760p.
1911. 732p. 1931. 1113p.
1914. 715p. 1940. 1215p.

‾‾‾‾‾‾‾‾•
Yearbook of Agriculture. "Farmers in a changing world".
U.S. Dept. of Agriculture. Washington, 1940. 1215p.
U.S. Internal Revenue Dept.
Guagers' Weighing Manual. U.S. Internal Revenue,
no. 11. Revised, supplement no. 1. Washington,
August 18, 1911. 646p.

‾‾‾‾‾‾‾‾•
Tax on distilled spirits. (Regulations and instructions
concerning the) No. 7. Washington, Government
Printing Office, 1908. 272p.
U.S. Treasury Dept.
Guaging Manual. Embracing instructions and tables for
determining the quantity of distilled spirits by proof and
weight. Washington, Bureau of Industrial Alcohol, 1933.
579p.
Urbana Wine Co.
Gold Seal Champagne. Urbana, New York, 1901.
(Cover title-The Gold Seal). 16p. Illus.
Ure, Andrew, MD
Dictionary of arts, manufactures, and mines. 2nd
edition. London, Longman, Orme, Brown, Green and
Longmans, 1840. 1334p. 1856. 2 vol. New York,
D. Appleton and Co., 998-1116p.

‾‾‾‾‾‾‾‾•
A dictionary of chemistry. 3rd edition. London,
Thomas Tegg, et al. 1927. 829p.
Urquhart, D. H.
British North Borneo. A review of the colony with
special reference to AGRICULTURAL DEVELOPMENT
and opportunities for investment in AGRICULTURE
ENTERPRISE. Bournville, Cadbury Brothers, Ltd.,
1959. 38p. Illus-photos. List of publications on
cocoa-growing.

Urquhart, D. H.
Cocoa. 2nd edition. London, Longmans, Green and Co., Ltd., 1962. 293p. Illus-photos. References.

_____.
Cocoa in some countries of South East Asia and the Pacific. Ceylon-Hawaii-Thailand-Malaya-Papua- and New Guinea. The Fiji group. Bournville, Cadbury Brothers, Ltd., 1957. 38p. Illus-photos.

_____.
Prospects for cocoa growing in Uganda and Zanzibar. Bournville, Cadbury Brothers, Ltd., 1958. 28p. Illus-photos.

_____.
Prospects of the growing of cocoa in the British Solomon Islands with notes on Malaya, Ceylon and Java. Bournville, Cadbury Brothers, Ltd., 1951. 44p. Illus-photos.

_____.
Report on an investigation into the prospects for growing cocoa and oil palms in India. Bournville, Cadbury Brothers, Ltd., 1959. 24p. Illus-photos.

_____.
Report on the cocoa industry in Sierra Leone. And notes on the cocoa industry of the Gold Coast. Bournville, Cadbury Brothers, Ltd., 1955. 43p. Illus-photos.

_____.
Report on the cocoa industry in the French Ivory Coast. Bournville, Cadbury Brothers, Ltd., 1955. 32p. Illus-photos.

_____.
Report on the expansion of the cocoa industry in Jamaica. Bournville, Cadbury Brothers, Ltd., 1957. 27p. Illus-photos.

_____.
Report on the possibilities of cocoa-growing in the protectorate of Nyasaland. Bournville, Cadbury Brothers, Ltd., 1958. 16p. Illus-photos.
Urquhart, D. H. and R.E.F. Dwyer
Prospects of extending the growing of cocoa in Papua and New Guinea. Bournville, Cadbury Brothers, Ltd., 1951. 39p. Illus-photos.
Urquhart, D. H. and G.A.R. Wood
Report on a visit to the cocoa zone of Bahia, Brazil. Bournville, Cadbury Brothers, Ltd., 1954. 32p. Illus-photos.

Uribe Compuzano, Andres
Brown gold; the amazing story of coffee. New York,
Random House, 1954. 237p. Illus.
Usher's Wiltshire Brewery, Ltd.,

Houses and ale. Cheltenham and London. Ed. J.
Burrows and Co., Ltd., n. d. 176p.
V., (pseud)
The vine and wine making in Victoria, by V. and
Beberrao. Melbourne, Wilson and M., 1861. 64p.
PLOSA
Vail, G. E.
See Justin, Margaret M.; Rust, Lucile Osborn and
Vail, Gladys E.
Foods. An introductory college course.
Vaillancourt, Emile
The history of the brewing industry in the province
of Quebec. Montreal, G. Ducharme, 1940. 47p.
References.
Vaizey, John
See Lynch, Patrick and Vaizey, John
Guinness's Brewery in the Irish economy. 1759-1876.

_____ .
The brewing industry, 1886-1951; an economic study,
for the Economic Research Council. London, Pitman,
1960. 173p. Bibliography.
Valaer, Peter
Blackberry, other berry and fruit wines, their methods
of production and analysis. Washington, Treasury
Dept., 1950. 53p.

_____ .
Wines of the world. New York, Abelard Press, 1950.
576p. Bibliography.
Valente-Perfeito, J. C.
Let's talk about port. Porto Instituto do Vinho do
Porto, 1948. 100p. Illus.
Van Ameringen-Haebler, Inc.
Alva flavors bottlers guide and price list. New York,
1946. 88p. Illus.

_____ .
Alva syrup making guide for vending machine
operators. New York, (1948). 13p.
Van Buren, J.
Scuppernong grape, its history and mode of culture

422

with a short treatise on manufacture of wine from it.
Memphis, Tenn., Published by author, 1868. 62p.
(National Agricultural Library)

Van Dyke, Mona
Cooking with wine. RECIPES. Lodi, Calif., Roma
Wine Co., Inc., 1935. 32p. Illus.

Van Dyk and Co.
Prices (Perfumery). New York, 1915. 8p.

Van Hall, J. J.
Cocoa. London, Abelard Press, 1914. 512p.   BM

Van Hook, Andrew
Sugar. Its production, technology and uses. New
York, Ronald Press, 1949. 155p.

Van Meter, Ralph A.
Bush fruit production. New York, Orange Judd
Publishing Co., Inc., 1928. 123p. Illus-photos.

Van Rensselaer, Stephen
Early American flasks and bottles. (Check list of)
Southampton, N. Y., Cracker Parrel Press, 1921.
109p. Illus-photos.

Vanderbilt, S. B.
See Vulte, Herman and Vanderbilt, Sadie B.
Food industries. 4th edition.

Vanstone, J. Henry
The raw materials of commerce. A descriptive
account of the vegetable, animal, mineral and synthetic
products of the world and of their commercial uses.
London, Sir Isaac Pitman and Sons, 1929. 2 vol.
792p. (consecutively) Illus.

Varounis, Georges
An introduction to French wines and spirits. Los
Angeles. Franco American Wine Co., 1933. 68p.
Illus.   LC

Vasey, Samuel A.
Guide to analysis of potable spirits. Bailliere, Tindall
and Cox, 1904. 87p.   (Boston   Public)

Vaughan, William
Natural and artificial directions for health. London,
R. Bradecke, 1626.   BM

Vecchi, Joseph
"The Tavern is my Drum". Autobiography. London,
Published by Odhams Press Ltd. Distributed by
Simpkin Marshall (1941), Ltd., 1948. 224p. Illus-
photos.

Vecki, Victor G.
Alcohol and prohibition. Philadelphia, J. P. Lippincott Co., 1923. 165p.

Vehling, Joseph D.
America's table. Chicago and Milwaukee, Hostaids,
1950. 882p. Dictionary.
Veley, Victor H. and Lillian J.
The mocro-organisms of faulty rum. London, H.
Frowde, 1898. 64p.   GBPOL
Venge, Per
Easy lessons in imported wines. Los Angeles,
Privately printed, 1961. 28p.   (NAPA)
Venner, Tobias
Via Recta ad via longam; or a plain philosophical
demonstration for the preservation of health. London,
Richard Moore, 1628. 226p.   BM
Verdad, Don Pedro (pseud)
A book about sherry (From vineyard to decanter.)
London, Edward Stanford, 1876. 121p.
Verdier, Paul
History of wine. When and how to drink it. San
Francisco, City of Paris, publisher, 1933. 42p.
                                                  (Davis)
Vermiere, Robert
See "Robert" (Robert Vermeire)
Cocktails. How to mix them.
Vernon, Charles
The Sweet Shop. A handbook for retail confectioners.
London. Sir Isaac Pitman and Sons Ltd., August
1939. 332p.
Vernon, H. M.
The alcohol problem. London, Bailliere, Tindall
and Cox, 1928. 252p.
Veronelli, Luigi
The wines of Italy. New York, 1964. 326p. Illus-
with labels.
Verrill, Alpheus Hyatt
Isles of spices and palm. New York and London,
D. Appleton and Co., 1915. 304p. Illus.

—————————.
Perfumes and spices, including an account of soaps and
cosmetics; the story of the history, source, preparation,
and use of the spices, perfumes, soaps, and cosmetics
which are in everyday use. Boston, L.C. Page and
Co., 1940. 304p. Illus.-photos, drawings.
Vespre, Francois S.
Dissertation on growth of vines in England. London,
1786. 69p.   BM

Viala, P. and L. Ravaz
American vines, their adaptation, culture grafting
and propagation. San Francisco, Published by the
translaters, 1903. 299p. Bibliography, glossary.
Vicaire, Georges
Bibliographie Gastronomique, 2nd edition. London,
Holland Press, 1954. 971p.
Vicary, Thomas
The Englishman's treasure. London, 1641. 115p.
(Kirkby)

Vickery, H. C. Comp.
The use of beer in foods. A cookery book.
Burpham, Guildford, 1938. 75p.
Victoria Wine Co., Ltd.
Here's how. Being a new symposium of recipes.
of good cheer. London, (1934). 79p. 1954, 84p.
Illus. n d, 61p. Illus.

———— .
Price list. London, Summer 1959. 20p.
Vigoureaux, Paul
See Wilcox, Barbara and Vigoureaux, Paul
Cook it the French Way.
Villanis., P.
Theoretical and practical notes upon wine-making,
and the treatment of wines, especially applied to
Australian wines. Adelaide, Reprinted from the
"Garden and Field". Webb, Vardon and Pritchard,
1884. 106p.
Villiars, Sir Thomas L.
Some pioneers of the tea industry. Colombo.
Colombo Apothecaries Co., 1951.
(Forrest-100 Years Ceylon Tea)
Villiers, O. W.
Handbook of brewing calculations. London, 1887.
48p.   GBPOL
Vilmorin, Louise de
Cognac. Remy Martin, Paris, 1962. unpaged (44).
Illus.
Vine, D. P.
Art of brewing explained. Gloucester, 1871. 59p.
BM
Vine, G.
Homemade wines. How to make and how to keep them.
London, Groomsbridge and Sons, n d. 48p.
(Brady Library-Fresno State College)

Viner, Richard
    See Criticos George (as told to Richard Viner)
    The life story of George of the Ritz.
Virginia Women's Christian Temperance Union.
    Thirst Aids for the charming hostess. Recipes
    compiled by Mrs. G.W. Custer director of Department
    of Natural Fruit Products. Roanoke, Va., 1952.
    24p.
Vizetelly, Ernest and Arthur
    Wines of France (The). London, Witherby and Co.,
    1908. 176p. Illus-photos.
Vizetelly, Henry
    Facts about champagne and other sparkling wines . . .
    London, Ward, Lock 1879. 235p. Illus.

———— Facts about port and madeira, with notices of the wines
    vintaged around Lisbon, and the wines of Tenerife.
    London, Ward, Lock and Co., New York, Scribner
    and Welford, 1880. 211p. Illus.

———— Facts about sherry, gleaned in the vineyards and bode-
    gas of the Jerez, Seville. Moguer and Montilla
    districts during the autumn of 1875. London, Ward,
    Lock and Tyler, Warwick House, 1876. 108p. Illus.

———— A history of champagne. With notes on the other
    sparkling wines of France. London, Vizetelly and Co.,
    New York, Scribner and Welford, 1882. 263p.
    Illus-engravings.

———— How champagne was first discovered and how the wine
    is now produced. Epernay, Moet and Chandon, 1890.
    90p.   (Crerar)

———— The wines of the world characterized and classed:
    with some particulars respecting the beers of Europe.
    London, Ward, Lock and Tyler, 1875. 202p.
Voegele, Marguerite C. and Grace H. Wooley
    Drink dictionary. New York, Ahrens Publishing Co.,
    Inc., 1961. 192p. Illus.
Vogel, Edward H.
    The practical brewer, a manual for the brewing
    industry, by Edward H. Vogel, Jr., and others.
    St. Louis Master Brewers Assn of America, 1947.
    228p. Illus.

Vogel, Max
On beer. A statistical sketch. London, Trubner and
Co., 1874. 73p. LC
Vom Endt, Rudi
See Heuckmann, Dr. Wilhelm and Vom Endt, Rudi
The grafted vine.
Vulte, Hermann T. and Vanderbilt, Sadie B.
Food industries. 4th edition. Easton, Pa., 1923.
323p. Bibliography.

W. (F.)
Warme beer, a treatise. London, Henry Overton,
1641. 143p. USBA
Wachtmeister, The Countess Constance and Davis, Kate
Buffington
Practical vegeterian Cookery. Minneapolis? Various
publishers, 1897. 179p.
Wagner, E.
Recipes for the preserving of fruit, vegetables and
meat. London, Scott, Greenwood and Son, 1908.
119p.
Wagner, Fritz
Das Getrankebuch. Giessen, Fachbuchverlag Dr.
Pfanneberg and Co., 1955. 226p. Illus. In German.
Wagner, Leopold
London Inns and Taverns. London, George Allen and
Unwin Ltd., 1924. 252p.

_____.
More London inns and taverns. London, George
Allen and Unwin Ltd., 1925. 256p.
Wagner, Philip Marshall
American wines and how to make them. New York,
Knopf, 1933. 295p. Illus. 2nd edition, rev., 1936.
367p. Bibliography.

_____.
American wines and wine-making. New York, Knopf,
1956. 264p. Illus. Bibliography.

_____.
Wine grapes; their selection, cultivation and enjoyment.
New York, Harcourt, Brace, 1937. 298p. Illus.
Bibliography.

————·————
A wine-grower's guide. Containing chapters on the
past and future of wine-growing in America, the
management of a vineyard, and the choice of suitable
wine-grape varieties. New York, Knopf, 1945. 230p.
Illus. 1965. 224p. Illus. Bibliography.

————·————
A wine-grower's guide. Revised edition. New York,
1965. 224p. Illus. Bibliography.
Wahl, Arnold Spencer
Wahl handybook of the American brewing industry . . .
by Arnold Spencer Wahl and Robert Wahl. Chicago,
Wahl Institute Inc., 1937. 4 volumes, Illus. "List
of publications and articles emanating from Robert and
Arnold Spencer Wahl".
Wahl, Robert
American handy-book of the brewing, malting and
auxiliary trades . . . by Robert Wahl., and Max
Henius. Chicago, Wahl and Henius, 1901. 1266p.
Illus. Bibliography. Dictionary of technical terms.
2nd edition, 1902.

————·————
Indian corn (or maize) in the manufacture of beer.
Washington, Gov't Printing Office, 1893. 21p.   LC

————·————
See Wahl, Arnold Spencer and Wahl, Robert
Wahl handybook of the American Brewing Industry.
Wahl, William H.
See Brant, William T. and Wahl, William H.
The Techno-Chemical Receipt Book.
Wahl Institute
Study of brewing and malting technique. Chicago,
1942. 106p.   NYPL
Wailes, Raymond B., Ed.
Manual of formulas. Recipes, methods and secret
processes. New York, Popular Science Publishing Co.,
1932. 250p.
Wait, Frona Eunice
Wines and vines of California; a treatise on the ethics
of wine-drinking. San Francisco, Bancroft, 1889.
215p. Illus.
Wakeman, Abram
History and reminiscences of lower Wall Street, etc.
New York, Spice Mill Publishing Co., 1914. 216p.
                                               NYPL

Wakeman, Rev. Joel
   The Maine law triumphant, etc., Boston, Albert
   Colby and Co., 1859. The mysterious parchment
   or the Satanic license. 323p.
Walbridge, William S.
   American bottles old and new. A story of the industry
   in the United States. Toledo, Ohio, The Owens Bottle
   Co., 1920. 113p. Illus.
Walch, Garnet
   A glass of champagne. Melbourne, Mc Carron, Bird
   and Co., 1885. 48p.   ANL
Waldo, Myra
   Beer and good food. Brighten your menus and recipes
   with beer and ale. Garden City, Doubleday, 1958.
   264p. Illus.

_____.
   The pleasures of wine, a guide to the wines of the
   world. New York, Crowell-Collier Press, 1963.
   190p. Illus.
Waldorf-Astoria. See Anon
   Food beverages and restaurant service.
Waldron, John
   Satyr against tea; or Ovington's essay upon the nature
   and qualities dissected and burlesqued. Dublin, 1733.
                                                          BM
Walker, A. Horace
   The inspection of fish, poultry, game, fruit, nuts and
   vegetables. London, Bailliere, Tindall and Cox, 1911.
   180p. Illus.
Walker, George
   The publican's and cellarman's guide for the manage-
   ment of spirits, ale and beer. London, 1871.   BM
Walker, James
   Hints to consumers of wine. Edinburgh, Peter Hill,
   1802. 57p.   NYPL
Walker, R. H.
   The rectifier's, compounder's and liquor dealer's manual.
   Wilkes-Barre, Penna., 1875. 32p.   LC
Walker, Hiram and Sons, Inc.,
   The Essential Guest. (cocktails). Detroit, n d.
   20p. Illus-drawings.

_____.
   The Hiram Walker outline of the distilled spirits
   business compiled as an aid to the salesmen. Detroit,
   1946. 120p. Illus.

Walker, John and Sons Limited
Around the world. Pictorial and descriptive of many
parts of the world. (Johnnie Walker whisky ads intersperced.) Kilmarnock, n d, (1924) 450p. Illus-photos.

Wall, Charles R. M.
United States practical brewing and malting interpreter.
New York, J. Axford, 1866. 176p.
(New York State Library)

Wallerius, Johan Gottschalk
Elementi di agricoltura Fisica E Chemica. Venice,
1791. 234p. Also in same volume L'Ortolano in villa
E L'Acurrato Giardiniere in citta. Venezia, 1779.
300p. Illus. (In Italian).

Wallerstein Company, Inc.
Forty years a-brewing. A record of Wallerstein
service to the brewing industry. New York, 1950.
64p. Illus. List of Wallerstein publications and
patents.

Wallerstein Laboratories
Alcohol tables based on the original extract of wort
(Balling) and balling of fermented beer. 2nd edition.
New York, 1933. 61p.

_____ .
Advances in beer quality. Part I. Beer and brewing
technology. Part II. Methodology for the brewing
laboratory. Staten Island, N. Y., 1961 and 1962.
176 and 240p. (2 vol.) Illus. Photos-drawings.

_____ .
Bottle beer quality, a 10-year research record. New
York, 1948. 161p. Illus. Bibliographies.

_____ .
The treatment of brewing water in the light of modern
chemistry. New York, Wallerstein Laboratories, 1935.
79p.

Wallerstein, Robert S.
Hospital treatment of alcoholism. Menninger Clinic
Monograph. Series no. 11. New York, Basis Books
Inc., 1957. 212p.

Wallis-Tayler, Alexander James
Tea machinery and tea factories; a descriptive treatise
on the mechanical appliances required in the cultivation
of the tea plant and the preparation of tea for the
market. London, C. Lockwood and Son, 1900. 452p.
Illus.

Walsh, J. H.
  The economical housekeeper, etc. London, G.
  Routledge and Co., 1857. 425p. Illus.
Walsh, Joseph M.
  Coffee; its history, classification and description.
  Philadelphia, Chicago, The John C. Winston Co., 1894.
  300p. Illus.

——————.
  "A cup of tea" containing a history of the tea plant,
  etc., Philadelphia, Published by author, 1884. 196p.
                                                        LC

——————.
  Tea-blending as a fine art. Philadelphia, Published
  by the author, 1896. 104p. Illus.

——————.
  Tea, its history and mystery. Philadelphia, Coates,
  1892. 265p. Illus.
Walter, Erich
  Manual for the essence industry. New York, John Wiley and
  Sons, 1916. 427p. Illus. 1933. 429p. Illus. 1922. 329p. Illus.
Walton, George Edward
  The mineral springs of the United States and Canada,
  with analyses and notes on the prominent spas of
  Europe, and a list of sea-side resorts. New York,
  D. Appleton and Co., 1874. 414p. Illus.
Walton, Howard R.
  Hiram Walker (1816-1899), and Walkerville from 1858.
  New York, Published by the Newcomen Society, 1958.
  24p. Illus.
Wandle, Jennie Taylor
  Extracts and beverages: the preparation of cordials,
  syrups, refreshing beverages, colognes, perfumes and
  various toilet articles. London and New York, The
  Butterick Publishing Co., Ltd., 1897. 46p.
Wanklyn, James Alfred
  Milk analysis. (A practical treatise.) London,
  Trubner and Co., 1874. 70p.

——————.
  Tea, coffee, and cocoa: a practical treatise on the
  analysis of tea, coffee, cocoa, chocolate, maté
  (Paraguay tea), etc., London, Trubner and Co., 1874.
  59p.

——————.
  Water-Analysis. A practical treatise on the examination of potable water. Revised by W. J. Cooper. 11th
  edition. London, Kegan Paul, Trench, Trubner and Co.,
  Ltd., 1907. 239p.

Warburton, Clark
The economic results of prohibition. New York,
Columbia University Press, 1932. 273p. Bibliography.
Warcollier, Georges
The principles and practice of cider-making, by Vernon
L. S. Charley, assisted by Pamela M. Mumford.
A translation of the 3d and last ed. (1928) of La
cidrerie by G. Warcollier, London, L. Hill, 1949.
367p. Illus. Bibliographies.
Ward, Artemas
The encyclopedia of food. New York, The Baker and
Taylor Co., 1929. 595p. Illus. Dictionary in 6
languages.

———————. The Grocer's encyclopedia. New York, Artemas Ward,
1911. (Cover title THE ENCYCLOPEDIA OF FOODS
AND BEVERAGES). 748p. Illus. Dictionary in 5
languages.

———————. The Grocer's hand-book and directory. Philadelphia,
The Philadelphia Grocer Publishing Co., 1886. 305p.
Ward, Ebenezer
Vineyards and orchards of South Australia. Adelaide.
South Australia Advertiser and Weekly Chronicle,
1867. 78p.   BM
Ward, H. W.
The book of the grape. London, (Reprinted), John
Lane, The Bodley Head Ltd., 1925. 97p. Illus.

———————. The book of the peach. London, The Walter Scott
Publishing Co., 1903. 113p.
Ward, John R.
Soda fountain profits. Stamford, Conn. Dahls, 1935.
32p.   LC
Ward, Maurice H.
Some brief records of brewing in South Australia.
Adelaide. Published by The Pioneers Ass'n of S. A.
1950. 22p.
Ward, Robert
Fallacies of teetotalism. London and Newcastle, 1872.
415p.   BM
Wardall, Ruth A. and White, Edna Noble
A study of foods. Boston, Ginn and Co., 1914.
174p. Illus.

Warder, John A.
    See Du Breuil A.
    Vineyard culture, improved and cheapened.
Waring, William G.
    Fruit growers handbook. Boalsburg, Pa. Boalsburg
    Centre Co., 1851. 134p.   NYPL
Warner, Charles K.
    The winegrowers of France and the Government since
    1875. New York, Columbia University Press, 1960.
    303p. Bibliography.
Warner, Harry S.
    The liquor cult and its culture. Columbus, Ohio. The
    Intercollegiate Association for study of the alcohol
    problem, 1946. 119p. Bibliography.

_____.
    See Johnson, F. Ernest and Warner, Harry S.
    Prohibition in outline.

_____.
    Social welfare and the liquor problem. Chicago, The
    Intercollegiate Prohibition Association, 1913. 298p.
Warner-Jenkinson Mfg. Co.
    The bottler's and ice cream maker's Handy Guide.
    St. Louis, 1921. 102p. Illus.

_____.
    Certified food colors. Booklet C-41. St. Louis, n d,
    1941. 38p. Illus. n d, 1960, 56p. Illus.

_____.
    Ice cream, carbonated beverages, with a short
    introduction to the study of chemistry and physics; a
    handbook for ice-cream makers, sodawater bottlers,
    and students taking short courses in dairying, etc.,
    written and published by Warner-Jenkinson Mfg., Co.,
    St. Louis, 1924. 134p. Illus.
Warre, James
    Past, present and possible future state of the wine
    trade. London, Hatcherd, 1823. 102p.   (Davis)
Warren, Chas.
    See Hamlin, Chas. E. and Warren, Chas.
    Hamlin's formulae or every druggist his own
    perfumer.
Warren, Cyprian A.
    Brewing waters. London, The Brewing Trade Review.
    (A reprint-after revision of a series of articles.), 1923.
    117p.

Warren, Geoffrey C.
    Elixir of Life. Being a slight account of the
    romantic rise to fame of a great house. Dublin,
    John Jamesson and Son, Ltd., 1925. (Liquor).
    17p. Illus.
Washburne, Chandler
    Primitive drinking. New York-New Haven, 1961.
    College and University Press, 1961. 282p.
    Bibliography.
Washburne, George B. and Bronner, Stanley
    Beverages de luxe. 2nd edition. (alcoholic) Louis-
    ville, The Wine and Spirit Bulletin, 1914. 93p.
    Illus-Advertising matter.   LC
Wassermann, Adeline, Comp.
    The Schenley Library Bibliography. New York,
    Schenley Distillers Corp., 1946. 98p.
Wasson, Rev. E. A.
    Religion and drink. New York, Burr Printing House,
    1914. 301p.
Water drinker
    Some enquiries into the effects of fermented liquors.
    London, J. Johnson and Co., 1814. 368p. 2nd ed.,
    1818. R. Hunter, 365p.
Watkins, George
    The compleat brewer. 2nd edition. London, J.
    Cooke. 1760. Also The compleat English brewer.
    London, J. Cooke, 1767. Compleat, 246p. (NYPL)
    Compleat English, 239p.   (Crerar)
Watkins, Michael
    Wining and dining in East Anglia. Ipswich. East
    Anglian Magazine, Ltd., 1969. 128p., Illus-drawings.
Watney Mann
    See Janes, Hurford
    The Red Barrel. A history of Watney Mann.
Watrous, Roberta C. Comp.
    Cacao. A bibliography on the plant and its culture and
    primary processing of the bean. Washington, Library
    list no. 53. U.S. Dept. Agri., October 1950. 49p.
    Bibliography.
Watson, John Forbes
    Culture and manufacture of tea in India. Calcutta,
    1871.   (Ukers-All about tea)
Watson, Margeret J. M.
    The home preservation of fruit and vegetables. London,
    Oxford University Press, 1926. 142p.

Watson, Richard
    Chemical essays. London, 1789. 5 vol. GBPOL
Watson, Rowland
    Merry gentlemen, A Bacchanalian scrapbook; being a
    curious, diverting and instructive miscellany of the
    Bacchanalian arts and sports. London, T. Werner
    Laurie, 1951. 296p. Illus.

――――――.
    A scrapbook of Inns. (England). London, T. Werner
    Laurie, Ltd., 1949. 218p. Illus.
Watt, Alexander
    Bordeaux and its wines. Paris. The Ministre des
    Travaux, Publics, etc., 1957. 20p. Illus-photos.
Watt, Bernice F. and Merrill, Annabel L.
    Composition of foods, raw, processed, prepared.
    U.S.D.A. Handbook (Agriculture) no. 8. Washington,
    June 1950. 147p.
Watt, Bernice K. See
    Merrill, Annabel L. and Watt, Bernice K.
    Energy value of foods.
Watt, James
    Description of a pneumatic apparatus with directions
    for production of factitious airs. Bristol, 1795.
    58p. GBPOL

――――――.
    Supplement to description of a pneumatic apparatus for
    preparing factitious airs. Birmingham, 1796. 48p.
                                                    GBPOL
Watts, Francis
    An introductory manual for sugar growers. London,
    Longmans, Green and Co., 1893. 151p.
Waugh, Alec
    In praise of wine. London, Cassell, 1959. 280p.
    Bibliography.

――――――.
    The Lipton Story. A centennial biography of England's
    great merchant sportsman. Garden City, N.Y.,
    Doubleday and Co., 1950. 277p.

――――――.
    Merchants of wine; being a centenary account of the
    fortunes of the House of Gilbey. London, Cassell,
    1957. 136p. Illus-photos.
Waugh, Evelyn
    Wine in peace and war. London, Saccone and Speed,
    1947. 77p. Illus. Bibliography.

Waugh, F. A.
  The American Apple Orchard. Sketch of the practice
  of apple growing in North America at the beginning
  of the 20th century. New York, Orange Judd Co.,
  1908. 215p. Illus.

———— The American peach orchard. New York, Orange
  Judd Co., 1913. 238p.

———— Plums and plum culture. New York, Orange Judd Co.,
  1901. 371p.
Waugh, Harry
  Bacchus on the wing. A wine merchant's travelogue.
  London, Wine and Spirits Publications, Ltd., 1966.
  203p. Illus-photos.

———— The changing face of wine. An assessment of some
  current vintages. London, Wine and Spirit Publications
  Ltd., 1968. 109p.
Weaver, John C.
  American barley production; a study in agricultural
  geography. Minneapolis, Burgess, 1950. 115p.
Webb, Sidney and Beatrice
  The history of liquor licensing in England principally
  from 1700 to 1830. London, Longmans, Green and
  Co., 1903. 162p.
Webber, Alexander
  Wine. A series of notes on this valuable product.
  London, Simpkin, Marshall and Co., 1888. 185p.
Weber, Frederick Parkes
  Climatology, health resorts, mineral springs.
  Philadelphia, P. Blakiston's Sons, 1901. 2 vol. Illus.
                                                    LC

Weber, Hermann
  The mineral waters and health resorts of Europe,
  by Hermann Weber, and F. Parkes Weber. London,
  Smith, 1898. 524p. Bibliography.

———— The spas and mineral waters of Europe, by Herman
  Weber, and F. Parkes Weber. London, Smith Elder,
  1896. 380p. Bibliography.
Weber, Sir Hermann and Weber, Parkes F.
  Climatotheraphy and Balneotheraphy. The climates and
  mineral water health resorts of Europe and North
  Africa. Third ed. of The Mineral waters and health
  resorts of Europe. London, Smith, Elder and Co.,
  1907. 833p. Bibliography.

Webster, Thomas
  An encyclopaedia of domestic economy, etc. assisted
  by late Mrs. Parkes from latest London edition. Notes
  and improvements by D. Meridith Reese. New York,
  Harper and Brothers, 1845. 1238p. Illus.
Wedgwood, Rev. G. R.
  The history of the tea-cup. London, Wesleyan
  Conference Office, n d, ca1878. 154p. Illus-engravings.
Weed, Raphael A.
  Silver wine labels. New York, New York Historical
  Society, 1929. 47 to 82 p. Illus.
Weeks, Courtenay C.
  Alcohol and human life. Being partly a revision of
  Horsley and Sturge, Alcohol and the human body.
  London, H. K. Lewis and Co., Ltd., 1929. 201p.

——————.
  Cocktails, their composition and mode of action.
  London, National Temperance League, 1933. 15p.
                                                    BM
Weeks, Morris
  Beer and brewing in America. New York, United
  States Brewers Foundation, 1949. 75p. Illus.
Wehman, Henry J.
  Wehman's bartender's guide. New York, 1891.
  95p.   LC
Weil, B. H. and Sterne, Frances
  Literature search on the preservation of food by
  freezing. Special report no. 23 State Engineering
  Experiment Station, Georgia School of Technology,
  Atlanta, June 1946. 409p.
Weiss, Harry Bischoff
  The history of applejack or apply brandy in New Jersey
  from colonial times to the present. Trenton, New
  Jersey Agricultural Society, 1954. 265p. Illus.
  Bibliography.
Weiss, Harry Bischoff and Grace M.
  The early breweries of New Jersey. Trenton, N.J.,
  N.J. Agricultural Society, 1963. 98p. Illus.
  References.
Weiss, Harry Bischoff and Kemble, Howard R.
  They took to the waters. (Mineral). Trenton, N.J.
  The Past Times Press, 1962. 232p. Illus.
Wekey, Sigismund
  The land, importance of its culture to the prosperity of
  Victoria with special reference to the cultivation of the
  vine. Melbourne, James G. Blundell, 1854. 45p.
                                                    ANL

Welby, Thomas Earle
  The cellar key. London, V. Gollancz, Ltd., 1933.
  160p.
Welch Grape Juice Co.
  Grape juice as a therapeutic agent. Westfield, N.Y.,
  1921. 28p.
Weld, C. R.
  Notes on Burgundy, 1869.
  (Massel-Applied Wine Chemistry and Technology)
Wellman, Frederick Lovejoy
  Coffee: botany, cultivation, and utilization. London,
  Hill; New York, Inter-science, 1961. 488p. Illus.
  Bibliography.
Wellman, Mabel Thacher
  Food study. Textbook. Boston, Little Brown and
  Co., 1917. 324p.
Wells, Guy
  An intoxicating hobby: the ABC of home-made sugar
  wines. New York, Comet Press Books, 1959.
  38p. Illus.   LC
Wells, Robert
  Pleasant drinks, effervescing mixtures, etc.
  Manchester, Abel Heywood and Son and Co., 1928.
  93p.   NYPL
Welsh, Herman
  Springs and baths of Kissingen. Kissingen.
  Published by author, 1888. 81p.
                              (Riley Memorial Library)
Wesley, John
  A letter to a friend concerning tea. (Reprint from
  1748, Printed by A. Macintosh). London, 1825.
  16p.

  ———————
  Primitive physic, etc., and General Receipt book.
  London, Milner and Sowerby, n d, (after 1780).
  126 p. Primitive physic.
  156 p. General Receipt book.
West, Horace J.
  Liquor making at home; how to make liquors without
  distillation, and how to make wines and beers. Los
  Angeles, Published by author, 1919. 36p.   LC
West, Trustham Frederick
  Synthetic perfumes, their chemistry and preparation,
  by T.F. West, H.J. Strausz and D.H.R. Barton.
  London, E. Arnold, 1949. 380p. Bibliographies.

Westergaard, Emil
On brewing. Edinburgh. Lectures at Royal Scottish
Society of Arts, 1908. 116p.   BM
A Western Grape Growers (pseud)
My vineyard at Lakeview. New York, Orange Judd
1866. 143p. Illus.
Westheimer, Ferdinand
See Anon
Red Top Rye Guide
Westney, R.
The wine and spirit dealer's and consumer's
Vade-mecum, etc. New edition, London, Published
by author, 1817. 162p.
Wetherill, Charles M.
The manufacture of vinegar: its theory and practice.
Philadelphia, Lindsay and Blakiston, 1860. 300p.
Wetmore, Charles A.
Propagation of the vine. San Francisco. Published
by author, 1880. 25p.   (Berkeley)

Treatise on wine production, and special reports
on wine examinations, the tariff and internal revenue
taxes, and chemical analyses. Appendix B to the
report of the Board of State Vitacultural Commissioner
for 1893-1894. Sacramento, State Office. 92p.
Weyl, Theodor
Coal tar colors. Philadelphia. P. Blakiston Son and
Co., 1892. 154p.   LC
Wheatley, Dennis
Seven ages of Justerini's 1749-1949 (The). London,
1949. Riddle Books Ltd., (Justerini and Brooks
liquor dealers). 85p. Illus.
Wheeler, C. V.
See Anon
Life and letters of Henry William Thomas,
mixologist.
Wheeler, L. B.
See Amerine, Maynard Andrew
A check list of books and pamphlets on grapes and
wine and related subjects, 1938-1948, by Maynard
A. Amerine and Louise B. Wheeler.
Whipple, O. B.
See Paddock, Wendell and Whipple, Orville B.
Fruit-growing in arid regions.

Whitaker, Mrs. Alma (Fullford)
Bacchus behave! The lost art of polite drinking.
New York, Frederick A. Stokes, 1933. 140p.
Whitaker, Tobias
The tree of humane life, or, The blood of the grape.
London, Printed for L. D. for H. O. 1638. 73p.
LC

Whitall, Tatum and Co.
Price list, Druggists sundries, 1881. Philadelphia.
New York. 80p. Illus. 1919. 168p. Illus.
Whitbread and Co., Ltd.
A book about beer. London, 1955. 24p. Illus.

——————— See Brown, B. Meredith
The Brewer's Art. 2nd edition.

——————— The Brewer's Art. Whitbread Library, no. 4.
London, 1948. 58p. Illus. Bibliography.

——————— The Brewer's Art. London, 1948. 58p. Illus.

——————— The Britannia Inn. Universal and International
Exhibition. 1958 Brussels. A description of the
house, with a catalogue of the collection. (Drunks
and drinking). London, 1958. 17p. Illus-photos-
drawings.

——————— Inn crafts and furnishing, Whitbread Library No. 10.
London, 1950. 58p. Illus. Bibliography.

——————— Inn-Signia, Whitbread Library No. 3. London, 1948.
58p. Illus. Bibliography. 2nd edition, 1949.

——————— Inns of Kent. Whitbread Library no. 6. London,
1948. 66p. Illus. 2nd edition, 1949.

——————— Inns of Sport, Whitbread Library No. 7. London,
1949. 54p. Illus. List of References.

——————— See Anon.
Receipts and relishes. Being a vade mecum for the
epicure in the British Isles.

——————— The story of Whitbread's. 3rd edition. London, 1964.
54p. Illus.

———— Whitbread's brewery, incorporating the Brewer's
art. London, 1951. 92p.

———— Whitbread's Brewery, Whitbread Library No. 1.
London, 1947. 54p. Illus. Bibliography.

———— Word for word; an encyclopaedia of beer, in which
are defined some of the many expressions, serious,
comic, colloquial, that have been used by the farmer
and the brewer, on both sides of the bar and in the
home, during the long and interesting history of this
country's traditional drink. London, 1953. 37p. Illus.
Dictionaries

———— Your club, Whitbread Library No. 9. London, 1950.
58p. Illus.

———— Your local . . . . London, Whitbread, 1947. 50p.
Illus.
White, Edward Forister
The Spatula soda water guide and book of formulas
for soda water dispensers. Boston, 1919. 204p. LC

———— Vest pocket sundae formulas. Boston, 1917. 199p.
LC
White, Edward Skeate
The Maltster's guide. London, W. R. Loftus, 1860.
236p.
White, Florence
Flowers as food; receipts and lore from many sources.
London, Jonathon Cape, 1934. 154p. LC
White, Frank James
The Hargreaves story, by Frank James White, alias
Eustace Hamilton Ian Stewart-Hargreaves including a
full history of the Cotswold Cider Company, London,
The Bodley Head, 1953. 191p. Illus.
White, Joseph J.
Cranberry culture. New and enl. edition. New York,
Orange Judd Co., 1885. 131p. Illus-drawings.
White, P. S. and Pleasants, H. R.
The war of four thousand years. Philadelphia,
Griffith and Simon, 1846. 295p.
White, Patricia
Perfumes and household fragrances to make at home.
New York, Home Institute, Inc., 1939. 39p. LC

441

White, Tony
  See Green, Martin and White, Tony
  Guide to London Pubs.

————————.
  How to run a pub. Advice to would-be publicans.
  London, Hamish Hamilton, 1969. 128p.
White Enamel Refrigerator Co.
  Housewives favorite recipes. (soft drinks). St. Paul,
  1916. 126p.   (Brown University)
White, Tompkins and Courage, Ltd.
  Brewing room diary and year book. 65th issue.
  London, 1963. 92p. plus diary. 1964, 66th issue,
  100p.
Whitebrook, William
  Art and mystery of brewing and receipts for English
  wines, laid open to every family. 3rd edition. London,
  Published for author, 1822. 16p.   BM
Whitehead, F. J.
  See Elliott, E. C. and F. J. Whitehead
  Tea planting in Ceylon
Whitehill, Dr. J. C.
  Cyclopedia of things worth knowing. St. Louis,
  International Publishing Co., 1879. 544p.
Whitfield, William Campbell
  Here's how; mixed drinks. Asheville, N. C.,
  Three Mountaineers, Inc., 1941. 76p. Illus.

————————.
  Just cocktails. 3rd edition. Asheville, N. C.
  Three Mountaineers, Inc., 1940. 49p. Illus.
Whitington, E.
  South Australian vintage. Adelaide. W. K. Thomas,
  1903. 74p.   ANL
Whitmore, Orin B.
  Bible wines versus saloon-keepers' bible. Seattle,
  Press of Alaska Printing Co., 1911. 115p.
                   (Brady Library-Fresno State College)
Whitney, Henry Martyn
  Hawaiian coffee planters' manual. Honolulu.
  Hawaiian Gazette Company's Press, 1894. 48p.   LC
Whitney, R.
  Complete treatise on distillation adapted to the use of
  grocers, farmers and families as well as distillers.
  Baltimore, Published by author, 1838. 168p. (Crerar)
Whittaker, Thomas
  Brighter England and the way to get it. London,
  Hodder and Stoughton, 1891. 322p.

Whitworth, E. W.
Wine labels. Collector's Pieces No. 8. London,
Cassell and Company, Ltd., 1966. 63p. Illus.

Whymper, Robert
Cocoa and chocolate, their chemistry and manufacture.
Rev. and enl. 2nd ed. Philadelphia, P. Blakiston's
Son, 1921. 568p. Illus. Bibliography.

Wickizer, Vernon Dale
Coffee, tea, and cocoa; an economic and political
analysis. Stanford, Stanford University Press, 1951.
497p. Bibliography.

―――――――.
Tea under international regulation. Stanford, Food
Research Institute, 1944. 198p.   LC

―――――――.
The World coffee economy with special reference to
control schemes. Stanford University, California.
Food Research Institute Stanford University, 1943.
258p.

Wickson, Edward J.
California fruits and how to grow them. 4th edition
revised and extended. Los Angeles, 1909. 433p.

Widmer's Wine Cellars Inc.
The promise of Widmer wines. Naples, N. Y. n d,
1964. Succeeded Widmer's Wine Manners. unpaged
(20), Illus.

―――――――.
Wine artistry. The story of Widmer's, Naples, N. Y.
n d, unpaged (16), Illus.

Wiggin, Henry and Co., Ltd.
Food manufacturing equipment. London, 1936.
88p. Illus.

Wiggins, L. F.
Sugar and its industrial applications. London, Royal
Institute of Chemistry no. 5., 1960. 44p. References.

Wigglesworth, E.
The brewers' and licensed victuallers' guide. Receipts
for brewing ales, porter, and black beer---managing
brandy, rum, gin---cider, etc. Leeds, Published
by author, n d, ca1880. 144p.

Wigney, George Adolphus
An elementary dictionary, or cyclopaediae, for the use
of maltsters, brewers, distillers, rectifiers, vinegar
manufacturers and others. Brighton, Printed for the
author by R. Sickelmore, 1838. 364p. Dictionary.

443

———— (An) introductory treatise on the theory and practice
of malting and brewing. Brighton, Published by
author, 1850. 196p.   BM

———— A philosophical treatise on malting and brewing.
Brighton, F. Wigney, 1823. 123p.   BM

———— Theoretical and practical treatise on malting and
brewing. 3rd edition. Brighton, Published by author,
1857. 253p. Illus.

Wilbraham, A.
See Drummond, Jack C. and Wilbraham, Anne
The Englishman's food. Five centuries of English diet.

Wilcox, Barbara and Vigoureaux, Paul
Cook it the French way. London and New York, Allan
Wingate, 1949. 135p.

Wilcox, Bettina
Simplified guide to table setting. New York, Home-
crafts, 1951. 94p. Illus.   LC

Wilcox, Earley Vernon
Tropical agriculture. The climate, soils, cultural
methods, crops, live stock, commercial importance
and opportunities of the tropics. New York and
London, D. Appleton and Co., 1926. 373p. Illus.
Reference Books.

Wilcox, J. K.
English, French and German periodicals on brewing,
distilling, wine and other alcoholic beverages. 30
items in English, 1933. 9p.   (Crerar)

Wilder, Louise Beebe
The fragrant path. A book about scented flowers and
leaves. New York, The Macmillan Co., 1932. 407p.
Bibliography.

Wildman, Frederick J.
A few wine notes. New York, M. Barrows and Co.,
1960. 32p. Illus. Bibliography.

Wiley, Harvey Washington
American wines at Paris exposition of 1900.
Washington, 1903. 40p.   NYPL

———— Autobiography. (Food and beverages). Indianapolis,
Bobbs-Merrill, 1930. 339p.   LC

444

Wiley, Harvey Washington
Beverages and their adulteration; origin, composition, manufacture, natural, artificial, fermented, distilled, alkaloidal and fruit juices. Philadelphia, P. Blakiston's Son and Co., 1919. 421p. Illus.

_____ Foods and their adulteration. Philadelphia, P. Blakiston's Son and Co., 1911. 638p.

_____ The history of a crime against the food law. Washington, Published by author, 1929. 413p.

_____ 1001 tests of foods, beverages and toilet accessories, good and otherwise; why they are so. New York, Hearst's International Library Co., 1916. 344p.

_____ Principles and practice of agricultural analysis. Easton, Pa. Chemical Publishing Co., 1895. 332p.

_____ Special report on the Beet-sugar Industry in the United States. Washington, Government Printing Office, 1898. 240p.
Wiley, James A. Comp.
The art of mixing; gathered and arranged by James A. Wiley, in collaboration with Helen M. Griffith. Philadelphia, Macrae Smith Co., 1932. 49p.
Wilkes, Don
The batchellor book. (Food and drink). London, A. J. White, 1903. 64p.   BM
Wilkinson, Albert E.
The encyclopedia of fruits, berries and nuts and how to grow them. Philadelphia, The Blakiston Co., 1945. 271p.
Wilkinson, Albert E.
Modern strawberry growing. Garden City, New York, Doubleday, Page and Co., 1913. 210p. Illus- photos drawings.
Wilkinson, Ronald and Frisby, Roger
They're open! London, The Harvill Press, 1950. 139p. Illus.
Wilkinson, W. Percy
An examination of the wines retailed in Victoria. Melbourne. Australasian Association for the Advancement of Science, 1901. 12p.
(State Library of Victoria)

See Dubois, Raymond and W. Percy Wilkinson
New methods of grafting and budding as applied to
reconstitution with American vines.

See Dubois, Raymond and W. Percy Wilkinson
Trenching and subsoiling for American vines.

Wilkinson, William P.
Nomenclature of Australian wines. Melbourne. T.
Urquhart and Co., 1919. 54p.   ANL

Willard, Francis E.
Woman and temperance; or the work and workers
of the W.C.T.U. Hartford, Ct. Park Publishing Co.,
1883. 653p.

Williams, C. Trevor
Chocolate and confectionery. London, Leonard Hill
Ltd., 1953. 240p. Illus.

Williams, Edward
Virginia's discovery of silk-vvormes with their
benefit. Also the dressing and keeping of vines,
for the rich trade of making wines there. London,
Printed by T.H. for J. Stevenson, 1650. 75p.
Illus.   LC

Williams, Edward Huntington
Alcohol, hygiene and legislation. New York, The
Goodhue Co., 1915. 134p.

The question of alcohol. New York, Goodhue Co.,
1914. 127p.

Williams, Ernest Edward
The new public house. London, Chapman and Hall
Ltd., 1924. 204p. Illus.

Williams, Florence
Dainties for home parties. A cook book for dance
suppers, etc. New York, Harper and Brothers, 1915.
89p.

Williams, George C.
The compounder. Williams' informer; or, Whiskey
buyer's guide. St. Louis, Published by author, 1898.
117p.   LC

Williams, George F.
Homemade wines. For family and medicinal use.
New Philadelphia, Ohio, 1915. 38p.

Williams, Mrs. H. Llewellyn
The book of ices. Iced beverages, ice cream and
ices. New York, Wehman Bros., 1891. 83p.

Williams, Harney Isham
    3 bottle bar; a miscellanea of those favored formulas
    that have been compiled. New York, M. S. Mill Co.,
    Inc., 1943. 64p. Illus.
    5th printing New York, 1945. 7th printing, New York,
    Barrows, 1956.

Williams, Henry Smith
    Alcohol. How it affects the individual, the community
    and the race. New York, The Century Co., 1909.
    151p.

Williams, Howard
    Home made wine and beer. The manufacture of wines
    and liquors without the aid of distillation. The art
    of distilling and rectifying spiritous liquors and
    alcohol. Home made beers. Cider and fruit brandies.
    Chicago, Charles T. Powner, 1944. 190p.

Williams, Iolo A.
    The firm of Cadbury. London, Constable and Co.,
    Ltd., 1931. 295p. Illus. List of Publications issued
    by Cadburys.

Williams, J. L.
    The manufacture of flor sherry. Adelaide, 1943.
                     (Location Unknown)

Williams, John W.
    Essay on the utility of sea bathing to preserve health
    and observations on mineral waters, natural and
    artificial. Portsmouth, England, J. S. Mills, 1820.
    224p.   (University of Missouri)

Williams, Lincoln
    Alcoholism. A manual for students and practitioners.
    Edinburgh and London, E. and S. Livingstone Ltd.,
    1956. 62p. Bibliography.

—————————.
    Tomorrow will be sober. 2nd edition. London,
    Cassell and Co., Ltd., 1961. 208p. Bibliography.

Williams, Llewelyn
    Tea. Chicago, Field Museum of Natural History, 1937.
    30p. Illus.

Williams, Peter Stanley, Comp.
    Recommended wayside Inns of England. 3rd edition.
    South Croydon, Surrey, Herald Advisory Services,
    (1965). 108p. Illus.

Williams, Richard Lippincott
    What, when, where, and how to drink, by Richard L.
    Williams and David Myers. New York, Bobbs-Merrill,
    1955. 159p. Illus.

Williams, Stephen
    See Mortlock, Geoffrey, Comp.
    The flowing bowl, a book of blithe spirits and blue
    devils, by Geoffrey Mortlock and Stephen Williams.
Williams, T.
    Accomplished housekeeper and universal cook.   London,
    Scatcherd, 1797.   274p.   LC
Williams, (Hounslow) Ltd.
    Edible colors.   (colour charts).   Hounslow, Middlesex,
    n d, (1938), 24p.
Williamson, G. C.
    Shakespeare's wine book, i. e. William Turner's new
    boke of nature and properties of wine.   London,
    Published by author, 1923.   20p.   BM
Williamson, Dr. George C.
    Everybody's Book on Collecting.   London, Herbert
    Jenkins Ltd., 1924.   324p.
Willis, Aubrey
    Our greatest enemy - beveraged alcohol.   New York,
    Exposition Press, 1958.   158p.
Willison, George F.
    Saints and Strangers.   New York, Reynal and
    Hitchcock, 1945.   (Food and drink of Pilgrims).
    513p.   Bibliography.
Willits, C. O.
    Maple Syrup Producers Manual.   Eastern Utilization
    Research and development Division.   U.S. Dept. Agri-
    Research Service.   Handbook no. 134.   Washington,
    Revised June 1965.   112p.   Illus.   References cited.
Willkie, Herman Frederick
    Beverage spirits in America.   A brief history.   New
    York, Published by The Newcomen Society of England,
    American Branch, 1949.   36p.   Illus.

————   Fundamentals of distillery practice; a handbook on the
    manufacture of ethyl alcohol and distillers' feed
    products from cereals.   By Herman F. Willkie and
    Joseph A. Prochaska.   Louisville, J.E. Seagram and
    Sons, Inc., 1943.   193p.   Illus.   Literature at end
    of each chapter.

————   An outline for industry (liquor).   Baltimore, C. C.
    Thomas, 1944.   260p.   LC
Willkie, Robert T.
    Distillers' grain manual, compiled by Robert T. Willkie
    and Rolland S. Mather.   Louisville, J.E. Seagram and
    Sons, Inc., 1942.   56p.   Illus.

Willoughby, Malcolm F.
Rum war at sea. Washington, Treasury Department
U.S. Coast Guard, 1964. 183p. Illus.
Wilson, A. M.
Wines of the bible. London, Hamilton Adams and Co.,
1877. 380p. NYPL
Wilson, Andrew
Our food and drinks. The Isobel Handbook no. 5.
London, C. Arthur Pearson, 1898. 118p.
Wilson, Charles Morrow
Empire in gold and green. The story of the American
Banana Trade. Henry Holt and Co., 1947. 303p.
Illus.
Wilson, James Boone
The spirit of old Kentucky. Louisbille, Glenmore
Distilleries Co., Inc., 1945. 49p. Illus.
Wilson, Robert Forrest
How to wine and dine in Paris. Indianapolis, The
Bobbs-Merrill Co., 1930. 122p.
Wilson, Ross
The House of Sanderson. London, Wm. Sanderson Ltd.,
(Whiskey makers), 1963. 108p. Illus.

_____.
Scotch made easy. London, Hutchinson, 1960.
336p.
Wilson Publishing Co.
Encyclopedia of state laws governing the sale of liquor
in the various states throughout the union. Cleveland,
1903. 136p. Illus. LC
Wilson, Salamon and Co., Ltd.
The advantages of saccharin in the manufacture of
aerated waters, cordials, etc. London, (1893).
7th edition. 61p. 10th edition, 1894. 48p.
Windle, E. G.
Modern coffee planting. London, J. Bale and Co.,
1933. 232p. NYPL
Wine Advisory Board
Adventures in wine cookery. San Francisco, 1965.
128p. Illus.

_____.
California Wine Cookery and drinks. San Francisco,
1967. 24p. Illus-colored drawings.

_____.
California's wine wonderland; a guide to touring
California's historic grape and wine districts. San
Francisco, 1962. 32p. Illus. Bibliography.

449

_____ Epicurean recipes of California winemakers. San
Francisco, 1969. 94p. Illus-drawings.

_____ Favorite recipes of California winemakers. San
Francisco, 1963. 128p.

_____ Gourmet wine cooking. The easy way. San Francisco,
1968. 128p. Illus-drawings.

_____ A guide to wines; California wine land of America.
San Francisco, 1958. 32p. Illus-photos. Bibliography.

_____ Hostess book of favorite wine recipes. Wartime
edition, n p, n d. 29p.

_____ Little wine cellar all your own. San Francisco, n d.
15p. Illus.

_____ Magic in your glass. An introduction to wine. San
Francisco. Prepared by Wine Institute, 1966. 24p.
Illus.

_____ Uses of wine in medical practice (a summary). 3rd
edition, San Francisco, 1960. 47p. Illus. Bibliography.

_____ Wine cook book (The). 57 thrifty home tested recipes,
etc. San Francisco, n d, (1945), 29p.

_____ The wine cook book. Fifty-four hometested recipes
for making good food taste better. San Francisco,
n d, (1955), 31p. Illus.

_____ Wine cookery, the easy way. San Francisco, Prepared
by Wine Institute, 1966. 24p.

_____ Wine handbook series, practical, non-technical handbooks on wines and wine-selling. San Francisco,
1943. 4 volumes, Illus. Bibliographies.

_____ Wines and wine serving. San Francisco, n d. 28p.
Illus.

✓ Wine and Food (Periodical)
London, Wine and Food Society. Originally a quarterly.
First issue, 1935. Various issues in library.

Wine and Food Society (The)
Lest we forget. Cellar book. London, n d. 63p.

———— .
Library of English and American books. Catalogue
no. 1. London, 1946. H-P have photo-prints of 16th,
17th, 18th centuries.

———— .
The Wine and Food Society's Library Catalogue no. 1.
English and American books. 16th thru 20th century.
London, 1946. 92p.
Wine and Spirit (Publishers)
The wine book of South Africa. The western province
of the Cape and its wine industry. Stellenbosch, 1936.
224p. Illus-photos.
Wine and Spirit Ass'n of Great Britain (The)
Spirits and Liqueurs. Their origin, method of
production, storage, preparation for sale and distribu-
tion. Lecture, n d, ca1950. 24p.

———— .
Wines; what they are, where they come from, how they
are made. London, (1952). 35p. Reprint ca1961.
Wine and Spirit Trade Review Trade Directory
Wine and spirit merchants and brewers. London,
William Reed, Ltd., 1965. (Annual). 386p.
Wine Institute
Selective bibliography of wine books. San Francisco,
1944. 40 numb. leaves. Bibliography.
Wine Trade Club
See Anon. Art of distillation (The).

———— .
The art of wine-making. A lecture delivered at
Vintner's Hall, by the Wine Trade Club on Friday,
the 22nd March, 1912. Crutched Friars, E.C.,
Palmer Sutton, 1912. 37p.

———— .
The vineyards of the world. Lecture delivered at
Vintner's Hall, London, Wyman, 1927. 54p.
Wines, Frederic H. and Koren, John
The liquor problem in its legislative aspects. 2nd
edition. Boston and New York, Houghton, Mifflin Co.,
1898. (Cover title The Liquor Problem. Committee
of Fifty.)
425p.
Wines and Vines
Directory of the wine industry. 1965-66. Vol. 46
no. 9-A. San Francisco, September 30, 1965.
146p. Advertising. Various Issues to 1969.

Winkler, A. J.
  General viticulture. Berkeley and Los Angeles,
  University of California Press, 1962. 633p. Illus.
  Bibliographies.

  See Amerine, Maynard A. and Winkler, A. J.
  Grape varieties for wine production.
Winskith, P. T.
  The comprehensive history of the rise and progress
  of the temperance reformation. Warrington, Published
  by the author, 1881. 876p.

  The temperance movement and its workers. London,
  Blackie and Son, Ltd., 1893. 4 volumes, 259, 292,
  288.
Winslow, E. A.
  See Prescott, Samuel Cate and Winslow, Charles-Edward
  Amory
  Elements of water bacteriology.
Winter, George
  How to mix drinks. Bar keepers' handbook. New
  York, Published by author, 1884. 52p. Advertising
                                                    LC
Winther, H.
  See Schlicting, Emil and Winther, H.
  Practical points for brewers.
Winton, Andrew L.
  A course in food analysis. New York, John Wiley,
  1917. 252p. Illus.
Winton, Andrew L. and Winton, Kate Barbara
  Analysis of foods. New York, John Wiley and Sons,
  1945. 999p.   LC

  The Structure and Composition of Foods. 4 vol.
  New York, John Wiley and Sons, Inc., 710p.
  Vol. 1. 1932, Cereals, starch, oil seeds, nuts, oils,
  forage plants. Vol. 2. 1935, 904p. Vegetables,
  legumes, fruits. Vol. 3. 1937, 524p. Milk, ice
  cream, etc. Vol. 4. 1939, 580p. Sugar, syrup,
  honey, tea, coffee, cocoa, spices, yeast, etc.
Wise, Dorothy, Ed.
  Homemade country wines. Beer, Mead and Metheglin.
  London, The Farmers Weekly-Longacre Press,
  reprint 1961. 78p. Illus.
Wishart, John
  Home and foreign alcoholic beverages. London, Richard
  C. James, 1908. 15p.   BM

Wister, Owen
Watch your thirst. A dry opera in three acts.
New York, The Macmillan Co., 1923. 175p. Illus.
Wittemann Brothers
Price current. Labels, bottle caps, etc., New York,
1883. 16p.
Wolf, Otto C. Engineer and Architect
Breweries and auxiliary buildings. Philadelphia,
G.M.S. Armstrong, 1906. 198p. Illus.
Wolfe, Udolpho
Elucidation of imposition in the imitation and
adulteration of Holland and English gin, 1857.   PM

_____.
Exposition of prevalent impositions and adulterations
practiced by dealers in wines and liquors. New York,
1851.   BM

_____.
Imposters unmasked, and the public protected in the
use of popular beverages. New York, Published by
author, 1859. 16p.
Wolley, Hannah
The Queen-like closet or Rich Cabinet. London,
Printed for R. Lowndes at the White Inn in Duck Lane
near West Smithfield, 1670. 383p.
Women's Christian Temperance Union of South Australia
Ideal Recipe Book. For use of currants, raisins,
sultanas and grapes. Also recipes for refreshing fruit
beverages and party drinks, 7th edition, Adelaide, 1952.
32p. Illus-photos.
Wood, A. D.
The truth and the wine interest! San Francisco,
Bacon and Co., 1883. 48p.   LC
Wood, Clement
See Goodard, Gloria and Wood, Clement
Let's have a good time tonight. An omnibus of party
games.
Wood, G.A.R.
Cocoa growing in India. Bournville, England, Cadbury
Brothers, Ltd., 1964. 27p. Illus. Publications on
cocoa growing.

_____.
Cocoa-growing in Venezuela, Columbia and Ecuador,
etc. Bournville, Cadbury Brothers, Ltd., 1959.
57p. Illus-photos, Literature cited.

―――――― See Urquhart, D. H. and Wood, G. A. R.
Report on a visit to the cocoa zone of Bahia, Brazil.

―――――― Report on cocoa growing in the Dominion Republic,
Mexico, Guatemala and Costa Rica. Bournville,
Cadbury Brothers, Ltd., 1957. 40p. Illus-photos.
Wood, Morrison
More recipes with a jug of wine. New York, Farrar,
Straus and Cudahy, 1956. 400p.

―――――― Specialty cooking with wine. New York, Signet Book,
New American Library. 1963. 224p.

√ ―――――― Through Europe with a jug of wine. New York, Farrar
Strauss and Co., 1964. 302p.

―――――― An unusual collection of recipes with a jug of wine.
New York, Farrar, Straus, 1949. 379p.
Wood and Selick Inc.
Ice Cream Supplies and Machinery. Catalog with
separate price list. New York, 1923. 76p. Illus.
Woodman, A. G.
See Richard, Ellen H. and Woodman, Alpheus G.
Air, water and food, from a sanitary standpoint.

―――――― Food analysis. 2nd edition. New York, McGraw-Hill
Book Co., 1924. 529p. 4th edition, 1941. London,
607p.
Woodman, Mary
Cocktails, ices, sundaes, jellies and American drinks.
How to make them. London, W. Foulsham and Co.,
Ltd., 1928. 155p. Illus.

―――――― See Hutchinson, Peggy.
Homemade wines and how to make them, by Peggy
Hutchinson and Mary Woodman.

―――――― Jams and preserves, bottled fruits and vegetables,
chutneys and pickles. London, Foulsham and Co.,
n d, 157p.
Woods, John
Brief history of tea. Richmond, 1850. 8p.   BM
Woodward, George E.
Woodward's graperies and horticultural building. New
York, Woodward, 1865. 139p. Illus.

Woolen, William W. and Thornton, William W.
Intoxicating liquors; the law relating to drunkenness.
Cincinnati, W. H. Anderson and Co., 1910. 2 vol.
LC
Wooley, G. H.
See Voegele, Marguerite C. and Wooley, Grace H.
Drink dictionary.
Wooley, S.W. and Forrester, G. P.
Pharmaceutical formulas. Being "The Chemist and
Druggist" book. 10th edition. London, The Chemist
and Druggist, 1929. (Volume 2 entitled The Chemist's
Recipe Book). 2 vol. 1146, 983.
Woolams, John
See Collingwood, Francis and Woolams, John
The Universal Cook.
Woolley, G. B.
Sweets and chocolates. London, Maclaren, 1935.
80p. BM
Woon, Basil
When it's cocktail time in Cuba. New York, Horace
Liveright, 1928. 284p.

——————— .
The Paris that's not in the guide books. New York,
Robert M. McBride and Co., 1931. 269p.
Wootton, James
Collection of valuable recipes. 104 recipes on wine
making, etc. Fort Scott, Kans. Pioneer Printing
House, 1876. 22p. LC
Worlidge, John
Dictionarium Rusticum (Gentlemen's companion).
London, S. Speed, 1669. 278p. BM

——————— .
Vinetum Britannicum or a treatise of cider, and other
wines and drinks extracted from fruits growing in this
Kingdom. London, Thomas Dring, 1691. 236p.
Wormwell, C. C.
Home wine-making. Your questions answered. London,
A Loftus Publication, The Borough Press Ltd., 1959.
6p.
Worthington, Richard
(An) invitation to inhabitants of England to manufacture
wines from fruits of their own country. Worcester,
Crosby and Co., 1812. 39p. BM
Wray, J. and Nephew Ltd.,
The story of Dagger Jamaica rum. Kingston, Jamaica,
n d, ca1940. 32p. Illus.

Wright, A. S.
American receipt book (The). Philadelphia, Lindsay and Blakiston, 1844. 359p.   LC

——— Wright's Book of 3000 Practical Receipts. New York, Dick and Fitzgerald, n d, 359p.

Wright, F. B.
Distillation of alcohol and denaturing. (Cover title A Practical handbook on the distillation of alcohol from farm products.) New York, Spon and Chamberlain, 1906. 194p. 2nd edition, 271p. Illus.

Wright, Helen Saunders (Smith)
Old-time recipes for home made wines, cordials and liqueurs from fruits, flowers, vegetables, and shrubs. Boston, Page, 1909. 155p. 4th impression, green binding. 4th impression, red binding.

Wright, Herbert
Theobroma cacao or cocoa, its botany, cultivation, chemistry and diseases. Colombo, Ferguson, 1907. 249p. Illus.

Wright, Herbert Edward
A handbook for young brewers. London, Crosby Lockwood and Co., 1877. 67p.

——— A handybook for brewers being a practical guide to the art of brewing and malting. London, Crosby, Lockwood and Son, 1892. 516p. Illus. 1897, same. 1907, New York, 562p.

Wright, Horace, J.
The Fruit grower's guide. New and revised edition of original published 30 years earlier written by John Wright. London, Virtue and Co., n d. 2 vol. 336, to 346.

Wright, John
An essay on wines (especially port). London, J. Barker, 1795. 68p.   BM

Wright, John S.
Pharmacology of the fluid extracts in common use. Indianapolis. Published by Eli Lilly and Co., 1905. 225p. Bibliography.

Wright, Richardson Little
The bed-book of eating and drinking. New York, Philadelphia, J.B. Lippincott Co., 1943, 320p. Illus.

Writner, George W.
American compounder (The). Davenport, Ia. H. L.
Wagner, 1887. 2 vol.   LC
Wunsch, Fery
ABC de cocktails. Rio de Janeiro, Irmoos Barthel,
1951. (In Portuguese). 148p.   (Cornell University)
Wyatt, Francis
Practical points for practical brewers. A reference
book for all interested in the arts of brewing and
malting. Editors, Francis Wyatt and Emil Schlicting.
New York, The National Brewers: Academy and
Consulting Bureau (Inc). 1909. 176p.
Wyatt, Victor
From sand-core to automation. A history of glass
containers. London, Glass Manufacturers Federation,
n d, (1966). 23p. Illus.
Wyman, Arthur Leslie
Chef Wyman's Daily health menus. Los Angeles,
Wyman Food Service, 1927. 502p.
Wyndham, Guy Richard C.
Port from grape to glass. London, Wine and Spirit
Publications, 1947. 66p.   BM
_____.
Sherry; from grape to glass. London, Wine and Spirit
Publications, (1949). 66p. Illus.
Wynn, Allan
The fortunes of Samuel Wynn. Winemaker, humanist,
zionist. North Melbourne, Cassell-Australia Ltd.,
1968. 236p. illus-photos.
Wynn, Elizabeth
See Necker, Walter L. and Wynn, Elizabeth, Compilers
List of periodicals currently received in the library
branch of the Institute. Chicago Quartermaster Food
and Container Institute.
Wynter, Andrew, MD
Our social bees or pictures of town and country life.
9th edition. London, Robert Hardwicke, 1869. 532p.

Yamasaki, Sankichi
Knowledge on flavor. Published Japan, n d. (In
Japanese). 237p. Illus-photos.

Yarros, V. S.
See Darrow, Clarence and Yarros, Victor S.
The prohibition mania. A reply to Irving Fisher and others.

Yasunosuke
See Fukukita, Yasunosuke
Tea cult of Japan. An aesthetic pastime.

Yates, Lucy H.
Successful jam making and fruit bottling. London, Rebman Ltd., 1909. 122p. Illus.

_____ .
The gardener and the cook. New York, McBride, Nast and Co., 1913. 260p. Illus.

Yeiser Brothers
A new method of making better home made wines, beers and invalid's drinks. Nehawka, Neb., 1934. 32p.   LC

Yeo, I. Burney
The therapeutics of mineral springs and climates. London, Cassell and Co., 1906. 760p.

Yeo, William
Method of ullaging and inching. (Brewing). London, 1749. 23p.   USBA

Yorba, J.
Mexican coffee culture. Its history, proper selection of land, cultivation and preparation of the bean. Mexico, Murguia Printing Office, 1894. 72p.

Yorke-Davies, N. E.
Wine and health. How to enjoy both. London, Chatto and Windus, 1909. 103p.

Youman, A. E. MD
A dictionary of every-day wants. New York, Frank M. Reed, 1872. 539p.

Youmans, Edward L.
Alcohol and the constitution of man. New York, Fowlers and Wells, 1854. 142p.

Young, Isabel Nelson
The coffee growing countries of North America, Mexico and Central America. New York, Bureau of Coffee Information, 1934. 23p. Illus.   LC

_____ .
The story of coffee. History, growing, preparation for market, characteristics, vacuum packing, brewing. 10th printing. New York, Bureau of Coffee Information, Sponsored by American Can Co., 1940. 40p. Illus. Bibliography.

Young, Mathew
    Tables of the weight of spirits, etc. London, 1830.
    15p.   GBPOL

Young, Thomas
    England's bane; or the description of drunkenness.
    London, 1617. 76p.   BM

———————·
    Epicure or a treatise on the essence, the age and the
    quality of foreign wines. London, 1815.
                         (Listed in Peddie)

Young's Market Company
    Wines, liquors and the like. Los Angeles, n d, (1933).
    32p. Illus.

Younge, C. D.
    Deipnosphists or banquet of the learned of Atheneaus.
    Translated literally by C. D. Younge. London, in
    3 volumes. Vol. 1. 1853, vol. 2. 1864, vol. 3.
    1854. (Henry G. Bohn). 1252p. Paged consecutively.

Younger, William
    Gods, men and wine. London, The Wine and Food
    Society and Michael Joseph, 1966. 526p. Illus.
    Bibliography.

Yoxall, Harry W.
    The wines of Burgundy. London, The International
    Wine and Food Society, 1968. 191p. Illus-drawings.
    Bibliography.

———————·
    Women and wine. The Saintsbury Oration, Privately
    printed, 1954. 9p.

Y-Worth, William
    Britannian magazine, or a new art of making above
    twenty sorts of English wines. London, Printed for
    N. Bodington, 1700. 155p.   LC

———————·
    Cerevisiarii comes or the new and true art of brewing.
    London, J. Taylor, 1691. 121p.   BM

———————·
    The compleat distiller. 2nd edition. London, J.
    Taylor, 1705. 300p.   (Yale University)

———————·
    Introitus apertus ad artem distillationis; or, The whole
    art of distillation practically stated. London, Printed
    for J. Taylor and S. Holford, 1692. 189p. Illus.
                                        LC

Zabriskie, George Albert, Comp.
   The bon vivant's companion; or, How to mix drinks,
   containing directions for mixing most of the beverages
   used in America, with the most popular British, French,
   German, Italian, and Spanish recipes embracing cocktails, punches, juleps, cobblers, etc., in endless
   variety. Ormond Beach, Florida, Privately printed,
   1948. 97p. Illus.
Zamarini, Guido
   Tested formulas for perfumes, cosmetics, soaps,
   liquors, wines and syrups. Mexico, Published by
   author, 1937. 525p.   NYPL
Zerr, George and Dr. R. Rubencamp
   A treatise on colour manufacture. London, Charles
   Griffin and Co., Ltd., 1908. (Authorised English
   edition by Dr. Charles Mayer). 605p. Illus.
Ziegler, O. L.
   Vines and orchards of the garden state. Adelaide,
   Mail Newspapers, 1929. 260p.   PLOSA
Zipperer, Paul
   The manufacture of chocolate and other cacao prepara-
   tions. 2nd edition., rearranged, thoroughly rev.,
   and largely rewritten. Berlin, M. Krayn; New York,
   Spon and Chamberlain, 1902. 277p. Illus.
   Bibliographical references.
Zubeckis, Edgar
   Fruit beverages in Ontario. Ontario Department of
   Agriculture, Toronto, 1960. Pages 132 to 144.
   Bibliography.
   _____ .
   Home production of fruit juices. Publication no. 357
   Ontario Department of Agriculture. Toronto, 1962.
   16p.

Anonymous Publications

ABC of cocktails. (The). Mount Vernon, N.Y. Peter
   Pauper Press, 1957. 60p. Illus.
About wines. New York. The Caxton Press, Privately
   printed, 1934. 54p. Illus-drawings.
                  (Brady Library-Fresno State College)
Accomplished housewife or the Gentlewoman's companion.
   London, J. Newberry, 1745. 431p.   GBPOL
Act (An) for laying a duty upon the retailers of spiritious
   liquors, and for licensing the retailers thereof, known
   as the Smugglers Act. London, Printed by John
   Basket, 1736. 42p.

Acts of Georgii III Regis.
　　CAP CXIII 1816 Licenses, beer, ale, cider, perry,
　　spirits.　p. 981-983.
　　CAP CIV 1815　Mfg. spirits in Ireland, p. 941-951.
　　CAP CLI 1815　Distilled spirits in Ireland, p. 1323-
　　1331.
　　CAP CV 1816　Trading spirits between Great Britain
　　and Ireland,　p. 914-918.
　　CAP　CLXIV　1815　Spirit intercourse of Great Britain
　　and Ireland　p. 1425-1427.
　　CAP　CLV 1815.　Duties on Scottish distilleries.
　　p. 1353-1354.
　　CAP　CXI　1816　Duties on spirits from Ireland,　p.
　　954-966.
　　London,　Printed by the government.
Address to such of the electors of Great Britain, as are
　　not makers of cyder and perry.　London,　Printed
　　for W. Nicoll, 1763.　59p.　　　　　　　　　　　LC
Adrian's International bar guide.　St. Louis, F. P. Aguardo,
　　1935.　　　　　　　　　　　　　(St. Louis Public)
Adulteration of food; drink and drugs.　Being the
　　evidence taken before the parliamentary committee.
　　London, David Bryce, 1855.　262p.
Adventures in soft drink land with "Zest" and "Sparkle".
　　n p, Published by Federal Council of Soft Drink
　　Manufacturers (Australia), n d, ca1957.　unpaged (16)
　　Illus.
Al-Anon Family Groups (The).　A guide for the families
　　of problem drinkers.　New York, 1955.　(Family
　　Group Literature) 112p.
Alcohol: its action on the human organism.　London, H. M.
　　Stationary Office, 1918.　133p.
Alcohol: its use and abuse.　Editors - J. Langdon Down,
　　Henry Power, J. Mortimer-Granville, John Tweedy.
　　London, Hardwicke and Bague, 1878.　95p.
Alcohol, science and society.　29 lectures in New Haven
　　Journal of Studies on Alcohol.　February, 1946.
　　473p.
Alcoholics Anonymous.　New York, World Publishing Co.,
　　1948.　400p.
Alcoholism.　A supervisory guide.　Washington.　Published
　　by the Department of the Navy, Office of Industrial
　　Relations, NAVSO, P-2498, 1966.　22p.
All-British Cookery Book (The).　London, The Goodship
　　House (Aldine), n d.　80p.

All in vue. 84 drinks for you. Recipe book with a great
deal of other information. Long Island City, N.Y.,
Ben Klein, n d, 36p.

Amateur Brewers-proceedings of the company of.
(Vrest Orten). n p, Privately printed for the members
of the Society. 1932. 159p. Illus-engravings. Glossary.

American Bottler, Blue Book Edition. The Bottlers'
Reference and Data Book. Atlanta, Annual publication.
Various dates and pages.

American Druggist Formula Compendium. New York,
Published by American Druggist, 1936. 128p.

American Library Directory. 24th edition. Compiled
by Eleanor F. Steiner-Prag. Published by R.R.
Bowker Co., 1964. 1282p.

American Prohibition Year-book for 1910. 256p. 1911,
288p. Campaign of 1912, 192p.

American Society for the promotion of Temperance. Annual
reports, 1st through 7th, 1828-1834. Andover, Mass.
Printed for the Society. Total pages 454.

Antidote against drunkenness being the drunkard's looking
glass, discussion of excessive use of strong drink.
London, No publisher, 1712. 119p.   BM

Appetizers, Hors D'Oeuvres, Canapes, Cocktails, Soups,
Salads, Sandwiches. 300 Recipes. Washington,
Frederick J. Haskins, 1937. 64p.

Art and mystery of vintners and wine, coopers, brief
discourse concerning various sicknesses and corruptions
of wines and their respective remedies. London,
Printed by W.R. and to be sold by A. Baldwin, 1703.
69p.   LC

Art of brewing on scientific principles, ale, beer and
porter, etc. London, Knight and Lacey, 1824. 204p.

Art of confectionery (The). Boston, J.E. Tilton and Co.,
1866. 346p.

Art of dispensing (The). Methods and practices involved
in the compounding of prescriptions. London, The
Chemist and Druggist, 1889. 280p. Illus.

Art of improving health and prolonging life by regulation
diet and regimen. London, J. Davy, printer, n d,
ca1828. 394p.

Art of making sugar. London, R. Willock, 1752. 34p.
                                                     BM

Art of mixing drinks (The). Based on Esquire Drink Book.
London, Transworld Publishers, 1963. 144p.

Art of tea blending. Hartford, Conn. N.P. Fletcher and
Co., n d, ca1893. 68p.

Art of tea blending (The). A handbook for the tea trade,
   guide to tea merchants, brokers, dealers and
   consumers in the secret of successful tea mixing.
   London, W.B. Whittingham and Co., 1893. 68p.
Arts revealed and Universal Guide.
Ash's Patent Piston Freezing Machine and wine cooler.
   (Recipes for ices, etc.) London, George Simpson,
   sole manufacturer, n d, ca1862. 54p.
Assam: sketch of its history, soil, and productions: with
   the discovery of the tea-plant. London, Smith Elder,
   and Co., 1839. 57p.   LC
Assize of bread and ale, and dyuers other thynges.
   London, n d, (1532). 40 leaves.   LC
Association of Special Libraries and Information. The
   Bureaux, Food and Beverages. London, 1949. 52p.
   List of Libraries.   (Brisbane Public Library)
Athenaeus Deipnosphists
   See Deipnosphists or banquet of the learned of
   Atheneaus.

Bar Florida Cocktails. Cocktail recipes in Spanish and
   English, n d. Habana, Published by Bar Florida,
   ca1915. 67p. Advertising matter.
Barkeepers' ready reference, containing one hundred
   recipes for mixed drinks, 1871.   LC
Barman's and barmaid's manual: or, how to mix all
   kinds of fancy drinks. London, International Publishing
   Co., n d, ca1880. 62p. Illus.
Bartender's guide. The art of mixing drinks. New York,
   New York Popular Publishing Co., 1882. 57p.   LC
Bartender's guide. How to mix drinks for home and
   professional use. Chicago, Stein Publishing House.
   1955 edition, 125p. 1957 edition, 125p.
Bartender's guide. How to mix drinks. "2 books in one"
   n p, Royal Publishing Co., 1914. Contains The
   Up-to-date bartender's guide, n p, L. and M.
   Ottenheimer, 1913. 62 and 64p.
Bartenders' manual: mixed drinks. Chicago, Bartenders'
   Ass'n of America, 1914. 58p.   LC
Beer and the beer traffic. Boston Alliance, 1874. 32p.
Beer, its importance as a beverage and an industry.
   Reprinted from Birmingham Post. Sponsored by
   Birmingham and Midland Counties Brewer's Ass'n,
   n d, ca1906. 50p.
Beer songs (Famous). A collection of favorite German,
   Scotch and English drinking songs. Evanston, Ill.,
   The Baker Publications, 1933. 24p. (with music).

The Beeread or progress of drink, 1736. Gosport.   PM
Before and after dinner beverages and a few sandwiches.
    New York, Meriden Co., n d. 40p. Illus.
Berlitz Diners' Dictionary. Edited by staff of Berlitz
    School of Languages. New York, Grosset and Dunlap,
    1961. 121p. Illus.
Best of everything. (Formulary). By author of "Enquire
    within". London, Frederick Warne and Co., n d,
    ca1865. 408p.
Bibliotheca Oenologica. Heidelberg, 1875.   BV
Bolton Letters (The). (Wine). Edited by A. L. Simon.
    Volume I, 1695-1700. Published 1928, 192p.
    Volume II, 1701-1714. Published 1960, 75p. London,
    T. Werner Laurie.
                    (Brady Library-Fresno State College)
Book about beer (A). By a drinker. London, Jonathan
    Cape, 1934. 112p. Illus.
Book for a cook (A). Devon, Conn. Compiled and
    published by Ladies Aid Society of the Devon Union
    Church, 1925. 151p.
Book of commerce by sea and land (The), and a history of
    commerce. (Formulas). Philadelphia, Uriah Hunt
    and Son, n d, ca1850. 185p.
Book of formulas prepared by editorial staff of Popular
    Science Monthly. New York, Grosset and Dunlap,
    1936. 250p.
Book of formulas. Recipes, methods and secret
    processes. New York, Popular Science Publishing
    Co., 1945. 250p.
Book of Simples (The). (from ms ca1700-1750).
    (Cookery). London, Sampson I ow, Marston and Co.,
    1908. 226p. Bibliography of herbals and cookery.
Book of the cheese (The). Traits and tales of a Johnsonian
    haunt. Compiled by T. W. Reid, London, T. Fisher
    Unwin, 1901. 200p. Illus.
Book of the cheese (The). Being traits and stories of
    "Ye Ole Cheshire Cheese". London, Published by
    Ye Ole Cheshire Cheese, 1882. 92p. Illus.
Book of wine. (by J. W.) Southport, England, 1881.
    144p. Glossary.
Booke of secrets (A). Annexed instructions for ordering
    wine, shewing how to make wine, etc. London, A.
    Islip for E. White, 1596. 40p. (facsimile)   LC
Bordeaux wine and liquor dealers' guide. A treatise on the
    manufacture and adulteration of liquors. By a practical
    liquor manufacturer. New York, Mabie and Co., 1857.
    146p.

Bottle washing. London, Published by Imperial Chemical
Industries, Ltd., 1939. 31p. Illus.
Bottlers and Beverage Manufacturers Universal Encyclopedia.
A complete reference book and guide with illustrations
of machines, utensils and supplies required by modern
bottlers and beverage manufacturers. Chicago,
Expositions Co. of America, 1925. 435p. Illus-
Advertising.
Bottler's Year Book. Published annually in London by B.Y.
B. Ltd., Guilford, Surrey. Library has complete
from 1937 to 1968. (32 editions). Dictionary.
Bottles and bins recipes. (Cookery). (Francis L. Gould,
Ed.). St. Helena, California. Published by G.
Mondavi and Sons, Charles Krug Winery. 1965. 129p. Illus.
Bottoms up! A guide to pleasant drinking. New York,
Published for Sutton Products Corp. by Leonard Wolf
and Associates, 1949. 46p. Illus.
Brasenose Ale: a collection of verses annualy presented
on Shrove Tuesday by the butler of Brasenose College,
Oxford, Boston, Linsolnshire, Robert Roberts,
1878. (Drinks and drinking). 264p.
Bratt system of liquor control in Sweden. Washington,
Association against the prohibition amendment, 1930.
32p.
Brew in your stew. (Cookery). Baltimore, Md.
Published by National Brewing Co., 1948. 32p.
Brewer (The). A familiar treatise on the art of brewing
with directions for selection of malt and hops--
instructions for making cider and British wines.
London, William R. Loftus, 1856. 192p. New ed.,
1857, 192p. 1863, 140p.
Brewer (The) in nine languages. Nurnberg, Verlag Hans
Carl, 1960. 215p. Dictionary.
Breweries and Texas politics. San Antonio, Passing
Show Publishing Co., 1916. 576p.
Brewer's Almanack and Wine and Spirit Trade Annual.
London, Review Press Ltd., Editions of 1911, 1913,
1915, 1917, 1925, 1933, 1941, 1951-52, 1954, 1962.
Brewers and bottlers universal encyclopedia. Chicago-
Philadelphia. The Brewers Publishing Co. of America
1910. 640p. Illus.
Brewer's, distiller's bottler's and licensed victualler's
diary for 1912. London, G.I. Hammond and Co.,
235p.   BM
Brewers Exhibition (Northern Counties). Official catalogue.
Manchester, 1931. 80p.

Brewers Exhibition, Official Catalogue, London. 13
editions from 1928, 45th year to 1957, 78th year.
Brewers' guide for the hotel, bar and restaurant. (by
Bacchus), n p. No publisher, n d. 185p.
Brewer's guide for U.S., Canada and Mexico. Supplement
to American Brewers Review, 1896-1898.   NYPL
Brewer's Handbook. Chicago, 1893. (26th year). (Scho)
Brewers' Journal and Hop and Malt Trades Review.
(Periodical). Volume XXIV. London, 1888. 716p.
Illus.
Brewer's Plea or a vindication of strong beer and ale, etc.,
London, 1647. 5p.   BM
Brewing, Bottling and Allied Trades Exhibition. Official
catalogue. London, Published by Trade Markets and
Exhibitions Ltd., 1960. 200p. Illus. 1964, 228p.
Illus.
Brewing plant and machinery. Frome, 1895. 92p.
                                              GBPOL
Brewing saccharometer with full instructions for its use.
London, W.R. Loftus, 1872. 31p.
Brewing Trade Review licensing law reports. London,
Butterworth Co., 1914. 356p.
Brief case of the distillers and the distilling trade, 1726.
                                              BV
Brigg's Maltsters working book. London, Mc Corquedale
and Co., 1895. 68p.   BM
British Guide or a directory to housekeepers and inn-
keepers--making and managing of choice British
wines. Compiled by "An experienced Gentleman".
Liverpool, Nuttall, Fisher and Dixon, 1808. 204p.
British Jewel (The), or compleat housewife's companion.
London, J. Miller, 1780. 104p.   BM
British National Formulary. London, British Medical Ass'n
and the Pharmaceutical Society of Great Britain, 1957.
226p. 1960, 272p.
British Pharmaceutical Codex. An Imperial dispensatory
for the use of medical practitioners and pharmacists.
London, The Pharmaceutical Press, 1934. 1768p.
British Pharmacopoeia. London, Published for General
Medical Council by Spottiswoode and Co., 2nd edition,
1867. 434p. 3rd edition, 1885, 536p. 6th edition,
1932, 723p. (Published by Constable).
Butler and publican: assistant in brewing. A practical
treatise on the nature of brewing fine wholesome
brilliant and rich high flavored Welch and scurvy grass
ales and strong beers, with London, Porter and brown
stout, fine table beer, etc. London, Printed for author,
1801. 20p.   466   GBPOL

The butler; his duties and how to perform them. London,
    Houlston and Sons, 1877. 111p.   LC

Cafe and Milk Bar Catering. Introduction by Joan N.
    Marks. London, Heywood and Co., 1952. 240p.
California Wine Association descriptive booklet. San
    Francisco, 1896. unpaged (40). Illus-photos.
Canner's Directory. Washington, The National Canner's
    Ass'n, 1954. 253p.
Carbonated Drinks. An illustrated quarterly gazette.
    Devoted to the interests of those engaged in making,
    bottling or dispensing sparkling beverages, including
    mineral waters both artificial and natural. Volumes I,
    II, III, IV, V. July 1877 to January 1882. Illus-
    advertising.
Catalogue (A) of all sorts of earth, the art of drawing,
    of brewing, etc. London, John Houghton, 1737.
                                              (Scho)
Cellar Book, 1763.   BG
Cellar work at a glance. Instructions to licensed
    victuallers, barmen, etc. (by a retired vinctualler).
    London, 1896.   BM
Centennial Temperance volume. A record of The Inter-
    national Temperance Conference held in Philadelphia
    June 1876. New York, National Temperance Society
    and Publication House, 1877. 900p.
Ceylon Tea Story (The). London, Ceylon Tea Centre,
    (1966). unpaged (16). Illus-drawings.
Chemist and Druggist diary and yearbook. London, 1938.
    420p. Advertising matter.
CHEERIO. One hundred and one best cocktail recipes.
    Chicago, 1933.   LC
Cherwell Wine Book. Oxford, Published by The Cherwell,
    n d, ca1932. 48p.
Children of the vineyards. (Portugal). Location Unknown.
Chocolate, its character, history and treatment. Paris,
    Compagnie Coloniale, 1869. 38p.   BM
Choosing and serving champagne. Paris, Editions
    Publicitaires, n d, unpaged (12), Illus.
Cider Cellar Songster. London, n d. 86p. Location
    Unknown.
Cider factory, plant and layout. See Charley, V.L.S. et
    al. London, Leonard Hill Ltd., 1953. 101p. Illus.
Cider of Somerset. London, Cheltenham, 1955. 21p.
                                              BM

Citric Acid USP. Elkhart, Indiana. Miles Chemical
Co., 1960. 30p. Illus-photos, drawings. Bibliography.
Citrus fruit juice control. History of the control.
Location Unknown.
Climates and Baths of Great Britain. Being a report of
the committee of the Royal Medical and Chirurgical
Society of London. London, Macmillan and Co., 1895
and 1902. 2 vol. 640, 608.
Closet for ladies and gentlewomen. Printed for John
Haviland, 1618. 96 leaves. Location Unknown.
Coca-Cola Bottler (The) Periodical. 50th anniversary
issue. Atlanta, 1959. Includes reprint of first issue
April 1909. 238p. Illus.
The Cocktail Book. A sideboard manual for gentlemen.
1900 Edinburgh Farrow and Jackson, 66p.
n d, London, John Hamilton, 80p.
1900 Boston L.C. Page and Co., 66p.
1902 London, John Macqueen, 60p. Index
1913 Boston (Paget, R.L. pseud). L.C. Page, 72p.
1925 Boston for St. Botolph Society, Page 80p.
1926 Boston for St. Botolph Page 1913, 72p.
1927 Boston for St. Botolph Page 80p.
1933 Boston for St. Botolph Page 80p. Repeal ed.
Cocktail Key (The). London, Herbert Jenkins Ltd.,
n d. 1 page fold-out.
Cocktail parade. Scarborough, N.Y., Canape Parade,
1933. 18p. Illus-drawings.
Cocktail Recipes. Sixth edition. Plymouth, England,
Published by Coates and Co., n d. 16p.
Cocktails, the great American drink, how to mix and
enjoy them. n p. Robinson and Miller, Inc., 1933.
16p.
Cocktails, wines and other drinks for the home. New
York, Reader Mail, Inc., 1935. 32p. Illus.   LC
Cocoa Bean Tests. Hamburg. Gordian Publishing House,
1962. 135p. Illus-photos.   GBPOL
Cocoa Grower's Bulletin. Bournville, England. Cadbury
Brothers Ltd., Publications Department, 1963-1966.
Each issue (7) about 28p. Illus. Abstracts.
Cocoa growing costs. (Reprints). Costs of cocoa
production by G.A.R. Wood. 14 pages. References.
Cocoa plantations in new areas, cost of establishment
and profitability, by L.J.C. Evans, T.A. Phillips,
A.D. Wadey, 12p. Cadbury Brothers Ltd., Bourn-
ville, 1967-1968. 26p.

Coffee and chicory, n p. Published by English and
Scottish Joint Co-operative Wholesale Society, n d.
63p.

Coffee from Puerto Rico, U.S.A., a Publication of the
government of Puerto Rico. Department of Agriculture
and Commerce, San Juan, 1942. 62p. Illus.

Cold-water man (The), or a pocket companion for the
temperate by Dr. Springwater of North America (pseud),
Albany, N.Y., Published by author and printed by
Packard and Van Benthuysen, 1832. 216p.

Collection of all of the statutes now in force relating to
excise upon beer, ale and other liquors. London, H.
and R. Tonson, 1737. 735p.

Compleat housewife or accomplished gentlewoman's companion,
by E---- S----. London, 3rd edition, J. Pemberton,
1729. 332p.

Complete brewer (The), by a brewer of extensive practice.
Dublin, 1766. (Listed by Lynch and Vaisey in Guinness.)

Complete Confectioner (The). Preston, G. Bateman, (1850).
60p.   GBPOL

Complete course in canning (A). Baltimore, 4th edition,
The Canning Trade, 1914. 272p.

Complete dealer's assistant or maltster's and mealman's
companion by a person of both callings. London,
1761.   (Scho)

Complete Distiller (The), by a gentleman of extensive
practice. Edinburgh, 1793. 151p.   BM

Complete family brewer (The), or the best method of
brewing or making any quantity of good strong ale and
small beer. Printed for J. Walker. London, 1789.
24p.   GBPOL

Complete family piece and country gentleman and farmer
BEST GUIDE. London, 2nd edition. A Bettesworth
and C. Hitch, etc., 1737. 525p.

Complete grocer, by an old distiller. New York,
Published for author, 1832. 204p.
                          (New York State Library)

Complete maltster and brewer. London, Printed for W.
Nicoll, 1765. 72p.   (Harvard University)

Complete planter and cyderist. London, T. Bassett,
1690. 256p.   (New York State Library)

Compounder's guide. Supplement to "Standard Blue Book
of mixed drinks." Milwaukee, Casper, 1933. 20p.
Location Unknown.

Confectioner (The). n p, Houlston and Wright, n d,
ca1850. 158p.

Confectionery Production Manual. Surbiton, Surrey,
England. Published by Confectionery Production, 1955.
241p. Bibliography cocoa, chocolate, etc.
Congress of Applied Chemistry. Original communications,
8th International. Washington and New York, September
4 to 13, 1912. Appendix Section VIa to Section XIb.
Vol. XXVI. 824p.
Connecticut Agricultural Experiment Station, 57th report on
Food Products (beverages) and 45th report on Drug
Products. New Haven, 1952. 77p.
Consequences (The) of the law reducing the dutys on French
wine, brandy, etc. London, W. Brand, 1713. 24p.
(Wormser, book dealer)
Conversations on chemistry, etc. The 15th edition from
last London edition. Hartford, Conn., John Beach,
1836. 356p.
Cook Book of the United States Navy. Washington, Navasanda
Publication no. 7, Revised 1944. 430p.
Cookery. Elizabeth Craig's Household Library. London,
Collings, n d. 256p.
Cooper (The). History and instruction. London, Houlston
and Stoneman, n d. 88p.
Corn distillery stated to the consideration of the landed
interest of England. London, 1784. 74p.
(Wormser, book dealer)
Cossart, Gordon and Co., The oldest and by far the
largest shippers of Madeira wine. London, Joseph
Causton and Sons, 1885. 39p. Illus.
Cottage brewer, by a retired brewer. Bolton, H.
Wherwell and Co., n d. 171p.   BM
Culpeper's Complete Herbal. London, W. Foulsham and
Co., n d, 430p.
Cyclopedia of practical receipts, by a practical chemist.
London, John Churchill, 1841. 281p.

D- C Druggists Circular formulary. 2896 formulas for
pharmacists. New York, The Druggists Circular,
Inc., 1928. 387p.
Deipnosphists or banquet of the learned of Atheneaus.
Translated by C.D. Younge. London, Henry G. Bohn,
In 3 volumes, 1853-1854. 1252p. (Consecutively in
3 volumes).
Descriptive account of wine industry of Italy. London,
W.M. Mills, 1889. 103p.   BM

Desultory notes on the origin, uses and effects of ardent
    spirit. By a physician. Philadelphia, Printed by
    A. Waldie, 1834. 126p.   LC
Dialogue between John and Thomas on the corn laws, the
    charter, teetotalism, etc. Paisley, Printed for author
    by G. Caldwell, 1842. 8p.
Dictionarie Oenonomique, 1735. Folio   BM
Dietetic canned foods. Washington, National Canners Ass'n.
    1953. 62p. Bibliography.
Digest of patents issued by the United States from 1790 to
    1839. Washington, Printed by Peter Force, 1839.
    670p.
Directions for brewing malt liquors. London, Printed for
    J. Nutt, 1700. 28p.   NYPL
Directions to be followed in determining the original gravity
    of beers, London, Jackson and Townson, 1869. 14p.
Dishes and drinks. Or philosophy in the kitchen. (by an
    old Bohemian). (G. L. M. Strauss, author). London,
    Ward and Downey, 1887. 285p.   BM
Dispenser Soda Water Guide. A collection of over 1300
    formulas for soda fountain, etc. Compiled by The Soda
    Fountain. 2nd edition, revised and enlarged. New
    York, D.O. Haynes and Co., 1909. 130p. Advertising.
Distiller of London (The). Compiled and set forth for the
    sole use of the Company of Distillers of London. Folio.
                                                    (Forbes)
Doctrine and discipline of the Methodist church. Reprint
    from Beverage Alcohol, etc. Washington, 1957.
    15p.
Domestic brewing. Handbook for families. London,
    Button and Reid, 1839. 60p.   POSL
Dr. Price's Delicious Desserts. Chicago, Price Flavoring
    Extract Co., 35th edition, 1904. 48p.
Drinks, cocktails and homemade wines. Good Housekeeping
    Library of cooking. London, Sphere Books, Ltd.,
    1969. 176p. Illus-photos.
"Drinks". Formulas for making "Ozonated" non-alcoholic
    drinks to resemble alcoholic cocktails and mixed drinks:
    New York, Manreh Publishers, 1921. 96p.
Drinks and how to make them. London, Ormond Press,
    1909. 47p.   BM
Duties of a butler, by a practical man with a guide to
    brewing and management of wine. London, 1858.
    136p.   BM
Economic aspects of the liquor problem, 12th annual report
    of the Commissioner of Labor 1897. Washington, 1898.
    275p.

"ECONOMIC" FORMULAE. Beverage flavor formulas
using gum arabic. Preface signed J.W.B. n d, n p.
England, ca1918. 24p.

Emulsion technology. Theoretical and applied. Brooklyn,
N.Y. Chemical Publishing Co., 1943. 290p. Illus.
References.

England's happiness improved. Containing the art of
making wine from English grapes, etc. London,
R. Clavill, 1697. 174p.   LC

English electric food mixer book. London, The English
Electric Co., Ltd., n d, ca1945. 82p.

English innkeeper's guide, containing one hundred and
Eighty receipts to make and manage wines and liquors.
Manayunk, Pa. S. Murphy, 1879. 120p.   LC

Enquire within upon everything. London, Simpkin,
Marshall, Hamilton Kent and Co., n d. 466p.

Enquiries into the effects of fermented liquors. By a
Water Drinker, London, Hunter, 1818. 365p.

Entertaining with wines of the Cape. Paarl, South Africa.
Published by Public Relations Department of K.W.V.
1959. 48p. Illus-drawings. 3rd edition, 1968,
79p. Illus-drawings.

Esquire's handbook for hosts. New York, Grosset and
Dunlap, 1953. 288p. Illus.

Essay on propriety and effect of malt liquors, 1727.
                                                        (Scho)

Essay on the nature, use and abuse of tea. By a physician.
London, R. Helsham, 1722. 63p.   BM

Essential oil forum. An exposition for non-technical
people. London, Published in Perfumery and Essential
Oil Review, March 1952 to April 1953. 9 installments.

European Brewery Convention. Proceedings of the
Congress held in Vienna, 1961. Amsterdam. Elsevier
Publishing Co., 1961. (In original languages with
English summaries.) 460p. Illus.

Every man his own brewer; or a compendium of the
English brewery. Of brewing London porter and ale,
amber, Burton, Western, and oat ales, good table
beer, etc. By a gentleman lately retired from brewing
business. London, Published by author, 1768. 256p.

Expert practical perfumery. London, Offices of British
and Colonial Druggist, 1898. 42p.   BM

Family dictionary and household companion. London, H.
Rhodes, 1695. unpaged.   BM

Family receipt book (The). London, Oddy and Co., n d, ca1817. 584p.

Family Save-all. A system of secondary cookery. By the editor of "Enquire within". London, W. Kent and Co., 1861. 292p.

Famous Highballs. Manhasset, N.Y., Published by Peeka Books, n d, ca1930. unpaged (16).

Famous old-time songs. New York, Padell Book Co., 1945. 96p.

Farmer's wife or complete country housewife. London Alex Hogg, n d, ca1780. 132p.   (Oxford)

Fifty doctors against alcohol. London, Issued under auspices of the literature committee of the National Brotherhood Council, n d, ca1911. 282p. Illus-photos.

Fine drinking. A booklet issued by Ayala champagne; Croizet brandy and Rocher liqueurs. London, n d, ca1944. 26p. Illus.-glossary.

Five-o'clock tea, cakes, cooling drinks, etc. London, K. Paul Trench, 1886. 78p.   LC

Flather's practical recipes for making artificial mineral waters. Manchester, England, 1897. 60p.   GBPOL

Flather's Trade Recipes. New edition. Manchester, Sam Flather, 1896. 136p.

Flavors and spices and flavor characterization. Hamman, Guenther and Chang. New York, Published by Fritzsche Bros., 1966. 45p. Bibliography.

Floral World. Garden guide and country companion. (brewing). London, Groombridge and Sons, 1877. 378p. Illus-drawings, etc.

Food-Beverages and restaurant service. New York, Waldorf-Astoria Hotel Corp., 1937. 118p. Glossary of culinary terms.

Food Industries manual. H.E. Cronshaw, editor. London, Leonard Hill, 1934. paged by sections. Bibliography. 15th edition, 1947, T. Crosbie-Walsh, ed., 1168p.

Food industry directory and grower's handbook. 7th edition. Published by Commercial Bulletin, Los Angeles, 1945. 136p.

Foods of the world. New York, Published by Association of Food Distributors, Inc., 1951. 158p.

For the best and most practicable plan for making the 18th amendment effective. Durant prize contest. Washington, Government Printing Office, 1929. 89p.

Formula book in manuscript form. (Flavors). England, No Author, n d, ca1927. 146p.

Formulary of the Parisian perfumer. Lyon, 1923. BM
Formulas of your favorite drinks (alcoholic). n p,
    No publisher, n d. 16p.
The French system of manufacturing management and
    adulteration of wines, brandies, cordials, etc. by an
    eminent wine dealer of Bordeaux. Alton, Ill., Clurier
    Printing Establishment, 1860. 50p. LC
French wines. Issued by French Government. Paris,
    Published for Sopexa and Comite National des vins de
    France, n d. 78p. Illus-photos.
Fruit Annual and Directory. H. F. Tysser, editor. London,
    British-Continental Press Ltd., 1937. First year-
    book and directory of the World's fruit trade.
    Dictionary of fruit terms in 4 languages. 355p.
Fruits and fruit products. Analysis, composition and
    manufacture. Washington, U.S. Department Agriculture,
    1900. paged by section.

G. Washington's coffee. New York, G. Washington Sales
    Co., n d. 24p.
Gentlemen's companion or tradesman's delight. London,
    J. Stone, 1735. 259p. LC
Gesellschaft fur die Geschichte und Bibliographia des
    Brauwesens E. V. Jahrbuch. Berlin, 1955. (in
    German). 237p. Illus. Bibliography.
Giggle water, including eleven famous cocktails of the most
    exclusive club of New York, as served before the war
    when mixing drinks was an art. New York, C. S.
    Warnock, 1928. 152p.
Gin Shop (The). London, 1795. BM
Glass of grog. London, Reed and Co., 1853.
                              (Wine and Food Society)
Glass of pale ale and a visit to Burton. London, Wyman
    and Sons, 1884. 32p. Illus.
Gleanings amongst the vineyards. (By an F.R.G.S.)
    London, Beeton, 1865. 170p. BM
Gleanings from Gloucestershire housewives. Gloucester.
    Published by the Gloucestershire Federation of Women's
    Institutes, 1939. 242p.
Good and cheap beer for the millions by the use of sugar
    and molasses in public breweries. London, P.
    Richardson, 1846. 35p. (Yale University)

Good Eating. A second book of wartime recipes.
Compiled by Daily Telegraph. London, Hutchinson
Co., ca1943. 129p.
Good Housekeeping's homemade wines. London, The
National Magazine Co., Ltd., 1963. 32p. Illus.
Good Wife's Cook Book. London, Published by Selfridge
and Co., Ltd., 1911. 323p.
Gourmet's book of food and drink. New York, Macmillan
Co., 1935. 278p. Illus.
Great Industries of the United States. Hartford and
Chicago. J.B. Burr and Co., 1874. (Liquors).
1304p. Illus-engravings.
Green and roasted coffee tests. Hamburg, Gordian
Publishing Co., 1963. 171p. Illus-photos. GBPOL
Grocer's Companion and Merchant's Handbook. Boston,
New England Grocer Office, 1883. 240p.
Grocer's guide (The). New York, Broderick and Ritter,
1820. 202p. (University Illinois)
Guager's weighing manual. Washington, U.S. Internal
Revenue no. 11, 1911. 646p.
Guide to art of manufacturing perfumes, artificial flavoring
extracts, etc., Washington, No Publisher, 1875.
161p. (Cincinnati Public)
Guide to cooling hot-weather drinks. n p, Printed in USA,
Calvert, 1935. 32p. Illus.
Guide to gentlemen and farmers for brewing finest malt
liquors. London, S. Popping, 1719. 37p. GBPOL
Guide to importers and purchasers of wines, containing a
topographical account of all of the known vineyards
of the world, etc. London, Henry Washburn, 1828.
248p. Vocabulary. GBPOL
Guide to young brewers, by a practical brewer. London,
1820. BM

Handbook on wines to all who drink them. An essay more
than passing useful. Melbourne, Vintners Co., 1888.
67p. (Harvard Univ.)
Handling empty deposit bottles. Suggestions on improved
methods for handling returnable deposit bottles in food
stores. Toledo. An industry report by the merchandising department of Owens-Illinois, 1954. 46p.
Illus-photos.

Harper's Export Wine and Spirit Gazette. Periodical.
3 times a year. London, Harper and Co., 11 issues
from 1956 to 1969.
Harper's Manual. Standard work of reference for the
wine and spirit trade. London, 1914. 495p.
Bibliography. LC
Health resorts of the south and summer resorts of New
England. Boston, George H. Chapin, 1895. 336p.
(Riley Library)
Health secrets from foreign lands. Emmaus, Penna.,
Rodale Books, Inc., 1961. 64p.
Health secrets of famous doctors. Emmaus, Pena.
J. I. Rodale, 1959. 96p.
Health secrets of famous people. Emmaus, Penna.
J. I. Rodale, 1961. 96p.
Here's How! A handbook of recipes of spiritous and non-
spiritous drinks. Gathered from authoritative sources,
n p. No Publisher, n d. 40p.
Hering's dictionary of classical and modern cookery.
Giessen, Germany. Trans. by Walter Bickel.
11th edition. Fachbuchverlag der Pfanneberg and Co.,
1958. 852p. Dictionary.
Hints on coffee planting. Ceylon. (Listed in Peddie).
History of brewing and liquor industry of Rochester.
Rochester, New York, 1907. 27p. LC
History of "Dirty Dick". A legend of Bishopsgate without.
Ye olde wein house of Dirty Dick. (By Nathaniel
Bentley). London, Published by proprietors of William
Barker and Son, n d. ca1940. 16p.
History of tea (A), by a proprietary planter (E. J. Adams).
Osborne, Ceylon, 1900. 8p. BM
History of William and Edward Willcocks, two servants
or, sobriety rewarded and drunkenness punished.
Dublin, 1824. 245p.
Holiday book of food and drink. New York, Hermitage
House, 1952. 341p. Illus.
Home industries; practical hints and suggestions (soft
drinks), suited to Indian conditions. Calcutta.
Industry Publishers, 1948. 186p. LC
Home-made beverages, by a practical brewer. New York,
Buyers Export Agency, 1919. 31p. LC
Home-made wines, beers, liqueurs, cordials, cups and
cocktails. London and Melbourne, Ward, Lock and Co.,
Ltd., 1937. 63p. LC
Hot water cure sought out in Germany in summer of 1844
(A). The journal of a patient. London, Saunders and
Otley, 1845. 284p. Illus.

476

Hotel and catering occupations. Choice of careers No. 33.
London, Central Youth Employment Executive. Her
Majesty's Stationary Office, 1959. 32p. Illus.
House and Garden Special Edition. Wine. London, Conde
Nast Publications, 1963. 117p. Illus.
House and Garden Wine Book. London, Conde Nast
Publications, 1959. 116p. Illus.
House of Dewar (The). 1846-1946. London, Published
by Dewar, 1946. unpaged (68), Illus-photos.
How Ceylon tea is grown and marketed. London, Ceylon
Tea Centre, 1966. 20p. Illus-photos, drawings.
How to make more than 100 summer and winter drinks,
etc. New York, 1870. 64p. (Brown University)
Huswifes jewell (the second part). London, Thomas
Dawson, 1585. BM

Importance of the brewery stated. Edinburgh, 1770.
74p. USBA
In vino veritas. An account of conversation betwixt Cup
the Cooper and Dash the Drawer. (Wine). London,
Printed for J. Nutt, 1698. 35p. (Columbia Univ.)
Jndian domestic economy and receipt book. (Dr. R.
Riddell). Bombay, 1849. 506p. LC
Influence of wholesome drink (The). n p, no Publisher,
186?. 36p. LC
Inns noted for good food in and around London. 3rd
edition. Published by British Travel, 1964. unpaged
(64).
Inns of Britain with accomodations for the visitor. n p,
Published by the British Travel Association in co-oper-
ation with Brewers' Society, 1965. 72p. Illus.
Inquire within for anything you want to know. New York,
Dick and Fitzgerald, 1858. 434p.
Internal Revenue Guager's Manual. Washington, Government
Printing Office, 1907. 612p. Illus.
Jnternal Revenue manual for information and guidance of
agents and officers. Washington, 1879. 429p.
International encyclopedia of food and drink. Leipsig.
(P.N. Bluher, ed.), 1901. (Jn German-English-
French). 2 vol. Encyclopedia. (Maggs Bros. Cat.)
It is smart to serve beer. Menus and recipes to assist
the gracious hostess, n p. Sponsored by Eastside Ale
and Beer. n d. 23p.

Italian wine. Supplement to Ridley's Wine and Spirit Trade
Circular. London, 1963. 42p.

Journal of the Institute of Brewing, containing the transac-
tions of the various sections, together with abstacts of
papers published in other journals, etc. Edited by
Arthur R. Ling. London, Harrison and Sons.
Vol. XIV   1908   647p.
Vol. XVI   1910   690p.
Vol. XVIII 1912   732p.

Knickerbocker, revised bartender's guide, or, how to mix
drinks. Seattle. Seattle Publishing and Printing Co.,
Inc., 1934. 104p.

Laboratory apparatus and materials Exhibition. Official
catalogue. London, 1960. 64p.
Lady's Companion (The). 5th edition. Printed for T.
Read. Vol. 2 only. London. 1751. 422p.
Land of coffee (The). New York. National Federation
of Coffee Growers of Columbia, 1939. 32p. Illus-
photos.
Lasche's Magazine for the practical distiller.
Periodical. Milwaukee, June 1903 to May 1904.
Laws of Massachusetts relating to intoxicating liquors,
etc. Boston, compiled and published by the Faxon
Political Temperance Bureau, 1902. 372p.
Lee's Priceless Recipes. Compiled by Dr. N. T. Oliver.
Edited by Dr. G. Van Zandt, Chicago, Laird and Lee,
1912. 368p.
Legend of liqueurs, wines and spirits Deluxe 4th edition.
Ginrum Alpha Co., Hastings, Nebr. Chicago, Reilly
and Lee Co., 1938. 229p. Illus-drawings. Glossary.
Leigh-Williams amateur winemaker's record book. Liver-
pool. Published by Leigh-Williams and Sons, n d.
blank forms in card folder.
Let's sell ice cream. Published by the Ice Cream
Merchandising Institute, Inc., Washington, 1947. 306p.

Letter to Elizium. (wine). London, W. Richardson, 1798. 8p.

Life and letters of Henry William Thomas, mixologist. 2nd edition, privately printed. Charles V. Wheeler. 64p. Illus.

Lifetime collection of 688 recipes for drinks. London, Herbert Jenkins Ltd., 1934. 124p.

Liqueuographic chart (The). Devised by Peter Hallgarten and S. P. E. Simon, 2nd edition. London, 1966. Chart.

Liquor dealer's silent partner. Containing tables of valuable information for liquor dealers and proprietors of hotels and saloons. New York, Warren V. D. Trott, 1899. 83p.

Liquor handbook (The). (Annual). New York, Cavan Jobson Associates, Inc., 1962. 232p. Illus.

Little book of sandwiches and beverages. London, G. Newnes, 1912. 95p. (Crerar)

Loftus' new mixing and reducing book. London, William R. Loftus, n d, ca1869. 96p.

London and Country Brewer. 5th edition, London, T. Astley, 1744. 332p.

London and Country cook. Charles Carter, Charles Hitch, John Hinton. Various names and editions. 1749 at Oxford University.

London Breweries Companies. London, 1906. 55p. BM

The London Complete art of cookery. (also the complete brewer). London, W. Lane, 1797. 232p. GBPOL

Lurie, A. N. Wine Merchants since 1892. (Illustrated price list.) New York, 1937. 40p. Illus.

Mackenzie's Five Thousand Receipts. Byan American Physician. Philadelphia, James Kay, Jr., 1830. 456p. 1864, T. Ellwood Zell and Co., 456p.

Mackenzie's ten thousand receipts in all the useful and domestic arts, etc. Philadelphia, T. Ellwood Zell, 1866. 496p.

Mc Monagle and Rogers' cooking recipes. (Flavorings). Middletown, New York, n d, ca1888. 44p.

Making and preserving apple cider. U.S.D.A. Farmer's bulletin no. 2125. Washington, 1964. 16p.

Malt Worms. See Vade mecum (A), or a guide to good fellows, etc.

Management in the hotel and catering industry. Choice of
careers No. 15. London, Her Majesty's Stationary
Office, Central Youth Employment Executive. 1961.
20p. Illus.
Manual for the inspector of spirits. Washington, Govern-
ment Printing Office, 1866. 169p.
Manufacture of syrups and cold drinks; with tried recipes
and practical hints. Calcutta, Industry Publishers,
19- -. 178p.   LC
Mastery of water (The). By the author of The Triumph of
Man. London, Sir Isaac Pitman and Sons, Ltd., n d,
ca1924. 202p. Illus.
Maxwell House coffee cookbook. New York, Simon and
Shuster, 1964. 274p.
Memorials prepared by Champagne merchants in Reims,
France on the subject of seizures made by the Custom-
House officers in San Francisco and New York,
New York. John W. Ammerman, printer, 1866. 33p.
Methods of analysis. Official and tentative of the Associa-
tion of Agricultural Chemists. Washington, 1919.
417p. 3rd edition, 1930. 4th edition, 1935.
Modern art of brewing splendid ale, porter and stout and
how to make cheap ginger beer, soda water, lemonade,
etc. London, n d. 16p.
Modern Baker, Confectionery and Caterer. Edited by John
Kirkland. London, Gresham Publishing Co., 1907.
6 volumes. Illus- photos.
Modern Brewery Age. Publication. Issues of July and
September 1945. 118 and 124p. Illus.
Modern methods of food industry management. Compiled
by editors of Food Engineering. Philadelphia, n d.
256p.
Mrs. Beeton's All about cookery. London, Ward Lock
and Co., Ltd., 1907. 584p. Illus.

National Bottlers Gazette, Periodical. Volume 1, No. 10-
1882; Volume XI, No. 127 and 129- 1892; Volume XIII
No. 146- 1894. New York. About 90 pages each.
Illus. Advertising material.
National Dairy and Ice Cream Exhibition Official Handbook.
London, 1934. 136p.
National Food and Beverage Exhibition. Official Catalogue.
Manchester, 1933. 60p.

National Temperance Mirror (The). Stories, sketches,
     music, etc. London, National Temperance Publication
     Depot, n d, ca1881. 308p. Illus.
Natural history of cocoa. 1724. (Listed in Peddie).
Natural history of coffee, thee, chocolate and tobacco,
     etc. and also a way of making MUM with some re-
     marks on that liquor. London, J. Chamberlayne,
     1682. 36p.   (Cornell University)
Nelson's Home Comforts. 23rd edition. London, G.
     Nelson, Dale and Co., Ltd., n d. 117p.
New Bartender's guide. Milwaukee, Ayl Publishing Co.,
     1933. (Location Unknown)
New bartender's guide. How to mix drinks. "2 books
     in one". New York, Padell Book and Magazine Co.,
     1957. Contains Harry Montague, Up-to-date bartender's
     guide, 1913. 62 and 64p.
New Bartender's guide. Telling how to mix all the standard
     and popular drinks called for every day. Baltimore,
     1914. Contains Harry Montague, Up-to-date bartender's
     guide, 1913. 62 and 64p.
New Delineator recipes. (cookery). Chicago, Butterick
     Publishing Co., 1929. 222p.
New school of arts, science and manufactures. Nottingham,
     R. Dawson, 1817. 2 vol.
New system of domestic cookery, etc. By a Lady.
     London, T. Allman Holborn, Hall, 1839. 419p.
New system of practical domestic economy. 3rd edition.
     London, Henry Colburn and Co., 1823. 402p.
Newest guide. How to mix drinks for man's pleasure.
     Milwaukee, Caspar, 1933. 161p.   NYPL
Notes on plants of "wineland the good." Published in
     RHODORA-Journal of the New England Botanical Club,
     1910. 21p.
Nutritional data. 3rd edition. Pittsburg, H.J. Heinz Co.,
     1956. 157p.

Observations and facts relative to public houses, etc.
     London, Charles Dilly, 1794. 48p.   BM
Observations on the art of brewing malt liquors. (by a
     practical brewer). A private course of lectures on
     brewing. London, I. Wilkie, 1775. 66p.   GBPOL
Off the shelf. A guide to the sale of wines and spirits.
     London, Brown and Pank, 1967. 128p. Illus-etchings.
     Bibliography and pronunciation guide.

Official bartender's guide and companion. St. Louis,
Bartender National Union, 1896. 20p.
(Missouri Historical Society)
Official handbook for the National Training School for
Cookery. London, Chapman and Hall Ltd., n d,
ca1890. 476p.
Old English coffee houses. London, The Rodale Press,
1954. 32p. Illus.
Old English drinking songs. Cincinnati, Bynams Press,
1903. 63p. LC
One hundred eleven tested methods of handling everyday
food problems. New York, McGraw-Hill Publishing Co.,
n d, 208p.
One hundred recipes for making beer and wine. Columbus,
Ohio, Big Features Publisity Co., 1919. LC
One hundred ways, especially prepared for connoisseurs and
well as the novitiate, by A. Traveller. Preface signed
by "J.B.S." New York, Stafford Brothers. 47p.
One hundred years of brewing: a complete history of the
progress made in the art, science and industry of
brewing in the world. Chicago, H.S. Rich M Co.,
1903. 718p. Illus.
One hundred years of progress of the United States, by
eminent literary men. Hartford, Conn. L. Stebbin,
1872. 546p.
One hundred years of temperance. A memorial volume
of the centennial Temperance Conference held in
Philadelphia, 1885. New York, National Temperance
Society and Publication House, 1886. 659p.
One thousand household hints. Elizabeth Craig's Household
Library. London, Collins, 1950. 248p.
Original documents respecting the injurious effects of the
impolicy of further continuance of the Port Royal
Wine Co., of Oporto. London, 1813. BV
Over a century of brewing tradition. The story of Tooth
and Co., Ltd., Sydney, Kent and Waverley Breweries,
1953. 78p. Illus.

Party book. Sponsored by Anton's Party Book, Inc.,
New York, 1958. 65p. Illus. Dictionary of California
Wine Terms.
Party Book. Sponsered by John Heller's Liquor Store.
New York, Party Book Publishers, 1961. 50p. Illus.

Patterson's Beverage Gazetteer. Periodical. Los Angeles, March and April 1951 issues. 160 and 184p. Illus- Advertising material.

Perfect cooking with Parkinson Renown gas cookers. Birmingham, n d. 287p.

Pfizer Products for the food and beverage industries. Brooklyn, N. Y., Chas. Pfizer and Co., Inc., 1952. 71p.

Piston Process of Freezing. 5th edition. London, Published by the Piston Freezing Machine and Ice Co., n d, ca1868. 130p.

Plain talk and friendly advice for domestics. Boston, Phillips, Sampson and Co., 1855. 214p.

Porter brewer digested (The). London, Ralph Green, 1768. (Scho)

Port wine and cookery. G.E.V.P. Tip. Rocha-Cara, 1968. 22p.

Practical treatise on brewing strong ales, beer, etc-- on nature of brewing fine wholesome brilliant and rich high flavoured ales and strong beers. 4th edition, London, n d. 22p. (Location Unknown)

Practical treatise on the nature of brewing fine, rich, brilliant, Welsh, Burton, scurvy-glass and Edinburgh high flavoured ales and Dorchester beers with London porter and brown stout. London, Printed for author by W. Smith, 1806. 35p. NYPL

Praise of the gout. London, 1617. BV

Price lists and catalogues from English manufacturers of flavours for beverages and for other uses, ca1930-1940. 20 items.

Prize essays on practical brewing, etc. Reprinted from Holmes Brewing Trade Gazette, Leeds, 1879. 3 issues 186p. each.

Professed cook (The). London, A. Davis and T. Caslon, 1769. (Oxford)

Prohibition Primer (A). New York, John Day and Co., 1931. 92p.

Public House Cellar Management. London, Published by B.Y.B. Ltd., Bottlers Year-book, n d. 32p.

Quarterly Journal of Studies on Alcohol. New Haven, Conn., Yale University, 1942 and 1943. 2 issues.

Queen's closet opened, by M. (W.). Many editions. London, Printed by N. Brook, 1655. BM

Queen's delight (A), or art of preserving, conserving
and candying, by M. W. Part 2 of Queen's closet,
London, 1668, Many editions. 106p. (Yale Univ.)

Ramrod Broken; or the bible, history and common sense
in favor of the moderate use of good spiritous liquors,
etc., by a New England journalist. Boston, Albert
Colby and Co., 1859. 300p.
Receipts and relishes, being a vade mecum for the epicure
in the British Isles. Part of Whitbread Library.
London, The Naldrett Press, 1950. 72p. Illus.
Recipes for the use of Huyler's cocoa and chocolate,
New York, 1913. 23p.
Recipes of various kinds in cooking, preserving, brewing,
etc. London, Herbert Jenkins, 1927. From original
ca1841. 230p.
Red Top Rye Guide, Cincinnati, Ferdinand Westheimer and
Sons, n d, (1900). 112p. Illus.
Red wine and blue water. A memento of a naval entente.
n p. Published by Saccone and Speed Ltd., (liquor
merchants). n d. 53p. Illus.
Regulation of the liquor traffic. Philadelphia, Annals of the
American Academy of Political and Social Science,
1908. 181p.
Report of the Commissioner of Patents for the year 1855.
Washington, 1859. 552p.
Report of the procedures of the commission of wine
merchants of London, London, 1812.   BV
Report of the Secretary of Agriculture for 1893.
Washington, 1894. 608p.
Report of the U. S. Commissioner of Agriculture for the
year 1878. Washington, Government Printing Office,
1879. 608p.
Report on the fermentation industries. Years of 1947,
1948, 1949, n p. Prepared for Society of Chemical
Industry and the Institute of Brewing. Various
compilers. 10, 27, 26p.
Review of discussions relating to the Oporto Wine Company.
London, Cadell and Davies, 1814. 106p.   NYPL
Rhode Island State Temperance Society. Proceedings at
its annual meetings. Providence, William Marshall and
Co., 1832. 24p. 3rd annual, 1833, 40p.

Rhodesian Bottle, Store and Hotel Review. Periodical,
    Salisbury, Southern Rhodesia. Centafrican Press (Pvt.)
    Ltd., 1955. 1 issue, 96p. Advertising material.
Richelieu Handbook. Wine cooking recipes and mixed
    drinks. Denver, Colo. Ambrose and Co., 1945.
    80p.
Ridley's Wine and Spirit Handbook. (Annual). London,
    Published by Ridley's Ltd., Issues from 1964 on.
Road (The). Leaves for the sketch book of a commercial.
    traveller by The Whistling Commercial. London,
    Smart and Allen, n d, ca1875. 323p.
Romance of tea (The). New York, etc. Published by
    Irwin-Harrison-Whitney, Inc., 1934. Presented by
    a world-wide tea organization. 119p. Illus.

S.D.I. Being an account of the soft drinks industry in
    Britain during the emergency years 1942-1948.
    London, Issued by Soft Drinks Industry Ass'n. Edited
    by Kenneth Penn, n d, ca1949. 106p. Illus.
Saccharin. Folder of articles on opinions as to
    physiological effects. Undated, 1920's, Mostly Europe.
    unpaged (38).
"Saloon secrets exposed"; the book of the hour, giving
    full instruction on how to prepare 151 tasty pre-war
    concoctions. Chicago, New Deal Syndicate, 1933.
    60p.   LC
Satyr against wine. With a poem in praise of small beer.
    St. Edmunds-Bury and Stamford. Printed by W.
    Thompson and T. Baily, 1712, 16p.   LC
Savoy Cocktail Book (The). New edition, revised and
    reset. London, Constable and Co., 1965. 251p.
    Glossary.
Schenley's encyclopedia of wines and liquors. New York,
    1938. 80p.   (Bourbon Institute)
Senn's war time cooking guide. London, The Food and
    Cookery Publishing Co., 1915. 76p.
Seppelt (The House of), (Wine). Adelaide, South Australia,
    B. Seppelt and Sons, Ltd., n d, ca1950. unpaged (16).
Shadow of the bottle (The). Washington, Review and
    Herald Publishing Ass'n, 1915. 128p.
Sheridan's Red Table. (Liquor). London, H.C. Lea and
    Co., 1950. 140p.   BM
Short guide to wine. London, The Friends of Wine, n d,
    ca1956. 19p. Illus-drawings.

Sike's tables of the concentrated spirits with directions for
use of Sike's hydrometer, n p, n d.
110p.

Silver dollar bar, how to mix drinks plain and fancy.
Chicago, Schiller and Eiseman, 1933. 75p.   LC

Soft Drink Industry Manual. New York, Magazine For
Industry, 1968-1969. 354p. Illus-photos, Advertising
material.

Songs of our grandfathers. Set in Guinness time. Dublin,
Guinness Brewery and St. James Gate, 1936. 24p.
Illus.

Souvenir Album of the Franco-British Exhibitions, London,
1908. Reduced facsimile. Presented to House of
Moet and Chandon, Epernay by Alfred M. Simon of
London, 1909. unpaged printed one side 120 sheets.
Illus.

Spanish Gem (A). Sherry. Jerez, Conejo Regulador, n d.
16p. Illus.

Spas of Britain (The). The official handbook of the British
Spa Ass'n. for use of the medical profession. Eath,
Printed by Pitman Press, n d, ca1913. 170p. Illus.

Spice Islands Cookbook (The). Menlo Park, Calif., Lane
Book Co., 1961. 208p.

Spirit tables of specific gravity at 60°-60° Alcohol tables.
London, Her Majesty's Stationary Office, 1961. 36p.

Spirit tables of specific gravity at 20° - 20° . (Alcohol
tables). London, Her Majesty's Sationary Office,
1965. 35p.

Spirit tables for Sike's hydrometer. Pocket edition.
London, Her Majesty's Stationary Office, 1962. 149p.

Spirit Trader's and Licensed Victualler's reducing table.
London, H.C. Lea and Co., 1937. 139p.   BM

Spirits. KTD (know the drink). London, Educational
Productions, Ltd., 1968. 48p. Illus-photos.

Standard Blue Book of Mixed Drinks. Supplement of
Compounder's Guide. Milwaukee, Casper, 1933. 20p.

Standard encyclopedia of the alcohol problem. E.H.
Cherrington, editor-in-chief. Westerville, Ohio,
American Issue Publishing Co., 1925-1930. 6 volumes,
Illus. Bibliographies.   LC

Story of chocolate and cocoa (The). Hershey, Pa. Published
by Hershey Chocolate Corp., 1964. 31p. Illus.

Story of Irish Whiskey (The). Dublin, United Distillers
of Ireland Ltd., n d. 19p. Illus-drawings.

Story of tea (The). Columbus, Ohio, American Educational
Press, 1948. 31p. (National Agricultural Library)

Story of tea (The). No author, publisher or date.
  Printed in Chinese and English. Accordian fold. 24p.
  printed on one side. 12 colored Chinese prints.
Story of the crown cork (The). Baltimore, Published
  by Crown Cork and Seal Co., Inc., 1949. 52p. Illus.
Syrups, extracts and flavorings, etc., by G.H. Dubelle.
  New York, Spon and Co., (U.S. Catalog 1902).

Table Topics. Periodical. Cooperstown, New York,
  Arthur A. Crist Co., July 1912.
Tables showing the relation between the specific gravity
  of spirits at 60° - 60° fahrenheit, etc. London,
  His Majesty's Stationary Office, 1918. 36p.
Tables to be used with Sike's A & B hydrometers.
  Strength of spirits, weight per gallon of spirits.
  London, His Majesty's Stationary Office, 1933. 68p.
                                                    GBPOL
Tales of old Inns. The history, legend and romance of
  some of our older hostelries. London, Trust Houses
  Ltd., 1927. 156p. Illus.
Taste of Kinloch. A handbook of wines and spirits based
  upon the experience of 100 years. London, Charles
  Kinloch and Co., Ltd., 1961. 42p. Illus-photos,
  drawings.
Tavern anecdotes and reminiscences of the origin of signs,
  clubs, coffee houses, etc. (By one of the old school).
  London, William Cole, 1825. 296p.
Tax on distilled spirits. Regulations and instructions.
  Washington, Government Printing Office, 1908.
  272p.
Tea, Journal of the United Kingdom Tea Council, n p,
  1967-1968. 4 issues. 16p. each. Illus-photos.
Tea and tea blending by a member of the firm of Lewis
  and Co., 4th edition. London, Eden Fisher and Co.,
  1894. 151p.
Tea cultivation in Ceylon. A series of letters.
  Colombo, A. and M. Ferguson, 1894. 44p.   BM
Tea encyclopedia (The). Calcutta, Indian Tea Gazette,
  1881. 355p. Illus-plates.
Tea estate practice. Nairobi. Tea Research Institute
  of East Africa. Tea Boards of Kenya, Tanganika and
  Uganda, 1966. 91p. Advertising material   GBPOL
Tea on service. London, The Tea Centre, 1947. 96p.
  Illus.

Tea plant of Assam, 1839. (Money)
Tea planter's vade mecum. London, W. B. Whittingham
and Co., 1886. 300p. LC
Tea purchaser's guide, by a friend of the public. London,
G. Kearsley, 1785. 46p. BM
Teetotalism and laws against the liquor trade. Article
in Edinburgh Review American edition July 1854. Vol.
XLI No. 1. Reprinted from No. CCIII. New York,
pgs. 23 to 41.
Theory and practice of malting and brewing, by a practical
brewer. Edinburgh, 1793. 72p. BM
This thirsty life. (Soft drinks). A "Schools publication".
n p. Published by Australian Council of Soft Drink
Manufacturers, 1966. 12p. Illus-drawings.
Three hundred and sixty five orange recipes. Philadelphia,
George W. Jacobs and Co., 1909. 158p. LC
Toast your friends in port. Oporto. Portugal,
Instituto do Vinho de Porte. 29p. Illus-photos, drawings.
Toasts and cocktails. St. Louis, Shallcross Printing and
Stationary Co., 1905. unpaged. Illus-drawings.
Toilet (The) of the flora or a collection of the most
simple and approved methods of preparing perfumes,
etc. London, J. Murray, 1779. 252p.
Trace ingredients and their influence on soft drink stability
and quality. London, Published in Mineral Water Trade
Review and Guardian, 1955. Four parts.
Traits and stories of Ye Olde Cheshire Cheese. London,
Beaufoy A. Moore, 1886. 133p. Illus.
Transactions of the Institute of Brewing. Volume VII
1893-1894. London, J. S. Phillips, 1894. 254p.
Treatise on brewing. London, Loftus, 1877. 176p.
GBPOL
Treatise on coffee, its properties, etc. London, 1831.
35p. (Specialty Book Concern-Oakville, Ont.)
Treatise on the manufacture, imitation, adulteration, and
reduction of foreign wines, brandies, gins, rums, etc.
Based on the "French system." Philadelphia,
Published for author, (John Stephen, MD), 1860. 208p.
Treatment of fruit juices and vegetables at Solo Feinfrost,
Hamburg. Published by Commonwealth of Australia,
1946. 10p.
Tricks of the trade, in the adulteration of food and physic
with directions for their detection and counteraction.
London, David Bogue, 1856. 191p.
True discovery of the projectors of the wine project.
London, Printed for Thos. Walkley, 1641. 28p.
(Chicago University)

A true relation of the proposing, threatning, and persuading
    the vintners to yield to the imposition upon wines.
    London, 1641. 10p.   LC
True way of preserving and candying and making several
    sorts of sweetmeats, 1681.   (Scho)
Truths about whisky. London, Published by four distilleries,
    John Jameson, William Jameson, John Power and
    George Roe, 1878. 103p. Illus. 1879, 103p. Illus.
Tuenda Bono Valetudine De. Paris, 1555 (In French).
    (Drinks and drinking). 151p.   USBA
Twining's in three centuries. (tea). London, Signed by
    A.B.M., 1910. 43p.   BM

United Beverage Bureau Book, Louisville, 36th edition, 1958.
    587p.
United States Practical Receipt Book. Philadelphia,
    Lindsay and Blakiston, 1844. 359p.
Universal instructor in art of brewing beer, etc. London-
    Bristol. By a brewer of upwards of 40 years
    experience, n d. 128p.
Unser Bier. Hannover. Steinbock Verlag, 1968. (In
    German). 214p. Illus-photos.
Up-to-date Bartender's Guide. See New bartender's guide.
    Telling how to mix all the standard and popular drinks
    called for every day. Baltimore, I. and M. Otten-
    heimer, 1914. Contains also Harry Montague's Up-
    to-date bartender's guide.
Use of preservatives and colouring matter in the preserva-
    tion and colouring of foods. London, His Majesty's
    Stationary Office, 1901. 497p.

Vade-Mecum (A). for MALT-WORMS. or a guide to good
    fellows. London, T. Bicketer, n d, ca1840. 104p.
    Illus.
Valuable secrets in arts, trades, etc. New York,
    Evert Duyckinck, 1815. 317p.
Vegetable substances used for man. London, Charles
    Knight, 1832. The Library of Entertaining Knowledge.
    396p. Illus-Engravings.

Vegetable substances (History and description of) used in
    the arts and domestic economy. London, 2nd edition,
    Charles Knight, 1830. Library of Entertaining Know-
    ledge. 422p. Illus-engravings.
Vest pocket pastry book (The). Evanston, Jll., 6th edition.
    The Hotel Monthly Press, 1905. 90p.
Vine Manual (The), or instructions for the cultivation of
    the grape vine, etc., 2nd edition. London, Journal of
    the Horticulture Office, n d, ca1865. 135p. Illus.
Vinetum Angliae: A new and easy way to make wine from
    English grapes and other fruit, equal to that of France,
    Spain, etc.   LC
Vineyard, being a treatise shewing nature of planting, etc.
    being the observations made by a gentlemen in his
    travels. (By S. J.)? London, Printed for W. Meers.
    1727. 192p.   (Brady Library-Fresno State College)
Vintners and tobacconists advocate. London, T. Reynolds,
    1733. 46p.   (Duke University)
Vintner's, brewer's, spirit merchant's and licensed
    victualler's guide, containing the history, theory and
    practice of manufacturing wines, foreign and domestic,
    malt liquors, etc. By a Practical Man. London,
    W. Weton, et al., 1826. 372p.
Vintner's mystery displayed or the whole art of the wine
    trade laid open. London, 1700.   BM
Vinum. Buyer's Guide for wines, spirits, liqueurs, etc.,
    9th edition. Paris, Les Editions de Chabassol, 1965.
    416p.
Vitaculture and viniculture in California. Sacramento, J.J.
    Ayres, Supt. State Printing, 1885. 42p.   LC

What's in a soft drink? London, Published by National
    Ass'n of Soft Drinks Manufacturers, Ltd., 1962.
    unpaged (8) illus.
Where German wine grows. Bad Gotesberg, Western
    Germany. Verband Deutscher Weinexporteure, 1960.
    unpaged (16).
Whitbread's Brewery. 1740-1920. An illustrated history.
    London, 1920. 39p. Illus.   BM
Whole art of confectionary (The). By an eminent confectione:
    London, Baldwin and Co., Longman and Co., etc.,
    1824. 84p.

"Wine-Australia". A guide to Australian wine. Written
and compiled by Australian Wine Board. Sydney,
Thomas Nelson Ltd., 1968. 94p. Illus-photos.
Glossary of wine terms.

Wine and cooking. New York, Dell Publishing Co., 1964.
65p.

Wine and Food Diary for 1966. London, Charles Letts
and Co., 1966. 47p. Illus.

Wine and food of Portugal and Madeira. London, Reprinted from Wine and Food Quarterly, n d. 28p.
Illus-drawings.

Wine and spirit adulterators unmasked. (By One of the
old school). London, J. Robins and Co., 1827. 215p.

Wine and Spirit Merchant (The). London, W.R. Loftus,
n d, ca1885. 357p. Illus-engravings. Glossary.

The Wine and spirit merchant. New and revised. London,
n d, ca1700. BG

Wine cooking recipes and mixed drinks. See Richelieu
Handbook for ----.

The wine-drinker's manual. London, Marsh and Miller,
1830. 296p. LC

Wine in America and American wine. Excerpt from
Harper's New Monthly Magazine, n p, n d. ca1869.
8p.

Wine manual. New York, Edited and published by E. H.
Glass, Inc., 1934. 94p.

Wine Record Book. London, Published by Wine and
Spirit Publications Ltd., 1969. unpaged.

Wine spirit adulterators, 1624. BG

Wine trade loan exhibition of drinking vessels, also
books and documents, etc. held at Vintners Hall.
London, J. Parry and Co., Printers, 1933. Book
section by Andre L. Simon. 92p. Illus-photos.
Bibliography.

Winemakers' Almanac. 1963-1964. Ed. by H.J. Ruzicka.
New Malden, Surrey, Published by Fermenta. 145p.
Illus-photos. (Brady Library-Fresno State College)

Wines, Beers and Liquors (How to make at home),
Old reliable home-made wines, beers and liquors.
Alcoholic and non-alcoholic for family consumption
only. n p. Published for the trade, 1919. 30p.

Wines. KTD (Know the drink). London, Educational
Productions Ltd., 1968. 48p. Illus-photos.

Wines. What they are, where they come from, how they
are made. Reprint of preliminary lecture of the
Wine and Spirit Ass'n of Great Britain. London, n d,
ca1961. 44p.

Wing's Brewers Handbook of United States and Canada,
    1884.   252p.   (Franklin Institute- Philadelphia)
Winslow's (Mrs.) domestic receipt book for 1862.   Printed
    in Boston, 32p.
Woman's Institute Library of Cookery.   Beverages, etc.
    Scranton, Pa. Women's Institute of Domestic Arts and
    Sciences, Inc., 1929.   156p.   Illus.
Woman's Institute Library of Cookery.   Fruit and fruit
    desserts, beverages.   Scranton, Pa.   Women's
    Institute of Domestic Arts and Sciences, Inc., 1929.
    paged by sections,   Illus-photos.
The World's Book of wines, spirits and liquors.   Paris,
    Edition Maurice Ponset, 1949.   (In French and Spanish)
    778p.   Illus-photos, Advertising.

Young brewer's monitor by a brewer of thirty years
    practical experience.   London, Printed for Baldwin,
    Cradoch and Joy, 1824.   119p.
Young Housewife's Daily Assistant.   London, Simpkin,
    Marshall and Co., 1864.   340p.

SUBJECT LIST

Description of Subject Categories

Beer and Brewing

Ale and porter; art of brewing; barley-malt-hops; beer cookery; brewed soft drinks; brewing industry; brewing operations; chemistry of brewing; distribution and consumption; exhibitions; gauging; history; homemade beer; licensing laws; literature; mead and metheglin; patents; serving; songs and ballads; statistics; stout.

Cider and Perry

Apple growing; cider making; chemistry; cider cookery; history; homemade cider; manuals; statistics; vinegar.

Cocktails

Bars and barkeeping; mixed drinks of all sorts; history; recipes; serving.

Cocoa and Chocolate

Bibliographies; botanical; composition and analysis; growing; history; nutritive values; recipes.

Coffee

Beverage making; bibliographies; botanical; coffee-houses; history; handling and marketing; planting and cultivation; properties of beverage; recipes, statistics.

Confectionery, Ices, Sherbets

Flavoring materials; historical; recipes; soda fountain formulas; syrup making.

Cookery

Drink recipes (specialty); food specialties to use with drinks; history; recipes and instructions for the use in cooking of beer, bitters; coffee foreign beverages, health beverages, medicinal beverages, milk, soft drinks, spirits, syrups, tea and wine.

Drinks and Drinking

Alcohol and alcoholism; description of beverages; drinking customs; drinking habits; drinking humor; drinking lore;

drinking utensils; drunkenness; historical; labels and
decorations; medicinal values of beverages; prohibition;
serving; pubs and publicans; songs; poetry; toasts.

Flavoring
Aroma; aromatic chemicals; colors; essential oils;
formulas; herbs and spices; materials used for flavoring;
processes; taste.

Foods
Adulteration; analysis; canning processes; drying; food
sources of beverage materials; food manufacturing; food
technology; food values; nutritional characteristics;
preserving; sweeteners.

Food and Drink
Canape and drink recipes; bibliographies; gastronomics;
serving; wining and dining; taste.

Formularies
Beverage making; flavor making; liquors; processing;
soft drinks; syrups.

Fruits
Beverage uses; botanical; composition and analysis;
culture; fruit products; processing.

Inns and Taverns
Coffee houses; English pubs; historical; tea houses.

Liquor (Spirits)
Alcohol, its properties, etc.; beverage distillation
and rectification of brandy, gin, rum, vodka, whiskey,
etc.; chemistry and technology; formulas and processes;
history; liqueurs and cordials; liquor cookery; liquor lore;
manufacture; marketing; raw materials; uses in other
products.

Mineral Water
Aerated water; carbonation; composition and analysis;
history; marketing; spas.

Miscellaneous
Air; bacteria; beverage containers; chemical tests;
chemistry; ferments and fermentation; general history of
beverage materials; glass; industrial distillation, measure-

ments; miscellaneous materials; national formularies; pH
and acidity; pharmacopoeias; yeast; water.

Perfumery
Formulas and instructions; history; raw materials; uses
in beverages.

Reference
Bibliographies and dictionaries on beer and brewing,
chocolate and cocoa, coffee, cookery and food, distillation
food and drink, soft drinks, tea, and wine; libraries.

Soft Drinks
Catalogues of beverage expositions, machinery, equipment and supplies; carbonation; formulas and processes;
historical; instruction books on making, bottling and canning;
making syrups; plant management; raw materials; recipes;
soda fountain drinks and management; soda fountain guides;
technical reports.

Tea
Bibliographies; culture; drinking customs; historical;
manufacture; marketing; tea houses; tea lore.

Temperance (Confined largely to specific beverages and
their consumption).
Action of alcohol; adulteration of liquor; history;
prohibition and repeal; regulation of sale of liquor; saloon
problem.

Wine (Includes grapes and grape culture).
Art of wine drinking; catalogues and price lists;
commercial production of wine in different countries;
consumer information about wine; cultivation of wine grapes
in different countries; descriptive information on wines;
historical; making wine at home; serving of wines;
technology; wines from fruits and herbs; wine in cookery;
winelore.

Subject List

For Full Description see Author List
or Anonymous Section at end of Author List

Beer and Brewing
Accum, F.   Treatise on the art of brewing . . .
Acton and Duncan.   Making mead . . .
Adcock, G.I.   Brewing for cordial makers
American Brewing Academy.   Tenth annual reunion
American Burtonizing Co.   Brewing water . . .
American Can Co.   History of packaged beer and its
     market in the United States
American Can Co.   Summer patterns of American beer
     consumption
American Society of Brewing Chemists.   Methods of
     analysis
_____ . Official and tentative methods of analysis
Amsdon, E.   Compl. system of bookkeeping for brewers
_____ . Guide brewer's bookkeeping
Amsinck, G.S.   Practical brewings
_____ . Statistics relate to brewing
_____ . Statistics relate to brewing trade
_____ . Statistical returns of brewers
Andrup, E.   Nogle Bidrug til pasteurisen
     (History of pasteruization)
Anheuser-Busch.   Hops - Rice - Malt
_____ . How to handle, serve draught beer
_____ . Men, material, equipment
_____ . Proper handling draught beer
_____ . Who has not heard of Budweiser
d'Appligny, Le Pileur. Instructions sur le art de faire la bière
Arnold, J.P.   History of brewing, etc.
_____ . Hist. brewing industry, etc.
_____ . Homemade beverages and vinegars.
_____ . Origin and history beer and brewing
Ashton and Green Ltd.   On use of slate in brewing
Atkinson, R.W.   Chemistry saki-brewing
Aufhammer, Bergal and Horne.   Barley varieties
Augenstein, M.   Man. instructions for brewers
Ault and Hudson.   Report on brewing, malt . . .

499

B., A. Some account rise and progress brewery
Bacchus. Guide for hotel, bar, restaurant
Bacchus and Cordon Bleu. New guide hotel . . .
Bailey, N. Dictionarium Domesticum . . .
Bailey, R.D. Brewer's analyst
Baker, J.L. Brewing industry
Barclay, J. Arts brewing and distillation
Barclay, Perkins. Anchor magazine
_____ . Three centuries
Barnard, A. Noted breweries Great Britain
Barnett and Foster. Aerated beverages, etc.
Baron, S. Brewed in America
Bass, Ratcliff and Gretton. Bass, story of ale
Bater, C.H. Brewing calculations
Baverstock, J. Practical observations . . .
_____ . Hydrometical observations . . .
_____ . Observations on state brewery
_____ . Short address to public . . .
_____ . J.H. Treatises on brewing . . .
Baxter, W.H. Repeal of malt tax . . .
Beadel, J. Instructions making beer . . .
Beaven, E.S. Barley. Fifty years observe
Beech, F.W. Homemade wines . . .
Beedell, S. Wine making and home brewing
Bennett, R. Guide to winemakers, brewers
Berry, C.J.J. Hints on home brewing
_____ . Homebrewed beers and stouts
Beverage Research Bureau. Manual on beers
Big Features Publ. Co. 100 recipes for beer
Birch, G.H. Gauging at breweries
Birch, L. Story of beer
Bird, W.H. Catalogue London section library
_____ . History Institute of brewing
Bickerdyke, J. Curiosities ale and beer
Black, J. Practical treatise brewing
Blake, G. Strictures on new mode brewing
_____ . Theoretical and practical remarks
Blake, W.H. Brewer's vade mecum
Bliss, R. Remarks and experiments . . .
Booth, D. Art of brewing
Boyle, P. Publican and spirits dealer . . .
Bradford, W. Brewery construction
Brande, W. Town and country brewery book
Brassieries de Pilson. Pilson Urguell
Bravery, H.E. Homebrewing without failures
_____ . The simple science of wine and beer
   making

Brewer's Ass'n. Brewing in Canada
Brewer's Digest. Buyers guide and directory
Brewer's Industrial Exhib. Essays . . .
Brewing Trade Review. Licensing laws . . .
Briant, L. Laboratory textbook for brewers
Briggs, R. English art of cookery . . .
Bristol Brewery Georges. 150 years of brewing
Brother Adam. Mead
Brown, A. J. Brewing and modern science
_____ . Lab. studies brewing students
Brown, P. M. The Brewer's Art
Brown, H. T. Reminiscences 50 years experience
Brown, R. C. Let there be beer!
Burgess, A. H. Hops. Botany, cultivation . . .
Burgoyne, Burbidges. Notes mfg. aerated waters
Bushman, J. S. Burton and its bitter beer
Byrn, M. L. Complete practical brewer

C. (P). Discourse preparation . . . malt liquors
Campbell, A. The book of beer
Carlsberg Brygerierne. Carlsberg Breweries
Carlson, A. J. et al. Studies action 3. 2 beer
Chadwick, W. A. Pract. treat on brewing
Champion, W. Maltster's Guide
Chapman, A. C. Brewing
_____ . Hop and its constituents
_____ . The industry of brewing
Child, S. Every man his own brewer
_____ . Pract. treat. art brewing . . .
Clark, George and Son. Brewing book reference
Clark, H. Beer gravity tables
Clark, E. W. Brewery bookkeeping
Clarkson, C. Instr. brewing porter, stout
Clausen, H. Souvenir 25th convention- USBA
Clinch, G. English hops . . .
Cobbett, W. Cottage economy
Cochran, T. C. Pabst Brewing Company
Cole, M. Ladies' complete guide
Collingwood and Woolams. Universal cook
Colman, J. Catechism of beer
Combrune, M. Essay on brewing . . .
_____ . Theory and pract. brewing
Comm. of Patents. Abridgements of specs
Cook, A. H. Barley and malt
Cook, C. H. See John Bickerdyke

Cooper, G. Modern domestic brewer
Cooper, I.M. References, ancient and modern
Coppinger, J. American pract. brewer . . .
Country Brewers Soc. 64th annual report
Crampton, C.A. Fermented alcoholic bev . . .
(Crewel, Dr.) Every man his own brewer
Cronk, A. English hops glossary
Crosfield, J. and Sons. Brewing in Soviet
Cunningham, J. and W. Co. Direction managing strong
    beer

Daraio, J.P. Healthful and therapeutic prop.
"Davenports" of Bath Row. 50 years progress
Davison, E. Beer in American home
Death, J. Beer of the Bible
_____ . Defects of beer
deClerck, J. de. Textbook of brewing
Denison, M. Barley and the stream
Dennis, C.B. Background mead making
Dixon, B. Redox methods
Dobell, D. Art of brewing exemplified
Dominion Brewers Ass'n. Facts brewing Industry in
    Canada
Donovan, M. Cabinet Cyclopaedia
Dougherty, J. General guager
Douglas, W. House of Shea
Dreesbach, P. Beer bottler's handybook

Edmonds, G. Country brewer's assistant
Edwards, W.N. Beverages we drink
Ehret, G. 25 years of brewing
Elivin, R.F. Essay toward improve brewing
Ellis, W. New art of brewing . . .
Elwell, F.H. Brewery accounting
(Ettlinger, J.) How make homebrewed ale

Faulkner, F. Art of brewing . . .
_____ . Malting, brewing . . .
_____ . Theory, pract. modern brewing
Feuchtwanger, L. Fermented liquors . . .
Fischer, I.W. Factworterbuch fur Braunei
Fisher and Son. Derbyshire instructor book
Fletcher, H.H. Instr. brew real beer at home

502

Flower, R. Observations on beer and brewers
Ford, W. Pract. treat. on malting . . .
Forsyth, J.S. Farmer, maltster, distiller
Fort, J.V. Let's talk beer
Foy, C.F. Princ. and pract. ale, beer botl'g
Franklin Brewery Hist. beer and Quaker beer

Gardner, J. Brewer, distiller, winemaker
Giles, S. Brewer's metcorological guide
Gilliland, R.B. et al. Brewing, malting . . .
Gillman and Spencer. Brewer's materials
Gneisieau, A. How brew beer and make wine
Geottsche, H.C. Brewery accounting
Goodwyn, H. Brewer's assistant
Gordon, E.B. When brewer had stranglehold
Graham, C. On lager beer
Gray and Co. Observations on vinous ferment.
Green, S.H. Beer gravity tables
Griesedieck, A. Falstaff story
Grindal, M. Warm beer, a treatise
Gross, E. Hops in botanical . . . aspects
Grossman, H.J. Guide to wines, beers . . .
Groves and Whitnall. Hist. of brewery. 1835-1949
Guinness, A. and Son. Guide St. James's Gate Brew.
_____ . Guinness - Dublin
_____ . Guinness's Brewery

Haas, J.J. Inc. Yakima Golding hop farms.
Hackstaff and Brenner. Analysis packing costs
Hall, H. The distiller
Ham (J.) Instr. for brewing new method
Ham, J. Theory, pract. brewing from corn . . .
Hantke's Brewers School. Letters on brewing
Hardings, G.N. Development, growth Courage Brew.
Hargraves, W. Malt liquors, nature, effects
Harris, W. Brewer's accounts
Hartley, A. Bottling English beers
Hartman, L.F. On beer and brewing Mesopatamia
Hartong, B.D. Elsivier's dictionary barley . . .
Hawkes, S.M. Historical notes beer and brewing
Hayman, E.N. Practical treatise render the art of brewing
    more easy
Hazelmore, M. Domestic economy
Henius, M. Danish beer and continental gardens

Herbert, J.   Art of brewing
Herter, R. B.   Back to work
Hind, H. L.   Brewing; science and practice
Hitchcock, T.   Pract. treatise on brewing
Hooper, E. G.   Manual of brewing
Hooper, E. G.   Manuel de brasserie
Hopkins, R. H.   Biochemistry applied to malting . . .
Houghton, A. G.   Brewing and malting.   Australasia
Houghton John.   Publ.   Art of brewing
Housekeeper, A.   Homebrewed ale
Hudson, J. R.   Development of brewing analysis
Hughes, E.   Treatise on brewing of beer
Hughey, G. W.   Beer as a beverage
Hulton, H. F. S.   Beer
Hunter, H.   Barley crop

Inc. Brewer's Guild.   Brewing scientific rev.
Institute of Brewing.   Brewing Ind. Research

Jack, F. B.   Homebrewed wines and beers
_____ .   100 homebrewed wines . . .
Janes, H.   The Red Barrel (Watney Mann)
Jeffrey, E. J.   Brewing, theory, practice
Johnson, C.   Modern brewery plant
Johnson, G.   Australian brew. stud. manual
_____ .   History brewing studies
_____ .   Practical studies for winemaker . . .
_____ .   Student's manual yeast culture
Johnson, R.   Bottling naturally matured beers
Johnson, Smith and Co.   Homebrewed wines and beers
Johnson's Saccharum Co.   Prod. brewer's worts

Keir, D.   Younger centuries
Keitel, A.   Government by brewers?
Keller, W. B.   Beer and ale bottlers' manual
Kelley, W. J.   Brewing in Maryland
Kelynack and Kirkby Arsenical poisoning in beer drinkers
Kent, R.   To thee: a toast
King, F. A.   Beer has a history
Klein, C. H.   Old Egyptian use of beer
Kloss, C. A. Art and science brewing
Krebs, R.   Making friends is our business

Lady (A). Art of cookery plain and easy
Lampray, J.H. Brewer's and distiller's diary
Lancaster, H. Practical floor malting
_____ . Maltster's materials and methods
Lance, E.J. The hop farmer . . .
Lanham, H. Brewers and bottlers accounts
Laufer, S. Standardizing methods analysis
Laurent, A. Dictionary of art of brewing
Lawlor, P. Froth-Blower's manual
Lawrence, J. Practical treatise on brewing
Leifchild, J. Compl. directions brewing . . .
Levesque, J. Art brewing and fermenting
Leyel, C.F. Summer drinks, winter cordials
Lightbody, J. Every man his own guager
Ling, A.R. Malting
Livesay, J. New lectures malt liquors
Loftus, W.R. The Maltster . . .
Long, J. Directions using saccharometer
_____ . Table specific gravity of worts
Loveless, R.D. Everyday wrinkles brewers
_____ . Every man his own brewer
Lovibond, T.H. Brewing with raw materials
Luker, H. and Co. Price list beer-ales
Luts, H.F. Vitaculture, brewing ancient orient
Lynch, P. and J. Vaisey Guinness's Brewing in Irish
    economy

M.A.L.T. What is beer?
Mac Cartie, J.C. Australian brewers
Mc Culloch, J. Distillation, brewing, malting
Mc Donald, J. The maltster, distiller . . .
MacDuff, I.M. Home-brewing for beginners
Mac Gregor, J. Beer making for all
M'Harry, S. The practical distiller
Manbre and Garten Ltd. 100 years progress
Maritzen, A. Illus. cat. architectural work for
    breweries
Master Brewers Ass'n. of America. Proceedings
_____ . Technical proceedings
Mathias, P. Brewing industry in England 1700
Matthews, C.G. Manual alcoholic fermentation
_____ . Microscope in the brewery
Max Henius Memoir Comm. Mac Henius-biography
May, R. Brewer and victualler guide
Meriton, G. Praise Yorkshire ale
Miller Frewing Co. Heritage born and pledged

_____ . Miller High-Life Centennial ed.

_____ . Quality since 1855

Mitchell's and Butler 50 years of brewing

Moir, W. Brewing made easy

Molyneaux, W. Burton-on-Trent. History . . .

Monckton, H.A. History English ale and beer

Moore, J. Whitbread craftsman

Moritz, E.R. Technology of brewing

Moritz, E.R. and G.H. Morris. Textbook on brewing

Morrice, A. Practical treatise brewing

Morrison, J. Beer duty tables

Moubray, B. Practical treatise instr. private brewery

_____ . Brewing ale and table beer

Munro, N.L. How to carve: how to brew

Myrick, H. The hop

Nash, J. Brewer's License, its history . . .

_____ . Facts, falacies, brewer's license tax

National Brewer's Academy. Practical points for
    practical brewers

Needham, J. Directions for brewing

Nettleton, J.A. Every man his own analyst

_____ . Preservation of hops

_____ . Study, history, art of brewing

Neville, S.O. 70 rolling years

Nichols, W.B. and Co. Brewing industry

Nithsdale, W.H. Practical brewing

_____ . and A.J. Manton. Practical brewing . . .

Noback, G. Tables of results of brewing

Noling, A.W. Brewing, Bottling . . . Exhibition

Nowak, C.A. Modern brewing

_____ . New fields for brewers

_____ . Selected practical methods mfg. low
    alcoholic beers

Nugey, A.L. Brewing formulas . . .

Nunn, F.J.R. Raw grain in brewing

O'Sullivan, H.D. Life work Cornelius O'S -

Pabst Brewing Co. Pamphlet 1893

Palmer, A.E. Brewer's pocket companion

Parker, H.H. Hop industry

Parkes, B. Domestic brewer . . .

Pasteur, L. Studies on fermentation
Pauls and White Ltd. Brewing room diary and year book
Peile, C.C. Handybook law relating to brewers
Perry, T. Method brewing English dry lager
Persons, W.M. Beer, brewing in America
Pickett, E.D. The wooden horse
Piesse, C.H. Chemistry in brewing room
Pitt, J. How to brew good beer
Ploughman, W. Economy in brewing
Pocock, J. Brewing non-excisable beers
Poole, T. The family brewer
_____ . Treatise strong beer and ale
Potter, J.G. Brewery manual
Potter and Clarke, Ltd. Botanic Brewers' Guide
Pozen, M.A. Successful brewing
Practical man. The butler, wine-dealer . . .
_____ . Innkeeper and public brewer
_____ . Publican, innkeeper and brewer guide
Preece, I. Biochemistry of brewing
_____ . Malting, brewing, allied processes

Rahr malting Co. To thee! a toast
Rawlinson, J. New method brewing malt liquor
Read Brothers. A bottle of beer
Reddington, W. Practical treatise on brewing
Reynoldson, J. Practical philosophical principles
    of making malt
Richardson, J. Philosophical principles of science of
    brewing
_____ . Remarks Baverstock's hydro. observations
_____ . Statistical estimates materials brewing
_____ . Theoretic hints improved practice
Ricketts, R.W. Cleaning in brewery
Ridgeway, J. Practical treatise enplain art and mystery
    brewing porter . . .
Riley, W.A. Brewery by-products
Roberts, A. Boake. Diary brew and syrup rooms
_____ . Technical materials for brewing
Roberts, W.H. British winemaker . . .
_____ . Scottish-ale-brewer . . .
Robinson, J. Whole art making British wines
Romer, F. Reviewing American brewing
Roose, S. New completed treatise on ullaging
Rosenthal, E. Tankards and traditions
Ross-Mackensie, J. Brewing and malting

_____ . Brew, malt and laboratory companion
_____ . Brewing and malting waters
Roundell, J. A. E.   The still-room
Ruff, D. G.   Bottling, canning beer
Ruppert, J.   Beer in the home
Ruswel, O. F.   Practical guide to malting

Saddington, T.   Plain directions family brewers
Salem, F. W.   Beer, its history . . .
Scammel, G.   Breweries and maltings
Scarisbrick, J.   Beer taxation
_____ . Beer manual, historical and technical
Schaefer, F. M.   Brew. Co. 100th year
Schlicting, E. and H. Winter Practical points
Schluter, H.   Brewing industry and workers
Schmidt, E.   Brewery architects . . . handbook
Schoellhorn, F.   Bibliographie Brauwesens
Scholefield, A. J. B.   Treatment brewing water
Schoppfer, T.   Philosophy of beer
Schwarz Laboratories.   Comparative analysis bottled,
    canned beers
_____ . Extract and alcohol tables
Serocold, W. P.   Story of Watneys
Seymour, W.   Practical treatise brewing . . .
Shales, K.   Brewing better beers
_____ . Short guide home brewing
Shannon, R.   Practical treatise brewing, distilling
Sheen, J. R.   Wines and other fermented liquors
Shih, K'O-ching American brewing industry
Shore, A.   Practical treatise on brewing
Siebel, J. E.   Beer and health
_____ . List of writings of Dr. Siebel
Sigsworth, E. M.   Brewing trade industrial revolution
Simmonds, P. L.   Hops; their cultivation . . .
Sleigh, G.   Brewer's assistant
Smith, W. S.   Extracts and how to increase them
Southby, E. R.   Brewing: practically considered
_____ . Practical brewing
Stansfield and Co.   How good beer is served
Statist.   All about beer
Steel, J.   Malting and brewing
_____ . Supplement to malting and brewing
Stevenson, J.   Advice, medical and economical
Stewart, W.   Practical instr. brewing porter . . .
Stopes, Harry Engineering of malting

_____ . Malt and malting
Stopes, Henry.   Barley and beer duty
_____ .   Brewing, malting machinery
_____ .   Drying malt . . .
Stratton, J.Y.   Hops and hop-pickers
Strong, L.A.G.   Brewer's progress 1757-1957
    (Charrington's Brewery)
Strong, S.   Romance of brewing
Sykes, W.J.   Princ., practice, brewing
_____ . and A.R. Ling Principles and practice of
    brewing

Taylor, F.   Hops and the hope trade
Taylor, J.   Tables calculating wine, beer . . .
Thatcher, F.   Brewing, malting, practically considered
_____ .   Treatise practical brewing, malting
Thausing, J.E.   Theory, practice preparation malt and
    fabrication beer
Thomann, G.   Alleged adulterations, liquors
_____ .   American beer . . .
_____ .   Documentary history USBA
_____ .   Effects of beer on those who make it and
    drink it
_____ .   Liquor laws of United States
_____ .   Real imaginary effects intemperance
Thomson, T.   Brewing and distillation
Thornton, F.W.   Brewery accounts
Thorpe, E. and H.T. Brown.   Report determination
    original gravity beers by distillation
Threale, T.   Compleat family brewer
Thurston, C.S.   Beer gravity tables
Times (The)   Beer in Britain
Tizard, W.L.   Rationale of malting
_____ .   Theory, practice of brewing
Tobe, J.H.   How to make own wines and beers
Tolman, L.M.   Study American beers and ales
Travers, G.W.   Century brewing Hudson ales
Tripp, C.H.   Brewery management
Tritton, S.M.   Successful wine, beer making
_____ .   Tritton's guide better wine . . .
Tryon, T.   New art brewing beer, ale . . .
(Tuck, J.)   Guide to young brewers . . .
Tuck, J.   Private brewer's guide . . .
Turner, B.C.A. and D.J. Moon.   Simple guide to home-
    made beer

United Brewers Industrial Foundation.   American beer
    and ale
————————.   Clean-up or close-up
————————.   What are the facts about beer
United States Brewers' Ass'n. Brewers almanac (various dates).
————————.   Brewers' Convention (26th) (34th)
————————.   Hist. brewing growth in United States
————————.   Proceedings 100th anniversary
————————.   Year book (various)
United States Brewers Foundation.   Barley, hops and
    history
————————.   Beer dispensing handbook
————————.   Brewers Almanac (various)
————————.   Questions, answers on beer
Usher's Wiltshire Brewery Ltd.   Houses and ale

Vaillancourt, F.   History of brewing industry Province
    of Quebec
Vaisey, J.   Brewing industry 1886-1951
Vickery, H.C.   Use of beer in foods
Villiers, O.W.   Handbook brewing calculations
Vine, D.P.   Art brewing explained
Vizetelly, H.   Wines of world classed . . .
Vogel, E.H.   Practical brewer
Vogel, M.   On beer

W. (F.) Warme beere, a treatise
Wahl, A.S.   Handybook. American brewing industry
————————.   American handybook brewing . . .
————————.   Indian corn in mfg. beer
Wahl Institute. Study brewing, malting technique
Wall, C.R.M. U.S. practical brewing and malting
Wallerstein Co.   40 years a-brewing
————————.   Alcohol tables on extract wort
————————.   Bottle beer quality
————————.   Treatment brewing water
Wallerstein Laboratories. Advances in beer quality. 1.
    Beer and brewing technology. 2. Methodology for the
    brewing laboratory.
Ward, M.H.   Brewing in South Australia
Warren, C.A.   Brewing waters
Watkins, G.   Compleat brewer

Weaver, J.C.   American barley production
Weeks, M.   Beer, brewing in America
Weiss, H.B. and G.M.   Early breweries in N.J.
Westergaard, E.   On brewing
Whitbread and Co.   Book about beer
_____.   Story of Whitbread's
_____.   Whitbread's brewery 1951
_____.   Whitbread's brewery 1740-1920
_____.   Word for word
Whitbread Library No. 4.   Brewer's art
_____.   No. 10 Inn crafts, furnishings
_____.   No. 3 Inn-signia
_____.   No. 6 Inns of Kent
_____.   No. 7 Inns of sport
_____.   No. 1 Whitbread's Brewery
_____.   No. 9 Your club
White, E.S.   Maltster's guide
White, Tompkins, Courage.   Brewing room diary and
   year book
Whitebrook, W.   Art and mystery brewing . . .
Wiggleworth, E.   Brewers' and Licensed Victuallers' guide
Wigney, G.A.   Elementary dictionary for maltster, brewers
_____.   Introductory treatise theory, practice malting
   and brewing
_____.   Philosophical treatise malting . . .
_____.   Theoretical and practical treat. on malting
   and brewing
Williams, H.   Home made wine and beer
Wise, D.   Homemade country wines, beer . . .
Wolf, O.C.   Breweries and aux. buildings
Wright, H.E.   Handybook for brewers . . .
Wright, H.E.   Handbook for young brewers
Wynter, A.   Our social bees . . .

Yeiser Brothers.   New method making better homemade
   wines, beers . . .
Yeo, W.   Method of ullaging and inching
Y-Worth, W.   Cerevisiarii comes or art of brewing

   Anonymous
Acts of Georgii - III
Amateur Brewers - proceedings
Art of brewing London.   New edition
Assize of bread and ale . . .

Beer, its importance as a beverage
Book about beer by a drinker
Bottler's Yearbook (Various)
Brewer (The) in nine languages
Brewer (The) Familiar treatise . . .
Brewer's Almanack and wine and spirit Trade Ass'n.
Brewer's, distiller's, bottler's and licensed victualler's
    diary 1912
Brewer's Guide. Chicago
Brewer's guide for the hotel, bar . . .
Brewer's Handbook. Chicago
Brewers' Journal and hop and malt Trades Review
Brewer's Journal Centenary Number
Brewer's Plea or vindication strong beer . . .
Brewers and Bottlers Universal Encyclopedia
Brewers, Exhibition (Northern Counties)
Brewers Exhibition Official Catalogue (Various)
Brewery Manual (Various Editions)
Brewing, Bottling and Allied Trades Expo. Cat.
Brewing Plant and machinery
Brewing saccharometer . . .
Brigg's Maltsters working book
Butler: his duties and how to perform
Butler and Publican's assistant in brewing

Carlsberg (The book of)
Catalogue (A) of all sorts of earth--of brewing . . .
Complete brewer (The) by brewer extensive practice
Complete dealer's assistant or maltster's companion . . .
Complete family brewer
Complete family piece and country gentleman and farmer's
    BEST GUIDE
Complete maltster and brewer
Cottage brewer, by a retired brewer

Directions for brewing malt liquors
Directions to be followed in determining original gravity
    of beers
Domestic Brewing. Handbook for families
Duties of a butler, by practical man

Essay on propriety and effect malt liquors
European Brewery Convention Proceedings
Every man his own brewer; or compendium

Floral World.   Garden guide and country companion
Formulas of your favorite drinks

Gesellschaft fur die Geschichte und Bibliographie des
    Brauwesens E.V.
Glass of pale ale and visit to Burton
Good and cheap beer for the millions . . .
Guide to gentlemen and farmers for brewing
Guide to young brewers

History of Brewing, liquor industry Rochester

Importance of the brewery stated
It is smart to serve beer

Journal of the Institute of Brewing.   Transactions of the
    various sections

London and Country brewer . . .
London Breweries Companies
London complete art of cookery

Modern art brewing splendid ale, porter . . .
Modern Brewery Age

Observations on art brewing malt liquors
One hundred years of brewing
Over century brewing tradition (Tooth and Co.)

Porter brewer digested (The)
Pract. treatise on nature brewing fine rich, brilliant Welsh,
    Burton . . . ales
Pract. treat. on brewing strong ales, beers
Prize essays on practical brewing
Public House cellar management

Report on the fermentation industries.   Years of 1947, 1948,
    1949.

Theory and practice malting and brewing
Transactions of Institute of Brewing
Treatise on brewing (Loftus)

United Beverage Bureau Book
Universal Instructor in art brewing beer
Unser Bier

Vintner's, brewer's, spirit merchants . . . guide

Wine and Spirit Trade Review Trade Directory
Wing's Brewers Handbook of U.S. and Canada

Young brewer's monitor

Cider
Alwood, W.B. et al. Chemical composition apples and
     cider
Alwood, W.B. Study of cider making in France . . .
Arnold, J.P. Homemade beverages, vinegar . . .
Atkinson, F.E. et al. Fruit juices, cider . . .

Beale, J. Treatise cyder and perry
Birkett, E. Golden vine of Old Britain
Board of Trade. Report British wines, cider
Booth, D. Art of winemaking . . .
Brannt, W.T. Pract. treatise mfg. vinegar, cider
_____ . Pract. treat mfg. vinegar . . .
Bravery, H.E. Homebrewing without failures
Buell, J.S. Cider makers' manual

Chapman, T. Cyder maker's instructor
Charley, V.L.S. Prin. and pract. cider-making
Cooke, C.W.R. Book about cider and perry
Coxe, W. View of cultivation fruit trees . . .
Crampton, C.A. Fermented alcoholic beverages
Curtis, J.H. As long as there is a single apple tree left

Ellis, W. Compleat cyderman

Evelyn, J.   Sylva, discourse of forest trees

Feuchtwanger, L.   Fermented liquors
Floyd, R. M.   Songs of the apple tree with kith and kin

Hall, H.   The distiller
Ham, J.   Mfg. cider and perry reduced to rules
Hopkins, A. A.   Homemade beverages . . .
Hydraulic Press, Mfg. Co.   Net price list
_____ .   Mount Gilead equipment

James, N. C.   Cooking in cider

Knight, T. A.   Treat. culture of apple and pear

Lloyd, F. J.   Report investigations cider-make
Luckwill, L. C. and A. Pollard.   Perry pears

M'Harry, S.   Practical distiller
Marshall, W.   Rural economy Gloucestershire
Ministry Agriculture.   Cider apple production
Moore, J.   England's interest
More, J.   Cyder book
Moubray, B.   Pract. treat. breeding . . .

National Fruit and Cider Institute Annual Reports

Parkes, B.   Domestic brewer, family winemaker
(Phillips, J.)   Cyder, a poem
Pollard, A. and F. W. Beech.   Cider-making

Roundell, J. A. E.   Still room

Saintsbury, G.   Notes on a cellar-book
Shannon, R.   Pract. treat. brewing . . .
Shirley, T.   Curious distillatory . . .
Stafford, H.   Treat. on cyder-making . . .
Stopes, Henry.   Cider, its history . . .

Taylor, J.   Tables for calculating beer . . .
Tritton, S.M.   Successful winemaking
Trowbridge, J.M.   Cider makers' handbook

Westney, R.   Wine and spirit dealer's and consumer's
    Vade-mecum
White, F.J.   Hargreaves story
Wigglesworth, E.   Brewers' and licensed guide
Worlidge, J.   Vinetum Britannicum, treat. on cider

    Anonymous
Act of Georgii - III
Address to such electors of Great Britain as are makers of
    cyder
Art of brewing, on scientific principles

Brewer (The) familiar treatise

Cider factory, plant and layout
Cider of Somerset (The)
Complete family piece (BEST GUIDE)
Complete planter and cyderist

Making and preserving apple cider

Cocktails
"Adrian" Cocktail fashions of 1936
Altshul, I.D.   Drinks as made before prohibition
Anderson, F.   Handbook of modern cocktails
_____ .   Modern cocktail manual 168 drinks
Anderson, R.   100 famous cocktails
Angostura Bitters Ltd.   For home use
Angostura-Wupperman.   Angostura recipes
Angostura-Wupperman.   Professional mixing guide
Anthony, N.   Here's how!
_____ .   Here's how again!
Applegreen, J.   Applegreen's new bar book
_____ .   Applegreen's barkeeper's guide
Armstrong, J. and V.I. Partch.   VIP's new bar guide
Arthur, S.C.   Famous New Orleans drinks

Atherton, E. Here's how
Auken, I. Dictionary scientific cocktail make

Bacchus and Cordon Bleu. New guide hotel, bar
Bacchus. Brewer's guide for the hotel . . .
Bailey, A.J. The mixologist
Banning, K. The Squire's recipes
Barclay, Jas. and Co. Corby's presents recipes
Barnes, A. Complete bartender
Beebe, L.M. Stork Club bar book
Beilenson, E. Holiday punches
Beilenson, P. Aquavit to zombie
_____ . Holiday drink book
_____ . King of hearts drink book
_____ . Merrie Christmas drink book
Bergeron, V.J. Bartender's guide
_____ . Trader Vic's Book food and drink
"Bernard" 100 cocktails. How to mix
Bird, A.E.P. and W. Turner. Cocktails, their kicks
    and sidekicks
Blochman, L.G. Here's how!
Blunier, O. Barkeeper's Golden Book
Boothby, W.T. Cocktail Boothby's American bartender
_____ . "Cocktail Bill" Boothby world drinks
_____ . World's drinks and how to mix
Booth's Distilleries Ltd. Anthology of cocktails
Bowen, H.E. The mixer
Bradley, J.F. Cocktails, wines and liquors
Brandimbourg, G. Guide des Bals et Soirees
Bredenbek, M. What shall we drink
Breen, M. and A. Lawson. Weekend companion
Brenner, F. 500 recipes. Cocktails . . .
Brown, B. Homemade hilarity. Country drinks
Brown, F.I. Bartender's friend
Brown, N.W. Liquor dealer's . . . companion
Browne, C. Gun Club drink book
Brunswick-Balke-Collender Co. Bk recipes
Buell, C.D. and J.T. Haughey. 110 drinks
Burke, H.B. Burke's compl. cocktail and drinking recipes
    (various dates)
Buzzo-Cardozo of Hollywood. Hollywood's favorite cocktail
    book
Byron, O.H. Mod. bartenders' guide

Calvert Distillers Co.   Party encylcopedia
Canada Dry Ginger Ale Co.   Masterly touch
Carrico, G.   Art mixing drinks
Carter, J. A.   Confessions of bartender
Casey, E.   Mixologist and compounder
Chapin and Gore.   Manual.   What to use
Charles, C.   Bartender's guide
"Charles".   The cocktail bar
Charles formerly of Delmonicos.   Punches and cocktails.
    (Book of)
Chicote, P.   Mis 500 cocktails
Clarke, E.   King cocktail
_____ .   Pract. bar management
_____ .   Shaking in the 60's
_____ .   Shaking with Eddie
Cobb, I. S.   Own recipe book
Coghill, J. A.   Cocktail recipes
Cohan, E.   Here's how! by Clegg
Concklin, J.   The bartender
Considene, J. H.   Buffet Blue Book
Consumers Union.   Wines and liquors
(Cook, R.)   Oxford night caps
Coombs, J. H.   Bar service
Cotton, L.   Old Mr. Boston Off.   Bartender's Guide.
    (Various)
Craddock, H.   Savoy cocktail book
Creek, D.   Cocktails for amateurs
Crockett, A. S.   Old Waldorf-Astoria bar book
Crockett, A. S.   Old Waldorf Bar Days
Culver, J. B.   Gentle art of drinking

Daly, T.   Daly's bartenders' encyclopedia
Davies, F.   Drinks of all kinds, hot and cold
Defay, S. G. M.   Professional bar management
Dey, S. Henry.   Merry mixer (The)
Didier, J. A.   The reminder
Diners' Club Magazine.   Diners' Club drink book
Dorf, B. B. and Co.   Cordial cocktail confidences
Doxat, J.   Booth's handbook cocktails . . .
Drex, A.   ABC of wines, cocktails . . .
Driscoll, J. F.   Bartender's friend
_____ .   Drink master
Du Brow, M.   Cocktails for two thousand
Duffy, P. G.   Bartender's guide (The Standard)
_____ .   Official mixer's manual
Durr, A.   Fashions in drinks

518

Edwards, W.M.　How to mix drinks by Bill Edwards
Elliott, V.　Quiet drinking
_____ .　Shake 'em up!
Embury, D.A.　Fine art mixing drinks
Engel, L.　American and other drinks
Ensslin, H.R.　Recipes for mixed drinks
Esquire.　Drink book

Farrow and Jackson, Ltd.　Recipes American and other
　　iced drinks
Feery, W.C.　Wet drinks for dry people
Field, S.S.　American drink book
Finch, Jos. S. and Co.　The Merry Mixer
Flanders, C.R.　Gourmet au Vatel
Fleishmann Distilling Co.　Mixer's manual
de Fleury, R.　1800 and all that
_____ .　1700 cocktails for man behind bar
Foughner, S.　Baron Foughner's bar guide

Gaige, C.　Cocktail guide, ladies companion
_____ .　Standard cocktail guide
Gale, H.　The how and when
Gammick, C.H.　Bartender and way to man's heart
Gavin, C.　Here's how
Gibson, J.W.　Scientific bar-keeping
Ginrum Alpha Co.　Legend of liqueurs . . .
Gooderham and Worts Ltd.　Souvenir Canadian National Fair
Gordon, H.J.　Cocktail and food recipes
Gorham Co.　Cocktail Book
Graham, S.　Melrose--honey of roses
Green, H.W.　Mixed drinks
Grohuska, J.A.　Jack's manual on vintage . . .
Grossman, H.J.　Practical bar management
Guyer, W.　The merry mixer

Haimo, O.　Cocktail and wine digest (in Spanish)
_____ .　Cocktail and wine digest
_____ .　Cocktail digest
Haney, J. and Co.　Steward and barkeeper's manual
"Harry" of Ciro's.　ABC mixing cocktails
Hayes, J.J.　Inside tip to man that came back
Haywood, J.L.　Mixology
Heath, A.　Good drinks
Heaton, N.　Wines, mixed drinks and savouries

Heaton, V. Cocktail party secrets
Held, J. Jr. Psychaud's New Orleans cocktails
_____. Ye Olde Mixer-Upper
Henderson, B. U. Pop's master mixer
Henninger, O. Reliable bartenders' guide
Hennessey, J. and Co. Hennessey is everywhere
Henseler, H. and B. Weichsel. Wir mixen
Herisko, C. Drinks and snacks for parties
Herrick, C. T. Modern domestic science
_____. Consolidated library mod. cooking
Hoffmann, H. The 'Count' reminisces
Hubbell, M. H. Art of mixing then
Huntington, R. T. Bar management and beverage profits

Iverson, J. R. Liquid gems

Jack, F. B. 100 drinks and cups
Jacquin, C et Cie. Jacquin's Cordials
Jayne, Dr. D. and Son. Bartender's guide
_____. Red J bartender's guide
Jimmy (pseud.) Green cocktail book
"Jimmy" late of Ciro's London. Cocktails
John. "Happy days!"
Johnson, H. New, impr. illus. bartenders' manual
Johnson Smith and Co. "Homebrewed" wines . . .
Jordon, J. Simple facts about wines . . .
Judge, Jr. (pseud.) Here's how!

"Kappa" Bartender's guide, best mixed drinks
Kappeler, G. J. Drinks and how to mix them
_____. Modern American drinks
Keen, A. G. Here's How
Koch, A. A. Official mixing guide
Kronlein, H. Handbuch fur mixer

Laird, W. H. American bartender
Lamore, H. The bartender
Larsen, N. 156 recettes de boissons Americaine
Lawlor, C. F. The Mixicologist
Lewis, V. B. Complete buffet guide
Loeb, R. Jr. Nip ahoy, picture bar guide
_____. Wolf in chef's clothing

London, R and A (pseud). Cocktails and snacks
Lowe, P.E. Bartender's quick reference man
_____ . Drinks. How to mix, serve
_____ . Drinks as they are mixed
Lupoiu, J. Cocktails (in French)
Lurie, G.A. Here's how

McDonough, P. Bar-keepers' guide
McGreal Bros. Co. Blue book
MacNiel, S.S. Zodiac cocktails
Mahoney, C.S. Hoffman House bartender's guide
Makus, E.W. Standard blue book mixed drinks
Maloney, J.C. Twentieth century guide
Manio, Jack, de. Jack de Manio's drinkards - cocktails
Mason, D. The art of drinking
_____ . Tipple and snack
Mayabb, J.E. International cocktail specialties
Meier, F. Artistry mixing drinks
Meyer, J.R. "Bottoms up"
Mills, J. Christmas in olden times or the Wassail bowl
Mouquin, Inc. Mouquin Epicure
Muckensturm, L.J. Louis' mixed drinks
Mueller, C.C. Experts' home compl. Amer.
     drink mixers' guide
_____ . Pioneers of mixing at elite bars
_____ . Pioneers of mixing cognac . . .
_____ . Pioneers of mixing gin . . .
_____ . Pioneers of mixing Irish and Scotch
_____ . Pioneers of mixing liqueurs . . .
_____ . Pioneers of mixing rums
_____ . Pioneers of mixing whiskeys . . .
_____ . Pioneers of mixing wines. All Pioneers with
     A.L. Hoppe
Myers, Fred L. and Son. Jamaica rum cocktails
_____ . Myers's Jamaica rum cocktails
_____ . Myers' Jamaica rum recipes

National Distiller Products Corp. Host's handbook
_____ . Mine Host's Handbook
Nelson, C.B. The instructor
Newell, R.C. Gin and bear it!
Newman, L.P. Book on scientific barkeeping
North, S. So red the nose

Odell, G.T. Beverages. Manual mixing cocktails
Other, A.N. Pick-me-up!

Paul, C. American and other iced drinks°
Peck, J.E. Fancy drinks and how to mix them
Perry, M.H. And to drink sir!
Portman, H. Harry's ABC of mixing cocktails
Powner, W.E. Complete bartender's guide
Proskauer, J.J. Fun at cocktail time
_____ . What'll you have?

Rawling, E.F. Book of mixed drinks
Reibstein, A. "Mixology" recipes
Reinhardt, C.N. "Cherrio!" Book of punches . . .
Richards, Rosen Associates Jnc. Guide to pink elephants
Ricket, E. and C. Thomas. Gentlemen's tableguide
"Robert" Cocktails. How to mix them
Rollat, E. Wine guide and cocktail book
Roos, H. New, standard mixed drinks
Roe, C and J Schwenck. Home bartender's guide and
    song book
Ryan's Liquor Shop. Bottoms up. Guide to pleasant
    drinking
De Salis, Mrs. Drinks a la mode

Sasena, J.P. Fine beverages and recipes mix drinks
Saucier, T. Bottoms up
Schell, J. H. Mixed drinks up to date
Schenley, Prod. Co. Merry mixer
Schmidt A.W. Fancy drinks and popular beverages
_____ . The flowing bowl
Seagram-Distillers Co. Vacation-time food and drink guide
Shane, T. Bar guide
_____ . Funny bar book and guide to mixed drinks
Sheridan, J.E. Complete buffet manual
Shore, W. Cups: how to make, why to take
Simons, S. Alcoholic drinks; easy way to make
Smith, C. Smacks and smiles
Smith, J.W. So mixe ich fur meine Freunde
Southern Comfort Corp. How to make 44 party drinks
Steele, S.F. My new cocktail book
Steedman, M.E. and C.H. Senn. Homemade summer and
    winter drinks

522

Steedman, M.E.   Homemade beverages and American
    drinks
Stiles, H.W.   Chapin and Gore manual
Stouffer Foods Corp.   Here's how by Stouffer's
Stouffer's Restaurants.   Nectars--Stouffer's
Straub, J.   Compl. manual mixed drinks
_____ .   Drinks
Stuart, T.   Fancy drinks and how to mix them
Sullivan, J.   Drinks of yesteryear.   A Mixology
Sundin, K.W.   200 selected drinks

Tarling, W.J.   Cafe Royal cocktail book
Thomas, J.   Bar-tender's guide
_____ .   Bon-Vivant's Companion
_____ .   How to mix drinks . . .
Tooze's, Minneapolis.   How? When? Where?
Torelli, A.   900 recettes de cocktails . . .
Townsend, J.   The bartender's book
Toye, N.   Drinks, long and short
_____ .   and A.H. Adair.   Petits and Grand Verres
Tuck, C.A.   Cocktails and mixed drinks

United Kingdom Bartender's Guide.   Approved cocktails
_____ .   The U.K.B.G. guide to drinks

Victoria Wine Co. Ltd.   Here's how

Walker, H. and Sons.   The essential guest
Wehman, H.J.   Bartender's guide
Wheatley, D.   7 ages of Justerini's
Whitfield, W.C.   Here's how; mixed drinks
_____ .   Just cocktails
Wiley, J.A.   Art of mixing
Williams, H.I.   3 bottle bar
Wilson Publ. Co.   Encyclopedia state laws
Winter, G.   How to mix drinks
Woodman, M.   Cocktails, ices, sundaes . . .
Wray, J. and Nephew Ltd.   Story of Dagger Jamaica rum
Wunsch, F.   ABC de cocktails

Young's Market Co.   Wine, liquors and like

Zabriskie, G.A.   Bon vivant's companion

Anonymous
The ABC of cocktails
Adrian's International bar guide
All in vue. 84 drinks for you
Art of mixing drinks

Bar Florida cocktails
Barkeepers' ready reference
Barman's and barmaid's manual
Bar-tender's Guide
Bartender's guide. How to mix drinks
Bartender's guide. For home and professional
Bartender's manual; mixed drinks
Before and after dinner beverages and a few sandwiches
Bottoms up! Guide to pleasant drinking

Cheerio, 101 best cocktail recipes
Cocktail Book. Sideboard manual (Various)
Cocktail key
Cocktail Parade
Cocktail recipes
Cocktails, the great American drink
Cocktails, wines and other drinks for the home

Drinks and how to make them
Drinks, cocktails and homemade wines
Drinks. Formulas for making . . .

Famous highballs

Giggle water
Good Cheer
Guide to cooling hot weather drinks

Here's How! Handbook of recipes
Here's How. (Maryland Wine Co.)

Knickerbocker, revised bartender's guide

Legend of liqueurs, wines and spirits
Life and letters of William Thomas, mixologist
Lifetime collection 688 recipes for drinks

Mary Elizabeth's Cocktail parade
524

New bartender's guide 1933
New Bartender's guide. How to mix drinks°
New Bartender's guide. Telling how to mix
Newest guide. How to mix drinks for man's pleasure

Official bartender's guide and companion
100 ways especially prepared for connoisseurs

Party Book Inc.

Red Top Rye Guide
Richelieu Handbook. Wine cooking, mixed drinks

"Saloon secrets exposed' book of the hour
Savoy cocktail book
Silver Dollar bar, how to mix drinks

Toasts and cocktails

Wehman Bros. bartenders' guide

Cocoa and chocolate
Alexander, H.C. Richard Cadbury, Birmingham
American Food Journal Institute. Bibliography
    nutritive values chocolate, cocoa

Baker, Walter and Co. Account mfg. and use cocoa . . .
_____ __. Best chocolate recipes
_____. Best chocolate and cocoa recipes
_____. Chocolate, cocoa recipes. Miss Parloa
_____. Chocolate plant
_____. Choice recipes by Miss Parloa
_____. Choice receipts (by Miss Parloa)
_____. Cocoa, chocolate, short history
_____. Description educational exhibit
_____. Famous chocolate recipes
_____. Famous recipes for Baker's Chocolate
Barber's C.A. Tropical agriculture research
Bareau, P. Cocoa: crop with future
Briton-Jones, H.R. Diseases and curing cacao
Broadbent, H. Domestick coffee man shewing
Brown, E. and H.H. Hunter Planting in Uganda
Browne, E. Cocoa

Brookes, R. Natural history of chocolate
Bywaters, H.W. Modern methods cocoa and chocolate

Cadbury Bros. Bournville, factory in garden
_____. Cadbury's of Bournville
_____. Cocoa and chocolate
_____. Cocoa and chocolate from grower to consumer
_____. Education and training
_____. Industrial challenge
Cadbury, R. Cocoa: all about it. (Historicus)
Chatt, E.M. Cocoa: cultivation, processing . . .
Chocolate Mfgrs. Ass'n. Story of chocolate
Colmenero, de L.A. Chocolate, Indian drinke
_____. Curious treat. nature chocolate
Compton, H. Chocolate and cocoa
Cook, L.R. Chocolate production and uses
Cross, G. Bar of chocolate

Dalgren, B.E. Cacao
Damblon, H. New method mfg. chocolate . . .
Deverson, H.J. Tree of golden pod
Dufour, P.S. Manner making coffee, tea . . .

Erneholm, I. Cacao production in So. Amer.
Evans, L.F.C. et al. Cocoa plantations

Finch, R.J. World-wide business
Frederick, Mrs. C. Hershey's helps for the hostess

Gardiner, A.G. Life of George Cadbury
General Foods Corp. My party book of tested chocolate
    recipes

Hamel-Smith, H. Cocoa planting West Indies
Hart, J.H. Cacao; manual cultivation . . .
Hatton, J. Cocoa
Hazelton, N.S. Chocolate!
Head, B. Food of the Gods
Hewitt, C. Chocolate and cocoa . . .
Hill, P. Gold Coast cocoa farmer . . .
"Historicus" see Richard Cadbury
Holm, J. Cocoa and its manufacture
Huggins, J.D. Hints to peasant proprietors . . .
Hughes, W. American physitian

Imperial College Tropical Agriculture.   Report on cacao
    research

Jacoutot, A.   Chocolate and confectionery mfg.
Jensen, H.R.   Chemistry, flavouring . . .
Johnson, W.H.   Cocoa.   Its cultivation . . .
Jordon, S.   Chocolate evaluation

Knapp, A.W.   Cocoa and chocolate industry
_____ .   Cocoa and chocolate, their history
_____ .   Cacao fermentation
_____ .   Scientific aspects cacao ferment.

Langseth-Christensen L. et al.   Chocolate and coffee
    cookbook

MacLaren, W.A.   Rubber, tea and cocoa
Mann, J.A.   Cocoa, its culture, mfg . . .
Mitchell, D.G.   The chocolate industry
Montgomery, E.G.   World trade in cocoa
Morris, Sir D.   Cocoa, how to grow and cure
Mueller, W.   Bibliographie des Käffee . . .
_____ .   Bibliographie de Kakao . . .

Nestle Co.   Perfect endings
"Nirvana" Chocolate making

Olivieri, F.E.   Cocoa planting and cultivation
_____ .   Treatise on cocoa
Organization for European Economic cooperation
    Main Products of the overseas territories: cocoa

Parloa, Miss Chocolate and cocoa recipes
_____ .   Choice recipes
Paulli, S.   Treat. on tobacco, tea . . .
Peattie, D.C.   Cargoes and harvests
Peck, A.M.   Coffee, tea, chocolate

Redmayne, P.   Cocoa and chocolate
Rieck, M.   Gordian essays on cocoa
Roberts, A.B. Co.   Handbook chocolate . . .
Rohan, T.A.   Processing raw cocoa . . .

Saint-Arroman, A.   Coffee, tea and chocolate
Shillington, D.F. and J.J. Bunting.   Book on breakfast
    beverages
Smith, H.H.   Fermentation of cacao
_____ .   Future of cacao planting

Smith, H. MD. Essay on foreign teas . . .
Steuart, M.E. Everyday life on Ceylon cocoa estate
Stevenson, J. Advice, medical and economical
Stubbs, H. The Indian nectar . . .

Urquhart, D.H. British North Borneo
_____ . Cocoa
_____ . Cocoa in South East Asia
_____ . Cocoa growing in Uganda . . .
_____ . Cocoa in British Solomon Islands
_____ . Cocoa growing--in India
_____ . Cocoa industry French Ivory Coast
_____ . Cocoa industry Sierra Leone
_____ . Cocoa industry in Jamaica
_____ . Cocoa growing Nyasaland
Urquhart, D.H. et al. Cocoa growing Papua
_____ . Cocoa zone of Bahia

Van Hall, J.J. Cocoa

Wanklyn, J.A. Tea, coffee and cocoa
Watrous, R.C. Cacao. Bibliography . . .
Whymper, R. Cocoa and chocolate . . .
Wikizer, V.D. Coffee, tea and cocoa . . .
Williams, C.T. Chocolate and confectionery
Williams, I.A. Firm of Cadbury
Wood, G.A.R. Cocoa growing in India
_____ . Cocoa growing Dominican . . .
_____ . Cocoa growing in Venezuela . . .
_____ . Costs cocoa production
Wooley, G.B. Sweets and chocolates
Wright, H. Theobroma cacao or cocoa . . .

Zipperer, P. Mfg. chocolate and cacao . . .

Anonymous
Cocoa bean tests
Cocoa grower's Bulletin
Cocoa growing costs
Chocolate, its character, history and treatment
Confectionery Production Manual

Natural history of cocoa
Natural history of coffee, thee . . .

Recipes for use of Huyler's cocoa . . .

Story of chocolate and cocoa

Coffee
Alcott, W.A.   Tea and coffee
Amer. Coffee Growers Ass'n.   Coffee by proxy
Anderson, G.   Jottings on coffee, Mysore
Arnold, E.L.   Coffee: its cultivation . . .
Arnold, E.L.L.   Coffee planting So. India
Axtell, F.P.   Standard coffee code

Benjamin, Count of Rumford.   Of the excellent qualities
    of coffee and the art of making it.
Boyes, E.   How to obtain ideal cup coffee
Bradley, R.   Short historical account coffee
—————— .   Virtue and use of coffee
Brazil.   The ABC of coffee
Brazilian Coffee Institute.   Coffee and Brazil
Breuckmann, F.E.   Treat. on coffee . . .
Broadbent, H.   Domestick coffee man shewing way of
    preparing . . .
Brown, A.   Coffee planter's manual
Brown, E. and H.H. Hunter.   Planting in Uganda
Burns, J.   The 'Spice Mill' companion

Campbell, L.   Tea, coffee, spice manual
Cauchois, F.A. and Co. Compiler.   Over the black coffee,
    history . . .
Chase and Sanborn.   Coffee
—————————— .   "To the household"
Cheek-Neal Coffee Co.   Story of coffee
Cheney, R.H.   Coffee: a monograph
Coffee Brewing Institute.   There's a story in your coffee
    cup.
Cook, O.P.   Shade in coffee culture
Costa Neves.   Story "King Coffee"
Cramer, P.J.S.   Review literature coffee research-
    Indonesia
Cross, G.   A cup of coffee
Cruwell, G.A. and A.S. Blackford.   Brazil as a coffee
    growing country

D. (N.) Virtues of coffee
Dahlgren, B.E.   Coffee
Dambaugh, L.N.   Coffee frontier-Brazil
Dignadice, N.D.   Vocational guide coffee culture
Doughty, C.M.   Travels in Arabian Deserta
Dufour, P.S.   Manner making coffee . . .

Elliot, R.M.   Gold, sport and coffee-Mysore
Ellis, J.   Historical account coffee
Embleton, W.K.   From plantation to cup

Ferguson, J.   Coffee planter's manual - Arabian and
    Liberian species
Foot, F.N.   Coffee, the beverage

Galland, A.   Treat. on origin of coffee
Gomez, G.   Cult. and prep. coffee
Gordon, J.   Coffee recipes
Graham, H.C.   Coffee, production . . .
Gray, A.   Over the black coffee

H. (M.) Coffee drinkers' manual
Haarer, A.E.   Modern coffee production
Hahnemann, S.   Treat. on effects of coffee
Hewitt, R.   Coffee; its history . . .
Hill, M.F.   Planters' progress
Hills Bros.   Art of coffee-making
Hockings, A.J.   Queensland garden manual
Hughes, J.   Ceylon coffee, soils, manures
Hull, E.C.P.   Coffee, its physiology . . .
_____ .   Coffee planting So. India, Ceylon

International Bureau Amer. Republics. Coffee

Jacob, H.E.   Coffee; epic of a commodity
_____ .   Saga of coffee
Johnston, E. and Co.   100 years of coffee

Kaufman, W.I.   Coffee cookbook
Keable, B.B.   Coffee, grower to consumer
Keen, W.   Coffee cultivation, Ceylon
Kirby, N. and E.   Aunt Martha's corner cupboard
Koehler, F.A.   Coffee for armed forces

Laborie, P.J.   Abridgement.   The Coffee Planter
_____ .   The Coffee Planter-Santo Domingo
Laerne, C.F.V.   Brazil and Java Coffee culture
Langseth-Christensen, L. et al.   Chocolate and coffee
    cookbook
Laroque, J. de.   Voyage to Arabia
Lascelles, A.R.W.   Treat. nature, cult. coffee
Law, W.   Hints on cooking coffee
_____ .   History of coffee

530

Lewis, G.C. Coffee planting, Ceylon
Lilly-White, B. London Coffee Houses
Lock, C.G.W. Coffee: its culture, commerce
Lockhart, E.E. et al. Survey world literature
Lodge, J.L. Coffee, history, preparation . . .

Mc Donald, J.H. Coffee growing: ref. E. Africa
Mackaye, P. Coffee man's manual
Marah, W.H. Essay, cult. mfg. coffee
Maxwell, J. ed. Gold Coast Handbook 1928
Middleton, W.H. Manual coffee planting Natal
Moreira, N.J. Brazilian coffee
Moseley, B. Treat. properties, effects, coffee
Mueller, W. Bibliographie des Kaffee . . .

Naironus, A.F. Discourse coffee, virtues . . .
National Coffee Dept. Brazil. Coffee facts . . .
National Federation Coffee Growers Columbia. Columbia--
____ land of coffee
_____ . Land of coffee
Nicholls, H.A. Cultivation Liberian coffee
Nicol (R.) Treatise on coffee

Owen, T.C. First years work coffee plantation

Pan Amer. Coffee Bur. Annual statistics
_____ . Coffee. Good neighbor product
_____ . Fun with coffee
_____ . Impact coffee on U.S. economy
Paulli, S. Treat. tobacco, tea, coffee . . .
Peattie, D.C. Cargoes and harvests
Peck, A.M. Coffee, tea and chocolate
Poore, G.V. Coffee and tea. Lecture
Prestoe, H. and M.F. Malepegne. Report coffee
    cultivation, Dominica
Pringle, W. Science and coffee

Q.M. Food, Container Institute. Horsford's The Army
    Ration 1864
Quinby, W.S. How to make perfect coffee
Quinn, J.P. Scientific market coffee

Ripperger, H.L. Coffee cookery
Rodriquez, D.W. Coffee, short history, Jamaica
Romero, M. Coffee and India rubber, Mexico
Rowe, J.W.F. The World's coffee
Rudy, P.O. Marketing of coffee

Sabonadiere, W. Coffee planter--Ceylon
Saint-Arroman, A. Coffee, tea and chocolate
Sanborn, H.J. Winter in Central Amer., Mexico
Schoffner, C.H. The coffee trade
Shillington, D.F. and J.J. Bunting. Book of breakfast
    beverages
Shortt, J. Handbook to coffee planting, South India
Simmonds, P.L. Coffee and chicory
Sivitz, M. and H.E. Foote. Coffee processing technology
Smith, H. Essay foreign teas . . .
Springett, L.E. Quality of coffee
Stainbank, H.E. Coffee in Natal: its cultivation . . .
Stevenson, J. Advice, medical and economical . . .
_____. Treat. tobacco, tea, coffee . . .
Syers, R. The coffee guide

Taylor, J.P. Coffee growing, Mexico
Thurber, F.B. Coffee: plantation to cup
Twining, S.H. House of Twining 1706-1956

Ugarte, J.P. Cult., prep., coffee for market
Ukers, W.H. All about coffee
_____. Coffee facts
_____. Coffee merchandising
_____. Romance of coffee
_____. 10 years coffee progress 1935-1944
Uribe, Compuzano, A. Brown gold. Amazing story of
    coffee

Walsh, J.M. Coffee; its history . . .
Wanklyn, J.A. Tea, coffee and cocoa
Wellman, F.L. Coffee: botany, cult . . .
Whitney, H.M. Hawaiian coffee planter's manual
Wickizer, V.D. Coffee, tea and cocoa
_____. World coffee economy
Windle, E.G. Modern coffee planting

Yorba, J. Mexican coffee culture
Young, I.N. Coffee growing countries N.A.
    North America, Mexico, and Central America
_____. Story of coffee

    Anonymous
Cafe and milk bar catering
Coffee and chicory
Coffee from Puerto Rico
532

G. Washington's coffee
Green and roasted coffee tests

Hints on coffee planting

Maxwell House Coffee cookbook

Natural history of coffee, thee . . .

Treat. coffee, its properties . . .

Uker's International Tea and Coffee Buyer's guide

Confectionery, Ices
Bell, J.   Treat. on confectionery
Bell, W.M.   Bell's "Pilot"
Berling, E.M.   Art in confectionery . . .
Blumenthal, S.   Food manufacturing
Bolton, M.   Homemade wines, confectionery . . .
Borella, Court and Country confectionery
Braum, E.   Frozen gems and dainty dishes
Butler, W.C.   Mod. pract. confectioner

Cameron, S.M.   Homemade ice cream and sherbets
Cardelli, M.   Manuel du Limonadier . . .
Carter, W.   Cook and confectionery guide
Charlotte.   Lets have a party
Colam, E.E.F.   Pract. milk bar operation
Craig, E.   Bubble and Squeak

Eales, M.   Compleat confectioner
_____ .   Eale's receipts

Farmer, J.A.   International sweetmaker and confectionery
Fisk, W.W.   Book of ice-cream
Francateli, C.E.   Cook's guide . . .
Frandsen, J.H. and E.A. Markham.   Mfg. ice creams and
    ices
Friedman, J.   Commonsense candy teacher

Gill, J.T.   Practical confectioner
_____ .   Compl. pract. confectioner
Glasse, H.   Compleat confectioner
Gouffe, J.   Book of preserves
Gratz, H.   Making ice cream, ices

Gunter, W. Confectioner's oracle
_____. Modern confectioner

Harris, H. G. and S. P. Borella. All about ices

Jacoutot, A. Chocolate and confectionery
Jarrin, W. A. Italian confectioner
Jeannes, W. Modern confectioner
Johnson, H. A. Co. Catalog baker, ice cream maker
Jordan, S. and K. E. Langwill. Conf. analysis

Knorr, W. L. Catalogue ice cream machinery

Lambert, E. Art of confectionery
Leon, S. I. Encyclo. candy, ice cream making
Lincoln, D. A. Frozen dainties

Mackenzie, E. L. Whole art confectionery
McNeill, F. M. Scot's kitchen
Mansur, C. E. Virginia hostess
Marshall, A. B. Fancy ices
_____. Book of ices
Masters, T. Ice book
Masurovsky, B. I. Sherbets, water ices . . .
Meserole, H. H. H. and O'N. Johnson, Ice cream
    at drug store fountain
Michael, P. Ices and soda fountain drinks
Miller, V. Stand. recipes ice cream makers

Newcombe, F. "Know-how" lollie ice mfg.
"Nirvana" Chocolate making . . .
Nott, J. Cook's and confectionery's dictionary
Nutt, F. Complete confectioner

Parkinson. Complete confectioner
Peddie, J. Dictionary of confectionery
Perfecto. Notes on American confectionery
Popp, C. W. Modern confectioner
Price, E. New Univ. and compl. confectioner

Read, G. Confectioner
Rigby, W. O. and F. Reliable candy teacher
Roberts, A. B. and Co. Handbook chocolate and conf.
Rorer, S. T. Ice creams, water ices . . .
Rylands, D. Complete catalogue of accessories . . .

Scarborough, N. F. Sweet manufacture

534

Senn, C. N.   Ices and how to make them
Skuse, E.   Confectioners' handbook . . .
Smith, J. H. et al.   Famous old recipes
Sommer, H. H.   Theory, pract. ice cream making
Stavely, S. W.   New whole art confectionery

Three Millers Co.   Supplies soda fountain
Turnbow, G. D. et al.   Ice cream industry

Vernon, C.   The sweet shop

Warner-Jenkinson Co.   Bottler's and ice cream maker's
    handy guide
_____ .   Ice cream, carbonated beverages
Williams, H. L.   Book of ices
Wood and Selick Inc.,   Ice cream supplies and machinery

    Anonymous
Art of confectionery
Ash's Patent Piston Freezing machine . . .

Complete confectioner (The)
Confectioner (The)
Confectionery Production manual

Dr. Price's delicious desserts

Lee's Priceless Recipes
Let's sell ice cream

National Dairy and Ice Cream Expo. Handbook
New Delineator recipes

Piston process of freezing

Table topics
True way preserving and candying . . .

Vest pocket pastry book

Whole art confectionery

Cookery
Abdullah, A. and J. Kenny.   For men only
Acton, E.   Modern cookery all branches

535

Adair, A. Kitchenette cookery
Adkins, T. H. Nautical cookery book
Ainsworth-Davis, J. R. Cooking through centuries
Allen, I. B. C. Wines and spirits cookbooi
_____ . Book sugar substitutes
Amer. Hominy Institute. Old favorite honey recipes
Angostura-Wupperman Corp. Ang. cookbook
_____ . Angostura recipes
_____ . For home use
_____ . 100 prize-winning West Indian recipes
_____ . Angostura Recipe Book
A. T. D. S. The cookery book
Atiyeh, W. Scheherazade cooks
Atkinson, A. and G. Holroyd. Pract. cookery
(Atkins, A.) Family magazine
Aylett, M. and O. Ordish. First catch your hare

Bacchus and Cordon Bleu. New guide hotel . . .
Baker, C. H. Jr. Esquire culinary companion
_____ . Gentlemen's companion
_____ . So. American gentlemen's companion
deBaralt, B. Z. Cuban cookery
Bazore, K. Hawaiian and Pacific foods
Beeton, I. Book household management
Beilenson, E. ABC of wine cookery
Bergeron, V. J. Trader Vic's book of food and drink
Bitting, K. Gastronomic bibliography
Blencowe, A. Receipt book
Booth, G. C. Food and drink of Mexico
Bourbon Institute. Bourbon Chef
Bradley, R. Country housewife
Bradshaw, P. Valuable family jewel
Briggs, R. English art cookery
Brown, C. L. Wine cook book
Brown, E. and B. Culinary Americana
Burnett, J. and Co. Dainty, artistic desserts

California Univ. Wine in cooking
Callahan, G. New California cook book
Carswell, D. and C. Scots weekend book
Carter, C. Compl. city, country book
_____ . Cook and confectioner's guide
Caruba, R. Cooking with wine and high spirits
Chambers, A. Ladies best companion
Chambers, M. D. One piece dinners
Charlotte. Let's have a party
Chase, E. Pleasures cooking with wine

Church, R.E. Mary Meade's Magic recipes
Claiborne, C. New York Times cook book°
Clarke, E. Plain cookery recipes
Cleland, E. New easy method cookery
Cleveland, B.A. California Mission recipes
Cole, M. Ladies complete guide
Collingwood, F. and J. Woollams. Universal cook
Courtney, M. Cocktail companions
Cox, H. Food, flowers, wine cookbook
Craig, E. Beer and vittels
_____ . Bubble and Squeak
_____ . Cook's guide to wine
_____ . Wine in the kitchen
_____ . Woman, wine and saucepan
Crang, A. Preserves for all occasions
Croly, J.C. Jennie June's Amer. cookery book
Culinary Arts Institute. Mixer, handmixer . . .
Cust, Lady. Invalid's own book

Davison, E. Beer in American home
De Gouy, L.P. Cooking with apple brandy
_____ . Derrydale game cook book
_____ . Master chef's best
Dietz, F.M. and A. Gay nineties cook book
Digby, K. Closet of Sir K-D opened
Director, A. Art wine cookery
_____ . Stand. wine cook book
Dodds, S.W. Health in household
Dods, M. (pseud). Cook and housewife's manual

Earle, M. Sickroom cookery . . .
Edwards, Mrs. Cookery book
Erlanger, B. and D. Pierce. Compl. Martini cookbook

Fairfax, A. Family's best friend
Farley, J. London art of cookery
Farmer, F.M. Food and cookery for sick . . .
Farmers Weekly. Farmhouse fare
Fedden, M. Nurse's invalid cookery book
Fink, R.B. Jr. Cooking with rum
Flexner, M.W. Cocktail-supper book
Flower, B. and E. Rosenbaum. Art cooking-Apicius
Folsom, A. Care, training husbands
Francateli, C.E. Cook's guide and housekeeper
Freeman, J.D. Confederate cook book
Frost, S.A. Our new cook book

Gammick, C.H. Bartender, way to man's heart
Gelleroy, W. London cook
Glasse, H. Art cookery, plain, easy
Gloeckner, J.T. Standard mixer
Goffinet, S. Cream, butter, wine
Goodhousekeeping Institute. Preserves, pickles
Goodwin, H. How to cook with wine
Gordon, J. Orange recipes
_____ . Rose recipes
Gouffe, J. Book of preserves
Greenberg, E. and M. Whiskey in the kitchen

Hale, D.E. Cook with beer
_____ . It's smart to cook with beer
Hall, T. Queen's royal cookery
Hallett, E.H. Hostess book
Harrison, M. Eeer cookery
Hastings, M. Physical culture food directory
Hatch, E.W. American wine cook book
Hazelmore, M. Domestic economy
Hazlett, W.C. Old cookery books . . .
Heath, A. and D.D. Cottington Taylor. National Mark
    Calendar of cooking
Heaton, N. St.J. Cooking with wine
Henderson, M.F. Diet for the sick
Henderson, W.A. Housekeeper's instructor
_____ . Modern Domestic Cookery
Herrick, C.T. Modern Domestic Science
_____ . Consolidated Library mod. cooking
Hooper, M. Little dinners
_____ . Nelson's home comforts
Howard, M.W. Lowney's cook book
Howe, Robin. Wine and food Society's guide to soups
Hume, R. Party food and drink
Hunter, A. Receipts in modern cookery

Jack, F.B. Cookery for every household
_____ . Good Housekeeping invalid cookery
James, N.C. Cooking in cider
Jenks, J. Complete cook
Johnstone, C.I. Cook and housewife manual

Kaufman, W.I. Coffee cookbook
Kirk, A.G. People's home recipe book
Kirk, E.W. Tried favorites cookery book
(Kitchener, W.) Apicius Redivivus or The Cook's Oracle

Kaufman, W.I.   Tea cookbook (The).   cookery
Ko- operatiewe Wignbouwers Verenging van Zuid- Afrika
    Beperkt.   Cooking with Cape wine
K.W.V.   Planning a wine and cheese party

Lady (A).   Art cookery made plain, easy
Lake, M.   Hunter wine
Lane, B.   ABC of spice cookery
Langseth- Christensen, L. and C.S. Smith.   Chocolate
    and coffee cookbook
Leigh, O. de L.   500 and one cocktail canapes
Lemery, L.   New curiosities in art and nature
Liebowitz, et al.   Cook to your heart's content on a low-
    fat, low- salt diet.
Lincoln, W.   American cookery books
Lindlahr, A.   Nature cure cookbook
Loeb, R. Jr.   How wine friends, affluent people
_____ .   Wolf in chef's clothing
Lowe, B.   Experimental cookery . . .
Luck, P.   Belgian cookbook
Luke, Sir H.   The tenth muse

MacDonald, D.   New London Family Cook
McDouall, R.   Cooking with wine
MacLaren, H.   Be your own guest
McNeill, F.M.   The Scots kitchen
Malone, D.   How mama could cook
Manoha, G.   Cooking with wine
Mansur, C.E.   Virginia hostess
Martin, E.   Cornish recipes
Massee, W.E.   Wine- food index
Mayabb, J.E.   International cocktail specialties
Meyer, E.L.   Art cooking with spirits
Miloradovich, M.   Art of cooking herbs and spices
Mirrlees, E.L. and M.R. Coker.   Wishful thinking
Mitchell, C.G.   Way to a man's heart
Mogen, David Wine Co.   Food, fun, festivity
Montagne, P.   Larousse gastronomique
Morel, J.J.   Progressive catering
Morton, B.   Catering for young
Mouquin, Inc.   The Mouquin Epicure
Moxon, E.   English housewifery

Nash, E.H.T. Dr.   Nash's cookery book
Neumann, R.V.   Cooking with spirits
Nott, J.   Cook's and confectionery's dictionary

O'Neill, Gil and Mercia.   Cooking in wine (a bachelor's guide to)
Old Bohemian (An).   Philosophy in the kitchen
Owen, J.   The Lejon cookbook
_____ .   Wine lover's cook book
Oxford, A.W.   English cookery books

Paddleford, C.   New easy ways to cook with rum
Pan American Coffee Bureau.   Fun with coffee
Parke, G.   Big chocolate cookbook
Patten, M.   Invalid cookery book
Pennell, E.R.   My cookery books
Pennington, Mrs.   The Royal cookbook
Petty, F.   Pudding Lady's recipe book
Platina.   Don Honesta Voluptate
Powell, J.   Complete book cookery . . .
Powell, M.L.   Eating for perfect health
Price, P.V.   Cooking with wine, spirits . . .°

Raper, E.   Receipt book
Ripperger, H.L.   Coffee cookery
_____ .   Spice cookery
Robertson, H.   Young ladies school
Rohde, E.S.   Rose recipes
Rundell, Mrs. Domestic cookery, private families
de Salis, Mrs. Housewife's referee
Sanderson, J.M.   Complete book
Senn, C.H.   Cookery for invalids . . .
Simon, A.L.   Madeira: wine, cakes, sauce
Smedley, J. and J.   Hangover cook book
Smith, J.H. et al.   Famous old recipes
Smith, J.   Vegetable cookery
Steel, F.A. and G. Gardiner.   Compl. Indian housekeeper and cook
Stegner, M.   Electric blender recipes
Suzanne, A.   La Cuisine Anglaise . . .

Taylor, E.   Lady's, housewife's and cook aid
Taylor, G.H.   Treasury of wine and wine cookery
Taylor Wine Co.   Wines for everyday enjoyment
Tolson, B. and E. McCaig.   Beer cookbook
Trahey, J. and D. Pierce.   Son of the Martini cookbook

Van Dyke, M.   Cooking with wine
Vickery, H.C.   Use of beer in foods
Victoria Wine Co.   Here's how. Recipes, good cheer

Wachtmeister, C. and K.B. Davis.   Pract. vegetarian
    cookery
Waldo, M.   Beer and good food
Wilcox, B. and P. Vigoureaux.   Cook it the French way
Williams, F.   Dainties for home parties
Williams, T.   Accomplished housekeeper . . .
Wine Advisory Board.   Adventures in wine cookery
_____ .   California wine cookery and drinks
_____ .   Epicurean recipes of California winemakers
_____ .   Favorite recipes of California winemakers
_____ .   Gourmet wine cooking
_____ .   Hostess book favorite wine recipes
_____ .   Wine cook book
_____ .   Wine cookery-easy way
Wood, M.   More recipes with jug of wine
_____ .   Specialty cooking with wine
_____ .   Through Europe with jug of wine
_____ .   Unusual collection recipes with a jug of wine
Wolley, H.   Queen-like closet of rich cabinet
Woman's Institute Library of cookery.   Beverages
Wyman, A.L.   Daily health menus

Yates, L.H.   Successful jam making . . .

    Anonymous
All-British cookery book
Appetizers, hors d'oeuvres, canapes . . .

Book for a cook (A)
Book of simples
Bottles and bins recipes
Brew in your stew
British Jewel or Compleat house-wife's companion

Closet for ladies and gentlemen
Compleat housewife . . .
Cook book of U.S. Navy
Cookery.   Elizabeth Craig's Household Library

Dr. Price's delicious desserts

English electric mixer book

Family Save-all.   Secondary cookery
Farmer's Wife
Five o'clock tea

Gleanings from Gloucestershire housewives
Good Eating.   2nd book wartime recipes
Good Wife's cook book

Hering's dictionary.   classical, modern cookery
Home industries (Calcutta)
Huswife's jewell (Second part)

Indian domestic economy . . .
It is smart to serve beer

London and Country cook
London complete art of cookery

Maxwell House coffee cookbook
Modern Baker, confectioner and caterer
Mrs. Beeton's All about cookery

Nelson's home comforts
New Delineator recipes
New system domestic cookery

Official hb. National Training School for cookery
One thousand household hints

Perfect cooking
Professed cook (The)

Queen's closet opened
Queen's (A) delight-or art preserving . . .

Recipes of various kinds in cooking
Receipts and relishes.   Vade mecum for epicure in
     British Isles
Richelieu Handbook.   Wine cooking recipes

Senn's War Time cooking guide
Spice Islands cook book

Table Topics

Vest Pocket pastry book

Wine and cooking
Mrs. Winslow's domestic receipt book
Woman's Institute Library of Cookery Beverages

Young housewife's daily assistant

Drinks and drinking
Abrahamson, E.M. and A.W. Pezet. Body, mind, sugar
Ackroyd, W. Hist., science drunkenness
Adams, L.D. Commonsense book of drinking
Ade, G. Old-time saloon
Ainsworth-Davis, J.R. Cooking through centuries
Allard, E. et al. Drinking and drinkers
Allen, H.W. No. 3 Saint James Street
_____ . Rum. Englishman's spirit
Amateur Brewers. Proceedings of company
Ames, R. Search after claret
Andre, G.G. Spon's encyclopedia industrial arts,
    manufactures . . .
Andrea, P. Prohibition movement
Angostura Bitters, Ltd. For home use
Anstie, F.E. Uses wines, health and disease
Anthony, N. Noble experiments
Anthony, N. and O. Soglow. Drunk's blue book
Arakelian K. Inc. Correct service Madera wines
    and brandies
Arthur, S.C. Famous New Orleans drinks
Ash, D. How identify Eng. drinking glasses
_____ . How identify Eng. silver drinking vessels
Ass'n. Amer. Railroads. Report on beverages
_____ . Beverages
Atkinson, J. Humour of drinking
Atwater, W.O. Physiological aspects liquor problem
Auken, I. Dict. scientific cocktail making

Bachchan, H. House of wine
Baines, M. What to drink
Baker, C.H. Gentlemen's companion
_____ . So. American gentlemen's companion
Baker, O. Black-jacks and leather bottels
Bangs, J.K. Coffee and repartee
Banning, K. Squire's recipes
Bayly, H.W. What we drink
Beach, F.H. 3 point 2, what goes with it
Beaumont, T. Nature, properties alcoholic drink
Bedford, J. Pewter

Bedford, John. Toby jugs
Beebe, L. Snoot if you must
_____ . Stork club bar book
Beilenson, P. Holiday drink book
Bensen, C (pseud). Anacreontics
Benstead, C.R. Hic, Haec, Hock!
Bergeron, V.J. Bartender's guide (Trader Vic)
_____ . Trader Vic's book of food and drink
Berkeley, T. We keep a pub
Beveridge, N.E. Cups of valor
Bickerdyke, J. (pseud) Curiosities of ale and beer
Birkett, E. Golden wine of old Britain
Bishop, G. The Booze Reader
Blaser, W. Japanese temples and tea houses
Blochman, L.G. Here's how!
Blumenthals Ltd. Let's have a party
Boothby, W. World's drinks and how to mix
Bowers, E.P. Alcohol, influence, mind and body
Boyle, P. Publican and spirit dealer's daily companion
Brathwait, R. Law of drinking
Breen, H. How to stop drinking
Bretzfield, H. Liquor marketing . . .
Brewers' Industrial Exhibition. Essays on malt liquor
    question
Brewster, H.P. Coffee houses and tea gardens of old
    London
Brodner, J. et al. Profitable food and beverage
    operation
Brooks, C. Tavern talk
Brooks, J. Whiskey Drips
Brooks, Johnny. My 35 years behind bars
Brown, B. Homemade hilarity
Brown, J.H. Early American beverages
Brown, R.C. Let there be beer!
Browne, C. Gun club drink book
Browne, P. Bishop of Cord and Ross. Of drinking to
    the memory of the dead
Bruun, K. Drinking behavior in small groups
Bruun, K. and R. Hauge. Drinking habits among
    Northern youth
Buck, T. But Daddy!
Burke, T. Will someone lead me to a pub?
Buring, L. Ltd. Art serving wine

Cain, A.H. Young people and drinking
Calkins, A. Opium and opium appetite . . .
Calkins, R. Substitutes for the saloon

Calvert Distillers Co.   Party encyclopedia
Camp, J.   Ocfordshire and Buckinghamshire pubs
Canada Dry Corp.   How to be a cordial host
Candler, C. H.   Asa Griggs Candler
Capper, W. B.   Licensed houses and management
Carlsberg Breweries.   Book of Carlsberg
Carpenter, W. B.   On use and abuse alcoholic liquors
Carroll, R. S.   What price alcohol?
Carson, G.   Social history bourbon
Carter, H.   Control of drink trade
Carter, J. A.   Confessions of a bartender
Cave, P. L.   Best drinking jokes
Chafetz, M. E. and H. W. Demone, Jr.   Alcoholism and
    society
Chafetz, M. E.   Liquor: servant of man
Chamberlain, A.   Speeches maintaining free discretion
    licensing justices
Charles (of Delmonicos) Punches and cocktails
Charters, J.   This must be the place!
Chase, E. L.   Waes Hael; book of toasts
Chesterton, G. K.   Wine, water, song
Chodowski, A. T.   Wine, its use and abuse: wines of the
    bible
Clarke, E.   Worship of Bacchus great delusion
Clarke, Eddie.   Shaking in the 60's
Clarke, T. E. B.   What's yours?
Clayton, D. and D. Langdon.   Wake up and die!
Clotho (pseud) Prosit; book of toasts
Cobb, I. S.   Red likker
Codman, T. L.   Was it a holiday?
Coffin, R. B.   Ale in prose and verse
Collier, J.   Cheers!
Cook, R.   Oxford night caps
Coombs, J. H.   Bar service
Cooper, R. W.   Drama of drink
Cotter, O.   Adulteration of liquors
(Cozzens, F. S.) Cozzens wine press
Craddock, H.   Savoy cocktail book
Crafts, W. F. et al.   Intoxicating drinks and drugs all
    lands and times
Crahan, M. E.   Early American inebrietatis
Crane, J. T.   Arts of intoxication
Crawley, A. E.   Dress, drinks and drums
Criticos, G.   Life story, George of Ritz
Crockett, A. S.   Old Waldorf bar days
_____ .   Old Waldorf-Astoria bar book
Crombie, M.   Infidel grape

_____ . The wassail bowl
Crosland, T.W.H. Beautiful teetotaler
Crowley, C.E. Compl. ritual conviviality . . .
Croze, A. de. What to eat and drink in France
Culver, J.R. Gentle art of drinking
Cust, Lady. Invalid's own book
Cutten, G.B. The psychology of alcoholism

Davis, J.I. Beginner's guide wine, spirits
Deighton, L. Drinks-man-ship
Depew, C.M. 100 years American commerce
De Voto, B. The hour
DeWitt, W.A. Drinking and what to do about it
Dick, W.B. Dick's book of toasts
Dodd, G. British manufacturers
_____ . Nature's gifts and how to use
Donovan, M. Cabinet encyclopedia
Doran, Dr. Table traits with something on them
Douglas, A. International hangover book
Downman, F. Not claret
Doxat, J. Booth's handbook of cocktails . . .
Drinkwater, C. How to serve wine and beer
Dugdale, J.N. How to keep healthy in tropics
Dulcken, H.W. Book of German songs
Duncan, D. Wholesome advice against use of hot liquors
Dunlop, J. Artificial drinking usages No. Britain
_____ . Philosophy artificial and compulsory
drinking usage, Great Britain, Ireland
Durfee, C.H. Should you drink?
_____ . To drink or not to drink

Edwards. H. Collection of old English customs
Ellis, A. Penny Universities
Ellis, C. Origin, nature and history of wine
Ellis, J. The wine question
Ellwanger, G.H. Meditations on gout
Elyot, T. Castle of Healthe
Emerson, E.R. Beverages, past and present
_____ . Lay thesis on Bible wines
Emerson, H. Alcohol and man
Emerson, Haven. Alcohol. Its effects on man
Entholt, H. Ratskeller in Bremen
Esquire. Drink Book

Fairburn, W.A. Man and his health: liquids
Fairchild, L. Tippler's vow
Felker, P.H. Grocers' manual

Fenton, F. Bible and wine (The).
Field, S. A. Vintage festival
Field, S. S. American drink book
Finn, T. Pub games
Fiske, J. Tobacco and alcohol
Flanders, C. R. Gourmet au Vatel
Flint, G. E. Whole truth about alcohol
Floyer, J. et al. History cold bathing . . .
de Focatiis, A. Main source alcoholism, U. S.
Forbes, P. Champagne, the wine, the land and the
    people
Ford, J. C. Man takes a drink
Foster and Ingle. Wine, what is it?
Foster, W. A. Short history cooper's company
Forsyth, J. S. Farmer, maltster, distiller
Fothergill, J. Confessions of Innkeeper
Foughner, S. Along the wine trail
Fowler, N. C. Stories and toasts, after dinner
Francis, G. R. Old English drinking glasses
Franklin, F. What prohibition has done Amer.
Free, J. L. Just one more
Freeland, J. M. Australian pub
French, R. V. History of toasting
_____ . 19 centuries drink in England
Froedtert Malt Corp. Motivation research beer
    consuming habits
Funk, W. If you drink
Furnas, J. C. Late demon rum

(Gallobeligicus) (pseud). Wine, Beere, Ale . . .
Gay, J. Wine. A poem
Gayre, G. R. Wassail! in mazers of mead
Gennery-Taylor, Mrs. Easy made wine country drinks
Gervinus, G. G. Art of drinking
Gibbs, E. Have a drink!
Gilbey, W. and A. Ltd. The Compleat Imbiber
Gillespie, J. L. The drinking driving man's diary
Gilmour, A. Our drinks, or nature fermented liquors . . .
_____ . Sacramental wines
Ginrum Alpha Co. Legend liquors, wines . . .
Girton, T. Come landlord!
Glasgow and District Licensed Trade Defense Ass'n.
    Summary of the Scottish licensing laws
Godwin, G. Hansons of Eastcheap
Gordon, J. Art of cooking with roses
Gorham, M. Back to the local
_____ . The local

Henshaw, D. Brush your teeth with wine
Herrick, C.T. Modern domestic science
_____. Consolidated Library mod. cooking
Herter, R.B. Back to work
Heywood, T. Philocathonista or Drunkard opened
Hindley, C. True hist. Tom and Jerry
Hirsh, Joseph. Problem drinker (The)
Hirshfield, A. Manhattan oases
Hitchcock, E. Essay on alcoholic and narcotic substances
Hocker, E.C. Alcoholic beverage encyclopedia
Holbrook, M.L. Eating for strength
Holding, E.M. What shall we drink?
Hooton, C.R. What shall we say about alcohol?
Hope, W.H. On English medieval drinking bowls
Horne, E. What the butler winked at
Horsley, V. and M.D. Sturge. Alcohol and human body
Horton, D. Functions alcohol primitive societies
Hospitality Guild. Catalog 500 books on foods, and
    beverages
Howitt, W. Student-life of Germany
Huie, J. Abridgement excise duties
Hume, R. Party food and drink
Hunt, E.M. Alcohol; as a food and medicine
Hunt, P. Eating and drinking
Hunt, R. Saloon in the home
Hutchinson, W.G. Songs of the vine

Jackson, H. Essay on bread, vile practices
    adulterations wines . . .
_____. Essay British isinglass, hints improvement
    malting, brewing . . .
Jacob, H.E. Coffee; epic of a commodity
_____. Saga of coffee
James, W. Antipasto
_____. Fear of wine
_____. Gadding vine
_____. Nuts on wine
Jarvis, D.C. Arthritis and folk medicine
Jelf, E.A. and C.J.B. Hurst. Law of innkeepers
Jellinek, E.M. Alcohol addiction and chronic alcoholism
Jessey, H. Lord's loud call to England, sin of drinking
    health
"Jimmy" late of Ciro's. Cocktails
Joelson, A. Memoirs of Kohler of K.W.V.
Johns, B. Ombibulous Mr. Mencken
Johnson, E. Drinks from drugs
Jones, H.W. What will you take to drink?

Jones, H. Alcoholic addiction
Juniper, W. Law of drinking
_____ . Merry, ingenius diverting work or true
    drunkard's delight

Karpman, B. The alcoholic woman
Kearney, P.W. Toasts and anecdotes
Kelynack, T.N. and W. Kirkby. Arsenical poisoning in
    beer drinkers
Kelynack, T.N. Drink problem of today
Kerr, N. Inebriety or Narcomania
Kerr, N.S. Wines of the Bible
King, A.R. Psychology of drunkenness
Kirby, J. Essays and poems (Brewing)
Kirton, J.W. Intoxicating drinks, hist.
Kitchener, W. Art of invigorating and prolonging life . . .
Knaggs, H.W. Healthy life beverage bk.
Koken, J.M. Here's to it. (Toasts)
Koren, J. Economic aspects liquor problem
Krout, J.A. Origin of prohibition

Landauer, B.C. Some alcoholic Americana
Langmead, F. and T.C. Hunt. Review effects of
    alcohol on man
Lane, J. Gin and bitters
Lariar, L. You've got me on the rocks
Laureat, J.S. Tunning of Elynour Rumming
Laver, James. Drinking in England
Laver, J. Victorian Vista
Law, E. King Henry VIII's newe wyne celler
Lawlor, C.F. Mixicologist
Lawlor, P. Froth-Blower's manual
_____ . Wholesale wine, spirit trade
Layton, T.A. Year at the Peacock
Leacock, S. Wet wit and dry humor
Leake, C. and M. Silverman. Alcoholic beverages in
    clinical medicine
Lemp, Wm. J. Brewing Co. Toasts
Lettsom, J.C. Hist. some effects hard drinking
Levy, H. Drink, economic and social study
Lewis, V.B. Complete buffet guide
Licensed Beverage Industries. ABC's of alcoholic
    beverages
Lindemann, E.H. Pract. guide and receipt book
Lindinger, F. Manual for the liquor trade
Lipton, T. Autobiography
Lolli, G. Alcohol in Italian culture

Marquis, D.   Her foot is on the brass rail
_____ . Old soak and Hail and Farewell
_____ . Old soak's hist. of the world
Martyn, C.   Foods and culinary utensils of the ancients
Mass-Observation.   The pub and the people
Maurice, A.B.   How they draw prohibition
Maynard, T.   Tankard of ale
Mendelsohn, O.A.   Dictionary of drink and drinking
_____ . Drinking with Pepys
_____ . The earnest drinker
_____ . Earnest drinker's digest
Meriton, G.   In praise Yorkshire ale
Merry, T.   Where to drink? (Irish bars)
Mew, J. and J. Ashton.   Drinks of the world
Middleton, S.   Dining, wining and dancing, N.Y.
Mitchell, S.W.   A Madeira party
Mlle. Mixer, (pseud.) Two hundred toasts.
Monahan, M.   Dry America
_____ . Text-bk. true temperance
Monroe, M.E. and J. Stewart.   Alcohol education for
    the layman
Monson-Fitzjohn, G.J.   Drinking vessels of bygone days
Morel, J.J.   Progressive catering
Morewood, S.   Essay on inventions, customs, ancient and
    modern, inebriating liquors
_____ . Philosophical and statistical hist. inventions
    and customs
Morgan, D.   Compl. bartender's joke book
Mortlock, G.   The flowing bowl
Mott, E.S.   The flowing bowl
Mowat, J.   Anthology of wine
Mulqueen, J.T. (Ed.)   Revenue Review (Periodical)
Murray, J.A.   Report by Thomas Tucker on revenues
    of excise and customs, Scotland
Murray, M.   Drink and the war

Nash, H.   Alcohol and caffeine
Nash, J.   Brewer's license, its history
_____ . Facts, falacies regard brewer's license tax
National Distiller Products Corp.   Host's hbk.
National Food, Beverage Exhibition.   Official Catalog
National Trade Development Ass'n.   Innkeeping
Nesbit, W.D.   After dinner speeches
Nettleton, J.A.   Adulteration, beer, by publicans
Newcombe, F.N.   Licensing question, its history
Newman, H.W.   Acute alcoholic intoxication
Newton, W. Teetotalism

Van Niekerk, J.A.H. Survey control alcoholic beverages
    other countries
Nisbet, W. Pract. treat. on diet
Noling, A.W. Hist. Hurty-Peck and Company
Noolas, R. Merry-go-down
North, S. So red the nose

Oaks, L.W. Medical aspects Latter-Day saint word of
    wisdom
Obsopaeo, V. De arte bibendi
Odell, G.T. Beverages. Manual mixing
Other, A.N. Pick-me-up!

Packer, J. Valley of the vines
Parker, H. Vintner's answer scandulous pamphl.
Parker, R.H. In praise of wine
Partch, V. and W. Mc Intyre. VIP tosses party
Partridge, B. History of orgies
Patrick, C.H. Alcohol, culture and society
Patrick, G.T.W. Psychology of relaxation
Patton, W. Laws of fermentation
Paul, E. and L. Quintanilla. Intoxication made easy
Payne, B. Story of Bacchus . . .
Peabody, R.R. Commonsense of drinking
Pearl, R. Alcohol and longevity
Peattie, D.C. Cargoes and harvests
Peddie, A. Hotel, innkeeper, vintner . . .
Peeke, H.L. Americana ebrietatis . . .
Pellegrini, A.M. Wine and the good life
Penzer, N.M. Book of wine label
Peter, Lord Bishop, Cork and Rosse. Discourse
    on drinking healths
Peterson, J. Intoxicating liquor licensing
Petulengro, Gipsy. Romany remedies, recipes
Phelps, I. Your health!
Pickett, D. Cyclopedia of temperance
_____ . Temperance and the changing liquor
    situation.
Pierce, S.S. Co. The Epicure
Pittman, D.J. and C.R. Snyder. Society, culture and
    drinking patterns
Plaisted, A.H. Ale feasts and country taverns
Portman, H. Harry's ABC mixing cocktails
Powell, A.M. The beer question
Pratt, E.A. The licensed trade
Prescott, H.P. Strong drink and tobacco smoke
Prince, W. Treat. on the vine

Proskauer, J.J.   Fun at cocktail time
_____ . What'll you have?
Prynne, W.   Healthes: sicknesse

Quarterly Journal of Studies on alcohol.   Cross cultural
    studies on alcohol

Ramsay, W.   Book of toasts
Ramsey, E.B.   Old Scottish conviviality
Rathbone, W. and E.L. Fanshowe.   Liquor legislation
    in U.S. and Canada
Ray, C. (Ed.)   The compleat imbiber (Various)
_____ . Gourmet's companion
Rea, F.B.   Alcoholism, its psychology, cure
Reach, A.B. Claret and olives, Garonne to Rhone
Reade, A.A.   Study and stimulants or the use of
    intoxicants and narcotics in relation to intellectual life?
Reinhart, C.   120 years of life . . .
Reinhardt, C.N.   "Cherrio"
Reynolds, B.   A cocktail Continentale
Rhoads, W.M. Poker.   Smoke and other things
_____ . Toasts
Rice, W. and F.   Toasts and tipple
Richardson, B.W.   Temperance lesson book
Riddell, P.   I was an alcoholic
Rivers, W.   Influence of alcohol
Roberts, G.E.   Cups and their customs
Robinson, J. Great evil of health drinking
Rodgers, H.A.   Toasts and cocktails
Roe, C. and J. Schwenck.   Home bartender's guide and
    song book.
Rogers, C.   Full and By (Praise of drinking)
Rogers, R.V. Jr.   Drinks, drinkers, drinking
Root, J.   Horrors of delerium tremens
Rosenthal, E.   Tankards and traditions
Roueche, B.   Alcohol.   Its history . . .
Roundell, J.A.E.   The still-room
Routh, J.   The Good Cuppa Guide
Ruppert, J.   Brewery.   Beer in the home

Sabine, H.   Complete cellarman . . .
Sadler, E. and C.R.L. Fletcher.   Wine ghosts of
    Bremen
Sadoun, R. et al.   Drinking in French culture
St. Sure, S.   Bohemian Life
(Sallengre, A.H. de) Ebrietatas enconium.   The praise
    of drunkenness

Saltus, F.S.   Flasks and flagons
Samson, G.W.   Divine law as to wines
Samuelson, J.   Drink, past, present, probable future
Samuelson, J.   History of drink
Sandeman, F.   History of Cognac, brandy
Sandford, W.   Remarks medicinal effects wine and spirits
Sanitas (pseud).   What to drink
Sargent, J.W.   Toasts for the times
Scarisbrick, J.   Spirit manual, historical and technical
Schoppfer, T.   Philosophy of beer
Scottish Licensed Trade Ass'n.   Handbook.   1968-1969
Seagram-Distillers Company.   Seagram's weekend bar . . .
Seagram, J.E. and Co.   Welcome to house of Seagram
Sedgwick, J.   New treat. on liquors . . .
Seldes, G.V.   Future of drinking
Seltman, C.T.   Wine in ancient world
Serjeant, R.   Man may drink
Scrivener, M.   Treat. against drunkenness
Shane Na Gael.   Irish toasts
Shannon, R.   MD.   Practical treatise on brewing, distilling
      and rectification
Shaw, P.   Juice of grape or wine preferable to water
Shaw, T.G.   Wine trade and its history
Shay, F.   Drawn from the wood
_____ .   More pious friends . . .
_____ .   My pious friends and drunken companions
Short, T.   Rational discourse on inward uses of water
Short, T.   View of prejudice arising from imposition tax on
      ale, beer . . .
Siebel, J.E. II.   Beer and health
Simmonds, P.L.   Popular beverages of various countries
Simon, A.L.   Bottlescrew days
_____ .   Concise encyclo. gastronomy
_____ .   Elixir of youth
_____ .   Wine maketh glad the heart . . .
Sinclair, J.   Code of health and longevity
Sinclair, U.   Cup of fury
Sinclair, W.J.   Beverages, water, tea . . .
Smith, A.   Bowl of punch
Smith, B.   Prohibition and the bible
Smith, W.H. and F.C. Helwig.   Liquor, servant of man
Snowden, P.   Socialism and drink question
Snyder, C.R.   Alcohol and the jews
Solis, V.   Drinking cups, ewers, vases . . .
Somerville, E.O.   In the vine country
Southern Comfort Corp.   Art of gracious tippling since
      800 B C

Spalding, W. B. and J. R. Montague. Alcohol and human affairs

Spencer, E. The flowing bowl (Mott)

Stamp, Lord. National Capital (Alcohol)

Stansfield and Co. How good beer is served

Starling, E. H. Action of alcohol on man

Steel, A. Custom of the room, early wine bks. of Christ's College

Steiner, P. Bottoms Up!

Stevenson, J. Advice, medical and practical

Stewart, D. A. The drinking patterns

Stewart, G. R. American ways of life

Stouffer's Restaurants. Nectars . . .

Strauss, R. and S. D. Bacon. Drinking in college

Street, J. L. Where Paris dines

Stuart, G. R. Saloon under searchlight

Sullivan, W. C. Alcoholism

Sutherland, D. Raise your glasses. A lighthearted history of drinking

Swan, F. W. Drink and service manual

Switzer, M. Who was the first toper?

Symonds, J. A. Wine, women, song

T., H. Dreadful character of drink

Takala, M. et al. Effects of distilled and brewed beverages

Taussig, C. W. Rum, Romance, Rebellion

Taylor, B. L. and W. C. Gibson. Log of water wagon

Taylor, J. Drinks and welcome

Taylor Wine Co. Wines everyday enjoyment

Tennent, J. E. Wine, its use and taxation

Terrington, W. Cooling cups and dainty drinks

Thomann, G. Effects of beer on those who make and drink it.

_____. Liquor laws of U. S.

_____. Real and imaginery effects of intemperance

Thompson, V. Drink

_____. Drink and be sober

Thompson, W. Control liquor-Sweden

Thorne, G. Great acceptance (Charrington)

Three Feathers Distillers, Inc. Life of the party

Tickner, J. Tickner's Pub

Tilley, F. Teapots and tea

Titterton, W. R. Drinking songs . . .

Tobe, J. H. How to make your own wines . . .

Tolles, D. Banquet libations of the Greeks

Tovey, C. Wit, wisdom and morals
Townsend, W.H. Lincoln and liquor
Trade Recipes. 100 secret, summer, winter
Travers, G.W. Century brewing Hudson ales
Tripp, C.H. Licensing act 1902
Tubbs, D.B. Kent pubs
Tucker, J. Impartial inquiry low priced spirits
Turnbull, G.H. Fruit of the vine
Turnbull, W.W. Law and liquor
Turner, F.G. Negligence with food, drinks . . .

United Kingdom Bartender's Guild. UKBG. Guide to drinks
United States Brewers' Ass'n. History brewing
United Brewers Industrial Foundation. American beer
    and ale

Verdier, P. History of wine . . .
Vernon, H.M. The alcohol problem
Voegele, M.C. and G.H. Wooley. Drink dictionary
de Voto, B. The hour

W. (F.) Warme beers, a treatise
Wagner, F. Das getrankebuch
Walker, G. Publican's and cellerman's guide
Walker, J. and Son. Around the world
Wallerstein, R.S. Hospital treatment of alcoholism
Ward, R. Fallacies of teetotalism
Washburne, C. Primitive drinking
Wassermann, A. Schenley Library bibliography
Water Drinker (A). Some enquiries effects, liquors
Watson, R. Merry gentlemen
Webb, S. and E. Hist. liquor licensing
Weed, R.A. Silver wine labels
Weeks, C.C. Alcohol and human life
Wheatley, D. Seven ages Justerini's
Wheeler, C.V. Life, letters, H.W. Thomas, mixologist
Whistling Commercial (The) The ROAD
Whitaker, A. Bacchus behave!
Whitbread and Co. The Brittania Inn
Whitbread Library. Inn crafts, furnishings
_____ . Inns of sport No. 7
_____ . Your club No. 9
Whitmore, O.B. Bible wines vs saloonkeepers' bible
Whitworth, E.W. Wine labels
Wilcox, J.K. List English, French, German periodical,
    brewing . . .

Wiley, H.W. Beverages and their adulteration
Wilkinson, R. and R. Frisby. They're open!
Williams, E.E. New public house
Williams, H.S. Alcohol. How effects individual
Williams, L. Alcoholism. A manual for students
_____ . Tomorrow will be sober
Williams, R.L. What, when, where, how drink
Williamson, G.C. Everybody's bk. collecting
Willison, G.F. Saints and strangers
Willouby, M.F. Rum war at sea
Wilson, A.M. Wines of the bible
Wilson, R. House of Sanderson
Wines, F.H. and J. Koren. Liquor problem in its
    legislative aspects
Wishart, J. Home and foreign alcoholic beverages
Wister, O. Watch your thirst
Wolfe, U. Exposition prevalent impositions and adulterations
    by dealers
_____ . Imposter unmasked . . .
Wood, A.D. Truth and wine interest
Woolen, W.W. and W.W. Thornton. Intoxicating liquors
Woon, B. When cocktail time in Cuba
Workers Educational Ass'n. Hatfield and people

Yorke-Davis, N.E. Wine and health
Youman's E.L. Alcohol and constitution man
Young, T. England's bane, description of drunkenesse

        Anonymous
Adulteration, food, drink, drugs
Al-Anon Family Groups, problem drinkers
Alcohol: its action on human organism
Alcoholism. Supervisory guide
Amateur Brewers - proceedings
Ancient Order of Froth Blowers
Antidote against drunkenness

Beer, its importance as a beverage and an industry
Beer songs (Famous)
Beeread (The) or progress of drink
Book of the cheese being traits and stories of "Ye Olde
    Cheshire Cheese)
Brasenose Ale. Collection of verses
Breweries and Texas politics
Brewer's, distiller's and licensed victualler's diary 1912

Cider cellar songster

Collection statutes relating excise on beer
Compleat Imbiber. (Various)

Deipnosphists or banquet learned Atheneasus

Economic aspects liquor problem
England's happiness improved - English wines . . .
Esquire's Handbk. for hosts

Famous old-time songs
For the best and most practicable plan for making the
    eighteenth amendment effective Durant prize contest

Glass of grog
Good and cheap beer for millions . . .

Harper's manual
History of "Dirty Dick"
Home-made wines, beers, liqueurs, cordial . . .
House of Dewar

Indian economy and receipt book
Influence of wholesome drink°
Internal Revenue manual

Life and letters of Henry William Thomas, mixologist
Liquor dealer's silent partner

Modern Baker, Confectioner, Caterer

National Food and Beverage Exhibition. Official
    Catalogue 1933

Off the shelf. (Brown and Pank)
Old English drinking songs

Party Book, Inc.
Praise of the gout

Quarterly Journal Studies on Alcohol

Red wine and blue water
Rhodesian Bottle, Store and Hotel Review
The ROAD. Leaves from sketch-bk. commercial traveller

Satyr against wine
Songs of our grandfathers

Souvenir album Franco-British Exhibition
Standard Encyclopedia alcohol problem
Story of the crown cork

Teetotalism and laws against liquor trade
Toasts and cocktails
Traits and stories of Ye Olde Cheshire Cheese
True relation vintners yield to imposition upon wines
Tuenda Bono Valetudine De
Twining's in three centuries

Vade-mecum (A) for Malt-worms
Vegetable substances used by man

Wehman Bros. Bartenders' Guide
Wine and spirit merchant
Wine Trade loan exhibition drinking vessels
Wines, beer, liquors. How to make at home
Wine and spirit adulterators unmasked
Wing's Brewers handbook of U.S. and Canada
Whitbreads Brewery 1740-1920
Woman's Institute Library Cookery-Beverages
_____ . Fruit and fruit desserts
World's book of wines, spirits and liquors

Flavors, odors, colors
Abbott Laboratories. Brominated oils
_____ . Sucaryl sweetened beverages
Airkem, Inc. Odors and sense of smell
Alexander, R.G. Plain plantain
Amer. Spice Trade Ass'n. History of spices
_____ . How to use spices
_____ . Manual of spices
_____ . Spices; what they are
_____ . Treasury of spices
Amoy Canning Co. Story of ginger
Arctander, S. Perfume and natural flavoring materials
_____ · Perfume and flavor chemicals

B.J.W. "Economic formulae. Beverage flavors
Bailey, E.H.S. Source, chemistry, use, food products
Beach and Clarridge. Concentrated extracts . . .
Belanger, E.J. Drug and specialty formulas
Bennett, H. Practical emulsions
Berghausen, E. Chem. Co. Flavor literature
Berliner, J.J. and Staff. Encyclopedia of alcoholic formulas

_____ . Syrup formulas
_____ . Survey on beverages
Berman, L.   Food and character
Bienfang, R.   The subtle sense
Blumenthal, S.   Food manufacturing
Brannt, W.T.   Pract. treat. animal, vegetable fats and
    oils
British Standards Institution.   Specs. Caramel
Bruce, E.M.   Detection common food adulterants
Burnett, J. and Co.   Dainty and artistic desserts
Bush, W.J. and Co.   Price list essential oils
Camp, C.D.   Laboratories.   Book of formulas . . .
Campbell Soup Co.   Proceedings Flavor Chemistry
    Symposium 1961
Chiris, Antoine Co.   Wholesale price list
Clair, C.   Of herbs and spices
Clarke, A.   Flavouring materials
Clarke, R.   Food colours
Clarkson, R.E.   Herbs, their culture and uses
Colburne, R.S.   Synthetic aromatics . . .
Colin, J.   Herbs and spices, health and beauty
Crocker, E.C.   Flavor

Dodge and Olcott Co.   Bases for summer drinks
_____ . Reference bk. and catalog . flavors
_____ . Story unique institution
_____ . Vanilla extracts . . .
Dupont, E.T.   Romance of flowers
Dussauce, H.   Treat. on coloring matters

Finnemore, H.   Essential oils
Firmenich and Cie.   Aromatic chemicals
Fisk, W.W.   Book of ice cream
Fogelsonger, M.L.   Secrets liquor merchant
Fox, H.M.   Gardening with herbs
Frandsen, J.H. and E.A. Markham.   Mfg. ice creams . . .
Fritzsche Bros. Catalogue, essential oils
_____ . Guide to flavoring ingredients
_____ . Pharmaceutical flavor guide
_____ . Pictorial record of present
_____ . Price list 1945
_____ . Wholesale price list 1940
Fujita, Y.   Fundamental studies essential oils

Gazan, M.H.   Flavours and essences
Gibbs, W.M.   Spices and how to know them

Gildemeister, E. and Fr. Hoffman. Volatile oils
Gill, J.T. Pract. confectioner
_____ . Compl. pract. confectioner
Gillett, E.W. Selling price list
Givaudan-Delawanna Inc. Givaudan Index
Grieve, M. Culinary herbs and condiments
deGroote, M. Mfg. emulsion flavors
Guenther, E. Essential oils
_____ . Lemon oil production

Hance Bros. and White. Pure fruit juices
Harris, F.L. Cooking with foreign flavor
_____ . Flavor's the thing
Harrop, J. Monograph flavoring extracts
Hay, W. Ltd. Story of ginger
Heine and Co. Perfumers raw materials
Hemphill, R. Fragrance and flavor
Hewitt, J.T. Synthetic colouring matter
Hires, C.E. Recipes mfg. flavoring extracts
Hollingsworth, H.L. and A. T. Poffenberger. Sense of
    taste
Hollingsworth, J. Modern extracter
Hopkins, A.A. Home made beverages . . .
Howe, S.E. In quest of spices

Idris, I.H.W. Notes on essential oils
India Council Scientific and Industrial Research. Essential
    oils and aromatic chemicals
von Isokovics, A. Modern aromatic chemicals

Jacobs, M.B. Synthetic food adjuncts
Jank, J.K. Spices, their botanical origin
Jaques, H.E. How to know economic plants
Judd, D.B. Colorimetry

Kesterson, J.W. and O.R. Mc Duff. Florida citrus oils
Kessler, E.J. Pract. flavoring extract maker
Knight, R.P. Analytical inquiry into the principles of
    taste

Lesparre, J.N. Herbs, spices . . .
Leyel, C.F. Elixirs of life
_____ . Herbal delights
_____ . Magic of herbs
Lieber, H. Use of coal tar colors
Linnaeus, C. Voyages . . . to Levant

Little, A.D. Inc. Flavor research, food acceptance
Lloyd, J.U. Elixirs and flavoring extracts
Loughlin, J.E. Rainbows in deserts (colors)
Lovell, R. Compleat herbal
Lucas, E.W. and H.B. Stevens. Bk. of receipts
Lunge, George. Treatise on the distillation of coal-tar
    and ammoniacal liquor . . .

(M., J.B.) Spices: Jamaica pepper to Zedoary
Mc Cormick and Co. Spices, their nature and the
    vanilla bean
_____ . Story of extracts
Mc Donough, E.G. Investigations in auto-oxidation
    aldehydes . . .
McKenzie, D. Aromatics and the soul
MacKinney, G. and A.C. Little. Color of foods
McNair, J.B. Spices and condiments
Mairet, E. Book vegetable dyes
Mariani and Co. Coca erythroxylon. Its uses in the
    treatment of disease
Martin, G. Perfumes, essential oils . . .
Menon, A.K. Indian essential oils
Merory, J. Food flavorings . . .
Mitchell, C.A. Oils, animal, vegetable, essential and
    mineral
Moncrieff, R.W. Chemical senses
_____ . Odour preferences
Morris, G.S. Bottlers' formulary
Muller, A. Internationsler Riechstoff-Kodex

Nat'l Analine and Chem. Co. National Certified food
    colors
deNavarre, M.G. Emulsions
Neergaard, W. Formula bk. elixirs, syrups . . .
Nelson, J.H. Druggist's handbk. private formulas
Noling, A.W. Aromatic chemicals
_____ . Beverage bases
_____ . Lemon. Notes
_____ . Soda water flavors

O'Connor, J.B. Vanilla, cult. in India

Parry, E.J. Chemistry essential oils . . .
Parry, J.W. Spice handbook
Peattie, D.C. Cargoes and harvests
Perkin, A.G. and A.E. Everest. Natural organic
    colouring matters

Pfizer, Chas. and Co.   Food preservatives

QM Food and Container Institute.   Chemistry natural food
     flavors
     _____ . Flavors, beverages and condiments

Redgrove, H. S.   Spices and condiments
Renner, H. D.   Origin of food habits
Ridley, H. N.   Spices
Romanne-James, C.   Herb-lore for housewives

Sawer, J. C.   Odorographia.   Hist. raw materials
Sawyer, G. F.   Bottlers' extracts: how to make
Schimmel and Co.   Annual report essential oils
     _____ . Schimmel Briefs
Schoengold, M. D.   Encyclopedia of substitutes
Schultz, A. W. et al.   Symposium on food
Scoville, W. L.   Extracts and perfumes
Seguin, A. C. Odoriferous formulary
Sievers, A. F.   Methods extracting volatile oils from plant
     materials
Sinclair, R.   Essential oils
Sluys Boechout (N. V.) Vade-mecum flavours, perfume
     oils . . .
Snell, F. D. Inc.   Report Aromanilla Co.
Standard Bottling and Extract Co.   Soda Water Flavors
Sulz, C. H.   Sulz's Compendium of flavoring

Taylor, N.   Cinchona in Java
     _____ . Color in garden
     _____ . Fragrance in garden
Teetgen, A. B.   Profitable herb-growing
Thurston, A.   Pharmaceutical and food analysis
Thurston and Braidich.   Water soluble . . . gums
Tidbury, G. E.   The clove tree
Tucker, S. A.   Pract. and scientific treat. on mfg.--
     extracts . . .
Tweed, E. J.   Economics of brewing

U. S. Industrial Chemical Co.   Ethyl alcohol handbook

Verrill, A. H.   Isles of spice and palm

Walter, E.   Manual for essence industry
Wandle, J. T.   Extracts and beverages
Warner-Jenkinson Mfg. Co.   Certified food colors

Weyl, T. Coal tar colors
Wilder, L. B. Fragrant path
Williams, Ltd. Edible colors

Yamasaki, S. Knowledge of flavor

Zerr, G. and R. Rubencamp. Treat colour mfg.

Anonymous
Chemist and druggist diary and yearbook, 1938

"Economic" Formulae. Beverage flavor formulas
Essential oil forum

Flavors and spices and flavor charerization
Formula book in manuscript form

Guide to art of manufacture perfumes

Mc Monagle and Rogers' Cooking Recipes. (Flavorings).
Morrissey, C. T. and Co. Catalogue. Preparations for
    making delicious drinks

Price lists and catalogues (England)

Syrups, extracts and flavorings . . .

Trace ingredients and influence on drinks

Food
Accum, F. Treat. adulteration food
Allen, I. C. B. Book of sugar substitutes
Amer. Can Co. Canned Food Manual
_____ . Canned food reference manual
_____ . Manual for institutional canning
Amer. Medical Ass'n. Accepted foods . . .
Amer. Sugar Refining Co. Annual reports
Amoy Canning Co. Story of Ginger
Anderson, O.E. Jr. Health of a nation
Andrea, A. L. Home bottling
_____ . Home canning, drying . . .
Appert, M. Art of preserving . . .
Arbuthnot, J. Essay concerning nature aliments
Ass'n. Food Distributors. Foods of the world

565

Bailey, E.H.S.   Food products, source . . .
Baker, E.A. and D.J. Fosdick.   Bibliography of food
Barber, C.A.   Tropical Agri.   Research in the Empire
Battershall, J.P.   Food adulteration . . .
Baumgartner, J.G. and A.C. Hersom.   Canned foods
Beck, B.F.   Honey and health
Bell, J.   Chemistry of foods
Bitting, A.W.   Appertizing, art of canning
Blumenthal, S.   Food manufacturing
_____ .   Food products
Blyth, A.W.   Analysis of foods
_____ .   Foods: composition and analysis
Boots Pure Drug Co. Saccharin
Bower, J.A.   Detecting food adulteration
Bradley, A.V.   Tables of food values
Brannt, W.T.   Animal and vegetable fats, oils
Bridges, M.A.   Food and beverage analysis
British Dairy Farmer's Ass'n.   Show catalogue
Brooks, R.O.   Critical studies, legal chemistry of foods
Brown, O.P.   Complete herbalist
Browne, W.A. and C.W. Browne.   Get back to nature
Bruce, E.M.   Detection common food adulterants
Bryan, A.H.   Maple-sap syrup; its mfg . . .
Burnett, J. Co.   About vanilla

Campbell, C.H.   C--bk. Manual on canning
_____ .   C--bk.   Canning, preserving . . .
Chatfield, C. and G. Adams.   Proximate composition
      American food materials
Chenoweth, W.W.   Food preservation
_____ .   How to preserve food
Church, A.H.   Food.   Brief account of source
Clark, Geo. and Co.   Technical Sugar data
Commissioner of Patents, Abridgements of specifications,
      preservation food . . .
Connecticut Agri. Exper. Sta.   57th report on food products
Cox, H.E.   Chemical analysis of foods
Cox, H.E. and D. Pearson.   Chem. analysis foods
Crookes, W.   On mfg. beet-root sugar . . .
Cussler, M. and M.L. DeGive.   'Twixt cup and lip

Davis, A.   Let's eat right to keep fit
Desrosier, N.W.   Technology of food preservation
Dickinson, D. and P. Goose.   Laboratory inspection canned
      and bottled foods
Dodge and Olcott.   Changing world of food

Dodoens, R.   A nievve herball
Dowd, M. T. and J. D. Jameson.   Food, composition . . .
Duckwall, E. W.   Canning, preserving . . .

Ellis, W.   The practical farmer
Elsdon, G. D.   Edible fats and oils

Fairrie, G.   Sugar
Fielding, C.   Food
Fiene, F. and S. Blumenthal.   Handbook food mfg.
Filby, F.   Hist. food adulteration
Fink, H. T.   Food and flavor
Folin, O.   Preservatives and other chemicals
Food Industries.   Successful quality control
Fowler, G.   How to bottle

Gardner, W. H.   Food acidulents
deGiacomi, R.   Food directory 1954
Gottlieb, D. and P. H. Rossi.   Bibliography . . .
    food and food habit research
Gould, W. A.   Quality control clinic
Grange, C.   Compl. bk. home food preserving
Grant, E. B.   Beet-root sugar
Gray, G. V.   Every step in canning
Greenish, H. G.   Microscopical examination of food and
    drugs

Haig, A.   Diet and food
Hassall, A. H.   Adulterations detected
_____ .   Food and its adulterations
Hastings, M.   Physical culture food directory
Hausner, A.   Mfg. preserved foods . . .
Hedrick, U. P.   Hist. agriculture State of N. Y.
Henderson, M. F.   Diet for the sick
Hill, J. M.   Canning, preserving . . .
Hinton, C. L.   Fruit pectins . . .
Hoffman, F.   Treat. nature aliments or foods
Hoffman, J. W.   Cyclopedia foods, condiments, beverage
Honig, P.   Principles of sugar technology
Hoynak, P. X. and G. M. Hollenback.   This is liquid sugar
Hughes, M. B.   Everywoman's canning book
Hughes, O.   Introductory foods
Hugill, J. A. C.   Sugar

Jackson, H.   Essay on bread, --practices of adulterating
    wines . . .
Jacobs, M. B.   Chemical analysis food . . .

Jaques, H.E. How to know economic plants
Jensen, L.B. Man's foods
Jones, T. Henry Tate 1819-1899 (Sugar)
Justin, M.M. et al. Foods

Kahn, A.R. Sugar. Popular treatise
Kallett, A. and F.J. Schlink. 100,000,000 guinea pigs
Keegan, L.M. Food values calculating diets
Kenwood, H.R. Public health laboratory work
Kirby, M. and E. Aunt Martha's corner cupboard
Kirshenbauer, H.G. Fats and oils
Knaggs, H.V. Romance of sugar

Lane-Clayton, J.E. Milk and its hygenic relations
Leffman, H. and W. Beam. Select methods food analysis
Lemery, M.L. Treat. all sorts of foods
Lethby, H. On food, its varieties . . .
Leyel, C.F. Magic of herbs
Linnaeus, C. Voyages . . . in Levant
Liverseege, J.F. Adulteration and analysis of food and
    drugs
Locke, E.A. Food values
von Loesecke, H.W. Drying and dehydration foods
_____. Outlines of food technology
Longwood, W. Poisons in your food
Lowe, B. Experimental cookery
Lyle, O. Technology sugar refinery workers

McCance, R.A. and E.M. Widdowson. Chemical
    composition of foods
Mackenzie, J.E. Sugars and simple derivatives
Manley, R.O.B. Honey production in Brit. Isles
Mariani, A. Coca and its therapeutic application
Marshall, J. Elbridge A. Stuart (Carnation)
Martindale, W. Coca and cocaine
May, E.C. The canning clan
Merrill, A.L. and B.K. Watt. Energy value foods
Ministry of food. Advertising, labelling and composition
    of food
Mitchell, C.A. Edible oils and fats
_____. Oils, animal, vegetable, essential mineral
_____. Vinegar: its mfg and examination
Mitchell, J. Treat. on falsifications of food
Mittelstaedt, O. Technical calculations for sugar works
Monier-Williams, G.W. Trace elements in food
Moor, C.G. and W. Partridge. Aids to analysis of food
    and drugs

568

Morgan, A. F. and I. S. Hall.   Experimental food study
Morris, T.   Principles of food preservation
Mortimer, W. G.   Peru.   History of Coca
Mottram, V. H. and G. Graham.   Hutchison's food and
    principles of diabetics

Neil, M. H.   Canning, preserving, pickling
Newlands, J. A. R. and B. E. R.   Sugar, handbook for
    planters and refiners
Nicholls, J. R.   Aids to analysis food and drugs

Olcott, H. S.   Sorgo and impee.   The Chinese and African
    sugar canes
Olsen, J. C.   Pure foods, their adulteration

Parker, M. E. et al.   Elements in food engineering
Parker, M. E.   Food plant sanitation
Parry, E. J.   Food and drugs
Peterson, M. E.   Preserving, pickling
Pfizer, C. and Co.   Food preservatives
_____ .   Pfizer products for food industry
Plimmer, R. H. A.   Analyses and energy value of foods
Pratt, J. T.   Food adulteration

Quelch, M. T.   Herbal remedies and recipes . . .
_____ .   Herbs for daily use
Quintus, R. A.   Cultivation sugar-cane-Java

Rector, T. M.   Scientific preservation food
Reed, W.   History of sugar
Refined Syrups.   This is liquid sugar
Reimund, D. A.   Bibliography tree nut production
Richards, E. H.   Food materials and adulterations
Riesenberg, E.   Preserving and canning
Rodale, J. I. and Staff.   Compl. bk. food and nutrition
Rohde, E. S.   Garden of herbs
Rolph, G. M.   Something about sugar
Rooker, W. A.   Fruit pectin
Rorer, S. T.   Canning and preserving

Savage, W. G.   Canned foods relation to health
_____ .   Food and the public health
Saxon, E. J.   Sensible food for all
Schlink, F. J.   Eat, drink and be wary
Schwaab, E. F.   Secrets of canning
Senn, C. H.   Dictionary of foods and culinary encyclopedia
Sherman, H. C.   Chemistry of food and nutrition

569

_____. and C.S. Lanford. Essentials of nutrition
_____. Food products
Simmonds, P.L. Tropical agriculture
Smith, E. Foods
Snyder, S.P. Treatise on food conservation
Soames, P. Treat. on mfg. sugar from cane
Sohn, C.E. Nutrition
Sommer, H.H. Market milk, related products
Spencer, G.L. and G.P. Meade. Sugar cane handbk.
Stewart, F.L. Sorgham, its products
_____. Sugar made from maize and sorgham
Sugar Information, Inc. Sugar as a food

Taylor, D.D.C. Jams, jellies fruit bottling
Thurston, A. Pharmaceutical and food analysis
Thurston and Braidich. Water soluble . . . (gums)
Tibbles, W. Food and hygiene
_____. Foods, their origin . . .
Tilden, J.H. Food, its composition . . .
_____. Food, Its influence in disease . . .
Tournefort, J.P. Compleat herbal
Travers, J. and Sons. Past, present in old firm
Tressler, D.K. and C.F. Evers. Freezing preservation
    of foods
Tressler, D.K. et al. Into freezer and out
Triebold, H.O. and L.W. Aurand. Food composition and
    analysis
Tryon, T. Treat. on cleanness meats and drinks
Tucker, J.H. Manual sugar analysis
Tudor, A.M. Little book of healing herbs

U.S. Commissioner Agri. Annual report 1897
U.S. Cuban Sugar Council. Sugar
U.S. Dept. Agri. Competitive relationships between
    sugar and corn sweeteners
_____. Foods and food adulterants
_____. Report of Secretary. 1893
_____. Sensory methods measure differences in food
    quality
_____. Spl. report on beet-sugar industry
_____. Yearbooks (Various)

VanHook, A. Sugar. Its production . . .
Vehling, J.D. America's table
Vulte, H.T. and S.B. Vanderbilt. Food industries

Wagner, E. Recipes for preserving fruit
570

Wanklyn, J. A.   Milk analysis
Ward, A.   Grocer's encyclopedia
_____.   Grocer's Handbk. and Directory
_____.   Encyclopedia of food
Wardall, R. A. and E. N. White.   Study of foods
Watt, B. K. and A. L. Merrill.   Composition of foods
Watts, F.   Introductory manual sugar growers
Weil, B. H. and F. Sterne.   Literature search on
    preservation food by freezing
Wellman, M. T.   Food study
Wetherill, C. M.   Mfg. vinegar . . .
Wiggin, H. and Co.   Food mfg. equipment
Wiggins, L. F.   Sugar, its industrial applications
Wilcox, E. V.   Tropical agriculture
Wiley, H. W.   Foods and their adulteration
_____.   Hist. crime against food law
_____.   1001 tests of food
_____.   Prin., pract. agri. analysis
Willits, C. O.   Maple syrup producers manual
Wilson, A.   Our food and drinks
Winton, A. L. and K. B.   Analysis foods
Winton, A. L.   Course in food analysis
Winton, A. L. and K. B. Structure, composition foods
Woodman, A. G.   Food analysis
Worlidge J.   Dictionarium Rusticum

Yates, L. H.   Gardener and cook

    Anonymous
Adulteration, food, drink and drugs
Art of making sugar

Canner's Directory
Citric Acid U. S. P.
Complete course in canning (A)
Culpeper's complete herbal

Dietetic canned foods

Emulsion technology

Food additives; what they are, how used
Food Industries manual
Food Industry Directory and Grocer's Handbk.
Foods of the world
Fruits and fruit products

Grocer's Companion and Merchants' handbk.

Health secrets from foreign lands
Health secrets of famous doctors
Health secrets of famous people

Modern methods food industry management

National Food and Beverage Expo. Off. Catalogue
Nutritional Data

111 tested methods food plant problems

Pfizer products for food and beverage industries

Report Comm. of Patents Year 1858 and 1860
Report of Commissioner of Agriculture for year 1878
Report Secretary Agri. 1893

Saccharin.   Folder of articles on opinions as to physiological
    effects

Use preservatives and colouring matters in preservation
    and colouring of food

Vegetable substances used for man
Vegetable substances used in arts and domestic economy

Food and drink
Alexis of Piedmont.   Secrets of Alexis
Allen, I.B.   When you entertain
Angostura-Wupperman Corp.   Angostura cookbook
Armitage, G.T.   Hawaiian hospitality

Baker, C.H. Jr.   Esquire culinary companion
_____.   Gentleman's Companion
_____.   South Amer. gentleman's companion
Baker, E.A. and D.J. Foskett.   Biblio. of food
Balfour, J.   Cocktail fare
Barber, E.M.   Party sampler
Barnes, A.   Successful entertaining for the modern hostess
Batchelor, D.   For what we are about to receive
Battiscombe, E.G.   English picnics
Beard, G.M.   Eating and drinking
Beard, J.A.   Hors d'oeuvre and canapes
Beilenson, E.   Christmas stocking book

572

Bitting, K. G.   Gastronomic bibliography
Bon Viveur.   London and British Isles
Book Club.   Bonanza banquets
Boorde, A.   Breviary of helthe
Booth, G. C.   Food and drink of Mexico
Borden's Condensed Milk Co.   Drinks and dishes
Boyle, P.   Publican's daily companion
Bradley, A. O.   Beverages and snadwiches
Breen, M. and A. Lawson.   Weekend companion
Brillat-Savarin, J. A.   Handbk. gastronomy
_____ .   Physiology of taste
Brodner, J. et al.   Profitable food and beverage operation
Brody, I.   The Colony (Restaurant)
Brown, C., R., and B.   Wining, dining quiz
Brown, H. E.   Book of appetizers
Bunyard, E. A.   Anatomy of dessert
Bunyard, E and L.   Epicure's companion
Burke, H. B.   Compl. cocktail and drinking recipes
_____ .   Cocktail and tastybite recipes
Buzzo-Cardozo.   Hollywood's favorite cocktail book

Calchestor-Wemyss, Sir Francis.   The pleasures of the
   table
Calvert Distillers Co.   Party encyclopedia
Capper, W. B.   Licensed houses, management
Carlisle, D. T.   Wining and dining with rhyme and reason
Cerwin, H.   Famous recipes of famous people
Chakravarty, T.   Food and drink in ancient Bengal
Chamberlain, N. G. and Narcisse.   Flavor of France
Chamberlain, S.   Bouquet de France
Clifton, F.   State of Physick, ancient and modern, briefly
   considered
Cogen, T.   The haven of health
Cole, A. K.   Fine food, wine and pickled pine
Conil, J.   For epicures only
(Cradock, J.)   Wining, dining in France with Bon Viveur
Croze, A de.   What to eat and drink in France
Cunynghame, F.   Reminiscences of an epicure

Davey, N.   Hungry traveller in France
Davies, J. B.   The butler
Davies, S. E.   English butler's canapes . . .
Deane, A. B.   Licensed victuallers' official annual
De Caux, J. W.   Licensed victualler's vade mecum
De Gouy, L. P.   The cocktail hour
Digby, Sir K.   Closet of - - - - opened

Drummond, J.C. and A. Wilbraham. The Englishman's food

Dunn, H.   Celebrity recipes
Durr, A.   Fashions in drinks
Dutton, T.   Food and drink rationally discussed
Dwyer, E.   Caviar to cordial: recipes

Elliott, V.   Quiet drinking
Ellwanger, G.H.   Pleasures of the table
Elphick, L.S.   Eat and drink to live

Fachiri, A.P.   Bacchus joins Lucullus
Faissole, C.A.   Restauranteers' handbook
Finch, Jos. S. Co.   Wilkin family home cooking
Finck, H.T.   Food and flavor
Fisher, M.F.K.   Here let us feast
Fitchett, L.S.   Beverages and sauces old Virginia
Fleishman, E.M.   Modern luncheonette mgt.
Floyer, Sir J.   Galenic art preserving old men's health
Foster, A.E.M.   Dining and wining
Foyles, C.   Party book
Froude, C.C.   Right food the right remedy
Furnivall, F.J.   Boke of Nurture . . .

Garrow, A.B.   Sideboard and cellar
Gavin, C.   Here's how
Gesner, C.   Newe Jewell of Healthe
Glozer, L.F. and W.K.   California in kitchen
Goddard, G. and C. Wood.   Let's have a good time tonight
Golding, L. and A.L. Simon.   We shall eat and drink again
Gordon, H.J.   Cocktail and food recipes
Gordon, R.I.   Cocktails and snack (R. and A. London)

Hackwood, F.W.   Good cheer
Hampson, J.   English at table
Harington, Sir J.   Englishman's doctor . . .
Harris, F.L.   Flavor's the thing
Hart, J.   Diet of the diseased
Hart, M.A.   Eating and drinking
Hartley, D.R.   Food in England
Hartman, G.   Curiosities art and nature
Haywood, E.   New present for serving maid
Heath, A.   Dining out. What to drink
Heaton, N. StJ.   Calendar of food, wine
_____ . Wines, mixed drinks and savouries

Herisko, C.   Drinks and snacks for parties
Hiller, E.O.   Calendar of sandwiches and beverages
Hispanus, Petrus.   Treasure of health
Hoy, A.H.   Eating and drinking
Hughes, J.E.   Licensed victualler's manual
Hunt, P.   Eating and drinking
Huntington, R.T.   Beverage service
Hyatt-Woolf, C.   Food, drink and drug frauds
_____ .   Truth about things

Irving, W.   Old Christmas in Merrie England

Johnson, H.   Best of vineyards is cellar
Jones, I.   High bonnet
Jones, J.   Arte and science preserving bodie and soule
    in healthe
Josephy, H. and M.M. McBride.   Beer and skittles
Judson, H.   Light entertaining

Keating, L.A.   Men in aprons
Kirwan, A.V.   Host and guest

Labarge, M.W.   Baronial household of 13th century
Lake Roland Garden Club.   Wine and dine with-
Lamb, R. de F.   Amer. Chamber of Horrors
Layton, T.A.   Dining 'round London
_____ .   Five to a feast
_____ .   Table for two
_____ .   Year at the Peacock
Lehrian, P.   The restaurant
Licensed Beverage Industries, Inc.   Time for hospitality
Lawlor, C.F.   The Mixicologist

Macauley, T.   The festive board
Mac Clure, V.   Good appetite, my companion
_____ .   Party fare
Mc Culloch-Williams, M.   Dishes and beverages of the
    old South
Mc Cully, H.   Nobody ever tells you these things
MacDougall, A.F.   Coffee and waffles
Maggs Bros.   Food and drink through the ages
Mario, T.   Playboy gourmet
Mason, D.   Tipple and snack
Massee, W.E.   Guide to eating and drinking in Europe
_____ .   Wine and food index
Massingham, H.J.   English countryman

Mead, W.E. English Medieval Feast
Medlock, A. Eat, drink and be healthy . . .
Melick, H.C.W. Sale food and drink common law
Montagne, P. Larousse Gastronomique
Monzert, L. Licensed victualler
Moor, S. Publican's friend and guide do well
Moore, L. Dictionary foreign dining terms
Moore, P. Hope of health
Morel, J.J. Progressive catering
Moufet, T. Healths improvement . . .
Moulton, T. This is the Myrrour of Glasse of health
    necessary

National Book League. Food and wine
National Distillers Prod. Corp. Mine host's handbook
National Food and Nutrition Institute. Proceedings
Nisbet, W. Pract. treat. on diet

Old Bohemian (An). Philosophy in the kitchen
O'Leary, A. Ingesta: Eating and drinking

Pascall, F. Old-time recipes
Paul, E. and L. Quintanilla. Intoxication made easy
Peddie, A. Hotel, innkeeper, vintner and spirit
    dealer's assistant
Pelligrini, A.M. Unpredujiced palate
Perry, M.H. And to drink, sir!
Price, P.V. France - food and wine guide

Rattray, B. Having a party
Ray, C. ed. Gourmet's Companion
Reboux, P. Food for the rich
Rhoads, W.M. Poker, smoke and other things
Richards, L. and N. Treat. Tea-room recipes
Richards, Rosen Associates. Guide to pink elephants
Robertson, J. and A. Food and wine of the French
    provinces
Robson, E.I. Guide to French Fetes
Ronay, E. 1965 guide 1000 pubs England
Root, W.L. Food of France
Rose, R.H. Eat your way to health
Rosen, R.C. POP, Monsieur
Ruppert, J. Beer in the home

St Sure, S. Bohemian life
Salmon, W. SEPLASIUM Compl. English physician

School Hotel Adm. Hotel mgt., related subjects
Seagram-Distillers Co. Vacation-time food and drink guide
Selivanova, N.N. Dining and wining in old Russia
Shand, P.M. Book of food
Shaw, C.G. Nightlife-New York
Simon, A.L. Art of good living
_____. Bibliotheca Gastronomica
_____. By request: autobiography
_____. English fare and French wines
_____. Gourmet's Week-end book
_____. Guide to good food and wines
_____. In praise of good living
_____. Menus for gourmets
_____. Partners. (Game and wine)
_____. Tables of content
_____. Wine and food menu book
Stanley-Wrench, M. Cocktail snacks and canapes
Stieff, F.P. Eat, drink, be merry, Maryland
Street, J.L. Table topics
Strom, S.A.E. And so to dine

Thomas, A. Wait and see (Butler)
Thompson, Sir H. Food and feeding
Tryon, T. Way to get health
_____. Way to get wealth
_____. Way to health

Vaughan, W. Natural and artificial directions for
    health . . .
Vecchi, J. "Tavern is my drum."
Venner, T. Via recta ad via Longam. Plain
    philosophical demonstration preservation of health
Vicaire, G. Bibliographie Gastronomique
Vicary, T. Englishman's treasure
Victoria Wine Co. Here's how

Watkins, M. Wining and dining in East Anglia
White, F. Flowers as food
Wilcox, B. Simplified guide to table setting
Wilkes, D. The batcheller book
Williams, F. Dainties for home parties
Wilson, R.F. How wine and dine in Paris
Wine and Food quarterly (Periodical)
Woon, B. The Paris not in guide books
Wright, R.L. Bed-book of eating and drinking

Beasley, H. Druggist's General receipt bk
Belanger, E.J. Drug and specialty Formulas
_____ . Modern mfg. formulary
Bennett, H. ed. Chemical Formulary (various)
_____ . Formulas for profit
_____ . Money-making formulas
_____ . New formulas for profit
Brannt, W.T. and W.H. Wahl. Techno-chemical receipt book
Brown, C.W. Stand. cyclopedia recipes
Burt, S.H. Universal household assistant

Chase, A.W. Dr. Chase's receipts (various)
_____ . New receipt bk. medical advisor
Corbyn, T.N. Compounder's pocket remembrancer

David, W.K. Secrets of wise men, chemists
Dick, W.B. Encyclopedia pract. receipts
Digby, Sir K. Closet opened
Doring, P. Money-saving formulas
Druggists Circular. Druggists Circular formula book

Ebert, A.E. and A.E. Hiss. Stand. formulary
Ellet, Mrs. Practical housekeeper

Freeman, J.D. Confederate cookbook

Griffiths, T.M. Non-secret formulas

Hamilton, A.V. Household cyclopedia practical receipts
Hiscox, G.D. ed. Henley's 20th century bk recipes
    (various)
_____ . and T.O'C. Sloane. Fortunes in formulas
Hiss, A.E. and A.A. Ebert. New stand. formulary
Hiss, A.E. Stand. manual soda and other beverages
Hopkins, A.A. Scientific Amer. cyclopedia

Kilner, W.B. Compendium modern pharmacy
Kinsley, C. Circle of useful knowledge

Lillard, B. Pract. hints and formulae . . .
Lucas, E.W. and H.B. Stevens. Book of pharmacopaes
    and unofficial formularies
_____ . Book of prescriptions

Mac Ewan, P. Pharmaceutical formulas

579

Mackenzie, C. 1000 experiments in chemistry
Markham, G. Country contentments
_____. Maison Rustique, or country farme
Meighn, M. Little bk conceited secrets . . .
Minrath, W. Van Nostrand's Practical formulary
Moore, R. Artizans' Guide, everybody's ass's
_____. Everybody's Guide
_____. Universal assistant

Parrish, E. Treatise on pharmacy

Ruthven, Lord P. Ladies cabinet opened

Salmon, W. Family dictionary . . .
Shaw Publishing Co. Mfgr's practical recipes
Shreve, F. 10000 secrets of rich and wise
Skinner, H. B. American prize book

Trade Recipes. How to make 300 secret trade recipes
Tuson, R. V. Cooley's cyclopedia of pract. receipts

Ure, A. Dictionary art, mfgs and mines

Wailes, R. B. Manual of formulas, recipes ...
Walsh, J. H. Economical housekeeper
Webster, T. Encyclopedia, domestic economy
Wesley, J. Primitive physic and general receipt book
Whitehill, J. C. Cyclopedia things worth knowing
Wooley, S. W. and G. P. Forrester. Pharmaceutical
    formulas
Wright, A. S. American receipt book
_____. Wright's bk of 3000 pract. receipts

Youman, A. E. Dictionary everyday wants

    Anonymous
Accomplished housewife . . .
Amer. Druggist Formula Compendium

Best of everything
Book of Commerce (The) sea and land
Book of formulas (Popular Science)
Book of formulas, Recipes, methods and secret processes

Complete family piece and country gentleman and farmer
    BEST GUIDE

Compleat housewife or accomplished Gentlewoman's
    companion
Cyclopedia of practical receipts

D and C Druggists Circular formulary

Enquire within upon everything

Family dictionary and household companion
Family receipt book
Flather's Trade Recipes

Lady's companion
Lee's Priceless Recipes

Mackenzie's 5000 receipts
Mackenzie's 10000 receipts . . .

U.S. Practical Receipt Book

Fruit
Aiken, G.D.   Pioneering with fruits and berries
Alderton, G.E.   Treat. and handbk. orange culture in
    Auckland and New Zealand
Allen, F.W.   Apple growing in California
Allen, W.J.   Citrus culture
Amer. Medical Ass'n.   Accepted foods . . .
Atkinson, F.E. et al.   Fruit juices, cider . . .
Auchter, E.C. and H.B. Knapp.   Orchard and small
    fruit culture

Bailey, L.H.   Principles of fruit-growing
_____ .   Pruning manual
_____ .   Sketch evolution native fruits
Barker, R.E.   Small fruits
Barrett, O.W.   Tropical crops
Barry, P.   Barry's fruit garden
_____ .   The fruit garden
Bartholomew, E.T. and W.B. Sinclair.   Lemon fruit
Bartrum, E.   Bk of pears and plums
Beach, S.A. et al.   Apples of New York
Beckett, E.   Fruit bottling and preserving
Beckett, Edwin.   Bk. of strawberry
Beeton, I.M.   Jam making . . .
Berry, R.M.F.   Fruit recipes

Biggle, J. Biggle berry book
_____ . Biggle orchard book
Blits, H.I. Canning fruits and vegetables
Bogert, L.J. Dietary uses of banana . . .
Bradley, E. and M. Crooke. Bk. fruit bottling
Brandt, J. The grape cure
Bridgeman, T. Fruit cultivator's manual
Brooks, R.M. et al. Register new fruit and nut varieties
Brooks, R.M. and C.O. Hesse. Western fruit gardening
Buchanan, R. Culture of the grape
Bunyard, E.A. Anatomy of dessert
Bunyard, G. Apples and pears
Bunyard, G. and O. Thomas. Fruit garden
Bush, R. Fruit-growers diary
_____ . Harvesting and storing fruit garden
_____ . Soft fruit growing
_____ . Treefruit growing
Butterfield, H.E. Scientific mfg. Jams and allied products
Butterfield, H.M. Bush berry culture in California

California, Board State Vitacultural Commissioners.
    Annual Report 1893
California Fruit Growers Exchange. Exchange citrus pectin
California State Board of Horticulture. Annual Report 1891
Card, F.W. Bush-fruits
Central Food Technological Research Institute. Mango
_____ . Papaya
Chase, E.M. et al. Citrus fruit products
Chandler, W.H. Fruit growing
Charley, V.L.S. Recent advances fruit juice production
Chatfield, C. and L.I. McLaughlin. Proximate composition
    fresh fruits
Clarke, J.H. Small fruits in home garden
Clinkard, C.E. Uses of juice extracted from raw fruits . .
Coit, J.E. Citrus fruits
Cole, S.M. American fruit book
Cooke, M. Injurious insects of orchard . . .
Coville, F.B. Directions for blueberry culture
Coxe, W. View cultivation of fruit trees and management
    of orchards and cider
Crang, A. Preserves for all occasions
Crichton, D.A. Australasian fruit culturist
Cruess, W.V. Commercial fruit and vegetable products
_____ and J.M. Irish. Fruit beverage investigations
Cruess, W.V. and A.W. Christie. Laboratory Manual
    fruit, vegetable products

Cruess, W. V. Preparation fruit juice in home

Demko, C. Growing grapes in Florida
Downing, A. J. Fruits and fruit trees, America
Dyal, S. Tropical fruits . . .

Eastwood, B. Complete manual for the cultivation of the
    cranberry
Elliott, F. R. Western fruit book or Amer. fruit-growers
    guide
Evelyn, J. French gardiner
_____. Sylva. A discourse with appendix concerning
    fruit trees in relation to cider

Fawcett, W. Banana
Field, T. A. Pear culture
Fletcher, S. W. Strawberry growing
Florida Citrus Commission. Citrus fruit in health and
    disease
Florida Citrus Exchange. Florida s food fruits
Forsyth, W. Treat. on culture, mgt. fruit trees
Fraser, S. American fruits
_____. The strawberry
Fuller, A. S. Small fruit culturist
Fulton, J. A. Peach culture

Gardner, V. R. Cherry and its culture
Garey, T. A. Orange cult. in California . . .
Giles, J. Ananas
Glendinning, R. Pract. hints culture pineapple
Goudiss, C. H. Give the grape its rightful food place
Gould, H. P. Peach growing
Green, S. B. Amateur fruit growing
_____. Popular fruit growing
Gregg, T. Handbk. fruit culture
Grindon, L. H. Fruits and fruit trees
Grubb, N. H. Cherries

Hall, Sir A. D. and M. B. Crane. The apple
Hedrick, U. P. Cherries of New York
_____. Cyclopedia hardy fruits
_____. Fruits for home garden
_____. Grapes of New York
_____. Peaches of New York
_____. Pears of New York
_____. Plums of New York

583

_____. Small fruits of New York
Hemlow-Merriam and Co. Fruit growers' manual
Henry, B.S. Studies of yeast and fermentation fruits
    and berries Washington
Hill, E. Water into gold
Hills, W.H. Small fruits
Hitt, Thomas. Treatise of fruit trees (A)
Hoare, A.H. Commercial apple growing
Hockings, A.J. Queensland garden manual
Hogg, R. Apple, pear as vintage fruits
_____. The fruit manual
Hooper, E.J. Western fruit book
Hoos, S. and R.E. Seltzer. Lemon and lemon products
Hoos, S. and J.N. Boles. Oranges and orange products
Hovey, C.M. Fruits of America
Hume, H.H. Citrus fruits and their culture
_____. Cultivation citrus fruits
Hydraulic Press Mfg. Co. Mount Gilead Equipment
    and supplies for cider . . .
Hydraulic Press Mfg. Co. Price list equipment

International Federation Fruit Juice Producers.
    Analyses . . .
_____. Results science and technology fruit juices
Irish, J.H. Fruit juice concentrates
_____. Fruit juices and fruit juice beverages

Jaques, G. Pract. treat. mgt. fruit trees
Johnston, J.C. Citrus fruit for home orchard
_____. Citrus growing in California
Jones, M.A. Publications of U.S. Citrus Products Sta.
    Winter Haven
Joslyn, M.A. and G.L. Marsh. Utilization of fruit in
    commercial production

Kenrick, W. New American orchardist
Kepner, C.D. Jr. and J.H. Soothill. The banana empire
Kesterson, J.W. and O.R. McDuff. Florida citrus oils
Knight, T.A. Treat. cult. apple, pear

Langford, T. Plain, full instructions raise all sorts fruit
    trees
Lansdell, J. Grapes, peaches, nectarines and melons
Laurence, John. Fruit Garden Kalendar (Mr. Laurence's)
Lelong, B.M. Treat. citrus culture in California
Lindley, G. Guide to orchard and kitchen garden

Linnaeus, C. Voyages, travels Levant
vonLoesecke, H.W. Bananas . . .
Lowe, T.A. Fruit farm in England
Lund, C.H. "Magic of the grape".
Lynch, S.J. and N.J. Mustard. Mangos in Florida

M'Ewen, G. Cult. peach and nectarine
McKenzie, W.F. Fruit culture for amateur
McNair, J.B. Citrus products (2 parts)
Mc Phee, J. Oranges
Manning, R. Book of fruits
Maril, L. Savor and flavor
Maynard, S.T. Practical fruit grower
Meech, W.W. Quince culture
Meehan, T. Gardner's monthly
Miller, C.D. and K. Bazore. Fruits, Hawaii
Miller, C.D. et al. Fruits of Hawaii. Description
    nutritive values, and recipes
Ministry Agri., Fisheries and Food. Cider apple
    production

Newland, H.O. Planting, expression, culture of coconuts
New York Agri. Experiment Sta. 14th annual report
Nicholls, H.A. Textbk. tropical agriculture
Noling, A.W. Lemon. Notes
Noling, L.J. Lemons and lemon processing

Oldham, C.H. Cultivation berried fruits in Great
    Britain
Otter-Swain Corp. Beverages, mfg. and sale Lesson No.
    8 - Fruit juices

Paddock, W. and O.B. Whipple Fruit-growing in arid
    regions
Peterson, M.G. How to know wild fruits
Poole, H.M. Fruits and how to use them
Porter, G. Tropical agriculturalist
Powell, E.P. Orchard and fruit garden

Quinn, G. Fruit tree and grape vine pruning

Reynolds, P.K. The banana . . .
Roe, E.P. Success with small fruits
Ruck, J.A. Chemical methods for analysis fruit and
    vegetable products

Sanders, T.W. Fruit and its cultivation

_____. and J. Lansdell.   Grapes; peaches; melons and how to grow them
Seabrook, W. P.   Modern fruit growing
Sears, F. C.   Productive small fruit culture
Shear, S. W. and R. E. Blair.   California fruit statistics
Shoemaker, J. S.   Small fruit culture
Simmonds, N. W.   Bananas
Sinclair, W. B.   The orange
Skinner, C. M. Myths and legends, flowers trees, fruits and plants
Skinner, H. B.   American Prize-book
Smith, J.   Fruits and farinacea
Smith, K. L.   Growing and preparing guavas
Smock, R. M. and A. M. Neubert.   Apples and apple products
Stambaugh, S. U.   The papaya . . .
Stark, W. P.   Inside facts of profitable fruit growing
Stennis, M. A.   Florida fruits and vegetables
Sunkist Growers Products Dept.   Exchange citrus pectin
Suttor, G.   Culture of wine grape and orange in Australia and New Zealand
Swartout, J. M.   Small fruits

Talbert, T. J. and A. E. Murneek.   Fruit crops
Taylor, A.   Treat. on ananas or pineapple
Taylor, F.   Annual report Nebraska State Horticultural Society 1895
Taylor, H. V.   Plums of England (The)
Taylor, N.   Fruit in the garden
Thacher, J.   The American Orchardist
Thomas, H. H.   Book of the apple
Thomas, J. J.   American fruit culturist
_____. The fruit culturist
Thomson, D.   Pract. treat. culture pine-apple
Todd, S. E.   The apple culturist
Tolkowsky, T.   Hesperides. Hist. cult. citrus fruits
Tressler, D. K. and C. F. Evers.   Freezing preservation of foods
Tuffin, H. R.   Grapes, peaches, nectarines

United Fresh Fruit and Vegetable Ass'n.   Bananas
U. S. Dept. Agri. Fruits -non-citrus by states

Van Meter, R. A.   Bush fruit production

Wagner, E.   Recipes for preserving fruit . . .
Ward, H. W.   Book of the peach

586

Waring, W. G.   Fruit growers Handbook
Watson, M. J. M.   Home preservation fruit . . .
Waugh, F. A.   American apple orchard
_____ .   American peach orchard
_____ .   Plums and plum culture
Welch Grape Juice Co.   Grape juice as a therapeutic agent
White, J. J.   Cranberry culture
Wickson, E. J.   California fruits and how grow
Wilcox, E. V.   Tropical agriculture
Wilkinson, A. E.   Encyclopedia, fruits, berries . . .
_____ .   Modern strawberry growing
Wilson, C. M.   Empire in gold and green
Woodman, M.   Jams, preserves, bottled fruits
Wright, H. J.   Fruit grower's guide

Yates, L. H.   Gardener and the cook
_____ .   Successful jam making, fruit bottling

Zubeckis, E.   Fruit beverages in Ontario
_____ .   Home production fruit juices

Anonymous
Citrus Juice fruit control

Fruit Annual and Directory (various)
Fruit and fruit products.   Analysis, composition and
    manufacture

Report Commissioner Patents 1854 and 1858

Three hundred sixty five orange recipes
Treatment fruit juices and vegetables

Vegetable substances used in arts . . .

Woman's Institute Library Cookery - Fruit and fruit
    desserts

Inns and taverns
Aldin, C.   Old inns

Ballentine and Sons.   Guests of an old time Inn
Brown, A. J.   I bought a hotel
Burke, T.   Book of the inn
_____ .   The English inn

Callow, E. Old London taverns
Camp, J. Oxfordshire and Buckinghamshire pubs

Delderfield E. R. Brief guide to inn signs
_____ . More about inn signs
Drake, S. A. Old Boston taverns and clubs

Earle, A. M. Stage-coach and tavern days
Elliot-Godsave, G. and A. C. Crouch. The Thames

Field, E. The Colonial tavern
Foster, D. S. Inns, taverns, alehouses . . .
Fothergill, J. Confessions of an innkeeper
_____ . An Innkeeper's diary
_____ . My three inns

Girtin, T. Come landlord!
Goodson, A. London's friendly inns and taverns
_____ . More friendly inns and taverns . . .
Gorham, M. Back to the local
_____ . The local
Green, M. and T. White. Guide to London pubs

Hackwood, F. W. Inns, ales and drinking customs of
    old England
Hall, E. H. Coffee taverns, cocoa houses . . .
Harper, C. G. Historic and picturesque inns of Old
    England
Heaton, V. A pub of your own
Hill, B. Inn-signia
Hindley, C. Tavern anecdotes . . .

Jones, V. East Anglian pubs

Keeble, R. Surrey pubs
Keverne, R. Tales of old inns

Lathrop, E. Early Amer. inns and taverns
Layton, T. A. Year at the Peacock
Lilly-White, B. London coffee houses

McNeish, J. Tavern in the town
Maskell, H. P. Taverns of old England
Matz, B. W. Dickensian inns and taverns
_____ . Inns and taverns of "Pickwick"
Monckton, H. Q. History of the English public house (A)

National Trade Development Ass'n.   Innkeeping

Oliver, B.   Renaissance of the English public house

Part, A.F.   Art and practice of innkeeping
Popham, H.E.   The taverns in the town

Rainbird, G.M.   Inns of Kent
Reeve-Jones, A.   London pubs
Richardson, A.E. and H.D. Eberlein.   English inn,
    past and present
Richardson, A.E.   Old inns of England
Robinson, E.F.   Early hist. coffee houses in England
Rogers, K.   Mermaid and Mitre taverns

Selley, E.   English public house as it is
Shelley, H.C.   Inns and taverns of old London
Stanley, L.T.   Old inns of London

Timbs, J.   Clubs and club life in London
Tozier, J.   Among English inns

Wagner, L.   London inns and taverns
_____ .   More London inns and taverns
Wakeman, A.   Hist. and reminiscences lower Wall Street
Watson, R.   Scrapbook of inns
Whitbread and Co. Ltd.   Story of Whitbread's
_____ .   Your local
_____ .   Library No. 3 Inn-signia
_____ .   Library No. 6 Inns of Kent
_____ .   Library No. 7 Inns of sport
_____ .   Library No. 10 Inn crafts and furnishings
White, Tony   How to run a pub.   Advice to would-be
    publicans
Williams, E.E.   New public house
Williams, P.S.   Recommended wayside inns of England

    Anonymous
Book of the Cheese

Inns noted for good food in and around London
Inns of Britain with accomodations for the visitor

Old English Coffee houses

Tales of old inns

Tavern anecdotes and reminiscences of the origin of
   signs, clubs, coffee houses . . .
Traits and stories of Ye Olde Cheshire Cheese

Liquor

Acker Merrill and Condit. Price list 1877
Adler, H.R. Handbk for retail liquor dealer
Allen, H.W. Rum. Englishman's spirit
_____ . White wines and cognac
Arechabala, J. S.A. On its 75th anniversary
Arroyo, R. Studies on rum
(Atkyns, A.) The Family Magazine
Augenstein, M. Manual instructions brewers, distillers
Austin, Nichols and Co. Wine, liquor handbk

B. (E.) Treatise on virtues of whisky
Baar, S. Beverage distilling industry
Bacchus. Brewer's guide for hotel, bar . . .
Bacchus and Cordon Bleu. New guide of hotel, bar,
   restaurant . . .
Balch, A.W. and Co. Price list wines, liquors
Baldwin, L.D. Whiskey rebels
Barclay, J. Arts of brewing and distillation
Barham, J.F. Considerations, prohibition corn in
   distillery
Barnard, A. Whisky distilleries in U.K.
Barron, H. Distillation of alcohol
Bate, R.B. Tables for patent saccharometer
_____ . Tables weight of spirits
Beastall, W. Useful guide for grocers . . .
Bedel, A. Traite complet fabrication liqueurs
Beech, F.W. Homemade wines, syrups and cordials
Bell, A. Inquiry policy prohibition grain in distilling
Bellew, J. Fermented goods
Belth, G. Household guide to wines, liquors
Beman, D. Mysteries of the trade
Bennett, R. Guide to winemakers, distillers
Benson, J. Licensed victualler's instructor
Benson, J. Spirit and licensed victualler's guide
Bernard, B.M. Liquor laws in 48 states
Beverage Research Bureau. Manual on beers
Black, H.C. Treat. on laws regulating mfg. sale
   intoxicating liquors
Bourbon Institute. Bourbon chef
Boyle, P. Publican and spirit dealer's daily companion

590

Bradley, J. F.   Cocktails, wines, liquors
Brande, W. T.   Experiments ascertain state in which
    spirit exists in fermented liquors
Brannt, W. T.   Pract. treat. raw materials and
    distillation liquors . . .
Bretzfield, H.   Liquor marketing and advertising
Brevans, J. M. de.   Mfg. liquors and preserves
Brunswyke, J.   Vertouse boke distyllacyon
Bryant, W. B.   19th century handbk. mfg. liquors
Bush, Baron de and R. A.   Recipes mfg. liqueurs
Bush, W. J. and Co.   Liqueur compounder's handbk.
_____ .   Recipes for mfg. liqueurs . . .
Byrn, M. La F.   Compl. pract. distiller

Cardelli, M.   Manuel du Limonadier et du confiseur
Carson, G.   Social history of bourbon
Caruba, R.   Cooking with wine and high spirits
Cary, S. F.   Liquor manufacture and traffic
"Clements" Homemade wines, liqueurs . . .
Collier, J.   Experiments and observations on fermentation
    and distillation spirit
Collingwood, F. and J. Woollams.   Universal cook
Consumers Union.   Report on wines and spirits
_____ .   Wines and liquors
Cook and Bernheimer and Co.   Liqueurs fines
Cooper, A.   Compl. domestic distiller
_____ .   Complete distiller
Corbyn, T. N.   Compounder's pocket remembrancer
Cotten, C. B.   Formula of N. Y. Phila. and Baltimore mfgrs.
    wines and liquors
Country Ass'ns.   Wines, spirits for all occasions
Cramond, W.   On Scots drink
Crampton, C. A.   Fermented alcoholic beverages . . .
Cross, C.   American compounder

Daiches, D.   Scotch whisky. Its past and present
Daraio, J. P.   Healthful and therapeutic properties wines,
    beer, whiskey . . .
Dejean, M.   Traite raisonne de la distillation . . .
Delavan, E. C.   Adulterations of liquors
Digby, Sir K.   Closet of Sir- -opened
Donovan, E. O.   On question whether alcohol product of
    fermentation or distillation
Donovan, M.   Cabinet cyclopedia
Doran, J. M.   Elementary chemistry whiskey manufacture
Dossie, R.   Essay on spiritous liquors in regard to
    health

591

Drahota, R.   Treat. on mfg. liquors . . .
Dubrunfaut, A. P.   Compl. treat. art distillation
Duffy Malt Whiskey Co.   Pure malt whiskey
Dunn, J. B.   Adulteration of liquors
Duplais, P.   Treat. on mfg. and distillation of alcoholic
    liquors

Edwards, W. N.   The beverages we drink
Eichler, Fr. A.   Treat. on mfg. liquors . . .
Elholtz, J. S.   Curious distillatory
Elliott, C.   Distillation in practice
_____ .   Distillation principles
Evans, G. C.   What shall we drink?
Evans, R.   Whiskey salesman's handbook

Fenton, S.   Excellent properties salted brandy
Feuchtwanger, L.   Fermented liquors . . .
Field, S. S.   The Amer. drink book
Finch, J. S. and Co.   Wilkin family home cooking album
Finchett, T.   Crosland's cordial and liqueur maker's
    guide and publican's instructor
Findlater, Mackie, Todd and Co. Ltd.   The home of
    Treble Diamond
Fink, R. B. Jr.   Cooking with rum
Fisher, M. I.   Liqueurs, a dictionary . . .
Fleishman, J.   Art blending and compounding liquors
    and wines
Fogelsonger, M. I.   Secrets of liquor merchant revealed
Forbes, R. J.   Short history of art distillation
Freels, S. C.   The X-Ray or compiled facts, . . .
    interest to retail liquor dealer
Freeman, H. E.   Retail liquor dealer's guide
French, J.   Art of distillation
_____ .   The London distiller
Fries and Fries Inc.   Manual for compounders
Fries, Alex. and Bro.   Manual for compounders . . .
Fries Bros.   Manual
Fritzsche Brothers.   Manual formulas suggestions
Furness, R.   Fermentation industry

Gardner, J.   Brewer, distiller and wine mfgr.
Gee, P.   Scotch whisky
Gesner, C.   Newe booke distillattyon . . .
Gilbey, Sir W.   Notes on alcohol
Gilbey, W. and A.   Complete list wines, spirits
_____ .   Treat. on wines and spirits

Ginrum Alpha Co. Legend of liqueurs, wines, spirits . . .
Glauber, J.R. Description philosophical furnaces, new
    art of distilling
Glenlivit Distillery. Glenlivit Distillery annals
Gold, Alec, ed. Wines and spirits of the world
Gooderham and Worts Ltd. Souvenir Canadian National
    Fair
_____. What is whiskey?
Graham, S. Melrose, honey of roses
Greenberg, E. and M. Whiskey in the kitchen
Griffin, J.J. Chem. testing wines, spirits
Grommes and Ulrich. Special price list (1915)
Grossman, H.J. Guide to wines and spirits
Gunn, N.M. Whisky and Scotland
Gutteridge, W. Ne Plus Ultra of assaying . . . spiritous
    liquors . . .

H. (M.) Young cook's monitor, distilling
Hallgarten, P. Liqueurs
Hamlin, C.E. and C. Warren. Formulae or every
    druggist his own perfumer
Hardy, J. Retail compounder . . .
Hartley, J. Wholesale and retail wine and spirit merchants
    companion
Hartley, W. Fermentation and distillation
Haskell, G. Wines, liqueurs and brandies
Hawkes, G. Publican's guide reducing spirits
Heering, P. History of Danish firm
Hennessy, J. and Co. Gift of taste (cognac)
_____. Hennessy is everywhere
Herstein, K.M. and T.C. Gregory. Chem and tech. of
    wines and liquors
Hester, J. These oils, water, extractions or essences
Higgins, B. Fragment or 4th part Dr. Higgins
    observations - sugar and rum
_____. Observations improvement and mfg.
    Muscovado sugar and rum St. Jago de la Vega
Hilsebusch, H.W. Thorough course rectifying and
    compounding
_____. Knowledge of a rectifier
Hiram-Walker and Sons. Plot against the people
Hirsh, I. Mfg. whiskey, brandy, cordials
Hirshfield, A.M. Stand. handbk. on wines and liquors
Hornsby, J.H. and T.S. Harrington. Successful liquor
    retailing
Howe, B.B. and A.H. Manual of liquor tests
Hu, Tun Yuan. Liquor tax U.S. 1791-1947

Hutton, J.B. Book of vodka

Isel, H. Blending at its best
Isaak, A. Distilled spirits industry

Jackson, G.B. Medicinal value French brandy
Jameson, J. and Son Ltd. "Sovereigne Liquor" (Irish
    whisky)
Jermyn, D. Story of gin
Jillson, W.R. Early Kentucky distillers
Johnson, G. Pract. studies, winemaker, brewer, distiller
Jonas, P. Distiller's guide
_____. Distiller's practical guide
_____. Distiller's wine and brandy merchant's vade
    mecum
Jones, G.C. and J.L. Baker. Original gravity tables
Joslyn, M.A. and M.A. Amerine. Commercial production
    of brandies

Kinross, Lord. The kindred spirit (Gin)
Kirshbaum, E. Distillation and rectification
Krafft, M.A. American distiller

L'Abbe, L. Liquor dealer's silent ass't.
Lacour, P. Mfg. liquors, wine and cordials
Lampray, J.H. Brewer's and distiller's diary
Laver, J. House of Haig
La-Vogue, B. Art and secrets in mfg. wines and liquors
Layton, T.A. Cognac and other brandies
Leroux and Co. Inc. Manual on cordials
Licensed Beverage Industries, Inc. ABC's of alcoholic
    beverages
_____. Facts about Licensed Beverage Industries
    in 1962
_____. That great American Spirit
Lichine, A. Encyclopedia wines and spirits
Lindemann, E.H. Pract. guide and receipt bk
Lindinger, F. Manual for liquor trade
Liquor Store Magazine. Knowing alcoholic beverages
_____. Pract. encyclopedia alcoholic beverages
Lockhart, Sir R.B. Scotch
Loftus (Publisher) Spirit merchant
Long, J. Tables strength spirits-Sykes hydrometer
Lo Pinto, M. Art making Italian desserts
Luker, H. Co. Ltd. Price List (spirits)

Mc Culloch, J. Distillation, brewing . . .

_____. Observations on mfg. rum
Mac Donald, A. Whisky
Mc Donald, J. Secrets of Great Whiskey Ring
Mc Dowall, R.J.S. Whiskies of Scotland
M'Harry, S. Practical distiller
Machet, L.J. Receipts for homemade wines, cordials . . .
McMullen, T. Handbk. wines, pract. and theor. and
    historical
MacNab, S. Under the black tiles
Manning, S.A. Handbk. wine and spirit trade
Marrison, L.W. Wines and spirits
Martin, B. Sure guide for distillers
Matthews, C.G. Manual alcoholic fermentation
Maxwell, Sir H. Half-a-century successful trade
_____. Three-fourths of a century of successful trade
Meyer, E.L. Art of cooking with spirits
Mida, Lee. Continous directory, spirits industry . . .
Mida, Wm. Handbook wholesale liquor dealers
Monzert, L. Independent liquorist
_____. Practical distiller
Morel, J.J. Progressive catering
Morewood, S. Philosophical and statistical hist.--
    inebriating liquors
Morgan, P.C. Handbk statistics relating to trade in
    alcoholic liquors
Moroney, J. Price list wines, spirits 1899
Morwyng, P. New booke of distillatyen of waters
Mueller, C.C. Pioneers mixing at elite bars

Nettleton, J.A. Condensing and cooling in distillation
_____. Flavour of whisky
_____. Mfg. whisky and plain spirit
_____. Mfg. spirit in various distilleries
Norton, C. Mod. blending and rectification
_____. Mod. manual for rectifiers . . .
_____. Mod. yeasting and distillation
Nutt, F. Receipts for homemade wines, cordials . . .

Packman, W.V. Gentlemen's own guide to wines and
    spirits
_____. Wine and spirit manual . . .
Paddleford, C. New easy ways to cook with rum
Park and Tilford. Wholesale price list 1894
Piaz, A. dal. Brandy distillation . . .
Plat, H. Divers conclusions concerning art of
    distillation

Practical Man (A) Innkeeper and public brewer
_____ . Publican, innkeeper and brewer guide
Prescott, A.B. Chem. exam. alcoholic liquors
Preyer, E.R. Information and guide liquor business

Rack, J. French wine and liquor mfgr.
Ramsden, J. Account experiments obtain strength spiritous
    liquors
Rhodes, J.B. Publican's handbk., calculator
Robb, M.J. Scotch whiskey
Roberts, W.H. British winemaker . . .
Robinson, J. Whole art making British wines
Robertson, H.M. Water of life
Roose, S. Wine and spirit dealer's guide
Rose, S. Spirit merchant's and excise officers assistant
Rosenbloom, M.V. Bottling for profit
_____ . The liquor industry
Ross, W. Present state distilleries Scotland
Rowndell, J.A.E. The still-room
Rudkin, W. Hints to liquor merchants

Sabin, A. Wine and spirit merchants accounts
Saintsbury, G. Notes on a cellar book
Sandeman, F. History of cognac-brandy
Scarisbrick, J. Spirit manual, historical and technical
Schimmel and Co. Praktische Vorschriften
Schultz, C. Manual for mfg. cordials, liquors . . .
Scotch Whisky Ass'n. Scotch whisky
Seagram, J.E. and Co. Welcome to house of Seagram
Sethness, C.O. et al. Mod., simple and pract. formulas
    pertaining cordials . . .
Shannon, R. Pract. treat. on brewing, distilling . . .
Shaw, Alex. D and Co. Simple facts about wines, spirits
Shaw, P. 3 essays-improvement of distillation
Sheen, J.R. Wines and other fermented liquors
Sheridan, J. Compl. treat. art distillation
Shevlin, J. and T. Hetherington. Alcoholic spirit testing
Shirley, J. Accomplished ladies rich closet
Shirley, T. Curious distillatory . . .
Sillett, S.W. Illicit Scotch
Simmonds, C. Alcohol. Its production . . .
Simon, A.L. Rum
Simons, S. Alcoholic drinks, easy way to make
Smith (?) The school of arts
Smith, G. Compl. body of distilling
_____ . Nature of fermentation explained

Smith, G. of Kendal. Practical distiller
Smyth, W.A. Publican's guide . . .
Steedman, M.E. Homemade beverages . . .
_____ . and C.H. Senn. Homemade summer and
  winter drinks
(Steinberg, L.) Dominion compounder's guide
Stevenson, P. Explanation process partial evaporation
Stone, J.W. Brief hist. beverage alcohol
Stone, S.L.E. Liquor buyers guide

Taylor, H.E. Handbk. wines and liquors
Thomas, J. Bar-tender's guide
_____ . How to mix drinks . . .
Thomson, T. Brewing and distillation
Tobe, J.H. How to make own wines and beers . . .
Tovey, C. British and foreign spirits
Tripp, C.H. Brewery management
_____ . Licensing act of 1902
Tritton, S.M. Successful winemaking
Tryon, T. Health's grand improvement
Tucker, J. Impartial inquiry benefits low priced spirits . . .
Tweed, E.J. Economics of brewing

Vasey, S.A. Guide analysis potable spirits
Veley, V.H. and L.J. Micro-organisms faulty rum
deVilmorin, L. Cognac

Walker, (Hiram) Inc. Outline of distilled spirits business
Walker, R.H. Rectifier's, compounder's and liquor dealer's
  manual
Walton, H.R. Hiram Walker and Walkerville
Warren, G.C. Elixir of Life
Weiss, H.B. Hist. of applejack
West, H.J. Liquor making at home
Westney, R. Wine and spirit dealer°s and consumer's
  Vade-mecum
_____ . Compl. treat. distillation
Wiggleworth, E. Brewer's and licensed victualler's guide
Williams, G.C. The compounder
Willkie, H.F. Beverage spirits of America
_____ . Fundamentals of distillery practice
_____ . Outline for industry
Willkie, R.T. Distiller's grain manual
Wilson, J.B. Spirit of Old Kentucky
Wilson Publ. Co. Encyclopedia state laws on sale of
  liquors
Wilson, R. House of Sanderson

_____ . Scotch made easy
Wine and Spirit Ass'n. Great Britain. Spirits and
  liqueurs
Wolfe, Adolphe. Elucidation, imposition in imitation
  and adulteration gin, rum
Wray, J. and Nephew Ltd. Story Dagger Jamaica rum
Writner, G.W. American compounder

Y-Worth, W. Britannian Magazine (art of distillation)
_____ . Compleat distiller
_____ . Introitus . . . . Whole art distillation
Young's Market Co. Wine, liquors and the like

Zamarini, G. Tested formulas, perfumes, liquors . . .

        Anonymous
Act for laying duty upon retailers of spiritous liquors
Acts of Georgii III
Art of distillation (The)

Bordeaux wine and liquor dealers' guide
Brewer's guide for hotel, bar and restaurant
Brewer's Almanack and Wine and Spirit Trade annual
  (various)
Brief case of the distillers and distilling trade

Complete distiller (The)
Complete family piece (BEST GUIDE)
Compl. grocer by an old distiller
Compounder's Guide
Consequences of law reducing Dutys on French wine, brandy
Corn distillery stated to consideration of landed interest
  of England

Desultory notes on origin uses and effects of ardent spirit
Distiller of London (The)

Economic aspects of liquor problem
England's happiness improved (Art and mystery distilling
  brandy)
English innkeeper's guide . . .
Essay on importance and best mode converting grain
  into spirits

Formulas of your favorite drinks
French system mfg. . . . wines, brandies . . .

Giggle water (homemade liquors)
Gin Shop (The)
Grocer's Guide
Guaging Manual.   (U.S. Bureau of Internal Rev.)

Harper's Wine and Spirit Gazette (Various)
Hist. liquor and brewing industry Rochester
Homemade beverages by practical brewer

Lasche's Magazine for practical distiller
Liqueurograph Chart (The)
Liquor handbook
Loftus's new mixing and reducing bk

Manual for inspector of spirits

Off the shelf.   Guide sale wines and spirits

Patterson's Beverage Gazetteer 1951
Party Book, Inc.   Party Book, N.Y.

Ridley's Wine and Spirit Handbook

Sheridan's Red Table
Sike's tables concentrated spirits . . .
Spirit Trader's and Licensed victualler's reducing table
Spirits. K.T.D. (Know the drink)
Story of Irish Whiskey (The)

Tables to be used with Sike's A and B hydrometers
Taste of Kinloch (Scotch whisky)
Tax on distilled spirits
Treat. on mfg. imitation, adulteration and reduction of
    foreign wines . . .
Truths about whisky

Vintner's, brewer's spirit merchant's and licensed
    victualler's guide

Wine and spirit merchant
Wine and spirit adulterators unmasked
Wines, beers and liquors (how to make at home)

Mineral water
Accum, F. Guide to Chalybeate spring Thetford

Addison, W. English Spas
Allen, B. Natural hist. mineral waters G.B.
_____ . Natural hist. Chalybeat and purging waters
   of England
Allen, R.L. Hist., chem. and therapeutical analysis
   fountains, Saratoga Springs
Althaus, J. Spas of Europe
Andree, J. Account of the Tilbury water
Ash, J. Experiments and observations mineral waters
   of Spa and Aix-la-Chapelle

Barry, Sir E. Observations, hist., critical and medical
   on wines . . . of ancients
Baylies, W. Pract. reflections on uses and abuses of
   Bath waters
Bell, A.N. Climatology and mineral waters U.S.
Bell, J. Mineral and thermal springs of U.S. and Canada
_____ . On baths and mineral waters
Bergman, T. Om Luftsyra (Acid in air)
_____ . On acid in air
Booth, A. On the natural chem. properties of water
   and on various British waters
Boyle, R. Short memoirs for natural experimental
   history of mineral waters
Bradshaw, B. Dictionary of mineral waters
Brownrigg, W. Use of knowledge of mephetic exhalations
   (Spa water)
Buchan, W. Cautions concerning--drinking mineral
   waters
Byfield, T. The artificial spaw or mineral waters to drink

Caledonia Springs. Grand Hotel Co.
Chancellor, C.W. Treat. on mineral waters
Charleton, R. Treat. on Bath waters
Coan, T.M. Home uses of mineral waters
Cotar, C. Treat. on mineral waters of Vichy
Crook, J.K. Mineral waters of U.S. and their therapeutic
   uses

Davis, T. Mineral waters. Price list 1759
Dawson, C.C. Saratoga: its mineral waters
Deane, E. Spadacrene Anglica or English Spa

Echols, P. and Sons. Bedford alum and iodine spgs
Elliot, J. Account nature, medicinal values mineral
   waters, G.B. and Ireland

Falconer, W. Account efficacy agua mephetics
_____ . Account use and application Bath waters
_____ . Essay on Bath waters
_____ . Pract. dissertation Bath waters
Firestone, C.B. Bubbling waters
Fitch, W.E. Mineral waters of U.S. and American spas
Floyer, J. and E. Baynard. Hist. cold bathing
Foord, A.S. Springs, streams and spas London
Fothergill, A. New experimental inquiry Cheltenham water
Franz, J.H.A. Treatise on mineral waters

Gairdner, M. Essay on natural hist . . . mineral and
    thermal springs
Garnett, T. Treat. mineral waters Harrogate
Glover, R.M. On mineral waters . . .
Graham, J. New, plain, rational, treat. true nature,
    uses, Bath waters
Granville, A.B. Spas of England (Midland)
_____ . Spas of England (Northern Spas)
_____ . Spas of England (Southern Spas)
_____ . Spas of Germany
_____ . Spas of Germany revisited
Grew, N. Treat. on nature salt in Epsom
Guidott, T. An apology for the Bath
_____ . Collection of treatises relating to city and
    water of Bath
_____ . Discourse of Bathe and hot waters
Gutmann, E. Watering places and mineral springs of
    Germany, Austria and Switzerland

Hales, S. Experiments on Chalybeate or Steel waters
_____ . Statical essays
Hawkins, J. Treat. on natural and artificial mineral
    waters
Haywood, J.K. Mineral waters of U.S.
Higgins, B. Analysis Tillbury alterative water
Hoffman, F. New experiments and observations on mineral
    waters

Ingram and Royle. Natural mineral waters . . .
Irwin, J.A. Hydrotheraphy at Saratoga

Jorden, E. Discourse natural Bathes and mineral waters

Kemp, J.F. Mineral springs of Saratoga
King, W. Observations on artificial mineral waters of
    Dr. Struve

601

Kirwan, R. Essay analysis mineral waters

Lee, E. The baths of Germany
_____ . Mineral springs of England
_____ . Watering places of England
Linden, D. Treat. on origin, natures ... of Chalybeate
waters . . .
Lucas, C. Analysis Dr. Rutty's methodical synopsis of
mineral waters
_____ . Cursary examination of methodical synopsis
of mineral waters
_____ . An essay on waters
Luke, T.D. Spas and health resorts of British Isles

Macpherson, J. Baths and Wells of Europe
_____ . Our baths and wells . . .
Madden, T.M. Principal health-resorts of Europe and
Africa . . .
Magalhaes, J.J. de. Description glass apparatus for
making mineral waters . . .
Molyneux, W. Burton-on-Trent, Hist. . . . .
Moncreiff, J. Inquiry into medicinal qualities . . . of
aerated alkaline waters
Monro, D. Treatise on mineral waters
Moorman, J.J. Mineral springs of No. Amer.
_____ . Mineral waters of U.S. and Canada
Myrtle, A.S. Practical observations on Harrogate
waters

Nessel, M. Treat. concerning medicinal Spaw water

Oliver, W. Pract. dissertation of Bathe waters
Owen, W. Account nature, properties and uses mineral
waters Great Britain

Peale, A.C. Lists and analyses mineral springs of U.S.
Peedle, T. and T. Coxbie. Fallacy water drinking
Pratt, E. Metallic and mineral waters
Priestley, J. Directions impregnating water with fixed
air . . .

Riley, J.J. Scientific and medical origin of carbonated
waters
Rouse, L. Tunbridge Wells
Russell, R. Dissertation on use of sea-water also on
mineral waters of Great Britain
Rutty, J. Methodical synopsis mineral waters

Satterly, J. and R. T. Elworthy. Mineral springs of Canada
Saunders, W. Treat. on chemical history, medical powers
    mineral waters
Scherer, P. and Co. List mineral waters . . .
Schultz, C. H. Mineral spring waters, composition, action,
    use
    _____. Schultz and Warker's mineral waters
Scudamore, Sir C. Treat. composition and medical
    properties mineral waters
Seaman, V. Dissertation mineral waters Saratoga
Short, R. Peri phychropsoias of drinking water
Short, T. Essay natural and medicinal history mineral
    waters Cumberland . . .
    _____. General treat. mineral waters England
    _____. Natural, experimental and medicinal history
    mineral waters Derbyshire . . .
Skinner, W. W. Amer. mineral waters . . .
Skrimshire, F. Popular chemical essays
Smith, H. Essay foreign teas, mineral waters
Smith, S. H. Some remarks on medicinal mineral waters
Spender, J. K. Bath thermal waters . . .
Steel, J. H. Analysis Congress Spring . . .
    _____. Analysis mineral water-Saratoga
Stone, W. L. Reminiscences Saratoga and Ballston
Sunderland, S. Old London's Spas, Baths, Wells
Swiss Exporter Ltd. Swiss Spas

Tichbourne, C. R. C. and P. James Mineral waters of
    Europe
Turner, G. Brief account mineral waters of Spa
    _____. Full, distinct account mineral waters Spa and
    Pyrmont
Turner, W. Booke natures and properties of bathes in
    England . . .
    _____. Pure treasure-English Bathes

Walton, G. E. Mineral springs of U. S. and Canada
Weber, F. P. Climatology, health resorts - mineral springs
Weber, H. and F. P. Weber. Climatotheraphy and
    Balnoetheraphy
    _____. Mineral waters and health resorts of Europe
    _____. Spas and mineral waters Europe
Weiss, H. D. and H. R. Kemble. They took to the
    waters (Springs-New Jersey)
Welsh, H. Springs and baths-Kissengen
Williams, J. W. Essay utility sea bathing and observations
    on mineral waters

Yeo, I.B.   Therapeutics mineral springs . . .

<u>Anonymous</u>
Climates and baths of Great Britain

Flather's pract. recipes artificial mineral waters

Health resorts of South and summer resorts of New
    England
Hot water cure sought in Germany 1844

Spa waters.   In Soft Drinks Trade Journal
Spas of Britain

<u>Miscellaneous</u>
Abrahamson, E.M. and A.W. Pezet.   Body, mind and
    sugar
American Perfumer and Aromatics.   First documentary
    edition
American Pharmaceutical Ass'n.   National Formulary
    (various)
Anstie, F.E.   Stimulants and narcotics
Anthony, D.   Guaging inspector . . .
Appleton, J.H.   Beginners' handbk. chemistry
Ass'n. Agri. Chemists.   Methods analysis
Attfield, J.   Water and water supplies

Bakewell, F.C.   Great facts (Water)
Baumgartner, J.G. and A.C. Hersom.   Canned foods
Beal, E.A. Information readers No. 1
Beddoes, T.   Considerations medical use factitious airs
Bedford, J.   Pewter
Berman, L.   Food and character
Bewley, R.   (pseud) Treatise on air
Birkett, E.L.   Thomson's conspectus British pharmacopoeias
Bishop, J.L.   Hist. Amer. manufacturers
Blunt, E.M.   Merchants . . . measurer
Bumstead, G.   Specimen bibliography mugs, glass . . .
Byrne, E.   Guaging
Byrne, O.   Pract. compl. and correct guager

Cavallo, T.   Essays on medical preparation factitious airs
Clark, H.   Beer gravity tables
Cobbett, W.   Cottage economy

Commissioner Patents. Abridgement specifications cutting
    cork, bottling liquids
_____ . Relating to preservation of food
Conant, J.B., ed. Pasteur's study of fermentation
Cosnett, T. Footman's Directory . . .
Cossley-Batt, J. and I. Baird. Elixir of life
Coxe, J.R. Emporium arts and sciences
Crane, E.J. et al. Guide literature chemistry
Crown Cork and Seal Co. Story of CCandS

Depew, C.M. 100 years American commerce
Dobson, M. Medical commentary on fixed air
Donovan, M. Domestic economy
Dougherty, J. General guager . . .

Eichlor, L. New book etiquette
Elville, E.M. English table glass

Fabre, J.H. Secret everyday things
Farmer, F.C. Guide wine, spirit merchant's rule
Fisher, M.F.K. A cordiall water
Folin, O. Preservatives and other chemicals in foods . . .
Forbes, R.J. Short history of art distillation
_____ . Studies in ancient technology
Furnas, C.C. and S.M. Story man of his food

Gilpin, G. Tables reducing weight mixtures spirits and
    water
Glass Mfgrs. Federation. Glass containers
Gobright and Pratt. Union Sketch-book
Greenwood, E. Classified guide technical and commercial
    books

Haggard, H.W. Devils, drugs and doctors
Hale, W.J. Prosperity beckons. Dawn of alcohol era
Hankerson, F.P. Cooperage handbook
Hartshorne, A. Old English glasses
Hawkes, G. Publican's guide reducing spirits
Hay, W.H. Health via food
Haynes, E.B. Glass through the ages
Hehner, O. Alcohol tables -proof spirit
Henry, B.S. Studies of yeast . . .
Henry, T. Experiments and observations on ferments and
    fermentation
Henry, W. Elements experimental chemistry
Higgins, B. Experiments and observations relating to
    acetous acid, fixable air

Hodges, E. Story of glass
Hollingworth, H. L. Influence caffein on efficiency
Holt, A. Life of Joseph Priestley
Hutchinson, W. H. and Son. Into Hutchinson's 2nd century

Imperial Chemical Industries. Bottle washing

James, D. J. Evolution glass container industry
Johnston, J. F. W. Chemistry common life
Jonas, P. Theory and practice guaging
Jones, T. P. New conversations on chemistry
Judson, L. V. Units and systems weights, measures

Keene, J. B. Handbook of hydrometry
_____ . Handbook of pract. guaging
Kent, J. C. Essay on nature . . . imitation of fine arts
Kentish, T. Guager's guide and measurer's manual
Kenwood, H. R. Public health laboratory work
Kirschbaum, E. Distillation and rectification
Krause, M. V. Food nutrition and diet theraphy

Latchford-Marble Glass Co. History glass containers
La Wall, C. H. Curious lore drugs and medicines
_____ . 4000 years of pharmacy
Leadbetter, C. Royal guager
Liebig, J. Chemistry in application agriculture and
    physiology
Lewis, J. S. Old glass and how to collect
London College. Essentials of pharmacy

McBride, D. Experimental essays on medical philosophical
    subjects (fermentation)
MacEwan, P. Art of dispensing
Mackenzie, C. 1000 experiments in chemistry
Maignen, P. A. Water, preventable disease and filtration
Mant, J. B. Pocket book mensuration
Martindale, W. H. Extra Pharmacopoeia
Meehan, T. Gardner's Monthly (wine)
Menzies, J. Common things made plain
Meyer, G. J. Mfg. Co. Bottle Scuffing and prevention
Miller, F. J. Carbon dioxide in water, wine . . .
Monson-Fitzjohn, G. J. Drinking vessels of bygone days
Moody, B. E. Origin of 'reputed quart' . . .
_____ . Packaging in glass
Moor, C. G. and W. Partridge. Aids to analysis of food
    and drugs
Morrison, Plummer and Co. Druggists ready reference

Muldoon, H. C.   Pharmaceutical latin (lessons)
Mulder, G.   Chemistry animal and vegetable physiology
Murray, J.   System Materica Medica and pharmacy
Muspratt, Dr. S.   Chemistry - theoretical practical applied
　　to arts and mfg. 1803

National Automatic Merchandising Ass'n.   Blue book of
　　of automatic merchandising
Necker, W. L. and E. Wynn.   List periodicals at QM
　　Food and Container Institute
Nesbit, W. D.   After dinner speeches
Nettleton, J. A.   Study hist. and meaning "original gravity"
Notter, J. L. and R. H. Firth.   Pract. domestic hygiene
Noyes, W. A.   Organic chemistry for laboratory
Nurnberg, J. J. Crowns-the complete story

Painter, O. C. Wm.   Painter and his father (crowns)
Papin, D.   New digester--making drinks . . .
Parrish, E.   Treatise on pharmacy
Patent Office Great Britain.   Subject list works domestic
　　economy
Percival, M.   Glass collector
Pereira, J.   Treatise on food . . .
Peters, L. H.   Diet and health . . .
Petulengro, Gipsy.   Romany remedies, recipes
Pfizer, Chas. and Co.   Our smallest servants
Pollack, A.   Botanical index to medicinal plants
Priestley, J.   Experiments and observations relating to
　　natural philosophy
＿＿＿＿＿＿＿＿ .   Experiments and observations relating to
　　analysis atmospherical air
＿＿＿＿＿＿＿＿ .   Lectures on experimental philosophy
Pringle, Sir. J.   Discourse on different kinds of air
Prudden, T. M.   Drinking water and ice supplies

Quinn, E. L. and C. Jones.   Carbon dioxide

Reed, A.   Old bottles and ghost towns
Reilly, J.   Distillation
Remington, J.   Practice of pharmacy
Renner, H. D.   Origin of food habits
Resuggan, J. C. L.   Cleaning and sterilization of bottles . . .
＿＿＿＿＿＿＿＿ .   Quaternary ammonium compounds
Rideal, S.   Carbohydrates and alcohol
Rose, A.   Carbonic acid in medicine
Rose, A. and E.   Bibliography literature distillation
Ruck, J. A.   Chemical methods analysis fruit and
　　vegetable products

Salzman, L. F. English industries in middle ages
Schittler, E. and B. Freres. Schweizerische Korkenfabrik
 (Corks)
Schmeiser, A. Have bottles . . . will "POP"
Schreiber, G. R. Concise history vending in U. S. A.
Schroeter, L. C. Sulphur dioxide
Schwartz, R. J. Dictionary business and industry
Scoville, W. L. Art of compounding
Shaw, D. Catalogue British scientific and technical books
Sibson, A. Agricultural chemistry
Silverman, M. Magic in a bottle
Simmonds, C. Alcohol. Its production . . .
_____ . Alcohol in commerce and industry
Skinner, C. M. Myths and legends flowers . . .
Sloane, T. O'C. Liquid air . . .
Solis, V. Drinking cups, ewers, vases . . .
Solvay Sales Corp. Solvay Blue Book
Stevenson, T. Spirit-gravities with tables
Sutheim, G. H. Introductions to emulsions
Symons, W. Practical gager

Tate, F. G. H. Alcoholometry (British method)
Thayer and Co. Fluid and solid extracts
Thorpe, T. E. Joseph Priestley
Thurston and Braidich. Water soluble and bulking gums
Tilden and Co. Formulas for making tinctures, infusions,
 syrups . . .
Turner, F. G. Negligence with food, drink . . .

U. S. Bottlers Machinery Co. Bottling engineer handbook
U. S. Bureau of Census. Statistical abstract of U. S. 1951
U. S. Treasury Dept. Guaging manual
Ure, A. Dictionary of chemistry

Van Rensselaer, S. Early American flasks and bottles
Vanstone, J. H. Raw materials of commerce

Walbridge, W. S. American bottles, old and new
Walker, A. H. Inspection fish, poultry fruit, nuts . . .
Wanklyn, J. A. Water analysis
Watson, R. Chemical essays
Watt, J. Description pneumatic apparatus with directions
 for prod. factitious airs
_____ . Supplement to "Description ----"
Wedgewood, R. G. R. History of tea cup
Welch Grape Juice Co. Grape juice as a therapeutic agent

Wesley, J. Primitive physic . . .
Whitall, Tatum and Co. Price list 1881 (Glass)
Wiley, H.W. An autobiography
Williamson, G.C. Everybody's bk. collecting
Willkie, H.F. Fundamentals of distillery practice
Witteman Bros. Price current 1883 (bottles)
Wright, F.B. Distillation of alcohol and denaturing
Wright, J.S. Pharmacology fluid extracts
Wyatt, V. From sand-core to automation (bottles)
Wynter, A. Our social bees (London stout)

Young, M. Tables of weight of spirits

Zuiderweg, F.J. Laboratory manual batch distillation

Anonymous
Adulteration of food, drink, drugs
Art of dispensing
Arts revealed and universal guide

Bottle washing
British National Formulary (various)
British Pharmaceutical Codex 1934
British Pharmacopoeia (various)

Conversations on chemistry
Cooper (The) History and instructions

Digest patents in U.S. 1790-1839

Emulsion technology

Family Receipt Book

Great Industries of U.S.
Guagers' weighing manual

Inquire within for anything . . .
Internal Revenue gauger's manual
Internal Revenue manual for information and guidance of
    agents

Laboratory apparatus and materials. Exhibition Official
    catalogue 1960

Mackenzie's 5000 receipts

Mastery of water

New school arts and sciences
New system practical domestic economy

100 years progress in U.S.

Plain talk and friendly advice . . .

Report Commissioner patents 1854, 1860

Spirit tables of specific gravity (Alcohol)
Spirit tables for Sike's hydrometer

Tables showing relation specific gravity spirits
Tricks of the trade--adulteration food . . .

U.S. Practical Receipt book
Use preservatives and colouring matters . . .

Valuable secrets in arts and trades

Perfumery
American Perfumer and Aromatics. First documentary
    edition
Askinson, G.W.   Perfumes and cosmetics
_____. Perfumes and their preparation

B (R).   The perfumers' legacy or the companion to the
    toilet
Bedoukian, P.Z.   Perfumery, synthetics and isolates
Burbidge, F.W.   Book of the scented garden

Clifford, F.S.   Romance of perfume lands
Cooley, A.J.   Handbook of perfumes, cosmetics. . .
_____. Toilet and cosmetic arts . . .
Cooper, A.   The complete distiller
_____. Complete domestic distiller
Cristiani, R.S.   Perfumery and kindred arts

Dayl, B.   World of fragrance
Deite, C.   Pract. treat. mfg. perfumery
Durvelle, J.P.   Preparation of perfumes
Dussauce, H.   Pract. guide for perfumer

Ellis, A.   Essence of beauty

Farkas, A. Perfume through the ages
Firmenich and Cie. Aromatic chemicals
Fritzsche Bros. Perfumer's handbook and catalog
Furnivall, F.J. Book quinte essence

Gattefosse, R.M. Formulary of perfumery . . .
Givaudan-Delawanna Inc. Givaudan index

Hamlin, C.E. and C. Warren H--formulae or every
    druggist his own perfumer
Hampton, F.A. Scent flowers and leaves
Harrison, O.W. Perfumery, history . . .
Heine and Co. Perfumers' raw materials

Jellinek, P. Practice modern perfumery
Jessee, J.E. Perfume album
Jude. Medicinal and perfumery plants

Lady (A). Art cookery, plain and easy
Le Gallienne, R. Romance of perfume
Lille, C. British perfumer
Lodge, E.A. Art manufacture perfumery

Martin, G. Perfumes, essential oils
Maurer, E.S. Perfumes and their production
Moncrieff, R.W. Chem. perfume materials
Morfit, C. Perfumery: its manufacture . . .

Naves, Y.R. Natural perfume materials

Owen, R.J. Practice of perfumery

Parry, E.J. Chem. essential oils and artificial perfumes
    _____ P---'s cyclopedia of perfumery
    _____ . Raw materials of perfumery
Perfumery and Essential Oil Record. Annual directory and
    buyer' guide
    _____ . Golden Jubilee Special number
Piesse, G.W.S. Art of perfumery
Poucher, W.A. Perfumes, cosmetics . . .
Pradel, P. Compl. treat on perfumery

Redgrove, H.S. Scent and all about it
Rimmel, E. Book of perfumes
Rohde, E.S. Scented garden

Sagarin, E. Science and art perfumery

Sawer, J.C. Odorographia, natural hist. raw materials,
    . . . in perfume industry
Scoville, W.L. Extracts and perfumes
Sinclair, R. Essential oils. Basis of nature's perfume
Snively, J.H. Treat. mfg. perfumes . . .
Soap, Perfumery and Cosmetics. SPC yearbk

Thompson, C.J.S. Mystery and lure perfume

Van Dyk and Co. Prices 1915
Verrill, A.H. Perfumes and spices . . .

West, T.F. Synthetic perfumes, chem . . .
White, P. Perfumes, household fragrances

    Anonymous
Expert practical perfumery

Formulary of the Parisian perfumer

Guide to art manufacturing perfumes

Toilet of the flora

Reference
American Food Journal Institute. Bibliography of
    nutritive values chocolate and cocoa
Amerine, M.A. Check list books, . . . grapes and
    wine
_____ . Short check list books . . . in
    English grapes, wines . . . 1949-1959
Aylett, M. and O. Ordish. First catch your hare

Baker, E.A. and D.J. Foskett Biblio. of food
Bird, W.H. Catalogue London section Institute of Brewing
    Library
Bitting, K.G. Gastronomic bibliography
Brown, E. and B. Culinary Americana

Cooper, I.M. References, ancient, modern to literature on
    beer and ale
Corbett, E.V. Libraries, museums and art galleries year-
    book 1964
Cramer, P.J.S. Review literature coffee research in
    Indonesia

Cusmano, G. Dizionario di vitaculture ed enologia

Faes, Dr. H. Lexique Viti-Vinicole International
Fischer, I.W. Factworterbuch fur braurei und maltzerei

Glozer, L.F. and W.K. California in kitchen
Goeldner, C.R. Automatic merchandising
Goettler, Dr. H. Lexikon der spirituosen-und alkoholfreien
    getranke-industrie
Greenwood, E. Classified guide technical and commercial
    books

Hartong, B.D. Elsivier's dictionary of barley, malting
    and brewing
Hazlitt, W.C. Old cookery books . . .
Hospitality Guild. Catalog 500 bks on food and beverages
Hurty-Peck and Co. Library. Bibliography books and
    booklets on beverages

International Library Directory. World directory of libraries

Lincoln, W. American cookery books

Maggs Bros. Food and drink through the ages 2500 B C
    to 1937
Mueller, W. Bibliographie des kaffee, des kakao . . .
_____ . Bibliographie des kakao . . .
Muldoon, H.C. Lessons in pharmaceutical latin
Muller, A. Internationaler Riechstoff-Kodex

National Book League. Food and wine

Oxford, A.W. English cookery books to 1850

Patent Office, Great Britain. Subject list works on
    domestic economy
Pennell, E.R. My cookery books
Prince, G. Current books about wine
Public Library of South Australia. Research Service
    Bibliographies Series 4 No. 82. Wine and vita-
    culture

Rose, A. and E. Bibliography distillation literature

Schoellhorn, F. Bibliographie des Brauwesens
Shaw, D. Catalogue British scientific and technical books
Simon, A.L. Bibliotheca Bacchica

_____. Bibliotheca castronomica
_____. Bibliotheca vinaria
Vicaire, G. Bibliographie gastronomique
Voegele, M. C. and G. H. Woolley. Drink dictionary

Wassermann, A. Schenley library bibliography
Wilcox, J. K. List English, French and German periodicals
    on brewing . . .
Wine and Food Society. Library catalogue No. 1
Wine Institute. Selective biblio. wine bks

Anonymous
American Library Directory
Association Special Libraries and Information
    The Bureaux. Food and beverages
Bibliotheca Oenologica
Brewer, (The) in nine languages

Dictionarie Oenonomique

Gesellschaft fur die Geschichte und bibliographie des
    brauwesens

Hering's dictionary classical and mod. cookery

International encyclopedia food and drink

Soft Drinks
Adcock, G. I. Cordial maker's syrups
_____. Jusfrute Book 1937 and 1957
_____. Pasteurization for cordial makers
_____. Preservatising beverages
Adkins, W. S. National soda fountain guide
Allen, I. B. When you entertain
American Bottler. Blue Book editions (various)
American Bottlers Carbonated Beverages. Air in bottled
    carbonated beverages
_____. Beverage production, plant operation
_____. Bibliography Research Fellowship
_____. Bottle washing
_____. Bottling plant maintenance
_____. Bottling plant sanitation
_____. Cost survey, suggested budgets
_____. Customer checking beverage bottles
_____. Development improved beverage cases

614

615

Bacchus and Cordon Bleu. New Guide of hotel . . . bar
Bailey, E. H. S. Source, chem. use of food
Bakewell, F. C. Great facts. History
Bancks, G. W. Mead, and how to make it
Barker (J. H.) and Co. 100 fountain formulas
Barnett and Foster. Aerated Beverages . . .
_____. Catalogue mineral water . . . machinery and
    appliances
_____. General catalogue No. 645
_____. Instructions erecting and working B and F
    machinery
_____. Recipes for mfg. aerated waters
_____. Some syrup suggestions
Beach and Clarridge. B and C concentrated extracts, juices
_____. B and C book of soda formulas
Beadle, S. C. Soda fountain guide
Beattie, G. B. ABC of soft drinks
_____. Brief hist. soft drinks
_____. Factory arrangement
_____. Mechanical side mineral water manufacture
    (Pyramid)
_____. Mineral water spoilage prevention (Pyramid)
_____. Plant for the smaller bottler
_____. Small bottlery problems
_____. Soft drink flavours, hist. . . .
_____. Soft Drink Bottler. Vol's I and II
_____. Squashes
_____. What the young bottler should study
Beech, F. W. Homemade wines, syrups . . .
Bernhard, W. Book of 100 beverages
Blue Seal Extract Co. Beverage flavor handbk
Blumenthal, M. L. Bottler's helper
Blumenthal, S. Food manufacturing
Board of Trade. Report census production soft drinks 1954
Boeglin, C. A. Sundaes, ices and cream sodas
Bonham, W. A. Guide for soda dispensers
Boots Pure Drug Co. Saccharin
Bowker, Dr. H. L. Co. Price list extracts 1879
Bratby and Hinchliffe, Ltd. Pract. mineral water maker
Braum, E. Frozen gems and dainty dishes
Brazilla Co. Soda fountains and supplies 1920
Brewery and Bottling Engineer's Ass'n. British brewery and
    soft drinks equipment
Briggs, J. Treat. on machinery used for soda water
Bryant, W. B. 19th century handbk. on mfg. wines,
    cordials . . .
Buchanan, J. H. and M. Levine. Bottle washing

Burgoyne, Burbidges and Co. Notes on mfg. aerated
    waters . . .
Burns Bottling Machine Works. Master Airfree bottling
    system
_____. 20 years plus "Burns" 1939
Bush, Baron de and R. A. Recipes for mfg. aerated and
    mineral waters (various)
Bush, W. J. and Co. Ltd. Bush catalogue and book reference
_____. Centenary album
_____. Citrus juice compounds
_____. Export price list 1947
_____. General Price List 1949
_____. Pract. recipes mfg. aerated beverages
_____. Price list for soft drinks industry 1957
_____. Products for soft drink industry
_____. Products for the beverage trade (various)
Byrn, M. L. Complete practical brewer

California Fruit Growers Exchange. Bottlers' handbook
    for use with juices
Campbell, W. T. Big beverage
Candler, C. H. Asa Griggs Candler
Cazaubon, D. Treat. and pract. guide of apparatus for
    fabrication gaseous drinks
Chain Store Research Bureau. Future of soft drink
    industry
Charlotte. Let's have a party
Chester, T. Carbonated beverages
Coca- Cola Co. Guide to proper cup machine operation
_____. Opinions, orders, injunctions . . .
_____. The Refresher. 75th anniversary
Colam, E. E. F. Pract. milk bar operation
Commissioner of Patents. Abridgements. Beverages
    (various)
_____. Abridgements. Unfermented beverages
Continental Can Co. ABC of canning soft drinks
Cordley and Hayes. Catalog coolers 1920
Craig, E. Sip softly
Crewe- Jones, F. 250 recipes delicious drinks
Cruess, W. V. and J. H. Irish. Fruit beverage investigations
Culinary Arts Institute. Ice cream and cool drinks
Curtis, K. J. Soft drinks industry legal handbook

Dahl, J. O. Soda fountain and luncheonette Management
_____. Soda fountain management
Dahlmann, W. Tafelwasser, limonaden und brausen
Daughters of Amer. Revolution. Book of beverages

Davies, F. Temperance drinks for summer and winter
DeCouy, L. P. Soda fountain-luncheonette drinks and
   recipes
Delineator Home Institute. Beverages for parties
De Lisser and Co. Book of formulas
Dennis, C. B. Background mead making
Digby, Sir K. Choice and experimental receipts
Doran, R. B. Prohibition punches
Dorf, B. B. and Co. Cordial cocktail confidences
Dows, C. D. and Co. Catalogue, price list soda water
   apparatus. 1873-74
Dubelle, G. H. "Non plus ultra" Soda fountain requisites of
   modern times
_____. Soda fountain beverages

Eberle, E. G. Soda water formulary
Edwards, W. H. Beverages we drink
Eichenlaub, J. E. Home tonics and refreshers
Elliott, J. Account nature and values mineral waters,
   Dr. Nooth's experiment air
Enkema, L. A. Acids used in soft drinks
_____. Bottlers prepare--protect your beverages
   against off-season changes
_____. Root beer . . .
_____. Syrup making for cup venders
_____. Use benzoate of soda as preservative

Farrow and Jackson. Recipes Amer. and other iced
   drinks
Feltham, L. R. Service for soda fountains
Fleishman Co. Excellent recipes, summer drinks
Food Engineering. Bottler's and glass packer's handbook
Food Standards Committee. Report on soft drinks
Foote and Jenks, Inc. Calculator for bottlers (various)
Forbes, B. A. Money making hints for soda fountains
Fritsch, J. Manual pratique fabrication eaux et poiseous
   gaseuses
Fuller, A. H. Bottle washing
_____. Jusfrute handbook for soft drink industry
   1. Factory design and layout 2. Plant sanitation
_____. Water treatment

Gardner, W. H. Food acidulants
Garrett, F. Coca-Cola 1886-1962 History
Ginsberg, B. Let's talk soft drinks
Goeldner, C. R. Automatic merchandising

618

Goold, J. Aerated waters and how to make
Goosmann, J.C. Carbonic acid industry
Great Britain Food standards Comm. Report on soft drinks
Green and Green Inc. Flavors of distinction
Groves, P.W. Microbiology

Hance Bros. and White. Advice and help
_____ . Pure fruit juices
Hancock G.C. Report British wines and cordials (alcoholic
    and non-alcoholic)
Hay, W. Ltd. Story of ginger
Hayward-Tyler and Co. Aerated water machinery . . .
Heath, A. Good drinks
Henry, T. Account--preparing mephetic julep
Hires, C.E. Co. Jingle jokes for little folks
Hollingworth, H.L. Influence caffein on mental and motor
    efficiency
Hopkins, A.A. Home made beverages . . .
Horton, C.H. Mineral Water Trade Yearbook 1939
Hoynak, P.X. and G.N. Hollenback. This is liquid sugar
Hurty-Peck and Co. How to make syrup soft drinks
_____ . Ice and ice-cold Tall-One
Hutchinson, P. Making soft drinks with P.H.

Institute (The) Good Housekeeping's book of cool drinks
Invictus. Guide to soda fountain
Irish, J.H. Fruit juices and beverages

Jack, F.B. Homebrewed wines and beers
Jacobs, M.B. Mfg. and analysis carbonated beverages
Jusfrute Ltd. Aerated water mfgrs. handbook
_____ . Jusfrute schools
_____ . Technique without tears No's 1-2-3

Kahn, E.J. Jr. The big drink
_____ . The Universal drink
Keller, W.B. Bottler's handbook
Kendrick, S.G. Preparation flavoured mineral waters
Kirkby, W. Evolution artificial mineral waters
Knaggs, H.V. Healthy life beverage book
Koonin, P.M. Health cocktails
Korab, H.E. Microbiological aspects of one-trip glass

Ladd, E.F. North Dakota Bulletin No. 69 Food and food
    products
Ladies Home Journal. Women's buying habits and attitudes
    toward soft drinks

Langden, A.   Dainty drinks and sherbets

Larson, C.R.   Fountain operator's manual

Levine, M. and J.H. Toulouse.   Suggestions elimination
spoilage beverages

Leyel, C.F.   Summer drinks and winter cordials

Lippincott, C. and Co.   Soda fountains 1890

_____.   Catalogue, price list soda fountains-1873

_____.   Catalogue apparatus making, bottling soda
water-1886

_____.   Catalogue apparatus making and dispensing
soda water

_____.   Instructions and sundry catalogue

_____.   Soda water apparatus

Liquid Carbonia Acid Mfg. Co.   Catalogue 1896

_____.   Catalog No. 37 Carbonating machinery

Liquid Carbonic Co.   ABC fountain profits

_____.   Catalog No. 36 1903

_____.   Dispenser's catalog no. 532 (1925)

_____.   "Goin to town"

_____.   History, organization, 50th anniversary 1938

_____.   1910 soda water guide and book recipes

_____.   Price list syrup tables . . . 1952

_____.   Sales manual 1934

_____.   Sanitation program for carbonated beverage
plants

_____.   Soda water, how to make and serve

Liquid Carbonic Company Ltd.   Study of effect of air on
carbonation (A)

Luhmann, E.   Die industrie der alkoholfreien getranke.
1905

Lund, J. and G.H. Richardson.   Mineral water manufacturer's
accounts

McClellan, W.S.   Utilization ingested carbon dioxide . . .

MacMahan, A.C.   Latest recipes and Amer. sodawater
dispenser's guide

MacSwiney, E.   Mineral water maker's vade-mecum

Manio, Jack de.   Jack de Manio's drinkards-Non-
alcoholic drinks

Manville, C.H.   Carbonated bottled beverages

Martin, M.W.   Twelve full ounces (Pepsi-Cola)

Masters, T.   Patent investions production ice and
artificial cold, soda water . . .

Masurovsky, B.I.   Sherbets, water ices, modern soda
fountain operation

Matthews, J.   Aerated beverages . . . 1876

_____. Frigid soda water apparatus catalogue-1889

Rawlings, H.D.   Sparkling draughts, mfg . . .
Rich, H.S. and Co.   Beverage Blue Book (various)
Ricket, E. and C. Thomas.   Gentlemen's table guide
Riley, J.J.   History Amer. soft drink industry
_____. Organization in soft drink industry
_____. Scientific and medical origin carbonated waters
_____. Twentieth century in bottled carbonated
   beverage industry
Roberts, A.B.   Diary for brewing and syrup rooms (various)
Rollin, B.   Non-drinker's drink book
Rose and Co.   Aerated water makers guide
Ruiz, I.J.Z.   Beverages (handbook)
Rylands, D.   Complete catalogue accessories making
   aerated water . . .

Sabin, B.C.   Wines and fresh fruit beverages
Sawyer, G.F.   Bottlers' extracts
Saxe, De F.W.   Saxe's guide.   Hints for soda water
   dispensers (various editions)
Schroeter, L.G.   Sulphur dioxide.   Applications
Seager, R.   Pract. treat. mfg. cheap non-alcoholic
   beverages
Smith, D.   Carbonated waters.   Guide to mfg.
Smith, J.G.   Aerator's and bottlers' cyclopedia.
_____. St. Paul's Bottling Co. bk. reference
Snively, J.H.   Soda water, what it is . . .
Society Soft Drink Technologists.   Your key to quality
Soda Fountain (The).   Dispenser's formulary
_____. Dispenser soda water guide
Southworth, M.E.   101 beverages
Standage, H.C.   Temperance and light drinks
Star Liquid Machinery Co.   Catalog 1949
State Laboratories, North Dakota.   Food and drug
   bulletins (various)
Steedman, M.E.   Homemade beverages and Amer. drinks
_____. Homemade summer and winter drinks
Stevenson and Howell Ltd.   Label booklet, price list,
   formulas (1897)
_____. Mfg. aerated beverages (various)
_____. Mineral water trade and
   food and drugs act
_____. Non-excisable fruit wines and cordials
_____. Non-alcoholic fruit wines and cordials
Stevenson, Wm. and R. Howell.   S and H gallonage table

Stockbridge, B.E.   What to drink; blue book of beverages
Sulz, C.H.   Treat. on beverages

Tall-One Co.   Merchandising plan
Taylor, N.   Cinchona in Java
_____ .   7500 case bottling plant
Thompson, E.C.   Long's portable soda fountain
Thompson, H.   Australian milk bar and soda fountain
Three Millers Co.   Catalog supplies for soda fountain 1924
Timm, H.   Limonaden und alkoholfreie getranke 1909
Toulouse, J.H. and M. Levine.   Suggestions maintaining
    quality . . . soft drinks
Towey, J.M.   Cherry.   Information about industry and
    flavors
_____ .   Orange.   Information about different
    varieties . . .
Trade Recipes.   100 secret trade and family recipes
    summer, winter drinks
Tripp, C.H.   Brewery management
Tucker, S.A.   Pract. and scientific treat. mfg.
    carbonated beverages
Tufts, J.W.   Advertising folder 1893
_____ .   Arctic soda water apparatus 1873
    also 1885, 1888, 1889
_____ .   Book of directions (various)
_____ .   Descriptive catalog Arctic soda-water
    apparatus (various)
_____ .   Illustrations soda water apparatus

United Amer. Soda Fountain Co.   Favorite fountain
    formulas
United Interest Soda Generator and Fountain Co.   A.D.
    Puffer's carbonic acid generator
U.S. Bottlers' Machinery Co.   Bottling and packaging
    engineer
_____ .   Bottling and engineer handbook

Van Ameringen-Haebler, Inc.   Alca flavors-bottlers
    guide and price list 1946
Virginia Woman's Christian Temperance Union.   Thirst
    aids for hostess

Wandle, J.T.   Extracts and beverages
Ward, J.R.   Soda fountain profits
Warner-Jenkinson Co.   Bottler's and ice cream maker's
    handy guide

_____. Ice cream, carbonated beverages
Wells, R. Pleasant drinks, effervescing mixtures
White, E. F. Spatula soda water guide
_____. W-vest pocket sundae formulas
White Enamel Refrigerator Co. Housewives favorite
    formulas
White, Tompkins and Courage. Brewing room diary and
    year book (various)
Wittemann Brothers. Prices. Labels, caps . . .
Woman's Institute Library Cookery. Beverages
Women's Christian Temperance Union So. Australia. Ideal
    recipe book
Woodman, M. Cocktails, ices, sundaes, American drinks

Anonymous
Adventures in soft drink land
American Cream Soda (G. B. B.)

Barman's and barmaid's manual
Blackpool and District Mineral Water Ass'n.
    Annual reports (various)
_____. Memorandum and articles of Ass'n.
Botanic Brewers' Guide (various)
Bottler's Yearbook (various)
Bottlers and Beverage Mfgrs Universal Encyclopedia
Brewers and Bottlers Universal Encyclopedia
Brewers Exhibition Official Catalogue (various)
Brewers' guide for hotel, bar . . .
Brewing, Bottling and Allied Trades Exhibition catalogues
    (various)

Cafe and milk bar catering
Carbonated Drinks. Periodical 1877-1881
"Coca-Cola Bottler". 50th anniversary
Cola drinks-American type (G. B. B.)
Compl. family piece and country gentleman

Dispenser Soda Water Guide (various)
Drinks. Formulas for making . . .

"Economic" Formulae (Beverage flavors)
Essential oil forum

Flather's pract. recipes artificial mineral waters
Flavoured cordials
Formula book in manuscript form

Good Cheer (Recipes)

Handling empty deposit bottles
Herbal Drinks. Operational techniques
Home industries (Indian)
How to make more than 100 summer . . . drinks

Mfg. syrups and cold drinks
Mineral Water Maker's Manual (various)

National Bottlers Gazette (various volumes)

Pfizer Products for the food and beverage industries
Price lists and catalogues (England)

Soft Drinks Industry-Britain 1942-48
Soft Drink Industry Manual 1968-1969
Spa Waters (G.B.B.)

Trace ingredients and influence

United Beverage Bureau Book

Tea
Alcott, W.A.   Tea and coffee effects
Andrews, W.   Over the tea cups
Antrobus, H.A.   History Assam Company
Armstrong, C.S.   Tea culture in Ceylon
Ash, O.M.   Ceylon tea from bush to teapot

B., (J.). In praise of tea
Baildon, S.   Tea in Assam
_____ . Tea industry in India . . .
Bald, C.   Indian tea: culture and mfg.
Ball, S.   Account cult. and mfg. tea in China
Bamber, E.F. and M. Kelway.   Account cult. and mfg.
    tea in India
Bamber, E.F.   Textbk. chem. and agri. of tea
Baring, F.   Principle commutation act . . .
Barker, G.M.   Tea planter's life in Assam
Blake, J.H.   Tea hints for retailers
Blaser, W.   Japanese temples and teahouses
Bonynge, F.   Future wealth of America
Broadbent, H.   Domestick coffee man, ways to make . . .
    tea

Browne, E.A. Tea
Bruce, C.A. Account mfg. black tea
_____. Report on mfg. tea . . . Assam
Buckingham, Sir J. Few facts about Indian tea

Campbell, L.E. Tea coffee and spice manual
Carpenter, P.H. and C.J. Harrison. Mfg. tea in
    Northeast India
Cave, H.W. Golden tips (Ceylon)
Chamney, M. Story of the tea leaf
Chandler, S.E. and J. McEwan. Tea, culture, manufacture
    and commerce
Chase and Sanborn. The tea table
Compton, H. Come to tea with us
Cottam, H. Tea cultivation in Assam
Crole, D. Tea; textbk. tea planting and mfg.
Crook, W. New relation, use, virtue tea

Dane, F. Sketch growth, history tea . . .
Davidson, J.W. Island of Formosa
Day, S.P. Tea, its mystery and history
Deas, F.T.R. Young tea planter's companion
Dowling, A.F. Indian tea
_____. Tea notes
Drake, F.S. Tea leaves (American colonies)
Drennen, G.T. Tea gardens' South Carolina
Dufour, P.S. Manner making coffee, tea . . .

Eden, T. Tea
Elliott, E.C. and F.J. Whitehead. Tea planting in Ceylon
Empire Tea Marketing Expansion Board. New essay on tea

Flockhart, W.B. Pure Indian tea
Forrest, D.H. 100 years Ceylon tea
Fortune, R. Journey to tea countries of China
_____. Report present condition . . . prospects tea
   cult. North-west provinces
         . Report tea plantations Northwest provinces
_____. Tea districts China and India
Fraser, F.M. Recollections of tea planter
Fakukita, Y. Tea cult of Japan

Gray, A. Little tea book
Griffith, W. Report tea planting upper Siam
Griffith, Sir. P. History Indian tea industry

Hamway, J. An essay on tea

Hanson, R. Short account tea and tea trade
Harington, J.E.M. Tea in Europe
Harler, C.R. Culture and marketing tea
_____ . Tea growing
_____ . Tea manufacture
Hauser, I.L. Tea: its origin, cult . . .
Henderson, J.A. and W.E. Account tea cultivation-Ceylon
Hockings, A.J. Queensland garden manual
Hope, G.D. Report aspects tea industry Java and Sumatra
Hope, G.D. and G.A. Carpenter. Some aspects modern tea
    pruning
Horsfield, T. Essay culture and mfg. tea-Java
Huxley, G. Talking of tea

Ibbetson, A. Tea from grower to consumer
Irwin-Harrissons and Crosfield. Trip to the Keemun tea district

Japan Tea Syndicate. Facts about tea
Johnson, R.J. Notebook for tea planters
Jones, K.B.W. Tea mfg.-Southern India
Jones, T. Tea
Kaufman, W.I. Tea cookbook (The).
Keegal, E.L. Tea mfg. in Ceylon
Kendo, T.A. Treat. silk and tea cultivation
Kingsford, A.C. Report tea industries-Java, Formosa,
    Japan
Kirby, M. and E. Aunt Martha's corner cupboard
Klaunberg, H.J. Tea, pharmacology . . .

Lancaster, O. Story of tea
Lees, W.N. Memo. tour tea districts-Eastern Bengal
_____ . Tea culture-India
Lettsom, J.C. Natural history tea-tree . . .
Linde, F. Tea in India
Lipton, Sir T. Autobiography
Lipton and Co. All about tea
Littlejohn, R.M. Tea
London Genuine Tea Co. History of tea plant
Loureiro, P. Tables, cost tea in New York

Mabson, R.R. 45 years history tea trade
Mc Calman, G. Natural commercial medicinal treatise
    on tea
McClelland, J. Report physical condition Assam tea plant
Mc Cormick and Co. Charm of tea
_____ . Tea, its cultivation, mfg . . .

Mc Cormick, K.R. Tea: its part in peace and war
McEwan, J. Commerce in tea
McGowan, A.T. Tea planting in outer Himalayah
Mac Laren, W.A. Rubber, tea and cocoa
Mann, H.H. Factor which determines quality of tea
_____ . Green manuring in tea culture in India
_____ . Tea soils of Cachar and Sylhet
_____ . Treatment deteriorated tea
Mark, G Tea plant, hist. and properties
Martin, R.M. Past, present state tea trade of England
Mason, S. Good and bad effects tea considered
Masters, J.W. Run through Assam tea gardens
Mennell, R.O. Tea. Historical sketch
Money, E. Cultivation and mfg. tea
Moppett, H.J. Tea manufacture. Theory and practice
    in Ceylon
Morrison, R.D. Tea, its production and marketing
_____ . Tea; memo relating to tea industry
    and tea trade of the world
Mowbray de, E.G.B. Notes on tea manufacture
Mueller, W. Bibliographie des kaffee-- des tea . . .

National Council of Applied Economic Research.
    Economically weak tea gardens in North-east India
Newnham, W. Some observations medical and dietary
    properties green tea
Newton, E.E. Short account Twinings
Nye, G. Tea: and the tea trade

Okakura, K. The book of tea (various)
Oriental Tea Co. The tea cup
Ovington, J. Essay on nature and qualities of tea
Owen, T.C. Tea planter's manual

Page-Croft, J. A talk on tea
Paulli, S. Treat. on tobacco, tea . . .
Peattie, D.C. Cargoes and harvests
Peck, A. Coffee, tea and chocolate
Pennington, B. Teas of the U.S.A.
Penny, F.E. Fickle fortune in Ceylon
Phelan, T.A. Book of tea secrets
Poore, G.V. Coffee and tea . . .

Ramsdan, A.R. Assam planter
Reade, A. Tea and tea drinking
Reid, C. Planting engineer

Repplier, A. To think of tea!
Roth, R. Tea drinking in 18th century America
Rous, T. B. Observations on commutation project- 1786
Routh, J. The good cuppa guide
Roy, K. K. Marketing of tea (The)
Royle, J. F. On cultivation tea Northwest provinces of
India
Rutherford, H. K. Ceylon tea planter's notebook

Saint-Arroman, A. Coffee, tea and chocolate
Salada Tea Company. Story of the tea plant
_____ . Five years of TEAMWORK
Saunders, W. Tea culture probable American industry
Scott, J. M. The great tea venture
_____ . The tea story
Shillington, D. F. and J. J. Bunting. Book on breakfast
beverages
Short, T. Discourses on tea . . .
_____ . Dissertation on tea
Sigmond, G. G. Tea; effects medicinal, moral
Skrine, E. H. and G. Brownen. Tea we drink
Smith. Tsiology; a discourse on tea
Smith, H. Essay on foreign teas . . .
Stables, W. G. Tea-drink of pleasure, health
Stanton, A. G. Report British grown tea
_____ . Tea
Staveacre, F. W. F. Tea and tea dealing
Stevenson, J. Advice, medical, economical purchase,
consumption tea . . .
_____ . Treat on tobacco, tea . . .
Stoker, T. G. Notes management tea plant
Sumner, J. Popular treat. on tea

Tea Ass'n. U. S. A. Tea
Tea Bureau, Inc. The cup that cheers
_____ . Memorandum on tea
_____ . Story of tea (The)
Tebb, W. Tea and effects of tea drinking
Tilley, F. Teapots and tea
Torgasheff, B. P. China as a tea producer
Travers, J. and Sons Ltd. Past and present in an old firm
Turner, H. A. Treatise on tea
Turnstall, A. C. Tea roots
Twining, S. H. House of Twining 1706-1956

Ukers, W. H. All about tea
_____ . Japan and Formosa

_____ . Java and Sumatra
_____ . Romance of tea
_____ . Tea in a nutshell
_____ . Trip to Brazil
_____ . Trip to Ceylon
_____ . Trip to China
_____ . Trip to India
_____ . What everyone should know about tea

Villiers, Sir T. L.   Some pioneers tea industry

Waldron, J.   A satyr against tea.   1733
Wallis-Taylor, A. J.   Tea machinery and tea factories
Walsh, J. M.   "A cup of tea"
_____ . Tea-blending as a fine art
_____ . Tea, it hist. and mystery
Wanklyn, J. A.   Tea, coffee and cocoa
Watson, J. F.   Culture and mfg. tea India
Waugh, A.   The Lipton story
Wedgewood, G. R.   History of the tea-cup
Wesley, J.   Letter to friend about tea
Wickizer, V. D.   Coffee, tea and cocoa
_____ . Tea under international regulation
Williams, L.   Tea
Woods, J.   Brief history of tea

Anonymous
Art of tea blending
Assam: sketch of its history . . . with discovery of tea
    plant

Cafe and milk bar catering
Ceylon tea story (The)

Essay on nature, use and abuse of tea

Five o'clock tea

History of tea by a propriety planter
How Ceylon tea is grown and marketed
Natural history of coffee, thee . . .

Romance of tea (The)

Story of tea (Chinese and English)
Story of Tea. (Columbus, Ohio)

Tea.   Journal of United Kingdom Tea Council
Tea and tea blending by member of firm of Lewis and Co.
Tea cultivation in Ceylon
Tea encyclopedia (The)
Tea Estate Practice (Nairobi)
Tea on service
Tea plant of Assam
Tea planter's vade mecum
Tea purchasers guide by a friend of the public
Twining's in three centuries

Uker's International Tea and Coffee Buyer's guide

Temperance
Agg-Gardner, J.T.   Compulsory temperance
D'Alonzo, C.A.   The drinking problem and its control
Amer. Academy Political and Social science
      Regulation of liquor traffic
Anderson, D.   The other side of the bottle
Andreae, P.   Prohibition movement
Armstrong, L.   Temperance revolution, history
Arthur, T.S.   Bar-rooms at Brantly
_____.   Grappling with the monster or curse, cure,
      strong drink
_____.   Six nights with Washingtonians
_____.   Ten nights in a bar-room

Baker, G.M.   Temperance drama
Balfour, C.L.   Morning dewdrops or juvenile abstainer
Bayly, H.W.   What we drink
Beard, G.M.   Stimulants and narcotics
Barrett, E.R.   Truth about intoxicating drinks
Beecher, L.   Six sermons on nature . . . intemperance
Hinkley, R.G.   Responsible drinking
Bishop, J.   Glass crutch
Blair, H.W.   Temperance movement
Blythe, S.G.   The old game (on water wagon)
Bodington, C.   Wines of the Bible
Bogen, E. and Lehmann, W.S.H.   What about alcohol?
Buckingham, J.S.   Hist. and progress temperance refor-
      mation in Great Britain
Burns, D.   Christendom and drink curse
_____.   Temperance history
Burns, Dawson.   Temperance in the Victorian age

Calkins, R. Substitutes for the saloon
Cambiaire, C.P. Black horse of Apocalypse
Cary, S.F. Liquor mfg. and traffic
_____ . National temperance offering
Cheever, G.B. Defense of judgement libel of "Inquire
  Amos Giles' distillery"
Cheraux, M.T.P. Daughter of an alcoholic
Cherrington, E.H. Ed. Anti-Saloon League year book
  (various)
_____ . Hist. Anti-saloon League
Clarke, E. Worship Bacchus-great delusion
Clubb, H.S. Maine liquor law
Colman, J.A. Catechism on beer
Colvin, D.L. Prohibition in U.S.
Cooper, R.W. Drama of drink
Cotter, O. Adulteration of liquors
Couling, S. Hist. temperance movement in Great Britain
  and Ireland
Crafts, W.F. et al. Intoxicants and opium
_____ . Intoxicating drinks and drugs in all lands
  and times
Crane, J.T. Arts of intoxication
Crooker, J.H. Shall I drink?
Crosfill, J. Historical survey temperance question
Cross, M.E. Mirror of intemperance

Daniels, W.H. Temperance reform and its great reformers
Darrow, C. and V.S. Yarros. Prohibition mania
Dearden, J. Brief hist. ancient and modern tee-totalism
Delavan, E.C. Adulterations of liquors
_____ . Temperance essays . . .
Dickey, J.M. Devil's mortgage cancelled
Dobyns, F. Amazing story of repeal
Dorchester, D. Liquor problem all ages
Dorf, R.C. Drink. Coercion or control
Douglass, E.L. Prohibition and commonsense
Dunn, J.B. Adulteration of liquors
Dupre, A. On elimination of alcohol

Eaton, E.L. Winning the fight against drink
Ellis, Mrs. Voice from the vintage
Ellis, J. Fruit of the vine
_____ . New Christianity
_____ . Pure wine-fermented wine and other alcoholic
  drinks . . .
_____ . Reply to "The wine question in light of new
  dispensation"

_____. The two-wine theory. Communion wine
Johnson, E. Drinks from drugs . . .
Johnson, F.E. and H.S. Warner. Prohibition in outline

Kerr, N.S. Inebriety or Narcomania
_____. Wines of the bible
_____. Wines, scriptural and ecclesiastical
Knott, H. The Destroyer
Knox, T.W. Teetotaler Dick. Temperance story
Koren, J. Alcohol and society
_____. Economic aspects liquor problem

Ladies of the Mission. Old brewery and new mission
    house at Five Points
Lees, F.R. Argument legal, historical, for legislative
    prohibition liquor traffic
_____. Textbook of temperance
_____. Textbook of true temperance
London, J. John Barleycorn
Lorenz, E.S. New Anti-Saloon songs

McAdoo, W.G. Challenge. Liquor and lawlessness vs
    constitutional government
Mc Auley, J. His life and work
McKenzie, F.A. "Pussyfoot" Johnson
M' Neil, D. The reformed drunkard
Malins, J. Professor Alcoholico
Mass-Observation. Pub and the people
Merz, C. The dry decade
Miller, J. Alcohol: its place and power
Moelman, C.H. When all drank and thereafter
Morrow, H.W. Tiger! Tiger! Life story of Henry B.
    Gough

National Temperance Society. Bible wines
Nesbit, W.B. Drink
Nye, N. What shall we drink?

Osborn, J. Vineyards in America
Oswald, F.L. Poison problem, cause, cure of intemperance

Parsons, B. Anti-bacchus, essay crimes . . .
    connected with use of intoxicating drinks
Patton, W. Laws of fermentation, wine of ancients
Penney, L. Readings and recitations
Pliny Moore Papers IV "Journal of Drink"
Poling, D.A. John Barleycorn

635

Porter, E. Fatal effects ardent spirits
Potter, A. Addresses by himself and others
Powell, A.M. The beer question
Powell, F. Bacchus dethroned

Raymond, I.W. Teaching of early church on use wine
    and strong drink
Reilly, H. Easy does it. Story of Mac
Rembaugh, A.C. Alcohol
Richardson, B.W. Brief notes for temperance teachers
_____. Dialogues on drink
_____. Temperance lesson book
Richmond, A.B. Leaves from diary old lawyer.
    Intemperance great source of crime
Root, J. Horror delerium tremens
Rountree, J. and A. Sherwell. Public control of the
    liquor traffic
Rush, B. Effects of ardent spirits upon human mind and
    body
Russell, J.V. Outlawing the Almighty

Seliger, R.V. Alcoholics are sick people
Shirley, C. Fetters on freedom
Smith, B. Prohibition and the bible
Smith, R.W. The sober world
Souttar, R. Alcohol: its place and power in legislation
Starke, J. Alcohol. The sanction for its use
Stebbins, J.E. 50 years hist. of temperance cause
Stevenson, T. Treatise on alcohol . . .
Stoddard, C.F. Handbk. modern facts alcohol
Stone, M.E. American liquor control
Story, C.A. Alcohol: its nature and effects
Strecker, E.A. and F.T. Chambers. Alcohol, one man's
    meat

Toledo Blade. Beer and the body
Turnbull, W.W. Law and liquor

United Brewers Industrial Foundation. Scientific
    moderation in drinking

Vecki, V. Alcohol and prohibition

Wakeman, J. Maine law triumphant
Warburton, C. Economic results prohibition
Ward, R. Fallacies of teetotalism

Warner, H.S.   Liquor cult and its culture
_____. Social welfare and liquor problem
Wasson, E.A.   Religion and drink
Weeks, C.   Cocktails, their composition and mode
  of action
White, P.S. and H.R. Pleasants.   War of 4000 years
Whittaker, T.   Brighter England and way to get it
Willard, F.E.   Woman and temperance: or work and
  workers of WCTU
Willcocks, W. and E.   History of William and Edward
  Willcocks, two servants
Williams, E.H.   Alcohol, hygiene and legislation
_____. Question of alcohol
Williams, H.S.   Alcohol.   How effects individual,
  community, race
Willis, A.   Our greatest enemy--beveraged alcohol
Wines, F.H. and J. Koren.   Liquor problem in its
  legislative aspects
Winskill, P.T.   Comprehensive history of rise, progress
  temperance reformation
_____. Temperance movement and its workers

      Anonymous
Alcohol: its use and abuse
Alcohol, science and society
Alcoholics Anonymous
American Prohibition Yearbook 1910
Amer. Society Promotion Temperance Annual reports
  (various)

Beer and the beer traffic
Bratt system liquor control.   Sweden

Centennial Temperance volume
Cold-water man; or pocket companion for the temperate

Desultory notes on origin, uses, effects of ardent spirit
Dialogue between John and Thomas on corn laws
Doctrine and discipline.   Methodist Church

Enquiries into effects fermented liquors

Fifty doctors against alcohol

History of William and Edward Willcocks, two servants

Influence of wholesome drink

Laws of Massachusetts relating to intoxicating liquors ...
    1902

National Temperance Mirror

One hundred years of temperance

Prohibition primer

Ramrod Broken: or bible, history commonsense in favor
    moderate use spirits
Regulation of liquor traffic.   Annals Amer. Academy
    Political, Social Science. 1908
Rhode Island State Temperance Society Proceedings 1832
    _____ . Third annual report 1833

Shadow of the bottle
Standard encyclopedia of alcohol problem

Wine
Accum, F.C.   Treat. art making wines from native fruits
Acker, Merrill.   Condit. Price list 1877
Acton, B. and P. Duncan.   Making wines like those you
    buy
Adams, L.D.   Commonsense book of wine
Addison, J.   Trial of wine-brewers
Adlum, J.   Memoir on cultivation of vine in America and
    best mode making wine
    _____ . On making wine
Akenhead, D.   Vitacultural research
Alanne, E.   Observations on development and structure
    English wine-growing terminology
Alexander, R.G.   Plain plantain.   Country wines 17th
    century
Allen, H.W.   Claret
    _____ . Contemplation of wine
    _____ . Gentlemen, I give you--wine!
    _____ . Good wine from Portugal
    _____ . History of wine
    _____ . Mr. Clerihew-Wine Merchant
    _____ . Natural red wines
    _____ . Number Three St. James' Street
    _____ . Romance of wine
    _____ . Sherry and port

_____ . Sherry
_____ . Through the wine-glass
_____ . White wines and cognac
_____ . Wines of France
_____ . Wines of Portugal
Allen, J. F. Culture of the grape
_____ . Pract. treat. culture and treatment of grape
vine
Allen, P. Burgundy: the splendid Duchy
Amateur, A. Home-brewed wines and unfermented
beverages
Amateur Winemakers National Guild of Judges. Judging
home-made wines
American School of Classical Studies at Athens. Amphoras,
and ancient wine trade
Amerine, M.A. Check list bks . . . on grapes and wine
. . .
_____ . Laboratory procedures for enology (various)
_____ . Short checklist books . . . in English on
grapes, wine 1949-1959
_____ . Wine
_____ . and W.V. Cruess. Technology of winemaking
_____ . and M.A. Joslyn. Commercial production
table wines
_____ . and M.A. Joslyn. Table wines . . .
_____ . and G.L. Marsh. Winemaking at home
_____ . and E.B. Roessler. Sensory evaluation of
wines
_____ . and V.L. Singleton. Wine, an introduction
for Americans
_____ . and A.J. Winkler. Grape varieties for wine
production
Andrae, E.H. Guide to cultivation grape-vine in Texas
Angostura Bitters Ltd. For home use
Anstie, F.E. On the uses of wines in health and disease
Appleyard, A. About home-made wines
_____ . Make your own wine
Arakelian, K. Inc. Correct service of Madera wines
and brandies
D'Armand, F. Jr. Key to the trade
Arnold, J.P. Home-made beverages . . .
Arnold of Villanova. Earliest printed book on wine
Arnaldus de V. Earliest printed book on wine
(facsimile 1943)
Atchison, Topeka and Sante Fe. Wine in California
Atkinson, F.E. et al. Fruit juices, cider and wines
Atkinson, J. Wine wisdom (buying, serving)

Atkinson, R.W. Chemistry saki-brewing
(Atkyns, A.) The Family Magazine
Austin, Cedric. Science of wine (The)
Austin, Nichols and Co. Wine and liquor handbk
Australian Wine Board. Wine, 1788-1939
Aye, J. Wine wisdom (see J. Atkinson)
Aylett, M. Encyclopedia home-made wines

Bacchus. Brewer's guide hotel, bar . . .
Bacchus and Cordon Bleu. New guide hotel, bar
Bacci, A. De naturali, Vinerum historia de vinis Italiae
Bachchan, H. House of wine
Batchelor, D. Wines great and small
Bagenall, B.W. Descendents of pioneer winemakers
    of South Australia
Bagnall, A.G. Wines of South Africa
Bailey, L.H. American grape training
Bailey, N. Dictionarium Domesticum
Balch, A.W. and Co. Price list. Wines . . . 1898
Balzer, R.L. Adventures in wine. Legends. History.
    Recipes
_____ . California's best wines
_____ . Pleasures of wine
Barclay, J. Arts of brewing and distillation
Barron, A.F. Vines and vine-culture
Barry, Sir E. Observations, historical, critical and
    medical wines of ancients
Battam, A. Collection scarce valuable receipts . . .
    for making wine
Bayard, L. Wine Guide Volume 1 through 5
Beach, S. New, compl. cellar bk. homemade wines
Bear, J.W. Vitacultural resources of Victoria
Beardsall, F. Treat. natural properties and composition
    ancient and modern wines
Beastall, W. Useful guide for grocers
Beatty-Kingston, W. Claret, its production . . .
Beck, E.J. Aesthetics of wine
Beck, F. The Fred Beck wine book
Beck, H. Meet the Cape wines
Beckwith, A.R. The vintner's story
Beckwith, E.L. Pract. notes on wine
Beech, F.W. Homemade wines, syrups, cordials
_____ . Wines and juices
Beedell, S. Wine making and home brewing
Beeton, I.M. Jam making--homemade wines
Belloc, J.H.P. Advice

Bellows and Co. Inc. Catalogue fine wines . . .
Belt, T.E. Preserving winemaking ingredients
Belth, G. Household guide wines, liquors
Bennett, R. Guide to winemakers, brewers . . .
Bentley, I. Wine with a merry heart
Benwell, W.S. Journey to wine in Victoria
Berliner, J.J. and Staff. Wine and fermented fruit
    products
    _____ . Wines
Berry, C.J.J. Amateur winemaker's recipes
    _____ . First steps in winemaking (various)
    _____ . Making wine is not difficult
    _____ . 130 new winemaking recipes
    _____ . Winemaking with canned and dried fruit
Berry, C.W. In search of wine
    _____ . A miscellany of wine
    _____ . Viniana
Berry Bros. Co. Tokay
    _____ . A wine cellar
Berry-Smith, F. Grape growing in home garden
    _____ . Vitaculture
Beverage Research Bureau. Manual on beers, wines . . .
Biddle, A.J.D. The land of wine
    _____ . The Madeira Islands
Big Features Publicity Co. 100 recipes for making beer
    and wine
Bijur, G. Wines with long noses
Bioletti, F.T. Bench grafting resistant vines
    _____ . Best wine grapes in California
    _____ . Elements of grape growing in California
    _____ . Grape culture in California
    _____ . Mfg. dry wines in hot countries
    _____ . New method making dry red wines
    _____ . New wine cooling machine
    _____ . Principles of wine making
    _____ . Wine making on small scale
Bird, W. French wines . . .
    _____ . Pract. guide to French wines
Bleasdale, J.I. On Colonial wines
    _____ . Pure native wine considered as article of food
    and luxury
Bloomfield, William. The servant's companion, or practical
    housemaid's and footman's guide
Blout, J.S. Brief economic history- California wine-
    growing industry
Blunno, M. Notes on winemaking

Bode, C.G. Wines of Italy
Bodington, C. Wines of the bible
Boireau, R. Wines, care, treatment cellar . . .
Bolitho, H. Wine of the Douro
Bolling, R. Jr. Sketch of vine culture
Bolton, M. Homemade wines . . .
Book Club of California. Wine in early California
Booth, D. Art of wine-making
Borella. Court and country confectioner . . .
Bosdari, C. de. Wine of the Cape
Bose, D.K. Wine in ancient India
Boswell, P. Wine makers manual
Boulestin, X.M. What shall we have to drink?
Bourke, A. Winecraft; encyclopedia . . .
Boyle, P. Publican and spirit dealer's daily companion
Bradford, Sarah. The Englishman's wine. The story of
    port
Bradley, J.F. Cocktails, wines, liquors
Bragato, R. Viticulture in New Zealand
Brandt, J. The grape cure
Brannt, W.T. Pract. treat. mfg. vinegar . . . fruit
    wines
Bravery, H.E. Amateur wine making
_____ . Home wine making
_____ . Home wine making without failures
_____ . The simple science of wine and beer
    making
_____ . Successful winemaking at home
Briggs, R. English art of cookery . . .
Bright, W. Bright on the grape question
Broadbent, J.M. Wine tasting
Brock, R.B. Outdoor grapes in cold climates
_____ . Progress with vines and wines
_____ . Starting a vineyard
Browne, C. Gun club drink book
Bryant, W.B. 19th century handbk. mfg. liquors, wines
    cordials without distillation
Buchanan, R. Culture of grape and winemaking
Bulos, Mons. Art of wine making
Burgess, Rev. H.T. Fruit of the vine
Buring, L. Ltd. Art of serving wine
Buring, H.P.L. Australian wines; 150th anniversary
    of the wine industry of Australia
Busby, J. Australian farmer's . . . guide culture wine
    in New South Wales
_____ . Grapes and wine

642

_____. Journal recent visit vineyards-Spain
_____. Manual plain directions planting cult. vine-
    yards-New South Wales
_____. Treat. culture of vine and art making wine
Bush and Son and Meissner. Catalogue American grape
    vines 1883
Butler, F.H. Wine and wine lands of world
Bynam, L.D. California wines, how to enjoy

California Board State Vitacultural Commissioners.
    Report-1893-94
California State Fair and Exposition. Wine awards
Campbell, I.M. Reminiscences of a vintner
_____. Wayward tendrils of the vine
Campbell, I.M. Wine: Post war problems and
    possibilities
deCaradeuc, H. Grape culture and winemaking in the
    South
Carling, T.E. Compl. book of drink
_____. Wine. Thumbnail sketches
_____. Wine aristocracy
_____. Wine drinker's aide-memoire
_____. Wine etiquette . . .
_____. Wine lore
_____. Wine wise
Carlisle, D.T. Wining and dining with rhyme and reason
Carnell, P.P. Treat. on family winemaking
Carosso, V.P. California wine industry
Carter, Y. Drinking Bordeaux
_____. Drinking Burgundy
_____. Drinking champagne and brandy
Caruba, R. Cooking with wine and high spirits
Cassagnac, P. de. French wines
Castella, F. de. Home wine making
Castella, H. de. Handbook vitaculture Victoria
_____. John Bull's vineyard
Catts-Patterson Co. Ltd. Proposed plan for the
    development of the Australian wine industry
Cazaubon, D. Treat. and pract. guide to apparatus for
    fabrication sparkling wines
Cazenave, A. Pract. manual culture vine in the Gironde
Chaloner, L. What the vintners sell
Chamberlain, B.P. Treat. on making palatable table
    wines
Champin, A. Vine grafting
Chappaz, G. and A. Herriot. Champagne vine country and
    champagne wine

Chappius, B. Manual Swiss vigneron
Chaptel, J.A.C. et al. Treat. upon wines
Charleton, W. 2 discourses- of mysterie of vintners
Chase, E. Pleasures of cooking with wine
Chodowski, A.T. Wine, its use and abuse
Chorlton, W. Amer. grape growers guide
_____ . Cold grapery
_____ C--grape growers guide
Christ, E.R. and F.R. Fisk. That bk about wine
Christian, R. Sherry
Chubb, W.P. Receipt book- nearly 1000 receipts for making
    British wine
Church, M.E. American guide to wines
Churchill, C. Notebook for wines of France
_____ . World of wines
Churchill, S.D. All sorts, condition, drinks
Clarke, Frank K. Make your wine at home
Clarke, Nick. Bluff your way in wine
Clarke, W. Compl. cellar manual . . .
Cleland, C. Abstracts of laws relating to import of wine.
    1737
"Clements". Homemade wines . . .
Cobb, G. Oporto, older and newer
Cockburn, E. Port wine and Oporto
Cocks, C. Bordeaux. Its wine and the claret country
Codman, C.R. Years and years; some vintage years in
    French wines
Codman, R.S. Vintage dinners
Colburn, F.E.W. In old vintage days
Collingwood, F. and J. Woollams. The Universal cook
Comite Interprofessionel du vin de Champagne. The
    Champagne wine
Consumer Union. The CU report, wines, spirits
_____ . Wines and liquors
Cook, Fred S. ed. The wines and wineriers of California
Cook, P. Wine merchant's assessment of Burgundy
C(osens), F.W. Sherryana
Cossart, Gordon and Co. Madeira Island
Costello, L.S. Summer amongst the Bocages and the
    vines
Cotten, C.B. Formula of N.Y., Phila., and Baltimore
    mfgrs of wines and liquors
Couche, D.D. Modern detection and treatment wine
    diseases
Country Ass'ns. Wines, spirits for all occasions
Courtenay, J.M. de. Canada vine grower

_____. Culture of vine and emigration
Cox, H.   Food, flowers and wine cookbook
Cox, Harry.   Wines of Australia
Cozzens, F.S.   C--wine press
Cradock, J.   ABC of wine drinking
Craig, E.   Wine in the kitchen
_____. Woman, wine and a saucepan
Crawford, I.   Make me a wine connisseur
_____. Wine on a budget
Cresta Blanca Wine Co.   Nature smiled and there was
    Cresta Blanca
Croft, J.   Treatise on wines of Portugal
Croft-Cocke, R.   Madeira
_____. Port
_____. Sherry
_____. Wine and other drinks
Crombie, M.   The infidel grape
Crotch, W.W.   Compl. yearbk.   French wines, spirits
    and liqueurs
Cruess, W.V. et al.   Laboratory exam. wines and other
    fermented fruit products
_____. Prin. and pract. wine making
Cusmano, G.   Dizionario di vitacultura edenologia

(D., S.) Vinetum Angliae.   New way to make wine of
    English grapes . . .
Daraio, J.P.   Healthful and therapeutic properties wine . . .
Davidson, W.R.   Wholesale wine trade in Ohio
D'Armand, F.   Art of fine wine drinking
Davies, J.   Innkeeper and butler's guide
Davis, J.I.   Beginner's guide to wines . . .
Davis, S.F.   History of the wine trade
Deering, C.   Muscadine grapes
Delavan, E.C.   Adulterations of liquors
Demko, C.   Growing grapes in Florida
Denman, J.L.   Brief discourse wine, historical and
    descriptive
_____. Pure wine and how to know it
_____. The vine and its fruit
_____. What should we drink?
_____. Wine and its adulterations
_____. Wine and its counterfeits
_____. Wine as it is drank in England
_____. Wine, the advantages of pure and natural
    wine . . .
Denniston, G.   Grape culture in Steuben Co.

Despeissis, A. Handbook horticulture and vitaculture-
Western Australia
Despeissis, K. A. Vineyard and the cellar
De Tassigny and Gauthier Ltd. Wines - whys and where-
fores
Dettori, R. G. Italian wines and liqueurs
Dewey, H. T. and Sons Co. 50th anniversary 1907 (wine
dealer)
Dewey, S. Wines for those who have forgotten and for
those who want to know
Dexter, P. Notes on French wines
Dicey, P. Wine in South Africa
Digby, Sir K. Closet of Sir K. D. opened
Director, A. Art wine cookery
Doblache, G. My first trip to Villa Neuva (Sherry
country)
Don, R. S. Wine
Donovan, M. Cabinet encyclopedia
Dornot, C. C. Wine and spirit merchants own book
Dorozynski, Alexander and Bibiane Bell. The wine book
Dougherty, J. General guager
Downey, A. J. Australian grape growers' manual for the
use of beginners
Downman, F. Not claret
Draz, F. and Co. Glimpse famous wine cellar
Driver, J. Letters from Madeira in 1834
Driver, S. C. Some principles of wine trade
Druitt, R. Report cheap wines from France, Italy,
Austria, Greece and Hungary
Dubois, R. and W. P. Wilkinson. New methods grafting
and budding
_____ . Trenching and subsoiling Amer. Vines
Du Breuil, M. Thomery system grape culture
_____ . Vineyard culture
Dufour, J. J. Amer. vine-dresser's guide
Dumbra, C. D. Forward American wines
Dumont, L. How you can make wines . . .
Duncan, Peter and Bryan Acton. Progressive winemaking
Dunlop, J. On the wine system of Great Britain
Du Pont, de Nemours, A. Cultivation vineyards
southwestern France

Eakin, J. R. Rudiments of grape culture
Edmonds, G. Country brewer's ass't and English
vintner's instructor
Edmonds, W. On wines. New way to make from herbs
fruit, flowers

Edwards, W. N. The beverages we drink
Ellis, C. Origin, nature, history wine
Ellwanger, G. H. Meditations on gout-cure through use
    of wine
Emerson, E. R. Lay treat. on bible wines
——————— . Story of the vine
Ermitano (pseud). Shillingsworth of sherry
Escritt, L. B. Small cellar
(Evans, Len) Guide to Australian wines

F. and I. Wine, what is it?
Fabre, J. H. C. Analysis wines and interpretations of
    analytical results
Fadiman, C. Dionysus; a case vintage tales
Faes, H. Lexique Viti-Vinicole International
Fallon, J. T. Handbk. Australian vines, wines
——————— . Wines of Australia
Farley, J. New, compl. cellar bk. . . .
Farmers Weekly. Homemade country wines
Feret, E. Bordeaux and its wines classified
Fessler, J. Art of wine making . . .
——————— . Guidelines pract. winemaking
Feuchtwanger, L. Fermented liquors . . .
Feuerheerd, H. L. Gentlemen's cellar . . .
Field, S. B. Vintage festival
Field, S. S. American drink book
Findlater, Mackie, Todd and Co. Ltd. Home of Treble
    Diamond (wines)
Fisher, M. F. Story of wine-California
Fisher, S. I. Observations on character and culture
    European vine
Fitchett, L. S. Beverages and sauces colonial Virginia
Flagg, W. J. Three seasons in European vineyards
Foote, E. J. Will you take wine?
Forbes, E. Wines for everyman
Forbes, P. Champagne: the wine, the land . . .
Fornachon, J. C. M. Bacterial spoilage of fortified
    wines
——————— . Studies on the sherry flor
Forrester, J. J. Port and wines-Portugal
——————— . Prize essay on Portugal
——————— . Word or two on port wine
——————— . Wine trade of Portugal
Foster and Ingle. Wine, what is it? See F and I.
——————— . Gatherings from wine-lands
Foster, A. E. M. Through wine list

Foster, C. Home winemaking
Foughner, S. Along wine trail
Franklyn, H. M. Glance at Australia in 1880
Franz, A. New wine book
_____ . Use of starters making sounder finer wines
Freels, S. C. The X- ray; or, facts, figures of interest
    to retail liquor dealer
Friends of wine (Publ.) Summer wine coolers
Frumkin, L. Science and technique of wine
Fuller, A. S. Grape culturist

Gardner, J. Brewer, distiller, wine mfgr.
Gardner and Son. Price list. Wines . . . 1910
Garey, T. A. Orange culture in California with appendix
    on grape culture
Garnsey, W. New wine tables
Garrett, P. Art serving wine
Garvin, F. French wines
Gayon, U. Studies on wine-sterilizing machines
Gennery- Taylor., Mrs. Easy made wine, country drinks
Geysius, J. J. Parastota, fablam Monte . . .
Gilbey, W. and A. Book prices 1870
_____ . Compl. list wines, spirits . . .
_____ . Treat. on wines and spirits of principal
    producing countries
Gilmour, A. Sacramental wines
Ginrum Alpha Co. Legend of liqueurs, wines and spirits
Gneisieau, A. How brew beer and make wine
Gold, E. ed. Wines and spirits of world
Gonzalez, Byass and Co. Ltd. Old sherry
Good Housekeeping Institute. Preserves . . . and home
    made wines
Gore- Browne, M. Let's plant a vineyard
Graham, M. E. Comp. Wine and Food Society of Southern
    California: a history with a bibliography of A. L. Simon
Graham, W. Art of making wines from fruits and flowers
Gramp, G. and Sons Ltd. 100 years of winemaking
Grant, C. W. Manual of the vine
Grants of St. James Ltd. Gateway to wine
Gratrix, Dawson. In pursuit of the vine
Gray, J. After repeal--serving wines
Grazzi-Soncini, G. Wine. Class-tasting
Greenwood, R. Vintage at Chateau Monbousquet
Greg, T. T. Through the glass lightly
Gregor, M. Notes upon pure and natural wines
_____ . Notes upon pure and natural wines of
    Hungary

Griffin, J.J. Chem. testing wines, spirits
Griswold, F.G. Old Madeiras
Grommes and Ulrich. Special price list whiskies, wines
    . . .1915
Grossman, H.J. Guide to wines, spirits . . .
Guthrie, W. Remarks on burgundy, claret, champagne
Guyot, J. Cultivation of the vine and winemaking
_____ . Growth of the vine and principles of winemaking
Gwynn, S. Burgundy
Gyrogy, P. Fine wines of Germany and all the World's
    Wine Lore

Haarlem, J.R. Variety tests for grapes for wine
Hack, F. Home brewed wines and beers
Hackett, F.M. English cottage wines
Haimo, O. Cocktail and wine digest
_____ . Cocktails and wine digest (Spanish)
Halasz, Z. Hungarian wine through ages
Hall and Nahler. Six best cellars
Hall, H. The distiller
Hall, J.J. and J. Bunton. Wines
Hallgarten, S.F. Alsace and its wine gardens
_____ . Rhineland wineland
Hammond, H. Notes on wine and vine culture in France
Hancock, G.C. Report composition commoner British
    wines and cordials
Hann, G.E. Some notes technical study and handling of
    wines
Haraszthy, A. Grape culture, wines and winemaking
Hardman, W. Wine-growers' and wine-coopers' manual
Hardwick, H. Winemaking at home
Hardy, T. and Sons, Lts. Hardy tradition (winemaking
    family)
Hardy, T. Note on vineyards Amer. and Europe
_____ . A vigneron abroad
Harrison, G. Bristol cream
Hartley, J. Wholesale and retail wine and spirit merchant's
    companion
Harvey, John and Sons Ltd. Harvey's wine guide
Harvey, J. and Sons Ltd. Wine list decorations
_____ . Wine list 1963-64
Haskell, G. Wines liqueurs and brandies
Haskell, Geo. Account various experiments for production
    new, desirable grapes
Hasler, G.F. Wine service in restaurant
Haszonics, J.J. and S. Barratt. Wine merchandising

Hawker, C.E.   Chats about wine
_____ . Wine and wine merchants
Hayne, A.P.   Control temperature in wine fermentation
Healy, M.   Bibulography of memorabilia, trivia,
jocosa, jocoseria . . . upon wine and lore
Healy, M.   Claret and white wine and Bordeaux
_____ . Stay me with flagons
Heath, A.   Home-made wines and liqueurs
Heaton, N.   Wines, mixed drinks, savouries
Heddle, E. M.   Story of a vineyard-Chateaux Tahbilk
Hedrick, U.P.   Grapes and wines from home vineyards
_____ . Hist. horticulture in America
_____ . Manual American grape-growing
Helmont, J.P. van.   Tennery of paradoxes (Tartar in
wine) 1650
Henderson, A.   Hist. ancient and modern wines
Henderson, J.F.   Startling profits from wine making
Henri, M.   Wines Ltd.   Your guide to imported wines of
Monsieur Henri
Herbemont, N.   Treat. on culture of vine
Herrick, C.T. and M. Harland.   Consolidated Library
modern cooking
_____ . Modern Domestic Science Vol. 5
Herod, W.P.   Introduction to wines
Herstein, K.M. and T.S. Gregory.   Chem. and technology
wines and liquors
Heuckmann, W. and R. Vom Endt.   Grafted vine
Hewitt, J.T.   Chemistry of winemaking
Heyne, E.B.   Compl. catalogue European vines . . .
Hilgard, E.W.   Reports experiments on fermenting red
wines
Hill, E.   Water into gold
Hills, W.H.   Small fruits
Hilsebusch, H.W.   Knowledge of rectifier
Hirshfield, A.M.   Stand. handbk. wines . . .
Hoare, C.   Descriptive account improved methods planting,
managing vines
_____ . Pract. treat. cultivation grape vine
Hofer, A.F.   Grape growing single pole system
Hogg, A. ed.   Wine mine (various)
Hoggson, T.   Squire's homemade wines
Holden, E.A.   History of vitaculture and winemaking in
Australia
Holland, V.   Drink and be merry
Hopkins, A.A.   Home made beverages
Hornickel, E.   Great wines of Europe

Hudson, W. Wines of Italy
Huggett, H. E. V. Rhenish. (Rhine wines)
Hughes, A. Cyprus wines
Hughes, J. M. Itinerary Provence and Rhone
Hughes, W. Compleat vineyard
Husenbeth, F. C. Wine merchant- Bristol
Husmann, G. Amer. grape growing and wine making
_____ . Cultivation of native grape . . .
_____ . Grape culture and wine- making California
_____ . Some uses of grapevine and its fruit
_____ . and C. Deering. Muscadine grape
Hutchinson, P. Do's and don'ts of winemaking
_____ . Home- made sparkling wine secrets
_____ . Home- made wine secrets
_____ . Home- made wines, how to make
_____ . More Peggy Hutchinson's homemade wine secrets
_____ . Tonic wine- making secrets
Hutton, I. G. The vigneron. Essay cultivation of grape
   and making wine
Hyams, E. Dionysus. Social hist. of wine vine
_____ . Grape vine in England
_____ . Grapes under clothes
_____ . Vin; wine country of France
_____ . Vineyard in England
_____ . Wine Country of France
Hyatt, T. H. Handbk. grape culture . . .

Imperial Economic Committee. Wine report No. 23 1932

Jack, F. B. Homebrewed wines and beers . . .
_____ . 100 homebrewed wines . . .
Jackson, H. Essay British isinglass- hints improvement,
   fermenting . . .
Jacob, H. E. Grape growing in California
Jacquelin, L. and R. Poulain. Wines and vineyards of France
Jagendorf, M. A. Folk wines, cordial . . .
James, W. Barrel and book
_____ . Fear of wine
_____ . What's what about wine
_____ . Wine; brief encyclopedia
_____ . Wine growers diary
_____ . Wine in Australia
_____ . Word book of wine
Jeffs, J. Sherry
Jerez Industrial Editions. Sherry as seen by the British
Joelson, A. Memoirs of Kohler of K. W. V.

Johnson, G.W. and R. Errington. The grape vine
Johnson, H. Best of vineyards is the cellar
_____ . Pan book of wine
_____ . Wine
Johnson, S. Indulgence in wine
Johnson Smith and Co. Homebrewed wines and beers
Jonas, P. Distiller's guide
Jones, I. Vines in the sun
_____ . The vineyard
Jordan, J.V. Simple facts about wines
Jordan, R. Quality in dry wines . . .
Joslyn, M.A. and M.A. Amerine. Commercial production
    dessert wines
_____ . Dessert, appetizer and related flavored
    wines
Joslyn, M.A. and W.V. Cruess. Elements of winemaking
Jullien, A. Topography of all known vineyards
_____ . Wine merchants companion

K., G.A. Clarets and sauternes
Keane, E. Penfold story (Wine-growing)
Keech, J. Grape grower's guide
Keir, U. The vintage
Kelly, A.C. Vine in Australia
_____ . Wine-growing in Australia
Kercht, J.S. Improved practical culture of the vine
    especially in regular vineyards
Kerr, N.S. Wines: scriptural and ecclesiastical
Kirk, A. Grape culture up-to-date
deKlerk, W.A. White wines South Africa
Knittel, J. Cyprus wine from my cellar
Koenen, A. From vineyard to table
Ko-operatiewe Wijnbouwers Verenging van Zuid-Afrika
    Beperkt. Cooking with Cape wine
Ko-operatiewe Wijnbouwers Vereniging van Zuid-Afrika
    Beperkt. Wine handbook for hoteliers
Kressmann, E. The wonder of wine
Krickauff, F. Future of our wine industry (Australia)
KWV Public Relations Dept. Entertaining with wines of the
    Cape
KWV Public Relations Dept. A handbook on wine
KWV. Planning a wine and cheese party
KWV. The South African wine industry. Its growth and
    development
KWV. Public Relations Dept. Survey. wine growing
    South Africa (Various)

Lacour, P. Mfg. liquors, wines . . . without aid of
    distillation
Lady (A). Art of cookery made plain, easy
Laffer, H.E. Wine industry of Australia 1938 and 1949
Lake, M. Classic wines of Australia
_____ . Hunter wine
_____ . Vine and scalpel
Lamb, D.L. Guide to Bordeaux wines and cognac
La Montagne and Sons. Wines of Bordeaux
Lamson-Scribner, F. Fungus diseases of the grape . . .
Landfield, J. California, America's vineyard
Langenbach, A. German wines and vines
Lansdell, J. Grapes: and how to grow them
Laumer, W.F. About wines
Launay, A. Merrydown book country wines
Laver, J. Victorian vista (anthology)
La-Vogue, E. Art and secrets in mfg. wines . . .
Law, E. King Henry VIII's newe wyne seller at Hampton
    Court
Layton, T.A. Choose your wine
_____ . Modern wines
_____ . Winecraft. Encyclopedia wines and spirits
_____ . Wines and castles of Spain
_____ . Wine's my line
_____ . Wines and Chateaux of Loire
_____ . Wines of Italy
Le Brocq, P. Description with notes of certain methods
    of planting
Leedom, W.S. Vintage wine book
Lees, F.R. First prize essay sacramental wine
Lefevre, N. Discourse Sir Rawleigh's great Cordial
Leggett, H.B. Early history wine production in
    California
Legrand, N.E. Champagne
Leipoldt, C.L. 300 years of Cape wine
Levett, J. Making wines at home
Lewis, R.A. Wines of Madeira
Leyel, C.F. Summer drinks and winter cordials
Libby Glass Mfg. Co. Notes for an epicure
Lichine, A. Encyclopedia wines and spirits
_____ . Wines of France
Lima, J.J. de C. Port wine
Lindegaard, P. New method forcing grapes and keeping
    them in winter
Lindemann, E.H. Pract. guide and receipt book for
    distillers, wine-growers . . .
Liquor Store Magazine. Pract. encyclopedia of alcoholic
    beverages

Lloyd, F. C.   Art and technique of wine
Locke, J.   Observation on growth and culture of wines
    and olives
Loeb, R. H. Jr.   How wine friends and affluence people
Loos, M. and W. Duranty.   Return to vineyard
Loubat, A   Amer. vine-dresser's guide
Loyd, J. F.   Wine as a beverage
Lucia, S. P.   Hist. wine as theraphy
_____.   Wine and health
_____.   Wine as food and medicine
Lukas, J.   Book of wine
Luker, H. and Co. Ltd.   Price list 1880
Lutz, H. F.   Vitaculture and brewing in the ancient orient

Maanen-Helmer, E. van.   What to do about wines
Mabon, M. F.   ABC of America's wines
(Mac Arthur, Sir W.)   Letters on the culture of the vine
McBride, D.   General instructions choice wines and
    spiritous liquors
Mac Collom, W.   Vines and how to grow them
Macculloch, J.   Remarks of the art of making wine . . .
Mc Douall, Robin.   Cooking with wine
Mc Ewin, G.   South Australian Vigneron and gardener's
    manual
Mc Gee, W.   From vineyard to decanter
Macgregor, J.   Wine making for all
M'Harry, S.   Practical distiller
(Machet, J. J.)   Receipts for homemade wines
Mc Indoe, D.   Chapman's New Zealand grape manual . . .
Mackay, M.   The Wine Princes (Novel)
Mc Laren, M.   Pure wine; or In Vino Veritos
McLean, J. M.   Book of wine
McMullen, T.   Handbk. of wines, pract. theoretical and
    historical
McWilliam, D. M.   Wine merchants bk recipes
Madden, J.   Shall we drink wine?
Maior, J. M.   Viniculture of claret
Malet, W. E.   Australian winegrowers' manual
Mallet., P.   Narrative of circumstances relating to excise
    bill on wine
Manning, S. A.   Handbook wine and spirit trade
Manoha, G.   Cooking with wine
Marcus, I. H.   Dictionary wine terms
Marks, R.   Wines; how, when, and what to serve
Marrison, L. W.   Wines and spirits
Martin, W.   Rough sketch renewal system, pruning grape
    vines

Martyn, C.   Wine steward's manual
Marvel, T.   Pocket dictionary of wines
Mascall, L.   Boke of arte and manor how to plant and
    graffe all sorts of trees
Massee, W.E.   Wine handbook
_____ .   Wines and spirits
Massel, A.   Applied wine chemistry and technology
_____ .   Dicta technica.   Modern techniques
Masters, J.E.   Old English wines and cordials
Maupin, M.   L'Art de la vigne 1780
Maveroff, P.A.   Enologia
Maxwell, G.A.   Winery accounting and cost control
Maxwell, K.   Fairest vineyards. (So. Africa)
(May, W.J.)   Vine culture for amateurs by a practical
    hand
Mazade, M.   First steps in ampelography
Mead, P.B.   Elementary treat. on American grape culture
    and winemaking
Mearns, J.   Treat. on pot culture of the grape
Melville, J.   Guide to California wines
Meredith, J.   Treatise on the grape wine
Meyden, T.A.   Trattato della natvra de vino
Mida, L.W.   Continous directory spirits industry . . .
Milbourn, T.   Vintner's Company .. .
Mills, F.C.   Wine guide
Mills, S.A.   Wine story-Australia
Misch, R.J.   Quick guide to wine
Misiatrus, P.   The honour of the gout
Mitchell, J.R.   Scientific winemaking-made easy
Mitchell, S.W.   A Madeira party
Mitchell, Sir T.L.   Notes on culture of vine and methods
    making wine-Southern Spain
Mitzsky and Co.   Our native grape
Mogen David Wine Co.   Food, fun and festivity
Mohr, F.   The grape vine.   Pract. scientific treatise on
    management
Molyneaux, E.   Grape growing for amateurs
Moodie-Heddle, E.   Story of a vineyard
Moonen, L.   Australian wines
Morel, J.   Progressive catering
Morgan, L.   Home-made wines
Moroney, J.   Price list finest old wines and spirits 1899
Morris, D.   The French vineyards
Morris, W.   Praise of wine
Morton, A.   Just what you want to know about wine
Moubray, B.   Pract. treat on breeding--instruction in
    British wine making 1834

Mouraille, L.P.   Pract. guide treatment wine in English
   cellars
Mournetas, A. and H. Pelisser.   Vade-mecum of the
   wine lover
Muir, A.   How to choose and enjoy wine
Mulder, G.J.   Chemistry of wine
Munch, F.   School for American grape culture
Munson, T.V.   Foundations American grape culture
Murphy, D.F.   Australian wine guide
Murray, S.W.   Wines of the USA.   How to know and choose
   them

National Wine Board Portugal.   Wines of Portugal
New York State Agri. Experiment Sta.   Grape varieties.
   Bulletin no. 794
Newhall, C.S.   Vines of northeastern America
Newmark, A.   Tannin and its uses in wine
Newton, J.C.   Homemade wines
Norris, S.   Your life is more pleasant with wine
Nutt, F.   Receipts for homemade wines . . .

Oechs, A. and Co.   Commentary on wines
Oesterreicher and Co.   Rational mfg. American wines
Oldham, C.F.   California wines
Olivier, S.   Wine journeys
Opperman, D.J. Editor.   Spirit of the vine: Republic of
   South Africa
Ordish, G.   Wine growing in England
Osborn, J.   Vineyards in America
Ott, E.   From barrel to bottle
Ough, C.S. and M.A. Amerine.   Effects of temperature
   on wine making
Ozias, B.   How modern hostess serves wine
_____ .   All about wine

Packer, J.   Valley of the vines
Packman, W.V.   Gentlemen's own guide to wines and
   spirits
_____ .   Wine and spirit manual . . .
Pacottet, P.   Vinification.   Vin, eau de vie, vinaigre . . .
Paguierre, M.   Classification and description wines of
   Bordeaux
Paige, W.V.   Is this your wine?
Palmer, J.S.   Popular receipts, proper guide for making
   wines
Park and Tilford.   Wholesale price list 1894

Parker, H.   Vintner's answer to scandulous pamphlets
Parkes, B.   Domestic brewer and family winemaker
Parsons, H. Grapes under glass
Patten, M.   500 recipes homemade wines . . .
Pearks, G.   Complete home wine-making
Pearkes, G.   Growing grapes in Britain
Pearson, J.R.   Vine culture under glass
Peixotto, E.C.   Bacchic pilgrimage: French wines
Pellicot, A.   Vine and wine-making in Southern France
Pelligrini, A.M.   Wine and the good life
Peninou, E.P. and S.S. Greenleaf.   Directory California
    wine growers . . . in 1860
_____ .   Winemaking in California
Penning-Rowsell, Edmund.   Wines of Bordeaux
Penzer, N.M.   Book of the wine label
Perkins, A.J.   Vine-pruning; its theory and practice
Perold, A.I.   Treat. on vitaculture
Perry, M.H.   And to drink sir!
Persoz, J.F.   New process of culture of vine
Petrar, M.F.   Chroni ca delle viti de Pontfici.   1526
Phelps, R.H.   The vine: its culture in U.S.
Phin, J.   Open air grape culture
Pierce, N.B.   California vine disease
Plimmer, R.H.A.   Chemical changes and products resulting
    from fermentation
Portuguese.   Wine question considered
Postgate, R.W.   Alphabet of choosing and serving wine
_____ .   Home wine cellar
_____ .   Plain man's guide to wine
_____ .   Portuguese wine
Poupon, P. and P. Porgeot.   Bk of Burgundy
Practical Brewer.   Publican, innkeeper and brewer's guide
Practical man.   Butler, wine-dealer and private brewer
_____ .   Innkeeper and public brewer
Pretyman, H.   Recipes for homemade wines
_____ .   33 recipes homemade wines
Price, P.V.   Winelover's handbook
Prince, G.   Current books about wine
Prince, W.R.   Treatise on the vine
Proskauer, J.J.   What'll you have?
Public Library of South Australia.   Research Service
    Bibliographies Series 4 No. 82.   Wine and vitaculture

Quinn, G.   Fruit tree and grape vine pruning

Rack, J.   French wine and liquor mfgr.
Rafinesque, C.S.   Amer. Manual grape vines

Rainbird, G. Pocket book of wine
_____ . Sherry and wines of Spain
Rainford, B. Sicily and its wine
Rawnsley, K. Health giving brews
_____ . Homemade wines . . .
Ray, Cyril. Lafite. The story of Chateau Lafite-Rothschild.
_____ . Introduction to wines
_____ . Wines of Italy
Ray, G. French wines
Reach, A.B. Claret and olives from Garonne to Rhone
Redding, C. Every man his own butler
_____ . French wines and vineyards . . .
_____ . Hist. and description modern wines
Reemelin, C. Vine-dresser's manual
_____ . Winemaker's manual
Reeve, L.E. Gift of the grape
Rendle, W.E. England a wine-producing country
Renner, H.D. Pocket guide to wine
Riker, D.H. Wine book of knowledge
Rittich, V.J. and E.A. European grape growing
Rixford, E.H. Wine press and the cellar
Reate, M.C. How to make wine in your kitchen
Roberts, J. Culture of vine under glass
Roberts, W.H. British wine-maker and domestic brewer
Robinson, J. Whole art making British wines
Robson, E.I. Wayfarer in French vineyards
Roger, J.R. Wines of Bordeaux
Rollat, E. Wine guide and cocktail book
Rolleston, Samuel. Dissertation on barley wine (A).
Rolli, O.C. Wine for home and medicinal use
_____ . Wines and cordials for home and medicinal
      use
Roos, L. Wine-making in hot climates
Roose, S. Wine and brandy dealer's complete guide
Rosatti, G. Wine industry of Italy
Rose, J. English vineyard vindicated
Rose, R.S. Wine making for amateur
Rosen, R.C. POP, Monsieur. Champagne recipes for
      everyday food and drink
Rudd, H.R. Hocks and Moselles

Sabin, B.C. Wines and fresh fruit beverages
Sabine, H. Compl. cellarman or innkeeper and publican's
      sure guide
St. Pierre, L. de. Art of planting, cultivating the vine ...
Saintsbury, G. Notes on a cellar book

Sala, G.A. In a wine cellar on Store St
deSalis, Mrs. Drinks ala mode. Cups and drinks every
    kind of season
Samson, G.W. Divine law as to wines
Sandeman, G.G. Sons Co. Jerez and its wine-sherry
Sandeman, P.W. Port and sherry
Sanders, J. Pract. treat. cultivation of vine under glass ...
Saunders, W. Essay on culture native and exotic grape
    and both sides of grape question
Schenck, H.A. New medical wine bk
Schenley, Import Corp. Introduction to wines
_____ . Wine without frills
_____ . Wines; how, when, and what to serve
Schmidt, J.A. Diseases of the vine . . .
Schoonmaker, F. American wines
_____ . Compl. wine book
_____ . Dictionary of wines
_____ . Encyclopedia of wine
_____ . Vintage chart 1945-1954
_____ . Wines of Germany
Scott, D. Winemakers of New Zealand
Scott, G. Wine
Scott, J.M. Man who made wine
_____ . Vineyards of France
Sellers, C. Oporto, old and new
Shand, P.M. Bacchus; or, wine today and tomorrow
_____ . Book of wine
_____ . Book of French wines
_____ . Bk of other wines than French
Shannon, R. Pract. treat. brewing--- and making wines . . .
Shaver, G.O. Wines and liquors from the days of Noah.
    A safe guide to sane drinking
Shaw, A.D. and Co. Simple facts about wines, spirits,
    ale and stout
Shaw, H. Vine and civilization
Shaw, P. Juice of the grape or wine prefereble to water
_____ . Three essays ---concentrating wine and
    other fermented liquors
Shaw, T.G. Wine, the vine and the cellar
_____ . Wine trade and its history
Sheen, J.R. Wines and other fermented liquors
Shepherd, C.W. Wine you can make
_____ . Wines, spirits and liqueurs
Sherrard-Smith, W. Make mine wine
_____ . Make your own wine
_____ . 222 reputed wine recipes
_____ . Wine book for beginners
_____ . Winemaking in earnest

Shirley, J.   Accomplished ladies rich closet of rarities
   1687
Short, T.   Discourses on tea, made wines . . .
Sichel, A.   Guide to good wine
_____ .   Penguin book of wines
Simon, A. L.   Bibliotheca Bacchia
_____ .   Bibliotheca vinaria
_____ .   Blood of the grape . . .
_____ .   Champagne 1949
_____ .   Champagne 1962
_____ .   Champagne.   Elixir of youth 1930
_____ .   Champagne; with appendices on corks:
  methods of keeping and serving . . .
_____ .   Commonsense of wine
_____ .   Concise encyclopedia gastronomy
_____ .   Dictionary of wine
_____ .   Dictionary wines, spirits, liqueurs
_____ .   Drink
_____ .   English wines and cordials
_____ .   German wines
_____ .   Great wines of Germany (with S. F. Hallgarten)
_____ .   Guide to good food and wines
_____ .   History of Champagne
_____ .   History champagne trade in England
_____ .   History wine trade in England
_____ .   How to enjoy wine in the home
_____ .   How to serve wine in hotels
_____ .   In the twilight
_____ .   In vino veritas, book about wine
_____ .   Know your wines
_____ .   Let mine be wine.   The philosophy of wine
_____ .   Madiera and its wines
_____ .   Madeira; wine, cakes and sauce (with E. Craig)
_____ .   Noble grapes and great wines of France
_____ .   Notes on late J. Pierpont Morgan's cellar book
_____ .   Port
_____ .   Supply, the care and sale of wine
_____ .   Vintagewise
_____ .   What about wine?
_____ .   Wine and spirits, connoisseur's textbook 1919
_____ .   Wine and the wine trade
_____ .   Wine connoisseur
_____ .   Wine connoisseur- s catechism
_____ .   Wine in Shakespeare's days . . .
_____ .   Wine maketh glad the heart and gladdens the
  heart of man
_____ .   Wine primer

         . Wines and liqueurs from A to Z
         . Wines and spirits; connoisseur's textbook 1961
         . Wines of France
         . 'Wines of the World' pocket library
         . Wines of the world 1967
         . Wines, vineyards and vignerons of Australia
Simon, S. P. and P. Hallgarten. Wineograph chart
Simpson, J. Grape vine, preparation, cultivation
Simpson, W. Philosophical discussion of fermentation 1675
Slater, L. G. Secrets making wine from fruits and berries
Slessor, K. Grapes are growing; story of Australian wine
Smeed, T. Wine merchant's manual
Smith, A. J. and Co. Ltd. Wine list 1963
Smith, G. Pract. distiller and treat. on making artificial
    wines
Smith, S. and Son Ltd. 100 years good earth (wine-
    Australia)
Smith, W. B. Bleasdale 1850-1950
Societe Hellenique de Vins et Spiritueux
    Production wines and spirits in Greece
Speechly, W. Treat. on culture of the vine . . .
Spinola, O. Martini Museum
Spooner, A. Cultivation American grape vines and making
    of wine
Steedman, M. E. and C. H. Senn. Homemade summer and
    winter drinks
Stern, G. B. Bouquet (wine-lore)
Stevenson, J. Advice, medical and economical relative
    purchase . . .--wines
Stiles, H. W. Chapin and Gore manual
Stoll, H. F. Grape districts of California
        . What wine to serve
        . Wine-wise, handbook judge, keep, serve,
    enjoy wines
Storm, J. Invitation to wines
Street, J. L. Civilized drinking
        . Wines, their selection, care and service
Stringer, C. Wines; what to serve . . .
Strong, W. C. Culture of the grape
Stuart, M. Scriptural view of wine question
Sutherland, G. South Australian wine-growers manual
Suttor, G. Culture of grape vine and orange
    Australia and New Zealand
Suydam, J. Treat. on culture and mgt. of grape vines
Swiss Wine Growers Ass'n. Bright and fragrant wines of
    Switzerland
Symington, J. D. Notes on port wine

Tait, G.M. Port. From vine to glass
_____. Pract. handbook on port wine
Taylor, A. What everybody wants to know about wine
Taylor, G.H. Treasury wine and wine cookery
Taylor, H.E. Handbook wines and liquors
Taylor, J. Tables calculating wine, beer, cider . . .
    (Excise duties)
Taylor, W.A. and Co. Art fine wine drinking
Taylor, S.B. ed. Wine, wisdon and whimsy
Taylor Wine Co. Wines for everyday enjoyment
Tennent, Sir J.E. Wine, its use and taxation
Terrington, W. Cooling cups and dainty drinks
Terry-Thomas. Festive guide to wine
Thenard, L.J. Memoir on vinous fermentation
Theron, C.J. and C.G. Niehaus. Wine making
Thiebaut, de B.A. Vine-dresser's theoretical and
    practical manual . . .
Thomas, F.A. Wines, Cocktails and other drinks
Thomson, W. Pract. treat. cultivation grape vine
Thudichum, J.L.W. On wines, their production, treatment
    and use
_____. Treat. on origin, nature and varieties of wine
_____. Treat. on wines, their origin . . .
Tobe, J.H. How to make your own wines and beers
Tod, H.M. Vine growing in England
Todd, F.D. Little red guide to homebrewed wines
Todd, W.J. Handbk of wine; how to buy . . .
_____. Port: how to buy, serve, store . . .
Tomes, R. Champagne country
Tovey, C. Champagne: its history, mfg and properties
_____. Wine and wine countries . . .
_____. Wine revelations
Tremlett, Rex. Homemade wine
Tripp, C.R. Brewery management
Tritton, S.M. Amateur winemaking
_____. Grape growing and wine making
_____. Successful winemaking
_____. Successful wine and beer making
_____. Guide to better wine and beer making for
    beginners
_____. Winemaking from pulps, fruits, juices and
    concentrates
_____. Wine making from fruit pulps and concentrates
Truman, B.C. See how it sparkles
Tryon, J.H. Pract. treat. on grape culture
Tryon, T. Way to get wealth (English wine)

Tudor, E. October dawn; treat. mfg. homemade wines New
    England
Turner, B.C.A. Enjoy your own wine
_____ . Improve your winemaking
_____ . Pan book winemaking
_____ . Pract. guide to winemaking
_____ and C.J.J. Berry. Winemaker's companion
_____ . and E.A. Roycroft. AB - Z winemaking
Turner, B.C.A. and P. Down. Behind the wine list
Turner, W. Book of wines (facsimile 1941)
_____ . New boke natures, properties all wines used
    in England 1568
Tutuola, A. Palm-wine drinkard and his dead palm wine
    tapster in Dead's Town

Urbana Wine Co. Gold Seal Champagne 1901

V., (pseud). Wine and wine making in Victoria (The)
Valaer, P. Blackberry and other berry and fruit wines
_____ . Wines of the world
Valente-Perfeito, J. Let's talk about port
Van Buren, J. Scuppernong grape, hist, culture, mfg wine
Van Dyke, M. Cooking with wine. Recipes
Varounis, G. Introduction to French wines and spirits
Venge, P. Easy lessons in imported wines
Verdad, Don P. Book about sherry (from vineyard to
    decanter)
Verdier, P. History of wine
Vernelli, L. Wines of Italy
Vespre, F.S. Dissertation on growth vines in England
Viala, P. and L. Ravaz. American vines . . .
Victoria Wine Co. Price list 1959
Villanis, P. Thoeretical and pract. notes upon wine-
    making . . .
Vine, G. Homemade wines. How to make and to keep
Vizetelly, E.A. and A. Wines of France
Vizetelly, H. Facts about champagne and other sparkling
    wines
_____ . Facts about port and madeira . . .
_____ . Facts about sherry . . .
_____ . History of champagne
_____ . How champagne was first discovered and how
    wine now produced
_____ . Wines of the world characterized and classed

Wagner, P.M. American wines and how to make

Wiley, H.W.   American wines at Paris exposition of 1900
Wilkinson, W.P.   An examination of the wines retailed in
  Victoria
Wilkinson, W.P.   Nomenclature Australian wines
Williams, E.   Virginia's discovery of silkevvormes, - - - -
  dressing vines, making wines
Williams, G.F.   Homemade wines.   Family and medicinal
  use
Williams, H.   Homemade wine and beer
Williams, J.L.   The manufacture of flor sherry
Williamson, G.C.   Shakespeare's wine book i e Wm.
  Turner's boke wine
Wine Advisory Board.   Adventures in wine cookery
_____ .   California's wine wonderland
_____ .   Epicurean recipes of California
  winemakers
_____ .   Favorite recipes- California winemakers
_____ .   Gourmet wine cooking.   Easy way
_____ .   Guide to wines; California wine land of
  America
_____ .   Little wine cellar all your own
_____ .   Magic in your glass.   Introduction to wine
_____ .   Uses of wine in medical practice
_____ .   Wine cook book (The).
_____ .   Wine handbook series
_____ .   Wines and wine serving
Wine and Food Society.   Lest we forget.   Cellar book
_____ .   W. and F.   Society Library Catalogue No. 1
  English and Amer. books
Wine and Spirit Ass'n of G.B.   Wines; what they are,
  where they come from . . .
Wine and Spirit, Publ. Wine book of South Africa
Wine Institute.   Selective bibliography of wine books
Wine Trade Club.   Art of wine- making
_____ .   Vineyards of the world
Wines and Wines Publ.   Directory of wine industry 1965- 66
Winkler, A.J.   General vitaculture
Wise, D.   Homemade country wines
Wood, M.   More recipes with jug of wine
_____ .   Specialty cooking with wine
_____ .   Through Europe with jug of wine
_____ .   Unusual collection recipes with a jug of wine
Wootton, J.   Collection valuable recipes.   104 recipes on
  wine making
Worlidge, J.   Vinetum Britanicum or treatice of cider
  and other wines
Wormwell, C.C.   Home wine- making

Worthington, R.   Invitation inhabitants England mfg. wines
    from own fruits
Wright, H. S.   Old-time recipes home made wines
Wright, J.   Essay on wines
Wyndham, G. R. C.   Port; from grape to glass
Wyndham, R.   Sherry; from grape to glass
Wynn, A.   Fortunes of Samuel Wynn

Yates, L. H.   Gardener and the cook
Yeiser Brothers.   New method making better homemade
    wines and beers . . .
Young, T.   Epicure - treatise on essence, age, quality
    foreign wines
Younger, W.   Gods, men and wine
Young's Market Co.   Wines, liquors and the like 1933
Y-Worth, W.   Britannian magazine.   New art making 20
    sorts British wines
Yoxall, H. W.   Wines of Burgundy
_____ .   Women and wine

Zamarini, G.   Tested formulas perfumes -- liquors, wines
    and syrups
Ziegler, O. L.   Vines and orchards of the garden state.
    Adelaide

    Anonymous
Art and mystery vintners and wine-coopers
Art brewing on scientific principles

Bibliotheca Oenologica
Bolton Letters (A. L. Simon, ed.)
Book of wine. (by J. W.)
Booke of secrets (wine annexed)
Bordeaux wine and liquor dealers' guide
Botanic Brewers' guide
Bottles and bins recipes
Brewer (The)   A familiar treatise on brewing--
    instructions making wine
Brewer's Almanack and Wine and Spirit Trade annual
    (various)
Brewers' guide for hotel, bar and restaurant
British Guide or directory to housekeepers and innkeepers,
    making . . . wines
Butler: his duties and how to perform

California Wine Ass'n.   Descriptive booklet

Cellar Book 1763
Cellar work at a glance
Cherwell Wine book
Children of the vineyards
Choosing and serving champagne
Cocktails, wines and other drinks for the home
Compleat housewife or accomplished gentlewoman's
    companion
Complete family piece and country gentleman and farmer
    BEST GUIDE
Consequences of a law reducing dutys on French wine . . .
    1713

Descriptive account wine industry in Italy
Dictionaire Oeconomique or Family dictionary
Dissertation concerning origin and antiquity of barley wine
Drinks, cocktails and homemade wines
Duties of a butler--by a practical man

England's happiness improved--art making wine of English
    grapes
English innkeeper's guide--180 receipts make and manage
    wines . . .
Entertaining with wines of the Cape

Fine drinking. Ayala Champagne . . .
Formulas of your favorite drinks
French System mfg. management and adulteration of wines
French wines

Giggle water. Homemade wines . . .
Gleanings amongst the vineyards
Good Housekeeping's homemade wines
Guide to importers and purchasers of wines

Handbk on wines to all who drink them
Harper's manual. Standard work reference for wine and
    spirit trade 1914 (1st)
Harpers Wine and Spirit Gazette (various)
Homemade country wines
Homemade wines, beers, liquors . . .
House and Garden Special Edition - Wine
House and Garden Wine Book

In Vino Veritas. Account conversation betwixt Cup the
    Cooper and Dash the Drawer

Italian wines.   Supplement Ridley's Wine and Spirit Trade
     Circular 1963

Leigh-Williams amateur winemaker's record bk
Letter to Elizium 1796
Liquor handbook
Lurie, A.N.   Wine merchants Price list 1937

Memorials by Champagne merchants in Reims on seizures
     at San Francisco and N.Y. 1866
Merrydown - Wine of Sussex

Notes on plants of Wineland and the Good

Off the shelf.   Guide to sale wines and spirits
Original documents respecting injurious effect impolicy
     Port Royal Wine Co.

Party Book, Inc.
Port wine and cookery

Report procedures on commission of wine merchants of
     London
Review of discussions relating to Oporto Wine Co.   1814
Richelieu handbook.   Wine cooking recipes . . .
Ridley's Wine and Spirit Handbk (various)

Satyr against wine (in praise small beer) (1712)
Schenley's Encyclopedia wines and liquors
Seppult (House of) 1851-1951
Short guide to wine
Souvenir album Franco-British Exhibition (Moet and
     Chandon 1908)
Spanish Gem (A). - Sherry

Taste of Kinloch.   Handbk. wines and spirits
Toast your friends in Port
Treat. on mfg., imitation, adulteration, reduction, foreign
     wines . . .
True discovery of projectors of wine project
True relation-perswading vintners yeeld to imposition upon
     wines 1641

Vine manual or instructions for cultivation of grape vine
Vinetum Angliae--easy way to make wine.   English grapes
     and other fruit

Vineyard-being treatise shewing nature of planting . . .
    1727
Vintners and tobacconists advocate 1733
Vintner's, brewer's spirit merchant's . . . guide
Vintner's mystery displayed or whole art of the wine
    trade laid open
Vinum. Buyer's guide for wines . . .

Where German wine grows
Wine and cooking
Wine and Food (Periodical)
Wine and Food Diary 1966
Wine and food of Portugal and Madeira
Wine and spirit adulterators unmasked
Wine and spirit merchant. (Loftus)
Wine and spirit merchant. New revised 1790
Wine and Spirit Trade Review Trade Directory (various)
"Wine--Australia". A guide to Australian wine
Wine-drinker's manual 1830
Wine in America and American wine
Winemakers Almanac 1963-64
Wine manual (Maison E.H. Glass, Inc.)
Wine record book
Wine and spirit adulterators 1624
Wine Trade Loan Exhibition of drinking vessels--also
    books and documents
Wines, K.T.D. (know the drink)
Wines. What they are, where come from . . .
Wines, beers and liquors. How to make at home

SHORT- TITLE LIST

Books Listed Alphabetically by Title
(See Author List for Complete Reference)

ABC of America's wine. M. F. Mabon
ABC de coctails. F. Wunsch
ABC of canning soft drinks. Continental Canning Co.
ABC of cocktails (The). Anon
ABC of coffee. Brazil. Departmento Nacional do Cafe
ABC of fountain profits. Liquid Carbonic Co.
ABC of mixing cocktails. Harry of Ciro's
ABC of prohibition. F. Franklin
ABC of soft drinks business. George B. Beattie
ABC of spice cookery. Petty Lane
ABC of wine cookery. E. Beilenson
ABC of wine drinking. Bon Viveur
ABC of wines, cocktails and liqueurs. A. Drex
ABC's of alcoholic beverages. Licensed Beverage Industries
AB-Z of wine-making. Turner and Roycroft
About home-made wines. A. Appleyard
About vanilla. Jos. Burnett Co.
About wines. Anon
About wines. W. F. Laumer, Jr.
Abridgement of excise duties. J. Huie
Abridgement of the coffee planter of Santo Domingo.
    P. J. Laborie
Abridgements of specifications Beverages. Commissioner
    of Patents
Abridgements of specifications relating to brewing, wine-
    making . . . Commissioner of Patents
Abridgements of specifications relating to preparing and
    cutting cork . . . Commissioner of Patents
Abridgements of specifications relating to preservation
    of food. Commissioner of Patents
Abridgements of specifications relating to unfermented
    beverages, aerated liquids . . . Commissioner of
    Patents
Abstracts of several laws relating importation, exportation
    wines . . . C. Cleland
Accepted foods and their nutritional significance.
    Amer. Medical Assn.

673

Accomplished housekeeper and universal cook. T.
Williams
Accomplished housewife or the Gentlewoman's companion.
Anon
Accomplished ladies rich closet of rarities. J. Shirley
Account of efficacy of the aguamephetica, alkalines . . .
W. Falconer
Account of experiments to determine specific gravity . . .
J. Ramsden
Account of preserving water at sea. T. Henry
Account of tea cultivation Ceylon. J. A. and W. E.
Henderson
Account of cultivation and mfg. tea in China . . . S. Ball
Account of the culture and mfg. tea in India . . . Bamber
and Kelway
Account of the mfg. and use of cocoa and chocolate . . .
W. Baker Co.
Account of mfg. of black tea. C. A. Bruce
Account of the nature and medicinal values principal
mineral waters . . . J. Elliott
Account of the nature, properties and uses mineral waters
Great Britain. W. Owen
Account of the Tillbury water. John Andree
Account of the use and application and success of Bath
waters . . . W. Falconer
Account of various experiments for production new and
desirable grapes. G. Haskell
Acids. Comparative uses of types in soft drinks.
L. A. Enkema
Act for laying a duty upon retailers of spiritous liquors.
Anon
Action of alcohol on man. E. H. Starling
Acts of Georgii III Regis. Anon
Acute alcoholic intoxication. H. W. Newman
Address to such electors of Great Britain as are makers
of cyder and perry. Anon
Addresses by himself and others. A. Potter
Adler's handbook for the retail liquor dealer. H. R. Adler
Adrian's International Bar Guide. Anon
Adulteration and analysis of food and drugs. J. F.
Liverseege
Adulteration of beer by publicans. J. A. Nettleton
Adulteration of food, drinks and drugs. Anon
Adulteration of liquors. O. Cotter
Adulteration of liquors with description of the poisons used
in mfg. J. E. Dunn

Adulterations detected. A.H. Hassell

Adulterations of liquors. E.C. Delavan

Advance circular 1890 Soda Fountains. Chas. Lippincott
and Co.

Advances in beer quality. Part I Beer and brewing
technology. Part II, Methodology for the brewing
laboratory. Wallerstein Laboratories

Advantages of saccharin in the manufacture of aerated
waters, cordials . . . (The). Wilson, Salamon and
Co., Ltd.

Adventures in soft drink land with "Zest" and "Sparkle".
Anon.

Adventures in wine. Legends. History. Recipes. R.L.
Balzer

Adventures in wine cookery. Wine Advisory Board

Advertising folder (16 pages) with illustrations of fountains
shown at Columbian Exposition. J.W. Tufts

Advertising, labelling and composition of food (The).
Ministry of Food

Advice (Wine). J.H.P. Belloc

Advice and help. (soda fountains). Hance Brothers and
White

Advice, medical and economical relative to the purchase
and consumption of tea, coffee and chocolate, wines and
malt liquors. J. Stevenson

Aerated beverages (including cordials, brewed beers . . .)
and all about them. Barnett and Foster

Aerated beverages. Instructions to operators . . .
John Matthews

Aerated water machinery and bottlers' appliances.
Hayward-Tyler and Co. Ltd.

Aerated water makers guide. Rose and Company

Aerated water manufacturers' hand book. Jusfrute, Ltd.

Aerated waters and how to make them; together with
receipts for non-alcoholic cordials, and a short essay
on the art of flavouring. Joseph Goold

Aerator's and bottler's cyclopaedia (The). J. Gilbert
Smith, Editor

Aesthetics of wine (The). History of wine in Australia.
E.J. Beck

After dinner speeches and how to make them. W.D.
Nesbit

After repeal; what the host should know about serving
wines and spirits, proper glassware and cocktail
recipes. James Gray

Agricultural chemistry. Alfred Sibson
Aids to the analysis of food and drugs. C.G. Moor and
    W. Partridge
Aids to the analysis of food and drugs. J.R. Nicholls
Air in bottled carbonated beverages. A.B.C.B.
Al-Anon Family Groups (The). A guide for the families
    of problem drinkers. Anon
Alcohol. Dr. A.C. Rembaugh
Alcohol addiction and chronic alcoholism. E.M. Jellinek
Alcohol and caffeine. A study of their psychological
    effects. Harvey Nash
Alcohol and civilization. S.P. Lucia
Alcohol and human affairs. W.B. Spalding and J.R.
    Montague
Alcohol and human life. C.C. Weeks
Alcohol and longevity. Raymond Pearl
Alcohol and man, on the scientific basis of total
    abstinence. William Hargreaves
Alcohol and man. The effects of alcohol on man in
    health and disease. Haven Emerson, Editor
Alcohol and prohibition. V.G. Vecki
Alcohol and Science, or Alcohol: what it is and what it
    does. William Hargreaves
Alcohol and social responsibility. R.H. McCarthy and
    E. M. Douglass
Alcohol and society. John Koren
Alcohol and the constitution of man. E.L. Youmans
Alcohol and the human body. Sir Victor Horsley and
    M.D. Sturge
Alcohol and the human race. R.P. Hobson
Alcohol and the Jews. C.R. Snyder
Alcohol; as a food and medicine. E.M. Hunt
Alcohol, culture and society. C.H. Patrick
Alcohol education for the layman. A bibiliography.
    M.E. Monroe and Jean Stewart
Alcohol explored; Haggard and Jellinek
Alcohol. How it affects the individual, the community
    and the race. H.S. Williams
Alcohol, Hygiene and Legislation. E.H. Williams
Alcohol in commerce and industry. Charles Simmonds
Alcohol in Italian culture. Giorgio Lolli, et al
Alcohol: its action on the human organism. Anon
Alcohol. Its effects on man. Haven Emerson
Alcohol. Its history, folklore, effect on the human body.
    Berton Roueche
Alcohol. Its influence on mind and body. E.F. Bowers

Alcohol: Its nature and effects.   C.A. Story
Alcohol: Its place and power.   James Miller
Alcohol: Its place and power in legislation.   Robinson
    Souttar
Alcohol. Its production, properties, chemistry and
    industrial applications.   Charles Simmonds
Alcohol: Its use and abuse.   W.S. Greenfield
Alcohol: Its use and abuse.   Anon
Alcohol: Its uses and abuses.   A syllabus for schools.
    K.W. Harkness and L.M. Fort
Alcohol, one man's meat.   E.A. Strecker and F.T.
    Chambers
Alcohol problem (The).   H.M. Vernon
Alcohol, Science and Society.   Anon
Alcohol tables based on the original extract of wort
    (Balling) and of fermented beer.   Wallerstein
    Laboratories Inc.
Alcohol tables, proof spirit.   Otto Hehner
Alcohol. The sanction for its use.   Dr. J. Starke
Alcoholic addiction.   A psycho-social approach to
    abnormal drinking.   Howard Jones
Alcoholic beverages in clinical medicine.   Dr. Chauncey
    Leake and Dr. Milton Silverman
Alcoholic beverage encyclopedia.   Hocker El Curtis
Alcoholic drinks; easy way to make them--cordials,
    liqueurs, cocktails . . . Simon Simons
Alcoholic spirit testing.   James Shevlin and Thomas
    Hetherington
Alcoholic to his sons.   H.B. Hough
Alcoholic woman (The).   Benjamin Karpman
Alcoholics Anonymous.   Anon
Alcoholics are sick people.   R.V. Seliger
Alcoholism.   A chapter in social pathology.
    W.C. Sullivan
Alcoholism.   A manual for students and practitioners.
    Lincoln Williams
Alcoholism and society.   M.E. Chafetz and H.W. Demone
Alcoholism.   A supervisory guide.   Anon
Alcoholism, its psychology and cure.   Frederick E. Rea
Alcoholometry.   Account of the British method of alcohol
    strength determination.   R.G.H. Tate
Ale feasts and country taverns.   A.H. Plaisted
Ale in prose and verse, by Barry Gray (pseud) and
    John Savage.   R.B. Coffin
Alexis Lichine's encyclopedia of wines and spirits.
    Alexis Lichine

All about beer. Portraits of a traditional industry.
The Statist

All about coffee. W.H. Ukers

All about ices, jellies, creams, and conserves. H.G.
Harris and S.P. Borella

All about tea. Lipton and Co.

All about tea. W.H. Ukers

All about wine. Blake Ozias

All-British Cookery Book (The). Anon

All in vue. 84 drinks for you. Anon

All sorts and conditions of drinks. S.D. Churchill

Alleged adulterations of malt liquors. Gallus Thomann

Along the wine trail; wines of the world. Selmer Fougner

Alphabet of choosing and serving wine. R.W. Postgate

Alsace and its wine gardens. S. Hallgarten

Alva Flavors. Bottlers Guide and price list. Van
Ameringen-Haebler, Inc.

Alva Syrup making guide for vending machine operators.
Van Ameringen-Haebler, Inc.

A Man may drink. Aspects of a pleasure. Richard
Serjeant

Amateur Brewers. (proceedings of the company of.) Anon

Amateur fruit growing. S.B. Green

Amateur winemaker's recipes. C.J.J. Berry

Amateur wine-making. H.F. Bravery

Amateur wine making; an introduction and complete guide
to wine, cider, perry, mead and beer making, and
to the cultivation of the vine. S.M. Tritton

Amazing story of repeal. Fletcher Dobyns

American and English drinks. Gabriel Brandimbourg

American and other drinks. Leo Engel

American and other iced drinks. Charlie Paul

American Apple Orchard. F.A. Waugh

American barley production; a study in agricultural
geography. J.C. Weaver

American Bartender. W.H. Laird

American beer and ale; a handbook of facts and figures.
United Brewers Industrial Foundation

American beer. Glimpses of its history and description
of its manufacture. Gallus Thomann

American Bottler- Blue Book edition. (Various dates).
Anon

American Bottles old and new. W.S. Walbridge

American brewing industry and the beer market.
K'O-Ching Shih and C.Y. Shih

American Chamber of Horrors. The truth about food and
drugs. R. deF. Lamb

678

American compounder; or Cross' guide for retail liquor
dealers (The).   Charles Cross
American compounder (The).   G.W. Writner
American Cookery Books 1742-1860.   Waldo Lincoln
American Cream Sodas.   G.B. Beattie
American dispensers book.   American Soda Fountain Co.
American distiller, or, The theory and practice of
distilling.   M.A. Kraft
American drink book (The).   S.S. Field
American Druggist Formula Compendium.   Anon
American Fruit Book.   S.W. Cole
American Fruit Culturist . . . J.J. Thomas
American Fruits.   Their propagation, cultivation,
harvesting and distribution.   Samuel Fraser
American grape growers guide.   William Chorlton
American grape growing and wine making.   George
Husmann
American grape training.   L.H. Bailey
American guide to wines.   M.E. Church
American handy-book of the brewing, malting and
auxiliary trades.   Robert Wahl
American Library Directory.   Anon
American Liquor control.   M.B. Stone
American manual of the grape vines and the art of
making wine.   C.S. Rafinesque
American mineral waters: the New England states.
W.W. Skinner
American orchardist.   James Thacher
American peach orchard (The).   F.A. Waugh
American Physitian.   Treatise on roots and plants.
William Hughes
American practical brewer and tanner.   Joseph Coppinger
American Prize-Book (The).   (Formulas).   H.B. Skinner
American Prohibition Year Book for 1910.   Anon
American receipt book.   A.S. Wright
American Society for the promotion of Temperance.
Annual Reports.   Anon
American Soda Book of receipts and suggestions.
American Soda Fountain Co.
American Soda Water Dispensers' Guide.   A.C. MacMahon
American vine-dresser's guide, being a treatise on the
cultivation of the vine, and the process of wine making.
J.J. Dufour
American vine-dresser's guide. (The).   Alphonse Loubat
American vines, their adaptation, culture, grafting and
propagation.   P. Viala and L. Ravaz

American ways of life. G. R. Stewart
American wine cook book (The). E. W. Hatch
American wines, by Frank Schoonmaker and Tom Marvel
American wines and how to make them. P. M. Wagner
American Wines and Wine-making. P. M. Wagner
American wines at Paris exposition of 1900. H. W. Wiley
Americana ebrietatis; the favorite tipple of our fore-
    fathers and the laws and customs relating thereto.
    H. L. Peeke
America's table. Joseph D. Vehling
Among English Inns (Little pilgrimages). Josephine Tozier
Amphoras and the ancient wine trade. American School
    of Classical Studies at Athens
Anacreontics. (Poetry about drinking.) Carl Benson (pseud)
Analyses. Analytical methods of determining fruit juice
    content. International Federation of Fruit Juice
    Producers
Analyses and energy value of foods. R. H. A. Plimmer
Analyses of foods and drugs, also Beverages . . .
    North Dakota Regulatory Department
Analysis of Dr. Rutty's methodical synopsis of mineral
    waters. Charles Lucas
Analys s of foods. A. L. and K. B. Winton
Analysis of foods and the detection of poisons. A. W. Blyth
Analysis of packaging costs in the brewing industry (An).
    B. W. Hackstaff and M. W. Brenner
Analysis of the Congress Spring with practical remarks on
    its medical properties (An). J. H. Steel
Analysis of the mineral waters of Saratoga and Ballston
    (An). J. H. Steel M. D.
Analysis of the Tilbury alterative water. Dr. Bryan
    Higgins
Analysis of wines and interpretation of analytical results
    . . . J. H. C. Fabre
Analytical inquiry into the principles of taste. R. P. Knight
Ananas. John Giles
Anatomy of dessert with a few notes on wine. E. A.
    Bunyard
Anatomy of drunkenness (The). Robert Mc Nish
Anchor Magazine (Beer . . .) 150th year commemoration.
    Barclay Perkins and Co. Ltd.
And so to dine. A brief account of the food and drink
    of Mr. Pepys. based on his diary. S. A. E. Strom
And to drink, Sir! M. H. Perry
Angostura Cook Book. Angostura-Wupperman Corp.
Angostura, Recipe Book. Angostura-Wupperman Corp.

Angostura Recipes. Angostura-Wupperman Corp.
Animal and Vegetable fats and oils. W. T. Brannt
Annual coffee statistics. Pan American Coffee Bureau
Annual directory and Buyers guide, 1956
    ed. Perfumery and Essential Oil Reoord
Annual report. 1891. California State Eoard of
    Hcrticulture
Annual report. 1893. Grape syrup. California Board
    of State Viticultural Commissioners
Annual report for 1878. U. S. Commissioner of
    Agriculture
Annual Report. 1885-1886. Country Brewers Society
Annual report. 1895. (14th). New York Agricultural
    Experiment Station
Annual Report on essential oils, aromatic chemicals and
    related materials. Schimmel and Co., Inc.
Annual Reports. American Sugar Refining Co.
Annual reports. Blackpool and District Mineral Water
    Mfgrs. and Bottler's Trades Protection Ass'n.
Annual reports. 1917 - 1947 - 1949. National Fruit
    and Cider Institute
Anthology of cocktails. Booth's Distilleries Ltd.
Anthology of wine. Jean Mowat
Anti-alcohol movement in Europe (The). Ernest Gordon
Anti-bacchus: an essay on the crimes, diseases and other
    evils connected with the use of intoxicating drinks.
    B. Parsons.
Antidote against drunkenness being the drunkards looking
    glass . . . discussion of excessive use of strong
    drink. Anon
Antipasto. Walter James
Antique drinking glasses. (Former title - Old English
    Glasses). Albert Hartshorne
Anti-saloon League Year-Book. E. H. Cherrington
Anti-saloon songs. W. F. Mc Cauley
Apicius Redivivus or cook's oracle. William Kitchener
Apology for disuse of alcoholic drinks. G. B. MacDonald
Apology for the bath. Thomas Guidott
Apparatus for making and dispensing soda water, mineral
    waters . . . Chas. Lippincott and Co.
Appertizing or art of canning; its history and development.
    A. W. Bitting
Appetizers, Hors D'Oeuvres, Canapes, cocktails, soups,
    salads, sandwiches. Anon
Apple (The). Sir A. D. Hall and M. B. Crane

Apple and Pear as vintage fruits (The). Robert Hogg
Apple Culturist (The). S.E. Todd
Apple Growing in California. F.W. Allen
Applegreen's Bar Book or how to mix drinks.
    John Applegreen
Applegreen's barkeeper's guide; or How to mix drinks.
    John Applegreen
Apples and apple products. R.M. Smock and A.M. Neubert
Apples and pears. George Bunyard
Apples of New York. S.A. Beach et al.
Applied wine chemistry and technology. A. Massel
Approved cocktails. United Kingdom Bartender's Guild
Aquavit to zombie; basic and exotic drinks.
    Peter Beilenson
Architectural and engineering work (Breweries). August
    Maritzen
Arctic Soda Water apparatus. J.W. Tufts
Arctic Soda Water Apparatus - Book of Directions.
    J.W. Tufts
Argument legal and historical for the legislative prohibition
    of the liquor traffic. F.R. Lees
Aromanilla Company, Inc. Comparative evaluation by
    the flavor profile method of Aromanilla, Pure
    vanilla extract, and a vanillan-coumarin blend as
    flavoring agents. F.D. Snell, Inc.
Aromatic Chemicals, Technical Booklet. Firmenich and Cie.
Aromatic Chemicals. A.W. Noling
Aromatics and the soul; a study of smells. Dan McKenzie
Around the world. John Walker and Sons Ltd.
Arsenical poisoning in beer drinkers. T.N. Kelynack
    and William Kirkby
Art and mystery of brewing and receipts for English wines.
    William Whitebrook
Art and mystery of making British Wines (See Whole
    Art . . .). James Robinson
Art and mystery of vintners and winecoopers. Anon
Art and practice of innkeeping (The). A.F. Part
Art and science of brewing (The). C.A. Kloss
Art and secrets in the manufacture of wines and liquors
    according to ancient and modern international methods
    requiring no machinery. Bruno Ia-Vogue
Art and technique of wine. F.C. Lloyd
Art de la vigne (L'). Mr. Maupin
Art in confectionery and pastry. E.M. Eerling
Art of Blending and compounding liquors and wines (The).
    Joseph Fleischman

Art of brewing . . . (The). David Booth
Art of brewing. John Houghton
Art of brewing and fermenting and making malt . . .
John Levesque
Art of brewing beer or every man his own guager.
James Lightbody
Art of brewing exhibiting the London practice of brewing
porter brown stout, ale, table beer . . . (A
treatise on the). Frederick Accum
Art of brewing explained. D.P. Vine
Art of brewing India pale ale and export ale, stock and₀
milk ales, porter and stout (The). James Herbert
Art of brewing on scientific principles . . . ale, table
beer and porter. Anon
Art of brewing practically exemplified. Instructions to
brew --ales, stout, porter, and India pale ales (The).
Daniel Dobell
Art of brewing; practical and theoretical (The). Frank
Faulkner
Art of coffee-making (The). Hills Bros.
Art of compounding (The). Wilbur L. Scoville
Art of confectionery. Edward Lambert
Art of confectionery. Anon
Art of cookery made plain and easy. Hannah Glasse
Art of cookery made plain and easy. Lady (A)
Art of cooking by Apicius (The). B. Flower and
E. Rosenbaum
Art of cooking with herbs and spices (The).
Milo Miloradovich
Art of cooking with roses (The). Jean Gordon
Art of cooking with spirits (The). E.L. Meyer
Art of dispensing (The). Peter MacEwan
Art of dispensing (The). Anon
Art of distillation . . . also the whole art of
rectification (A complete treatise on the).
A.P. Dubrunfaut
Art of distillation (The). John French
Art of distillation (The). Wine Trade Club
Art of distillation --also the whole art of rectification
(A complete treatise on the). John Sheridan
Art of drinking. A historical sketch. G.G. Gervinus
Art of drinking; or, what to make with what you have
(The). Dexter Mason
Art of fine wine drinking. F. D'Armand.
Art of good living; a contribution to the better understanding
of food and drink (The). A.L. Simon

Art of gracious tippling since 800 B.C. (The).
Southern Comfort Corp.
Art of improving health and prolonging life by regulation
diet and regimen. Anon
Art of invigorating and prolonging life by food, clothes,
air, exercise, wine . . . (The). William Kitchener,
MD
Art of making Italian desserts. Maria Lo Pinto
Art of making sugar. Anon
Art of making wines from fruits and flowers (The).
William Graham of Ware
Art of manufacture of perfumery (The). E.A. Lodge
Art of mixing (The). J.A. Wiley
Art of mixing drinks. G. Carrico
Art of mixing drinks (The). Based on Esquire Drink Book.
Anon
Art of mixing then. M.H. Hubbell
Art of perfumery (The). G.W.S. Piesse
Art of planting and cultivating the vine and also of making,
fining and preserving wines. Louis de St. Pierre
Art of preserving of all kinds of animal and vegetable
substances for several years. M. Appert
Art of serving wine. Leo Buring Ltd.
Art of serving wine. Paul Garrett
Art of tea blending. A handbook for the tea trade. Anon
Art of Wine Cookery. Anne Director
Art of Wine making. Mons. Bulos
Art of wine-making. Wine Trade Club
Art of wine making and wine vinegar. Julius Fessler
Art of wine-making, in all its branches. David Booth
Arte and science of preserving bodie and soule in healthe.
John Jones, M.D.
Arte bibendi. (De). Libri tres. Vincentio Obsopaeo
Artificial drinking usages of North Britain. John Dunlop
Artificial spaw, or mineral-waters to drink; imitating the
German Spaw-water in its delightful and medicinal
operations on humane bodies . . . T. Byfield
Artistry of mixing drinks. Frank Meier
Arthritis and folk medicine. D.C. Jarvis
Artizans' Guide and everybody's assistant. R. Moore
Articles and By-Laws. Blackpool and District Mineral Water
Mfgrs. and Bottler's Trade Protection Assn.
Arts of brewing and distillation. J. Barclay
Arts of intoxication. The aim and results. Rev. J.T.
Crane
Arts revealed and universal guide. Anon

As long as there is a single apple tree left, New England
never can be made bone dry. J.H. Curtis
Asa Griggs Candler. C.H. Candler
Ash's Patent Piston Freezing Machine and wine cooler.
Anon
Assam Planter. Tea planting and hunting in the Assam
jungle. A.R. Ramsden
Assam: sketch of its history, soil, and productions; with
the discovery of the tea-plant. Anon
Assize of bread and ale, and dyuers other thynges. Anon
Association of Special Libraries and Information. The
Bureaux. Food and beverages. Anon
Aunt Martha's corner cupboard, or stories about tea,
coffee . . . Mary and Elizabeth Kirby
Australasian Fruit Culturist. D.A. Crichton
Australian brewing student's manual. Grove
Johnson
Australian farmer's and land owner's guide to the profitable
culture of wine in New South Wales. James Busby
Australian grape growers' manual for the use of beginners.
A.J. Downey
Australian milk bar and soda fountain practice. Harry
Thompson
Australian Pub (The). J.M. Freeland
Australian wine guide. D.F. Murphy
Australian winegrowers' manual. W.E. Malet
Australian wines. L. Moonen
Australian wines: 150th anniversary of the wine industry
of Australia. H.P.L. Buring
Autobiography. H.W. Wiley
Autobiography and personal recollections. J.B. Gough
Automatic merchandising. A selected and annotated
bibliography. C.R. Goeldner

B. and C. book of hot soda formulas. Beach and
Clarridge
Bacchic pilgrimage--French wines. E.C. Peixotto
Bacchus. An essay on the nature, causes, effects and
cure of intemperance. R.B. Grindrod
Bacchus behave! The lost art of polite drinking.
Mrs. Alma Whitaker
Bacchus dethroned. Frederick Powell
Bacchus joins Lucullus. A.P. Fachiri
Bacchus on the wing. A wine merchant's travelogue.
Harry Waugh

Bacchus; or, Wine today and to-morrow. P.M. Shand
Back to the Local. Maurice Gorham
Back to work; an old industry leads the way (Beer).
    R.B. Herter
Background to mead making. C.B. Dennis
Background to the crown. C.J. Parker
Bacterial spoilage of fortified wines. J.C.M. Fornachon
Baker's Best Chocolate Recipes. Baker, Walter and
    Co.
Banana Empire. A case study in American imperialism.
    C.D. Kepner and J.H. Soothill
Banana (The). Its cultivation, distribution and commercial
    uses. William Fawcett
Banana (The). Its history, cultivation and place among
    staple foods. Philip Reynolds
Bananas. United Fresh Fruit and Vegetable Ass'n.
Bananas. Chemistry, physiology, technology. H.W.
    von Loesecke
Bananas. Tropical Agriculture Series. N.W. Simmonds
Banquet libations of the Greeks. Delight Tolles
Bar Florida Cocktails. Anon
Bar Guide. Cartoons by Vip. pseud. Ted Shane
Bar Management and beverage profits. R.T. Huntington
Bar of chocolate. Gwen Cross
Bar Service. A non-technical manual for male and
    female bar-staff. J.H. Coombs
Barflies and cocktails. Harry McElhone
Barkeeper's Golden Book. O. Blunier
Barkeepers' ready reference, containing one hundred
    recipes for mixed drinks. Anon
Barley. Fifty years of observation and experiment.
    E.S. Beaven
Barley and malt. Biology, biochemistry, technology.
    A.H. Cook
Barley and the beer duty. Henry Stopes
Barley and the Stream. The Molson Story. Merrill
    Denison
Barley Crop (The). Herbert Hunter
Barley, hops and history. United States Brewers
    Foundation
Barley varieties - EBC - G. Aufhammer, P. Bergal,
    F.R. Horne
Barman's and Barmaid's manual. or how to mix all
    kinds of fancy drinks. Anon
Baron Foughner's bar guide. Selmer Foughner
Baronial household of the thirteenth century (A)-
    M.W. Labarge

Barrel and book; a winemaker's diary.   Walter James
Bar-rooms at Brantly, or the great hotel speculation.
    T.S. Arthur
Barry's Fruit Garden.   P. Barry
Bartender (The).   Harry Lamore
Bartender and the way to a man's heart.   C.H. Gammick
Bartender; or, How to mix drinks.   Jerry Concklin
Bartender's book (The); being a history of sundry alcoholic
    potations, libations, and mixtures.   Jack Townsend
Bartender's friend; a compilation of the best in mixicology
    from reliable sources.   F.I. Brown
Bartender's friend.   J.F. Driscoll
Bartender's guide, by Trader Vic pseud.   V.J. Bergeron
Bartender's guide.   C. Charles
Bartender's Guide (The Standard).   P.G. Duffy
Bartender's guide . . . Harry Johnson
Bartender's guide to the best mixed drinks.   "Kappa"
Bartender's guide.   W.E. Powner
Bar-tender's guide; or, How to mix all kinds of plain
    and fancy drinks--embracing punches, juleps, cobblers,
    . . . (The).   Jerry Thomas
Bartender's joke book (The complete).   Dan Morgan (pseud)
Bartender's guide.   The art of mixing drinks.   Anon
Bartender's Guide.   How to mix drinks.   For home and
    professional use.   Anon
Bartender's Guide.   How to mix drinks.   "2 in one".
    Anon
Bartender's manual; mixed drinks.   Anon
Bartender's manual . . . (New and improved illustrated.)
    Harry Johnson
Bartender's quick reference manual.   P.E. Lowe
Bass. The story of the world's most famous ale.   Bass,
    Ratcliffe and Gretton Ltd.
Batchellor book.   Don Wilkes
Bath Thermal Waters, historical, social and medical
    (The).   J.K. Spender
Baths and Wells of Europe (The).   John MacPherson
Baths of Germany.   Edwin Lee
Be your own guest.   Hale MacLaren
Beach and Clarridge, makers concentrated extracts,
    fruit juices, ess. Oils, vegetable colors and fruit
    acids.   Beach and Clarridge
Beautiful teetotaler.   T.W.H. Crosland
Bed-book of eating and drinking.   R.L. Wright
Bedford Alum and Iodine Springs near New London,
    Bedford County, Virginia.   P. Echols and Sons

Beer. H.F.E. Hulton
Beer and ale bottlers' manual. W.B. Keller
Beer and brewing in America. Morris Weeks
Beer and brewing in America; an economic study.
  W.M. Persons
Beer and good food. Brighten your menus and recipes
  with beer and ale. Myra Waldo.
Beer and health. J.E. Siebel II
Beer and skittles. H. Josephy and M.M. McBride
Beer and the beer traffic. Anon
Beer and the body. Blade, Toledo
Beer and vittels. Elizabeth Craig
Beer as a beverage. G.W. Hughey
Beer bottlers' handy book. Philip Dreesbach
Beer bust songbook, or, pictures to look at while others
  are singing (The). Frank Lynn
Beer cookbook. Tolson, B. and E. McCaig
Beer cookery; 101 traditional recipes. Michael Harrison
Beer dispensing handbook (A). United States Brewers
  Foundation, Inc.
Beer duty tables for use of members of excise branch
  John Morrison
Beer Gravity tables. Herbert Clark
Beer gravity tables. S.H. Green
Beer gravity tables and ready reckoner. C.S. Thurston
Beer has a history. F.A. King
Beer in Britain. The Times, London
Beer in the American home. Eloise Davison
Beer in the home. Jacob Ruppert
Beer, its history and its economic value as a national
  beverage. F.W. Salem
Beer, its importance as a beverage and an industry.
  Anon
Beer making for all. James Macgregor
Beer manual: Historical and technical. Joseph Scarisbrick
Beer of the Bible (The). James Death
Beer question (The). A.M. Powell
Beer songs (Famous). A collection of favorite German,
  Scotch and English drinking songs. Anon
Beer taxation. Joseph Scarisbrick
Beeread (The). Or progress of drink. Anon
Beet-Root Sugar and cultivation of the beet. E.B. Grant
Beet-sugar industry in the United States. U.S. Dept. of
  Agriculture
Before and after dinner beverages and a few sandwiches.
  Anon
Beginner's guide to wines and spirits. J.I. Davis

Beginners' handbook of Chemistry. J.H. Appleton
Behind the wine list. B.C.A. Turner and Peter Down
Belgian Cookbook (The). Mrs. Brian Luck
Bench grafting resistant wines. F.B. Bioletti et. al.
Bennett's guide to winemakers, brewers, distillers . . .
    containing tables arranged to specific gravity . . .
    R. Bennett
Berlitz Diners' Dictionery. Anon
Best chocolate and cocoa recipes. Walter Baker and Co.
Best drinking jokes. P.L. Cave
Best of everything, by author of "Inquire within". Anon
Best of vineyards is the cellar (The). Hugh Johnson
Best wine grapes of California. F.B. Bioletti
Beverage base inventory control. A.W. Noling
Beverage bases. A.W. Noling
Beverage Blue Book (The). H.S. Rich and Co. Publishers
Beverage dictionary. H.J. Grossman
Beverage distilling industry. Stanley Baar
Beverage Flavor Handbook and Catalog. Blue Seal Extract
    Co., Inc.
Beverage flavoring materials in the bottled carbonated
    beverage industry. A.W. Noling
Beverage Flavors. A.W. Noling
Beverage manufacture (non-alcoholic). R.H. Morgan
Beverage production and plant operation. A.B.C.B.
Beverage Service. R.T. Huntington
Beverage Spirits in America. A brief history.
    H.F. Willkie
Beverages. Ass'n of American Railroads
Beverages. J.A. Murray
Beverages. A manual for mixing cocktails. G.T. Odell
Beverages and sandwiches to your husband's friends.
    Mrs. A.O. Bradley
Beverages and sauces of colonial Virginia. L.S. Fitchett
Beverages and their adulteration. H.W. Wiley
Beverages de luxe. G.B. Washburne
Beverages for parties. Delineator Home Institute
Beverages - Manufacture and sale. Lesson 8. Fruit
    Juices. Otter-Swain Corp.
Beverages, past and present. E.R. Emerson
Beverages. Soft drink bottlers handbook. I.J.Z. Ruiz
Beverages, water, tea, cocoa . . . W.J. Sinclair
Beverages we drink (The). W.N. Edwards
Bible and wine (The). F. Fenton
Bible wines. National Temperance Society
Bible wines versus saloon-keepers' bible. O.B. Whitmore

Bibliographie des Brauwesens. Fritz Schoellhorn
Bibliographie des Kaffee, des Kakao, des Schokolade,
    des Tee . . . Wolf Mueller
Bibliographie des Kakao . . . Wolf Mueller
Bibliographie Gastronomique. Georges Vicaire
Bibliography, A. B. C. B. Research Fellowship and Technical
    Publications. A. B. C. B.
Bibliography and bibliographic review of food and food
    habit research. D. Gottlieb and P. H. Rossi
Bibliography of books and booklets on beverages, their
    history and manufacture (A). Hurty-Peck and Company
Bibliography and distillation literature. Arthur and E. Rose
Bibliography of food. E. A. Baker and D. J. Foskett
Bibliography of nutritive values of chocolate and cocoa.
    American Food Journal Institute
Bibliography of the writings of Anton Schwarz.
    Anton Schwarz
Bibliography of tree nut Production and marketing
    research. D. A. Reimund
Bibliotheca Bacchica. A. L. Simon
Bibliotheca Gastronomica. A. L. Simon
Bibliotheca Oenologica. Anon
Bibliotheca vinaria. A. L. Simon
Bibliography of memorabilia, trivia jocosa, jocoseria
    and other odd notes upon wine and its lore.
    M. "Prattler" Healy
Big Beverage. W. T. Campbell
Big chocolate cookbook. G. Parke
Big drink (The). The story of Coca-Cola. E. J. Kahn Jr.
Bibble berry book. Jacob Biggle
Biggle orchard book. Jacob Biggle
Biochemistry applied to malting and brewing. R. H. Hopkins
Biochemistry of brewing (The). I. A. Preece
Black horse of the Apocalypse. C. P. Cambiaire
Black Jacks and leather bottels. Oliver Baker
Blackberry, other berry and fruit wines. Peter Valaer
Bleasdale 1850-1950. W. B. Smith
Blending at its best; thousands of new creations. Harry
    Isel
Blue Book of automatic merchandising. National Automatic
    Merchandising Ass'n.
Bluff your way in wine. Nick Clarke
Blood of the grape (The); the wine trade text book.
    A. L. Simon
Body, mind and sugar. Key to understanding alcoholism
    . . . E. M. Abrahamson and A. W. Pezet

Bohemian life. Savarin St. Sure (Pseud?)

Boke of nurture . . . F. J. Furnivall

Boke of the arte and manor how to plant and graffe
all sort of trees . . . (wine). Leonard Mascall

Bolton letters (The). Edited by A. L. Simon (Wine).
Bolton

Bonanza banquets. Book Club of San Francisco

Bon-Vivant's companion; or, How to mix drinks (The).
Jerry Thomas

Bon vivant's companion; or, How to mix drinks (The).
G. A. Zabriskie

Bon Viveur's London and the British Isles. Bon Viveur

Book about beer (A). Whitbread and Co., Ltd.

Book about beer, by a drinker. Anon

Book about cider and perry. C. W. R. Cooke

Book about sherry (A). (From vineyard to decanter.)
Don Pedro Verdad (Pseud).

Book for a cook (A). Anon

Book of appetizers. With a number of drinks by
Philip S. Brown. H. E. Brown

Book of beer (The). Andrew Campbell

Book of beverages (A). Daughters of the American
Revolution

Book of Burgundy (A). Pierre Poupon and Pierre
Forgeot

Book of commerce (The) by sea and land, and a history
of commerce. Anon

Book of directions. Arctic Soda water Apparatus.
J. W. Tufts

Book of directions for carbonated beverages. John Mathews
Apparatus Co.

Book of directions for setting and operating soda water
apparatus. J. W. Tufts

Book of food (A). P. M. Shand

Book of food and nutrition (The complete). J. I. Rodale
and staff

Book of formulas and manufacturers guide. C. D. Camp
Laboratories

Book of formulas. For the manufacture of carbonated
beverages. De Lisser and Co.

Book of formulas. (Popular Science Monthly). Anon

Book of formulas. Recipes, methods and secret
processes. Anon

Book of French wines (A). P. M. Shand

Book of fruit bottling. Edith Bradley and May Crooke

Book of fruits. Robert Manning

Book of German songs (The). H.W. Dulcken
Book of household management. Mrs. Isabella Beeton
Book of Ice-cream (The). W.W. Fisk
Book of Ices (The). A.B. Marshall
Book of Ices (The). Iced beverages, ice cream and ices.
    Mrs. H.L. Williams
Book of instructions and sundry catalogue. American
    Soda Fountain Co.
Book of 100 beverages. William Bernhard
Book of One Hundred beverages for family use.
    William Bernhard
Book of other wines--than French (A). P.M. Shand
Book of pears and plums. Edward Bartrum
Book of perfumes (The). Eugene Rimmel
Book of pharmacopoaes and unofficial formularies.
    E.W. Lucas and H.B. Stevens
Book of prescriptions. E.W. Lucas and H.B. Stevens
Book of preserves (The). Jules Gouffe
Book of prices. Walter and Alfred Gilbey
Book of quinte essence. F.J. Furnivall
Book of recipes. How to mix fancy drinks --
    BARTENDER's GUIDE. Brunswick-Balke-Collender Co.
Book of receipts. E.W. Lucas and H.B. Stevens
Book of Simples (The). Anon
Book of Tea (The). A Japanese harmony of art culture
    and the simple life. Kakuzo Okakura
Book of tea secrets; being a little treatise on "The cup
    that cheers". T.A Phelan
Book of the apple (The). H.H. Thomas
Book of the Cheese (The). Anon
Book of the Cheese (The). Being traits and stories of
    "Ye Ole Cheshire Cheese". Anon
Book of the grape (The). H.W. Ward
Book of the inn (The). Thomas Burke
Book of the peach (The). H.W. Ward
Book of the scented garden. F.W. Burbidge
Book of the Strawberry. With sections also on the
    raspberry, blackberry, loganberry and Japanese wine-
    berry. Edwin Beckett
Book of the wine-label (The). N.M. Penzer
Book of toasts (A). William Ramsay
Book of vegetable dyes (A). Ethel Mairet
Book of Vodka. J.B. Hutton
Book of wine. Jan Lukas
Book of wine. J.M. McLean
Book of wine. P.M. Shand

Book of wine. (by J. W.)

Book of wines (A). William Turner

Booke of secrets (A). (Shewing dieurs waies to make and prepare). Annexed instructions for ordering wine . . . shewing how to make wine . . . Anon

Booke of the natures and properties as well as the bathes in England and of other bathes in Germany, Italy . . . William Turner

Booth's handbook of cocktails and mixed drinks. John Doxat

Booze Reader (The). A soggy sage of a man in his cups. George Bishop

Bordeaux and its wines classed by order of merit. Edouard Feret

Bordeaux: its wines and the claret country. C. Cocks

Bordeaux and its wines. A. Watt

Bordeaux wine and liquor dealers' guide. Anon

Botanic brewers' guide. Potter and Clarke, Ltd.

Botanical index to all the medicinal plants (A). Allan Pollock

Bottle beer quality, a 10-year research record. Wallerstein Laboratories

Bottle of beer (A). Read Brothers

Bottle scuffing and its prevention. George J. Meyer Mfg. Co.

Bottle Washing. A. H. Fuller

Bottle washing. A. B. C. B.

Bottle washing. Anon

Bottle washing and its control in the carbonated beverage industry. J. H. Buchanan and Max Levine

Bottlers and beverage manufacturers universal encyclopedia. Anon

Bottler's and Glass Packers' Handbook. Food Engineering

Bottler's and ice cream maker's handy guide (The). Warner-Jenkinson Co.

Bottlers' extracts: How to make them. G. F. Sawyer

Bottlers' formulary; practical recipes, formulas and processes for making the soluble flavors used in the manufacture of carbonated beverages. G. S. Morris

Bottlers Handbook for the use of EXCHANGE Bottlers juices. California Fruit Growers Exchange

Bottler's helper; a practical encyclopedia for the bottler of soft drinks. M. L. Blumenthal

Bottler's Reference and Data Issue. American Soft Drink Journal

Bottlers' requisites. (catalogue). R. Powley and Sons Ltd.

Bottlers prepare--protext your beverages against off-
season changes. L. A. Enkema
Bottler's Sales Manual. National Bottlers' Gazette
Bottler's Year Book. (Yearly from 1937). Anon
Bottles and Bins Recipes. Anon
Bottling and canning of beer. D. G. Ruff
Bottling and packaging engineer. U. S. Bottlers
Machinery Co.
Bottling engineer handbook. U. S. Bottlers Machinery Co.
Bottling for profit; a treatise on liquor and allied industries.
M. V. Rosenbloom
Bottling of English beers (The). Arthur Hartley
Bottling of naturally matured beers. R. Johnson
Bottling plant maintenance. A. B. C. B.
Bottling plant sanitation. A. B. C. B.
Bottlescrew days; wine drinking in England during the
eighteenth century. A. L. Simon
Bottoms up! A Guide to pleasant drinking. Anon
"Bottoms up". J. R. Meyer
BOTTOMS UP. Ryan's guide to pleasant drinking.
Ryan's Liquor Shop
Bottoms up. Ted Saucier
Bottoms Up! Paul Steiner
Bouquet. G. B. Stern
Bouquet de France. Samuel Chamberlain
Bourbon Chef (The). Bourbon Institute, Publ.
Bournville, the factory in a garden. Cadbury Brothers
Bowl of punch (A). Albert Smith
Bradshaw's dictionary of mineral waters. B. Bradshaw
Bradshaw's valuable family jewel. Penelope Bradshaw
Brandy distillation. (Part I). Cognac distillation and
manufacture (Part II). Antonio dal Piaz
Brasenose Ale: a collection of verses. Anon
Bratt system of liquor control in Sweden. Anon
Brazil and Java. Report on coffee-culture in America,
Asia and Africa. C. F. Van D. Laerne
Brazil as a coffee growing country. G. A. Cruwell and
A. S. Blackford
Brazilian coffee. Nicolau J. Moreira
Breviary of helthe. Andrew Boorde
Brew in your stew. Anon
Brewed in America; a history of beer and ale in the
United States. Stanley Baron
Brewer and victualler guide. Richard May
Brewer, distiller and wine manufacturer. John Gardner

Brewer, (The). A familiar treatise on the art of brewing
with directions for selection of malt and hops--instruc-
tions for making cider and British wines. Anon
Brewer (The). In nine languages. Anon
Brewer's accounts. William Harris
Brewers Almanac. The Brewing Industry in the United
States. (Various editions). United States Brewers
Foundation
Brewer's Almanack and Wine and Spirit Trade Annual.
(Various editions). Anon
Brewer's Analyst. R. D. Bailey
Brewers and bottlers accounts. Herbert Lanham
Brewers and bottlers universal encyclopedia. Anon
Brewer's distiller's diary and text-book. J. H. Lampray
Brewer's and licensed victuallers' guide (The).
E. Wigglesworth
Brewer's Art. B. M. Brown
Brewer's Art. Whitbread Library
Brewer's assistant. G. Sleigh
Brewer's assistant. Henry Goodwyn
Brewers' Convention. (Various years). United States
Brewers' Ass'n.
Brewer's, distiller's, bottlers, and licensed victualler's
diary for 1912. Anon
Brewers Exhibition (Northern Counties). Anon
Brewers Exhibition Official Catalogue. (Various years).
Anon
Brewers' guide for the hotel, bar and restaurant. Anon
Brewer's Guide for U.S., Canada, and Mexico. Anon
Brewer's Guide for the Hotel, Bar and Restaurant.
Bacchus
Brewer's Handbook. Anon
Brewer's Journal Centenary number.
Brewer's Journal and Hop and Malt Trades Review
Brewers' Journal and Hop and Malt Trades Review - 1888.
Anon
Brewer's license, its history . . . John Nash
Brewer's materials. A. W. Gillman and S. Spencer
Brewer's meterological and statistical guide (The).
Samuel Giles
Brewer's Plea or a vindication of strong beer and ale
. . . Anon
Brewer's pocket companion. A. E. Palmer
Brewer's progress 1757-1957. L. A. G. Strong
Brewer's Vade Mecum. W. H. Blake

Breweries and auxiliary buildings. O.C. Wolf
Breweries and maltings: their arrangement, construction,
    and machinery. George Scammel
Breweries and Texas politics. Anon
Brewery accounting. F.H. Elwell
Brewery accounting. H.C. Goettsche
Brewery accounts. F.W. Thornton
Brewery architects and engineers hand-book. E. Schmidt
Brewery bookkeeping. E.W. Clarke
Brewery by-products. W.A. Riley Jr.
Brewery construction. William Bradford
Brewery management. C.H. Tripp
Brewery Manual (The). J.G. Potter
Brewing. A.C. Chapman
Brewing. A Book of reference. George Clark and Son,
    Ltd.
Brewing and distillation. Thomas Thomson
Brewing and malting. J. Ross-Mackenzie
Brewing and malting and laboratory companion. Ross-
    Mackenzie J.
Brewing and malting in Australasia. A.G. Houghton
Brewing and malting machinery and appliances.
    Henry Stopes
Brewing and malting practically considered. Frank Thatcher
Brewing and malting waters. J. Ross-Mackenzie
Brewing and modern science. A.J. Brown
Brewing better beers. Ken Shales
Brewing, Bottling and Allied Trades Exhibition (The)
    A.W. Noling
Brewing, Bottling and Allied Trades Exhibition
    (Catalogue of). Anon
Brewing calculations. C.H. Bater
Brewing for cordial makers. G.I. Adcock
Brewing formulas practically considered. A.L. Nugey
Brewing in Canada. Brewers Assn. of Canada
Brewing in Maryland. W.J. Kelley
Brewing in the Soviet Union. Joseph Crosfield and Sons
    Ltd.
Brewing industry (The). J.L. Baker
Brewing industry; a brief survey of markets, distribution
    methods, operating costs, and capital requirements.
    W.B. Nichols and Co.
Brewing industry, 1886-1951 (The); an economic study.
    John Vaisey
Brewing industry and the brewery workers' movement
    in America (The). Hermann Schlüter

Brewing industry in England, 1700-1830 (The). Peter Mathias

Brewing industry of United States. United States Brewing Ass'n.

Brewing industry research foundation. Institute of Brewing

Brewing made easy. William Moir

Brewing, malting and allied processes 1956. R.B. Gilliland, G.A.F. Harrison and E.C. Knight

Brewing of non-excisable beers (The). J. Pocock

Brewing Plant and machinery. Anon

Brewing; practically and scientifically considered. E.R. Southby

Brewing room diary and year book. Pauls and White Ltd.

Brewing room diary and year book. White, Tompkins and Courage, Ltd.

Brewing Saccharometer. Anon

Brewing; science and practice. H.L. Hind

Brewing Scientific Reviews. Incorporated Brewers' Guild

Brewing; theory and practice. E.J. Jeffrey

Brewing trade during the industrial revolution. E.M. Sigsworth

Brewing Trade Reviews Licensing law reports 1914. Anon

Brewing water, its defects and their remedy. American Burtonizing Co.

Brewing waters. C.A. Warren

Brewing with raw grain: a practical treatise. T.W. Lovibond

Brief account of the mineral waters of Spa. G. Turner

Brief case of the distillers and the distilling trade. Anon

Brief economic history of the California wine-growing industry (A). J.S. Blount

Brief guide to innsigns. E.R. Delderfield

Brief history of beverage alcohol and of Kentucky bourbon whiskey. J.W. Stone

Brief history of soft drinks. G.B. Beattie

Brief history of tea. John Woods

Brief history of the ancient and modern Tee-totalism with a short account of drunkenness. J. Dearden

Brief notes for temperance teachers. B.W. Richardson

Brief records of brewing in South Australia. M.H. Ward

Brigg's Maltsters Working Book. Anon

Bright and fragrant wines of Switzerland. Swiss Wine Growers Assn.

Bright on the grape question. William Bright

Brighter England and the way to get it. Thomas Whittaker

Bristol cream. Godfrey Harrison
Britannia Inn. Whitbread and Co. Ltd.
Britannian magazine. William Y-Worth
British and foreign spirits. Charles Tovey
British Brewery and soft drinks equipment. Brewery
    and Bottling Engineer's Ass'n.
British Guide or a directory to housekeepers and inn-
    keepers--making and managing of choice British Wines.
    Anon
British Jewel (The). or compleat housewife's companion.
    Anon
British manufactures. (Formulas). George Dodd
British National Formulary. Anon
British North Borneo. (Cocoa). D.H. Urquhart
British Perfumer. Charles Lille
British Pharmaceutical Codex. Anon
British Pharmacopoeia. Anon
British wine-maker, and domestic brewer (The). W.H.
    Roberts
Brominated Oils (basic formulas for use of). Abbott
    Laboratories
Brown gold; the amazing story of coffee. C.A. Uribe
Brush your teeth with wine. Dennis Henshaw
Bubble and Squeak. Elizabeth Craig
Bubbling waters. C.B. Firestone
Buffet Blue Book. 322 mixed drinks. J.H. Considine
Bunting's book on breakfast beverages. D.F. Shillington
    and J.J. Bunting
Burgundy. Stephen Gwynn
Burgundy. The splendid Duchy. Percy Allen
Burns Master Air-Free Bottling system. Burns Bottling
    Machine Works
Burton and its bitter beer. J.S. Bushman
Burton-on-Trent; its history, its waters, and its breweries.
    Wm. Molyneux
Bush berry culture in California. H.M. Butterfield
Bush fruit production. R.A. Van Meter
Bush-Fruits. F.W. Card
But Daddy! (Drinking). Tom Buck
Butler (The). J.B. Davies
Butler and publican s assistant in brewing (practical
    treatise on). Anon
Butler (The). His duties, and how to perform them.
    Anon
Butler, the wine-dealer and private brewer (The).
    A Practical Man

Butler's modern practical confectioner. W.C. Butler
Buyers' guide and Directory. 1965. Brewers' Digest
By request; an autobiography. A.L. Simon

Cabinet encyclopaedia (The). Domestic Economy Volume I.
    Michael Donovan
Cacao. B.E. Dahlgren
Cacao. A bibliography on the plant and its culture and
    primary processing of the bean. R.C. Watrous
Cacao: a manual on the cultivation and curing. J.H. Hart
Cacao fermentation. A.W. Knapp·
Cacao production in South America. Ivar Erneholm
Cadbury, George (Life of). Alfred G. Gardiner
Cadbury's of Bournville. The building of a modern
    business. Cadbury Brothers Ltd.
Cafe and Milk Bar Catering. Anon
Cafe Royal Cocktail book. W.J. Tarling
Cakes and ale; a dissertation on banquets interspersed
    with various recipes . . . E.S. Mott
Calendar of food and wine (A). N. St.J. Heaton
Calendar of sandwiches and beverages. E.O. Hiller
Calculator for bottlers (The). Foote and Jenks Inc.
California, America's Vineyard. Jerome Landfield
California fruit statistics and related data. S.W. Shear
    and R.E. Blair
California fruits and how to grow them. E.J. Wickson
California in the kitchen. L.F. and W.K. Glozer
California Mission Recipes. B.A. Cleveland
California vine disease. Newton B. Pierce
California Wine Association. Descriptive booklet. Anon
California wine cookery and drinks. Wine Advisory
    Board
California wine industry, 1880-1895. V.P. Carosso
California's best wines. R.L. Balzer
California's wine wonderland. Wine Advisory Board
California wines. C.F. Oldham
California wines; how to enjoy them. L.D. Bynum
Campbell's book. A manual on canning, pickling and
    preserving. C.H. Campbell
Campbell's book of canning, preserving and pickling.
    C.H. Campbell
Campbell's tea, coffee and spice manual. L.E. Campbell
Canada vine grower. J.M. de Courtenay
Cane Sugar Handbook. G.L. Spencer and G.P. Meade

Canned Foods. An introduction to their microbiology.
J.G. Baumgartner and A.C. Hersom
Canned Food Manual. American Can Co.
Canned Foods in relation to health. W.G. Savage
Canned foods reference manual. American Can Co.
Canner's Directory. The National Canners Association.
Anon
Canning and preserving. Mrs. S.T. Rorer
Canning and preserving of food products with bacteriological
techniques. E.W. Duckwall
Canning Clan (The). E.C. May
Canning fruits and vegetables by hot air and steam. H.I.
Blits
Canning, preserving and jelly making. J.M. Hill
Canning, preserving and pickling. M.H. Neil
Carbon dioxide in water, in wine, in beer, and in other
beverages. F.J. Miller
Carbonated beverages. The art of making, dispensing,
and bottling soda-water . . . Thomas Chester
Carbonated bottled beverages. C.H. Manville
Carbonated Drinks. An illustrated quarterly gazette. Anon
Carbonated waters; a guide to their manufacture. David
Smith
Carbohydrates and alcohol. Samuel Rideal
Carbon dioxide. E.L. Quinn and C. Jones
Carbonic acid in medicine. Achilles Rose
Carbonic acid industry. J.C. Goosmann
Care and training of husbands. Anne Folsom
Cargoes and harvests. D.C. Peattie
Carl Schultz's mineral spring waters, their chemical
composition, physiological action . . . C.G. Schultz
Carlsberg (The book of). Carlsberg Ereweries
Carlsberg Brygerierne. Carlsberg Ereweries
Case of whiskey (The). G.C. Howell
Castle of Healthe. Sir Thomas Elyot
Catalog no. 36. Liquid Carbonic Company
Catalog no. 37. Carbonating machinery and supplies.
Liquid Carbonic Acid Manufacturing Co.
Catalog no. 96. American Soda Fountain Co.
Catalog of everything for the baker, confectioner and
ice cream maker. H.A. Johnson Co.
Catalog of 500 books on foods and beverages.
Hospitality Guild
Catalog of the London section of the Institute of Erewing
Library. William H. Bird
Catalog of XXth Century Coolers. Cordley and Hayes

Catalogue and book of reference for the bottler. W.J.
    Bush and Co.
Catalogue and price list of apparatus, machinery and
    materials for making and serving carbonated
    beverages. John Mathews Apparatus Co.
Catalogue and price list of soda water apparatus.
    Charles Lippincott and Co.
Catalogue - gas machinery-flavors. Liquid Carbonic
    Acid Mfg. Co.
Catalogue (A) of all sorts of earth, the art of drawing,
    of brewing, . . . Anon
Catalogue of American grape vines. Bush and Son and
    Meissner
Catalogue of apparatus for making and bottling soda water.
    Chas. Lippincott and Co.
Catalogue of apparatus for making and dispensing soda
    water, mineral waters . . . Chas. Lippincott and Co.
Catalogue of British scientific and technical books (A).
    Daphne Shaw
Catalogue of essential oils, aromatic chemicals, fine
    drugs and fruit flavors. Fritzsche Bros. Inc.
Catalogue of fine wines and spirits. Bellows and Co.
    Inc.
Catalogue of mineral water and ice making machinery and
    appliances. Barnett and Foster
Catalogue (with prices) of Puffer's Frigid Soda and Mineral
    Water Apparatus. A.D. Puffer and Sons
Catalogue of soda water apparatus. John Matthews
Catechism on beer. Julia Colman
Catering for the young. Dorothy Morton
Cautions concerning cold bathing and drinking mineral
    waters. William Buchan
Caviar to cordial; a book of recipes. Eleanor Dwyer
Celebrity recipes. Helen Dunn
Cellar Book. Anon
Cellar key (The). T.E. Welby
Cellar work at a glance. Instructions to licensed victuallers,
    barmen . . . Anon
Centenary Album. 1851-1951. W.J. Bush and Co. Ltd.
Centennial Temperance Volume. Anon
Century of brewing Hudson ales and the Evans brewery.
    G.W. Travers
Century of drink reform in the United States. A.F.
    Fehlandt
Cerevisiarii comes or the new and true art of brewing.
    William Y-Worth

Certified Food Colors. Warner-Jenkinson Mfg. Co.
Ceylon coffee, soils and manures. J.F. C.S. Hughes
Ceylon tea from the bush to the teapot. O.M. Ash
Ceylon tea planter's notebook. H.K. Rutherford
Ceylon Tea Story (The). Anon
Challenge (The). Liquor and lawlessness versus
    constitutional government. W.G. McAdoo
Champagne. N.E. Legrand
Champagne. (1962). A.L. Simon
Champagne. (1949). A.L. Simon
Champagne country (The). Robert Tomes
Champagne: its history, manufacture, properties.
    Charles Tovey
Champagne. The Elixir of youth. A.L. Simon
Champagne, the wine, the land and the people. Patric
    Forbes
Champagne vine country and champagne wine. G. Chappaz
    and A. Henriot
Champagne wine. Comite Interprofessionnel du Vin de
    Champagne
Champagne; with appendices on corks . . . A.L. Simon
Changing face of wine. Harry Waugh
Changing world of food. Dodge and Olcott, Inc.
Chapin and Gore manual (guide to barkeeping).
    H.W. Stiles
Chapman's New Zealand grape manual. David McIndoe,
    Ed.
Charm of tea. McCormick and Co.
Chats about wine. C.E. Hawker
Check list of books and pamphlets on grapes and wine
    and related subjects. M.A. Amerine
"Cheerio!". A book of punches and cocktails.
    C.N. Reinhardt
CHEERIO. 101 best cocktail recipes. Anon
CHEERS! Jim Collier
Chef Wyman's daily health menus. A.L. Wyman
Chemical analysis of food and food products. M.B. Jacobs
Chemical analysis of foods. H.E. Cox
Chemical analysis of foods. H.E. Cox and D. Pearson
Chemical changes and products resulting from
    fermentation. R.H.A. Plimmer
Chemical essays. Richard Watson
Chemical composition of apples and cider. W.B. Alwood
    et al.
Chemical composition of foods (The). R.A. McCance and
    E.M. Widdowson

Chemical examination of alcoholic liquors. A.B. Prescott
Chemical Formulary. (Various editions). H. Bennett
Chemical Industry facts book. Manufacturing Chemists'
    Assn.
Chemical methods for analysis of fruit and vegetable
    products. J.A. Ruck
Chemical Senses (The). R.W. Moncrieff
Chemical testing of wines and spirits. J.J. Griffin
Chemist and Druggist diary and year book. Anon
Chemistry and pharmacy of vegetable drugs. N.L. Allport
Chemistry and Physiology of flavors (The). H.W. Schultz
    et al.
Chemistry and technology of food and food products (The).
    M.B. Jacobs
Chemistry and technology of wines and liquors.
    K.M. Herstein and T.C. Gregory
Chemistry and technology of wines and liquors.
    H.M. Herstein and M.B. Jacobs
Chemistry, flavouring and manufacture of chocolate
    confectionery and cocoa. H.R. Jensen
Chemistry in its application to agriculture and physiology.
    Justus Liebig
Chemistry in the brewing-room. C.H. Piesse
Chemistry of animal and vegetable physiology. Gerardus
    Mulder
Chemistry of Common Life (The). J.F.W. Johnston
Chemistry of essential oils and artificial perfumes.
    Ernest J. Parry
Chemistry of food and nutrition. H.C. Sherman
Chemistry of Foods. James Bell
Chemistry of natural food flavors, a symposium.
    Quartermaster Food and Container Institute for the
    Armed Forces
Chemistry of perfumery materials (The). R.W. Moncrieff
Chemistry of saki-brewing. R.W. Atkinson
Chemistry of wine (The). G.J. Mulder
Chemistry of winemaking. J.T. Hewitt
Chemistry, theoretical, practical and analytical.
    Dr. Sheridan Muspratt
Cherries. N.H. Grubb
Cherries of New York (The). U.P. Hedrick et al.
Cherry and its culture. V.R. Gardner
Cherry. Information about industry and flavors. J.M.
    Towey
Cherwell Wine Book. Anon
Children of the vineyards. (Portugal). Anon

China as a tea producer. B. P. Torgasheff
Chocolate! N. S. Haxelton
Chocolate and cocoa. Information book. Henry Compton
Chocolate and cocoa, its growth and culture. Charles
Hewitt
Chocolate and cocoa recipes. Miss Maria Parloa
Chocolate and cocoa recipes by Miss Parloa.
Walter Baker and Co., Ltd.
Chocolate and coffee cookbook. L. Langseth-Christensen
and C. Smith
Chocolate and confectionery. C. T. Williams
Chocolate and confectionery manufacture. Auguste Jacoutot
Chocolate evaluation. Stroud Jordan
Chocolate Industry (The). D. G. Mitchell
Chocolate, its character, history and treatment. Anon
Chocolate making. "Nirvana"
Chocolate-or an Indian drinke . . . L. A. de Colmenero
Chocolate plant (The). (Theobroma Cacao). Walter
Baker and Co.
Chocolate production and uses. L. R. Cook
Choice and experimental receipts in Physick and Chirurgy
. . . Sir Kenelm Digby
Choice recipes by Miss Maria Parloa. Walter Baker and
Co.
Choice receipts. Walter Baker and Co.
Choice receipts. (by Miss Parloa). Walter Baker and Co.
Choice recipes. Miss Maria Parloa
Choose your wine. T. A. Layton
Choosing and serving champagne. Anon
Chorlton's grape growers' guide. A handbook of the
cultivation of the exotic grape. W. Charlton
Christendom and the drink curse . . . Dawson Burns
Christmas in the olden times or the Wassail Bowl.
John Mills
Christmas Stocking Book. Edna Beilenson, Comp.
Chroni ca delle viti de Pontefici (Wine). M. F. Petrar
Chymical Essays. F. Skrimshire
Cider apple production. Ministry of Agriculture, Fisheries
and Food. Great Britain
Cider Cellar Songster. Anon
Cider Factory, plant and layout. Anon
Cider, its history, manufacture and properties. Henry
Stopes
Cider makers' hand book. J. M. Trowbridge
Cidermakers' manual. J. S. Buell
Cidermaking. A. Pollard and F. W. Beech

Cider of Somerset.   Anon
Cinchona in Java.   The story of Quinine.   Norman Taylor
Circle of useful knowledge (The).   (Formulas`.   Charles
    Kinsley
Citric Acid U S P.   Anon
Citrus Culture.   W.J. Allen
Citrus fruit in health and disease.   Florida Citrus
    Commission
Citrus fruit for the home orchard.   J.C. Johnston
Citrus Fruit Juice Control.   History of the control.   Anon
Citrus Fr uit Products.   E.M. Chace, H.W. Von Loesecke
    and J.L. Heid
Citrus Fruits.   J.E. Coit
Citrus Fruits and their culture.   H.H. Hume
Citrus growing in California.   J.C. Johnston
Citrus juice compounds for the soft drinks industry.
    W.J. Bush and Co. Ltd.
Citrus Products.   J.B. McNair
Civilized drinking.   J.L. Street
Claret.   H.W. Allen
Claret and olives from the Garonna to the Rhone.
    A.B. Reach
Claret and the white wine of Bordeaux.   Maurice Healy
Claret, its production . . . W. Beatty-Kingston
Clarets and Sauternes.   G.A.K.
Clarke's complete cellar manual.   William Clarke
Classic wines of Australia.   Max Lake
Classification and description of the wines of Bordeaux.
    M. Paguierre
Classified guide to technical and commercial books.
    Edgar Greenwood
Cleaning and sterilization of bottles and other glass
    containers.   J.C.L. Resuggan
Cleaning in the brewery, bottling store and licensed house.
    R.W. Ricketts
Clean-up or close-up.   A self-regulation program unique
    in industry.   United Brewers Industrial Foundation
Climates and Baths of Great Britain.   Anon
Climatology and mineral waters of the United States.
    A.N. Bell
Climatology, health resorts--mineral springs.   F.P. Weber
Climatotheraphy and Balneotheraphy.   Si r H. Weber and
    F.P. Weber
Closet for ladies and gentlewomen.   Anon
Closet of Sir Kenelme Digby opened.   Sir Kenelme Digby
Cloudy beverages.   What they are and how to handle them.
    A.W. Noling

Clove tree (The). G.E. Tidbury
Clubs and club life in London. John Timbs
Coal tar colors. Theodor Weyl
Coca and cocaine. W. Martindale
Coca and its therapeutic application. Angelo Mariani
Coca-Cola Bottler (The). Anon
Coca-Cola 1886-1962. A chronological history.
    Franklin Garrett
Cocktail and drinking recipes. (Various editions).
    H.B. Burke
Cocktail and food recipes. H.J. Gordon
Cocktail and wine digest (Spanish). Oscar Haimo
Cocktail and wine digest; encyclopedia and guide for
    home and bar. Oscar Haimo
Cocktail Bar. "Charles"
Cocktail Boothby's American bartender. W.T. Boothby
"Cocktail Bill" Boothby World drinks and how to prepare
    them. W.T. Boothby
"Cocktail Bill" Boothby's World drinks and how to mix
    them. W.T. Boothby
Cocktail Book (The). A sideboard manual for gentlemen.
    (Various editions). Anon
Cocktail Companions. Marion Courtney
Cocktail Continentale (A). Bruce Reynolds.
Cocktail digest. Oscar Haimo
Cocktail fare. Jean Balfour
Cocktail fashions of 1936. "Adrian"
Cocktail guide and ladies' companion. Crosby Gaige
Cocktail hour (The). L.P. De Gouy
Cocktail Key (The). Anon
Cocktail Parade. (Mary Elizabeth?). Anon
Cocktail party secrets. V. Heaton
Cocktail recipes. J.A. Coghill
Cocktail Recipes. (Coates). Anon
Cocktail snacks and canapes. Mollie Stanley-Wrench
Cocktail-supper book. M.W. Flexner
Cocktails. "Jimmy" late of Ciro's
Cocktails. Jean Lupoiu
Cocktails and mixed drinks. C.A. Tuck
Cocktails and snacks. R.I. Gordon
Cocktails and tastybite recipes. H.B. Burke
Cocktails for amateurs. Douglas Creek
Cocktails for two thousand. Maxwell Du Brow
Cocktails. How to mix them (Various editions). "Robert"
Cocktails, ices, sundaes, jellies and American drinks.
    Mary Woodman

Cocktails, the great American drink, how to mix and
enjoy them.   Anon
Cocktails, their composition and mode of action.
C. C. Weeks
Cocktails, their kicks and sidekicks.   A. E. P. Bird
and W. Turner
Cocktails, wines and other drinks for the home.   Anon
Cocktails, wines and liquors.   J. F. Bradley
Cocoa.   E. A. Browne
Cocoa.   Joseph Hatton
Cocoa.   J. J. Van Hall
Cocoa.   D. H. Urquhart
Cocoa; a crop with a future.   Paul Bareau
Cocoa; all about it.   Richard Cadbury (Historicus, pseud)
Cocoa and chocolate.   Paul Redmayne and T. Insull
Cocoa and chocolate from grower to consumer.   Cadbury
Brothers Ltd.
Cocoa and chocolate industry; the tree, the bean, the
beverage (The).   A. W. Knapp
Cocoa and chocolate.   A short history of their production
and use.   Walter Baker and Co. Ltd.
Cocoa and chocolate, their chemistry and manufacture.
R. Whymper
Cocoa and chocolate, their history from plantation to
consumer.   A. W. Knapp
Cocoa and its manufacture.   John Holm
Cocoa Bean Tests.   Anon
Cocoa: cultivation, processing, analysis.   E. M. Chatt
Cocoa Grower's Bulletin (Various editions).   Anon
Cocoa growing costs.   (Reprints).   Anon
Cocoa growing in India.   G. A. R. Wood
Cocoa-growing in Venezuela, Colombia and Ecuador . . .
G. A. R. Wood
Cocoa, how to grow and how to cure.   Sir Daniel Morris
Cocoa in some countries of Southeast Asia and the Pacific.
Ceylon- Hawaii- Thailand- Malaya- Papua- and New Guinea-
The Fiji Group.   D. H. Urquhart
Cocoa, its cultivation and preparation.   W. H. Johnson
Cocoa, its culture, manufacture and uses.   J. A. Mann
Cocoa planting and its cultivation.   F. E. Olivieri
Code of health and longevity . . . (The).   Sir John Sinclair
Coffee.   Chase and Sanborn
Coffee.   B. E. Dahlgren
Coffee.   The story of a good neighbor product.   Pan
American Coffee Bureau
Coffee; a monograph of the economic species.   R. H. Cheney

Coffee and Brazil. Brazilian Coffee Institute
Coffee and chicory. Anon
Coffee and chicory: their culture, chemical composition,
    preparation for market, and consumption.
    P. L. Simmonds
Coffee and India rubber culture in Mexico. Matias Romero
Coffee and repartee. J.K. Bangs
Coffee and tea. G.V. Poore
Coffee and waffles. A.F. MacDougall
Coffee. A short economic history with special reference
    to Jamaica. D.W. Rodriquez
Coffee: botany, cultivation, and utilization. F.L. Wellman
Coffee cookbook. W.I. Kaufman
Coffee Cookery. H.L. Ripperger
Coffee cultivation in Ceylon. W. Keen
Coffee drinkers manual. H. (M).
Coffee. Extensive information and statistics. Inter-
    national Bureau of the American Republics
Coffee facts. W.H. Ukers
Coffee facts and fancies. National Coffee Department of
    Brazil
Coffee for the Armed Forces. F.A. Koehler
Coffee, from grower to consumer. B.B. Keable
Coffee: from plantation to cup. F.B. Thurber
Coffee frontier in Brazil. L.N. Dambaugh
Coffee from Puerto Rico, U.S.A. Anon
Coffee growing. A.E. Haarer
Coffee growing by proxy. American Coffee Growers Ass'n.
Coffee growing countries of North America, Mexico,
    and Central America. I.N. Young
Coffee growing in Mexico. J.P. Taylor
Coffee growing: with special reference to East Africa.
    J.H. McDonald
Coffee houses and tea gardens of old London. H.P.
    Brewster
Coffee guide (The). R. Ryers
Coffee in Natal: its culture and preparation. H.E.
    Stainbank
Coffee: its culture and commerce in all countries.
    C.G.W. Lock
Coffee: its cultivation and profit. E.L. Arnold
Coffee; its history, classification and description.
    J.M. Walsh
Coffee: its history, cultivation, and uses. Robert Hewitt, Jr.
Coffee: its history, preparation . . . J.L. Lodge
Coffee, its physiology, history and culture. E.C.P. Hull

Coffee man's manual. Payson Mackaye
Coffee merchandising. W.H. Ukers
Coffee planter in Ceylon. William Sabonadiere
Coffee Planter of Santo Domingo. P.J. Laborie
Coffee planter's manual. Alex Brown
Coffee planter's manual for both Arabian and Liberian
    species. John Ferguson
Coffee planting in Ceylon, past and present. G.C. Lewis
Coffee planting in Southern India. E.L.L. Arnold
Coffee planting in southern India and Ceylon. E.C.P. Hull
Coffee processing technology. M. Sivitz and H.E. Foote
Coffee, Production, trade, and consumption by countries.
    H.C. Graham
Coffee recipes, Customs, Facts, Fancies. Jean Gordon
Coffee taverns, cocoa houses and coffee palaces.
    E.H. Hall
Coffee, tea and chocolate. A.M. Peck
Coffee, tea and chocolate: their influence upon health,
    the intellect, and the moral nature of man.
    A. Saint-Arroman
Coffee, tea, and cocoa: an economic and political
    analysis. V.D. Wickizer
Coffee, the beverage. F.N. Foot
Coffee; the epic of a commodity. H.E. Jacob
Coffee trade. C.H. Schöffer
Cognac. (Remy Martin). Louise de Vilmorin
Cognac and other brandies. T.A. Layton
Cognac distillation and manufacture (Part II) see
    Brandy distillation (Part I). Antonio dal Piaz
Cola drinks. American Type. G.B. Beattie
Cold Grapery. William Chorlton
Cold-Water man (The), or a pocket companion for the
    temperate. Anon
Collection of all of the statutes now in force relating to
    excise upon beer, ale and other liquors. Anon
Collection of old English customs and bequests. Henry
    Edwards of Hoxton
Collection of scarce valuable receipts together with directions
    for making several sorts of wine. Anne Battam
Collection of treatises relating to the city and water of
    Bath. Thomas Guidott
Collection of valuable recipes. James Wootton
Colloid chemistry. Jerome Alexander
Colonial Tavern (The). A glimpse of New England town life
    in the 17th and 18th centuries. Edward Field
Colonial wines (On). J.I. Bleasdale

Colony (The). Portrait of a restaurant and its famour recipes. Iles Brody
Color in the garden. Norman Taylor
Color of foods. G. Mackinney and A.C. Little
Colorimetry. D.B. Judd
Colorimetry for chemists. M.G. Mellon
Columbia, land of coffee. National Federation of Coffee Growers of Columbia
Come landlord! Tom Girtin
Come to tea with us. Herbert Compton
Coming, Sir! The autobiography of a waiter. Dave Marlowe
Commentary on Wines. Anthony Oechs and Co.
Commerce in tea. John McEwan
Commercial apple growing. A.H. Hoare
Commercial Fruit and Vegetable products. W.V. Cruess
Commercial production of brandies. M.A. Joslyn and M.A. Amerine
Commercial production of dessert wines. M.A. Joslyn and M.A. Amerine
Commercial production of table wines. M.A. Amerine and M.A. Joslyn
Commonsense book of drinking. L.D. Adams
Commonsense book of wine. L.D. Adams
Common-sense candy teacher. Jacob Friedman
Commonsense of drinking (The). R.R. Peabody
Commonsense of wine (The). A.L. Simon
Common things made plain. James Menzies
"Communion Wine". A Review. John Ellis
Comparative analysis of bottled and canned beers. Schwarz Laboratoties, Inc.
Compendium of flavoring. C.H. Sulz
Compendium of Modern Pharmacy and Druggists' Formulary. W.B. Kilner
Competitive relationships between sugar and corn sweeteners. U.S. Dept. of Agriculture
Compleat body of distilling, explaining the mysteries of that science . . . George Smith
Compleat brewer. George Watkins, Brewer
Compleat confectionery. Mary Eales
Compleat confectioner. Hannah Glasse
Compleat cyderman . . . (The). Wm. Ellis
Compleat distiller. William Y-Worth
Compleat family brewer. Thos. Threale
Compleat herbal. Robert Lovell
Compleat herbal. J.P. Tournefort

Compleat housewife or accomplished gentlewoman's
    companion. Anon
Compleat imbiber (The). (Various editions) Cyril Ray
Compleat Imbiber. A centenary exhibition of drinking
    through the centuries. W. and A. Gilbey Ltd.
Compleat Martini cookbook. B. Erlanger and D. Pierce
Compleat vineyard. William Hughes
Complete bartender. The art of mixing cocktails, punches
    egg noggs . . . Albert Barnes
Complete bartender's guide, how to mix drinks; a manual
    of quick reference (The). W.E. Powner
Complete bartender's joke book. D. Morgan (pseud)
Complete body of distilling . . . G. Smith
Complete book of drink; a guide to the buying, storing,
    service and selling of all alcoholic liquors. T.E. Carling
Complete book of food and nutrition. J.I. Rodale and
    Staff
Complete book of home food preservation (The).
    Cyril Grange
Complete brewer (The), by a brewer of extensive practice.
    Anon
Complete buffet Guide or how to mix all kinds of drinks
    (The). V.B. Lewis
Complete buffet manual; or, How to mix fancy drinks.
    J.E. Sheridan
Complete catalogue of all accessories for making
    aerated waters, cordials, ices . . . Dan Rylands
Complete catalogue of European vines with their
    synonyms and brief description. E.B. Heyne
Complete cellarman or innkeeper and publican's sure
    guide. H. Sabine
Complete city and country book. Charles Carter
Complete Confectioner (The). Frederick Nutt
Complete Confectioner (The). Anon
Complete Cook. J.M. Sanderson
Complete cook. James Jenks
Complete course in canning (A). Anon
Complete dealer's assistant or master's and mealman's
    useful companion, by a person or both callings.
    Anon
Complete directions for brewing fine, rich and wholesome
    ale and beer . . . J. Leifchild
Complete Distiller (The). Anon
Complete distiller (The). A. Cooper
Complete domestic distiller (The). A. Cooper, Distiller
Complete family brewer (The). Anon

Complete family piece and country gentleman and farmer
BEST GUIDE. Anon
Complete grocer, by an old distiller. Anon
Complete Herbalist. O. P. Brown
Complete home wine-making. G. Pearks
Complete Indian Housekeeper and cook. F. A. Steel and
G. Gardiner
Complete list of mineral waters, foreign and domestic,
with their analysis, uses and sources. P. Scherer
and Co.
Complete list of wines, spirits, liqueurs . . . (A).
W. and A. Gilbey
Complete maltster and brewer. Anon
Complete manual for the cultivation of the cranberry.
B. Eastwood
Complete manual of mixed drinks. Jacques Straub
Complete planter and cyderist. Anon
Complete practical brewer. Instructions art of brewing,
ale, beer and porter; and small beers, root,
sarsaparilla . . . M. L. Byrn
Complete practical confectioner in eight parts.
J. T. Gill
Complete practical distiller . . . M. L. Byrn
Complete ritual of conviviality, hospitality and hilarity
. . . C. E. Crowley
Complete system of bookkeeping for brewers . . .
Edward Amsdon
Complete treatise on distillation adapted to the use of
grocers, farmers and families as well as distillers.
R. Whitney
Complete treatise on perfumery: containing notices of the
raw material used in the art. P. Pradal and M. F.
Malepeyre.
Complete treatise on the art of distillation. A. P.
Dubrunfaut
Complete treatise on the art of distillation. J. Sheridan
Complete wine book (The). Frank Schoonmaker and
Tom Marvel
Complete year book of French quality wines, spirits and
liqueurs (The). W. W. Crotch
Composition of foods - Raw, processed, prepared
B. K. Watt and A. L. Merrill
Compounder (The). Williams' informer; or, Whiskey
buyer's guide. G. C. Williams
Compounder's Guide. Anon
Compounder's pocket remembrancer; a treatise on the
manufacture of liquors, syrups, cordials . . . T. N.
Corbyn

Comprehensive history of the rise and progress of the
    temperance reformation (The). P. T. Winskill
Comprehensive view of the culture of the vine under glass
    (A). John Roberts
Compulsory temperance. J. T. Agg-Gardner
Concise encyclopedia of gastronomy. A. L. Simon
Concise history of vending in the U. S. A. G. R. Schreiber
Condensing and cooling in distillation. J. A. Nettleton
Confectioner (The). George Read
Confectioner (The). (Houston and Wright). Anon
Confectioners' hand-book and practical guide to the art of
    sugar boiling in all its branches (The). E. Skuse
Confectioner's oracle. William Gunter
Confectionery analysis and composition. S. Jordan and
    K. E. Langwill
Confectionery Production Manual 1955. Anon
Confederate Cook Book. J. D. Freeman
Confessions of a bartender. J. A. Carter
Confessions of a decanter. Mrs. C. L. Balfour
Confessions of an Innkeeper. John Fothergill
Congress of Applied Chemistry. Original communications.
    8th International. Anon
Connecticut Agricultural Experiment Station. (57th).
    report on Food Products. (Beverages). Anon
Consequences (The) of a law reducing the duties on
    French wine, brandy . . . Anon
Considerations of the medical use of factitious airs.
    Thomas Beddoes
Considerations on the late act for continuing the
    prohibition of corn in the distillery. J. F. Barham
Consolidated Library of modern cooking and household
    recipes. Vol. V. Beverages . . . C. T. Herrick and
    M. Harland
Consumers Union repcrt on wines and spirits. Consumer
    Union
Contemplation of wine. H. W. Allen
Contribution to the classification of the species of the grape
    vine, with hints on culture. J. M. McMinn
Control of liquor in Sweden. Walter Thompson
Control of temperature in wine fermentation. A. P. Hayne
Control of the drink trade. Henry Carter
Convention of drunkards: a satirical essay on intemperance,
    (The). Rev. Charles Giles
Conversations on chemistry . . . Anon
Cook and confectioner's guide. W. Carter
Cook and housewife's manual (by C. I. Johnston).
    Mistress Margaret Dods (pseud).

Cook Book of the United States Navy. Anon
Cook it the French way. B. Wilcox and P. Vigoureaux
Cook to your heart's content on a low-fat, low-salt diet.
    D. Liebowitz, et al.
Cook with beer; real old-country cooking. D.E. Hale
Cook's and confectioner's dictionary. John Nott
Cook's Guide and housekeeper's and butler's assistant.
    C.E. Francatelli
Cook's guide to wine. Elizabeth Craig
Cookery. Elizabeth Craig's Household Library. Anon
Cookery Book (The). A.T.D.S.
Cookery for every household. F.B. Jack
Cookery for invalids and the convalescent. C.H. Senn
Cooking in cider. N.C. James
Cooking in wine (a bachelor's guide to). Gil and Mercia
    O'Neill
Cooking through the centuries. J.R. Ainsworth-Davis
Cooking with spirits. R.V. Neumann
Cooking with apple brandy. L.P. DeGouy
Cooking with Cape wine. Ko-operatiewe Wignbouwers
    Verenging van Zuid-Afrika Beperkt
Cooking with rum. R.B. Fink
Cooking with wine. N. St.J. Heaton
Cooking with wine. Robin McDouall
Cooking with wine. G. Manoha
Cooking with wine. Recipes. Mona Van Dyke
Cooking with wine and high spirits. Rebecca Caruba
Cooking with wine, spirits, beer and cider. P.V. Price
Cook's oracle. William Kitchener
Cooley's cyclopedia of practical receipts. R.V. Tuson
Cooling cups and dainty drinks. Wm. Terrington
Cooper (The). (History and instructions). Anon
Cooperage handbook (The). F.P. Hankerson
Corby's presents ten superb recipes. Jas. Barclay
    and Co. Ltd.
Cordial cocktail confidences. B.B. Dorf and Company
Cordial makers' syrups. G.I. Adcock
Cordiall Water. M.F.K. Fisher
Corn distillery stated to the consideration of the landed
    interest of England. Anon
Cornish recipes. Ancient and modern. Edith Martin
Correct service of Madera wines and brandies. K.
    Arakelian Inc.
Cossart, Gordon and Co. The oldest and by far the
    largest shippers of Madeira wine. Anon

Cost survey and suggested operating budgets for the
    carbonated beverage industry. A. B. C. B.
Cottage Brewer, by a retired brewer. Anon
Cottage Economy. William Cobbett
'Count' reminisces, presenting in authentic, concise
    form famous drink mixing recipes and data.
    Henry Hoffmann
Country brewer's assistant, and English vintner's instructor.
    George Edmonds
Country contentments or the English Housewife.
    G. Markham
Country housewife. Richard Bradley
Country housewife's family companion. William Ellis
Country wines. Mary Aylett
Course in food analysis (A). A. L. Winton
Court and country confectioner . . . distilling, making
    fine flavoured English wines. Borella
Cozzens Wine Press. F. S. Cozzens
Cranberry culture. J. J. White
Cream, butter and wine. Sybil Goffinet
Critical studies in the legal chemistry of foods.
    R. O. Brooks
Crosland's Cordial and liqueur maker's guide and
    publican's instructor. Thomas Finchett
Cross-cultural study of drinking (A). Quarterly Journal
    of Studies on alcohol
Crowns--the complete story. J. J. Nurnberg
Cuban Cookery. B. Z. deBaralt
Cuisine Anglaise et la Patisserie. Alfred Suzanne
Culinary Americana. Cookbooks 1860
    through 1960. E. and B. Brown
Culinary herbs and condiments. Maud Grieve
Culpeper's complete herbal. Anon
Cultivation and manufacture of tea (The). Edward Money
Cultivation and manufacture of tea in China. Samuel Ball
Cultivation and preparation of coffee. Gabriel Gomez
Cultivation and preparation of coffee for the market (The)
    J. Ugarte
Cultivation of American grape vines and the making of
    wine. Alden Spooner
Cultivation of berried fruits in Great Britain (The).
    C. H. Oldham
Cultivation of citrus fruits (The). H. H. Hume
Cultivation of fruit trees and management of fruit trees
    and management of orchards and cider . . . William
    Coxe
Cultivation of the native grape, and manufacture of
    American wines (The). George Husmann

Cultivation of sugar-cane in Java (The). R.A. Quintus
Cultivation of tea in Northwest provinces of India.
    J.F. Royle
Cultivation of the strawberry. See Buchanan, R.
    Culture of the grape and wine-making. N. Longworth
Cultivation of the vine and wine-making. Jules Guyot
Cultivation of vineyards in southwestern France- Alicia
    DuPont de Nemours
Culture and manufacture of tea in India. J.F. Watson
Culture and marketing of tea. C.R. Harler
Culture of the apple and pear, and the manufacture of
    cider and perry. T.A. Knight
Culture of the grape. J.F. Allen
Culture of the grape. W.C. Strong
Culture of the grape, and wine-making. Robert Buchanan
Culture of the grape vine and the orange in Australia
    and New Zealand. George Suttor
Culture of the peach and nectarine (The). George M'Ewen
Culture of the vine and emigration. J.M. deCourtenay
Cup of coffee. Gwen Cross
Cup of fury (The). Upton Sinclair
Cup that cheers. Handbook of tea (The). Tea Bureau, Inc.
"Cup of tea (A)", containing a history of the tea plant
    . . . J.M. Walsh
Cup that cheers but not inebriates (The). Oriental Tea
    Company
Cups and their customs. G.E. Roberts
Cups; how to make, why to take. William Shore
Cups of valor. N.E. Beveridge
Curious distillatory or the art of distilling coloured
    spirits, liquors, cyder . . . from vegetables.
    Thomas Shirley, M.D.
Curious lore of drugs and medicines. (Four thousand
    years of pharmacy). C.H. La Wall
Curious treatise on the nature and quality of chocolate.
    Colmenero de Ledesma
Curiosities of ale and beer: an entertaining history.
    C.H. Cook
Curiosities of ale and beer. (Charles Cook). John
    Bickerdyke (Psued).
Curiosities of art and nature or the true preserver and
    restorer of health. George Hartman
Current books about wine. Guy Prince
Cursary examination of the methodical synopsis of mineral
    waters . . . Charles Lucas

Custom of the room or early winebooks of Christ's College,
    Cambridge (The).   Anthony Steel
Customer checking of beverage bottles - some preliminary
    ideas.   A. B. C. B.
Cyclopedia of foods, Condiments and beverages.
    J. W. Hoffman
Cyclopedia of hardy fruits.   U. P. Hedrick
Cyclopedia of perfumery; a handbook on the raw materials
    used by the perfumer.   E. J. Parry
Cyclopedia of practical receipts, by a practical chemist.
    Anon
Cyclopedia of temperance, prohibition and public morals.
    Dean Pickett
Cyclopedia of things worth knowing.   Dr. J. C. Whitehill
Cyder, a poem.   John Phillips
Cyder book (Compleat cyderman).   Jonas More
Cyder-maker's instructor.   Thomas Chapman
Cyprus wines.   An island industry.   A. Hughes
Cyprus wine from my cellar.   John Knittel

D- C- Druggists Circular Formulary.   2896 formulas
    for pharmacists.   Anon
Dainties for home parties.   A cook book for dance
    suppers . . .   Florence Williams
Dainty and artistic desserts.   Joseph C. Burnett and Co.
Dainty drinks and sherbets.   Amelie Langden
Dairy Show catalogue.   British Dairy Farmer's Assn.
Dairyman's guide to Orange Drink Production (The).
    F. Newcombe
Daly's bartenders' encyclopedia.   Tim Daly
Danish beer and continental beer gardens.   Max Henius
Das Getrankebuch.   Fritz Wagner
Daughter of an alcoholic.   Dr. M. T. Cheraux
Defects of beer (The).   James Death
Defense in abatement of judgement for an alleged libel
    in the story entitled "Inquire at Ames Giles'
    Distillery".   G. B. Cheever
Definition of an intoxicating beverage.   L. A. Greenberg
Deipnosphists or banquet of the learned of Atheneaus.
    Anon
Derbyshire instruction book, How to brew splendid ale.
    Fisher and Son
Derrydale game cook book.   L. P. DeGouy
Descendents of the pioneer winemakers of South Australia.
    B. W. Bagenall

Description of a glass-apparatus for making in a few
    minutes, and at a very small expense, the best
    mineral waters of Pyrmont, Spa. Seltzer, Seydschutz,
    Aix-la-Chapelle.   J.J. Magalhaes
Description of a penumatic apparatus with directions for
    production of factitious airs.   James Watt
Description of new philosophical furnaces, or, A new art
    of distilling.   J.R. Glauber
Description of the educational exhibit of cocoa and chocolate.
    Walter Baker and Co.
Description with notes of certain methods of planting . . .
    (wine).   Philip LeBrocq
Descriptive account of an improved method of planting
    and managing roots of grape vines.   Clement Hoare
Descriptive account of wine industry of Italy.   Anon
Descriptive catalogue and price list of soda water
    apparatus.   C.D. Dows and Co.
Descriptive catalogue of Arctic Soda-Water Apparatus.
    J.W. Tufts
Descriptive catalogue of James W. Tufts soda apparatus.
    J.W. Tufts
Dessert, appetizer and related flavored wines.   The
    technology of their production.   M.A. Joslyn and
    M.A. Amerine
Destroyer (The).   Henry Knott
Desultory notes on the origin, uses and effects of ardent
    spirit by a physician.   Anon
Detection of common food adulterants.   E.M. Bruce
Detergents and sterilizers for the brewing industry.
    Reddish Chemical Co. Ltd.
Development and growth of Courage's Brewery.
    G.N. Hardinge
Development of brewing analysis.   A historical review.
    J.R. Hudson
Development of improved beverage cases.   A.B.C.B.
Devils, drugs and doctors.   H.W. Haggard
Devil's Mortgage cancelled.   J.M. Dickey
Dialogue between John and Thomas on the corn laws,
    the charter, teetotalism . . . Anon
Dialogues on drink.   B.W. Richardson
Diary for the brewing and syrup rooms (various editions).
    A. Boake Roberts and Co.
Dick's book of toasts.   W.B. Dick
Dicta technica.   Modern techniques in the beverage industry.
    A. Massel
Dickensian inns and taverns.   B.W. Matz

Dictionarie Oeconomique. Anon
Dictionarium Domesticum being a new and compleat
    household dictionary. N. Bailey
Dictionarium Rusticum. (Gentleman's Companion).
    John Worlidge
Dictionary of arts, manufactures and mines. Andrew Ure
Dictionary of business and industry (The). R.J. Schwartz
Dictionary of chemistry. Andrew Ure, M.D.
Dictionary of confectionery. James Peddie
Dictionary of drink and drinking. O.A. Mendelsohn
Dictionary of every-day wants. A.E. Youman, M.D.
Dictionary of foods and culinary encyclopedia.
    C.H. Senn
Dictionary of foreign dining terms. A concise guide to
    the food and wines of 15 nations. Lew Moore
Dictionary of scientific cocktail making. I. Aucken
Dictionary of the art of brewing, malting and vinegar
    making. A. Laurent
Dictionary of wine. A.L. Simon
Dictionary of wine terms. I. Marcus
Dictionary of wines. Frank Schoonmaker
Dictionary of wines, spirits and liqueurs. A.L. Simon
Die Industrie der Alkoholfreien Getranke. Dr. E. Luhmann
Diet and food. Alexander Haig
Diet and health with key to the calories. L.H. Peters
Diet for the sick; a treatise on the values of foods.
    M.F. Henderson
Diet of the diseased. James Hart, M.D.
Dietary uses of the banana in health and disease.
    L.J. Bogert
Dietetic Canned Foods. Anon
Digest of Patents issued by the United States from 1790.
    Anon
Diners' Club drink book. Diners' Club Magazine
Diners' dictionary of foreign terms. Lew Moore
Dining and wining. A.E.M. Foster
Dining out. How and what to order. What to drink.
    Ambrose Heath
Dining 'round London. T.A. Layton
Dining, wining and dancing in New York. Scudder
    Middleton
Dining and wining in old Russia. N.N. Selivanova
Dionysus; a case of vintage tales about wine. Clifton
    Fadiman, ed.
Dionysus. A social history of the wine vine. Edward
    Hyams

Directions for blueberry culture. Frederick V. Coville
Directions for brewing malt liquors. Anon
Directions for brewing with Needham-Rawlings Co.
    patent machine. J. Needham
Directions for impregnating water with fixed air. Joseph
    Priestley
Directions for managing strong beer exported to America
    . . . J. and W. Cunningham Co.
Directions for using Mathew's machines for making soda
    water. John Mathews
Directions for using the new patent saccharometer for
    brewing ale and beer . . . (Blake's). Joseph Long
Directions, suggestions and rules for setting up and
    operating the various machinery for manufacturing,
    dispensing and bottling carbonated beverages.
    A.D. Puffer and Sons Mfg. Co.
Directions to be followed in determining the original
    gravity of beers. Anon
Directory of California wine growers and wine makers in
    1860. E.P. Peninou and S.S. Greenleaf
Directory of the wine industry. Wines and Vines
Discourse of Bathe and the hot waters there.
    Tho. Guidott
Discourse of drinking healths. Lord Peter Bishop of
    Cork and Rosse
Discourse of forest-trees (cyder) (A). John Evelyn
Discourse of natural Bathes and mineral waters.
    Edward Jorden
Discourse of Sir Rawleigh's Great Cordial.
    Nicholas Lefevre
Discourse on coffee, its description and virtues.
    A.F. Naironus
Discourse on different kinds of air. Sir John Pringle
Discourse on the preparation, preservation . . . of malt
    liquors. C. (P.)
Discourse on wine embracing an historical and
    descriptive account of the vine . . . J.L. Denman
Discourses on tea, --wines--spirits with rules for gouty
    people. Thomas Short, M.D.
Discussion of the One Trip Container. A.B.C.B.
Diseases and curing of cocao. H.R. Briton-Jones
Diseases of the vine (The). How to prevent and cure
    them, according to doctrines of M. Pasteur.
    J.A. Schmidt
Dishes and beverages of the old south. Martha-McCulloch-
    Williams

Dishes and drinks. Or philosophy in the kitchen (by an old Bohemian). Anon
Dispenser's catalog no. 532. Liquid Carbonic Company
Dispenser's formulary; or, soda water guide. Soda Fountain (The)
Dispenser soda water guide. Anon
Dissertation on barley wine (A). Samuel Rolleston
Dissertation on growth of vines in England. F. Vespre
Dissertation on the mineral waters of Saratoga . . . Valentine Seaman
Dissertation on tea. Thomas Short
Dissertation on the properties and the efficacy of the Lisbon diet drink . . . J.H. Leake
Dissertation on the use of sea-water . . . also an account of the nature and properties of all the remarkable mineral waters of Great Britain. Richard Russell, M.D.
Dissolving caustic before addition to bottle washer (Schemes for). A.B.C.B.
Distillation. Joseph Reilly
Distillation and rectification. Emil Kirschbaum
Distillation, brewing and malting. John McCulloch
Distillation in practice. Cyril Elliott
Distillation of alcohol. Harry Barron
Distillation of alcohol and denaturing. F.B. Wright
Distilled spirits industry and contributions to distilling science. Alexander Izaak
Distiller (The). Harrison Hall
Distiller of London (The). Anon
Distillers' grain manual. R.T. Willkie and R.S. Mather
Distiller's Guide (The). Peter Jonas
Distiller's Practical Guide. Peter Jonas
Distiller's, wine and brandy merchant's vade mecum. Peter Jonas
Divers chemical conclusions concerning the art of distillation - also known as Jewel House of art and nature. Sir Hugh Plat
Divine law as to wines. G.W. Samson
Dizionario di Viticultura ed Enologia. G. Cusmano
Dr. Chase's new receipt book and medical advisor. A.W. Chase
Dr. Chase's third, last and complete receipt book. A.W. Chase
Dr. Chase's recipes. (Various editions) A.W. Chase
Dr. Eichenlaub's home tonics and refreshers for daily health and vigor. J.E. Eichenlaub

Dr. Nash's Cookery Book. Dr. E.H.T. Nash
Dr. Price's Delicious Desserts. Anon
Doctrine and discipline of the Methodist Church. Anon
Documentary history of the United States Brewers'
    Association. Gallus Thomann
Domestic brewer and family wine maker. B. Parkes
Domestic brewing. Handbook for families. Anon
Domestic cookery for the use of private families.
    Mrs. Rundell
Domestic economy. Michael Donovan
Domestic economy-- also the complete brewer.
    Maximillian Hazelmore
Domestic coffee man shewing the true way of preparing
    and making of chocolate, coffee and tea.
    Humphrey Broadbent
Dominion compounder's guide. I. Steinberg
Do's and dont's of wine making. Peggy Hutchinson
Down from Canada came tales of a wonderful beverage.
    R.W. Moore
Dragons in the wind. Ethel Hubler
Drama of drink. Its facts and fancies through the ages
    until now. R.W. Cooper
Drawn from the wood. Frank Shay
Dreadful character of drink. H.T.
Dress, drinks, and drums. A.E. Crawley
Drink. W.B. Nesbit
Drink. A.L. Simon
Drink. A revised and enlarged edition of Drink and be
    Sober. Vance Thompson
Drink. An economic and social study. Hermann Levy
Drink and be sober. Vance Thompson
Drink and be merry. Vyvyan Holland
Drink and drug evil in India. Badrul Hassan
Drink and service manual. F.W. Swan
Drink and the war. Marr Murray
Drink book. Esquire
DRINK: Coercion or control. R.C. Dorr
Drink dictionary. M.C. Voegele and G.H. Woolley
Drink master; how to prepare and mix all popular
    American alcoholic drinks. J.F. Driscoll
Drink, past, present and probable future. J. Samuelson
Drink problem of today. T.N. Kelynack
Drinking and drinkers. Alcohol research in northern
    countries. Erik Allardt, Touko Markkanen,
    Martti Takala°
Drinking and intoxication. R.G. McCarthy

Drinking and what to do about it. W.A. DeWitt
Drinking behavior in small groups. Kettil Bruun
Drinking Bordeaux. Youngman Carter
Drinking Burgundy. Youngman Carter
Drinking champagne and brandy. Youngman Carter
Drinking cups, ewers, vases . . . Virgil Solis
Drinking driving man's diary (The). J.L. Gillespie
Drinking habits among northern youth. Kettil Bruun
    and Ragnar Hauge
Drinking in college. Robert Strauss and S.D. Bacon
Drinking in England. James Laver
Drinking in French culture. R. Sadoun et al
Drinking patterns. D.A Stewart
Drinking problems (The) and its control. C.A. D'Alonzo
Drinking songs and other songs. W.R. Titterton
Drinking usages of society. Alonzo Potter
Drinking vessels of bygone days. G.J. Monson-Fitzjohn
Drinking with Pepys. O.A. Mendelsohn
Drinking-water and ice supplies. T.M. Prudden
Drinks. Jacques Straub
Drinks ala Mode. Cups and drinks of every kind for
    every season. Mrs. DeSalis
Drinks and dishes. Borden's Condensed Milk Co.
Drinks and how to make them. Anon
Drinks and how to mix them. G.J. Kappeler
Drinks and snacks for parties. Clarence Herisko
Drinks and welcome; or, The Famous historie of the most
    part of drinks, in use now in the Kingdomes of Great
    Britaine and Ireland . . . John Taylor
Drinks as they are mixed. P.E. Lowe
Drinks as they were made before prohibition. I.D. Altshul
Drinks, cocktails and homemade wines. Anon
Drinks, drinkers and drinking; or the law and history
    of intoxicating liquors. R.V. Rogers
"Drinks". Formulas for making "Ozonated" non-alcoholic
    drinks to resemble alcoholic cocktails and mixed drinks.
    Anon
Drinks from drugs. Eli Johnson
Drinks. How to mix and how to serve. P.E. Lowe
Drinks--long and short. Nina Toye
Drinks-man-ship. Town's album of fine wines and high
    spirits. Len Deighton
Drinks of all kinds, hot and cold, for all seasons.
    Frederick Davies
Drinks of the world. James Mew and John Ashton
Drinks of yesteryear. Jere Sullivan

Drug and specialty formulas. E. Belanger
Druggists circular formula book. The Druggists Circular
Druggist's General Receipt book . . . Henry Beasley
Druggist's Hand-Book of Private Formulas.
J. H. Nelson
Druggists Ready Reference. Morrison, Plummer and Co.
Drunkard's Cup. Robert Harris
Drunk's blue book (The). N. Anthony and O. Soglow
Dry America. Michael Monahan
Dry decate (The). Charles Merz
Drying and dehydration of foods. H. W. von Loesecke
Drying malt; practically considered. Henry Stopes
Duffy's Pure malt whiskey. Medicine for all mankind.
Duffy Malt Whiskey Co.
Duties of a butler--by a practical man-- With a guide to
brewing and management of wine. Anon

Eale's receipts. Mrs. Mary Eales
Earliest printed book on wine (The). Arnold of Villanova
Early American Beverages. J. H. Brown
Early American flasks and bottles. Stephen Van Rensselaer
Early American inebrietatis. M. E. Crahan
Early American inns and taverns. Elise Lathrop
Early breweries of New Jersey. H. B. and G. M. Weiss
Early history of coffee houses in England. E. F. Robinson
Early history of wine production in California.
H. B. Leggett
Early Kentucky distillers 1783-1800. W. R. Jillson
Earnest drinker (The). A short and simple account of
alcoholic beverages. O. A. Mendelsohn
Earnest drinker's digest (The). O. A. Mendelsohn
East Anglian pubs. Vincent Jones
Easy does it. The story of Mac. Hugh Reilly
Easy lessons in imported wines. Per Venge
Easy made wine and country drinks. Mrs. Gennery-Taylor
Eat and drink to live. L. S. Elphick
Eat, drink and be healthy . . . Addison Medlock
Eat, drink and be merry in Maryland. F. P. Stieff
Eat, drink and be wary. F. J. Schlink
Eat your way to health. R. H. Rose, M. D.
Eating and drinking. G. M. Beard
Eating and drinking. A. H. Hoy, M. D.
Eating and drinking, A Miscellany. M. A. Hart
Eating and drinking. An anthology for epicures.
Peter Hunt

Eating for perfect health. Mrs. M. P. Powell
Eating for strength. M. L. Holbrook
Ebrietatas enconium: or The praise of drunkenness . . .
    by Boniface Oinophilia, de Monte Fiascone (pseud)
    A. H. Sallengre
Economic aspects of the liquor problem.   John Koren
Economic aspects of the liquor problem.   Anon
"ECONOMIC" FORMULA.   Beverage flavor formulas
    using gum arabic.   Anon
Economic history of the California wine-growing industry.
    J. S. Blout
Economic results of prohibition.   Clark Warburton
Economical housekeeper . . . (The).   J. H. Walsh
Economically weak tea gardens in Northeast India.
    National Council of Applied Economic Research
Economics of brewing (The).   Remarks on distillation
    and rectifying.   E. J. Tweed
Economy in brewing.   William Ploughman
Edible colours.   Williams, (Hounslow) Ltd.
Edible oils and fats.   C. A. Mitchell
Edible oils and fats.   Their substitutes and adulterants.
    G. D. Elsdon
Education and training in office and factory. (cocoa).
    Cadbury Brothers Ltd.
Edwards (Mrs). cookery book.   Mrs. Edwards
Effects of ardent spirits upon the human mind and body
    (The).   Benjamin Rush
Effects of beer upon those who make and drink it.
    Gallus Thomann
Effects of distilled and brewed beverages.   Martti Takala,
    Toivo A. Pihkanen, Touko Markkanen
Effects of temperature on wine making. C. S. Ough
    and M. A. Amerine
1800 and all that.   Drinks ancient and modern.
    R. deFleury
Elbridge A. Stuart.   Founder of the Carnation Company.
    James Marshall
Electric blender recipes.   Mabel Stegner
Elementary chemistry of whiskey manufacture.   James M
    Doran
Elementary dictionary, or cyclopaedia for the use of
    maltsters, brewers, distillers, rectifiers, vinegar
    manufacturers and others.   G. A. Wigney
Elementary treatise on American grape culture and wine
    making.   P. N. Mead
Elementi di agricoltura Fisica E Chemica.   J. G. Wallerius

Elements in winemaking. M.A. Joslyn and W.V. Cruess
Elements of experimental chemistry (The). William Henry
Elements of food engineering. M.E. Parker et al
Elements of grape growing in California. F.T. Bioletti
Elements of water bacteriology. S.G. Prescott and C.E.A.
    Winslow
Elimination of spoilage in the carbonated beverage industry.
    Max Levine and J.H. Toulouse
Elixir of Life. Dr. Jill Cossley-Batt and Dr. Irvin Baird
Elixir of Life. Being a slight account of the romantic
    rise to fame of a great house (Whiskey). G.C. Warren
Elixir of Youth. Andre Louis Simon
Elixirs and flavoring extracts. J.U. Lloyd
Elixirs of life. Mrs. C.F. Leyel
Elizabeth Hallett's Hostess Book. E.H. Hallett
Elsevier's dictionary of barley, malting and brewing.
    in six languages. B.D. Hartong
Elucidation of imposition in the imitation and adulteration
    of Holland and English gine. Udolpho Wolfe
Empire in Gold and Green. The story of the American
    Banana Trade. C.M. Wilson
Emporium of Arts and Sciences. J.R. Coxe
Emulsion Technology. Anon
Encyclopedia of alcoholic beverages (Practical). Liquor
    Store Magazine
Emulsions. M.G. de Navarre
Encyclopaedia of alcoholic essence formulas. J.J.
    Berliner and Staff
Encyclopedia of candy and ice cream making. S.I. Leon
Encyclopaedia of domestic economy .. . Thomas Webster
Encyclopedia of food (The). Artemas Ward
Encyclopedia of foods and beverages. Artemas Ward
Encyclopedia of fruits, berries and nuts and how to
    grow them. A.E. Wilkinson
Encyclopedia of gastronomy. A.L. Simon
Encyclopedia of home-made wines. Mary Aylett
Encyclopedia of practical receipts and processes containing
    over 6400 receipts. W.R. Dick
Encyclopedia of state laws governing the sale of liquor in
    the various states throughout the union. Wilson
    Publishing Co.
Encyclopedia of substitutes and synthetics. M.D. Schoengold
Encyclopedia of wine. Frank Schoonmaker
Encyclopedia of wines and spirits. Alexis Lichine
Energy value of foods . . . basis and derivation.
    A.L. Merrill and B.K. Watt

England, a wine-producing country. W.E. Rendle
England's bane; or the description of drunkennesse.
    Thomas Young
England's happiness improved. Containing the art of
    making wine of English grapes . . . the whole art
    and mystery of distilling brandy . . . To make all
    sorts of plain and purging ales . . . Anon
England's interest, or the gentlemen and farmer's
    friend. John Moore
English art of cookery according to the present practice
    . . . Richard Briggs
English at table (The). From Roman times.
    John Hampson
English butler's canapes, salads, sandwiches, drinks
    . . . S.E. Davies
English Cookery Books to the year 1850. A.W. Oxford
English Cottage Wines. The art of making wine in the
    home. F.M. Hackett
English countryman. H.J. Massingham
English drinking glasses and decanters. Douglas Ash
English Electric Food Mixer Book. Anon
English fare and French wines. A.L. Simon
English, French and German periodicals on brewing,
    distilling, wine and other alcoholic beverages.
    J.K. Wilcox
English hops. A history of cultivation and preparation
    for the market from the earliest times. George
    Clinch
English hops glossary. Anthony Cronk
English housewifery. Elizabeth Moxon
English industries in the middle ages. L.F. Salzman
English inn (The). Thomas Burke
English inn, past and present. A.E. Richardson
    and H.D. Eberlein
English innkeeper's guide, containing one hundred and
    eighty receipts to make and manage wines and liquors.
    Anon
English medieval drinking bowls and other vessels such
    as Standing Cups, Chalices . . . W.H. St. J. Hope
English Medieval Feast. W.E. Mead
English picnics. E.G. Battiscombe (Harwood)
English Public House as it is. Ernest Selley
English Spas. William Addison
English tableglass. E.M. Elville
English vineyard vindicated. John Rose
English wines and cordials. A.L. Simon

Englishman's doctor or School of Salerne. Sir John
Harington
Englishman's food. Five centuries of English diet.
J. C. Drummond and Anne Wilbraham
Englishman's treasure. Thomas Vicary, M. D.
Englishman's wine (The). The story of port.
Sarah Bradford
Enologia. P. A. Maveroff
Energy value of foods -- basis and derivation.
A. L. Merrill and B. K. Watt
Engineering of malting. H. Stopes
Enjoy your own wine; a beginner's guide to making wine
at home. B. C. A. Turner
Enquire within upon everything. Anon
Enquiries into the effects of fermented liquors. By a
water drinker. Anon
Entertaining with wines of the Cape. Anon
Entertaining with wines of the Cape. KWV Public
Relations Dept.
Epicure (The) (periodical). S. S. Pierce Co.
Epicure (The) or a treatise on the essence, the age and
the quality of foreign wines. Thomas Young
Epicure's (The) Companion. E. and L. Bunyard
Era Formulary (The). W. C. Alpers and E. J. Kennedy
Instructions for Erecting and working B and F patent
improved aerated water and beer carbonating machinery.
Barnett and Foster
Esquire Culinary Companion (The). C. H. Baker
Esquire's Handbook for hosts. Anon
Essay concerning that nature of aliments and the choice
of them. John Arbuthnot
Essay on alcoholic and narcotic substances (An).
Edward Hitchcock
Essay on analysis of mineral waters. Richard Kirwan
Essay on Bath waters. William Falconer
Essay on bread; . . . explaining the vile practices
committed in adulterating wines, cider, porter, punch,
. . . (An). Henry Jackson
Essay on brewing with a view of establishing the principles
of the art. (An). Michael Combrune
Essay on British isinglass intersperced with hints for
further improvement of malting, brewing, fermenting
. . . (An). Henry Jackson
Essay on culture and manufacture of tea in Java . . .
Thomas Horsfield

Essay on foreign teas with observations on mineral waters,
    coffee, chocolate . . . Hugh Smith
Essay on medical preparation of factitious airs.
    Tiberius Cavallo
Essay on propriety and effect of malt liquors.   Anon
Essay on spiritous liquors with regard to their effects
    on health.   Robert Dossie
Essay on tea.   Jonas Hamway
Essay on the analysis of mineral waters.   Richard Kirwan
Essay on the cultivation and manufacture of coffee.
    W. H. Marah
Essay on the culture of the native and exotic grape,
    also both sides of the grape question.   Wm. Saunders
Essay on the importance spirits and best mode of
    converting grain into spirits . . . Anon
Essay on the inventions and customs of both ancient and
    modern in the use of inebriating liquors . . .
    S. Morewood
Essay on the natural history, origin, composition and
    medicinal effect of the mineral and thermal springs.
    Meridith Gairdner
Essay on the nature and properties of Alcoholic drinks.
    Thomas Beaumont
Essay on the nature, the end and the means of imitation
    in the fine arts.   J. C. Kent
Essay on the nature, use and abuse of tea.   Anon
Essay on the utility of sea bathing to preserve health
    and observations on mineral waters, natural and
    artificial.   J. W. Williams
Essay on waters.   Charles Lucas
Essay on wines (especially port).   John Wright, M. D.
Essay toward improvement of Brewing.   R. F. Elivin
Essay towards a natural and medicinal history of principal
    mineral waters of Cumberland, Northumberland,
    Sheffield.   Thomas Short
Essay upon tea, addressed to the medical profession
    (A new).   Empire Tea Market Expansion Board
Essay upon the nature and qualities of tea (An).
    J. Ovington
Essays and poems (Domestic Brewing).   Jeremiah Kirby
Essays on the malt liquor question.   Brewer's Industrial
    Exhibition.
Essence of Beauty (The).   A history of perfume . . .
    Aytoun Ellis
Essential Guest.   Hiram Walker and Sons, Inc.
Essential Oil Forum.   An exposition for non-technical
    people.   Anon

Essential oils, (price list) . . . Antoine Chiris Company
Essential oils (The). Horace Finnemore
Essential oils (The). Ernest Guenther
Essential oils. The basis of nature's perfume.
    Robert Sinclair
Essential oils and aromatic chemicals. India (Republic)
    Council of Scientific and Industrial Research
Essential of nutrition. H.C. and C.S. Sherman
Essentials of pharmacy for students. London College
Ethyl alcohol handbook. U.S. Industrial Chemicals Co.
European Brewery Convention. Anon
European grape growing in cooler districts where winter
    protection is necessary. V.J. and E.A. Rittich
Every brewer his own analyst. J.A. Nettleton
Every man his own brewer (see Town and Country Brewery
    Book). W. Brande
Every man his own brewer. Samuel Child
Every man his own brewer. Dr. Crewel
Every man his own brewer. Bonington Moubray (pseud)
Every man his own brewer; or a compendium of the
    English brewery. Anon
Every man his own brewer, or the ABC of brewing
    clearly explained for the amateur and the household.
    R.D. Loveless
Every man his own butler. Cyrus Redding
Every man his own guager. James Lightbody
Every step in canning. G.V. Gray
Everybody's Book on Collecting. Dr. G.C. Williamson
Everybody's Guide; or, things worth knowing. R. Moore
Everyday wrinkles for brewers. R.D. Loveless
Everyday life on a Ceylon cocoa estate. M.E. Steuart
Every woman's Canning Book. M.B. Hughes
Evolution of artificial mineral waters. William Kirkby
Evolution of the glass container industry. R.J. James
Examination of the wines retailed in Victoria (An).
    W.P. Wilkinson
Excellent properties of salted brandy as a most efficacious
    medicine and sedative (The). Rev. Samuel Fenton
Excellent recipes for baking raised breads, also directions
    for making summer drinks. Fleishman Company
Exchange Citrus Pectin. California Fruit Growers Exchange
Experimental cookery from the chemical and physical
    viewpoint. Belle Lowe
Experimental essays on medical and philosophical subjects.
    The fermentation elementary mixtures. Nature .. .
    of fixed air. David Mc Bride

Experimental Food Study. A. F. Morgan and I. S. Hall
Experiments and observations on different kinds of air.
    Joseph Priestley
Experiments and observations on fermentation and the
    distillation of ardent spirits. Joseph Collier
Experiments and observations relating to acetous acid,
    fixable air . . . Bryan Higgins
Experiments and observations relating to different kinds
    of air and other branches of natural philosophy.
    Joseph Priestley
Experiments and observations relating to the analysis of
    atmospherical air. Joseph Priestley
Experiments and observations on ferments and fermentation.
    Thomas Henry
Experiments and observations to investigate by chemical
    analysis the medical properties of mineral waters of
    Spa and Aix- la- Chapelle, in Germany . . . John Ash
Experiments on Chalybeate or Steel waters. Stephen Hales
Experiments to ascertain the state in which spirit exists
    in fermented liquors. W. T. Brande
Expert practical perfumery. Anon
Experts home complete American drink mixers guide.
    C. C. Mueller
Explanation of the partial process of evaporation.
    P. Stevenson
Export price- list No. 1. - W. J. Bush and Co. Ltd.
Exposition of prevalent impositions and adulterations
    practiced by dealers in wines and liquors.
    Udolpho Wolfe
Extra Pharmacopoeia of Martindale and Westcott (The).
    W. H. Martindale
Extract and alcohol tables. Schwarz Laboratories, Inc.
Extracts and beverages . . . J. T. Wandle
Extracts and how to increase them. W. S. Smith
Extracts and perfumes. W. L. Scoville

Factor which determines the quality of tea. H. H. Mann
Factory arrangement. G. Beattie
Facts about champagne and other sparkling wines . . .
    Henry Vizetelly
Facts about port and madeira. Henry Vizetelly
Facts about sherry. Henry Vizetelly
Facts about soft drinks. A. B. C. B.
Facts about tea. Japan Tea Syndicate (The'
Facts about the Licensed Beverage Industries 1962.
    Licensed Beverage Industries Inc.

Facts and falacies regarding brewer's.   John Nash
Facts on the brewing industry in Canada.   Dominion
    Brewers Association
Facts on worterbuch fur braurei and maltzerei.
    Ing. Walther Fischer
Fairest vineyards.   Kenneth Maxwell
Fallacies of teetotalism.   Robert Ward
Fallacy of water drinking.   Thomas Peedle and Thomas
    Coxbie
Falsifications of food . . . John Mitchell
Falstaff story (The). Alvin Griesedieck
Family brewer (The).   T. Poole
Family Dictionary (The).   Wm. Salmon
Family dictionary and household companion.   Anon
Family Magazine (The).   Arabella Atkyns
Family physitian (The).   George Hartman
Family Receipt Book (The).   Anon
Family Save-all.   A system of secondary cookery (The).
    Anon
Family's best friend, or the whole art of cookery made
    plain and easy (The).   Arabella Fairfax
Famous chocolate recipes.   Walter Baker and Company, Inc.
Famous chocolate recipes selected by Frances Lee Barton.
    Walter Baker and Co.
Famous Highballs.   Anon
Famous New Orleans drinks and how to mix them.
    S. C Arthur
Famous old recipes.   J.H. Smith, and S.M.M. Halsey
Famous old-time songs.   Anon
Famous recipes by famous people.   Herbert Cerwin
Famous recipes for Baker's chocolate and breakfast cocoa.
    Walter Baker and Co. Inc.
Fancy drinks, and how to mix them.   J.E. Peck
Fancy drinks and popular beverages; how to prepare
    and serve them.   A.W. Schmidt
Fancy Ices.   Mrs. A.B. Marshall
Farmer, maltster, distiller and brewer's practical memo
    book.   J.S. Forsyth
Farmer's Yearbook of Agriculture.   U.S. Dept. of
    Agriculture
Farmer's Wife or complete country housewife.   Anon
Farmhouse Fare.   Farmers Weekly (The)
Fashions in drinks.   Alfina Durr
Fatal effects of ardent spirits (The).   Ebenezer Porter
Fats and oils.   An outline of their chemistry and
    technology.   H.G. Kirshenbauer

Favorite fountain formulas. United American Soda
    Fountain Co.
Favorite Recipes of California Winemakers. Wine
    Advisory Board
Fear of wine (The). Walter James
Fermentation and distillation. William Hartley
Fermentation industry. Rex Furness
Fermentation of cacao. H.H. Smith
Fermented alcoholic beverages, malt liquors, wine, and
    cider. C.A. Crampton
Fermented goods. John Bellew
Fermented liquors: a treatise on brewing, distilling,
    rectifying. Lewis Feuchtwanger
Festive Board (The). Thurston Macauley
Festive guide to wine. Thomas Terry
Fetters on freedom. The story of prohibition in America.
    Cecil Shirley
Few facts about Indian tea. Sir J. Buckingham
Few practical remarks on the Medicinal effects of wine
    and spirits . . . (A). William Sandford
Few wine notes (A). F.J. Wildman
Fickle fortune in Ceylon. F.E.K. Penny
Fiftieth anniversery. H.T. Dewey and Sons Co.
Fifty doctors against alcohol. Anon
Fifty years history of the temperance cause.
    J.E. Stebbins
Fifty years of brewing. Mitchells and Butlers Ltd.
Fifty years of progress. Davenports of Bath Row
Findlater's - the home of Treble Diamond. Wine and
    liquor price list. Findlater, Mackie, Todd and Co.
    Ltd.
Fine art of mixing drinks (The). D.A. Embury
Fine art of wine drinking. W.A. Taylor and Co.
Fine beverages and recipes for mixed drinks. J.P. Sasena
Fine drinking. Booklet issued by Ayala Champaigne
    . . . Anon
Fine food, wine and pickled pine. A.K. Cole
Fine wines of Germany and all the world's wine lore.
    Paul Gyrogy
Firm of Cadbury (Cacao). I.A. Williams
First annual Soda Fountain Handbook. Mal. Parks
First catch your hare. Mary Aylett and Olive Ordish
First documentary edition. American Perfumer and
    Aromatics
First prize essay on sacramental wine.
    Rev. F.R. Lees

First steps in Ampelography. Marcel Mazade
First steps in wine making. C.J.J. Berry
First steps in wine making. C.J.J. Berry (Canadian
    Edition)
First years work on a coffee plantation. T.C. Owens
Five hundred and one easy cocktail canapes.
    Olga de L. Leigh
500 recipes. Cocktails and mixed drinks. Felix Brenner
500 recipes for home-made wines and drinks.
    Marguerite Patten
Five o'clock tea; cakes, cooling drinks . . . Anon
Five to a feast. T.A. Layton
Flasks and flagons. F.S. Saltus
Flather's practical recipes for making artificial
    mineral waters. Anon
Flather's Trade Recipes. Anon
Flavor. E.C. Crocker
Flavor Chemistry Symposium 1961. Campbell Soup Company
Flavor literature. Berghausen, E. Chemical Co.
Flavor of France in recipes and pictures. N.G. Chamberlain
    and Narcisse
Flavor research and food acceptance. Arthur D. Little Inc.
Flavor's the things. F. La G. Harris
Flavors and spices and flavor characterization. Anon
Flavors, Beverages and Condiments. Quartermaster Food
    and Container Institute for the Armed Forces
Flavor of whisky. J.A. Nettleton
Flavored Cordials. G.B. Beattie
Flavoring materials, natural and synthetic. A. Clarke
Flavours and essences; a handbook of formulas.
    M.H. Gazan
Fleishmann's mixer's manual. Fleishmann Distilling
    Corp. (The)
Floral World (Brewing) Garden guide and country
    companion. Anon
Florida citrus oils, Commercial production methods and
    properties of essential oils. J.W. Kesterson and
    O.W. Mc Duff
Florida's Food Fruits. Florida Citrus Exchange
Florida fruits and vegetables in the commercial menu.
    M.A. Stennis
Flower scent. F.A. Hampton
Flowers as food; receipts and lore from many sources.
    Florence White
Flowing Bowl (The). Charley Grapewin
Flowing bowl, a book of blithe spirits and blue devils
    . . . Geoffrey Mortlock

Flowing bowl; a treatise on drinks of all kinds and of
all periods. E.S. Mott

Flowing Bowl. A treatise on drinks of all kinds and of
all periods. E. Spencer
Flowing bowl; when and what to drink. A. Schmidt
Fluid and solid extracts with formulas and receipts.
Thayer and Company
Folk wines, cordials, and brandies. M. Jagendorf
Food. Sir Charles (Agricola) Fielding
Food. A brief account of its sources, constituents and
uses. A.H. Church
Food acidulants. Wm. Howlett Gardner
Food Additives. What they are. How they are used.
Manufacturing Chemists Ass'n.
Food adulteration. J.T. Pratt
Food adulteration and its detection. J.P. Battershall
Food analysis. A.G. Woodman
Food and beverage analysis. M.A. Bridges
Food and character. Louis Berman M.D.
Food and cookery for the sick and convalescent.
F.M. Farmer
Food and Drink in ancient Bengal. Taponath Chakravarty
Food and Drink of Mexico. G. Booth
Food and drink rationally discussed. Thomas Dutton
Food and drink through the ages, 2500 B.C. to 1937 A.D.
Maggs Bros.
Food and Drug Bulletins. (Various editions). North
Dakota State Laboratories Dept.
Food and drugs. E.J. Parry
Food and feeding. Sir. Henry Thompson
Food and Flavor. H.T. Finck
Food and hygiene. William Tibbles
Food and its adulterations . . . A.H. Hassell
Food and nutritional values of bottled carbonated beverages.
A.B.C.B.
Food and the public health. W.G. Savage
Food and wines. An exhibition of rare printed books
assembled and annotated by Andre L. Simon.
National Book League
Food and wine of the French provinces. J. and A.
Robertson
Food Beverages and restaurant service. Anon
Food colours. Ronald Clarke
Food composition and analysis. H.O. Triebold and L.W.
Aurand
Food Directory 1954. R. De Giacomi

Food, drink and drug frauds and the law of adulteration. Charles Hyatt-Woolf
Food flavoring. Joseph Merory
Food, flowers and wine cookbook. Helen Cox
Food for the rich. Paul Reboux
Food, fun and festivity with Mogen David wines and champagnes. Mogen David Wine Co.
Food in England. Complete historical and practical treatise on the English Kitchen. D.R. Hartley
Food industries. H.T. Vulte and S.B. Vanderbilt
Food Industries Manual. Anon
Food Industry Directory and Growers Handbook. Anon
Food, its composition and preparation. M.T. Dowd and J.D. Jameson
Food, its composition, preparation, combination. J.H. Tilden
Food. Its influence as a factor in disease and health. J.H. Tilden
Food manufacturing. A compendium of food information in the canning, flavoring, beverage, confectionery, essence . . . industries. Saul Blumenthal
Food manufacturing equipment. Henry Wiggin and Co. Ltd.
Food materials and their adulterations. E.H. Richards
Food microbiology. W.C. Frazier
Food, nutrition and diet theraphy. M.V. Krause
Food of France (The). W.L. Root
Food of the gods . . . (The). Brandon Head
Food plant sanitation. M.E. Parker
Food preservation. W.W. Chenoweth
Food preservatives. Chas. Pfizer and Co., Inc.
Food Products, their chemistry, and use. E.H.S. Bailey and H.S. Bailey
Food Products. Saul Blumenthal
Food Products. H.C. Sherman
Food study. M.T. Wellman
Food Values. E.A. Locke
Food values for calculating diabetic and nepfritic diets. L.M. Keegan
Foods. M.M. Justin; L.O. Rust, and G.E. Vail
Foods. Edward Smith
Foods and culinary utensils of the ancients. Charles Martyn
Foods and food adulterants. U.S. Dept. Agriculture
Foods and food products, Whiskey and other beverages. E.F. Ladd

Foods and their adulteration. H.W. Wiley
Foods of the World. Anon
Foods; their composition and analysis. A.W. Blyth
Foods. Their origin, composition and manufacture.
    William Tibbles
Footman's Directory and butler's remembrancer (The).
    Thomas Cosnett
For epicures only. Jean Conil
For home use. Angostura Bitters
For MEN ONLY. A cookbook. Achmed Abdullah and
    John Kenny
For the best and most practicable plan for making the
    eithteenth amendment effective. Durant prize contest
    Anon
For what we are about to receive. Denzil Batchelor
Formula Book manuscript form (Flavors). Anon
Formulas book of elixirs, syrups, wines . . . William
    Neergaard
Formula of the New York, Philadelphia and Baltimore
    manufactures of wines and liquors. C.B. Cotten
Formulas for making tinctures, infusions, syrups,
    wines, mixtures, pills . . . Tilden and Company
Formulary of perfumery and of cosmetology.
    R.M. Gattefosse
Formulary of the Parisian Perfumer. Anon
Formulas for Profit. H. Bennett
Formulas of your favorite drinks. Anon
Fortunes in formulas. G.D. Hiscox and T. O'Conner
    Sloane
Fortunes of Samuel Wynn. Winemaker, humanist,
    Zionist. (The). Allan Wynn
Forty five years history of the tea trade. R.R. Mabson
Forty years a-brewing. Wallerstein Company, Inc.
Forty years' fight with the DRINK DEMON.
    Charles Jewett
Foundations of American grape culture. T.V. Munson
Fountain operator's manual. C.R. Larson
Four Thousand years of pharmacy. C.H. La Wall
Forward American wines, including wine producers
    formulae. C.D. Dumbra
Fragment of the 4th part of Dr. Higgins observations
    and advices for the improvement of - - - sugar and rum.
    Bryan Higgins
Fragrance and flavor. The growing and use of herbs.
    Rosemary Hemphill
Fragrance in the garden. Norman Taylor

Fragrant path (The). A book about scented flowers and
    leaves. L.B. Wilder
France-a food and wine guide. P.V. Price
Fred Beck Wine Book. Fred Beck
Freezing preservation of foods (The). D.K. Tressler
    and C.F. Evers
French Gardiner (The). John Evelyn
French system of manufacturing, management and
    adulteration of wines, brandies, cordials . . . Anon
French vineyards (The). Denis Morris
French wine and liquor manufacturer (The). John Rack
French wines. Anon
French wines. Paul de Cassagnac
French wines. Fernande Garvin
French Wines. (The). Georges Ray
French wines; a practical guide for the cellarman,
    winebutler and connoisseur. William Bird
French wines and Havana cigars. F.G. Griswold
French wines and vineyards; and the way to find them.
    Cyrus Redding
Frigid Soda Water Apparatus. (Catalogue of). Puffer,
    A.D. and Sons Mfg. Co.
Friendly admonition to drinkers of gin, brandy and
    other distilled spiritous liquors. Stephen Hales
Fritzsche's manual, containing practical formulas and
    suggestions for the application of essential oils, essences
    and aromatic products for the preparation of liquors,
    cordials, flavorings . . . Fritzsche Brothers
From barrel to bottle (notes on the home bottling of wine).
    Edward Ott
From plantation to cup. W.K. Embleton
From sand-core to automation. A history of glass
    containers. Victor Wyatt
From vineyard to decanter. W. Mc Gee
From vineyard to table. Anton Koenen
Froth-Blower's Manual. Beer ballads and stories.
    A beer encyclopedia to settle all arguments.
    Pat Lawlor
Frozen dainties. Mrs. D.A. Lincoln
Frozen gems and dainty dishes. Recipes for the general
    use of fine and fancy drinks, plain and fancy soda
    waters, syrups, phosphates . . . and everything
    pertaining to the soda fountain. Emil Braum
Fruit and fruit desserts-beverages . . . Anon
Fruit and its cultivation. T.W. Sanders
Fruit and its cultivation in garden and orchard.
    T.W. Sanders

Fruit Annual and Directory.   Anon
Fruit beverage investigations.   W.V. Cruess and
    J.H. Irish
Fruit Beverages in Ontario.   Edgar Zubeckis
Fruit bottling and preserving.   Mrs. E. Beckett
Fruit crops.   Principles and practices of orchard
    and small fruit culture.   T.J. Talbert and A.E.
    Murneek
Fruit cultivators manual.   Thomas Bridgeman
Fruit culture for the amateur.   W.F. McKenzie
Fruit culturist (The).   J.J. Thomas
Fruit farm in England.   T.A. Lowe
Fruit garden (The).   P. Barry
Fruit Garden (The).   George Bunyard and Owen Thomas
Fruit garden calendar (Mr. Laurence's). John Laurence
Fruit- growers dairy (A).   Raymond Bush
Fruit Grower's Guide (The).   H.J. Wright
Fruit Growers Handbook.   W.G. Waring
Fruit growers manual.   Hemlow- Merriam and Co.
Fruit growing.   W.H. Chandler
Fruit- growing in arid regions.   Wendell Paddock and
    O.B. Whipple
Fruit in the Garden.   Norman Taylor
Fruit juice concentrates.   J.H. Irish
Fruit juices and fruit juice beverages.   J.H. Irish
Fruit juices, cider and wines.   F.E.Atkinson, et al
Fruit Manual: A guide to the fruits and fruit trees of
    Great Britain.   Robert Hogg
Fruit of the vine.   Rev. H.T. Burgess
Fruit of the vine as seen by many witnesses of all times.
    G.H. Turnbull
Fruit of the vine (The) (Unfermented or fermented, which?)
    John Ellis
Fruit Pectin.   Its commercial manufacture and uses.
    W.A. Rooker
Fruit pectins, their chemical behavior and jellying
    properties.   C.L. Hinton
Fruit Recipes.   Manual of the food values of fruits and
    nine hundred different ways of using them.
    R.M.F. Berry
Fruit tree and grape vine pruning.   George Quinn
Fruits and Farinacea.   The proper food of man . . .
    John Smith
Fruits and Fruit Products Analysis, composition and
    manufacture.   Anon
Fruits and fruit- trees.   L.H. Grindon

Fruit and Fruit trees of America. A.J. Downing
Fruits and how to use them. Mrs. H.M. Poole
Fruits for the home garden. U.P. Hedrick
Fruits- Non- Citrus- by States 1960 and 1961. U.S. Dept.
    of Agriculture
Fruits of America (The). Charles M. Hovey
Fruits of Hawaii. C.D. Miller and Katherine Bazore
Fruits of Hawaii. Description, nutritive values, and
    recipes. C.D. Miller et al.
Full and By- being a collection of verses by persons
    of quality in praise of drinking. Cameron Rogers
Full and distinct account of the mineral waters of Spa
    and Pyrmont. G.Turner
Fun at cocktail time. J.J. Proskauer
Fun with coffee. Pan American Coffee Bureau
Functions of alcohol in privative societies: a cross-
    cultural study. Donald Horton
Fundamental studies in essential oils. Y. Fujita
Fundamentals of distillery practice. H.F. Willkie
Fungus diseases of the grape and other plants and their
    treatment. F. Lamson-Scribner
Funny bar book and guide to mixed drinks. Ted Shane
Future of cacao planting (The). H.H. Smith
Future of drinking (The). G.V. Seldes
Future of our wine industry and the results of manuring
    vineyards in Europe and Australia. F.E.H.W.
    Krickauff
Future of the soft drink industry. (The). Chain Store
    Research Bureau
Future wealth of America; agricultural advantages of
    cultivating tea, coffee, and indigo. Francis Bonynge

Gadding vine. Walter James
Galenic art of preserving old men's health. Sir John
    Floyer
Garden of herbs (A). E.S. Rohde
Gardener and the cook (The). L.H. Yates
Gardener's Monthly (The). Thomas Meehan
Gardening with herbs. For flavor and fragrance.
    H.M. Fox
Garnsey's new wine tables. William Garnsey
Gastronomic Bibliography. K.G. Bitting
Gateway to wine. Grants of St. James Ltd.
Gatherings from the wine-lands. Foster and Ingle
Gay Nineties cook book. F.M. Dietz and A. Deitz Jr.

General catalogue No. 645 (soft drinks). Barnett
    and Foster
General gauger or the principles and practice of guaging
    beer, wine, and malt (The). John Dougherty
General instructions for the choice of wines and spiritous
    liquors. Duncan Mc Bride
General Price List No. 1 (soft drinks). W.J. Bush and
    Co. Ltd.
General receipt book (See primitive physic . . .)
    John Wesley
General treatise on different sorts of cold mineral waters
    of England. Thomas Short
General vitaculture. A.J. Winkler
Gentle art of drinking (The). J.B. Culver
Gentlemen, I give you--wine! H.W. Allen
Gentlemen's cellar and butler's guide. H.L. Feuerheerd
Gentleman's companion (The). C.H. Baker
Gentlemen's companion or tradesman's delight (The).
    Anon
Gentlemen's own guide to wines and spirits. W.V.
    Packman
Gentlemen's table guide. (The). E. Ricket and C. Thomas
George of the Ritz. George Criticos (as told to Richard
    Viner)
G. Washington's coffee
German wines. A.L. Simon
German wines and vines. Alfred Langenbach
Gesellschaft fur die Geschichte and Bibliography des
    Brauwesens E.V. Anon
Get back to nature and live. W.A. Browne and C.W.
    Browne
Gift of taste. Jas. Hennessy and Co.
Gift of the grape. L.E. Reeve
Giggle water, including eleven famous cocktails of the
    most exclusive club of New York. Anon
Gin and bear it. R.C. Newell
Gin and bitters (A novel about gin trade 1700's).
    Jane Lane
Gin Shop (The). Anon
Givaudan Index. Specifications of synthetics and isolates
    for perfumery. Givaudan-Delawanna Inc.
Give the grape its rightful food place. C.H. Goudiss
Giving a party. Brenda Rattray
Glance at Australia in 1880 or Food from the South (A).
    H.M. Franklyn
Glass collector (The). Maciver Percival

Glass containers. Glass Manufacturers Federation
Glass Crutch (The). The biographical novel of William
    Wynne Wister. Jim Bishop
Glass of champagne (A). Garnet Walch
Glass of grog. Anon
Glass of pale ale and a visit to Burton. Anon
Glass through the ages. E.B. Haynes
Gleanings amongst the vineyards. By an F.R.G.S. Anon
Gleanings from Gloucestershire housewives. Anon
Glenlivit-being the annals of Glenlivit. Glenlivit Distillery
Glimpse of a famous wine cellar (A). Francis Draz
    and Co.
Gods, men and wine. William Younger
"Goin' to Town". A resume of the sound film by the
    same name (soft drinks). Liquid Carbonic Corp.
Gold coast cocoa farmer (The). Polly Hill
Gold Coast handbook 1928 (The). John Maxwell
Gold Seal Champagne. Urbana Wine Co.
Gold, sport and coffee planting in Mysore. R.H. Elliot
Golden Jubilee Special number. Perfumery and Essential
    Oil Record
Golden Tips. A description of Ceylon and its great tea
    industry. H.W. Cave
Golden wine of Old Britain. E. Birkett
Good and bad effects of tea considered. Simon Mason
Good and cheap beer for the millions by the use of sugar
    and molasses in public breweries. Anon
Good appetite my companion. Victor Mac Clure
Good Cuppa Guide (The). Where to have tea in London.
    Jonathan Routh
Good cheer. Anon
Good cheer. The romance of food and feasting.
    F.W. Hackwood
Good drinks. Ambrose Heath
Good Eating. A second Book of wartime recipes. Anon
Good Housekeeping invalid cookery book. F.B. Jack
Good Housekeeping's Book of cool drinks-Institute (The)
Good Housekeeping's home-made wines. Anon
Good Wife's Cook Book. Anon
Good wine from Portugal. H.W. Allen
Gordian Essays on cocoa. Max Rieck
Gordon's cocktail and food recipes. H.J. Gordon
Gorham Cocktail Book (The). Gorham Company
Gourmet (The). F.G. Griswold
Gourmet au Vatel. An authoritative guide to the proper
    selection, handling, mixing and serving of wines and
    liqueurs. C.R. Flanders

Gourmet wine cooking. The easy way. Wine Advisory
    Board
Gourmet's Book of food and drink. Anon
Gourmet's Companion (The). Cyril Ray
Gourmet's week end book (The). A. L. Simon
Government by the brewers? Adolph Keitel
Grafted wine (The). Dr. Wilhelm Heuckmann and
    Rudi Vom Endt
Grand Hotel Company of Caladonia Springs- Caladonia Springs
Grape, Information about grapes, history, uses . . .
    L. J. Noling
Grape culture and winemaking in the South. H. De Caradeuc
Grape culture in California. F. T. Bioletti
Grape Culture in Steuben County. G. Denniston
Grape culture and wine- making in California. G. C. F.
    Husmann
Grape culture up- to- date. Alexander Kirk
Grape culture, wines, and winemaking with notes upon
    horticulture and agriculture. A. Haraszthy
Grape culturist, a treatise on the cultivation of the native
    grape (The). Andrew S. Fuller
Grape cure (The). Johanna Brandt
Grape districts of California (The). H. F. Stoll
Grape grower's guide. J. Keech
Grape growing, a simple treatise on the single pole system.
    A. F. Hofer
Grape growing and wine making. S. M. Tritton
Grape growing for amateurs. E. Molyneaux
Grape growing in California. H. E. Jacob. Revised
    by A. J. Winkler
Grape growing in the home garden, by F. Berry- Smith.
    New Zealand. Dept. of Agriculture
Grape juice as a therapeutic agent. Welch Grape Juice Co.
Grape syrup. Annual report. California. Board of State
    Viticultural Commissioners
Grape varieties . . . New York (State) Agricultural
    Experiment Station
Grape varieties for wine production. M. A. Amerine and
    A. J. Winkler
Grape wine (The). G. W. Johnson and Robert Errington
Grape vine; its preparation and cultivation (The).
    John Simpson
Grape vine in England. E. S. Hyams
Grape vine (The). Practical scientific treatise on its
    management. Frederick Mohr
Grapefruit. Published in Soft Drinks Trade. G. B. Beattie

Grapes: and how to grow them.   J. Lansdell
Grapes and wine.   A visit to the principal vineyards
    of Spain and France.   James Busby
Grapes and wines from home vineyards.   U. P. Hedrick
Grapes are growing; the story of Australian wine. (The).
    Kenneth Slessor
Grapes of New York (The). U. P. Hedrick, et al.
Grapes: peaches: melons: and how to grow them.
    T. W. Sanders and J. Lansdell
Grapes, peaches, nectarines. H. R. Tuffin
Grapes, Peaches, Nectarines and Melons.   J. Lansdell
Grapes under cloches.   Howard Hyams
Grapes under glass.   H. Parsons
Grappling with the Monster or the curse and cure of
    strong drink.   T. S. Arthur
Great acceptance (The).   The life story of F. N. Charrington.
    Guy Thorne
Great American Band Wagon.   Charles Merz
Great evil of health drinking.   Jonathan Robinson
Great Facts.   A popular history of the most remarkable
    inventions during the present century.   F. C. Bakewell
Great Industries of the United States.   Anon
Great Tea Venture (The).   J. M. Scott
Great wines of Europe (The).   Ernest Hornickel
Great wines of Germany and its famed vineyards (The).
    A. L. Simon and S. F. Hallgarten
Green and roasted coffee tests.   Anon
Green and Green presents- Flavors of distinction.   Green
    and Green Inc.
Green cocktail book.   Jimmy (pseud)
Green manuring in tea culture in India.   H. H. Mann
Grocer's Companion and Merchant's handbook.   Anon
Grocer's encyclopedia (The).   Artemas Ward
Grocer's Guide (The).   Anon
Grocer's hand book and directory (The).   Artemas Ward
Grocers' Manual (The).   P. H. Felker
Grossman's guide to wines, spirits and beers.   H. J.
    Grossman
Growing and preparing guavas.   K. L. Smith
Growing grapes in Britain.   G. Pearkes
Growing grapes in Florida. Dr. Charles Demko
Growth and economic status of the bottled soft drink
    industry, 1957; a statistical summary.   A. B. C. B.
Growth of the vine and principles of winemaking.
    Jules Guyot
Gauger's guide and measurer's manual (The).   Thomas
    Kentish

Gauger's weighing manual. Anon
Gauging. E. Byrne
Gauging inspector and measures assistant (The).
    Daniel Anthony
Gauging Manual. Embracing Instructions.
    U.S. Treasury Dept.
Guests of an old time Inn. Ballantine and Sons
Guide des Bals et Soirees. (American and English
    drinks). Gabriel Brandimbourg
Guide for proper cup machine operation. (A). The
    Coca-Cola Co.
Guide for soda dispensers. W.A. Bonham
Guide for the perfumer. Hippolyte Dussauce
Guide to analysis of potable spirits. S.A. Vasey
Guide to art of manufacturing perfumes. Anon
Guide to Australian Wines (Ben Evans). Cellarmaster
    of The Bulletin
Guide to Bordeaux wines and cognac. D.L. Lamb
Guide to brewer's bookkeeping. Edward Amsdon
Guide to California wines. John Melville
Guide to cooling hot-weather drinks. Anon
Guide to drinks. United Kingdom Bartender's Guild
Guide to eating and drinking in Europe. W.E. Massee
Guide to Farmar's wine and spirit merchant's rule.
    F.C. Farmar
Guide to French Fetes (A). E.I. Robson
Guide to gentlemen and farmers for brewing finest malt
    liquors. Anon
Guide to good food and wines; a concise encyclopedia
    of gastronomy. A.L. Simon
Guide to good wine (A). Allan Sichel
Guide to importers and purchasers of wine. Anon
Guide to inn signs. E.R. Delderfield
Guide to London pubs. Martin Green and Tony White
Guide to pink elephants (A). Richards Rosen Associates
Guide to St. James's Gate brewery. Arthur Guinness
    and Son and Co. Ltd.
Guide to the Chalybeate spring of Thetford. Frederick
    Accum
Guide to the cultivation of the grapevine in Texas and
    instructions for winemaking. E.H. Andrae
Guide to the flavoring ingredients as classified under the
    Federal Food, Drug and Cosmetic Act.
    Fritzsche Brothers, Inc.
Guide to the Orchard and Kitchen garden . . . George
    Lindley

745

Guide to the literature of chemistry (A). E.J. Crane
    A.M. Patterson and E.B. Marr
Guide to the soda fountain. Invictus
Guide to wines; California wine land of America (A).
    Wine Advisory Board
Guide to young brewers (A). Anon
Guide to young brewers particularily adapted to the
    families of the nobility, and gentry, farmers
    and private brewers. John Tuck
Guidelines to practical winemaking. J.H. Fessler
Guinness-Dublin. Arthur Guinness Son and Co.
Guinness's Brewery. Arthur Guinness Son and Co.
Guinness's Brewery in the Irish economy. Patrick Lynch
    and John Vaisey
Gun Club drink book. Charles Brown
Gunter's Confectioner's oracle. William Gunter
Gunter's modern confectioner. William Jeannes

Hail and farewell (see The Old Soak). Don Marquis
Half-A-Century of Successful Trade. Sir Herbert Maxwell
Hamlin's formulae or every druggist his own perfumer.
    C.E. Hamlin and Chas. Warren
Hance's Pure fruit juices. Hance Brothers and White
Handbook. 1968-1969. Scottish Licensed Trade Ass'n.
Handbook Australian vines and wines. J.T. Fallon
Handbook for Australian brewers. J.C. Mac Cartie
Handbook for young brewers (A). H.E. Wright
Handbook of brewing calculations. O.W. Villiers
Handbook of chocolate and confectionery. A. Boake
    Roberts and Co.
Handbook of food manufacture. Dr. F. Fiene and Saul
    Blumenthal
Handbook of fruit culture. Fruit culture for the millions.
    Thomas Greggs
Handbook of Gastronomy (A). J.A. Brillat-Savarin
Handbook of grape culture; or, why, where, when, and
    how to plant and cultivate a vineyard, manufacture
    wines . . . T.H. Hyatt
Handbook of gauging at breweries. George Birch
Handbook of horticulture and vitaculture of Western
    Australia (The). A. Despeissis
Handbook of hydrometry. J.B. Keene
Handbook of modern cocktails. Frederick Anderson
Handbook of modern facts about alcohol. C.F. Stoddard

Handbook of perfumes, cosmetics and other toilet articles.
    A.J. Cooley
Handbook of practical guaging. J.B. Keene
Handbook of practical guaging with instructions in the use
    of Syke's hydrometer. James B. Keene
Handbook of statistics and information. P.C. Morgan
Handbook of the wine and spirit trade (A). S.A. Manning
Handbook of wine; how to buy, serve, store, and drink it.
    (A). W.J. Todd
Handbook of wines and liquors (The). H.E. Taylor
Handbook of wines, practical, theoretical, and historical;
    with a description of foreign spirits and liqueurs.
    Thomas McMullen
Handbook on vitaculture for Victoria. Hubert de Castella
Handbook on wine (A). (For retail licensees).
    KWV Public Relations Dept.
Handbook on wines to all who drink them. An essay
    more than passing useful. Anon
Handbook to coffee planting in Southern India. John Shortt
Handling Empty Deposit Bottles. Suggestions on
    improved methods for handling returnable deposit bottles
    in food stores. Anon
Handybook for brewers being a practical guide to the art
    of brewing and malting (A). H.E. Wright
Handybook of law relating to brewers. C.C. Peile
Handybook of the American brewing industry. A.S. Wahl
Handbuch fur mixer. Hans Kronlein
Haney's steward and barkeeper's manual. Jesse Haney
    and Co.
Hangover Book (The). Prevention, preparation, treatment
    and cure. Jonathon Routh
Hangover cook book. J. and J. Smedley
Hansons of Eastcheap. 1747. George Godwin
"Happy Days!" A book of good cheer, of cocktails . . .
    John
Hardy tradition; tracing the growth and development of a
    great winemaking family through its first hundred years
    (The). Thomas Hardy and Sons
Hargreaves story (The) (Cider). F.J. White
Harper's Export Wine and Spirit Gazette. Anon
Harper's Manual. Anon
Harry's - ABC of mixing cocktails. Harry Portman
Hartman's curiosities of art and nature of the true
    preserver and restorer of health. George Hartman
Harvesting and storing garden fruit. Raymond Bush
Harvey's wine guide. John Harvey and Sons

Hatfield and its people. Hatfield Workers Educational
    Ass'n.
Have a drink! Ed. Gibbs
Have bottles . . . will "POP". A. Schmeiser
Haven of health (The). Thomas Cogan
Hawaiian and Pacific foods. Katherine Bazore
Hawaiian coffee planters' manual. H.M. Whitney
Hawaiian hospitality. G.T. Armitage
Health and liquids. A.B.C.B.
Health cocktails (from fruit and vegetables.)
    Dr. P.M. Koonin
Health giving brews. Kenneth Rawnsley
Health in the household. S.W. Dodds
Health of a nation (The). Harvey W. Wiley and the
    fight for pure food. O.E. Anderson, Jr.
Health resorts of the south and summer resorts of
    New England. Anon
Health secrets from foreign lands. Anon
Health secrets of famous doctors. Anon
Health secrets of famous people. Anon
Health via food. W.H. Hay
Healthes: Sicknesse . . . William Prynne
Healthful and therapeutic properties of wine, beer,
    whiskey, bitters, liquors in general. J.P. Daraio
Health's grand preservative or the Woman's best doctor.
    Thomas Tryon
Healths improvement or rules . . . Thomas Moufet
Healthy life beverage book (The). H.V. Knaggs
Henley's Twentieth Century book of Recipes, Formulas
    and Processes. G. Hiscox
Hennessy is everywhere. Jas. Hennessy and Co.
Henry Tate 1819-1899. (Food). Tom Jones
Her foot is on the brass rail. Don Marquis
Herb-lore for housewives. Mrs. J.C. Romanne
Herbal delights. Mrs. C.F. Leyel
Herbal Drinks-operational techniques. G.B. Beattie
Herbal remedies and recipes and some others. M.T. Quelch
Herbs and spices for health and beauty. Jane Colin
Herbs for daily use. M.T. Quelch
Herbs, spices and seasonings. J.N. Lesparre
Herbs. Their culture and uses. R.E. Clarkson
Here let us feast. M.F.K. Fisher
Here's how. Emmett, Atherton (pseud)
Here's how. Clark Gavin
Here's how! Judge, Jr.
Here's How. Maryland Liquor Co.

Here's How . . . a book of recipes for the mixing of
    beverages. G.A. Lurie
Here's How! A handbook of recipes of spiritous and
    non-spiritous drinks. Anon
Here's How! A round-the-world bar guide. L.G. Blochman
Here's How. Being a new symposium of recipes of good
    cheer. G.A. Keen
Here's How. Being a new symposium of recipes of good
    cheer. Victoria Wine Co.
Here's how by Clegg (pseud). Erwin Cohan
Here's how, by Souffer's. Stouffer Foods Corp.
Here's how; mixed drinks. W.C. Whitfield
Here's how! New and rev. ed. By Judge, Jr. (pseud)
    Norman Anthony
Here's how again! by Judge, Jr. (pseud). Norman Anthony
Here's how to be healthy. B.G. Hauser
Here's to it! (toasts). J.M. Koken
Hering' Dictionary of classical and modern cookery. Anon
Heritage born and pledged anew. Miller Brewing Co.
Hershey's helps for the hostess. Mrs. C. Frederick
Hesperides. A history of the culture and use of citrus
    fruits. T. Toldowsky
Hic, Haec, Hock! C.R. Benstead
High Bonnet. Idwal Jones
Hilsebusch's thorough course of rectifying and compounding.
    H.W. Hilsebusch
Hints on coffee planting. Anon
Hints on home brewing. C.J.J. Berry
Hints on the cooking of coffee. William Law
Hints to consumers of wine. James Walker
Hints to liquor merchants. William Rudkin
Hints to peasant proprietors and others engaging in
    cultivation of cocoa. J.D. Huggins
Hiram Walker (1816-1899) and Walkerville from 1858.
    H.R. Walton
Hiram Walker outline of the distilled spirits business.
    Hiram Walker Inc.
His life and work. Jerry Mc Auley
Historic and picturesque inns of old England.
    C.G. Harper
Historical account of coffee (An). John Ellis
Historical, chemical and theurapeutical analysis of the
    principal mineral fountains at Saratoga Springs (A).
    R.L. Allen
Historical notes on beer and brewing. S.M. Hawkes
Historical survey of the temperance question. John
    Crosfill

History and description of modern wines (A). Cyrus
    Redding
History and progress of the temperance reformation,
    in Great Britain. J.S. Buckingham
History and reminiscences of lower Wall St. . . .
    Abram Wakeman
History and science of drunkenness (The). William Ackroyd
History of a brewery (The). 1835-1949. Groves and
    Whitnall, Lt d.
History of a crime against the food law (The). H.W. Wiley
History of a Danish Firm during 125 years (The). Peter
    F. Heering
History of a zoological convention held in Central Africa.
    Edward Hitchcock
History of Agriculture in the State of New York (A).
    U.P. Hedrick
History of American manufactures. J.L. Bishop
History of ancient and modern wines (The). Alexander
    Henderson
History of applejack or apple brandy in New Jersey from
    colonial times to the present (The). H.B. Weiss
History of Assam Company (A). H.A. Antrobus
History of beer and Quaker beer. Franklin Brewery
History of brewing and liquor industry of Rochester. Anon
History of brewing and the growth of the United States
    Brewers Association (The). United States Brewers'
    Ass'n.
History of brewing in the United States. J.P. Arnold
History of brewing studies. Grove Johnson
History of Champagne (The). A.L. Simon
History of Champagne. With notes on the other
    sparkling wines of France (A). Henry Vizetelly
History of coffee . . . (The). William Law
History of cognac-brandy. F. Sandeman
History of cold bathing both ancient and modern. John
    Floyer First part 1702 Dr. Edward Baynard Second
    part 1706
History of "Dirty Dick". A legend of Bishopsgate without.
    Ye olde wien house of Dirty Dick (National Bentley).
    Anon
History of dri nk (The). A review, social scientific and
    political. James Samuelson
History of English ale and beer (A). H.A. Monckton
History of food adulteration and analysis. (A). F.A. Filby
History of glass containers (The). Latchford-Marble Glass
    Company

History of horticulture in America to 1860 (A).
　　U. P. Hedrick
History of Hurty- Peck and Company.　Its first 50 years.
　　1903- 1953.　A. W. Noling
History of Hurty- Peck and Co.　Its first fifty years.
　　Abridged edition.　A. W. Noling
History of liquor licensing in England principally from
　　1700 to 1830 (The).　Sidney and Beatrice Webb
History of orgies (A).　Burgo Partridge
History of packaged beer and its market in the United
　　States (A).　American Can Co.
History of pasteurization (The).　Ernst Andrup
History of soda fountain industry.　C. J. Palmer
History of some effects of hard drinking.　J. C. Lettson
History of spices (A).　American Spice Trade Ass'n.
History of sugar (The).　William Reed
History of tea (A).　by a proprietary planter.　Anon
History of the ancient and modern Tee- Totalism with a
　　short account of drunkenness (A).　Joseph Dearden
History of the Anti- saloon league.　E. H. Cherrington
History of the brewing industry and brewing science in
　　America.　J. P. Arnold
History of the brewing industry in the province of Quebec
　　(The).　Emile Vaillancourt
History of the champagne trade in England.　A. L. Simon
History of the English Public House.　H. A. Monckton
History of the Indian tea industry (The).　Sir Percival
　　Griffiths
History of the Institute of Brewing (The).　W. H. Bird
History of the tea cup (The).　Rev. G. R. Wedgwood
History of the tea plant; from the sowing of the seed,
　　to its package for the European market (The).
　　London Genuine Tea Co.
History of the temperance movement in Great Britain
　　and Ireland.　Samuel Couling
History of the wine trade.　S. F. Davis
History of the wine trade in England (The).　A. L. Simon
History of toasting; or, Drinking of healths in England
　　(The).　R. V. French
History of vitaculture and winemaking in Australia.
　　Edgar A. Holden
History of William and Edward Willcocks, two servants
　　or, sobriety rewarded and drunkenness punished.　Anon
History of wine as theraphy (A).　S. P. Lucia
History of wine; great vintage wines from the Homeric age
　　to the present day.　H. W. Allen

History of wine in Australia (The). E.J. Beck (see
    Aesthetics of wine)
History of wine. When and how to drink it. Paul Verdier
Hocks and Moselles. H.R. Rudd
Hoffman house bartender's guide; how to open saloon and
    make it pay (The). C.S. Mahoney
Holiday Book of food and drink. Anon
Holiday drink book (The). Peter Beilenson
Holiday punches, party bowls, and soft drinks. Edna
    Beilenson
Hollywood's favorite cocktail book. Buzzo-Cardozo of
    Hollywood
Home and foreign alcoholic beverages. John Wishart
Home bartender's guide and song book (The). Charlie
    Roe and Jim Schwenck
Home bottling, drying and preserving. A.L. Andrea
Home-brewed ale; or plain instructions . . . A. House-
    keeper
Homebrewed beers and stouts. Canadian Edition.
    C.J.J. Berry
Homebrewed wines and beers and bartenders' guide.
    Johnson Smith and Co.
Home brewed wines and beers. F. Hack
Homebrewed wines and beers including cordials and
    syrups. F.B. Jack
Home-brewed wines and unfermented beverages for all
    seasons of the year. Anne Amateur (pseud)
Home-brewing for beginners. I.M. Macduff
Home brewing without failures. H.E. Bravery
Home canning, drying and preserving. A.L. Andrea
Home industries; a sheaf of practical hints and
    suggestions on a few remunerative home industries
    suited to Indian conditions with lots of tried recipes.
    Anon
Homemade beverages and American drinks. M.E. Steedman
Home-made beverages and vinegars, temperance and light
    drinks. J.P. Arnold
Home-made beverages, by a practical brewer. Anon
Home made beverages, the manufacture of non-Alcoholic
    and alcoholic drinks in the household. A.A. Hopkins
Home-made country wines. Farmers Weekly (magazine)
Homemade country wines, beer, mead and Metheglin.
    Dorothy Wise, ed.
Homemade Hilarity. Country drinks both hard and soft.
    Bob Brown
Homemade ice cream and sherbets. S.M. Cameron

Home-made sparkling wine secrets. Peggy Hutchinson
Homemade summer and winter drinks. Cups, liqueurs,
    cocktails and invalid drinks. M. E. Steedman
    and C. H. Senn
Homemade wine. Rex Tremlett
Home made wine and beer. The manufacture of wines
    and liquors without the aid of distillation. Howard
    Williams
Home-made wine secrets. Peggy Hutchinson
Home-made wines. Louise Morgan
Homemade wines. J. C. Newton
Home-made wines and liqueurs; how to make them.
    Ambrose Heath
Home-made wines, beers, liqueurs, cordials, cups and
    cocktails. Anon
Homemade wines, confectionery and sweets. Mary Bolton
Homemade wines. For family and medicinal use.
    G. F. Williams
Homemade wines. How to go about it. Kenneth Rawnsley
Homemade wines. How to make and how to keep. G. Vine
Home-made wines; how to make them. Peggy Hutchinson
    and Mary Woodman
Homemade wines, liquors and vinegars. "Clements".
Homemade wines, syrups and cordials. F. W. Beech, ed.
Home made wines, syrups, and cordials . . . National
    Federation of Women's Institutes
Home preservation of fruit and vegetables. M. J. M. Watson
Home production of fruit juices. Edgar Zubeckis
Home tonics and refreshers for daily health and vigor.
    J. E. Eichenlaub
Home uses of mineral waters. T. M. Coan
Home wine cellar with chapters on home bottling and
    other advice on the care of wine. R. W. Postgate
Home wine-making. H. E. Bravery
Home wine making. F. de Castella
Home winemaking. Charles Foster
Home wine-making. Gillian Pearks
Home wine-making. Your questions answered.
    C. C. Wormwell
Home wine-making without failures. H. E. Bravery
Honesta Voluptate (de). (Indulgence and good health).
    Platina (i.e. Bartolomeo de Sacchi di Piadena)
Honey and health; a nutrimental, medicinal and historical
    commentary. B. F. Beck
Honey production in the British Isles. R. O. B. Manley
Honour of the Gout. Philander Misiatrus (pseud)

Hop (The).   Herbert Myrick
Hop and its constituents (The).   Alfred C. Chapman
Hop farmer--hop culture--embracing its history, laws
    and uses . . . E.J. Lance
Hop industry (The).   H.H. Parker
Hope of health.   Philip Moore
Hops and hop-pickers.   Rev. J.Y. Stratton
Hops and the hop trade.   F. Taylor
Hops.   Botany, cultivation and utilization.   A.H. Burgess
Hops in their botanical, agricultural and technical aspects.
    Emanual Gross
Hops.   Rice.   Malt.   Anheuser-busch
Hops; their cultivation, commerce, and uses in various
    countries.   P.L. Simmonds
Horrors of delerium tremens.   J. Root
Hors d'oeuvres and canapes, with a key to the cocktail party.
    J.A. Beard
Horsford's THE ARMY RATION OF 1864.   (Coffee).
    Quartermaster Food and Container Institute for the
    Armed Forces
Hospital treatment of alcoholism.   R.S. Wallerstein
Hospitality recipes out of a Pepsi-Cola bottle.
    Pepsi-Cola Co.
Host and guest.   A book about dinners, dinner-giving,
    wines, and desserts.   A.V. Kirwan
Hostess book of favorite wine recipes.   Wine Advisory
    Board
Host's handbook.   National Distiller Products Corp.
Hot water cure sought out in Germany in the summer of
    1844 (A).   Anon
Hotel and catering occupations.   Anon
Hotel, innkeeper, vintner and spirit dealer's assistant.
    Alexander Peddie
Hotel Management and related subjects.   A selected list
    of books, pamphlets and periodical articles (Various
    editions).   School of Hotel Administration
Hour (The).   Bernard De Voto
House and Garden special edition - wine.   Anon
House and Garden Wine Book.   Anon
House of Dewar.   1846-1946.   Anon
House of Haig.   James Laver
House of Sanderson.   (Whiskey).   Ross Wilson
House of Shea (Beer).   William Douglas
House of Twining 1706-1956.   (Tea).   S.H. Twining
House of wine.   (Madhushala).   Harivanshrai Bachchan
Household Cyclopedia of practical receipts and daily
    wants.   A.V. Hamilton

Household guide to wines and liquors. George Belth
Houses and ale. Usher's Wilshire Brewery Ltd.
Housewife's Referee. Mrs. de Salis
Housekeeper's instructor or universal family cook.
   W.A. Henderson
Housewives favorite recipes. White Enamel Refrigerator Co.
How and when (Cocktails). H. Gale and G.E. Marco
How Ceylon tea is grown and marketed. Anon
How champagne was first discovered and how the wine
   is now produced. Henry Vizetelly
How good beer is served. Stansfield and Co.
How Mama could cook! Dorothy Malone
How the modern hostess serves wine. Blake Ozias
How they draw prohibition. A.B. Maurice
How to be a oordial host. Canada Dry Corp.
How to bottle. George Fowler
How to brew beer and make wine. Arthur Gneisieau
How to brew good beer. John Pitt
How to brew splendid ale. See The Derbyshire instruction
   book. Fisher and Son
How to carve, and how to serve a dinner. (And brew).
   N.L. Munro
How to choose and enjoy wine. Augustus Muir
How to cook with wine. Harriet Goodwin
How to enjoy wine in the home. A.L. Simon
How to handle and serve bottled and draught beers.
   Anheuser-Busch, Inc.
How to make more than 100 summer and winter drinks
   . . . Anon
How to identify English drinking glasses and decanters.
   Douglas Ash
How to identify English silver drinking vessels 600-1830.
   Douglas Ash
How to keep healthy in the tropics. J.N. Dugdale
How to know the economic plants. H.E. Jaques
How to know wild fruits. A guide to plants when not in
   flower by means of fruit and leaf. M.G. Peterson
How to make 44 favorite party drinks. Southern Comfort
   Corp.
How to make home-brewed ale. John Ettlinger
How to make perfect coffee. W.S. Quinby
How to make syrup for soft drinks. Hurty-Peck and Co.
How to make 300 secret trade recipes. Trade Recipes
How to make wine in your own kitchen. M.C. Roate
How to make your own wines and beers. J.H. Tobe
How to mix drinks. W.M. Edwards

How to mix drinks. Bar keepers' handbook. George
Winter
How to mix drinks, or, Bon-Vivant's companion.
Jerry Thomas
How to obtain an ideal cup of coffee . . . E. Boyes
How to preserve foods. W.W. Chenoweth
How to protect stainless steel beverage processing
equipment from corrosion. A.B.C.B.
How to run a pub. Tony White
How to serve wine and beer. Caleb Drinkwater
How to serve wine in hotels. A.L. Simon
How to settle in Victoria. Rusticus (pseud)
How to stop drinking. Herbert Breen
How to use spices. American Spice Trade Ass'n.
How to wine and dine in Paris. R.F. Wilson
How to wine friends and affluent people. R.H. Loeb, Jr.
How? When? Where? (Cocktails). Tooze's, Minneapolis
How you can make wines . . . Louis Dumont
Humour of drinking, by John Aye (pseud).
John Atkinson
Hundred years of Ceylon Tea. 1867-1967. D.M. Forrest
Hungarian wine through the ages. Zoltan Halasz
Hungry traveller in France. Norman Davey
Hunter wine. Max Lake
Huswifes jewell. Anon
Hutchinson's Food and the principles of dietetics.
V.H. Mottram and George Graham
Hydrometrical observations and experiments in the
brewery. J.H. Baverstock
Hydrotheraphy at Saratoga. A treatise on natural mineral
waters. J.A. Irwin
Hygiene in soft drinks manufacture. R.H. Morgan

I bought a hotel. A.J. Brown
I was an alcoholic. The story of a cure. Patrick Riddell
Ice and artificial cold, soda water, lemonade and all
aerated beverages . . . Thomas Masters
Ice and Ice-cold Tall-One. Hurty-Peck and Co.
Ice book (The). Thomas Masters
Ice cream and cool drinks. Culinary Arts Institute
Ice cream at the drug store soda fountain. H. H. H. Meserole
and O'Neal Johnson
Ice cream, carbonated beverages. Warner-Jenkinson Co.
Ice cream industry. G.D. Turnbow et al.
Ice cream Supplies and Machinery (Catalog). Wood and
Selick, Inc.

Ice creams, water ices, frozen puddings. Mrs. S. T.
    Rorer
Ices and how to make them. C. H. Senn
Ices and soda fountain drinks. P. Michael
Ida Bailey Allen's wines and spirits cook book.
    Mrs. I. C. B. Allen
Ideal bartender. Thomas Bullock
Ideal Recipes Book. For use of currants, raisins,
    sultanas and grapes. Also recipes for refreshing
    fruit beverages and party drinks. Women's Christian
    Temperance Union of South Australia
Identification of organic compounds. G. B. Neave and
    I. M. Heilbron
If you drink. Wilfred Funk
Illicit Scotch. S. W. Sillett
Illustrated Catalogue and price list No. 1. of apparatus
    for making, cooling and dispensing soda water and
    other aerated beverages. John Mathews
Illustrations of James W. Tuft's Soda-Water Apparatus
    J. W. Tufts
Impact of coffee on the U. S. Economy. Pan-American
    Coffee Bureau
Imperial drug trade. Josiah Rowntree
Impartial inquiry into the benefits arising to the nation from
    the present use of low priced spirits . . . Josiah
    Tucker
Importance of the brewery stated. Anon
Imposters unmasked, and the public protected in the use
    of popular beverages. Udolpho Wolfe
Improve your winemaking. B. C. A. Turner
Improved practical culture of the vine especially in
    regular vineyards. J. S. Kercht
Improving maintenance operations. A. B. C. B.
In a wine cellar in Store Street. G. A. Sala
In old vintage days. F. E. W. Colburn
In praise of ale. W. T. Marchant
In praise of good living. A. L. Simon
In praise of tea. A poem. J. B., Writing master
In praise of wine. R. H. Parker
In praise of wine. Alec Waugh
In praise of Yorkshire ale. George Meriton
In pursuit of the Vine. Dawson Gratrix
In quest of spices. S. E. Howe
In search of wine . . . C. W. Berry
In the twilight. A. L. Simon
In the vine country. E. OE. Somerville and Martin Ross

In vino veritas, a book about wine. A.L. Simon
In Vino Veritas. An account of conversation betwixt
    Cup the Cooper and Dash the Drawer. Anon
Independent liquorist. Leonard Monzert
Indian corn (or maize) in the manufacture of beer.
    Robert Wahl
Indian domestic economy and receipt book. Anon
Indian essential oils; a review. A.K. Menon
Indian Housekeeper and cook. F.A. Steel and G. Gardiner
Indian nectar or a discourse concerning chocolate. Henry
    Stubbs (Stubbe)
Indian tea. A.F. Dowling
Indian tea: its culture and manufacture. Claud Bald
Indulgence and good health. (See De Honesta Voluptate)
    Platina
Indulgence in wine. Samuel Johnson
Industrial Challenge (Cocoa). Cadbury Brothers, Ltd.
Industrial fermentations. Paul W. Allen
Industrial Relations Guide. A.B.C.B.
Industry of brewing. A.C. Chapman
Inebriety or Narcomania, its etiology, pathology, treatment
    and jurisprudcence. Norman Kerr
Infidel grape (The). An anthology in miniature IN PRAISE
    of WINE. Max Crombie, Ed.
Influence of alcohol and other drugs on fatigue. W.H.R
    Rivers
Influence of caffein on mental and motor efficiency.
    H.L. Hollingworth
Influence of wholesome drink. Anon
Information for bottlers. Penrith, Akers Mfg. Co.
Information readers Number 1. Food and beverages.
    E.A. Beal
Ingesta: Eating and drinking. As an art instead of more
    animal indulgence. A. O'Leary
Injurious insects of the orchard, vineyards . . .
    Matthew Cooke
Inn crafts and furnishings. Whitbread Library
Innkeeper and butler's guide. John Davies
Innkeeper and public brewer. A practical Man
Innkeeper's Diary. John Fothergill
Innkeeping. A manual for licensed victuallers. National
    Trade Development Ass'n.
Inn-signia. Brian Hill
Inn-Signia. Whitbread and Co.
Inns, ales, and drinking customs of old England.
    F.W. Hackwood

Inns and taverns of old London. H.C. Shelley
Inns and Taverns of "Pickwick". B.W. Matz
Inns noted for good food in and around London. Anon
Inns of Britain with accomodations for the visitor. Anon
Inns of Kent. G.M. Rainbird
Inns of Kent. Whitbread and Co.
Inns of sport. Whitbread and Co.
Inns, taverns, alehouses, coffee houses in and around
    London. D.S. Foster
Inquire within for anything you want to know. Anon
Inquiry into the medicinal qualities and effects of the
    aerated alkaline water. John Moncreiff
Inquiry into the nature and object of the several laws
    for restraining and regulating the retail sale of
    alcohol, beer, wines and spirits. Robert Henderson
Inquiry into the policy and justice of the prohibition of
    the use of grain in distilling. Archibald Bell
Insect control in the beverage plant. A.B.C.B.
Inside facts of profitable fruit growing. W.P. Stark
Inside tip to the man that came back, the bar tender.
    J.J. Hayes
Inspection of fish, poultry, game, fruit, nuts and
    vegetables. A.H. Walker
Instructions and sundry catalog. Information regarding
    setting up and operating machinery employed on mfg.,
    disp., and bottling carbonated beverages. Chas.
    Lippincott and Co.
Instructions for brewing by new method from unmalted
    corn. J. Ham of Westeokers, Somerset
Instructions for brewing porter and stout. Charles
    Clarkson
Instructions for erecting and working B and F patent
    improved aerated water and beer carbonating
    machinery. Barnett and Foster
Instructions for making beer and ale in all temperance
    specially adopted for tropical climates. J. Beadel
Instructions for manufacture of aerated beverages, mineral
    waters, fruit syrups (or wines) and cordials. W.
    Meadowcroft and Son Ltd.
Instructions for operators of Matthews' apparatus, for
    manufacturing, dispensing and bottling soda water
    John Matthews
Instructions sur l'art de faire la biere. Le Pileur
    d'Appligny
Instructions to brew real beer at home. H.R. Fletcher
Instructor (The). Recipes, how to mix, handle and serve
    . . . contains over 500 drinks. C.B. Nelson

Internal Revenue Guager's Manual. Anon
Internal Revenue Manual for information and guidance
    of Internal-Revenue Agents and officers. Anon
International cocktail specialties, from Madison Avenue
    to Malaya. J.E. Mayabb
International Encyclopedia of food and drink. Anon
International hangover book. A. Douglas
International sweetmaker and confectioner. J.A. Farmer
Internationsler Riechstoff-Kodex. International
    compendium of aromatic materials. Arno Muller
Into Hutchinson's second century. (Crowns). W.H.
    Hutchinson and Son
Into the freezer-and out. D.K. Tressler et al.
Intoxicants and opium. In all lands and times. Dr.
    and Mrs. W.F. Crafts et al.
Intoxicating drinks and drugs in all lands and times.
    Dr. and Mrs. W.F. Crafts and Misses Mary and
    Margaret W. Leitch
Intoxicating drinks, their history and mystery. J.W. Kirton
Intoxicating hobby (An). the ABC of homemade sugar
    wines. Guy Wells
Intoxicating liquor licensing acts. 1872-1874.
    J. Peterson
Intoxicating liquors: the law relating to and drunkenness.
    W.W. Woolen and W.W. Thornton
Intoxication made easy. Elliot Paul and Luis Quintanilla
Introduction to French wines and spirits. Georges Varounis
Introduction to wines. Cyril Ray
Introduction to wines, by Oscar J. Wile. Schenley
    Import Corp.
Introduction to wines. W.P. Herod
Introductory foods. Osee Hughes
Introductory manual for sugar growers. Francis Watts
Introductory treatise on the theory and practice of malting
    and brewing. G.A. Wigney
Introitus apertus ad artem distillationis; or, The whole art
    of distillation practically stated. William Y-Worth
Invalid cookery book. Marguerite Patten
Invalid's own book. Lady Cust
Inventions and customs of both ancient and moderns in the
    use of inebriating liquors . . . Samuel Morewood
Inventions at your service. A.J. Kramer
Investigations in the autoxidation of aldehydes used in
    perfumery. E.G. McDonough
Invitation to inhabitants of England to manufacture wines from
    fruits of their own country. Richard Worthington

Invitation to wines; an informal guide to the selection,
care, and enjoyment of domestic and European
wines. John Storm
Invitations to dine in London and Greater London.
A.G. Hall
Irish toasts. Shane Na Gael
Irvin S. Cobb's own recipe book. I.S. Cobb
Is this your wine? W.V. Paige
Island of Formosa. Past and present. J.W. Davidson
Isles of spice and palm. A.H. Verrill
It is smart to serve beer. Menus and recipes to assist
the gracious hostess. Anon
Italian Confectioner. W.A. Jarrin
Italian wine. Anon
Italian wines and liqueurs. R.G. Dettori
Itinerary of Province and the Rhone. John Hughes
It's history, organization, production and markets.
Liquid Carbonic Company
It's smart to cook with beer. D.E. Hale

Jack De Manio's drinkards. Cocktails. J. De Manio
Jack De Manio's drinkards. Non-alcoholic drinks.
J. De Manio
Jack's manual on the vintage, care and handling of
wines, liquors . . . J.A. Grohusko
Jacquin's cordials. C. Jacquin et Cie
Jam making . . . including homemade wines. I.M.
Beeton
Jamaica rum cocktails. Fred L. Myers and Son
Jams and preserves, bottled fruits . . . M. Woodman
Jams, jellies and fruit bottling. D.D.C. Taylor
Japan and Formosa. W.H. Ukers
Japanese temples and tea-houses. W. Blaser
Java and Sumatra. W.H. Ukers
Jayne's bartender's guide. D. Jayne and Son
Jennie June's American cookery book. J.C. Croly
Jerez and its wine, sherry. Geo. G. Sandeman, Sons
and Co.
Jewel house of art and nature. H. Plat
Jingle jokes for little folks. C.E. Hires Co.
John Barleycorn. J. London
John Barleycorn. His life and letters. D.A. Poling
John Bull's vineyard. H. Castella
Jolly toper. M. Hardwick
Joseph Priestley. T.E. Thorpe

Jottings on coffee, its culture in Mysore. G. Anderson
Journal of a recent visit to the vineyards of Spain and
    France . . . J. Busby
"Journal of drink". Pliny Moore papers
Journal of the Institute of Brewing. Anon
Journey to the tea countries of China, including Sung-lo
    and the Bohee Hills . . . R. Fortune
Journey to wine in Victoria. W.S. Boswell
Judging home-made wines. Amateur Winemakers National
    Guild of Judges
Juice of the grape or wine preferable to water. P. Shaw
Jusfrute Book. A text book of aerated water
    manufacturers. G.I. Adcock
Jusfrute handbook for soft drink industry. A.H. Fuller
Jusfrute schools - topic sheets. Jusfrute Ltd.
Just cocktails. W.C. Whitfield
Just one more. J.L. Free
Just what you want to know about wine. M. Alexander

Keller's bottler's hand book. W.B. Keller
Kent Pubs. D.B. Tubbs
Distiller's guide (The). Key to the distillery. P. Jonas
Key to the trade. F. D'Armand Jr.
Kindred spirit. A history of gin and the House of Booth.
    Lord Kinross
King Henry VIII's newe wyne sellar at Hampton Court.
    E. Law
King of hearts drink book. P. Beilenson
Kitcheonette cookery. A. Adair
Knickerbocker, revised bartender's guide or how to mix
    drinks. Anon
Knorr's catalogue of ice cream machinery. W.L. Knorr
Know-how of lollie ice manufacture. F. Newcombe
Know your wines. A.L. Simon
Knowing alcoholic beverages. Liquor Store Magazine
Knowledge of a rectifier. H.W. Hilsebusch

Label booklet, price list and formulas. Stevenson and
    Howell Ltd.
Laboratory Apparatus and Materials Exhibition. Official
    catalogue. Anon
Laboratory examination of wines and other fermented
    products. W.V. Cruess
Laboraroty inspection of canned and bottled foods. D.
    Dickinson and P. Goose

Laboratory manual of fruit and vegetable products.
W. V. Cruess and A. W. Christie
Laboratory procedures for enology. M. A. Amerine
Laboratory studies for brewing students. A. J. Brown
Laboratory text book for brewers. L. Briant
Ladies best companion. A. Chambers
Ladies cabinet enlarged and opened. P. Ruthven
Ladies complete guide. Includes the complete brewer.
M. Cole
Lady's Companion (The). Anon
Lady's, housewife's and cook-aids assistant. E. Taylor
Lafite. Story of Chateau Lafite-Rothschild. C. Ray
Land, importance of its culture to the properity of
Victoria (The). S. Wekey
Land of coffee (The). Anon
Land of coffee. National Federation of Coffee Growers
of Columbia
Land of the wine; being an account of the Madeira Islands.
A. J. D. Biddle
Larousse Gastronomique. P. Montagne
Lasche's Magazine for the practical distiller. Anon
Latimers (The). Tale of whiskey insurection.
H. C. Mc Cook
Law and liquor. W. W. Turnbull
Law of drinking. R. Brathwait
Law of drinking. W. Juniper
Law of innkeepers. E. A. Jelf and C. J. B. Hurst
Laws of fermentation and the wines of the ancients.
W. Patton
Laws of Massachusetts relating to intoxicating liquors
. . . Anon
Lay thesis on bible wines. E. R. Emerson
Leasing vs owning of trucks and equipment. ABCB
Leaves from the diary of an old lawyer. A. B. Richmond
Lectures on experimental philosophy. J. Priestley
Lee's Priceless Receipts. Anon
Legend of liqueurs, wines and spirits. Anon
Leigh-Williams' amateur winemaker's record book. Anon
Lejon Cookbook. J. Owen
Lemon. Information about lemons and lemon processing.
L. J. Noling
Lemon Notes from various trade references on its use.
A. W. Noling
Lemon and lemon products. S. Hoos and R. E. Seltzer
Lemon fruit (The). E. T. Bartholomew and W. B. Sinclair
Lemon oil production around the world. E. Guenther

Lesson in pharmaceutical latin.   II. C. Muldoon
Lest we forget.   Cellar book.   Wine and Food Society
Let mine be wine.   The philosophy of wine.   The anatomy
   of wine.   The geography of wine.   The choice of
   wine.   The service of wine.   A. L. Simon
Let there be beer.   R. C. Brown
Let's eat right and keep fit.   A. Davis
Let's have a good time tonight.   G. Goddard and C. Wood
Let's have a party.   Blumentals Ltd.
Let's have a party.   Charlotte
Let's plant a vineyard.   M. Gore-Browne
Let's sell ice cream.   Anon
Let's talk about port.   J. C. Valente-Perfeito
Let's talk beer.   J. V. Fort
Let's talk soft drinks.   B. Ginsberg
Letter to a friend concerning tea (A).   J. Wesley
Letter to Elizium.   Anon
Letters from Madeira in 1834.   J. Driver
Letters on brewing.   Hantke's Brewers' School and
   Laboratories.
Letters on the culture of the vine.   W. MacArthur
Lexikon der spirituosen - und alkoholfreien - industrie.
   H. Goettler
Lexique Viti-Vinicole International.   H. Faes
Libraries, museums and art galleries year-book 1964.
   E. V. Corbett
Library of English and American books.   Wine and Food
   Society
License-holder's handy guide.   A. J. Harris
Licensed houses and their management.   W. B. Capper, ed.
Licensed trade (The).   E. A. Pratt
Licensed victualler (The).   L. Monzert
Licensed victualler's instructor and spirit dealer's
   companion.   J. Benson
Licensed victualler's manual.   J. E. Hughes
Licensed victualler's vade mecum.   J. W. DeCaux
Licensed victualler's official annual legal text-book . . .
   A. B. Deane
Licensing act of 1902.   G. H. Tripp
Licensing question, its history . . . F. N. Newcombe
Life and letters of Henry William Thomas, mixologist.
   Anon
Life and times of THE LATE DEMON RUM.   J. C. Furnas
Life and work of Cornelius O'Sullivan. H. D. O'Sullivan
Life of George Cadbury.   A. G. Gardiner
Life of Joseph Priestley.   A. Holt
Life of the party.   Three Feathers Distillers

Life story of George of the Ritz. G. Criticos
Lifetime collection of 688 recipes for drinks.   Anon
Light entertaining; a book of dainty recipes for special
    occasions.   H. Judson
Limonaden und alkokolfreie getranke.   H. Timm
Lincoln and liquor.   D. C. Milnor
Lincoln and liquor.   W. H. Townsend
Lipton story (The).   A. Waugh
Lipton's autobiography.   T. Lipton
Liqueur compounder's handbook of recipes for manufacture
    of liqueurs . . . W. J. Bush and Co.
Liqueurograph Chart (The).   Anon
Liqueurs.   P. Hallgarten
Liqueurs, a dictionary and survey.   M. I. Fisher
Liqueurs fines.   Cook and Bernheimer and Co.
Liquid air and the liquidation of gases.   T. O'C. Sloane
Liquid Gems.   A book of drinks for the fastidious drinker.
    J. E. Iverson
Liquor buyers' guide.   S. L. E. Stone
Liquor cult and its culture.   H. S. Warner
Liquor dealer's and bartender's companion.   N. W. Brown
Liquor dealer's silent assistant.   L. L'Abbe
Liquor dealer's silent partner.   Anon
Liquor handbook (The).   Anon
Liquor industry (The).   M. V. Rosenbloom
Liquor laws in 48 states.   B. M. Bernard
Liquor laws of the United States.   G. Thomann
Liquor legislation in U. S. and Canada.   W. Rathbone
    and E. L. Fanshowe
Liquor license.   An ethnography of bar behavior. S. Cavan
Liquor making at home . . . H. J. West
Liquor manufacture and traffic.   S. F. Cary
Liquor marketing and liquor advertising.   H. Bretzfield
Liquor problem in all ages.   D. Dorchester
Liquor problem in its legislative aspects.   F. H. Wines
    and J. Koren
Liquor, the servant of man.   M. E. Chafetz
Liquor: The servant of man.   W. H. Smith and F. C. Helwig
Liquor tax in U. S. 1791-1947.   T. Y. Yu
List of members.   National Ass'n of Soft Drink
    Manufacturers.
List of periodicals currently received in library branch
    of the Institute.   W. L. Necker and E. Wynn
List of references to authoritative writings on the
    carbonated beverage industry.   ABCB
List of the writings of Dr. Siebel.   J. E. Siebel

List of U.S., British and German patents covering the
   manufacture of non-alcoholic beers . , . Mock and
   Blum
List of wines, spirits and liqueurs. W. and A. Gilbey
Lists and analyses of the mineral springs of the U.S.
   A.C. Peale
Literature search on the preservation of food by freezing.
   B.H. Weil and F. Sterne
Little book of healing herbs. A.M. Tudor
Little book of sandwiches and beverages. Anon
Little booke of conceited secrets and delightes for ladies.
   M. Meighn
Little dinners. M. Hooper
Little red guide to home brewed wines. F.D. Todd
Little tea book (The). A. Gray
Little wine cellar all your own. Wine Advisory Board
Local (The). M. Gorham
Loftus' new mixing and reducing book. Anon
Log of the water wagon. B. Taylor and W.C. Gibson
London and country brewer. Anon
London and country cook. Anon
London and the British Isles. Bon Viveur
London art of cookery. J. Farley
London Breweries Companies. Anon
London Coffee Houses. B. Lillywhite
London complete art of cookery. Anon
London Cook (The). W. Gelleroy
London Distiller, the way to draw spirits and strong
   waters . . . (J. French)
London inns and taverns. L. Wagner
London Pubs. A. Reeve-Jones
London's friendly inns and taverns. A. Goodson
Long's portable soda fountain. E.C. Thompson
Lord's loud call to England . . . H. Jessey
Louis' mixed drinks, with hints for care and serving
   of wines. L.J. Muckensturm
Lowney's cook book. M.W. Howard
Lurie (A.N.) wine merchants. Anon

Mc Donough's bar-keepers' guide. P. McDonough
McGreal's blue book. McGreal Bros. Co.
Mackenzie's five thousand receipts. Anon
Mackenzie's ten thousand receipts in all the useful and
   domestic arts. Anon
MacMahan's latest recipes and American soda-water
   dispensers' guide. A.C. MacMahon

McMonagle and Rogers' cooking recipes.   Anon
Madeira.   R. Croft-Cooke
Madeira and its wines.   A.L. Simon
Madeira: wine, cakes and sauce.   A.L. Simon and E.
    Craig
Madeira Islands.   A.J.D. Biddle
Madeira party (A).   S.W. Mitchell
Madera wines and brandies.   K. Arakelian, Inc.
Magic in a bottle.   M. Silvermann
Magic in your glass.   Wine Advisory Board
Magic of herbs.   C.F. Leyel
"Magic of the grape".   C.H. Lund
Main products of overseas territories - Cocoa.
    Organization for European Economic Cooperation
Main source of alcoholism in the U.S. and suggested
    remedial legislation.   A. de Focatus
Maine law triumphant . . .   J. Wakeman
Main liquor law, its origin, history . . .   H.S Clubb
Maison Rustique, or the country Farme.   G. Markham
Make me a wine connisseur.   I. Crawford
Make mine wine.   W. Sherrard-Smith
Make your own wine.   A. Appleyard
Make your own wine.   W Sherrard-Smith
Make your wine at home.   Frank K. Clarke
Making and preserving apple cider.   Anon
Making friends is our business.   R. Krebs
Making mead, metheglin, hippocras, melomel, pymont,
    cyser.   B. Acton and P. Duncan
Making of ice creams, ices . . .   H. Gratz
Making soft drinks with Peggy Hutchinson.   P. Hutchinson
Making wine is not difficult.   C.J.J. Berry
Making wines at home.   J. Levett
Making wines like those you buy.   B. Acton and
    P. Duncan
Malt and malting.   H. Stopes
Malt liquors: their nature and effects.   W. Hargreaves
Malting.   A.R. Ling
Malting, brewing and allied processes.   I.A. Preece, ed.
Malting, brewing vinegar-making and distilling.
    F. Faulkner
Maltster (The).   W.R. Loftus
Maltster, distiller and spirit dealers' companion.
    J. Mc Donald
Maltster's guide.   W. Champion
Maltster's guide.   E.S. White
Maltster's materials and methods.   H.M. Lancaster

Malt-worms. (see Vade-mecum for ----.) Anon
Man and his health; liquids. W.A. Fairburn
Man takes a drink. Facts and principles about alcohol.
    J.C. Ford
Man who made wine (The). J.M. Scott
Management and cost control in the carbonated beverage
    industry. A.H. Bolte and A.E. Low
Management for profit in the bottled soft drink industry.
    ABCB
Management in the hotel and catering industry. Anon
Mango. Central Food Technological Research Institute
Mangos in Florida. S.J. Lynch and M.J. Mustard
Manhattan oases. A. Hirschfeld
Manner of making of coffee, tea and chocolate.
    P.S. Dufour
Man's foods. L.B. Jensen
Manual (Liquor). Fries Brothers
Manual for compounders, rectifiers and cordial
    manufacturers. Alex. Fries
Manual for compounders. Fries and Fries
Manual for institutional canning. American Can Co.
Manual for profit planning for the bottled carbonated
    beverage industry. ABCB
Manual for the essence industry. E. Walter
Manual for the inspector of spirits. Anon
Manual for the liquor trade. F. Lindinger
Manual for the manufacture of cordials, liquors, fancy
    syrups . . . C. Schultz
Manual of alcoholic fermentation . . . C.G. Matthews
Manual of American grape growing. U.P. Hedrick
Manual of brewing. E.G. Hooper
Manual of coffee planting in Natal. W.H. Middleton
Manual of formulas . . . R.B. Wailes, ed.
Manual of instructions for brewers and distillers.
    M. Augenstein
Manual of liquor tests. B.B. and A.H. Howe
Manual of plain directions for planting and cultivating
    vineyards and for making wine in New South Wales.
    J. Busby
Manual of spices. American Spice Trade Ass'n.
Manual of sugar analysis. J.H. Tucker
Manual of the Swiss vigneron. B. Chappius
Manual of the vine. C.W. Grant
Manual on beers, wines and liquors for everybody.
    Beverage Research Bureau
Manual on cordials. Leroux and Co. Inc.

Manual pratique de la fabrication des eaux et boissons,
   gazeuses. J. Fritsch
Manual. What to use. How to mix. How to serve.
   Chapin and Gore
Manuel de brasserie. E. G. Hooper
Manuel du Limonadier et du Confiseur. M. Cardelli
Manufacture and analysis of carbonated beverages.
   M. B. Jacobs
Manufacture of aerated beverages, cordials ... Stevenson
   and Howell
Manufacture of beet-root sugar in England and Ireland.
   W. Crookes
Manufacture of bottled carbonated beverages. H.E. Medbury
Manufacture of chocolate and other cacao preparations.
   P. Zipperer
Manufacture of cider and perry reduced to rules. J. Ham
Manufacture of dry wines in hot countries. F.T. Bioletti
Manufacture of emulsion flavors. M. de Groote
Manufacture of flor sherry. J. L. Williams
Manufacture of ice creams and ices. J.H. Frandsen
   and E.A. Markham
Manufacture of liquors and preserves. J.M. de Brevans
Manufacture of liquors, wines and cordials without the
   aid of distillation. P. Lacour
Manufacturers of machinery for beverage, food and
   chemical industries. Star Liquid Machinery Corp.
Manufacture of preserved foods and sweetmeats.
   A. Hausner
Manufacture of spirit as conducted at various distilleries
   of the United Kingdom. J.A. Nettleton
Manufacture of syrups and cold drinks: with tried recipes
   and practical hints. Anon
Manufacture of tea in Northeast India. P.H. Carpenter
   and C.J. Harrison
Manufacture of vinegar: its theory and practice.
   C.M. Wetherill
Manufacture of whiskey, brandy and cordials. I. Hirsch
Manufacture of whisky and plain spirit. J.A. Nettleton
Manufacture of wine in California. H. Lachman
   (see H.W. Wiley-American wines at Paris)
Manufacturers' practical recipes. Shaw Publ. Co.
Maple-Sap Syrup: its manufacture, composition . . .
   A.H. Bryan
Maple syrup producers' manual. C.O. Willits
Market milk and related products. H.H. Sommer
Marketing of coffee. P.O. Rudy

769

Marketing of tea. K.K. Roy
Martini Museum (The). O. Spinola
Mary Meade's magic recipes. R.E. Church
Master chef's best. L.P. De Gouy
Masterly touch (The). Canada Dry GingerAle Co.
Mastery of water (The). Anon
Matthews' catalogue and price list of apparatus . . .
    J. Matthews Apparatus Co.
Matthews sirup book. J. Matthews
Max Henius - a biography. Max Henius Memoir Committee
Maxwell House Coffee cookbook. Anon
Mead. Brother Adam
Mead, and how to make it. G.W. Bancks
Measuring the sugar content of syrup and beverages.
    A.W. Noling
Measuring the acid content of soft drinks. A.W. Noling
Mechanical side of mineral water. G.B. Beattie
Medical aspects of the Latter-day saint Word of
    Wisdom. L.W. Oaks
Medical commentary on fixed air. M. Dobson
Medicinal and perfumery plants and herbs of Ireland.
    Jude
Medicinal value of French brandy. G.H. Jackson
Meditations on gout with a consideration of its cure
    through use of wine. G.H. Ellwanger
Meet the Cape wines. H. Beck
Melrose, honey of roses. S. Graham
Memoir on the cultivation of the vine in America and
    best mode of making wine. J. Adlum
Memoir on vinous fermentation. L.J. Thenard
Memoirs of Kohler of the KWV. A. Joelson
Memorandum on sweetening agents for carbonated
    beverages. ABCB
Memorandum on tea. Tea Bureau Inc.
Memorandum written after a tour through the tea districts
    of Bengal in 1864-65. W.N. Lees
Memorials prepared by Champagne merchants in Reims
    . . . Anon
Men in aprons. L.A. Keating
Men, materials, equipment. Anheuser-Busch
Menus for gourmets. A.L. Simon
Merchandising plan. The Tall-One Co.
Merchant and seaman's expeditious measurer . . .
    E.H. Blunt
Merchants of wine. A. Waugh
Mermaid and Mitre taverns of old London. (The).
    K. Rogers

Merrie Christmas drink book. P. Beilenson
Merrydown book of country drinks. A. Launay
Merrydown-wine of Sussex. Merrydown Wine Co.
Merry gentlemen, a Bacchanalian scrapbook. R. Watson
Merry-go-down. A gallery of gorgeous drunkards through
    the ages. R. Noolas
Merry, ingenious and diverting work entitled Liber
    compotorum felicium: or The true drunkard's delight.
    W. Juniper
Merry mixer. Jos. S. Finch and Co.
Merry mixer. H.S. Lev
Merry mixer. Schenley Products Co.
Merry mixer. A booklet of mixtures and mulches . . .
    Schenley Products Co.
Merry mixer; or, cocktails and their ilk. W. Guyer, ed.
Metallic and mineral waters. E. Pratt
Method of brewing English dry lager beer (The).
    T. Perry
Method of ullaging and inching. W. Yeo
Methodical synopsis of mineral waters . . . J. Rutty
Methods of analysis. American Society of Brewing
    Chemists
Methods of analysis. Official and tentative of the Ass'n.
    of Agricultural Chemists. Anon
Methods of extracting volatile oils from plant material.
    A.F. Sievers
Mexican coffee culture. J. Yorba
Microbiological aspects of one-trip glass bottles.
    H.E. Korab
Microbiology. P.W. Groves
Micro-organisms of faulty rum. V.H. and L.J. Veley
Microscope in the brewery and malt-house (The).
    C.G. Matthews and F.E. Lott
Microscopical examination of food and drugs. H.G. Greenish
Mida's continuous directory and merchandiser for the
    spirits and vinous industries. L.W. Mida
Mida's handbook for wholesale liquor dealers. W. Mida
Milk analysis. J.A. Wanklyn
Milk and its hygenic relations. J.E. Lane-Clayton
Miller High-Life centennial edition. Miller Brewing Co.
Mine Host's handbook. National Distillers Products Corp.
Mineral and aerated waters. C.A. Mitchell
Mineral and thermal springs of U.S. and Canada. J. Bell
Mineral springs of Canada. J. Satterly and T. Elworthy
Mineral springs of England. E. Lee
Mineral springs of North America; how to reach and how
    to use them. J.J. Moorman

Mineral springs of Saratoga. J. F. Kemp
Mineral springs of the United States and Canada.
    G. E. Walton
Mineral Water Maker's Manual. J. G. Smith
Mineral water maker's Vade Mecum. E. Mac Swiney
Mineral water manufacturer's accounts. J. Lund and
    G. H. Richardson
Mineral water manufacturer's guide to bookkeeping.
    E. Amsdon
Mineral water spoilage prevention. "Pyramid"
    (G. B. Beattie)
Mineral water trade and the food and drugs act.
    Stevenson and Howell
Mineral water trade year book. C. H. Horton
Mineral waters and health resorts of Europe. H. and F. P.
    Weber
Mineral waters of Europe. C. R. C. Tichborne and P. Jones
Mineral waters of the United States. J. K. Haywood
Mineral waters of the United States and American spas.
    W. E. Fitch
Mineral waters of the United States and Canada.
    J. J. Moorman
Mineral waters of the United States and their therapeutic
    uses. J. K. Crook
Mineral waters. Price-list and invoice. T. Davis
Mirror of intemperance. M. E. Cross
Mis 500 cocktails. P. Chicote
Miscellany of wine (A). C. W. Berry
Mixed drinks. A manual for bar clerks. H. W. Green
Mixed drinks up to date. H. J. Schell
Mixer (The). H. E. Bowen
Mixer, handmixer and blender cookbook (The).
    Culinary Arts Institute
Mixologist (The). C. F. Lawlor
Mixologist (The). A. J. Bailey
Mixologist and compounder (The). E. M. Casey
"Mixology" recipes for old and new mixed drinks.
    A. Reibstein
Mixology; the art of preparing all kinds of drinks.
    J. L. Haywood
Modern aerated water machinery and appliances.
    W. Meadowcroft and Son
Modern American drinks. G. J. Kappeler
Modern aromatic chemicals. A. von Isokovics
Modern art of brewing splendid ale, porter, stout . . .
    Anon

Modern Baker, Confectioner and Caterer.   Anon
Modern bartenders' guide . . . O.H. Byron
Modern blending and rectification.   C. Norton
Modern brewery plant.   C. Johnson
Modern brewing.   C.A. Nowak
Modern Brewery Age.   Anon
Modern cocktail manual of 168 drinks.   F. Anderson
Modern coffee production.   A.E. Haarer
Modern coffee planting.   E.G. Windle
Modern confectioner (Gunter's).   W. Jeannes
Modern confectioner.   C.W. Popp
Modern cookery in all its branches.   E. Acton
Modern detection and treatment of wine diseases.
     D.D. Couche
Modern domestic brewer (The).   G. Cooper
Modern domestic cookery.   W.A. Henderson
Modern Domestic Science Vol. 5. Beverages.
     G.T. Herrick and M. Harland
Modern extracter (The).   J. Hollingworth
Modern fruit growing.   W.P. Seabrook
Modern handbook of wine and liquor control.
     R.M. Grinstead
Modern luncheonette management E.M. Fleishman
Modern manual for rectifiers, compounders, and all
     dealers in whiskies, wine and liquors.   C. Norton
Modern manufacturing formulary.   E.J. Belanger
Modern methods of cocoa and chocolate manufacture.
     H.W. Bywaters
Modern methods of food industry management.   Anon
Modern, simple and practical formulae, pertaining to
     the manufacture of cordials, bitters, gins . . .
     C.O. Sethness et al.
Modern strawberry growing.   A.E. Wilkinson
Modern water treatment.   ABCB
Modern wines.   T.A. Layton
Modern yeasting and distillation.   C. Norton
Molson Story (The).   M. Denison (see Barley and the
     stream)
Money-making formulas.   H. Bennett
Money making hints for soda fountains.   B.A. Forbes
Money-saving formulas.   P. Doring
Monograph on flavoring extracts with essences, syrups
     and colorings.   J. Harrop
Monzert's practical distiller.   L. Monzert
More about inn signs.   E.R. Delderfield
More friendly inns in and around London.   A. Goodson

More London inns and taverns. L. Wagner
More Peggy Hutchinson's home-made wine secrets.
P. Hutchinson
More pious friends and drunken companions. F. Shay
More recipes with a jug of wine. M. Wood
Morning dewdrops of the juvenile abstainer. C.L. Balfour
Morrissey's catalogue and net wholesale pricelist.
C.T. Morrissey and Co.
Motivation research of beer consuming habits. Froedtert
Malt Corp.
Mount Gilead equipment and supplies for cider, vinegar
and grape juice manufacturers. Hydraulic Press
Mfg. Co.
Mouquin Epicure (The). An unusual recipe book. Mouquin,
Inc.
Mr. Clerihew - wine merchant. H.W. Allen
Mrs. Allen's book of sugar substitutes. I.C.B. Allen
Mrs. Beeton's all about cookery. Anon
Muscadine grapes. C. Deering
Muscadine grapes. G.C. Husmann and C. Deering
My cookery books. E.R. Pennell
My first trip to Villa Nueva. G. Doblache
My new cocktail book. G.F. Steele
My party book of tested chocolate recipes. General
Foods Corp.
My pious friends and drunken companions. F. Shay
My three inns. J. Fothergill
My 35 years behind bars; memories and advice of a
bartender. J. Brooks
My vineyard at Lakeview. Western Grape Grower (pseud)
Myers's Jamaica rum cocktails . . . Fred L. Myers and
Son
Myers' Jamaica rum recipes. Fred L. Myers and Son
Mystery and lure of perfume (The). C.J.S. Thompson
Mysteries of the trade. D. Beman
Myths and legends of flowers, trees, fruits, plants.
C.M. Skinner

Narrative of circumstances relating to the excise bill
on wine. P. Mallet
National Bottlers Gazette (periodical). Anon
National Capital (The). And other statistical studies.
Lord Stamp
National Certified Colors. National Analine Division.
Allied Chemical and Dye Corp.

National Certified food colors. National Aniline and
    Chemical Company, Inc.
National Certified Food-drug and cosmetic colors-
    National Analine Division
National Dairy and Ice Cream Exhibition. Official
    Handbook. Anon
National Food and Beverage Exhibition Official
    Catalogue. Anon
National Formulary of unofficial preparations (The).
    American Pharmaceutical Ass'n.
National Mark Calendar of cooking. Ambrose Heath and
    D.D.C. Taylor
National Soda Fountain Guide (The). W.S. Adkins
National Temperance Mirror (The). Anon
National Temperance Offering (The). S.F. Cary
National Mineral Water Trade Guild (The). National
    Union of Mineral Water Mfgs. Ass'ns. Ltd.
Natural and artificial directions for health. William Vaughan
Natural chemical properties of water and on various
    British mineral waters. Abraham Booth
Natural, commercial and medicinal treatise on tea (A).
    Godfrey Mc Calman
Natural experimental and medicinal history of the mineral
    waters of Derbyshire, Lincolnshire and Yorkshire.
    Thomas Short
Natural history of chalybeat and purging waters of England.
    Benjamin Allen
Natural history of chocolate-being an account of the cocoa
    tree . . . Richard Brookes
Natural history of cocoa. Anon
Natural history of coffee, thee, chocolate and tobacco
    . . . Anon
Natural history of mineral waters of Great Britain.
    Benjamin Allen
Natural history of the tea-tree with observations on the
    medical qualities of tea and effects of tea drinking (The).
    J.C. Lettsom
Natural mineral waters, their properties and uses. Ingram
    and Royle
Natural organic colouring matters. A.G. Perkins and
    A.E. Everest
Natural perfume materials. Y.R. Naves and G. Mazuyer
Natural red wines. H.W. Allen
Naturali, vinorum historia de vinis Italiae. Andreae Bacci
Nature cure cook book and ABC of natural dietetics (The).
    Anna Lindlahr

Nature of fermentation explan'd (The).   George Smith
Nature smiled . . . and there was Cresta Blanca.
    Cresta Blanca Wine Co.
Nature's gifts and how to use them.   George Dodd
Nautical Cookery Book (The).   T. F. Adkins
Ne Plus Ultra of assaying, weighing and valuing of
    spiritous liquors (The).   William Gutteridge
Nebraska State Horticultural Society for year of 1895
    (Annual Report).   Frederick Taylor
Nectars- Stouffer's.   Stouffer's Restaurants
Negligence with food, drink, drugs.   F. G. Turner
Nelson's Home Comforts.   Mary Hooper
Nelson's Home Comforts.   Anon
Net price list of equipment and supplies.   Hydraulic
    Press Mfg. Co.
New American Orchardist (The).   William Kenrick
New and complete cellar book for homemade wines.
    S. Beach
New and complete cellar book or butler's ass't.   James
    Farley
New and complete treatise on ullaging.   Samuel Roose
New and easy method cookery.   Elizabeth Cleland
New and improved illustrated bartenders' manual; or,
    How to mix drinks of the present style (The).
    Harry Johnson
New and standard mixed drinks.   Henry Roos
New Anti- Saloon Songs.   E. S. Lorenz
New art of brewing and improving malt liquors (The).
    William Ellis (Brewer).
New art of brewing beer, ale and preparing all sorts of
    liquors.   Thomas Tryon
New art of making above twenty sorts of English wines
    (A).   William Y- Worth
New book of the natures and properties of all wines
    that are commonly used here in England (A).
    William Turner
New Bartender's Guide.   Anon
New Bartender's Guide.   Telling how to mix all the standard
    and popular drinks called for everyday.   Anon
New book of etiquette (The).   Lillian Eichler
New book of distillatyen of waters . . . Peter Morwyng
New California Cook Book (The).   Genevieve Callahan
New and easy way to make wine of English grapes and
    other fruit (A).   Anon
New Christianity (The).   John Ellis
New Crusade including a report concerning prohibition . . .
    (The).   Leslie Gordon

New curiosities in art and nature.   Louis Lemery
New deal in Liquor (A).   A plea for dilution.   Yandell
    Henderson
New Delineator Recipes.   Anon
New digester or engine for softning bones. (A).
    Denys Papin, M. D.
New easy ways to cook with rum.   Clementine Paddleford
New experimental inquiry into the nature and qualities of
    the Cheltenham waters (A).   Anthony Fothergill
New experiments and observations on mineral waters.
    F. Hoffman
New fields for brewers and others active in the fermentation
    and allied industries.   C. A. Nowak
New formulas for profit.   H. Bennett
New guide of the hotel, bar, restaurant, butler and chef.
    Bacchus and Cordon Bleu
New lecture on malt liquors.   Joseph Livesay
New London Family Cook.   Duncan Mac Donald
New medical wine book (The).   H. A. Schenk
New method in manufacture chocolate, cocoa powder and
    confectionery.   Heinrich Damblon
New method of brewing malt liquors in small quantities
    for domestic use (A).   J. Rawlinson
New method of forcing grapes and keeping them in winter.
    P. Lindegaard
New method of making better home made wines, beers
    and invalid's drinks (A).   Yeiser Brothers
New method of making dry red wines.   F. B. Bioletti
New methods of grafting and budding as applied to
    reconstitution with American vines.   Raymond Dubois
    and W. P. Wilkinson
New plain rational treatise on the true nature and uses on
    Bath waters.   James Graham
New present for serving maid (A).   Mrs. Eliza Haywood
New primer on alcoholism.   How people drinks, how to
    recognize alcoholics and what to do about them.
    Marty Mann
New process of the culture of the vine.   J. F. Persoz
New public house (The).   E. E. Williams
New relation of use and virtue of tea.   W. Crook
New results in science and technology of fruit juices.
    International Federation of Fruit Juice Producers
New school of arts, science and manufactures.   Anon
New standard formulary (The).   A. E. Hiss and
    A. A. Ebert
New system of domestic cookery . . . by a Lady.   Anon

New system of practical domestic economy.   Anon
New treatise on liquors where-in the use and abuse of
    wine, malt drinks, water . . . are particularily
    considered in many diseases . . . (A).
    James Sedgwick
New universal and complete confectioner (The).
    Elizabeth Price
New wine book (The).   Arnulf Franz
New wine cooling machine.   F.T. Bioletti
New whole art of confectionery (The).   S. W. Stavely
New York Times Cook Book.   Craig Claiborne
New book of distillation of water (A).   Conrad Gesner
New Jewel of Health.   Conrad Gesner
Newest Guide.   How to mix drinks for man's pleasure.
    Anon
Newman's book on scientific barkeeping.   L. P. Newman
Nievve Herball (A).   R. Dodoens
Nightlife.   Vanity Fair's intimate guide to New York
    after dark.   C. G. Shaw
900 recettes de cocktails et boissons Americaines.
    A. Torelli
Nineteen centuries of drink in England.   R. V. French
1965 guide to 1000 pubs and inns in England and Wales
    . . . Egon Ronay
1910 soda water guide and book of recipes.   Liquid
    Carbonic Co.
Nineteenth century handbook on the manufacture of liquors,
    wine, and cordials without the aid of distillation.
    W.B. Bryant
Nip ahoy; the picture bar guide.   R.H. Loeb
"Noble Experiment".   Irving Fisher
Noble experiments.   Norman Anthony (Judge Jr.) pseud
Noble grapes and the great wines of France (The).
    A. L. Simon
Nobody ever tells you these things.   Helen Mc Cully
Nogle Bidrag Til Pasteuriseringens historie.   (The
    history of pasteurization).   Ernst Andrup
Nomenclature Australian wines.   W. P. Wilkinson
Non-alcoholic fruit wines and cordials.   Stevenson and
    Howell Ltd.
Non-Drinker's Drink Book (The).   Betty Rollin
Non-excisable fruit wines and cordials.   Stevenson and
    Howell Ltd.
Non-intoxicants; a practical manual on the manufacture
    of soft drink extracts and cereal beverages.
    C.A. Nowak

"Non Plus Ultra" (The). Soda Fountain requisites of
modern times. G.H. Dubelle
Non-secret formulas. T.M. Griffiths
Norwesco hand book (The). Northwestern Extract Co.
Norwesco 1947 Catalog. Northwestern Extract Co.
Not claret. Francis Downman
Notebook for Tea Planters. R.J. Johnson
Notebook for the wines of France. Creighton Churchill
Note on the vineyards of America and Europe. Thomas
Hardy
Noted breweries of Great Britain and Ireland (The).
Alfred Barnard
Notes for an epicure. A Handbook on the traditions and
service of wine and other beverages. Libbey Glass
Mfg. Co.
Notes on a cellar book. G.E. Saintsbury
Notes on alcohol. Sir Walter Gilbey
Notes on American confectionery with methods of working
different branches of candy making, ice cream and
soda water. Perfecto
Notes on Burgundy. C.R. Weld
Notes on essential oils. T.H.W. Idris
Notes on French wines. Philip Dexter
Notes on port wine. J.D. Symington
Notes on the culture of the vine and the olive and methods
of making wine and oil . . . Sir. T.L. Mitchell
Notes on tea manufacture. E.G.B. de Mowbray
Notes on the late J. Pierpont Morgan's cellar book.
A.L. Simon
Notes on the management of the tea plant. T.G. Stoker
Notes on the manufacture of aerated waters, cordials,
brewed beers . . . Burbidges Burgoyne and Co.
Notes on the plants of wineland the good. Anon
Notes on wine and vine culture in France. H. Hammond
Notes on winemaking. Michele Blunno
Notes upon pure and natural wines. M. Gregor
Notes upon pure and natural wines of Hungary. M. Gregor
Number three Saint James's Street; a history of Berry's,
the wine merchants. H.W. Allen
Nurse's invalid cookery book (The). Marguerite Fedden
Nutrition. C.E. Sohn
Nutritional Data. Anon
Nuts on wine. Walter James

Observations and advices for the improvement and manufacture
of Muscovado sugar and rum. Bryan Higgins

Observations and facts relative to public houses . . . Anon
Observations, historical, critical, and medical, on the
    wines of the ancients. Sir Edward Barry
Observations on beer and brewers in which the inequalities,
    injustice and impolicy of the malt and beer tax
    are demonstrated. Richard Flower
Observation on growth and culture of wines and olives.
    John Locke
Observations on the art of brewing malt liquors. Anon
Observations on the artificial mineral waters of Dr. Struve.
    William King
Observations on the character and culture of the European
    vine. S.I. Fisher
Observations on the commutation project. T.B. Rous
Observations on the development and structure of English
    wine-growing terminology. Eero Alanne
Observations on the manufacture of rum. John Mc Cullouch
Observations on the state of the brewery and on the
    saccharine quality of malt. James Baverstock
Observations on the vinous fermentations advantages to the
    process of brewing. Gray and Co. Brewers
October dawn; a short and practical treatise on the
    manufacture of home made wine. Emma Tudor
Odoriferous formulary (The). How to prepare flavoring
    extracts, cordials, syrups . . . A. Seguin
Odorographia, a natural history of raw materials and drugs
    used in the perfume industry. J.C. Sawer
Odors and sense of smell. Airkem, Inc.
Odour preferences. R.W. Moncrieff
Of drinking to the memory of the dead. Peter Browne
    (Bishop of Cork and Ross)
Of drinking water . . . R. Short
Of herbs and spices. Colin Clair
Of the excellent qualities of coffee and art of making it.
    Benjamin, Count of Rumford
Off the shelf. A guide to the sale of wines and spirits.
    Anon
Official and tentative methods of analysis of the society.
    American Society of Brewing Chemists.
Official bartender's guide and companion. Anon
Official handbook for the National Training School for Cooker
    Anon
Official mixing guide, a complete guide to the popular
    system of how to make fancy and mixed drinks.
    A.A. Koch
Official mixer's manual (The). P.G. Duffy

Offizieller Katalog. Deutsche Brauerei Austellung.
Oils, Animal, vegetable, essential and mineral. C.A. Mitchell
Old Boston taverns and tavern clubs. S.A.D. Drake
Old Bottles and Ghost Towns. Adele Reed
Old brewery and the new mission house, at the five points. (The). Ladies of the Mission
Old Christmas in Merrie England. Washington Irving
Old cookery books and ancient cuisine. W.C. Hazlitt
Old Egyptian use of beer, as a food, as a beverage and as a medicament (The). C.H. Klein
Old English Coffee Houses. Anon
Old English drinking glasses, their chronology and sequence. G.R. Francis
Old drinking songs. Anon
Old English glasses. Albert Hartshorne
Old English wines and cordials. J.E. Masters
Old Favorite Honey Recipes. American Honey Institute
Old Game (The). A retrospect after three years on the wagon. Samuel Blythe
Old glass and how to collect it. J.S. Lewis
Old inns. Cecil Aldin
Old inns of England (The). A.E. Richardson
Old Inns of London (The). L.T. Stanley
Old London taverns. Edward Callow
Old London's Spas, Baths and Wells. Septimus Sunderland
Old Madeiras. F.G. Griswold
Old Mr. Boston; deluxe official bartender's guide. Leo Cotton
Old Scottish conviviality. E.B. Ramsey
Old sherry; the story of the first hundred years. Gonzalez Byass and Co.
Old Soak and Hail and farewell (The). Don Marquis
Old Soak's history of the World (The). Don Marquis
Old-time recipes for home made wines, cordials and liqueurs from fruits, flowers, vegetables and shrubs. H.S. Wright
Old-time recipes. wines, bitters, preserves confections. Frank Pascall
Old-time saloon; not wet--not dry, just history (The). George Ade
Old Waldorf-Astoria bar book (The). A.S. Crockett
Old Waldorf-Astoria bar book with amendments due to the repeal of the XVIII (The). A.S. Crockett
Old Waldorf Bardays. A.S. Crockett
Oliveira prize-essay on Portugal (The). J.J. Forrester

Ombibulous Mr. Mecken. B. Johns
On Luftsyra. (On acid in air). Tobern Bergman
On acid of air. Treatise on bitter, seltzer, spa and
    pyrmont waters and their synthetical preparation.
    T.O. Bergman
On baths and mineral waters. John Bell
On Beer. A statistical sketch. Max Vogel
On beer and brewing techniques in ancient Mesopotamia.
    L.F. Hartman
On brewing. Emil Westergaard
On cultivation of Liberian coffee in West Indies.
    H.A. Nicholls
On elimination of alcohol. August Dupre
On food; its varieties . . . H. Letheby
On its 75th anniversary (Rum). Jose S.A. Arechabala
On lager beer. C.Graham
On making wine. John Adlum
On mineral waters; their physical and medicinal properties.
    Robert Mortimer Glover
On mixing wine cups. Friends of Wine (The).
On Scots drink. W. Cramond
On the economical production of brewer's worts. Johnson's
    Saccharum Co. Ltd.
On the question whether alcohol is the product of
    fermentation or distillation. E.O. Donovan
On the use and abuse of alcoholic liquors, in health and
    disease. W.B. Carpenter
On the use of slate in breweries. Ashton and Green Ltd.
On the uses of wines in health and disease. F.E. Anstie
On the wine system of Great Britain. John Dunlop
On Uncle Sam's water wagon; 500 recipes for delicious
    drinks. H.W. Moore
On wines. New Way of making wines from herbs fruits and
    flowers. W. Edmonds
On wines, their production, treatment and use. J.L.W.
    Thudichum
One hundred and fifty years of brewing. Bristol Brewery
    Georges and Co. Ltd.
One hundred and one beverages. M.E. Southworth
100 and 10 most popular American drinks. O.D. Buell
    and J.T. Haughey
One hundred cocktails. How to mix them. "Bernard"
One hundred drinks and cups. F.B. Jack
One hundred eleven tested methods of handling everyday
    food plant problems. Anon

100 famous cocktails; the romance of wines and liquors, etiquette, recipes.   Russell Anderson

156 recettes de boissons Americaines.   N. Larson

One hundred fountain formulas.   J.H. Barker and Co.

One hundred home-brewed wines including cordials, beers and syrups.   F.B. Jack

100, 000, 000 guinea pigs.   Arthus Kallett and F.J. Schlink

One hundred prize winning West Indian recipes.   Angosturs Bitters, Ltd.

One hundred recipes for making beer and wines.   Anon

One hundred secret trade and family recipes for summer and winter drinks.   Trade recipes

One hundred thirty new winemaking recipes. C.J.J. Berry

120 years of life and how to obtain them.   Charles Reinhardt, M.D.

One hundred ways-especially prepared for connoiseurs as well as the novitiate   by A. Traveller.   Anon

One hundred years of American Commerce.   C.M. Depew, Ed.

One hundred years of brewing; a complete history of the progress made in the art, science, and industry of brewing in the world.   Anon

One hundred years of coffee.   E. Johnston and Co. Ltd.

One hundred years of good earth (Wine).   S. Smith and Son Ltd.

One hundred years of progress.   Manbre and Garten Ltd.

One hundred years of progress of the United States by Eminent Literary Men.   Anon

One hundred years of Temperance.   Anon

100 years of wine-making.   G. Gramp and Sons

One-piece dinners.   M.D. Chambers

One thousand experiments in chemistry and practical observations on the manufacturing and chemical processes persued in the successful cultivation of the useful arts.   Colin Mac Kenzie

One thousand household hints.   Anon

1001 tests of foods, beverages . . .   H.W. Wiley

Open air grape culture---and manufacture of domestic wine . . . John Phin

Opinions, orders, injunctions and decrees relating to unfair competition and infringement of trademark. Coca-Cola Co.

Opium and opium appetite with notices of alcoholic beverages, cocoa, tea, coffee and the like.   Alonzo Calkins

Oporto, old and new; being a historical record of the port
wine trade. Charles Sellers
Oporto, older and newer. Gerald Cobb
Orange. Information about different varieties . . .
J.M. Towey
Orange (The). Its biochemistry and physiology.
W.B. Sinclair, Ed
Orange cultivation in California with an appendix on grape
culture. T.A. Garey
Orange Recipes. Jean Gordon
Oranges. John McPhee
Oranges and orange products. Changing economic relation-
ships. Sidney Hoos and J.N. Boles
Orchard and fruit garden (The). E.P. Powell
Orchard and small fruit culture. E.C. Auchter, and H.B.
Knapp
Organic chemistry for the laboratory. W.A. Noyes
Organization in the soft drink industry; a history of the
American Bottlers of Carbonated Beverages. J.J.
Riley
Organization of the mineral water industry and the National
Mineral Water Trade Guild. National Union of Mineral
Water Mfgrs. Ass'ns Ltd.
Origin and history of beer and brewing. J.P. Arnold
Origin, nature and history of wine. Charles Ellis
Origin of food habits (The). H.D. Renner
Origin of prohibition (The). J.A. Krout
Origin of the 'reputed quart' and other measures.
B.E. Moody
Original documents respecting the injurious effects of the
impolicy of further continuance of the Port Royal Wine
Co. of Oporto. Anon
Original gravity tables. G.C. Jones and J.L. Baker
Origins of alcoholism. W. Mc Cord and J. Mc Cord
Other side of the bottle (The). Dwight Anderson
Our baths and wells. The mineral waters of the British
Islands. John Macpherson
Our drinks - or the nature and physical effects of fermented
liquor as an ordinary beverages. Andrew Gilmour
Our food and drinks. Andrew Wilson
Our greatest enemy - beveraged alcohol. Aubrey Willis
Our native grape. C. Mitzsky and Co.
Our new cook book. S.A. Frost
Our smallest servants. The story of fermentation. Chas.
Pfizer and Co.
Our one hundredth year. 1842-1942. F.M. Schaefer
Brewing Co.

Our social bees or pictures of town and country life.
Andrew Wynter, M. D.
Our wasted resources; the missing link in the temperance
reform. William Hargreaves
Outdoor grapes in cold climates. R. B. Brock
Outlawing the Almighty. J. V. Russell
Outline for industry (An). H. F. Willkie
Outlines of food technology. H. W. (Von) Loesecke
Over a century of brewing tradition. The story of Tooth
and Co. Limited. Anon
Over the black coffee. Arthur Gray
Over the black coffee, History . . . F. A. Cauchois and Co.
Over the tea cups. W. Andrews
Ovington's essay upon nature and qualities-dissected and
burlesqued. John Waldron
Oxford night caps, a collection of receipts for making
various beverages used in the University. Richard Cook
Oxfordshire and Buckinghamshire pubs. John Camp

Pabst Brewing Co. History of an American business.
T. C. Cochran
Pabst Brewing Co. Pamphlet. Anon
Packaging in glass. B. E. Moody
Palm-wine drinkard and his dead palm wine tapster in
the Dead's town. A. Tutuola
Palmer's popular receipts, proper guide for making wines.
J. S. Palmer
Pan book of wine (The). H. Johnson
Pan book of winemaking (The). B. C. A. Turner
Papaya. Central Food Technological Research Institute
Papaya. A fruit suitable to South Florida. S. U. Stambaugh
Parallel between intemperance and the slave-trade. H.
Humphrey
Parastota, Fabylam Monte Fiasconium . . . J. J. Geysius
Paris that's not in the guide books. B. Woon
Partners. A guide to the game of wine and food
matching. A. L. Simon
Party book. C. Foyles
Party Book, Inc. Anon
Party encyclopedia. Calvert Distillers Co.
Party fare. V. Mc Clure
Party food and drink. R. Hume
Party sampler. E. M. Barmer
Passing of the saloon. G. M. Hammell
Past and present in an old firm. Joseph Travers and Sons

Past and present state of the tea trade of England . . .
R.M. Martin
Past, present and probable future state of the wine trade.
J. Warre
Pasteur's study of fermentation. J.B. Conant
Pasteurization for cordial makers. G.I. Adcock
Patent inventions and apparatus for production of ice and
artificial cold, soda water . . . T. Masters
Patterson's Beverage Gazetteer. Anon
Peach culture. J.A. Fulton
Peach growing. H.P. Gould
Peaches of New York. U.P. Hedrick et al
Pear culture. T.A. Field
Pears of New York. U.P. Hedrick
Penfold story (The). E. Keane
Penguin book of wines. A. Sichel
Penny Universities. A history of coffee houses.
A. Ellis
People versus the liquor traffic. S.D. Hastings
People's home recipe book. A.G. Kirk
Perfect cooking with Parkinson Renown gas cookers. Anon
Perfect endings: chocolate dessert and beverage cookbook.
Nestle Co.
Perfume album. J.E. Jessee
Perfume and flavor chemicals. S. Arctander
Perfume and natural flavoring materials. S. Arctander
Epicurean recipes of California winemakers. Wine
Advisory Board
Perfume through the ages. A. Farkas
Perfumer's handbook and catalog. Fritzsche Brothers
Perfumer's legacy or the companion of the toilet (R). B.
Perfumer's raw materials, essential oils . . . Heine and
Co.
Perfumery and kindred arts. R.S. Cristiani
Perfumery, its history, character and use. A.W. Harrison
Perfumery: its manufacture and use. C. Morfit
Perfumery synthetics and isolates. P.Z. Bedoukian
Perfumery and cosmetics, their preparation and manufacture.
G.W. Askinson
Perfumes and spices. A.H. Verrill
Perfumes and their preparation. G.W. Askinson
Perfumes and their production. E.S. Maurer
Perfumes and household fragrances to make at home.
P. White
Perfumes, cosmetics and soaps. W.A. Poucher
Perfumes, essential oils and fruit essences. G. Martin

786

Peri phychropsoias of drinking water.   R. Short
Perry pears.   L. C. Luckwill and A. Pollard
Peru.   History of coca.   G. W. Mortimer
Peterson's preserving, pickling . . . M. E. Peterson
Petition for exemption of bottled carbonated beverages from
    ingredient labeling . . . ABCB
Petits and grande verres choix des meilleurs cocktails.
    N. Toye and A. H. Adair
Pewter.   J. Bedford
Peychaud's New Orleans cocktails.   J. Held, Jr.
Pfizer products for the food and beverage industries.   Anon
Pharmaceutical and food analysis.   A. Thurston
Pharmaceutical flavor guide.   Fritzsche Bros.
Pharmaceutical formulas.   P. Mac Ewan
Pharmaceutical formulas.   S. W. Wooley and G. P. Forrester
Pharmaceutical recipe book.   American Pharmaceutical Ass'n.
Pharmacology of the fluid extracts in common use.
    J. S. Wright
Philocathonista or drunkard opened . . . T. Heywood
Philosophical and statistical history of the inventions and
    customs of ancient and modern nations in the manufacture
    and use of inebriating liquors.   S. Morewood
Philosophical discussion of fermentation.   W. Simpson
Philosophical principles of the science of brewing . . .
    J. Richardson
Philosophical treatise on malting and brewing.   G. A. Wigney
Philosophy in the kitchen.   Old Bohemian
Philosophy of artificial and compulsory drinking usage in
    Great Britain and Ireland.   J. Dunlop
Philosophy of beer.   T. Schoppfer
Physical culture food directory.   M. Hastings
Physiological aspects of alcoholic beverages.
    A. Guinness and Son
Physiological aspects of the liquor problem.   W. O. Atwater
    et al
Physiography in its application to grape culture.   F. J. Cope
    (see Essay on the culture of native and exotic grape.
    W. Saunders)
Physiology of taste.   J. A. Brillat-Savarin
Pick-me-up!   A. N. Other
Pictorial record of the present.   Fritzsche Brothers
"Pilot".   W. M. Bell
Pilson Urguell.   Brasseries de Pilson Entreprise Nationale
Pioneering with fruits and berries.   G. D. Aiken
Pioneers of mixing cognac . . . C. C. Mueller and
    A. L. Hoppe

Pioneers of mixing gin . . . C.C. Mueller and A.L. Hoppe
Pioneers of mixing Irish and Scotch whiskys. C.C.
    Mueller and A.L. Hoppe
Pioneers of mixing liqueurs and cordials. C.C. Mueller
    and A.L. Hoppe
Pioneers of mixing rums. C.C. Mueller and A.L. Hoppe
Pioneers of mixing whiskeys, ryes and bourbons. C.C.
    Mueller and A.L. Hoppe
Piston process of freezing (The). Anon
Plain and full instructions to raise all sorts of fruit trees.
    T. Langford
Plain cookery recipes. E. Clarke
Plain directions for family brewers. T. Saddington
Plain man' s guide to wines. R.W. Postgate
Plain plantain. R.G. Alexander
Plain talk and friendly advice for domestics. Anon
Plant for the smaller bottler. G.B. Beattie
Plant operation manual. ABCB
Planter's progress. Story of coffee in Kenya. H.F. Hill
Planting engineer. C. Reid
Planting, expression and culture of coconuts. H.O.
    Newland
Planting in Uganda. E. Brown and H.H. Hunter
Playboy gourmet, the food and drink handbook for the
    host at home. T. Mario
Pleasant drinks, effervescing mixtures . . . R. Wells
Pleasures of cooking with wine. E. Chase
Pleasures of the table. Sir Francis Colchester-Wemyss
Pleasures of the table. G.H. Ellwanger
Pleasures of wine. R.L. Balzer
Pleasures of wine, a guide to the wines of the world.
    M. Waldo
Plot against the people (A). An attempt to pervert the food
    law. Hiram-Walker and Sons
Plums and plum culture. F.A. Waugh
Plums of England. H.V. Taylor
Plums of New York. U.P. Hedrick et al
Pocket book of mensuration. J.B. Mant
Pocket book of wine. G. Rainbird
Pocket dictionary of wines. T. Marvel
Pocket book to wine. H.D. Renner
Poison problem, or the cause and cure of intemperance.
    F.L. Oswald
Poisons in your food. W. Longwood
Poker, smoke and other things. W.M. Rhoads
POP, Monsieur. Champagne recipes for everyday food
    and drink. R.C. Rosen

Pop's master mixer. B.U. Henderson
Popular beverages of various countries. P.L. Simmonds
Popular fruit growing. S.B. Green
Popular treatise on tea. J. Sumner
Port. R. Croft-Cooke
Port. A.L. Simon
Port and sherry. The story of two fine wines. P.W.
  Sandeman
Port and the wines of Portugal. J.J. de Forrester
Port from grape to glass. G.R. Wyndham
Port. From the vine to the glass. G.M. Tait
Port: how to buy, serve, store and drink it. W.J. Todd
Port wine. J.J. da Costa Lima
Port wine and cookery. Anon
Port wine and Oporto. E. Cockburn
Porter brewer (The) digested. Anon
Portuguese (A). Royal Oporto Wine Co.
Portuguese wine. R. Postgate
Powell's complete book of cookery . . . J. Powell
Practical aerated water maker and book of English recipes.
  J. Pocock
Practical and philosophical principles of making malt.
  J. Reynoldson
Practical and scientific treatise on the manufacture of
  pure high class carbonated beverages . . . S.A. Tucker
Practical bar management. E. Clarke
Practical bar management. H.J. Grossman
Practical brewer. E.H. Vogel
Practical brewing. W.H. Nithsdale and A.J. Manton
Practical brewing and the management of British beers.
  W.H. Nithsdale and A.J. Manton
Practical brewings. G.S. Amsinck
Practical complete and correct gager. O. Byrne
Practical confectioner. J.T. Gill
Practical cookery. A. Atkinson and G. Holroyd
Practical direction, receipts and processes for production
  of various kinds of liquors. Busch Products Co.
Practical dissertation of Bathe waters. W. Oliver
Practical dissertation on Bath waters. W. Falconer
Practical distiller and a treatise of making artificial wines.
  G. Smith
Practical distiller . . . S.M' Harry
Practical domestic hygiene. J.L. Notter and R.H. Firth
Practical emulsions. H. Bennett
Practical encyclopedia of alcoholic Beverages. Liquor
  Store Magazine
Practical farmer. W. Ellis

Practical flavoring extract maker. E.J. Kessler
Practical floor malting. H. Lancaster
Practical fruit grower. S.T. Maynard
Practical gager. W. Symons
Practical guide and receipt book . . . E.H. Lindemann
Practical guide for the perfumer . . . H. Dussauce
Practical guide to French wines. W. Bird
Practical guide to malting. O.F. Ruswel
Practical guide to treatment of wine in English cellars.
    L.P. Mouraille
Practical guide to winemaking. B.C.A. Turner
Practical handbook on port wine. G.M. Tait
Practical handbook on the distillation of alcohol from farm
    products. F.B. Wright
Practical hints and formulas for busy druggists.
    B. Lillard
Practical hints on the culture of the pine-apple.
    R. Glendinning
Practical housekeeper. Mrs. Ellet
Practical instructions for brewing porter and ales
    according to English and Scottish methods.
    W. Stewart
Practical instructions in brewing ale and table beer for
    the use of private families. B. Moubray (pseud)
Practical manual for the culture of the vine in the Gironde.
    A. Cazenave
Practical milk bar operation. E.E.F. Colam
Practical mineral water maker (The). Bratby and
    Hinchliffe
Practical notes on wine. E.L. Beckwith
Practical observations on Harrogate waters. A.S. Myrtle
Practical observations or prejudices against the brewery
    with hints to sugar colonists. J. Baverstock
Practical points for brewers. National Brewers'
    Academy
Practical points for brewers. E. Schlicting and H.W.
    Winther
Practical points for practical brewers. National Brewers'
    Academy
Practical prohibition. V.W. Grubbs
Practical recipes for the manufacture of aerated waters
    . . . W.J. Bush and Co.
Practical reflections on the uses and abuses of Bath
    waters. W. Baylies
Practical studies in fermentation . . . E.C. Hansen
Practical studies for winemaker, brewer and distiller.
    G. Johnson

Practical treatise explaining the art and mystery of brewing
parter, ale, two-penny . . . S. Child
Practical treatise explaining the art and mystery of brewing
porter, ale, two-penny and table beer. J. Ridgeway
Practical treatise on animal and vegetable fats and oils
. . . W.T. Brannt
Practical treatise on breeding . . . with instructions for
the private brewery. B. Moubray
Practical treatise on brewing . . . W.A. Chadwick
Practical treatise on brewing . . . T. Hitchcock
Practical treatise on brewing. J. Lawrence
Practical treatise on brewing . . . W. Reddington
Practical treatise on brewing . . . A. Shore
Practical treatise on brewing and after-management of malt
liquors. W. Seymour
Practical treatise on brewing and on storing of beer . . .
W. Black
Practical treatise on brewing based on chemical and
economical principles. W. Black
Practical treatise on brewing, distilling and rectification.
R. Shannon
Practical treatise on brewing strong ales . . .
Anon
Practical treatise on brewing the various sorts of malt
liquors. A. Morrice
Practical treatise on diet (A). W. Nisbet
Practical treatise on grape culture. J.H. Tryon
Practical treatise on malting and brewing. W. Fort
Practical treatise on manufacture of cheap non-alcoholic
beverages. R. Seager
Practical treatise on the cultivation of the grape vine.
C. Hoare
Practical treatise on the cultivation of the grape vine.
W. Thomson
Practical treatise on the cultivation of the vine under
glass as well as in the open air. J. Sanders
Practical treatise on the culture and treatment of the
grape vine. J.F. Allen
Practical treatise on the culture of the pine-apple.
D. Thomson
Practical treatise on the management of fruit trees.
G. Jaques
Practical treatise on the manufacture of vinegars, acetates,
cider . . . W.T. Brannt
Practical treatise on the manufacture of perfumery.
C. Deite

Practical treatise on the nature of brewing fine, rich,
brilliant Welsh, Burton, scurvy glass---ales. Anon
Practical treatise on the raw materials and the distillation
and rectification of alcohol. W. T. Brannt
Practical treatise to render the art of brewing more easy.
E. N. Hayman
Practical vegetarian cookery. Countess Wachmeister and
K. B. Davis
Practice of modern perfumery. P. Jellinek
Practice of perfumery. R. J. Owen
Practice of pharmacy. J. P. Remington
Praise of drunkenness. A. H. deSallengre (See Ebrietatas
enconium . . .)
Praise of the gout. Anon
Praise of wine. W. Morris
Praktische Vorschriften. Schimmel and Co.
Preparation of flavoured mineral waters. S. G. Kendrick
Preparation of fruit juice in the home. W. V. Cruess
Preparation of perfumes and cosmetics. J. P. Durvelle
Present state of the distilleries of Scotland (The). W. Ross
Preservation of hops (The). J. A. Nettleton
Preservatising beverages . . . G. I. Adcock
Preservatives and other chemicals in food. O. Folin
Preserves handbook. Sunkist Growers. (see Exchange
citrus pectin)
Preserves for all occasions. A. Crang
Preserves, pickles, salads and homemade wines. Good
Housekeeping Institute
Preserving and canning. E. Riesenberg
Preserving winemaking ingredients. T. E. Belt
Preyer's information and guide for the liquor business.
E. R. Preyer
Price current - labels, bottles, caps . . . Wittemann
Brothers
Price list. Henry Luker and Co.
Price list and descriptive catalogue of extracts, colors
. . . H. J. Bowker and Co.
Price list 1881. Whitall, Tatum and Co.
Price list for the soft drinks industry. W. J. Bush and Co.
Price list 1915. Fritzsche Brothers
Price list 1959. Victoria Wine Co.
Price list of essential oils . . . W. J. Bush and Co.
Price list of finest old wines and spirits. James Moroney
Price list of wines and liquors. 1898 A. W. Balch and Co.
Price list of wines and liquors. 1877 Acker, Merrill
and Condit

Price list, syrup tables, directions . . . Liquid Carbonic
    Corp.
Price list. Wine and spirit merchants, maltsters.
    Gardner and Son
Price lists and catalogues. English manufacturers of
    flavors . . . Anon
Prices. Van Dyk and Co.
Priestley, Joseph (A life of). A. Holt
Primer on alcoholism. M. Mann
Primitive drinking. C. Washburne
Primitive physic . . . and general receipt book.
    J. Wesley
Principal health-resorts of Europe and Africa . . . T.M.
    Madden
Principle of the commutation act . . . F. Baring
Principles and practice of agricultural analysis. H.W.
    Wiley
Principles and practice of ale, beer and stout bottling.
    C.F. Foy
Principles and practice of brewing. W.J. Sykes and
    A.R. Ling
Principles and practice of cider-making. V.L.S. Charley
Principles and practice of wine making. W.V. Cruess
Principles of food preservation. T. Morris
Principles of fruit-growing. L.H. Bailey
Principles of sugar technology. P. Honig
Principles of wine-making. F.T. Bioletti
Private brewer's guide. J. Tuck
Prize essays on practical brewing. Anon
Problem drinker (The). J. Hirsch
Proceedings - Flavor Chemistry Symposium. Campbell
    Soup Co.
Proceedings 1953. National Food and Nutrition Institute
Proceedings of annual conventions. Master Brewers'
    Ass'n of America
Proceedings of the company of Amateur Brewers.
    O. Vrest
Proceedings of 100th anniversary convention. United States
    Brewers' Ass'n.
Processing of raw cocoa for the market. T.A. Rohan
Producing of wines and spirits in Greece. Societe
    Hellenique de Vins et Spiritueux
Productive small fruit culture. F.C. Sears
Products for the beverage trades. W.J. Bush and Co.
Products for the soft drinks industry. W.J. Bush and Co.
Professed cook (The). Anon

Professional bar management. S. G. M. Defay
Professional mixing guide. Angostura-Wupperman Corp.
Professor Alcoholico. J. Malins
Profitable food and beverage operation. J. Brodner, et al.
Profitable herb growing and collecting. A. B. Teegen
Progress with wines and vines. R. B. Brock
Progressive catering. J. J. Morel
Progressive winemaking. Peter Duncan and Bryan Acton
Prohibition and christianity. J. Erskine
Prohibition and commonsense. E. L. Douglass
Prohibition and the bible. B. Smith
Prohibition at its worst. I. Fisher
Prohibition in outline. F. E. Johnson and H. S. Warner
Prohibition in United States. D. L. Colvin
Prohibition, its economic and industrial aspects.
    H. Feldman
Prohibition mania. C. Darrow and V. S. Yarros
Prohibition movement (The). P. Andreae
Prohibition primer (A). Anon
Prohibition punches, a book of beverages. R. B. Doran
Prohibition the enemy of temperance. J. A. Homan
Promise of Widmer's wines. Widmer's Wine Cellars Inc.
Propagation of the vine. C. C. Wetmore
Proper handling of Anheiser-Busch draught. Anheuser-Busch
Proposal showing profit possibilities in development of
    organization to operate a number of bottling plants.
    A. W. Noling
Proposed plan for the development of Australian wine
    industry. Catts Patterson Co.
Prosit; a book of toasts. Clotho (pseud)
Prospects for cocoa growing in Uganda and Zanzibar.
    D. H. Urquhart
Prospects for extending the growing of cocoa in Papua and
    New Guinea. D. H. Urquhart and R. E. P. Dwyer
Prospects for the growing of cocoa in the British Solomon
    Islands . . . D. H. Urquhart
Prosperity beckons. Dawn of the alcohol era. W. J. Hale
Proximate composition of American food materials.
    C. Chatfield and G. Adams
Proximate composition of fresh fruits. C. Chatfield and
    L. I. McLaughlin
Prudent housewife. Mrs. Fisher
Pruning manual. L. H. Bailey
Psychology of alcoholism. G. B. Cotten
Psychology of drunkenness. A. R. King
Psychology of relaxation. G. T. W. Patrick
PUB. A celebration. A. Mc Gill

Pub and the people (The).   Mass-Observation
Pub games.   T. Finn
Pub of your own (A).   V. Heaton
Public control of the liquor traffic.   J. Rountree and
     A. Sherwell
Public health laboratory work.   H. R. Kenwood
Public House Cellar Management.   Anon
Public ownership of the liquor trade.   A. Greenwood
Public and an innkeeper's practical guide.   W. Clarke
Publican and spirit dealer's daily companion.   P. Boyle
Publican and cellarman's guide for the management of
     spirits, ale and beer.   G. Walker
Publican's daily companion.   P. Boyle
Publican's friend and sure guide to do well.   S. Moor
Publican's guide for reducing spirits.   G. Hawkes
Publican's guide, or key to the distill-house.   W. A. Smyth
Publican's handbook and general spirit calculator.
     J. B. Rhodes
Publican, innkeeper and brewer's guide.   A Practical
     Brewer
Publications and patents of U. S. Citrus Products Station,
     Winter Haven, Fla.   M. A. Jones
Puborama.   I. Mackay
Pudding lady's recipe book.   F. Petty
Puffer's approved and simplified carbonic acid generator.
     United Interest Soda Generator and Fountain Co.
Punches and cocktails (Book of).   "Charles"
Pure foods, their adulteration.   J. C. Olsen
Pure fruit juice.   Hance Brothers and White
Pure Indian tea or the tea we drink.   W. B. Flockhart
Pure native wine considered as an article of food and
     luxury.   J. I. Bleasdale
Pure treasure of the English Bathes.   W. Turner
Pure wine.   Fermented wine and other alcoholic drinks
     in the light of the new dispensation.   J. Ellis
Pure wine and how to know it.   J. L. Denman
Pure wine or - in Vino Veritas.   M. McLaren
"Pussyfoot" johnson.   F. A. Mc Kenzie

Quality control clinic.   W. A. Gould
Quality in dry wines through adequate fermentations . . .
     R. Jordan
Quality in coffee.   L. E. Springett
Quality since 1855.   Miller Brewing Co.
Quarterly Journal of Studies on Alcohol.   Anon

Quaternary ammonium compounds in chemical sterilization.
J. C. L. Resuggan
Queen's Closet opened by M. (W.).   Anon
Queen's delight (A) or art of preserving by (M., W.).   Anon
Queen's royal cookery.   T. Hall
Queensland garden manual.   A. J. Hockings
Queen-like closet of Rich Cabinet.   H. Wolley
Question of alcohol.   E. H. Williams
Questions and answers on beer.   United States Brewers'
Foundation
Quick guide to wine.   R. J. Misch
Quiet drinking: a book of beer wines and cocktails and
what to serve with them.   V. Elliott
Quince culture.   W. W. Meech

Rainbows in deserts.   J. Loughlin
Raise your glasses.   D. Sutherland
Ramrod broken; or the bible, history and common sense
in favor of the moderate use of good spiritous liquors
. . . Anon
Rational discourse on the inward uses of water.
T. Short
Rational manufacture of American wines.   Oesterreicher
and Co.
Rationale of malting . . . W. L. Tizard
Ratskeller in Bremen (The).   H. Entholt
Raw grain in brewing.   F. J. R. Nunn
Raw materials of commerce.   J. H. Vanstone
Raw materials of perfumery, their nature, occurance and
employment.   E. J. Parry
Rawling's book of mixed drinks.   E. P. Rawling
Readings and recitations.   L. Penney
Readings for winter gatherings.   J. Fleming
Real and imaginery effects of intemperance.   G. Thomann
Recent advances in fruit juice production.   V. L. S.
Charley, et al°
Receipt Book of Elizabeth Raper.   E. Raper
Receipt book of Mrs. Ann Blencowe.   A. Blencowe
Receipt book or Oracle of Knowledge . . . W. P. Chubb
Receipts and relishes being a vade mecum for the epicure
in the British Isles.   Anon
Receipts for homemade wines, cordials . . .
J. J. Machet
Receipts for homemade wines, cordials . . . F. Nutt
Receipts in modern cookery with a medical commentary.
A. Hunter

Recipes for homemade wines. H. Pretyman
Recipes for mixed drinks. H.R. Enselin
Recipes for the manufacture of aerated waters, cordials
    . . . Barnett and Foster
Recipes for the manufacture of aerated and mineral waters
    and cordials. R. A. and Baron de Bush
Recipes for the manufacture of flavoring extracts . . .
    C.E. Hires
Recipes for manufacture of liqueurs, alcoholic cordials,
    spirits . . . W.J. Bush and Co.
Recipes for the manufacture of liqueurs, spirits . . .
    Baron de Bush and R.A. Bush
Recipes for the preserving of fruit, vegetables and meat.
    E. Wagner
Recipes for the use of Huyler's cocoa and chocolate. Anon
Recipes of American and other iced drinks. Farrow and
    Jackson
Recipes of various kinds in cooking. Anon
Recollections of a tea planter. W.M. Fraser
Recommended wayside inns of England. P.S. Williams
Rectifier's, compounder's and liquor dealer's manual.
    R.H. Walker
Red barrel (The). A history of Watney Mann. H. Janes
"Red J". Jay bartender's guide. D. Jayne and Son
Red likker. I.S. Cobb
Red Top Rye Guide. Anon
Red, white and rosé. A guide to wines and spirits . . .
    E. (Penning) Rowsell
Red wine and blue water. Anon
Redox methods. B. Dixon
Reference book and catalog of flavors and seasonings.
    Dodge and Olcott
References, ancient and modern to the literature on beer
    and ale. I.M. Cooper
Reformed drunkard with other poems and songs.
    D. M'Neil
Refresher (The). Magazine of Coca-Cola Co. Coca-Cola
    Co.
Register of new fruit and nut varieties
    R.M. Brooks et al
Regulation of the liquor traffic. Anon
Reliable bartenders' guide. O. Henninger
Reliable candy teacher. W.O. and F. Rigby
Religion and drink. E.A. Wasson
Remarks and experiments on the different parts of the
    process of brewing. R. Bliss
Remarks of the art of making wine . . . J. Macculloch

Report on the census of production for 1954. Board of
    Trade
Report on the cheap wines from France, Italy, Austria,
    Greece and Hungary. R. Druit
Report on the cocoa industry in Sierra Leone.
    D. H. Urquhart
Report on the cocoa industry in the French Ivory Coast.
    D. H. Urquhart
Report on the composition of commoner British wines and
    cordials. G. C. Hancock
Report on the expansion of the cocoa industry in Jamaica.
    D. H. Urquhart
Report on the fermentation industries. Anon
Report on the manufacture of tea and on the extent and
    produce of tea plantations in Assam. C. A. Bruce
Report on the possibilities of cocoa growing in the
    Protectorate of Nyasaland. D. H. Urquhart
Report on the present condition and future prospects of
    tea cultivation in the northwest provinces. R. Fortune
Report on the tea industries of Java, Formosa, and Japan.
    A. S. Kingsford
Report on the tea plantations of northwest provinces.
    R. Fortune
Report on wine and fermented fruit products. J. J. Berliner
    and Staff
Report to the Aromanilla Company. F. D. Snell Inc.
Reports on experiments on fermenting red wines.
    E. W. Hilgard
Research Service Bibliographies Series 4 Public Library
    of South Australia
Responsible drinking. R. C. Binkley
Restaurant (The). P. Lehrian
Restaurant roundabout. T. A. Layton
Restauranteers handbook. C. A. Faissole
Retail compounder or publican's friend. J. Hardy
Retail liquor dealers' guide of information. H. E. Freeman
Return to the vineyard. M. Loos and W. Duranty
Revenue Review. J. T. Mulqueen
Review of discussions relating to Oporto Wine Company.
    Anon
Review of Rev. Edward H. Jewett's "Communion wine".
    J. Ellis
Review of the effects of alcohol on man. F. Langmead
    and T. C. Hunt
Review of the literature on coffee research in Indonesia.
    P. J. S. Cramer

Reviewing American brewing. F. Romer
RHENISH. A paper on Rhine wines. H.E.V. Huggett
Rhineland wineland. S.F. Hallgarten
Rhode Island Temperance Society. Proceedings at its
    annual meetings. Anon
Rhodesian Bottle, Store and Hotel Review. Anon
Richard Cadbury of Birmingham. H.C. Alexander
Richelieu Handbook. Wine cooking recipes and mixed drinks.
    Anon
Ridley's Wine and Spirit Handbook. Anon
Right food the right remedy. C.C. Froude
Road (The). Leaves from the sketch book of a commercial
    traveller. Anon
Romance of brewing. S. Strong
Romance of candy (The). A.H. Austin
Romance of coffee (The). W.H. Ukers
Romance of flowers. E.T. Dupont
Romance of perfume. R. Le Gallienne
Romance of perfume lands. F.S. Clifford
Romance of sugar. H.V. Knaggs
Romance of tea. W.H. Ukers
Romance of tea (The). Anon
Romance of wine (The). H.W. Allen
Romany remedies and recipes. G. Petulengro
Root beer. How it got its name . . . L.A. Enkema
Rose recipes. J. Gordon
Rose recipes. E.S. Rohde
Rough sketch of renewal system, pruning grape vines.
    W. Martin
Royal cookbook (The). Mrs. Pennington
Royal guager. C. Leadbetter
Rubber, tea and cocoa. W.A. MacLaren
Rudiments of grape culture. J.R. Eakin
Rules - 1946. National Ass'n of Soft Drinks Manufacturers
Rum. A.L. Simon
Rum in the kitchen. I. Syrett
Rum, romance, rebellion. C.W. Taussig
Rum. The Englishman's spirit. H.W. Allen
Rum war at sea. M.F. Willoughby
Run through Assam tea gardens. J.W. Waters
Rural economy of Gloucestershire. W. Marshall

S. and H. gallonage table. Stevenson and Howell
S.D.I. Being an account of the soft drinks industry in
    Britain during the emergency years 1942-1948. Anon

Saccharin. Articles and opinions as to physiological
    effects. Anon
Saccharin. Its uses in foods and beverages of all kinds
    and in pharmacy. Boots Pure Drug Co.
Sacramental wines. Andrew Gilmour
Saga of coffee, the biography of an economic product.
    H. E. Jacob
St. Pauls Bottling Co. Book of reference. J. G. Smith
Saints and strangers. G. F. Willison
Sale of food and drink at common law and under the uniform
    sales act. H. C. W. Melick
Sales manual. Liquid Carbonic Co.
Saloon in the home (The). R. Hunt and G. S. Chappell
Saloon secrets exposed; the book of the hour - giving full
    instructions on how to prepare 151 tasty pre-war
    concoctions. Anon
Saloon society. Bill Manville
Saloon under the searchlight. G. R. Stuart
Sandwiches and beverages. Priscilla Publishing Co.
Sanitary code. Extra part to ABCB training course.
    ABCB
Sanitation program for carbonated beverage plants. Liquid
    Carbonic Corp.
Saratoga: its mineral waters, and their use in preventing
    and eradicating disease, and as a refreshing beverage.
    C. C. Dawson
Satyr against tea; or Ovington's essay upon nature and
    qualities - dissected and burlesqued. John Waldron
Satyr against wine. With a poem in praise of small beer.
    Anon
Savor and flavor. Lee Maril
Savoy cocktail book (The). H. Craddock
Savoy Cocktail Book. Anon
Saxe's guide, or, Hints to soda water dispensers.
    de F. W. Saxe
Saxe's new guide or hints to soda water dispensers.
    de F. W. Saxe
Scent and all about it; a popular account of the science
    and art of perfumery. H. S. Redgrove
Scent of flowers and leaves. F. A. Hampton
Scented garden (The). E. S. Rohde
Scheherazade cooks. W. Atiyeh
Schenley's encyclopedia of wines and liquors. Anon
Schenley Library Bibliography 1946. A. Wasserman
Schimmel Briefs. Schimmel and Co.
School for American grape culture. F. Munch
School of arts. Smith?

Schultz and Warker's mineral spring waters . . .
   Carl Schultz
Schweizerische Korkenfabrik. E.B. Schlitter Freres
Science and art of perfumery. E. Sagarin
Science and coffee. W. Pringle
Science and technique of wine. L. Frumkin
Science of wine. C. Austin
Scientific American cyclopedia. A.A. Hopkins
Scientific and medical origin of carbonated waters.
   J.J. Riley
Scientific aspects of cocao fermentation. A.W. Knapp
Scientific bar-keeping. J.W. Gibson
Scientific manufacture of jams and allied products.
   H.E. Butterfield
Scientific marketing of coffee. J.P. Quinn
Scientific moderation in drinking. United Brewers
   Industrial Foundation
Scientific preservation of food. T.M. Rector
Scientific winemaking-made easy. J.R. Mitchell
Scotch. The whisky of Scotland in fact and story.
   R.B. Lockhart
Scotch made easy. R. Wilson
Scotch whisky. M.J. Robb
Scotch whisky. Questions and answers. P. Gee
Scotch whisky. Scotch Whisky Ass'n.
Scotch whisky. Its past and present. D. Daiches
Scots cellar, its traditions and lore. F.M. McNeill
Scots kitchen. F.M. McNeill
Scots weekend book. D. and C. Carswell
Scottish ale-brewer . . . W.H. Roberts
Scottish ale-brewer and practical maltster. W.H. Roberts
Scrapbook of inns. R. Watson
Scriptural view of the wine question. M. Stuart
Scuppernong grape, its history and mode of culture with
   a short treatise on manufacture of wine from it.
   J. Van Buren
S.D.I. Being an account of the soft drinks industry in
   Britain 1942-1948. Soft Drinks Industry Ass'n.
Seagram's vacation-time food and drink guide. Seagram-
   Distillers Co.
Seagram's weekend bar and barbecue book. Seagram-
   Distillers Co.
Search after claret . . . R. Ames
Second part of good Huswifes jewell. Anon
Secret of everyday things. J.H. Fabre
Secret of Santa Vittoria (The). R. Crichton

Secrets of Alexis. Alexis of Piedmont (pseud. for G. Ruscelli)
Secrets of canning. E.F. Schwaab
Secrets of making wine from fruits and berries. L.G. Slater
Secrets of the great whiskey ring. J. Mac Donald
Secrets of the liquor merchant revealed. M.L. Fogelsonger
Secrets of wise men, chemists and great physicians. W.K. David
See how it sparkles. B.C. Truman
Select methods of food analysis. H. Leffmann and W. Beam
Selected practical methods of manufacturing low alcoholic malt and maltless beverages and beers. C.A. Nowak
Selection of the practical points of malting and brewing. J. Steel
Selective bibliography of wine books. Wine Institute
Selling price-list (flavors). E.W. Gillett
Senn's War-time Cooking Guide. Anon
Sense of taste. H.L. Hollingworth and A.T. Poffenberger, Jr.
Sensible food for all in Britain and the temperate zones. E.J. Saxon
Sensory evaluation of wines. M.A. Amerine and E.B. Roessler
Sensory methods for measuring differences in food quality. U.S. Dept. Agriculture
Seppelt (The House of) Anon.
SEPLASIUM. The compleat English physician. W. Salmon
Servant's companion, or practical housemaid's and footman's guide. W. Bloomfield
Service for soda fountains, ice cream parlours and milk bars. L.R. Feltham
Set 'em up! J. Madden
Seven ages of Justerini's. D. Wheatley
Seventeen hundred cocktails for the man behind the bar. R. de Fleury
Seventy-five thousand case bottling plants. Costs and organization. The Tall-One Co.
Seventy rolling years. S.O. Neville
Shade in coffee culture. O.P. Cook
Shadow of the bottle (The). Anon
Shake 'em up! A practical handbook of polite drinking. V. Elliott and P.D. Strong
Shakespeare's wine book i e Wm. Turner's new boke of nature and properties of all wines. G.C. Williamson

Shaking in the 60's. E. Clarke
Shaking with Eddie. E. Clarke
Shall I drink? J.H. Crooker
Shall we drink wine? J. Madden
Sherbets, water ices. Modern soda fountain operation.
    B.I. Masurovsky
Sheridan's Red Table. Anon
Sherry with appendix on shippers. H.W. Allen
Sherry. R. Christain
Sherry. R. Croft-Crook
Sherry. J. Jeffs
Sherry and port. H.W. Allen
Sherry and the wines of Spain. G. Rainbird
Sherry as seen by the British. Jerez Industrial
Sherry; from grape to glass. R. Wyndham
Sherryana (by F.W.C.) F.W. Cosens
Shillingsworth of sherry. Ermitano (pseud)
Shop notes for soft drink bottling plant operators. ABCB
Short account of tea and tea trade. R. Hanson
Short account of Twinings in the Strand. E.E. Newton
Short address to the public on the prejudices against the
    breweries. J. Baverstock
Short check list of books and pamphlets in English on
    grapes, wines and related subjects 1949-1959. M.A.
    Amerine
Short guide to home brewing. K. Shales
Short guide to wine. Anon
Short historical account of coffee. R. Bradley
Short history of Cooper's Company. W. Foster
Short history of the art of distillation. R.J. Forbes
Short memoirs for the natural experimental history of
    mineral waters. R. Boyle
Short treatise concerning some patent inventions applicable
    to ice, artificial cold, soda water . . . T. Masters
Should you drink? C.H. Durfee
Sicily and its wine. B. Rainford
Sickroom cookery and hospital diet. M. Earle
Sideboard and cellar. A.B. Garrow
Sike's tables of the concentrated spirits with directions for
    use of Sike's hydrometer. Anon
Silver dollar bar, how to mix drinks plain and fancy.
    Anon
Silver wine labels. R.A. Weed
Simple costings in the soft drinks industry. National
    Ass'n of Soft Drinks Mfgrs.
Simple facts about wines, spirits, ale and stout. Alex.
    D. Shaw and Co.

Simple facts about wines-spirits, liqueurs, . . .
J.V. Jordan
Simple guide to home-made beer. B.C.A. Turner and
D.J. Moon
Simple methods of detecting food adulteration. J.A. Bower
Simple science of wine and beer making. H.E. Bravery
Simplified guide to table setting. B. Wilcox
Sip softly. E. Craig
Six best cellars. H. Hall and H. Nahler
Six nights with the Washingtonians; and other temperance
tales. T.S. Arthur
Six sermons on the nature, occasions, signs, evils,
remedy of intemperance. L. Beecher
Sketch of the evolution of our native fruits. L.H. Bailey
Sketch of the growth and history of tea and the science
of blending particularily adopted to Canadian trade.
F. Dane
Sketch of vine culture. R. Bolling Jr.
Smacks and smiles. Fancy drinks and how they are mixed.
C. Smith
Small bottlery problems. G.B. Beattie
Small cellar. L.B. Escritt
Small fruit culture. J.S. Shoemaker
Small fruit culturist. A.S. Fuller
Small fruits. R.E. Barker
Small fruits. W.H. Hills
Small fruits. J.M. Swartout
Small fruits for your home garden. J.H. Clarke
Small fruits of New York. U.P. Hedrick
Smuggling in the Highlands. I. Macdonald
Snoot if you must. L. Beebe
So red the nose; or, Breath in the afternoon. S. North
So mixe ich fur meine Freunde. Ein cocktail buch.
J.W. Smith
Sober world (The). R.W. Smith
Social drinking. How to enjoy drinking without being hurt
by it. G. Lolli
Social history of bourbon. G. Carson
Social welfare and the liquor problem. H.S. Warner
Socialism and the drink question. P. Snowden
Society, culture and drinking patterns. D.J. Pittman and
C.R. Snyder
Soda fountain and luncheonette management. J.O. Dahl
Soda fountain and luncheonette supplies. Pick, Barth
and Co.
Soda fountain beverages. A practical receipt book.
G.H. Dubelle

Soda fountain guide. S.C. Beadle
Soda fountain handbook. M. Parkes, editor
Soda fountain luncheonette drinks and recipes.
    L.P. De Gouy
Soda fountain management. J.O. Dahl
Soda fountain profits. J.R. Ward
Soda fountains and supplies. The Brazilla Co.
Soda water apparatus. C. Lippincott and Co.
Soda water apparatus and machinery . J. Matthews
Soda water flavors. Description of what they are and
    instructions in their care and use. A.W. Noling
Soda water formulary. E.G. Eberle
Soda water, how to make and how to serve with profit.
    Liquid Carbonic Co.
Soda water. Is it a wholesome beverage? J. Matthews
Soda water, what it is and how it is made.
    J.H. Snively
Soft Drinks Bottler Volume I. G. B. Beattie
Soft Drinks Bottler Volume II. G.B. Beattie
Soft drink flavours, their history and characteristics.
    G.B. Beattie
Soft Drink Industry Manual. 1968-1969. Anon
Soft Drink industry legal handbook. J.K. Curtis
Soft Drinks Trade Manual. K. Penn, Editor
Soft fruit growing. R. Bush
Solvay Sales Bluebook. Solvay Sales Corp.
Some account of rise and progress and present state of
    the brewery. B., A.
Some alcoholic Americana. B.C. Landauer
Some aspects of modern tea pruning. G.D. Hope and
    G.A. Carpenter
Some brief records of brewing in South Australia.
    M.H. Ward
Some enquiries into the effects of fermented liquors.
    "Water drinker"
Some notes on cocoa planting in West Indies. H. Hamel-
    Smith
Some notes on the technical study and handling of wines.
    G.E. Hann
Some observations on the medical and dietary properties
    of green tea. W. Newnham
Some pioneers of the tea industry. T. Williams
Some principles of the wine trade. S.C. Driver
Some remarks on medicinal mineral waters, natural and
    artificial. S.H. Smith
Some syrup suggestions. Barnett and Foster Ltd.

Some uses of the grapevine and its fruit. G.C.F. Husmann
Something about sugar. Its history, growth, manufacture
    and distribution. G.M. Rolph
Son of the Martini cookbook. J. Trahey and D. Pierce
Songs of our grandfathers. Anon
Songs of the apple tree with kith and kin. R.M. Floyd
Songs of the vine. With a medley for maltworms.
    W.G. Hutchison
Sorgham and its products. F.L. Stewart
Sorgo and imphee. Chinese and African sugar canes.
    H.S. Olcott
Source, chemistry and use of food products. E.H.S.
    Bailey
South African wine industry. Its growth and development.
    K.W.V.
South American gentlemen's companion. C.H. Baker
South Australian vigneron and gardner's manual.
    G. Mc Ewin
South Australian vintage. E. Whitington
South Australia wine-grower's manual. G. Sutherland
Souvenir Album of the Franco-British Exhibition. Anon
Souvenir of Canadian International Fair. Gooderham
    and Worts, Ltd.
Souvenir of 25th convention of United States Brewers
    Ass'n. H.J. Clausen Jr.
Souvenir volume, being an account of 10th annual convention
    held in Baltimore 1898. American Bottlers'
    Protective Ass'n.
"Soverigne Liquor". A brief investigation into the making
    and maturing of good Irish whiskey. John Jameson
    and Son Ltd.
Spa waters. G.B. Beattie
Spadacrene Anglica, or the English Spa fountain. E. Deane
Spanish Gem (A). Sherry. Anon
Sparkling draughts, their introduction, manufacture and
    consumption. H.D. Rawlings
Spas and health resorts of British Isles. T.D. Luke
Spas and mineral waters of Europe. H. Weber
Spas of Britain. Official handbook of British Spa Ass'n.
    for use of the medical profession. Anon
Spas of England. Midland spas. A.B. Granville
Spas of England. Northern spas. A.B. Granville
Spas of England. Southern spas. A.B. Granville
Spas of Europe. J. Althaus
Spas of Germany. A.B. Granville
Spas of Germany revisited. A.B. Granville

Spatula soda water guide, and book of formulas for soda
water dispensers.   E. F. White
SPC Year Book 1961.   Soap, Perfumery and Cosmetics
Special price list of whiskies, wines . . .
Grommes and Ulrich
Special report on beet sugar industry in the United States.
H. W. Wiley
Specialty cooking with wine.   M. Wood
Specifications for Caramel for use in food-stuffs.   British
Standards Institution
Specimen of a bibliography of old books and pamphlets
illustrative of the mug, loving cup, bottle . . .
G. Bumstead
Speeches in Leeds, Cardiff and Hull in favour of maintain-
ing free discretion for the licensing justices.
A. Chamberlain
Speeches of the Flying Squadron.   J. F. Hanly and
O. W. Stewart
Spice cookery.   H. Ripperger
Spice handbook; spices, aromatic seeds and herbs.
J. W. Parry
Spice Islands Cook Book (The).   Anon
"Spice Mill" Companion.   J. Burns
Spices.   Jamaica pepper to zeduary.   (M., J. B.)
Spices.   H. N. Ridley
Spices and condiments.   J. B. Mc Nair
Spices and condiments.   H. S. Redgrove
Spices and how to know them.   W. M. Gibbs
Spices: their botanical origin . . . J. K. Jank
Spices, their nature and growth and the vanilla bean.
Mc Cormick and Co.
Spices; what they are--where they come from.   American
Spice Trade Ass'n.
Spirit and licensed victualler's guide.   J. Benson
Spirit gravities with tables.   T. Stevenson
Spirit manual, historical and technical.   J. Scarisbrick
Spirit merchant (The).   Loftus (Publ.)
Spirit merchant's and excise officer's assistant.   S. Rose
Spirit of old Kentucky (The).   J. B. Wilson
Spirit of the vine: Republic of South Africa.   D. J. Opperman
Spirit tables of specific gravity 60°-60°.   Anon
Spirit tables at 20°-20°.   Anon
Spirit tables for Sike's hydrometer.   Anon
Spirit Trader's and Licensed victualler's reducing table.
Anon
Spirits.   K. T. D. (Know the drink) London.   Educational
Productions Ltd.   Anon

Spirits and liqueurs. Their origin, method of production, storage, preparation for sale and distribution. Wine and Spirit Ass'n of Great Britain
Spon's encyclopedia of industrial arts, manufactures, raw commercial products. G. G. Andre
Springs and baths of Kissengen. H. Welsh
Springs, streams and spas of London; history and associations. A. S. Foord
Squashes. G. B. Beattie
Squire's homemade wines. T. Hoggson
Squire's recipes. K. Banning
Stage-coach and tavern days. A. M. Earle
Standard Blue Book of mixed drinks. E. W. Makus
Standard Blue Book of Mixed Drinks. Supplement of Compounder's Guide. Anon
Standard cocktail guide. C. Gaige
Standard coffee code. F. P. Axtell
Standard cyclopedia of recipes. C. W. Brown
Standard encyclopedia of the alcohol problem. Anon
Standard formulary. A. E. Ebert and A. E. Hiss
Standard handbook on wines and liquors. A. M. Hirshfeld
Standard manual of soda and other beverages. A. E. Hiss
Standard mixer; the American bartenders' guide. J. T. Gloeckner
Standard recipes for ice cream makers. V. Miller
Standard soda water flavors. Standard Bottling and Extract Co.
Standard wine cook book. A. Director
Standardizing methods of analysis. S. Laufer
Starting a vineyard. R. B. Brock
Startling profits from wine making, in combination with wine, spirit, and aerated water trades. J. F. Henderson
State of physick, ancient and modern. F. Clifton
Statical essays. S. Hales
Statical estimates of the materials of brewing. J. Richardson
Statistical Abstract of United States 1951. U. S. Bureau of the Census
Statistical returns of brewers, victuallers, beersellers . . . G. S. Amsinck
Statistics relating to the brewing trade. G. S. Amsinck
Stay me with flagons; a book about wine and other things. M. Healy
Sterile filling. G. Osgood
Steward and barkeeper's manual. Jesse Haney and Co.
Still-room (The). J. A. E. Roundell and H. Roberts

Stimulants and narcotics. G.M. Beard
Stimulants and narcotics, their mutual relations with
    special researches on the action of alcohol.
        F.E. Anstie
Stories and toasts for after dinner. N.C. Fowler
Stork Club bar book (The). L.M. Beebe
Story of a vineyard. E.M. Heddle
Story of an unique institution. Dodge and Olcott
Story of Bacchus and centennial souvenir. B. Payne
Story of beer. L. Birch
Story of chocolate. Chocolate Mfgrs. Ass'n of U.S.A.
Story of chocolate and cocoa. Anon
Story of coffee. I.N. Young
Story of coffee and how to make it. Cheek-Neal Coffee Co.
Story of Crown Cork and Seal. Crown Cork and Seal Co.
Story of Dagger Jamaica rum. J. Wray and Nephew Ltd.
Story of extracts. Mc Cormick and Co.
Story of gin. D. Jermyn
Story of ginger (The). Amoy Canning Co.
Story of ginger. W. Hay Ltd.
Story of glass. E. Hodges
Story of Irish Whiskey (The). Anon
Story of "King Coffee". Costa Neves
Story of man and his food. C.C. and S.M. Furnas
Story of tea (The). Anon
Story of tea (The). O. Lancaster
Story of tea (The). The Tea Bureau
Story of tea. Anon
Story of the crown cork (The). Anon
Story of the tea leaf. M. Chamney
Story of the tea plant. Salada Tea Co.
Story of the vine. E.R. Emerson
Story of Watney's. W.P. Serocold
Story of Whitbread's. Whitbread and Co.
Story of wine in California. M.F.K. Fisher
Strawberry (The). S. Fraser
Strawberry growing. S.W. Fletcher
Strictures on new mode of brewing . . . G. Blake
Strong drink and tobacco smoke; the structure, growth,
    and uses of malt, hops, yeast and tobacco.
        H.P. Prescott
Structure and composition of foods (The). A.L. and K.B. Winton
Stuart's fancy drinks and how to mix them. T. Stuart
Student-life in Germany. W. Howitt
Student's manual of yeast culture. G. Johnson
Studies in ancient technology. R.J. Forbes

Studies of yeasts and the fermentation of fruits and berries
of Washington. B.S. Henry
Studies on fermentation. The diseases of beer . . .
L. Pasteur
Studies on rum. R. Arroyo
Studies on the possible intoxicating action of 3.2% beer.
A.J. Carlson, et al.
Studies on the sherry flor. J.C.M. Fornachon
Studies on wine-sterilizing machines. U. Gayon
Study and stimulants: or, the use of intoxicants and
narcotics . . . A.A. Reade
Study of American beers and ales. L.M. Tolman
Study of brewing and malting technique. Wahl Institute
Study of cider making in France, Germany and England . . .
W.B. Alwood
Study of effect of air on carbonation (A). Liquid Carbonic
Co. Ltd.
Study of foods (A). R.A. Wardell and E.M. White
Study of history and meaning of expression "original
gravity". J.A. Nettleton
Study of the history and of the art of brewing.
J.A. Nettleton
Study of the lost art of brewing . . . J.A. Nettleton
Subject list of works on domestic economy. Patent Office
Library Great Britain
Substitutes for the saloon. R. Calkins
Subtle sense (The). R. Bienfang
Sucaryl sweetened beverages. Abbott Laboratories.
Success with small fruits. E.P. Roe
Successful brewing. M.A. Pozen
Successful entertaining for the modern hostess. A. Barnes
Successful jam making and fruit bottling. L.H. Yates
Successful liquor retailing. J.H. Hornsby and
T.S. Harrington
Successful quality control in food processing. Food
Industries
Successful wine and beer making. S.M. Tritton
Successful winemaking. Including mead, vermouth and
liqueurs. S.M. Tritton
Successful wine making. Mead, perry, cider, fruit wines,
sparkling wines, vegetable wine, wine recipes.
S.M. Tritton
Successful winemaking at home. H.E. Bravery
Sugar. G. Fairrie
Sugar. J.A.C. Hugill
Sugar. A.R. Kahn
Sugar. U.S. Cuban Sugar Council

Sugar. A handbook for planters and refiners.
J. A. R. and B. E. R. Newlands
Sugar and its industrial applications. L. F. Wiggins
Sugar as a food. Sugar Information, Inc.
Sugar. Its production, technology and uses. A. Van Hook
Sugar made from maize and sorgham, a new discovery.
F. L. Stewart
Sugar substitutes. I. C. B. Allen
Sugar technology. P. Honig
Sugars and their simple derivitives. J. E. Mackenzie
Suggested bottlers syrup formulas using other than cane
or beet sugar. H. G. Pfafflin
Suggestions for maintaining quality and uniformity of bottled
carbonated beverages. J. H. Toulouse and Max
Levine
Suggestions for preparing flavor bases for summer drinks,
home drink concentrates . . . Dodge and Olcott
Suggestions on elimination of spoilage in the carbonated
beverage industry. M. Levine and J. H. Toulouse
Sulphur dioxide. Applications in foods, beverages . . .
L. C. Schroeter
Summary of the Scottish licensing laws. Glasgow and
District Licensed Trade Defense Ass'n.
Summer amongst the Bocages and the vines. L. S. Costello
Summer drinks and winter cordials. C. F. Leyel
Summer patterns of American beer consumption.
American Can Co.
Summer wine coolers. Friends of Wine (The).
Sundaes, ices and cream sodas . . . C. A. Boeglin
Sunlight and shadow. J. B. Gough
Sunlight and soft drinks. ABCB
Sunstruck off-flavor in soft drinks. A. W Noling and
J. M. Towey
Supplement to description of a pneumatic apparatus for
preparing factitious airs. J. Watt
Supplement to Steel on malting and brewing. J. Steel
Supplies for the soda fountain, ice cream and confectionery
mfgrs. Three Millers Co.
Supply, the care and sale of wine (The). A. L. Simon
Sure guide for distillers. B. Martin
Surrey Pubs. R. Keeble
Survey of the control on alcoholic beverages in other
countries. J. A. H. van Niekerk
Survey of wine growing in South Africa. K. W. V. Public
Relations Dept.
Survey of world literature on coffee. E. E. Lockhart
and F. B. Bloomhardt

Survey on beverages. J.J. Berliner and Staff
Sweet dry and dry or see America thirst (The).
    J.P. Mc Evoy
Sweet manufacture. Practical handbook on manufacture
    of sugar and confectionery. N.F. Scarborough
Sweet Shop. A handbook for retail confectioners.
    C. Vernon
Sweets and chocolates. G.B. Woolley
Swiss spas. Swiss Exporter Ltd.
Sylva, or a discourse of forest trees . . . J. Evelyn
Symposium on food: the chemistry and physiology of
    flavors. H.W. Schultz, et al
Synthetic aromatics, perfumes, isolates. R.S. Colbourne
Synthetic colouring matter . . . J.T. Hewitt
Synthetic food adjuncts. M.B. Jacobs
Synthetic perfumes, their chemistry and preparation.
    T.F. West
Syrup formulas. J.J. Berliner and Staff
Syrup making for cup venders. L.A. Enkema
Syrup suggestions. Barnett and Foster
Syrups, extracts and flavorings . . . Anon
System of Materica Medica and pharmacy. J. Murray
Systematic handbook of practical brewing . . .
    E.R. Southby

Table for two. T.A. Layton
Table Topics (periodical). Anon
Table topics. J.L. Street
Table traits with something on them. Dr. Doran
Table wines; the technology of their production in
    California. M.A. Amerine and M.A. Joslyn
Tables for ascertaining the strength of spirits with Sykes
    hydrometer. J. Long
Tables for Bate's patent saccharometer. R.B. Bate
Tables for calculating wine, beer, cider . . . J. Taylor
Tables for reducing quantities of weight in any mixture of
    spirits and water. G. Gilpin
Tables of content; leaves from my diary. A.L. Simon
Tables of food values. A.V. Bradley
Tables of results of brewing. G. Noback
Tables of specific gravity of wash, worts . . . J. Long
Tables of the weight of spirits . . . M. Young
Tables of the weight of spirits in the Imperial measure
    . . . R.B. Bate
Tables showing the approximate cost of tea lain down in
    New York. P. Loureiro

Tables showing the relation between the specific gravity
of spirits at 60° - 60° Fahrenheit . . . Anon
Tables to be used with Sike's A and B hydrometers. Anon
Tafelwasser, limonaden und brausen. W. Dalhmann
Tales of old inns. The history, legend and romance of
some of the older hostelleries. Anon
Tales of old inns. R. Keverne
Talk of tea (A). J. Page-Croft
Talking of tea. G. Huxley
Tankard of ale; an anthology of drinking songs.
T. Maynard
Tankards and traditions. E. Rosenthal
Tannin and its uses in wine. A. Newmark
Taste of Kinloch. A handbook of wines and spirits . . .
Anon
Tavern anecdotes and reminiscences of the origin of signs,
clubs . . . Anon
Tavern anecdotes and sayings including origin of signs.
C. Hindley
Tavern in the town. J. Mc Neigh
"Tavern is my drum (The)". J. Vecchi
Tavern Talk. C. Brooks
Tavern in the town (The). H. E. Popham
Taverns of old England (The). H. P. Maskell
Tax on distilled spirits. Regulations and instructions.
Anon
Tea. E. A. Browne
Tea. T. Eden
Tea. Trevor Jones of the Tea Bureau
Tea. R. M. Littlejohn
Tea. A. G. Stanton
Tea. Tea Ass'n. of U. S. A.
Tea. L. Williams
Tea. An historical sketch. R. O. Mennell
Tea; a symposium on the pharmacology and the physiologic
effects of tea. H. J. Klaunberg
Tea; a textbook of tea planting and manufacture. D. Crole
Tea and coffee. W. A. Alcott
Tea and coffee: their physical, intellectual and moral
effects on the human system. W. A. Alcott
Tea and effects of tea drinking. W. Tebb
Tea and tea blending by a member of the firm of Lewis
and Co. Anon
Tea and tea dealing. F. W. E. Staveacre
Tea and tea drinking. A. Reade
Tea: and the tea trade. G. Nye
Tea blending as a fine art. J. M. Walsh

Tea, coffee and cocoa: a practical treatise on the analysis
    of tea, coffee, cocoa, chocolate, maté . . .
    J.A. Wanklyn
Tea cookbook (The). W.I. Kaufman
Tea cult of Japan. Y. Fukukita
Tea culture as a probable American industry. W. Saunders
Tea culture in Ceylon. C.S. Armstrong
Tea-culture in India. W.N. Lees
Tea cultivation in Ceylon. Anon
Tea cultivation in Assam. H. Cottam
Tea encyclopedia (The). Anon
Tea-districts of China and India. R. Fortune
Tea drinking in 18th century America: its etiquette and
    equipage. R. Roth
Tea estate practice. Anon
Tea from grower to consumer. A. Ibbetson
Tea gardens of South Carolina. G.T. Drennen
Tea growing. C.R. Harler
Tea hints for retailers. J.H. Blake
Tea in Assam. S. Baildon
Tea in a nutshell. W.H. Ukers
Tea in Europe. J.E.M. Harington
Tea in India. F. Linde
Tea industry in India . . . S. Baildon
Tea, its culture, manufacture and commerce.
    S.E. Chandler and J. Mc Ewan
Tea; its cultivation, manufacture and packing.
    Mc Cormick and Co.
Tea, its effects, medicinal and moral. G.G. Sigmond
Tea, its history and mystery. J.M. Walsh
Tea, its mystery and history. S.P. Day
Tea: its origin, cultivation, manufacture and use.
    I.L. Hauser
Tea: its part in peace and war. K.R. Mc Cormick
Tea, its production and marketing. R.D. Morrison
TEA. Journal of United Kingdom Tea Council. Anon
Tea leaves; being a collection of letters relating to
    shipment of tea to American colonies. F.S. Drake
Tea machinery and tea factories. A.J. Wallis-Taylor
Tea manufacture. C.R. Harler
Tea manufacture in Ceylon. E.L. Keegal
Tea manufacture in Southern India. K.B.W. Jones
Tea manufacture. Its theory and practice. H.J. Moppett
Tea; memorandum relating to the tea industry and tea trade
    of the world. R.D. Morrison
Tea notes. A.F. Dowling

Tea on service.   Anon
Tea plant, its history and properties.   G. Mark
Tea plant of Assam.   Anon
Tea planter's life in Assam.   G.M. Barker
Tea planter's manual.   T.C. Owen
Tea planter's vade mecum.   Anon
Tea planting in Ceylon.   E.C. Elliott and F.J. Whitehead
Tea planting in outer Himalayah.   A.T. Mc Gowan
Tea purchaser's guide by a friend of the public.   Anon
Tea-room recipes.   L. Richards and N. Treat
Tea roots.   A.C. Turnstall
Tea soils of Cachar and Sylhet.   H.H. Mann
Tea story (The).   J.M. Scott
Tea table (The).   Chase and Sanborn
Tea - the drink of pleasure and health.   W.G. Stables
Tea under international regulation.   V.D. Wickizer
Tea we drink (The).   E.H. Skrine and G. Brownen
Teaching of the early church on the use of wine and
    strong drink.   I.W. Raymond
TEAMWORK (Five years of).   Employee monthly.
    Salada Tea Co.
Teapots and tea.   F. Tilley
Teas of the U.S.A.   B. Pennington
Technical aspects of cans and canning of carbonated
    beverages.   American Can Co.
Technical calculations for sugar works.   O. Mittelstaedt
Technical materials for brewing.   A. Boake Roberts and Co.
Technical problems of the bottled carbonated beverage
    manufacture.   ABCB
Technical proceedings.   Master Brewers Ass'n. of
    America
Technical sugar data.   George Clark and Son
Technique without tears.   Jusfrute Ltd.
Techno-chemical Receipt Book.   W.T. Brannt and
    W.H. Wahl
Technology of brewing.   E.H. Moritz
Technology of wine making.   M.A. Amerine and
    W.V. Cruess
Technology for sugar refinery workers.   O. Lyle
Technology of food preservation.   N.W. Desrosier
Teetotaler Dick: his adventures, temptations and
    triumphs.   T.W. Knox
Teetotalism.   An essay on the impropriety of making and
    useing intoxicating liquors.   W. Newton
Teetotalism and laws against the liquor trade.   Anon
Temperance and light drinks.   H.C. Standage

Temperance and the changing liquor situation. D. Pickett
Temperance drama (The). G. M. Baker
Temperance drinks for summer and winter. F. Davies
Temperance essays, and selections from different authors.
    E. C. Delavan
Temperance history. D. Burns
Temperance in the Victorian age. D. Burns
Temperance lesson book. Alcohol and its action on the
    body. B. W. Richardson
Temperance movement and its workers. P. T. Winskill
Temperance movement. Conflict between man and alcohol.
    H. W. Blair
Temperance reform and its great reformers.
    W. H. Daniels
Temperance reformation, its history . . . L. Armstrong
Ten nights in a bar-room. T. S. Arthur
Ten thousand secrets of the rich and wise. F. Shreve
Ten years of coffee progress. 1935-1944. W. H. Ukers
Tennery of paradoxes. J. B. van Helmont
Tenth anniversary reunion, alumni and former students,
    American Brewing Academy
Tenth Muse (The). H. Luke
Tested formulas for perfumes, cosmetics, soaps, liquors,
    wines and syrups. G. Zamarini
Testing of washing solutions. J. H. Buchanan and
    M. Levine
Text book on brewing. J. de Clarck
Text book of temperance. F. R. Lees
Tectbook of tropical agriculture. H. A. Nicholls
Tect-book of true temperance. F. R. Lees
Textbook of true temperance. M. Monahan
Textbook on chemistry and agriculture of tea including the
    growth and manufacture. E. F. Bamber
Text-book on the science of brewing. E. R. Moritz and
    G. H. Morris
Thames (The). G. Elliot-Godsave and A. C. Crouch
That book about wine. E. R. Christ and F. R. Fisk
That great American spirit. Licensed Beverage Industries,
    Inc.
Theobroma cacao or cocoa, its botany, cultivation,
    chemistry and diseases. H. Wright
Theoretic hints on improved practice of brewing malt
    liquors . . . J. Richardson
Theoretical and practical notes upon winemaking especially
    applied to Australian wines. P. Villanis
Theoretical and practical remarks on G. Blake's system
    of malting and brewing. G. Blake

Theory and practice of malting and brewing. Anon
There's a story in your coffee cup. Coffee Brewing
    Institute, Inc.
Therapeutics of mineral springs and climates. I.B. Yeo
Theory and practice of brewing. M. Combrune
Theory and practice of brewing. W.L. Tizard
Theory and practice of brewing from malted and unmalted
    corn and from potatoes. J. Ham
Theory and practice of guaging. P. Jonas
Theory and practice of ice cream making. H.H. Sommer
Theory and practice of modern brewing. F. Faulkner
Theory and practice of the preparation of malt and
    fabrication of beer. T.E. Thausing
These oils, water, extractions or essences. J. Hester
They took to the waters. H.B. Weiss and H.R. Kemble
They're open! R. Wilkinson and R. Frisby
Thirst aids for the charming hostess. Virginia Woman's
    Christian Temperance Union
Thirty-three recipes for homemade wines. H. Pretyman
This is liquid sugar. Refined Syrups and Sugars
This is liquid sugar. P.X. Hoynak and G.N. Hollenback
This is the Myrrour of Glasse of health necessary.
    T. Moulton
This must be the place! J. Charters
This thirsty life. Anon
Thomery system of grape culture. M. Du Breuil
Thomson's conspectus of the British pharmacopeas.
    E.L. Birkett
Three bottle bar. H.I. Williams
Three centuries. The story of our ancient breweries.
    Barclay, Perkins and Co.
Three essays in artificial philosophy or unusual chemistry.
    An essay for improvement of distillation . . . P. Shaw
Three fourths of a century of successful trade.
    H. Maxwell
Three hundred sixty five orange recipes. Anon
Three hundred years of Cape wine. C.L. Leipoldt
Three point two, and what goes with it. F.H. Beach
Three seasons in European vineyards. W.J. Flagg
Three thousand practical receipts. A.S. Wright
Thirty-fourth brewers' convention. U.S.B.A.
Through Europe with a jug of wine. M. Wood
Through the glass lightly. T.T. Greg
Through the wine-glass. W.H. Allen
Through the wine list, by "Diner-Out". A.E.M. Foster
Tickner's Pub. J. Tickner

Tiger! Tiger! The life story of Henry B. Gough.
    H.W. Morrow
Time for hospitality.   Licensed Beverage Industries
Tipple and snack, good things to eat and better things to
    drink. D. Mason
Tippler's Vow (The). L. Fairchild
To drink or not to drink. C.H. Durfee
To the household. Chase and Sanborn
To thee! a toast. Rahr Malting Co.
To think of tea. A. Repplier
Toast your friends in port. Anon
Toasts. Wm. J. Lemp Brewing Co.
Toasts. W.M. Rhoads
Toasts and anecdotes. P.W. Kearney
Toasts and cocktails. Anon
Toasts and tipple: a book of conviviality. W. Rice
Toasts and tributes. A. Gray
Toasts of the times. Pictures and rhymes. J.W. Sargent
Tobacco and alcohol. J. Fiske
Toby jugs. John Bedford
Toilet and cosmetic arts in ancient and modern times.
    A.J. Cooley
Toilet of the flora or a collection of the most simple and
    approved methods of preparing perfumes . . . Anon
Tokay. Berry Brothers and Rudd Ltd.
Tom and Jerry's bartender's guide. W.E. Powner
    (See Complete bartender's guide)
Tomorrow will be sober. L. Williams
Tonic wine-making secrets. P. Hutchinson
Topography of all the known vineyards. A. Jullien
Toward liquor control. R.B. Fosdick and A.L. Scott
Town and country brewery book. W. Brande
Trace elements in food. G.W. Monier-Williams
Trace ingredients and their influence on soft drink stability
    and quality. Anon
Trader Vic's book of food and drink. V.J. Bergeron
Training course in beverage production and plant
    operation. ABCB
Traite complet de la fabrication des liqueurs . . .
    A. Bedel
Traite raisonne de la distillation ou la distillation reduite
    en principes. M. Dejean
Traits and stories of Ye Olde Cheshire Cheese. Anon
Transactions of the Institute of Brewing. Anon
Trattato della natvra de vino. T.A. Meyden
Travels in Arabian Deserta. C.M. Doughty

Treasure of health. P. Hispanus
Treasury of Spices. American Spice Trade Ass'n.
Treasury of wine and wine cookery. G.H. Taylor
Treatise against drunkenness. M. Scrivener
Treatise and handbook of orange culture in Auckland, N. Z.
    G.E. Alderton
Treatise and practical guide of the apparatus for the
    fabrication of gaseous drinks, sparkling wines . . .
    D. Cazaubon
Treatise concerning the medicinal Spaw waters . . .
    M. Nessel
Treatise concerning the properties and effects of coffee.
    B. Moseley
Treatise of all sorts of foods . . . M. L. Lemery
Treatise of cyder and perry. J. Beale
Treatise of fruit trees. T. Hitt
Treatise of practical brewing and malting. F. Thatcher
Treatise of the pot culture of the grape. J. Mearns
Treatise on adulterations of food and culinary poisons.
    F. Accum
Treatise on air . . . R. Bewley (pseud)
Treatise on alcohol . . . T. Stevenson
Treatise on Bath waters. R. Charleton
Treatise on beverages or the complete practical bottler.
    C.H. Sulz
Treatise on breeding . . . with instructions for the
    private brewery on cider, perry, and British wines.
    B. Moubray (pseud)
Treatise on brewing. Anon
Treatise on brewing . . . T. Hitchcock
Treatise on brewing. A, Morrice
Treatise on citrus culture in California . . . B.M. Lelong
Treatise on cleanness of meats and drinks. T. Tryon
Treatise on cocoa. F.E. Olivieri
Treatise on coffee. (R). Nocol
Treatise on coffee and condemnation of its use.
    F.E. Breuckmann
Treatise on coffee, its properties . . . Anon
Treatise on colour manufacture. G. Zerr and
    R. Rubencamp
Treatise on confectionery. J. Bell
Treatise on cyder-making. H. Stafford
Treatise on family wine making . . . P.P. Carnell
Treatise on food and diet. J. Pereira
Treatise on food conservation. S. P. Snyder
Treatise on malting and brewing. G. A. Wigney

Treatise on manufacture of sugar from sugar cane.
P. Soames
Treatise on mineral waters. J.C.A. Franz
Treatise on mineral waters. D. Monro
Treatise on mineral waters and sea-side resorts,
descriptive and medical. C.W. Chanceller
Treatise on mineral waters of Harrogate. T. Garnett
Treatise on natural and artificial mineral waters.
J. Hawkins
Treatise on origin, natures and virtues of Chalybeate waters
. . . D. Linden
Treatise on pharmacy. E. Parrish
Treatise on silk and tea cultivation and other Asiatic
industries adopted to soil of California. T.A. Kendo
Treatise on strong beer and ale fully explaining the art
of brewing. T. Poole
Treatise on tea. H.A. Turner
Treatise on the ananas or pineapple. A. Taylor
Treatise on the art of brewing exhibiting the London
practice of brewing porter, brown stout, ale, table
beer . . . F.C. Accum
Treatise on the art of making wines from native fruits.
F.C. Accum
Treatise on the brewing of beer. E. Hughes
Treatise on the chemical history and medical powers of
some of the most celebrated mineral waters.
W. Saunders
Treatise on the coloring matters derived from coal tar.
H. Dussauce
Treatise on the composition and medical properties of the
mineral waters of 12 different springs. C. Scudamore
Treatise on the culture and management of fruit trees.
W. Forsyth
Treatise on the culture and management of grape vines.
J. Suydam
Treatise on the culture of the vine. N. Herbemont
Treatise on the culture of the vine . . .
W. Speechly
Treatise on the culture of the vine and art of making wine.
J. Busby
Treatise on the distillation of coal-tar and ammoniacal
liquor. G. Lunge
Treatise on the effects of coffee. S. Hahnemann
Treatise on the falsification of food . . . J. Mitchell
Treatise on the grape vine. J. Meredith
Treatise on the laws regulating the manufacture and sale
of intoxicating liquors. H.C. Black

Treatise on the machinery used in making and preparation
of soda water. J. Briggs
Treatise on the making of palatable table wines.
B. P. Chamberlain
Treatise on the manufacture and distillation of alcoholic
liquors. P. Duplais
Treatise on the manufacture, imitation, adulteration and
reduction of foreign wines, brandies . . . Anon
Treatise on the manufacture of liquors, syrups, cordials
and bitters. R. Drahota
Treatise on the manufacture of liquors, syrups, cordial,
and bitters. A. Eichler
Treatise on the manufacture of perfumes . . . J.E. Snively
Treatise on the mineral waters of Harrogate, containing
history . . . T. Garnett
Treatise on the mineral waters of Vichy . . . C. Cotar
Treatise on the natural properties and composition of
ancient and modern wines. F. Beardsall
Treatise on the nature and cultivation of coffee; with some
remarks on the management and purchase of coffee
estates. A. R. W. Lascelles
Treatise on the nature and use of bitter purging salt
contained in Epsom . . . N. Grew
Treatise on the nature of aliments or foods. F. Hoffman
Treatise in the origin, nature and varieties of wine.
J. L. W. Thudichum
Treatise on the origin of coffee. A. Galland
Treatise on the true nature and uses of Bath waters.
J. M. Graham
Treatise on the vine; embracing its history from earliest
ages to present day. W. R. Prince
Treatise on the virtues of whisky considered in its physical
and political uses . . . (E). B.
Treatise on the wines of Portugal. J. Croft
Treatise on tobacco, tea, coffee and chocolate. S. Paulli
Treatise on tobacco, tea, coffee and chocolate. J. Stevenson
Treatise on vitaculture. A. I. Perold
Treatise on wine production and special reports on wine
examinations. C. A. Wetmore
Treatise on wines and spirits of the principal producing
countries. W. and A. Gilbey
Treatise on wines, their origin, nature and varieties . . .
J. L. W. Thudichum
Treatise upon vines. J. A. C. Chaptal
Treatises on brewing. J. Baverstock
Treatment of brewing water. A. J. B. Scholefield
Treatment of brewing water in the light of modern chemistry.
Wallerstein Labs.

Treatment of deteriorated tea. H.H. Mann
Treatment of fruit juices and vegetables at Solo Feinfrost,
    Hamburg. Anon
Tree fruit growing. R. Bush
Tree of humane life, or, The Blovd of the grape.
    T. Whitaker
Tree of the Golden Pod. Story of cocoa farmers and
    chocolate workers. H.J. Deverson
Trenching and sub-soiling for American vines. R. Dubois
    and W.P. Wilkinson
Trial of Sir Jasper: a temperance tale in verse.
    S.C. Hall
Trial of the wine-brewers. J. Addison
Tricks of the trade . . . Anon
Tried favorites cookery book. E.W. Kirk
Trip to Brazil. W.H. Ukers
Trip to Ceylon. W.H. Ukers
Trip to China. W.H. Ukers
Trip to India. W.H. Ukers
Trip to the Keemun tea district. Irwin-Harrissons and
    Crosfield
Tritton's guide to better wine and beer making for
    beginners. S.M. Tritton
Tropical agriculturalist. G. Porter
Tropical agriculture. P.L. Simmonds
Tropical agriculture. E.V. Wilcox
Tropical agriculture research in the empire. C.A. Barber
Tropical crops (The). O.W. Barrett
Tropical fruits. S. Dyal
Truck operation data. ABCB
True discovery of the projectors of the wine project. Anon
True drunkard's delight (The). W. Juniper
True history of Tom and Jerry. C. Hindley
True relation of the proposing, threatning, and persuading
    the vintners to yield to the imposition on wine. Anon
True way of preserving and candying . . . Anon
Truth about intoxicating drinks. E.R. Barrett
Truth about things. C. Hyatt-Woolf
Truth and the wine interest. A.D. Wood
Truths about whisky. Anon
Tsiology; a discourse on tea. Smith(?)
Tuenda Bono Valetudine De. Anon
Tunbridge Wells, or a directory for drinking those waters.
    L. Rouse
Tunning of Elynour Rumming. J.S. Loureat
Twelve full ounces. M.W. Martin

Twentieth century book of toasts. P.E. Lowe
Twentieth century guide. How to mix drinks.
    J.C. Maloney
Twentieth century in the bottled carbonated beverage
    industry. J.J. Riley
Twenty-five years of brewing . . . G. Ehret
Twenty four hour drink book. R. Maloney
Twenty years plus Burns equals profits to you. Burns
    Bottling Machine Co.
Twining's in the Strand. E.E. Newton
Twining's in three centuries. Anon
'Twixt the cup and the lip. Psychological and socio-
    cultural factors affecting food habits. M. Cussler
    and M.L. DeGive
Two discourses. (of mysterie of vintners.)
    W. Charleton
Two hundred fifty recipes for delicious drinks.
    F. Crewe-Jones
Two hundred selected drinks. K.W. Sundin
Two hundred toasts. Mlle. Mixer (pseud)
Two hundred twenty two reputed wine recipes.
    M. Sherrard-Smith
Two-wine theory. "Communion wine". E.H. Jewett

Uker's International Tea and Coffee Buyer's Guide. Anon
Under the black tiles. S. Macnab
Unflavored carbonated and mineralized waters. ABCB
Union Sketch-Book. Gobright and Pratt
United Beverage Bureau Book. Anon
United States, British and German patents covering the
    manufacture of non-alcoholic beers and similar malt
    beverages. Mock and Blum
United States practical brewing and malting interpreter.
    C.R.M. Wall
United States Practical Receipt book. Anon
Units of systems of weights and measures. Their origin,
    development and present status. L.V. Judson
Universal assistant. R. Moore
Universal cook. F. Collingwood and J. Woollams
Universal drink (The). E.J. Kahn Jr.
Universal household assistant. S.H. Burt
Universal instructor in art of brewing beer . . . Anon
Unprejudiced palate (The). A.M. Pellegrini
Unser Bier. Anon
Unusual collection of recipes with a jug of wine. M. Wood

Use of beer in foods. H. C. Vickery
Use of benzoate of soda as a preservative. L. A. Enkema
Use of coal tar colors in food products. H. Lieber
Use of invert syrup. ABCB
Use of knowledge of mephetic exhalations. W. Brownrigg
Use of preservatives and colouring matter in the preserva-
    tion and colouring of foods. Anon
Use of starters in making sounder and finer wines.
    A. Franz
Useful guide for grocers, distillers . . . making and
    managing all kinds of wines and spiritous liquors.
    W. Beastall
Uses of juice extracted from raw fruits and vegetables.
    C. E. Clinkard
Uses of wine in medical practice. Wine Advisory Board
Utilization of fruit in commercial production of fruit
    juices. M. A. Joslyn and G. L. Marsh
Utilization of ingested carbon dioxide. W. S. McClellan

Vade-Mecum (A) for Malt-worms or a guide to good
    fellows . . . Anon
Vade-mecum for the user of Sluy's flavours, perfumer oils,
    raw materials . . . Sluys Boechout (NV)
Vade-mecum of the wine lover. A. Mournetas and
    H. Pelisser
Valley of the vines. J. Packer
Valuable secrets in arts, trades . . . Anon
Vanilla extracts, flavors and sugars . . . Dodge and
    Olcott
Vanilla, its cultivation in India. J. B. O'Connor
Van Nostrand's practical formulary. W. R. Minrath
Variety tests for grapes for wine. J. R. Haarlem
Vegetable cookery. J. Smith
Vegetable substances used for man. Anon
Vegetable substances used in the arts and domestic
    economy. Anon
Vertouse boke of distyllacyon. J. Brunswyke
Vest pocket pastry book. Anon
Vest pocket sundae formulas. E. F. White
Via Recta Via Longam. T. Venner
Victorian vista. J. Laver
View of the cultivation of fruit trees and management of
    orchards and cider. W. Coxe

View of the prejudice arising both to the country and
    the revenue from imposition on ale, beer . . .
    T. Short
Vigneron (The). I. Hutton
Vigneron (A) abroad. T. Hardy
Vin; the wine country of France. E.S. Hyams
Vindication of strong beer and ale . . . Anon
    (see Brewer's Plea)
Vine and civilization (The). H. Shaw
Vine and its fruit; more especially in relation to the
    production of wine . . . J.L. Denman
Vine and scalpel. M. Lake
Vine and wine-making in Southern France. A. Pellicot
Vine and wine making in Victoria. V. (pseud)
Vine culture for amateurs - by a practical hand.
    (W.J. May)
Vine culture under glass. J.R. Pearson
Vine-dresser's manual. C. Reemelin
Vine dresser's theoretical and practical manual or the
    art of cultivating the vine. A. Thiebaut de Berneaud
Vine grafting. A. Champin
Vine growing in England. H.M. Tod
Vine in Australia (The). A.C. Kelly
Vine in early California (The). Book Club of California
Vine: its culture in the United States. R.H. Phelps
Vine manual (The) or instructions for the cultivation of
    the grape vine. Anon
Vine-pruning. Its theory and practice. A.J. Perkins
Vinegar; its manufacture and examination. C.A. Mitchell
Vines and how to grow them. W. MacCollom
Vines and orchards of the Garden State. O.L. Ziegler
Vines and vine culture . . . A.F. Barron
Vines in the sun. I. Jones
Vines of Northeastern America. C.S. Newhall
Vinetum Angliae: or, A new and easy way to make wine of
    English grapes and other fruit . . . Anon
Vinetum Britannicum or a treatise of cider . . .
    J. Worlidge
Vineyard (The). I. Jones
Vineyard and the cellar (The). J.A. Despeissis
Vineyard-being a treatise shewing nature of planting . . .
    Anon
Vineyard culture, improved and cheapened. A. Du Breuil
Vineyards and orchards of South Australia. E. Ward
Vineyards in America . . . J. Osborn
Vineyards in England. E.S. Hyams

Vineyards of France. J. M. Scott
Vineyards of the world. Wine Trade Club
Viniana. C. W. Berry
Viniculture of claret. J. Maior
Vinification. Vin, ear-de-vie, vinaigre. P. Pacottet
Vintage (The). U. Keir
Vintage at Chateau Monbousquet. R. Greenwood
Vintage chart. 1945-1954. F. Schoonmaker
Vintage dinners. R. S. Codman
Vintage festival (The). S. B. Field
Vintage wine book (The). W. S. Leedom
Vintagewise. A. L. Simon
Vintner's and tobaconists' advocate. Anon
Vintner's answer to some scandulous pamphlets.
     H. Parker
Vintner's, brewer's spirit merchant's and licensed
     victualler's guide. Anon
Vintner's Company (The), their muniments, plate . . .
     T. Milbourn
Vintner's mystery displayed or the whole art of the wine
     trade laid open. Anon
Vintner's story (The). A. R. Beckwith
Vinum. Buyer's guide for wines, spirits, liqueurs . . .
     Anon
VIP's new bar guide. J. Armstrong and V. I. Partch
VIP throws a party. V. Partch and W. McIntyre
Virginia hostess 17th and 18th centuries. C. Mansur
Virginia's discovery of silke-vvormes, also dressing and
     keeping wines. E. Williams
Virtue and use of coffee . . . R. Bradley
Virtues of coffee. (N.), D
Vitaculture and brewing in the ancient Orient. H. F. Lutz
Vitaculture and viniculture in California. Anon
Vitaculture. F. Berry-Smith
Vitaculture in New Zealand. R. Bragato
Vitacultural research. D. Akenhead
Vitacultural resources of Victoria (The). J. W. Bear
Vocational guide in approved coffee cultivation practices.
     N. D. Digadice
Voice from mash-tun. W. L. Tizard
Voice from the vintage. Mrs. Ellis
Volatile oils (The). E. Gildemeister and Fr. Hoffmann
Voyage to Arabia the happy. J. de Laroque
Voyages and travels in the Levant in years 1749-50-51-52.
     C. Linnaeus

Waes Hael; the book of toasts. E. L. Chase
Wait and see (Butler to principle . . .). A. Thomas
Wake up and die! D. Clayton and D. Langdon
War of 4000 years. P. S. White and H. R. Pleasants
Warm beer, a treatise. With observations on cold water
    . . . M. Grindal
Warme beere, a treatise. (F.) W.
Was it a holiday? T. L. Codman
Wassail bowl (The). An anthology in miniature of
    conviviality. M. Crombie
Wassail! in mazers of mead. G. R. Gayre
Watch your thirst. A dry opera in three acts. O. Wister
Water analysis. J. A. Wanklyn
Water and water supplies and unfermented beverages.
    J. Attfield
Water into gold. E. Hill
Water of life. H. M. Robinson
Water, preventable disease and filtration. P. A. Maignen
Water soluble; and bulking gums. Thurston and Braidich
Water treatment. A. H. Fuller
Watering places and mineral springs of Germany, Austria
    and Switzerland. E. Gutmann
Watering places of England. E. Lee
Way to a man's heart - choice recipes (The). C. G. Mitchell
Way to get health. T. Tryon
Way to get wealth. Directing how to make 23 sorts of
    English wine . . . T. Tryon
Way to health (The). T. Tryon
Wayfarer in French vineyards (A). E. I. Robson
Wayside inns of England (Recommended). P. S. Williams
Wayward tendrils of the vine. I. M. Campbell
We keep a Pub. T. Berkeley
We shall eat and drink again. A wine and food anthology.
    L. Golding and A. L. Simon
Wehman's bartender's guide. H. J. Wehman
Wehman Bros. bartenders' guide. Anon
Weekend Companion (The). M. Breen and A. Dawson
Welcome to house of Seagram. Jos. E. Seagram Co.
Western fruit book. J. W. Hooper
Western fruit-book or American fruit growers guide.
    F. R. Elliott
Western fruit gardening. R. M. Brooks and C. O. Hesse
Wet drinks for dry people. W. C. Feery
Wet wit and dry humor. S. Leacock
What about alcohol? E. Bogen and L. W. S. Hisey
What about wine? All the answers. A. L. Simon

What are the facts about beer?   United Brewers Industrial
    Foundation
What everybody wants to know about wine.   A. Taylor
What everyone should knowe about tea.   W. H. Ukers
What is beer?   M. A. L. T.
What is whiskey?   Gooderham and Worts Ltd.
What is wrong with the bottled carbonated beverage
    industry.   Millis Advertising Co.
What price alcohol?   A practical discussion of the causes
    and treatment of alcoholism.   R. S. Carroll
What prohibition has done for America.   F. Franklin
What shall we drink?   M. Bredenbeck
What shall we drink?   G. G. Evans
What shall we drink?   E. M. Holding
What shall we drink?   N. Nye
What shall we have to drink?   X. M. Boulestin
What should we drink?   J. L. Denman
What shall we say about alcohol?   C. R. Hooten
What the butler winked at.   E. Horne
What the vintners sell.   L. Chaloner
What the young bottler should study.   G. B. Beattie
What to do about wines.   E. van Maanen-Helmer
What to drink.   M. Baines
What to drink.   Sanitas (pseud)
What to drink: recipes and directions for making and
    serving non-alcoholic drinks for all occasions.
    B. E. Stockbridge
What to eat and drink in France.   A. deCroze
What we drink.   Various authors.   H. W. Bayly, ed.
What wine to serve.   H. F. Stoll
What, when, where, and how to drink.   R. L. Williams
    and D. Myers
What will you take to drink?   H. W. Jones
What'll you have?   A not too dry textbook about cocktails.
    J. J. Proskauer
What'll you have boys?   J. Madden
What's in a soft drink?   Anon
What's what about wine; an Australian wine primer.
    W. James
What's yours?   The student's guide to Publand.
    T. E. B. Clarke
What all drank and thereafter.   C. H. Moehlman
When it's cocktail time in Cuba.   B. Woon
When the brewer had a stranglehold.   E. B. Gordon
When you entertain.   I. B. Allen
Where German wine grows.   Anon

Where Paris dines. J.L. Street
Where to drink? T. Merry
Whiskey Drips. Interesting sketches illustrating operations
    of whiskey thieves . . . J. Brooks
Whiskey in the kitchen. E. and M. Greenberg
Whiskey rebels. L.B. Baldwin
Whiskey salesman's handbook. R. Evans
Whiskies of Scotland. R.J.S. Mc Dowall
Whisky. A. Mac Donald
Whisky and Scotland. N.M. Gunn
Whisky distilleries of the United Kingdom. A. Barnard
Whisky galore. C. Mackenzie
Whitbread's brewery. incorporating the brewer's art.
    Whitbread and Co.
Whitbread's brewery. Whitbread and Co.
Whitbreads Brewery. 1740-1920. Anon
Whitbread craftsman. J. Moore
White wines and cognac. H.W. Allen
White wines of South Africa. W.A. deKlerk
Who has not heard of Budweiser beer? Anheruser-Busch
Who was the first toper? Being a dry discourse on a wet
    subject. M. Switzer
Whole art of confectionery. Anon
Whole art of confectionery. E.L. Mackenzie
Whole art of distillation. W.Y-Worth
Whole art of making British wines . . . J. Robinson
Whole truth about alcohol. G.E. Flint
Wholesale and retail wine and spirit merchant's companion.
    J. Hartley
Wholesale price list. Essential oils . . . Antoine Chiris
    Co.
Wholesale price list. Park and Tilford
Wholesale price list. Fritzsche Brothers
Wholesale wine and spirit trade. A Wellington history
    P. Lawler, ed.
Wholesale wine trade in Ohio. W.R. Davidson
Wholesome advise against the use of hot liquors.
    D. Duncan
Why be teetotal? Scientific evidence regarding alcoholic
    beverages and their effects on life. J. Mankey
Wilkin family home cooking album. Jos. S. Finch and Co.
Will someone lead me to a pub? T. Burke
Will you take wine? E.J. Foote
William Painter and his father. O.C. Painter
Wine. M.A. Amerine
Wine. R.S. Don

Wine. H. Johnson
Wine. G. E. Scott
Wine; a brief encyclopedia. W. James
Wine, a poem. J. Gay
Wine. A series of notes on this valuable product.
     A. Webber
Wine, an introduction for Americans. M. A. Amerine
     and V. L. Singleton
Wine and cooking. Anon
Wine and dine with the Lake Roland garden Club.
     Lake Roland Garden Club
Wine and food (Periodical). Wine and Food Society
Wine and food of Portugal and Madeira. Anon
Wine and food menu book. A. L. Simon
Wine and food Society's guide to soups. Robin Howe
Wine and Food Society's Library catalogue No. 1. English
     and American books. The Society.
Wine and Food Society of Southern California; a history
     . . . M. E. Graham
Wine and health. S. P. Lucia, Ed.
Wine and health. How to enjoy both. N. E. Yorke-Davies
Wine and its adulterations. J. L. Denman
Wine and its counterfeits. J. L. Denman
Wine and liquor handbook. Austin, Nichols and Co.
Wine and other drinks. R. Croft-Cooke
Wine and spirit adulterators unmasked - by one of the old
     school. Anon
Wine and spirit dealer's and consumer's vade-mecum.
     R. Westney
Wine and spirit dealer's guide. S. Rouse
Wine and spirit manual and Packman's handy agency list.
     W. V. Packman
Wine and spirit merchant (The). Anon
Wine and spirit merchants accounts. A. Sabin
Wine and spirit merchant's companion. J. Hartley
Wine and spirit merchants own book together with the most
     approved methods of making British wines. C. C. Dornot
Wine and spirit merchants and brewers. Wine and Spirit
     Trade Review Trade Directory
Wine and spirits; the connoisseur's textbook. A. L. Simon
Wine and the good life. A. M. Pelligrini
Wine and the wine lands of the world. F. H. Butler
Wine and the wine trade. A. L. Simon
Wine and vitaculture. Public Library of South Australia.
     (see Research Service Biblio.)
Wine and wine countries: a record and manual for wine
     merchants and wine consumers. C. Tovey

Wine and wine merchants. C.E. Hawker
Wine aristocracy; a guide to the best wines of the world.
    T.E. Carling
Wine artistry. The story of Widmer's. Widmer's Wine
    Cellars, Inc.
Wine as a beverage. J.F. Loyd
Wine as food and medicine. S.P. Lucia
Wine as it is drank in England. J.L. Denman
"Wine Australia". A guide . . . Anon
Wine awards. California. State Fair and Exposition
Wine, Beere, Ale and Tobacco; a seventeenth century
    interlude. (Gallobelgicus) (pseud)
The wine book. Alexander Dorozynski and Bibiane Bell
Wine book of knowledge. D.H. Riker
Wine book of South Africa. Wine and Spirit
Wine cellar book. Berry Brothers and Rudd
Wine. Classification - wine tasting - qualities and defects.
    G. Grazzi-Soncini
Wine connoisseur. A.L. Simon
Wine connoisseur's catechism. A.L. Simon
Wine cook book. Cora, Rose and Bob Brown
Wine cook book. Wine Advisory Board
Wine cookery - the easy way. Wine Advisory Board
Wine cooking recipes. Anon (see Richelieu Handbook)
Wine country of France. E.S Hyams
Wine data. T.E. Carling (see Wine drinkers aide-
    memoire)
Wine drinker's aide-memoire. T.E. Carling
Wine drinker's manual (The). Anon
Wine etiquette . . . T.E. Carling
Wine - food index. W.E. Massee
Wine for home and medicinal use. O.C. Rolli
Wine for the vintage. E. Perdix
Wine ghosts of Bremen. E. Sadler and C.R.L. Fletcher
Wine grapes; their selection, cultivation and enjoyment.
    P.M. Wagner
Wine-growers and wine-coopers' manual. W. Hardman
Wine-grower's guide. P.M. Wagner
Wine growers diary. W. James
Winegrowers of France and the government since 1875.
    C.K. Warner
Wine-growing in Australia. A.C. Kelly
Wine growing in England. G. Ordish
Wine guide (The). F.C. Mills
Wine guide (The). L. Bayard
Wine guide and cocktail book. E. Rollat

Wine handbook. W.E. Massee
Wine handbook for hoteliers. K.W.V.
Wine handbook series. Wine Advisory Board
Wine in America and American wine. Anon
Wine in ancient India. D.K. Rose
Wine in Australia. W. James
Wine in cooking. California. Agricultural Extension
    Service
Wine in peace and war. E. Waugh
Wine in Shakespeare's days and Shakespeare's plays.
    A.L. Simon
Wine in South Africa. P. Dicey
Wine in the ancient world. C.T. Seltman
Wine in the bible. J.P. Hansen
Wine in the kitchen. E. Craig
Wine industry in Australia. H.E. Laffer
Wine industry of Italy. G. Rosatti
Wine, its use and abuse: wines of the bible.
    A.T. Chodowski
Wine, its use and abuse: the fermented wines of the
    bible. A.T. Chodowski
Wine its use and taxation. J.E. Tennent
Wine journeys. S. Olivier
Wine labels. E.W. Whitworth
Wine list decorations. J. Harvey and Sons
Wine list. 1963-1964. J. Harvey and Sons
Wine list 1963. A.J. Smith and Co.
Wine lore; a critical analysis of wine dogma.
    T.E. Carling
Wine lover's cook book. J. Owen
Wine-maker's manual. C. Reemelin
Wine makers manual; a guide for the home wine maker
    and the small winery. P. Boswell
Winemakers Almanac. Anon
Wine maketh glad the heart and gladdens the heart of man.
    A.L. Simon
Wine making. C.J. Theron and C.G. Niehaus
Wine making at home. M.A. Amerine and G.L. Marsh
Wine making for all. J. Macgregor
Wine making for the amateur. R.S. Rose
Wine making from fruit pulps and concentrates.
    S.M. Tritton
Winemaking in earnest. W. Sherrard-Smith
Wine-making in hot climates. L. Roos
Wine making on a small scale. F.T. Bioletti
Wine manual. (E.H. Glass Co.) Anon
Wine merchandising. J.J. Haszonics and S. Barratt

Wine merchant - Bristol. Guide for the wine cellar.
    F. C. Husenbeth
Wine merchant's assessment of Burgundy. P. Cook
Wine merchants' book of recipes. D. M. McWilliam
Wine merchants companion. A. Jullien
Wine merchant's manual. T. Smeed
Wine Mine. A. Hogg, ed.
Wine of California. Atchison, Topeka and Santa Fe
    Railroad
Wine of the Cape. C. de Bosdari
Wine of the Douro. H. Bolitho
Wine on a budget. I. Crawford
Wine: Post war problems and possibilities.
    I. M. Campbell
Wine press and the cellar. E. H. Rixford
Wine primer. A. L. Simon
Wine Princess (The). M. Mackey
Wine question considered. Portuguese
Wine question (The) in the light of the new dispensation.
    J. Ellis
Wine record book. Anon
Wine report No. 23. Imperial Economic Committee
Wine revelations. C. Tovey
Wine service in the restaurant. G. F. Hasler
Wine spirit adulterators. Anon
Wine, 1788- 1939. Australian Wine Board
Wine steward's manual. C. Martyn
Wine story of Australia (Penfold). S. Mills
Wine tasting. J. H. Broadbent
Wine, the advantages of pure and natural wine . . .
    J. L. Denman
Wine, the vine, and the cellar. T. G. Shaw
Wine. Thumbnail sketches of wine of the world . . .
    T. E. Carling
Wine trade (The) and its history. T. G. Shaw
Wine trade loan exhibition of drinking vessels, also books
    and documents . . . Anon
Wine trade of Portugal. Proceedings of a meeting.
    J. J. de Forrester
Wine, water and song. G. K. Chesterton
Wine, what is it? Foster and Ingle
Wine wisdom, a simple and concise guide on what to buy
    and what to serve by John Aye (pseud). J. Atkinson
Wine, wisdom and whimsy. S. B. Taylor, Ed.
Wine - wise, a popular handbook on how to correctly
    judge, keep, serve and enjoy wines. H. F. Stoll

Wine-wise. How to know, choose and serve wine.
    T.E. Carling
Wine with a merry heart. I. Bentley
Wine without frills; everyday enjoyment of imported wines
    and spirits. Schenley Import Corp.
Wine, women and song. Medieval Latin student's songs.
    J.A. Symonds
Wine you can make. C.W. Shephard
Winebook for beginners. W. Sherrard-Smith
Winecraft; the encyclopedia of wines and spirits.
    A. Bourke
Winecraft. The encyclopedia of wines and spirits.
    T.A. Layton
Winelovers' handbook. P.V. Price
Winemaker's companion; a handbook for those who make
    wine at home. B.C.A. Turner and C.J.J. Berry
Winemakers of New Zealand. D. Scott
Winemaking at home. H. Hardwick
Winemaking in California. E. Peninou and S. Greenleaf
Winemaking from pulps, fruits . . . S.M. Tritton
Winemaking with canned and dried fruit. C.J.J. Berry
Wineograph chart (The). S.P.E. Simon and P. Hallgarten
Winery accounting and cost control. G.A. Maxwell
Wines. J.J. Berliner and Staff
Wines. J.J. Hall and J. Bunton
Wines and castles of Spain. T.A. Layton
Wines and Chateaux of the Loire. T.A. Layton
Wines and cordials for home and medicinal use.
    O.C. Rolli
Wines and fresh fruit beverages. B.C. Sabin
Wines and juices. F.W. Beech
Wines and liqueurs from A to Z. A.L. Simon
Wines and liqueurs, what, when, how to serve.
    D. Hartman
Wines and liquors. Consumers Union
Wines and liquors (Price list of) 1898. A.W. Balch and Co.
Wines and liquors from the days of Noah. A safe guide
    to sane drinking. G.O. Shaver
Wines and other fermented liquors; from the earliest ages
    to the present time. J.R. Sheen
Wines and spirits. L.W. Marrison
Wines and spirits; a complete buying guide. W.E. Massee
Wines and spirits; the connoissuer's textbook. A.L. Simon
Wines and spirits of the world. A. Gold, ed.
Wines and vines of California. F.E. Wait
Wines and vineyards of France. L. Jacquelin and
    R. Poulain

Wines and wineries of California. Fred S. Cook, ed.
Wines and wine serving. Wine Advisory Board
Wines, beers and liquors (How to make at home). Anon
Wines, cocktails and other drinks. F. A. Thomas
Wines for everyday enjoyment. Taylor Wine Co.
Wines for everyman. E. Forbes
Wines for those who have forgotten and those who want
     to know. S. Dewey
Wines great and small. Denzil Batchelor
Wines; how, when and what to serve. R. Marks
Wines; how when and what to serve. Schenley Import Corp.
Wines. K. T. D. (Know the drink). London Educational
     Productions Ltd.,
Wines, liqueurs and brandies. G. Haskell
Wines, liquors and the like. Young's Market Company
Wines, mixed drinks and savouries. N. Heaton
Wine's my line. T. A. Layton
Wines of Australia. Harry Cox
Wines of Australia. J. T. Fallon
Wines of Bordeaux (The). La Montagne and Sons
Wines of Bordeaux. J. R. Roger
Wines of Bordeaux. Edmund Penning-Rowsell
Wines of Burgundy (The). H. W. Yoxall
Wines of France (The). H. W. Allen
Wines of France. A. Lichine
Wines of France (The). A. L. Simon
Wines of France. E. and A. Vizetelly
Wines of Germany (The). F. Schoonmaker
Wines of Italy. C. G. Bode
Wines of Italy. W. Hudson
Wines of Italy. T. A. Layton
Wines of Italy (The). C. Ray
Wines of Italy (The). L. Veronelli
Wines of Madeira (The). R. A. Lewis
Wines of Portugal (The). H. W. Allen
Wines of Portugal. National Wine Boards of Portugal
Wines of South Africa. A. G. Bagnall
Wines of the bible. C. Bodington
Wines of the bible. N. S. Kerr
Wines of the bible. A. M. Wilson
Wines of the U. S. A., how to know and choose them.
     S. W. Murray
Wines of the world. A. L. Simon
Wines of the world-pocket library. A. L. Simon
Wines of the world. P. Valaer
Wines of the world characterized and classed.
     H. Vizetelly

Wines: scriptural and ecclesiastical. N.S. Kerr
Wines, spirits and liqueurs. C.W. Shepherd
Wine, spirits for all occasions. Country Ass'ns.
Wines, their care and treatment in cellar and store.
    R. Boireau
Wines, their selection, care and service. J.L. Street
Wines, vineyards and vignerons of Australia. A.L. Simon
Wines. What they are, where they come from, and
    how they are made. Anon
Wines; what they are, where they come from, how they
    are made. Wine and Spirit Ass'n.
Wines; what to serve, when to serve, how to serve.
    C. Stringer
Wines with long noses. G. Bijur
Wines, whys and wherefores. De Tassigny and Gauthier
Wing's Brewers Handbook of U.S. and Canada. Anon
Wining and dining in East Anglia. M. Watkins
Wining and dining in France with Bon Viveur.
    J. Cradock
Wining and dining quiz. C., R., B., Brown
Wining and dining with rhyme and reason. D.T. Carlisle
    and E. Dunn
Winning the fight against drink . E.L. Eaton
Winslow's (Mrs) domestic receipt book 1862. Anon
Winter in Central America and Mexico. H.J. Sanborn
Wir mixen. H. Henseler and B. Weichsel
Wishful cooking. E.L. Mirrless and M.R. Coker
Wit wisdom and morals. Distilled from Bacchus.
    C. Tovey
Wolf in chef's clothing. R.H. Loeb
Woman and temperance. F.E. Willard
Woman, wine and saucepan. E. Craig
Woman's Institute Library of Cookery-Beverages. Anon
Woman's Institute Library of Cookery-Fruit and fruit
    desserts-beverages. Anon
Women and wine. H.W. Yoxall
Women's buying habits and attitudes toward soft drinks.
    Ladies Home Journal
Wonder of wine (The). E. Kressmann
Wooden horse (The); or, America menaced by a
    Prussianized trade. E.D. Pickett
Woodward's graperies and horticultural buildings.
    G.E. Woodward
Word book about wine (A). W. James
Word for word; an encyclopedia of beer. Whitbread and Co.
Word or two about port wine (A). J.J. de Forrester

World coffee economy with special reference to control
    schemes. V.D. Wickizer
World directory of libraries (A). International Library
    Directory
World of fragrance (The). B. Dayl
World of wines (The). C. Churchill
World trade in cocoa. E.G. Montgomery and A.M. Taylor
World-wide business (A). R.J. Finch
World's coffee. A study of the economics and politics
    of the coffee industries. J.W.F. Rowe
World's drinks and how to mix them. W. Boothby
Worship of Bacchus, a great delusion. E. Clarke
Wright's book of 3000 practical receipts. A.S. Wright
Writings of Dr. Siebel. J.E. Siebel

X-ray; or, compiled facts and figures of interest to the
    retail liquor dealer. S.C. Freels

Yakima Golding Hop Farms. J.I. Haas, Inc.
Ye Olde Mixer-Upper. J. Held
Year at the Peacock (A). T.A. Layton
Year Book (The). U.S Brewers' Ass'n.
Yearbook. U.S. Dept. Agriculture
Years and years; some vintage years in French wines.
    C.R. Codman
Young brewer's monitor - by a brewer of 30 years
    practical experience. Anon
Young cook's monitor (The) or directions for cookery and
    distilling. (M.) H.
Young housewife's daily assistant. Anon
Young ladies school of arts (The). H. Robertson
Young people and drinking. The use and abuse of beverage
    alcohol. A.H. Cain
Young tea planter's companion. F.T.R. Deas
Younger centuries (The). D. Keir
Your club. Whitbread and Co.
Your guide to the imported wines of Monsieur Henri.
    Monsieur Henri Wines, Ltd.
Your health! I. Phelps
Your life is more pleasant with wine. S. Norris
Your key to quality. Society of Soft Drink Technologists
Your local. Whitbread and Co.
You've got me on the rocks. L. Larier, ed.

Zodiac cocktails; cocktails for all birthdays. S.S. MacNiel

APPENDICES

Standard Works Consulted

American Bibliography, 1639-1800.   Charles Evans
American Bibliography, 1801-1819.   Ralph Shaw and
      Richard Shoemaker
American Catalog of Books, 1876-1910.   (Cummulates
      Annual American Catalog, 1886-1910).
      Publishers' Weekly
American Catalogue of Books . . . 1861-1871.
      James Kelley
American National Trade Bibliography.   (Supplemented by
      Annual American Catalogue and currently by Publishers'
      Weekly.)
Astor Library Catalogue, 1857-1866.

Bibliographer's Manual of English Literature.
      T.W. Loundes, 1864
Bibliotheca Americana, 1820-1861.   O.A. Roorbach
Bibliotheca Britannica.   Robert Watt, 1824
Bibliotheca Lindesiana.   1910
Bibliotheca Osleriana.   1929
Book Review Digest.   Current
British Museum Catalog,
      Subject Index.   1901-1950
British Museum General Catalogue of Printed Books
British National Bibliography.   1950-

Cambridge Bibliography of English Literature, 600-1900
Catalogue of Printed Books in the Library of the
      University of Edinburgh to 1923
Catalogue of the Books in the Library of the British
      Museum . . . to the year 1640.   1884
Catalogue of the Books, Pamphlets, Pictures, and Maps
      in Library of Parliament to 1911.   (Australia)
Cumulative Book Index (C.B.I.).   1928-

Dictionary of Books Relating to America . . .
      (1868-1892).   Joseph Sabin

Early English Books at Cambridge, 1475-1640
English Catalogue of Books . . . 1801-

Great American Trade Catalogs. Romaine

Incunabula and Americana, 1450-1800.
    Margaret Stillwell, 1931
Incunabula in American Libraries. Frederick Goff, 1964
Incunabula Medica. Osler. 1467-1480

John Carter Brown Library Catalog

Lamont Library (Catalogue of). Harvard. 1953
Library of Congress, Washington, D. C.
    Catalog of books by subjects
    Catalog of the Library of the United States, 1815
    Catalog of the Library of Congress to 1869
    Catalog of Books Represented by the Library of
        Congress Printed Cards to 1942.
        Supplements to 1963
    National Union Catalog of the Library of Congress.
        1953-1962

Morton's Medical Bibliography. 1954

Oxford Books. 1468-1680

Peabody Institute Catalog. Baltimore

Reference Catalogue of Current Literature. London

Short-title Catalogue . . . 1475-1640.
    Alfred W. Pollard and G. R. Redgrave
Short-title Catalogue . . . 1641-1700.
    Donald G. Wing
Standard Catalog for Public Libraries
Subject Guide to Books in Print. 1957-
Subject Index of Books Printed Before 1880. R. A. Peddie
Subject Index of London Library
Subject Index of Modern Works. Fortescue

U. S. Catalog; Books in Print. 1899-1928

Whitaker's Cumulative Book List. 1925-1957

Guide to Books in Author List
Which Contain Bibliographies,
Dictionaries, Glossaries, Vocabu-
laries or Other Helpful Sections

BEER AND BREWING

Andrup, E.   History of pasteurization
Arnold, J. P.   History of the brewing industry
Ault and Hudson.   Report on brewing
Baron, S.   Brewed in America
Beaven, E. S.   Barley - 50 years observ.
Berry, C. J. J.   Hints on home brewing
_____ .   Home brewed beers and stouts
Bird, W. H.   Catalogue- London section Institute of Brewing
Bravery, H. E.   Home brewing without failures
Brewer's Ass'n.   Brewing in Canada
Brown, B. M.   The brewer's art
Burgess, A. H.   Hops
Carlson, A. J. et al.   Studies on possible intoxication from
   3. 2 beer
Chapman, A. C.   Brewing
Clinch, G.   English hops
Cochran, T. C.   Pabst Brewing Co.
Cook, A. H.   Barley and malt
Cooper, I. M.   References, ancient and modern brewing
Cronk, A.   English hops (glossary)
Davison, E.   Beer in American home
Dominion Brewers Ass'n.   Facts on brewing
Fischer, I. W.   Factworterbuch . . .
Gordon, E. B.   When brewer had stranglehold
Grossman, H. J.   Guide to wines . . .
Hartman, L. F.   On beer and brewing technique
Hartong, B. D.   Elsivier's dictionary
Hind, H. L.   Brewing, science, practice
Hopkins, R. H.   Biochemistry applied
Jahrbuch 1955.   Biblio. brauwesens
Janes, H.   Red barrel
Kelynack and Kirkby.   Arsenical poison in beer
King, F. A.   Beer has a history
Kloss, C. A.   Art and science brewing
Lancaster, H.   Pract. floor malting

843

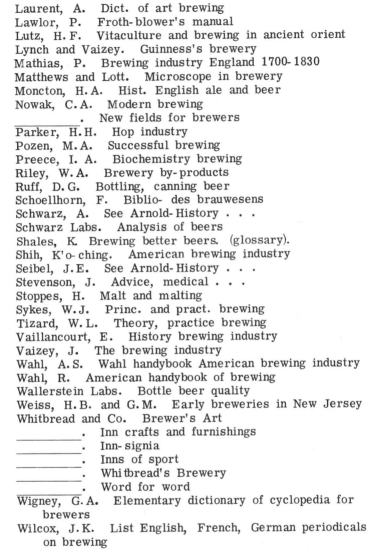

Laurent, A.   Dict. of art brewing
Lawlor, P.   Froth-blower's manual
Lutz, H. F.   Vitaculture and brewing in ancient orient
Lynch and Vaizey.   Guinness's brewery
Mathias, P.   Brewing industry England 1700-1830
Matthews and Lott.   Microscope in brewery
Moncton, H. A.   Hist. English ale and beer
Nowak, C. A.   Modern brewing
_____ .   New fields for brewers
Parker, H. H.   Hop industry
Pozen, M. A.   Successful brewing
Preece, I. A.   Biochemistry brewing
Riley, W. A.   Brewery by-products
Ruff, D. G.   Bottling, canning beer
Schoellhorn, F.   Biblio- des brauwesens
Schwarz, A.   See Arnold-History . . .
Schwarz Labs.   Analysis of beers
Shales, K.   Brewing better beers. (glossary).
Shih, K'o-ching.   American brewing industry
Seibel, J. E.   See Arnold-History . . .
Stevenson, J.   Advice, medical . . .
Stoppes, H.   Malt and malting
Sykes, W. J.   Princ. and pract. brewing
Tizard, W. L.   Theory, practice brewing
Vaillancourt, E.   History brewing industry
Vaizey, J.   The brewing industry
Wahl, A. S.   Wahl handybook American brewing industry
Wahl, R.   American handybook of brewing
Wallerstein Labs.   Bottle beer quality
Weiss, H. B. and G. M.   Early breweries in New Jersey
Whitbread and Co.   Brewer's Art
_____ .   Inn crafts and furnishings
_____ .   Inn-signia
_____ .   Inns of sport
_____ .   Whitbread's Brewery
_____ .   Word for word
Wigney, G. A.   Elementary dictionary of cyclopedia for
   brewers
Wilcox, J. K.   List English, French, German periodicals
   on brewing

Anonymous

Brewer (The) in nine languages
Gesellschaft fur die Geschichte und bibliographie des
   brauwesens E. B

CIDER, PERRY . . .
Alwood, W. B.   Study of cider-making
Curtis, J. H.   As long as single apple tree left . . .
Luckwell and Pollard.   Perry pears
National Fruit and Cider Inst.   Annual reports
Warcollier, G.   Prin. and pract. cider-making

COCKTAILS
Anderson, F.   Modern cocktail manual
Aucken, I.   Dict. scientific cocktail making
Blunier, O.   Barkeeper's Golden Book
Brenner, F.   500 recipes
Clarke, E.   Pract. bar management
Coombs, J. H.   Bar Service
Crockett, A. S.   Old Waldorf-Astoria bar book
Diners' Club Magazine.   Drink Book
Doxat, J.   Booth's handbook of cocktails
Duffy, P. G.   Bartender's guide
Gavin, C.   Here's How!
Heath, A.   Good drinks
Huntington, R. T.   Bar management
Perry, M. H.   And to drink, Sir!
Tarling, W. J.   Cafe Royal cocktail book
U. K.   Bartender's guild.   Approved cocktails

Anonymous

Savoy cocktail book

COCOA AND CHOCOLATE
Amer. Food Journal Institute.   Bibliography of food values
Briton-Jones, H. P.   Diseases and curing of cocoa
Chatt, E. M.   Cocoa: cultivation, processing, analysis
Chocolate Mfgrs. Ass'n.   Story of chocolate
Cook, L. R.   Chocolate production and uses
Ernholm, I.   Cocoa production South America
Hill, P.   Gold Coast cocoa farmer
Jordon, S.   Chocolate evaluation
Knapp, A. W.   Cocoa and chocolate industry
_____ .   Cocoa and chocolate, history
_____ .   Scientific aspects cocoa fermentation
MacLaren, W. A.   Rubber, tea and cocoa
Mueller, W.   Bibliographie des kaffee . . .
_____ .   Bibliographie des kakao
Peattie, D. C.   Cargoes and harvests
Redmayne, P.   Cocoa and chocolate

Rohan, T.A.   Processing of raw cocoa
Stevenson, J.   Advice, medical . . .
Urquhart, D.H.   British North Borneo Cocoa
Watrous, R.C.   Cacao
Whymper, R.   Cocoa and chocolate . . .
Wickizer, V.D.   Coffee, tea and cocoa
Williams, I.A.   Firm of Cadbury
Wood, G.A.R.   Cocoa growing in India
Zipperer, P.   Mfg. chocolate . . .

<u>Anonymous</u>
Cocoa Grower's Bulletins
Confectionery Production manual

<u>COFFEE</u>
Cheney, R.H.   Coffee, a monograph
Cramer, P.J.S.   Review literature coffee research in
     Indonesia
Doughty, C.M.   Travels in Arabia Deserta
Gordon, J.   Coffee recipes
Graham, H.C.   Coffee. Production . . .
Haarer, A.E.   Coffee growing
_____ .   Modern coffee production
International Bureau of American Republics.   Coffee
Jacob, H.E.   Coffee: epic of a commodity
_____ .   The saga of coffee
Lock, C.G.W.   Coffee: its culture . . .
Lockhart and Bloomhardt.   Survey of world literature on
     coffee
Peattie, D.C.   Cargoes and harvests
Rodriquez, D.W.   Coffee. Short economic history
Rudy, P.O.   Marketing of coffee
Ukers, W.H.   All about coffee
Wellman, F.L.   Coffee, botany . . .
Wickizer, V.D.   Coffee, tea and cocoa
Young, I.N.   Story of coffee

<u>CONFECTIONERY, ICES</u> . . .
Blumenthal, S.   Food manufacturing
Colam, E.E.F.   Pract. milk bar operation
Mansur, C.E.   Virginia hostess
Masurovsky, B.I.   Sherbets, water ices
Sommer, H.H.   Theory, practice ice cream making

<u>Anonymous</u>
Confectionery Production manual

COOKERY
Ainsworth-Davis, J.R.   Cooking through centuries
Aylett and Ordish.   First catch your hare
Bazore, K.   Hawaiian and Pacific foods
Brown, E. and B.   Culinary Americana
Francatelli, C.E.   Cooks's guide . . .
Hatch, E.W.   American wine cookbook
Hazlitt, W.C.   Old cookery books
Heaton, N.S.   Cooking with wine
Howard, M.W.   Lowney's cook book
Lincoln, W.   American cookery books 1742-1860
Lowe, B.   Experimental cookery
Mansur, C.E.   Virginia hostess
Oxford, A.   English cookery books
Pennell, E.R.   My cookery books

Anonymous

Book of simples
Hering's dictionary classical and modern cookery

DRINKS AND DRINKING
Abrahamson and Pezet.   Body, mind and sugar
Adams, L.D.   Commonsense book of drinking
Allardt-Markkanen-Takala.   Drinking and drinkers
Ash, D.   How to identify English drinking glasses
_____.   How to identify English silver drinking vessels
Benstead, C.R.   Hic, Haec, Hock
Bishop, G.   The Booze Reader
Blaser, W.   Japanese temples and teahouses
Breen, H.   How to stop drinking
Bretzfield, H.   Liquor marketing . . .
Brodner-Carlson-Maschal.   Profitable food and beverage
    operation
Bruun, K.   Drinking behavior small groups
Bruun and Hauge.   Drinking habits . . .
Brown, J.A.   Early American beverages
Cain, A.H.   Young people and drinking
Calkins, R.   Substitutes for the saloon
Candler, C.H.   Asa Griggs Candler
Carson, G.   Social history Bourbon
Chafetz and Demone.   Alcoholism and society
Chafetz, M.E.   Liquor: servant of man
Collier, J.   CHEERS!
Crahan, M.E.   Early American inebrietatis
Crawley, A.E.   Dress, drink and drums
Crockett, A.S.   Old Astoria-Waldorf bar book

Croze, A. de. What to eat and drink in France
Davis, J. I. Beginner's guide to wines
Dewitt, W. A. Drinking and what to do about it.
Durfee, C. H. To drink or not to drink
Emerson, H. Alcohol. Its effects on man
_____ . Alcohol and man
Fairburn, W. A. Man and his health: liquids
Forbes, P. Champagne, the wine, the land and the people
Ford, J. C. Man takes a drink
Freeland, J. M. The Australian pub
French, R. V. 19 centuries drink in England
Furnas, J. C. Late Demon Rum
Gayre, G. R. Wassail! In mazers of mead
Gorham, M. Back to the local
_____ . The local
Greenberg, L. A. Definition of intoxicating beverage
Greenfield, W. S. Alcohol: its use, abuse
Guinness, A. Physiological aspects of alcoholic beverages
Goettler, Dr. H. Lexikon der spirituosen (Dictionary)
Hammell, G. Passing of the saloon
Harkness and Fort. Alcohol: uses and abuses
Heath, A. Good drinks
Hindley, C. True history Tom and Jerry
Horsley and Sturge. Alcohol and human body
Horton, D. Functions of alcohol in primitive societies
Hunt, P. Eating and drinking
Jacob, H. E. Saga of coffee
Jellinik, E. M. Alcoholic addiction . . .
Jones, H. Alcoholic addiction
Kelynack, and Kirkby. Arsenical poisoning
Koren, J. Economic aspects liquor problem
Krout, J. A. Origin of prohibition
Leake and Silverman. Alcoholic beverages in clinical
    medicine
Licensed Beverage Industries. ABC's of alcoholic beverages
Lolli, G. Alcohol in Italian culture
Lucia, S. Alcohol and civilization
_____ . History wine as theraphy
_____ . Wine as food and medicine
Lutz, H. F. Vitaculture, brewing ancient orient
Mc Carthy and Douglass. Alcohol and social responsibility
Mc Cord, W. and J. Origins of alcoholism
Madden, Joe. Set 'em up!
_____ . What'll you have boys?
Mann, Marty. New Primer on alcoholism
_____ . Primer on alcoholism

Mass-Observation. Pub and the people
Mendelsohn, O.A. Dictionary of drinks and drinking
_____. Ernest drinker
_____. Ernest drinker's digest
Monroe and Stewart. Alcohol education for the layman
Nash, H. Alcohol and caffeine
Newman, H.W. Acute alcoholic intoxication
Van Niekerk, J.A.M. Survey of control alcoholic beverages
    other countries
Oaks, L. Medical aspects Latter-day Saints-Word of
    wisdom
Patent Office, Great Britain. Subject list of works on
    domestic economy
Peabody, R.R. Commonsense of drinking
Pearl, R. Alcohol and longevity
Peattie, D.C. Cargoes and harvests
Penzer, N.M. Book of wine label
Sadoun, R. et al. Drinking in French culture
    (Bibliography)
Seltman, C.T. Wine in ancient world
Serjeant, R. A man may drink
Sinclair, U. The cup of fury
Smith and Helwig. Liquor. The servant of man
Starling, E.H. Action of alcohol on man
Stone, J.W. Brief history beverage alcohol and of
    Kentucky Bourbon whiskey
Sutherland, D. Raise your glasses.
Takala-Pihkanen-Markkanen. Effects of distilled and
    brewed beverages
Taussig, W.H. Rum, Romance, Rebellion
Townsend, W.H. Lincoln and liquor
Voegele and Woolley. Drink dictionary
Wallerstein, R.S. Hospital treatment of alcoholism
Washburne, C. Primitive drinking
Wassermann, A. Schenley library biblio.
Whitbread and Co. Inn crafts and furnishings
_____. Inns of sport
Williams, L. Alcoholism
_____. Tomorrow will be sober
Willison, G.F. Saints and strangers

Anonymous
Standard encyclopedia of the alcohol problem

FLAVORS, COLORS, AROMA
Airkem, Inc. Odors and sense of smell

American Spice Trade Ass'n. History of spices
Arctander, Steffen. Perfume and natural flavoring materials.
    (Bibliography)
Bienfang, R. The subtle sense
Blumenthal, S. Food manufacturing
Clair, Colin. Of herbs and spices.
Crocker, E.C. Flavor
Fox, H.M. Gardening with herbs
Gildemeister and Hoffman. Volatile oils
Guenther, E. The essential oils
    _____. Lemon oil production around the world
Howe, S.E. In quest of spices
India (Republic). Essential oils, aromatics
von Isokovics, A. Modern aromatic chemicals
Jacobs, M.B. Synthetic food adjuncts
Jaques, H.E. How to know economic plants
Judd, J.B. Colorimetry
Kesterson and McDuff. Florida citrus oils
Leyel, C.F. Magic of herbs
Little A.B., Inc. Flavor research and food acceptance
McDonough, E.G. Investigations in auto-oxidation of
    aldehydes
Mackinney and Little. Color of foods
Mairet, E. Book of vegetable dyes
Martin, G. Perfumes, essential oils . . .
Nenon, A.K. Indian essential oils
Merory, J. Food flavorings . . .
Moncrieff, R.W. Chemical senses
    _____. Odour preferences
Muller, A. Internationaler Riechstoff-Kodex
Parry, J.W. Spice handbook
Peattie, D.C. Cargoes and harvests
Quartermaster Food and Container Inst.
    Chemistry of natural food flavors, beverages,
    condiments
Redgrove, H.S. Spices and condiments
Schimmel and Co. Annual report essential oils
Schultz, H.W. et al. Symposium on food
Taylor, N. Cinchona in Java
    Color in the garden
    Fragrance in the garden
Tidbury, G.E. The clove tree
Wilder, L.B. The fragrant path
Thurston and Braidich. Water soluble and bulking gums

Anonymous

Flavors and spices and flavor characterization

FOOD

American Can Co.   Canned foods reference manual
Anderson, O.E.   Health of a nation
Baker and Foskett.   Bibliography of food
Battershall, J.P.   Food adulteration and detection
Baumgartner and Herson.   Canned foods
Beck, B.F.   Honey and health
Bitting, K.G.   Gastronomic bibliography
Blumenthal, S.   Food manufacturing
————————.   Food products
Blyth, A.W.   Analysis food and detection of poisons
    Foods, composition . . .
Bridges, M.A.   Food and beverage analysis
Bryan, A.H.   Maple-sap syrup
Campbell, C.H.   Book of canning, preserving
Dowd and Jameson,   Food, its composition
Fairrie, G.   Sugar
Filby, F.A.   History food adulteration
Gardner, W.H.   Food acidulents
Hinton, C.L.   Fruit pectins
Honig, P.   Principles of sugar technology
Hughes, O.   Introductory foods
Jensen, L.B.   Man's foods
Jones, T.   Henry Tate
Kirshenbauer, H.G.   Fats and oils
Lane-Clayton, J.E.   Milk and its hygenic relations
Leffman and Beam.   Select methods of food analysis
Leyel, C.F.   Magic of foods
von Loesecke, H.M.   Drying and dehydration of foods
————————.   Outlines food technology
Longwood, W.   Poisons in your food
Lowe, B.   Experimental cookery
Mc Cance and Widdowson.   Chemical composition of foods
Manufacturing Chemists Ass'n.   Food additives
May, E.C.   Canning clan
Mitchell, C.A.   Edible oils and fats
Monier-Williams, G.W.   Trace elements in food
Mortimer, W.G.   Peru. History of cocoa
Refined Syrups.   This is liquid sugar
Richards, E.H.   Food materials . . .
Rohde, E.C.   Garden of herbs
Savage, W.G.   Canned food in relation to health
Schlink, F.J.   Eat, drink, be wary
Sherman, H.C.   Chemistry food and nutrition
    Essentials of nutrition; Food products
Simmonds, P.L.   Tropical agriculture
Sugar Information, Inc.   Sugar as food
Tressler and Evers.   Freezing preservation of foods

Triebold and Aurand. Food composition and analysis
U.S. Cuban Sugar Council. Sugar
U.S. Dept. Agri. Sensory methods
Vehling, J.G. America's table
Vulte and Vanderbilt. Food industries
Ward, A. Encyclopedia of food
_____. Grocer's encyclopedia
Wiggins, L.F. Sugar, industrial applications
Wilcox, E.V. Tropical agriculture
Willits, C.O. Maple syrup producers' manual

Anonymous

Citric Acid U.S.P. (Miles Labs.)
Dietetic canned foods
Food Industries manual

FOOD AND DRINK

Brodner, et al. Profitable food and beverage operation
Carlisle, D.T. Wining and dining with rhyme and reason
Chakravarty, T. Food and drink of ancient Bengal
Croze, A. de. What to eat and drink in France
Ellwanger, G.H. Pleasures of the table
Glozer, L.F. and W.K. California in the kitchen
Heath, A. Dining out
Hospitality Guild. Catalog of 500 books on food and drink
Huntington, R.T. Beverage service
Labarge, M.W. Baronial household of 13th century
Lamb, R. American chamber of horrors
Maggs Bros. Food and drink through the ages,
    2500 B.C. to 1931
National Book League. Food and wine
Perry, M.H. And to drink, Sir!
Simon, A.L. Guide to good food and wines
Street, J.L. Table topics
Vicaire, G. Bibliographie gastronomique
White, F. Flowers as food

Anonymous

Ass'n Special Libraries and Information.
    The Bureaux, Food and beverages
Food-beverages. Restaurant service
International encyclopedia of food and drink

FRUITS

Bartholomew and Sinclair. Lemon fruit
Beach, S.A. Apples of New York

852

Bailey, L. H.   Sketch of evolution of our native fruits
Card, Fred W.   Bush fruits . . .
Chace, E. M. et al.   Citrus fruit products
Charley, V. L. S.   Recent advances fruit juice production
Coit, J. E.   Citrus fruits
Cruess, W. V.   Commercial fruit and vegetable products
Cruess and Christie.   Laboratory manual fruit and
   vegetable products
Florida Citrus Commission.   Citrus fruit in health and
   disease
Grubb, N. H.   Cherries
Hall and Crane.   The apple
Hedrick, U. P.   Cherries of New York
_____ .   Cyclopedia hardy fruits
_____ .   Grapes of New York
_____ .   Peaches of New York
_____ .   Plums of New York
_____ .   Small fruits of New York
Hoare, A. H.   Commercial apple growing
Hume, H. H.   Citrus fruits and their culture
Johnston, J. C.   Citrus growing in California
Joslyn and Marsh.   Utilization of fruit
Kepner and Soothill.   Banana empire
Kesterson and McDuff.   Florida citrus oils
Lelong, B. M.   Treatise citrus culture in California
Lindley, G.   Guide to orchard and kitchen garden
von Loesecke, H. W.   Bananas
Lynch and Mustard.   Mangos in Florida
Miller, C. D. et al.   Fruits of Hawaii.   Description,
   nutritive values, and recipes.
Oldham, C. H.   Cultivation berried fruits- Great Britain
Reynolds, K. P.   The banana
Simmonds, N. W.   Bananas
Sinclair, W. B.   The orange
Talbert and Murneek, Fruit crops
Taylor, H. V.   Plums of England
Taylor, B.   Fruit in the garden
Tolkowsky, T.   Hesperides
Zubeckis, E.   Fruit beverages in Ontario

Anonymous

Fruit annual and directory

INNS AND TAVERNS
Hill, B.   Inn- signia
Lathrop, E.   Early American inns and taverns

Maskell, H.P. Taverns of old England
Stanley, L.T. Old inns of London
Whitbread and Co. Inn crafts and furnishings
_____ . Inn-signia
_____ . Inns of sport

LIQUOR
Arroyo, R. Studies on rum
Baar, S. Beverage distilling industry
Bretzfield, H. Liquor marketing and advertising
Daiches, David. Scotch whisky. Its past and present.
   (Bibliography)
Digby, K. Closet opened
Fisher, M.I. Liqueurs, a dictionary
Forbes, R.J. Short history art of distillation
Herstein and Gregory. Chemistry and technology wines
   and liquors
Hornsby and Harrington. Successful liquor retailing
Licensed Beverage Industries. ABC's of alcoholic
   beverages
_____ . Facts about licensed beverage industries
Lichine, A. Encyclopedia of wines and spirits
McDowall, R.J.S. Whiskies of Scotland
MacNab, S. Under the black tiles
Manning, S.A. Handbook wine and spirit trade
Marrison, L.W. Wines and spirits
Matthews, C.G. Manual alcoholic fermentation
Rosenbloom, M.V. Liquor industry
Sillett, S.W. Illicit scotch
Simmonds, C. Alcohol
Weiss, H.B. History of applejack and apple brandy
Willkie, H.F. Fundamentals of distillery practice

Anonymous
Off the shelf. Guide to sale wines and spirits
Party book. (Anton's)

MINERAL WATER
Bergman, T.O. On acid of air
Firestone, C.B. Bubbling waters
Fitch, W.E. Mineral waters of U.S. and American spas
Priestley, J. Directions impregnating water with fixed air
Sunderland, S. Old London spas, baths and wells
Weber, H. and F.P. Climatotheraphy and balneotheraphy
_____ . Mineral waters and health resorts of Europe

_____ . Spas and mineral waters of Europe

MISCELLANEOUS
Abrahamson and Pezet. Body, mind, sugar
Alexander, J. Colloid chemistry
Baumgartner and Hersom. Canned foods
Corbett, E.V. Libraries, museums and art galleries
    yearbook 1964
Elville, E.M. English table glass
Forbes, R.J. Short history art of distillation
_____ . Studies in ancient technology
Glass Mfgrs. Federation. Glass containers
Goeldner, C.R. Automatic merchandising
Greenwood, E. Classified guide technical and commercial
    books
Hankerson, F.P. Cooperage handbook
International Library Directory. World directory of
    libraries
La Wall, C.H. Curious lore of drugs and medicines
Miller, F.J. Carbon dioxide in water, wine . . .
Moody, B.E. Packaging in glass
Muldoon, G.C. Lessons in pharmaceutical latin
Percival, M. The glass collector
Pfizer, Chas and Co. Our smallest servants
Resuggan, J.C.L. Quarternary ammonium compounds
Rose, A. and E. Bibliography distillation literature
Shaw, D. Catalogue British scientific and technical books
Silverman, M. Magic in a bottle
Simmonds, C. Alcohol
Tate, F.G.H. Alcoholometry
Wright, J.S. Pharmacology of fluid extracts in common use

Anonymous

Emulsion technology

PERFUMERY
Arctander, S. Perfume and flavor chemicals
Bedoukian, P.Z. Perfumery synthetics and isolates
Burbidge, F.W. Book of scented garden
Hampton, F.A. Scent of flowers and leaves
Jessee, J.E. Perfume album
Martin, G. Perfumes, essential oils
Moncrieff, R.W. Chemistry perfume materials
Naves, Y.R. Natural perfume materials
Redgrave, H.S. Scent and all about it.

Sagarin, E. Science and art perfumery
West, T. F. et al. Synthetic perfumes and preparation

SOFT DRINKS
A. B. C. B. Bibliography of research fellowship and
    tech. publications
_____ . Health and liquids
_____ . Memo on sweetening agents
_____ . Use of invert sugar
Beattie, G. B. ABC soft drink business
_____ . Soft drink flavours
_____ . Soft Drink Bottler Vol. II
Blumenthal, S. Food manufacture
Candler, C. H. Asa Griggs Candler
Colam, E. E. F. Pract. milk bar operation
Gardner, W. H. Food acidulents
Hurty- Peck Library. Bibliography books on beverages
Jacobs, M. B. Manufacture and analysis carbonated
    beverages
Kirkby, W. Evolution artificial mineral waters
McClellan, W. S. Utilization of ingested carbon diozide
MacSwiney, E. Mineral water maker's vade mecum
Medbury, H. E. Mfg. bottled carbonated beverages
Mitchell, C. A. Mineral and aerated waters
Noling, A. W. Beverage flavors
_____ . Measuring the acid content of soft drinks
Noling, L. J. Lemon
Nowak, C. A. Non- intoxicants
Penn, K. Soft Drinks Trade Manual
Priestley, J. Directions for impregnating water with
    fixed air
Riley, J. J. Scientific and medical origin of carbonated
    waters
Schroeter, L. C. Sulphur dioxide
Society of Soft Drink Technologists. Your key to quality
Taylor, N. Cinchona in Java

TEA
Crole, D. Tea
Forrest, D. M. 100 years of Ceylon Tea
Fukukita, Y. Tea cult of Japan
Griffiths, P. History Indian tea industry
Harler, C. R. Tea manufacture
Keegel, E. L. Tea mfg. in Ceylon
Klaunberg, H. J. Tea, a symposium
MacLaren, W. A. Rubber, tea and cocoa

Peattie, D. C.　Cargoes and harvests
Ramsden, A. R.　Assam planter
Scott, J. M.　The tea story
Stevenson, J.　Advice medical and economical relative
　　to tea . . .
Torgasheff, B. P.　China as tea producer
Ukers, W. H.　All about tea
Wickizer, V. D.　Coffee, tea and cocoa

WINE
Adlum, J.　Memoir on cultivation of vine in America
Akenhead, D.　Vitacultural research
Allen, H. W.　Natural red wines
＿＿＿＿＿＿.　Wines of Portugal
Amerine, M. A.　Check list books on grapes and wine
＿＿＿＿＿＿.　Commercial production table wine
＿＿＿＿＿＿.　Sensory evaluation of wines
＿＿＿＿＿＿.　Short check list books on wine
＿＿＿＿＿＿.　Table wines
Amerine and Cruess.　Technology of winemaking
Amerine and Singleton.　Wine, an introduction for
　　Americans
Amerine and Marsh.　Wine making at home
Atkinson, J.　Wine wisdom
Beck, E. J.　Aesthetics of wine
Beck, F.　Fred Beck book of wine
Beech, F. W.　Wines and juices
Benwell, W. S.　Journey to wine-Victoria
Berry, C. J. J.　First steps in winemaking
Bioletti, F. M.　Elements of grape growing in California
Boswell, P.　Wine makers' manual
Bradford, Sarah.　The Englishman's wine.　The story of
　　port.
Broadbent, J. M.　Wine tasting
Carling, T. E.　Complete book of drink
＿＿＿＿＿＿.　Wine lore
Carosso, V. P.　California wine industry
Carter, Y.　Drinking Bordeaux
＿＿＿＿＿＿.　Drinking Burgundy
Churchill, C.　Notebook for wine-France
＿＿＿＿＿＿.　World of wines
Clarke, Nick.　Bluff your way with wine.
Cockburn, E.　Port wine-Oporto
Codman, C. R.　Years and years
Cook, Fred S.　Ed.　The wines and wineries of California

857

Crawford, I.   Wine on a budget
Crotch, W.   Complete yearbook French wines
Cruess, W.V.   Prin. and pract. winemaking
Cusmano, G.   Dizionario di viticultura
Davis, J.I.   Beginner's guide to wine
Dicey, P.   Wine in South Africa
Don, R.S.   Wine
Escritt, L.B.   The small cellar
Faes, M.   Lexique viti-vinicole International
Feret, E.   Bordeaux and its wines
Forbes, P.   Champagne . . .
Fornachon, J.C.M.   Studies on sherry flor
Garvin, F.   French wines
Gold, A.   Wines and spirits of the world
Graham, M.E. (Comp.)   Wine and Food Society of
     Southern California.   A history with a bibliography
     of A.L. Simon.
Grants of St. James Ltd.   Gateway to wine
Grossman, H.J.   Guide to wine . . .
Gyrogy, P.   Fine wines of Germany
Halasz, Z.   Hungarian wine through ages
Hallgarten, S.F.   Rhineland wineland
Hardwick, H.   Winemaking at home
Hedrick, U.P.   History of horticulture in America
Herod, W.P.   Introduction to wines
Herstein and Gregory.   Chemistry and technology of wines
Hyams, E.   Grapes under clothes
Jagendorf, M.A.   Folk wines and cordials
James, W.   Wine in Australia
Jeffs, J.   Sherry
Johnson, H.   Pan book of wine
Joslyn and Amerine.   Dessert, appetizer and related
     flavored wines
Jullien, A.   Topography of known vineyards
Lake, M.   Classic wines of Australia
KWV Public Relations Dept.   A handbook on wine.
     (For retail licensees).
Langenbach, A.   German wines and vines
Layton, T.A.   Winecraft
_____ .   Wines of Italy
Leedom, W.S.   Vintage wine book
Leggett, H.B.   Early history wine production in California
Lichine, A.   Encyclopedia of wines
Lucia, S.P.   History wine as theraphy
_____ .   Wine and health

_____. Wine as food and medicine
Manning, S. A.   Handbook of wine and spirit trade
Marcus, I. H.   Dictionary of Wine Terms
Marks, R.   Wines, How, when . . .
Marrison, L. W.   Wines and Spirits
Massee, W. E.   Wines and spirits
Massel, A.   Applied wine chemistry and technology.
    (Bibliography and Glossary)
_____. Dicta technica
Melville, J.   Guide California wines
Morris, D.   French vineyards
Muir, A.   How to choose and enjoy wine
Murphy, D. F.   Australian wine guide
Newhall, C. S.   Vines of northeastern America
Ordish, G.   Wine growing in England
Ott, E.   From barrel to bottle
Ough and Amerine.   Effects of temperature on winemaking
Penning-Rowsell, Edmund.   The wines of Bordeaux.
    (Bibliography)
Penzer, N. M.   Book of the wine label
Perold, A. I.   Treatise on vitaculture
Perry, M. H.   And to drink, Sir!
Phin, J.   Open air grape culture
Prince, G.   Current books about wine
Public Library South Australia
_____. Research Service bibliography
_____. Wine and vitaculture
Rainbird, G.   Pocket book of wine
_____. Sherry and wines of Spain
Ray, C.   Lafite
_____. Wines of Italy
Rixford, E. H.   Wine press and the cellar
Roger, J. R.   Wines of Bordeaux
Schenley Import Corp.   Wines, how, when . . .
Shand, P. M.   Book of wine
_____. Book of French wine
_____. Book of other wines than French
Simon, A. L.   Bibliotheca Bacchia
_____. Bibliotheca Gastronimica
_____. Bibliotheca Vineria
_____. Champagne
_____. Great wines of Germany
_____. History of Champagne
_____. History of wine trade in England
_____. In the twilight
_____. Noble trapes and great wines of France

_____. Wines and liqueurs from A- Z
_____. Wines of the world 1967
_____. Wines, vineyards . . . of Australia
Storm, J. Invitation to wines
Taylor, Allan. What everybody wants to know about wine.
    (Bibliography)
Thomas, F. A. Wines, cocktails and other drinks
Todd, W. J. Handbook of wine
Turner and Roycroft. AB- Z of winemaking
Valaer, P. Wines of the world
Viala and Ravas. American vines . . .
Wagner, P. M. American wines, how to make
_____. American wines and winemaking
_____. Wine grapes . . .
_____. Wine- growers guide
Warner, C. K. Winegrowers of France . . .
Waugh, A. In praise of wine
Waugh, E. Wine in peace and war
Wildman, F. J. Few wine notes
Wine Advisory Board. California's wine wonderland
_____. Guide to wines
_____. Uses of wine in medical practice
_____. Wine handbook series
Wine and Food Society. Library Catalogue No. 1
Wine Institute. Selective bibliography of wine books
Winkler, A. J. General viticulture
Younger, W. Gods, men and wine
Yoxall, H. W. The wines of Burgundy

Anonymous

Bibliotheca Oenologica
Book of wine (by J. W.)
Dictionaire Oenonomique
Fine drinking - Ayala Champagne
Harper's Manual
Legend of liqueurs, wines and spirits
Off the shelf (Brown and Pank)
Party Book (Anton's)
Wine - Australia. Guide to Australian wines
Wine and spirit merchant (1885)
Wine trade loan exhibition of drinking vessels- also books

Libraries Which Specialize in Fields Related
to Beverages or Have Better than Average Collections

American Cocoa Research Institute. Washington
Anheuser-Busch, Inc. St. Louis, Mo.
  (Beer and Brewing)
Babson Institute Library, Babson Park, Mass. (General)
Bourbon Institute (The). New York
British Museum Library. London
Canada Dry Research Laboratories. Greenwich, Ct.
Cincinnati Public Library (Beer and Brewing)
Crahan, Dr. Marcus. Los Angeles. (Wine)
Distilled Spirits Institute. Washington
Falstaff Brewing Corp. St. Louis. Mo.
Filson Club Library, Louisville, Ky. (Bourbon Whiskey)
Fleishman Malting Co. Library. Chicago (General)
Fleishman Research Laboratory Library. Stamford, Ct.
  (General)
Franklin Institute, Philadelphia (General)

Fresno State College of Library, Fresno, Calif.
  (Brady Wine Library)
General Foods Marketing Library. White Plains, N.Y.
  (General)
General Foods Public Relations Library. White Plains,
  N.Y. (General)
General Foods Research Library. Tarrytown, N.Y.
  (General)
Institute of Brewing Library. London
Institute of Brewing Research Library. Nutfield, Surrey,
  England
John Crerar Library. Chicago (General)
Jordan Wine Co. Toronto
Library of Congress. Washington
Licensed Beverage Bureau Library. New York
Linda Hall Library. Kansas City, Mo.
Little, Arthur D. and Co. Cambridge, Mass.
Lloyd Library. Cincinnati (Botanicals)
Merory, Joseph. Lake Hiawatha, N.J.
  (Technical and general)
Missouri Historical Society. St. Louis, Mo.
  (Mineral water)

Napa Valley Wine Library. St. Helena, Calif.
National Agriculture Library. Washington
National Soft Drink Ass'n. Washington
New York Agricultural Experiment Station. Geneva, N.Y.
New York Public Library
Patent Office Library. London
Pepsi-Cola Co. Long Island City, N.Y.
Pepsi-Cola Co. New York City (moved)
Schenley Distillers Library. Lawrenceburg, Indiana
     (General)
Schenley Distillers Library. New York
Schlitz, Jos. E. Brewing Co. Milwaukee
Schwarz Laboratories. Mt. Vernon, N.Y. (General)
Seibel Institute Library. Chicago (Brewing)
Simon, Andre L. London. (Wine)
Standard Brands, Inc. Library. Stamford, Ct.
Sugar Research Institute Library. New York
Sunkist Library. Ontario, Calif.
U.S. Brewers' Ass'n. Library. New York
U.S. Dept. Commerce Library. Washington
U.S. Internal Revenue Dept. Library. Washington
Univ. of California at Berkeley.
Univ. of California at Davis
Univ. of California at Los Angeles
Wallerstein Laboratories Library. Staten Island, N.Y.
Wine and Food Society Library. London
Wine Institute Library. San Francisco

Major Libraries Visited or Checked for
Titles in the Beverage Literature Field

State and National
Alexander Turnbull Library
  Wellington, N. Z.
Australian National Library
  Canberra, Australia
British Museum Library
  London
California State Library
  Sacramento
Canadian Nat'l Library
  Ottawa
Florida State Library
  Tallahassee
House of Parliament Library
  Canberra, Australia
Houses of Parliament
  Library. Ottawa
Indiana State Library
  Indianapolis
Kentucky State Library
  Frankfort
Library of Congress
  Washington
Library of Parliament
  Cape Town, S. A.
Michigan State Library
  Lansing
Missouri State Library
  Jefferson City
Mitchell Library   Sydney,
  Australia
National Library
  Wellington, N. Z.
Nevada State Library,
  Carson City
New South Wales State
  Library. Sydney,
  Australia

New York State Library
  Albany
No. Carolina State Library
  Raleigh
No. Dakota State Library
  Bismarck
Ohio State Library. Columbus
Oklahoma State Library
  Okla. City
Oregon State Library. Salem
Patent Office Library. London
Patent Office Scientific
  Library. Washington
State Library of Victoria
  Melbourne, Australia
Tennessee State Library
  Nashville
Washington State Library
  Olympia
Wisconsin State Library
  Madison

City Public Libraries
Atlanta, Ga.
Auckland, N. Z.
Berkeley, Calif.
Boston, Mass.
Brisbane, Australia
Brooklyn, N. Y.
  (Business branch)
Buffalo, N. Y.
Cape Town, South Africa
Chattanooga, Tenn.
Chicago, Ill.
Cincinnati, Ohio
Cleveland, Ohio

Columbus, Ohio
Dallas, Texas
Dayton, Ohio
Detroit, Mich.
District of Columbia
Durban, Natal, S. A.
Edinburgh, Scotland
Flint, Mich.
Fresno, Calif.
Indianapolis, Ind.
Knoxville, Tenn.
Los Angeles, Calif.
Louisville, Ky.
Milwaukee, Wisc.
Minneapolis, Minn.
Nairobi, Kenya
Nashville, Tenn.
New York, N. Y.
Oakland, Calif.
Ontario, Calif.
Orange, Calif.
Oshkosh, Wisc.
Peoria, Ill.
Philadelphia, Penn.
Pittsburg, Penn.
Portland, Ore.
Sacramento, Calif.
St. Louis, Mo.
St. Paul, Minn.
San Diego, Calif.
San Francisco, Calif.
Santa Ana, Calif.
Santa Barbara, Calif.
Santa Rosa, Calif.
Seattle, Wash.
Somerville, Mass.
Spokane, Wash.
Sydney, Australia
Toledo, Ohio
Toronto, Ontario
Vancouver, Brit. Columbia
Wellington, N. Z.
Wilkes-Barre, Penn.

University, School, and Other
Semi-Public Libraries
Amherst College. Amherst,
    Mass.
Arizona Univ. Tucson, Ariz.
Bodleian Library. Oxford
B-C University. Vancouver
    B. C.
Brown University. Providence
Butler Univ. Indianapolis
California (Univ. of)
    at Berkeley
    at Davis
    at Los Angeles
    at Santa Barbara
Calif. State Polytechnic Institute
    at Pomona, Calif.
    at San Luis Obispo, Calif.
Cambridge University
Carnegie Technical Inst.
    Pittsburg
Chicago (Univ. of)
Cincinnati (Univ. of)
Columbia University, N. Y.
Cornell Univ. Hotel Adm.
    School Library. Ithaca, N. Y.
Cornell Univ. Library (Olin)
    Ithaca, N. Y.
Dartmouth College, Hanover,
    N. H.
Dayton Univ. Dayton, Ohio
Dept. Commerce Library.
    Washington
Dept. Agriculture Library.
    Washington
Drexel Institute. Philadelphia
Duke Univ. Durham, N. C.
Filson Club Library.
    Louisville, Ky.
Franklin Institute. Philadelphia
Fresno State College. Fresno,
    Calif.
Honolulu Univ. Honolulu,
    Hawaii

Hoover Library. Palo Alto, Calif.

Howard Univ. Washington

Harvard Univ. Cambridge, Mass.

Illinois (Univ. of). Champaign

Illinois Inst. Technology. Chicago

Indiana Univ. Bloomington

Internal Revenue Dept. Library. Washington

Kentucky (Univ. of) Lexington

Leland Stanford Univ. Palo Alto, Calif.

Los Angeles State College

Mc Gill Univ. Montreal, Que.

Marquette Univ. Milwaukee, Wisc.

Massachusetts Inst. Technology. Cambridge, Mass.

Melbourne Univ. Melbourne, Australia

Miami Univ. Coral Gables, Fla.

Michigan State Univ. East Lansing

Michigan (Univ. of). Ann Arbor

Minnesota (Univ. of). Minneapolis

Missouri (Univ. of). Columbia

Natal Univ. Durban, South Africa

New South Wales Univ. Sydney, Australia

North Carolina (Univ. of) Chapel Hill

New York Univ.

Northwestern Univ. Evanston, Ill.

Notre Dame Univ. Notre Dame, Ind.

Ohio State Univ. Columbus

Oregon State College, Corvallis

Pennsylvania (Univ. of). Philadelphia

Pennsylvania State Univ. University Park

Pittsburg (Univ. of). Pittsburg

Puget Sound College. Tacoma, Wash.

Princeton Univ. Princeton, N. J.

Purdue Univ. Lafayette, Ind.

Rensselaer Polytechnic Inst. Troy, N. Y.

Royal Melbourne Inst. of Technology. Melbourne, Australia

Rutgers, the State Univ. New Brunswick, N. J.

St. Louis Univ. Missouri

San Francisco (Univ. of) Calif.

Southern California (Univ. of). Los Angeles

Sydney Univ. Sydney, Australia

Tennessee (Univ. of). Knoxville

Texas (Univ. of). Austin

State of New York Agricultural and Technical College, Morrisville, N. Y.

Vanderbilt Univ. Nashville, Tenn.

Victoria Univ. Wellington, N. Z.

Virginia Polytechnic Inst. Blackburg, Va.

Washington Univ. St. Louis, Mo.

Washington (Univ. of). Seattle

Wisconsin (Univ. of). Madison

Yale Univ. New Haven, Ct.

865

ה